Günther Feuerstein

Urban Fiction

Strolling through Ideal Cities from Antiquity to the Present Day

Edition Axel Menges

Published with support of the Österreichisches Bundesministerium für Bildung, Wissenschaft und Kultur, the Hochschuljubiläumsstiftung der Stadt Wien and by the group U.M.R.A.U.M. – Urbanismus. Medien. Research. Architektur. Utopie. Metropole.

© 2008 Edition Axel Menges, Stuttgart/London
ISBN 978-3-930698-26-4

Prepress work: Doris Grassl (assistant of the author)
Reproductions: Sebastian Michalski
Printing and binding: Everbest Printing Co., Ltd., China

Translation into English: Ilze Müller
Editing: Dorothea Duwe, Nora Krehl-von Mühlendahl, Ilze Müller
Design: Axel Menges

»Utopias are often nothing but premature truths.«
(Alphonse de Lamartine, 1823)

»Utopias are often nothing but premature truths.«
(Alphonse de Lamartine, 1823)

Introduction

Journeys. Interpretations

This study tells: truths and untruths (and yet not lies), dreams, experiences, visions, thoughts, fictions, fantasies, the real, the unreal. Let me tell you about my journeys through the cities of Utopia as many have done before me, more brilliantly, I'm sure. Let me tell my story as if all the cities had already been built, as did Thomas More and Antonio Filarete, Denis Veirasse and Giacomo Casanova, William Morris and Edward Bellamy, and many others. I believe I am justified in sometimes continuing the dream, adding something, bringing into play my own imagination.

May a work of art be freely interpreted? That question was answered long ago: In recent decades there has been tremendous leeway in interpreting music and literature, or, more specifically, dramatic literature. Indeed, variation, modification, mutation are given free rein. Thus I feel justified in claiming the same freedom for architectural projects that were never built. There have been attempts to complete Schubert's *Unfinished Symphony* and Kafka's *Castle* – can this be justified? The Cologne Cathedral and Gaudi's Sagrada Familia were actually »completed« – does that make sense?

The book does not claim to be strictly academic. It continues the tradition of utopias: A bold mixture of reality, probability, wishful thinking, and impossibility is the food of utopias as well.

Theories. Terms. Definitions

Relevant philosophies and theories are dealt with only briefly – only as long as is possible during a walk.

An inhabitant, a user of the city, a pedestrian, driver, passenger in an express car – does not have books about urban theories or social philosophies open in front of him but is directly confronted with the city, must come to terms with it. And we as travelers do not verbally get to hear more than our guides are willing to tell us.

For the same reason, the remarks of the architects and artists in this book are modest: They unfold no grand theories, but simply make comments, suggest backgrounds, ideas, concepts that help one to understand the organization and the society of the city. Let me quote a few terms, which will then no longer be repeated in the book.

U-topos is a non-place, probably not a very appropriate collective term for all these narratives, for many did find their place – in reality, in the planning stage, in a concept, in imagination, in a hypothesis, in fiction.

Eu-topos is a fortunate, blessed place. That would be an appropriate term for many of the narratives – the place of dreams, of desires, for which we long, yet not entirely without hope; perhaps it is even the dream of a perfect world.

Dis-topos is a vanishing, vanished place, a place we encounter in myths, fairy tales, legends. It will be of interest to us occasionally.

Dys-topos is a terrible, horrifying, fearful place – so often mentioned in connection with the New City, the city of the future – and so we cannot ignore it during our journeys.
Related to this term are the following:

Anti-utopia, negative utopia, devolutionist dystopia, counterutopia, horror utopia, inverted utopia, cacotopy, apotropaic utopia.

Real-topos is a place that really exists, that was transferred from the imagination into tangible, concrete reality.

To systematize things in another way, it is place and time that characterize utopias and fantasies. As we classify our journeys, we see that in most cases we have been separated from the place where we live or transported to a different period, or that place and time are completely changed (see the table at the end of the introduction).

How do we define Utopia? There are hundreds of definitions and explanations of the term »utopia«, and I don't intend to add any more. Let me simply quote two. Admittedly these are not complete in the context of this book.

Here is how Norbert Elias defines the term (1982):

»A utopia indicates how a person wishes to redesign the life of his society or what a person fears as the potential future of his society.

»A utopia is a vision of a society that contains proposals for solving very definite unsolved problems of a particular society.«

Karl Mannheim has a similar view (1965): »A utopian consciousness is one that is not in agreement with the surrounding reality. Because the concrete determination of what utopia is is always effected from a particular stage of reality, it is possible that the utopias of today may become the realities of tomorrow.«

There may not be a need for a definition, since we are actually wandering through the cities und experience them, with their buildings, people, landscapes. From viewing them, from our dynamic tours of them, from the conversations, we gain insights about the cities, into the cities.

Delimitations

Even if I do not add any further definitions, I believe it is necessary to differentiate, to explain which cities we are going to visit, and to give a few criteria for our travels.

This study is about the city – that is, in the broadest sense of the word, about any complex architectural configuration, independent of the size in which society and space are manifested in specific structures. At the same time, like people in antiquity, we do not want to make distinctions between a city and a state, and the polis and the politei, the city and its citizens, may become almost identical.

Accordingly, we are going to visit those imaginary cities that
– are interesting because of their societal, social, political, religious, reformative, philanthropic structure and
– those whose spatial layout, architecture and urban planning, art and design are of interest.
Above all, however, we are interested in cities that
– are interesting in terms of both their social and spatial structure.

Accordingly we will primarily visit:
– legendary, lost, destroyed cities,
– holy cities,
– ideal cities, primarily in the Renaissance,
– cities we discover on journeys, far away, during adventures,
– island cities, island states,
– great literary utopias,
– revolutionary cities, the cities of reformers and philanthropists,
– urban experiments,
– artists' cities, cities in art,
– visionary cities of the modern period,
– cities in drawings and paintings,
– fictional cities, cities in novels,
– naïve cities,
– recent urban visions.

With a few exceptions, some related themes need to be excluded, for instance:
– myths and fairy tales,
– exclusively technically and mechanically oriented concepts of science fiction,
– adventure novels and light novels, satires,
– fables and animal societies,
– stories of desert islands à la Robinson Crusoe,
– political novels,
– purely religious societies, sects,
– specific, ethnic societies, tribes,
– ecological utopias, dystopias,
– necropoles,
– apocalyptic themes, stories of catastrophes,
– tales of robots,
– prognoses.

In addition, from an architectural perspective – again with a few exceptions – the following need to be excluded:
– a priori concrete city planning, realistic plans for urban expansions,
– city-like exhibition grounds,
– rural settlements and communities,
– cities raised above the ground,
– interplanetary cities,
– entertainment cities, leisure worlds,
– communities of extraterrestrials, other living creatures (animals),
– cloud-cuckoo-land / Cockaigne,
– gardens, paradises.

On the other hand, the following do not, in general, need to be excluded:
– implementations of ideal cities, imaginary cities, visions,
– concrete urban planning that goes far beyond the bounds of reality,
– implementations that started out as visions and are represented in terms of the original concepts,
– implementations that failed after a relatively short time.

These delimitations show that utopias do not predict the future but call the present into question, and that it is not technological sensations, such as those often found in science fiction, but the city, architecture, and society that are of interest.

Travel program

I am traveling with my anonymous companion, and in each location the architect, artist, author, politician, or reformer, as the case may be, accompanies us. All the cities have already been built.

The title names the main responsible planner, artist, or politician.

The first date after the city's name indicates when the utopia, the concept, the fantasy was written as literature or planned; the second, italicized, date indicates when the fictional or actual implementation occurred. In most cases this date is missing, and then it must be assumed that the fictional implementation took place in the years directly following the conception of the utopia.

The architects, artists, or reformers explain the cities, the intentions, the history to us.

The original quotations are written in italics.

Quotations in Roman letters and in quotation marks (»...«) give the gist of the speaker's words, or are not direct quotes, or are fictional quotes.

We ask questions, express reservations, touch on problems.

Our direct speech is not in quotation marks.

After our tour we draw back, return to the reality of the present and reflect on what we have seen. Primarily we wonder which aspects, phenomena, plans, drafts have left their mark on reality – and to what degree.

The concluding comments do not represent an interpretation or an academic reflection; rather, they are an attempt to show the ideal city's relevance today. Frequently, these comments can be no more than rudimentary, speculative, or associative.

Utopia and reality

We have always been surprised to find that many »utopian ideas« have influenced the real world – a number of ideal cities were actually built, and ideal communities were established. The purpose of this study is to show that all these »topoi« can become places in our lives, realities of a specific kind. There are enough examples to show that bold ideas, rigorous systems, and theoretical concepts are also manifested in real cities – frequently only partially, rudimentarily.

Thus one could also maintain the opposite: Utopias are places. Even if it is only trace elements, glimpses that left their mark on our reality, they deserve our interest.

There are no utopias! Perhaps we only make this assertion in order to refute the term, perhaps only because the term is so familiar, perhaps to understand it in a completely new way?

From a technological perspective, almost all the projects we are going to visit could be implemented today. Indeed, many could have been implemented using existing technology at the time when they were first conceived. It is only economic, political, and social barriers that banish many of the projects to the realm of utopia. This is still true today. Or perhaps it is especially true today? Our study primarily wanted to demonstrate that utopias are by no means merely impossible, irrational fantasies, but that they are ideas with a past and a future, integrated in an inseparable historical continuity. That means they stand out from the isolation of utopia and always acquire a dimension of the real, however that may be defined.

Utopias **are** places.
Utopias **are** realities.

Possible place-time combinations

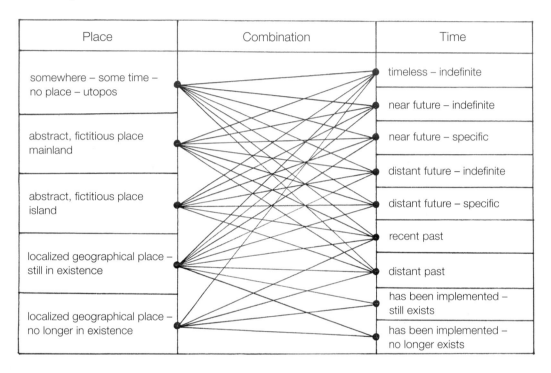

Place	Combination	Time
somewhere – some time – no place – utopos		timeless – indefinite
		near future – indefinite
abstract, fictitious place mainland		near future – specific
		distant future – indefinite
abstract, fictitious place island		distant future – specific
		recent past
localized geographical place – still in existence		distant past
		has been implemented – still exists
localized geographical place – no longer in existence		has been implemented – no longer exists

1. Myths and legends

Plato (428/427–348/347 BC). The submerged city of Atlantis, 9000 BC

We are deeply impressed by this imposing city. Plato begins by explaining to us the peculiar society of Atlantis, which is structured according to status and class: »*First there is the class of the priests or guardians, separate from the rest, then that of the craftsmen, each of whom, separate from the others, pursues his own business. The herdsmen, hunters, and farmers form one class, and finally there are the warriors.*«

However, the ruling class are the »guardians«: They have enjoyed a special education by their peers, but they also have specific duties. And, surprisingly, they have no property of their own. They own no assets, no housing or store rooms, and each has only as much money as he absolutely needs – and that is little, for their life is completely determined by society: The meals are communal, and all women have equal rights in every respect. For »*the male and female sex live in community, and each is by nature competent to practice communally that which each gender is intended for*«. No woman may live together with an individual man and vice versa. Thus it also goes without saying that the children are communal property – for no child knows its father and vice versa.

Atlantis was founded at the whim of an impetuous god: Poseidon created it in memory of his love for Cleito, a country girl.

The city is situated on a plateau whose slopes are inhabited by craftsmen and farmers. The latter can farm their land near the houses where they live. In the upper part of the city, grouped around the temple of Athene and Hephaistos, live the warriors in simple but attractive houses. They have surrounded their settlement with a circular wall.

The city on the hill is well fortified and circular in design. It is surrounded by five rings, two of land and three of water, which are, as it were, carved out of the island. The circular walls are faced with copper, pewter, and rock crystal, and gleam in the sunlight.

The first and second land rings measure three stadia (550 m) each. The third and fourth water rings measure two stadia each (370 m), and the fifth water ring is one stadium (185 m) wide.

Two springs, one hot, the other cold, have their source in the center of the island. They are utilized for indoor pools, separate ones for the kings, and for the women of the people. There is also a pond for the horses and draft animals. Surrounding the fountains there are impressive buildings and plantings of trees.

The island supplies all human needs in abundance: Mining provides various kinds of ores, there are large forests providing wood, fields and pastures for the animals, and even elephants are raised there. An exotic flora and fauna give the island its specific character.

1. Peter Connolly, Atlantis. Attempt at a reconstruction, 2003.

»On the island of Atlantis there was also united a great, wonderful power of kings whom the whole island obeyed, as did many other islands and parts of the mainland.«

In the center of the island there is a large fortress, and this is the royal residence. In its center is a sanctuary dedicated to Cleito and Poseidon. On the outside, the temple is plated with silver, while the battlements are plated with gold. The arches are ivory, richly adorned with gold, silver, and rock crystal. The golden statues of the rulers proclaim their power. The fortress and the houses of the city sparkle with rich colors, being built of white, red, and black stone.

The island has a number of other interesting features, such as the magnificent gardens, the racetrack that stretches around the entire island, and the athletic facilities, including large arenas – all serving the pleasure and physical fitness of the citizens.

Later, we visit the bustling shipyard and harbors. On the docks, we admire the roofed passages, bridges fortified with turrets, with gates that could close them off, and the subterranean water reservoirs.

Plato, *Critias*, 4th century BC, 1482, 1909; Mavor 1969, 1974; Servier 1971; Manguel 1981; Brentjes 1993; *Utopie* 1969.

But Atlantis sank below the sea 9,000 years before Plato – claims the philosopher. That is why the ongoing search for Atlantis postulating its once-real existence, is futile. Added support is constantly given to hypotheses of the island's actual site – a few arguments are often sufficient to fire the imagination. Thus the island has been located in the North Sea, near the Bahamas or in the East Indies, in South America or near Spain, west of the Gibraltar, by the coast of Yucatan as a Mayan city, in the Black Sea, in the East Indian Ocean. In recent times researchers believed they had found scientific proof: Atlantis was located in the Aege an Sea, on one of the Cyclades Islands, and the island of Thera, the present-day Santorin, which was destroyed by a volcanic eruption around 1500 BC, might be a remnant of Atlantis.

In the meantime Atlantis has become a myth, and the submerged continent feeds the theses and speculations of esoteric cults.

Whatever research and hypotheses may postulate, Atlantis will probably always remain a legend. Perhaps Plato meant to celebrate the city of Athens, its population, and system of government with his story, and his imagination was fired by the close proximity of the Dorians in Crete and by Sparta. The drawings – attempts to reconstruct Atlantis – are also only figments of the imagination.

Géza Marótl (1875–1941). The city of Atlantis, 9000 BC and 1937

Once more, we revisit Atlantis – but this time it was Géza Maróti, a Hungarian architect, who had a part in building the city. And again we need to look at the city from a bird's-eye perspective if we are to understand its nature and system.

Huge rings, precisely concentric, form the basic plan of the city. The total exterior diameter is close to 20 km, and the center is about 1,000 m

The outermost structural ring is at least 3,000 m wide and is formed by an incredibly compact, rigidly geometrical ring city. A wide, undeveloped field follows as a second ring, and another built-up area forms a third, a watercourse a fourth, a narrow ring a fifth, and finally, a second moat is the sixth ring. These rings of water have enormous dimensions: the innermost zone is 9 km long and 400 m wide, and the outermost is 16 km long and also 400 m wide. And an even more sizable watercourse, a canal, leads directly to the sea and a carefully laid-out harbor.

The center, the Acropolis, towers steeply above the rest: the magnificent and monumental center of Atlantis.

»A circular city plan is older than a square one«, explains Maróti. *»The symbolic rings of the sun explain the ground plan of the city of Atlantis, it is the city of the sun.«*

Now we walk through the Acropolis-like city center – but the steep high walls, which resemble a sculpture, remind us of the cliffs of the Acropolis in Athens – and in fact sections of the walls are natural bedrock: art and nature merge.

As we now enter the city center, the first thing that strikes us is the incredibly lavish use of gold and silver in the buildings. Indeed, some even seem to be coated with these noble metals. And, not least, the masterful stone and bronze statues attract our attention.

We discover a rich architectural program in this compact and monumental city center. A mighty stepped tower (though one with only small gradations) forms the center, and is visible from a great distance. The highly developed culture of the city of Atlantis is confirmed by the manifold

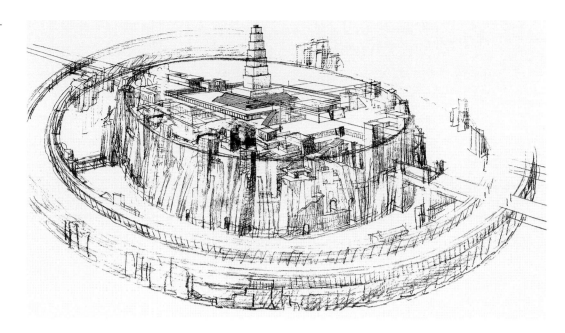

2. Géza Maróti, Janos Gerle, György Szegö, Atlantis. Free interpretation of the submerged city, 1937.

buildings: Beside the royal palace and the baths we find the astronomical observatories, libraries, temples, and tombs.

Almost exclusively, the basic architectural motif is a square, and a strict geometrical relationship of the lines creates tight order.

»*We should all build a kind of Atlantis today*«, concludes Maróti. And his friends Janos Gerle and György Szegö add: »*Our spiritual and emotional unity with the earth must be restored. Let us understand and respect the emotional, psychological, and spiritual sphere in order to create our inner peace. Circumstances in the cities and the landscape are directly linked with the quality of personal and community life. The key to the architecture of the coming century is communication between human beings and the Earth, between people and their neighbors, people and their own past, tradition, city, and landscape, which form their environment, and above all between human beings and their human selves, between human beings and God-given future potentials.*«

Naturally, this too is not an archaeological reconstruction – how could it be when Atlantis never existed? But it is an opulent, precise fantasy developed from the few details given by Plato. Maróti makes interesting comparisons: Many circular cities have been conceived, but only a few have been actually implemented, and Maróti includes Orvieto in Italy among them. Even the cliff formations of that city are an analogy to Maróti's Atlantis.

Marduk and Yahweh, and Pieter Breughel the Elder (1525/30–1569). Babylon, c. 1600 BC and 1563 AD

Approaching from the direction of the Euphrates, we enter the city of Babylon and are at once surrounded by busy construction workers. Next to the modest houses, we see a towering construction of gigantic size. And a hardworking stonemason informs us: »We're building a tower that will rise into the sky. Coming from many nations, we want to make a name for ourselves. And all of us work wonderfully in harmonic teams.«

And in fact the building, stepped toward the top, rises above a circular ground plan with hundreds of arches, windows, niches, arcades, figures, and stairs. Already, people are about to take possession of it.

On the tower ramp there is a huge crane with a clever device for raising heavy loads: Three men tread in place in a drum in the foreground, while three tread in a drum in the back. These are treadmills, and it is by this means that they can raise many times the weight of their own body. Just now, a cut block of stone is being heaved aloft. On a small balcony stands a man who, with a rope, keeps the block from swinging to and fro.

On the ramps there are a few shacks for the guilds, and as we approach, the construction workers have stopped for a snack as they engage in cheerful banter.

3. Pieter Bruegel the Elder, The Building of the Tower of Babel, 1563.

Let us look at the city, which seems almost minuscule. It is surrounded by a wall encircling pretty little houses with gables, turrets, and gates. In the harbor, ships are ready to set sail. Now we meet mighty King Nimrod. His huge build and powerful stature could almost qualify him as a giant. He wears a scepter and crown, and the stonemasons fall on their knees before him. He is visiting, watching, surveying the gigantic structure; he seems satisfied with the progress of the construction – he has every reason to be satisfied, after all. Let's take a look at the daring building. There are outstanding masters at work here. But, we wonder, can this construction – so incredibly complicated and complex – ever be completed at all? Isn't it clear from the very start that this plan cannot be completed?

The construction has already made a lot of progress, yet at the base we still find sections that have not been completed. Indeed, it appears as though a great wound will keep the building gaping open for all time. The exterior of the large spiral seems to have nothing at all to do with the interior, the core that is exposed here. And the further we look upward, the more dubious the entire construction becomes, the more comical, the more grotesque seems the connection between the form and the construction of the building. And so we gradually begin to question our first impression that the masons are erecting this magnificent work in well coordinated, fine teamwork. Our skepticism is confirmed from a completely different direction, however. Yahweh has been displeased by the human presumption of building a tower that would rise into the sky, into his domain. And suddenly we hear the mighty voice of Yahweh from on high: »*Behold, they are one people and they have all one language and this is only the beginning of what they will do; and nothing that they propose to do will now be impossible. Come, let us go down and there confuse their language, that they may not understand one another's speech.*«

And all at once none of them understands the speech of the other and thus they must stop building their great work, for they are scattered over the face of the earth and the mighty tower is ruined.

Old Testament, Moses 11, 1–9; Baumer 1967; Tod / Wheeler 1978; Minkowski 1991; Vercelloni 1994; Hagen 2001; *Visionen und Utopien* 2002; Seipel 2003.

Language, communication, is the precondition for any work – and most especially for a building project. Thus all nations – and particularly architects – have suffered the consequences of the confusion of languages to this very day. Babylon is the imposing symbol for this.

Babylon was the mighty city on the Euphrates, which flowed through it. The metropolis had 300,000 inhabitants. Three- and four-story houses lined the straight, wide streets that ran at right angles to the river. The area of the city center was 4 km². It was surrounded by massive walls protecting the temple district and the palace of Nebuchadnezzar. The hanging gardens of Semiramis transformed a section of the city into blooming, verdant oases.

But did the tower of Babylon really exist? Certainly not in Babylon and not in the form familiar to us from more than 200 depictions from the 15th century to the present day. Today there is clear archaeological evidence that one of numerous ziggurats existed in the city of Etemenanki. It was a temple tower consisting of six tiers; open-air stairs led to the top, and an inner staircase was a link to the temple, built on the topmost terrace. We can reconstruct its ground plan – a square measuring roughly 92 by 92 m – with some certainty. It was probably about 94 m high.

If we carefully reread Genesis, there is never a mention of Yahweh destroying the tower. Here the actual history of this ziggurat has obviously affected the interpretations. The ziggurat underwent numerous destructions, for instance, under Xerxes. It was rebuilt time after time, only to be finally destroyed definitively in the second century BC, after which it was no longer reconstructed. The King Nimrod who is portrayed in most of the depictions of the building of the Tower of Babel as the ruler who commissioned the building is a legendary invention.

Thus we are faced with the interesting fact that reality and utopia, artistic depictions and the real world, fantasy and fact intersect and overlap – a fact that will be the recurrent theme of this study. A reconstruction today tries to show the appearance of the above-mentioned ziggurat with some certainty.

But the building of the Tower of Babel and the short passage in the Bible have far more significance for generations past and to this very day. It is the symbol of presumption, it is the metaphor for a city that cannot be mastered. And thus it is not so very surprising that in the past and in the present century the building of the Tower of Babel was depicted repeatedly, greatly modified, that it kept arousing the interest of historians, visionaries, and artists. To mention only two examples: Fritz Lang in his magnificent film *Metropolis* portrayed a kind of Babel and drew on historical depictions in his production.

The architect and artist Constant (cf. chap. 13.3) calls his grandiose urban visions New Babylon, one more indication that the idea of confusion, diversity, differentiation, but also the idea of building as a profoundly human action continues to preoccupy us to this day. And naturally it is inevitable that in this context we think of September 11, 2001, legendary by now, and of the greatest destruction of a building ever experienced by the human race, the destruction of the World Trade Center in New York (cf. chap. 13.6). But the new Babylonian towers are rising once more, and the record height of 450 m reached only recently by the Petronas Towers in Kuala Lumpur has today been topped by the tower in Dubai, which is close to 700 m high. However, substantially higher towers are being planned already, and Frank Lloyd Wright's fantastic idea of building the 1,400-meter One-Mile-High Skyscraper is coming closer and closer: A Spanish architect wants to reach a height of 1,200 m with the Bionic Tower, and Japanese architects imagine 4,000-m-high tower cities.

Herodotus (c. 485–425 BC). Ekbatana, 715 BC

But Ekbatana, the capital of the Median empire, did actually exist, didn't it? Yes, though probably not as Herodotus shows it to us:

It is located on a pleasant hill from which there is a view of the surrounding landscape. If we want to reach the center of town, we must pass through seven walls, which grow taller the closer they are to the center.

Each of the concentric walls represents the social strata in a strict hierarchy, and at the same time they symbolize the planets known at the time and are painted in symbolic colors: white for Jupiter, black for Mercury, purple for Saturn, blue for Venus, orange for Mars, green for the Moon, and gold for the Sun.

Brentjes 1993.

One additional basic motif recurs throughout the entire history of the city: the wall. Its original function was material: protection, initially from animals, but later from attacking, advancing enemies. But even in Herodotus there is an added, symbolic, significance that occasionally replaces that of the wall as fortification: In Herodotus, the seven walls represent society, the sky, the cosmos. Later the wall becomes a metaphor for protection, security, safety, autonomy, power.

2. Antiquity

Plato (428/427–348/347 BC). *The Republic* (*Politeia*, c. 400 BC)

Plato at first explains the idea of the city, of society, to us. For one thing, in *The Republic* we are not moving through streets and squares, past splendid, ornate houses and temples. The form of what Plato considers the best state is architecturally invisible, it is a building of human virtues. The foremost of these is justice, which will bring well-being to the politei – the citizen. The state also needs to exist as an idea.

And Plato teaches us the manifold nature of Eros in society: a thoughtful love for beauty, the urge for truth and knowledge, the passion of the senses. Human beings must emulate the fundamental virtues that correspond to the three parts of the psyche: The attribute of the rational part is the striving for knowledge, the virtue of wisdom; the attribute of the will to self-assertion is bravery, manliness; and that of the capacity for desire is presence of mind and justice. To correspond to the three parts of the psyche there are three estates: craftsmen, farmers, warriors, or, seen from a different perspective, the teaching profession, agriculture, and the military profession.

Another trinity is based on the tripartite nature of the function of the psyche to which the estates and the parts of the bodies are assigned: Spirit – head – ruler, courage – breast – guardian, desire – belly – worker. And Plato offers us yet another synopsis: Learning – truth – knowledge – philosophy. Wanting – power – fame – victory. Love – desire – enjoyment – public spirit.

The wellsprings of all human evils are the craving for money and possessions, and the struggle for women. In principle authority must not be abolished – but we ask ourselves who is to be the ruler. Plato gives us the answer: »*If philosophers do not become kings in the states, or those who are now called kings and rulers do not become true and genuine philosophers, and if state power and philosophy are not one and the same, then there will be no end to evils for the states and probably also for the human race, and the state, too, will probably fail to thrive and see the light of day.*«

Although Plato's state primarily exists as an idea, the city-state takes a concrete shape, though only as a utopia, and Plato guides us through a perfectly planned city.

We are on the island of Crete, amazed that the city has no defense wall. Yet this is understandable: It is a city of peace. Yet in principle Plato is not opposed to the building of walls: »*If people absolutely have to have a wall, the construction of private housing may, from the outset, be designed in such a way that the entire city forms a single ring of wall in which all the residential buildings have the same design and stand on the same line, thus providing good protection in the direction of the streets; on the one hand, when the entire city looks like a single building, the view is very lovely, and also this makes it easier to guard the city and thus gives each individual and the community as a whole considerably more security.*«

As for the form of the city, Plato places great confidence in the artists: »*A city can never attain bliss if it is not designed by painters who follow the divine model.*«

Plato imagines the city as having simple geometry and above all the circle as its formal basis. The city is inhabited by 5,040 families and no more – admittedly that includes the suburbs. It is organized in concentric circles. The residential areas and agricultural areas are equally apportioned. Each family has a house in the city or nearby with a piece of land, but in the country the family owns a second house with a piece of land.

The state is led by regents or »guardians«, and these possess outstanding physical and intellectual qualities. They share their goods, houses, and meals, and know no avarice or greed – that would create division among them and distract them from their duties. They own only what is absolutely necessary, but in no case do they have individual housing and storerooms. Rather, everyone has access to their rooms. They also own no gold or silver, indeed they never even touch it, for they carry it in their heart.

But what about partnership and family in the ideal state? Plato explains the system to us. Admittedly it appears very rigid to us. »The ruler selects the couples suitable for procreation. The women range in age from 20 to 40, the men between 40 and 55.«

And we find the eugenic practice more than disconcerting: »*The best women shall have sexual relations with the best men as often as possible, while the constitutionally weakest men shall have sex with the constitutionally weakest women as infrequently as possible. The children of the former must be reared, but not those of the latter, if the herd is to be absolutely thoroughbred. Special holidays and sacrificial festivals have been designated, when brides and bridegrooms are brought together. The number of marriages is determined by the government.*«

Children do not belong to the parents, but to everyone. All elders are their educators and the state itself educates the children – it does so in public institutions – thus guaranteeing that education includes not only learning and knowledge, but that the idea of what is good and justice are its basis. However, if children are born of unauthorized unions, they are killed. Chronically ill persons are also killed, with their consent.

The goal of all education is nobility of mind, and consequently a harmonious personality, with genuine love for beauty. We are surprised to realize that men and women receive the same education, and that no profession is exclusively the domain of men. »*If women are to be educated for the same types of work as men, they must also receive the same training*«, argues Plato. Accordingly women, too, must be given training in the fine arts and gymnastics. Women, including older women, train naked on the wrestling grounds, and there is nothing ridiculous about it.

Training in the fine arts and gymnastics continues until the age of 20, while education in mathematics goes on till 30. By that age, young people understand the idea of good. The philosopher kings have been gathering experience in the civil service and in warfare until their 50th year.
We are taken aback when we see that the chosen women belong to all men jointly and that the children, too, belong to the entire community: A father does not know his child, nor the child its father. And, again with astonishment, we learn that women and children join the men to go to war, because war is a good education for the children. Those who distinguish themselves in battle receive the victor's laurels. They may kiss everyone, and are kissed by everyone. And during the campaign, no one they want to love, male or female, refuses them.

Lack of possessions, the fact that women and children are shared by the community, and equal education and professional opportunities for everyone guarantee the social existence of the state, we learn in *The Republic*.

Servier 1971; Freyer 1936; Berneri 1950, 1971; Plato 1974; Brentjes 1993; Eaton 2001.

In the journeys that follow we will constantly encounter the fact that utopias arise from a critique of specific social, political, and cultural conditions: They are ideal positions that counter prevailing circumstances. That is also true of the work of Plato. We must not overlook the similarity of *The Republic* and Plato's Atlantis. We can hardly fail to see the influence of Plato's ideas of the state. Especially the idea of communally shared property is like a red thread running through many utopias up to the present day. The city's simple geometry, and particularly the form of the circle, along with the square which is of Roman origin, is an archetype that is not characteristic of utopian city builders alone. These geometric forms have also been the basic premises in architectural planning through the ages, with very different motivations.

Euhemeros (c. 340–260 BC). Sacred History (*Hiera anagrapha*, c. 300 BC)

We now go on a distant journey, even further than Alexander the Great as he roamed through the world, further east on the oceans.

From »Arabia felix« we put to sea and sail south. We pass many islands, and land on one of them. Later we discover its name: It is called Panchaia.

People here live very differently than we are accustomed to living. They have a strictly hierarchical social structure, consisting of three strata, a kind of castes: Priests are at the head, and strangely enough this group also includes artists and craftsmen. Farmers are the next group, followed finally by warriors and herdsmen. Nevertheless, no land is privately owned, everything belongs to everybody, but each individual owns a house and garden. Manufactured goods and the produce of the fields are collected and fairly redistributed by the priests. What is wonderful here is that the soil produces crops without sowing and cultivation.

The laws that lead to bliss and the rules that govern life come directly from Zeus. They are recorded on a golden pillar in the temple.

Freyer 1936; Brentjes 1993.

During the centuries that follow, we keep encountering the idea that the ideal society can develop only on an island. The ideal city, the ideal state, must be separate, apart from the rest of the world. In this case, the island is assigned a specific locality – it is present-day Yemen – but many of these islands, like the legendary Atlantis, cannot be tied to a geographic locale, or not exactly.

Euhemeros from Messene was one of the Cyrenaicans. They do not reject the intellect, but primarily seek physical pleasure and trust only the perceptions of their own senses.

Iambulos. The Seven Islands of the Sun, 2nd century BC

The Seven Islands are in the Indian Ocean, in an »Arabia felix«, a peaceful country where it is always summer. They are surrounded by sweet water, and day and night resemble each other. An abundant nature, fertile and generous, ensures a carefree lifestyle. Oil and wine are plentiful, rare plants and fruit delight the eye and the palate. And because nature is healthful, all the people also have beautiful physiques. They are much taller than we are and live for up to 150 years. They live in a community where property is shared and groups of 400 form a kind of village led by an elder, a type of king. However, they are divided into three castes.

The people are free of hatred and war, for they are all equal: In the community, none is another's master, all crops and manufactured goods are distributed equally and fairly, and all people have access to knowledge and to faith. Marriage and family are considered to be superfluous, for they all live together with all the others and the children are raised by the entire community. After birth babies are switched so that the mothers do not know their children.

The children must submit to a test of courage, and only if they pass are they permitted to continue living in the community. Old and sick people choose death voluntarily: They lie down on a poisonous plant and pass away.

People have a split tongue that enables them to carry on two conversations at the same time, in all human languages. What is more, they can also imitate the voices of all the birds. However, when they have heard enough, they can clap their ears shut and stop listening.

On the islands of the sun there are no law courts, and since everyone lives peacefully together, there are no poor people.

Every islander is obliged to work, but there are no slaves. People take regular turns doing the work, and there is no such thing as division of work.

The people know that they owe everything to the sun, and so they worship a sun god as the state religion prescribes.

In the middle of the island there is also a temple to Zeus Triphyios, and the history of the Hellenic gods is recorded on a golden pillar.

Freyer 1936; Mohl 1960; Manguel 1981; Brentjes 1993.

The above outline makes it clear that frequently enough »ideal« communities – from a present-day perspective – are endowed with all kinds of cruelty, and we shall often encounter eugenic processes that seem inhuman to us. We feel there is an obvious contradiction in the fact that all people are completely equal, and yet are divided into three castes.

Marcus Vitruvius Pollio (c. 84 BC– ?). The real city (*De architectura libri decem*, 33/22 BC)

In the Vitruvian city we are in an absolutely healthy and rational city. Vitruvius instructs us in his own words how to plan a city: »When planning a city the first thing to keep in mind is choosing a healthy location. A place is healthy when it is located high above sea level, exposed neither to fog nor hoarfrost, facing neither hot, nor cold, but rather moderate directions. In planning a city one must be very careful to avoid regions where hot breezes blow.«

Vitruvius also gives clear reasons for the fundamental form of a city: »One must plan cities neither in the form of a square, nor with projecting corners, but rather in a circle, so that one can see the enemy from several points. The towers must be made round or many-cornered. Square towers are quickly wrecked by machines, for the battering ram damages the corners, while machines have no effect on round towers. In a harbor town the marketplace must be close to the harbor, but in an inland town it must be placed in the middle of town.«

With all these clear considerations, however, significance and symbol are not excluded.

»Depending on the gods to whom they are dedicated, the temples are to be erected with deliberation and care in the city and outside it. Basilicas are to be placed near the markets, facing the warmest directions. The treasury, prison, and council house are to be connected to the market. Once the market is laid out, a very healthy location is to be chosen for the theater.«

The many practical suggestions of Vitruvius also include the most important instructions regarding civil engineering as well as the description of ingenious machines and astronomical data. Now we'd like to hear about the actual nature of architecture from the master's own lips, and he is happy to oblige:

4. Vitruvius, design of a city. Illustration by Cesare Cesariano, 1521.

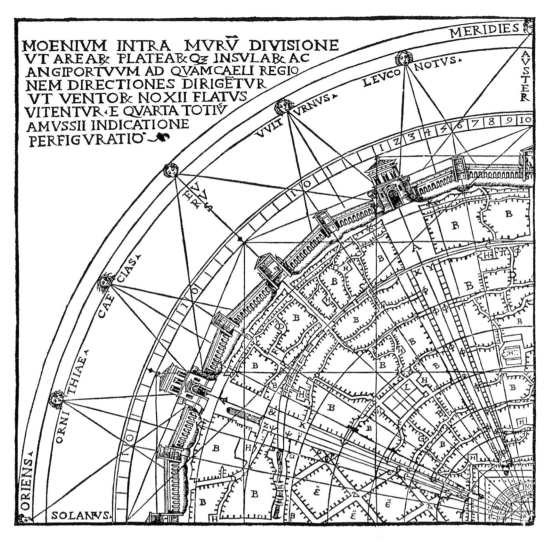

»The essence of architecture consists of six points: arrangement – ordinatio, disposition – dispositio, harmony – eurythmia, symmetry – symmetria, decorum – decor, and scale – distributio.«
Vitruvius 1826, 1960.

We get to know Vitruvius as the first »functionalist« of the city, and his elementary systematology has remained fascinating and valid to this day.

To call Vitruvius a »theoretician« is hardly justified. He does not develop a scholarly theory, but offers us a practical architectural handbook. No drawings, sketches, or illustrations by Vitruvius have been handed down to us, and thus a wide field of interpretations was open from the 16th to the 18th century, and we can see how far views diverge. Among the most important illustrations are those by Jocundus (Fra Giocondo) 1511; Cesariano 1521; Barbaro 1556; Perrault 1684; Galiani 1758; and Newton 1791.

5. Beatus of St. Severin, The New Jerusalem according to the Revelation of St. John, c. 776.
6. Hartmann Schedl, *Jerusalem*, from the *Weltchronik*, Nuremberg, 1493.
7. Herbert Boeckl, *Apocalypse*, Seckau Abbey, Austria, 1952–60.

3. The Middle Ages, c. 50–1300

Saint John the Baptist (c. 50). Patmos: Apocalypse
Saint Beatus of St. Severin (c. 776). The heavenly Jerusalem
Hartmann Schedl (1440–1514). Jerusalem, 1493
Herbert Boeckl (1894–1966). The Apocalypse in Seckau, 1952–1960

Saint John is given a revelation of the City of God. It is Jerusalem and at the same time it is Heaven – and yet the account provides the facts and figures of its construction. For the moment, however, John sees the horrors of the fateful horsemen:

>»Now I saw when the Lamb opened one of the seven seals, and I heard one of the living creatures say, as with a voice of thunder, Come! And I saw, and behold, a white horse, and its rider had a bow; and a crown was given to him, and he went out conquering and to conquer.
>
>When he opened the second seal, I heard the second living creature say, Come! And out came another horse, bright red; its rider was permitted to take peace from the earth, so that men should slay one another; and he was given a great sword.
>
>When he opened the third seal, I heard the third living creature say, Come! And I saw, and behold, a black horse, and its rider had a balance in his hand.
>
>When he opened the fourth seal, I heard the voice of the fourth living creature say, Come! And I saw, and behold, a pale horse, and its rider's name was Death, and Hades followed him; and they were given power over a fourth of the earth, to kill with sword and with famine and with pestilence and with wild beasts of the earth.«

However, we see not only the horrifying horsemen of the Apocalypse. We are granted a most glorious sight. With St. John and one of the seven angels we catch sight of the ideal city, heavenly Jerusalem.

And here is the vision of the holy city that is like Heaven: »*Then came one of the seven angels who had the seven bowls full of the seven plagues, and spoke to me, saying, Come, I will show you the Bride, the wife of the Lamb. And in the Spirit he carried me away to a great, high moun-*

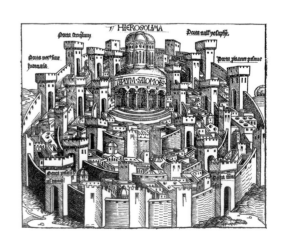

tain and showed me the holy city Jerusalem coming down out of heaven from God, having the glory of God, its radiance like a most rare jewel, like a jasper, clear as crystal. It had a great, high wall, with twelve gates, and at the gates twelve angels, and on the gates the names of the twelve tribes of the sons of Israel were inscribed; on the east three gates, on the north three gates, on the south three gates, and on the west three gates. And the wall of the city had twelve foundations, and on them the twelve names of the twelve apostles of the Lamb.

And the angel who talked to me had a measuring rod of gold to measure the city and its gates and walls. The city lies foursquare, its length the same as its breadth; and he measured the city with his rod, twelve thousand stadia [c. 2,5 km]. And He measured its wall, a hundred and forty cubits [c. 100 m] by a man's measure, that is, an angel's. The wall was built of jasper, while the city was pure gold, clear as glass. The foundations of the wall of the city were adorned with every jewel; the first was jasper, the second sapphire, the third agate, the fourth emerald, the fifth onyx, the sixth carnelian, the seventh chrysolite, the eighth beryl, the ninth topaz, the tenth chrysoprase, the eleventh jacinth, the twelfth amethyst. And the twelve gates were twelve pearls, each of the gates made of a single pearl, and the street of the city was pure gold, transparent as glass.

And I saw no temple in the city, for its temple is the Lord God Almighty and the Lamb. And the city has no need of sun or moon to shine upon it, for the glory of God is its light, and its lamp is the Lamb.«

St. Beatus of St. Severin very conscientiously reproduced John's city. It is a geometric city, an intimation of the earthly city, the »urbs quadrata« of sinful Rome, so despised by John. Here, however, we are in the promised, divine city that is to come. And we see the twelve gates with the twelve apostles, and the angels look over the city wall. In the center, though, there is no building, for it is reserved for the Lamb of Christ.

Much later, at the end of the 15th century, Hartmann Schedl introduces us to a completely different Jerusalem.

The city plan, now round, signifies cosmic perfection, and the Temple of Solomon in the middle is protected by three concentric walls between which the houses press forward.

And in the most recent past, yet another artist examines the apocalypse: In the Angel Chapel of the Basilica of Seckau, Styria, Austria, Herbert Boeckl shows us his version of the Secret Revelation, 1952–1960.

Will this heavenly Jerusalem remain closed to us forever here on earth? No: There is the magnificent anticipation of the city of God in this world – the medieval cathedral. It is more than a building, indeed, more than a city. It is the divine cosmos. And this heaven is inhabited by the Trinity, by the innumerable throng of saints, and, at their head, the Queen of Heaven, the Mother of God.

Almost exclusively associated with the concept of the »Apocalypse«, to this day, are prophecies of horror, particularly the visions of the horsemen of the Apocalypse. For centuries, artists, led by Albrecht Dürer, have been preoccupied with the Apocalypse, though mostly only with the sinister horsemen. If we view them as a prophetic utopia, there is no doubt that they have long since become a reality a thousand times over. Yet Saint John gives us great hope: His heavenly Jerusalem is filled with splendor and magnificence.

Saint Augustine (354–430). *The City of God (De civitate dei, 426)*

There are two cities, as it were, two kingdoms of the spirit, and two wills as well, and time after time Augustine was forced to experience the conflict between them within himself. Two interwoven *civitates* exist: one earthly, the other celestial. Here is how Augustine expresses this conflict: »*Two kinds of love have founded the two kingdoms: the worldly kingdom was founded by a self-love intensified to the point of contempt for God, while the celestial kingdom was founded by a love of God heightened to the point of contempt for oneself.*«

The Civitas Dei exists in tension to the Civitas terrenum, the earthly kingdom. True, the latter is a power structure willed by God, and yet also an unnatural realm of evil. For only »*in the divine kingdom is there no other human wisdom but piety*«.

»Of all that is visible, the world is the largest. We can see that the world exists; we believe that God exists.«

Two different kingdoms which are opposed to each other have evolved. Some live according to the flesh, others according to the spirit, or else some live according to human beings, the others according to God.

One person seeks fame among human beings, while for another the highest praise of God is the witness of conscience.

Only after the Judgment Day will the blessed create the Civitas Dei, opposed to which there is the worldly kingdom, an order that is necessary only for the fallen and is destined to perish. »Mother Church« is not yet the kingdom of God. It still comprises the just and the unjust, but it is the imperfect image of the kingdom of God and prepares the way for it.

The kingdom of God is made visible in the Church, but is not identical with its external form. And once more Augustine explains the dualistic area of conflict: »*These two different tendencies (amores), one directed toward God, the other in the reverse direction; one selfless, the other fixated on private things; one submissive to God, the other lusting to be like him; one peaceful, the other full of turmoil; one wishing equal benefit for oneself and one's neighbor, the other scheming to make the neighbor submissive to oneself; one intent on the benefit of one's neighbor, the other on one's own; – these two tendencies began with the angels and make up the difference between the two types of citizenry (civitates) founded in the human race, that of the just and that of sinners. Since the beginning of world time, both groups have been intermingled. At the Last Judgment both will be separated from each other.*«

The kingdom of God is not a place of refuge from worldly passions. Rather, it is a mission to act for those who are strong enough to fight the good fight.

Even if we live in expectation of the future kingdom, we must nevertheless strive for justice in this world as well, Augustine states: »*If each person is not granted what is his, if in other words justice is brushed aside, then what are kingdoms but big bands of robbers and what are bands of robbers but small kingdoms that can grow large when desperate men join them? Such a band of robbers after a conquest calls itself a kingdom, which name does not grant them absolution for their misdeed, but does give them impunity.*«

Augustine knows that the kingdom of God cannot be manifested on earth, not in the kingdoms of this world: »*There will always be this worldly kingdom and a society of people who live according to human beings, and it will not stop until the end of this world. However, a rebirth will take the kingdom of God, which is in exile in this world, to another world whose children neither beget nor are born.*«

Yet even in the worldly state, community is of elementary significance: »*There are three stages of human community: the house, the state, the earth. Thus in the worldly kingdom all use of worldly things aims at the enjoyment of earthly peace, while in the heavenly kingdom the aim is the enjoyment of eternal peace.*«

Even on earth, peace is a central concern: »*The highest good of the kingdmom of God is eternal, perfect peace. This is not the peace that mortals experience between cradle and grave; this is a peace in which immortals live, above all suffering. Happiness is found in peace, peace in justice, justice in love, love in virtue.*«

Augustinus 1963; *Visionen und Utopien* 2002/03; Baumann 1967; Servier 1971.

People have always tried to create »kingdoms of God« – but how »godly« were these kingdoms really? The Catholic Papal States were a strong political reality, but have long since shrunk to a symbolic dimension. The Islamic kingdom of God, Iran, is a powerful factor in today's world, and Hinduism, too, shows tendencies toward a kingdom of God. But how far are these states from St. Augustine's idea? For Augustine does not expect the true kingdom of God to be perfected in time and on earth: Seen from this perspective he is a realist, believing that the true kingdom of God will be realized at the end of time.

Along with Plato it was Augustine who influenced many subsequent ideas about the ideal society. In Augustine's dualisms, there may be echoes of Manichaeism, which Augustine subscribed to for a while.

Augustine's »two different tendencies« have become a reality a hundred times over in the constantly recurrent dualisms of the human race: the emperor and the pope, Christendom and Islam, East and West, capitalism and communism – to name only a few.

Saint Brendan (?–577/583). The holy, promised land (*Terra repromissionis sanctorum*), the good land (Bona Terra, 6th century)

»In an old book I read of wonders on an island in the West«, St. Brendan from Ireland tells us, »but I burned the book because I did not believe the stories. Now, as punishment, I have been roaming the oceans and islands for seven years.«

We're glad to accompany the saint on his adventures. Our ship plows through the oceans for many days and nights, we sail from island to island, and we lost our way a long time ago. We are sailing through total darkness across the thick, viscous »Liver Ocean«, just as it says in the old book. And we seek paradise on earth. What unbelievable adventures, what strange experiences during our journey, on the ocean and the islands! We are beset by devils, and saints console us, dragons and griffins attack us, volcanoes erupt and icebergs bar our way, flying fish and sea-horses threaten our ship. Yet with God's help we overcome all perils. Finally, after fifteen days, land is in sight!

Even before we arrive on the »Terra repromissionis sanctorum«, we see the bottom of the sea shining with gold and jewels, and there countless precious stones lie on the beach. The ocean surges against tall marble cliffs. In the distance gleams a mountain, no doubt of pure gold. We see a high wall that appears to be topped with gold, and topaz, emeralds, and sardonyxes flash on its stones. And we land on a wonderful island. It must be the island of the blessed: Happiness and beauty dwell here, no doubt. And now we hear the voice of an angel of God, saying: »God has given you what you are seeking – the promised land.«

The gate to the city that lies on a mountaintop is guarded by two dragons and over the archway a sword balances, swaying alarmingly. Now the gate opens and a young man of great beauty comes toward us: This is an angel of God giving us permission to enter. Led by him, we enter a city with beautiful gardens: We have found paradise. In the middle of the gardens is the palace. We enter unhindered and find a table lavishly set with food and drink. Invisible hands serve us and we seem to be welcome. Every day we discover new wonders, new glories, a succession of gardens and palaces. The miracles of the natural world delight us.

In spite of all this splendor, we stay only seven months, when the journey continues and we arrive at an island that has big flocks of sheep. Our crew wants to roast a sheep on the fire. Suddenly, the island sinks – it was the back of an enormous whale.

The journey continues as we reach a terrifying island: Here is the entrance to hell and poisonous fish, fire-breathing sea serpents, and diabolical birds are part of the pack of infernal creatures from whom we manage to escape.

Far away in the Atlantic Ocean, on a tiny island, lives a hermit who gives us strength and edification. And he also gives us directions to the true Promised Island. It is the insula uvarum, the island of wine and Bacchus, and we are able to take on board a rich load of grapes. On this island, too, we meet saints, and in a cave we awaken a giant from sleep. This is another kind of earthly paradise.

After seven years we again return to our home country – have we really discovered paradisiac islands?

Traum 2003.

Saint Brendan was the abbot of Clonfert near Galway, and he describes his image of earthly paradises. He does so in the form of »adventures«, which were popular even in his day, and the idea of the lovely, peaceful island will accompany us to the present day. It is impossible to determine the locality of many of them, and they will forever remain utopias. Pagan Celtic traditions are mingled with Christian elements and were the reason for the book's popularity in Brendan's time.

A Benedictine abbot. The Monastery of St. Gallen, 719, 747, 820

»You're right«, agrees the venerable abbot, »when you include a monastery in your study of urban planning – and of course this is particularly true of St. Gallen. I'll be happy to take you on a tour.« Naturally we begin in the spiritual and architectural center, in the wonderful and yet so simple Carolingian church.

»We built a double choir, and thus God and the world, pope and emperor are present simultaneously«, continues the abbot. The magnificent church has three naves and two altars. While we are accustomed in early Christian churches to visit the church by following a consistent axial path, here we enter a semicircular vestibule that leads us to the entrances into the side aisles.

8. St. Brendan visits the Bona Terra, illumination, 6th century.

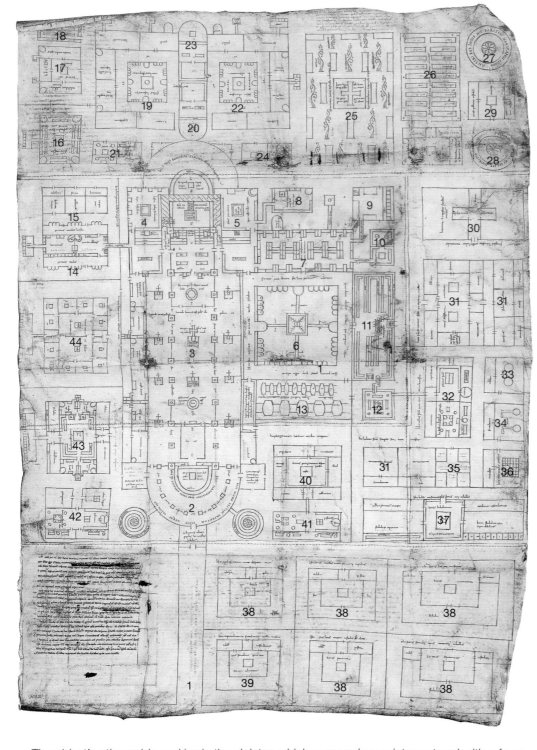

9. Early medieval ideal plan of a monastery, St. Gallen, Switzerland, c. 820. 1 entrance, 2 reception hall, 3 basilica, double-choir church with towers, 4 writing room (upper floor: library), 5 sacristy (upper floor: paraments), 6 cloister, 7 common room (*pisalis*; top floor: dormitory), 8 bakery for consecrated wafers, oil press, 9 privy, 10 laundry and bath house, 11 dining hall (refectory; top floor: vestiary), 12 kitchen, 13 storeroom for wine and beer, 14 abbot's house, 15 kitchen, cellar, bath of abbot's house, 16 house for bloodletting and purging patients, 17 doctors, apothecary, critically ill patients, 18 medicinal herb garden, 19 hospital, 20 hospital chapel, 21 hospital bath and kitchen, 22 novitiate 23 novitiate chapel, 24 novitiate bath and kitchen, 25 cemetery and orchard, 26 kitchen garden, 27 henhouse, 28 poultry house, 29 chicken and geese keeper, 30 granary, threshing floor, 31 workshops, 32 monks' bakery and brewery, 33 mill, 34 pounding floor, 35 granary, 36 drying kiln, 37 stable for horses and oxen, 38 stables for sheep, goats, and cows; pig pens, 39 servants' quarters, 40 inn for pilgrims, shelter for the poor, 41 brewery, bakery for the pilgrims and the poor, 42 kitchen, bakery, brewery for aristocratic guests, 43 house for aristocratic guests, 44 external school, for oblates.

The abbot's other pride and joy is the cloister, which surrounds a quiet courtyard with a fountain in its center. Adjacent to this spiritual architecture as it were is the worldly, or rather communal architecture: refectory, dormitory, parlatory, and, directly connected to these, the kitchen with adjoining rooms and storerooms, and access to the cellar.

Then comes the social part: a house and kitchen for the poor and for pilgrims.

»We must also fulfill a social mission outside the monastery community«, explains the abbot. »We provide room and board for the pilgrims on one hand and the poor on the other hand, and there's a separate kitchen for this purpose.«

There are special provisions for aristocratic guests: They have a comfortable house, their own kitchen and bakery, and a special beer is brewed for them.

»You will believe that we are completely autonomous when I show you the farm buildings«, says the abbot. And indeed what we have here is like a well-run farm, a fine little town: stables for horses and oxen, for geese and chickens, then barns and storerooms. Workshops and bakeries are cleverly located in close proximity, sizable areas are provided for the vegetable garden and medicinal herbs. We have now passed the hospital and the novitiate building and have reached the north side of the church. Here there are well-designed and friendly places where teaching and the healing of the sick take place. The house of the doctors is located between the house where bloodletting is performed and the herb garden.

To conclude the impressive tour, the abbot invites us to visit his beautiful house. As the man in charge of this fine institution with hundreds of monks he can afford his own wing, including a kitchen, cellar, and bath.

Stadt und Utopie 1982; Hecht 1982.

The plan does not represent the monastery of St. Gallen. Its name comes from the place where it was stored. This plan shows an ideal type. But hundreds of monasteries and convents were built in accordance with this type, exactly according to the particular rules of the orders, and so what we are looking at are worldwide and large-scale implementations of an idea.

In addition to the Benedictines, it was particularly the Cistercians who perfected the monastery plan worldwide in accordance with the reforms of Bernard of Clairvaux, developing a prototype with regional variations.

During the Baroque period, monasteries are considerably expanded, particularly in southern Germany and Austria, with additional functions: libraries, schools, collections, research centers, observatories, imperial suites, and more added to the monastic complex.

Honorius Augustodunensis. The Nova Terra of the Elucidarium, early 12th century

We are in the Nova Terra, in the new world – and it is now no longer the mirror of our sin. We live happy lives in a world free of sin, a wonderful enchanted garden. Roses and lilies and fragrant violets bloom eternally without wilting. In the center of the Nova Terra grows a huge mound of flowers.

There are no troubles and no pain – we are in the new paradise.

Vercelloni 1994.

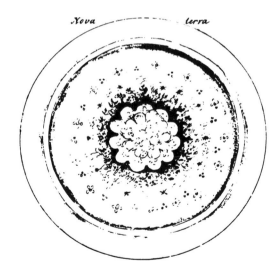

The monk's handbook, written in Latin, covers the sum total of 12th century Christian theology in the form of a dialogue. It has three main chapters: dogmatics, ethics, and eschatology. Not quite as paradisiacal is the division of the Church into three social strata: the good worshippers and teachers of the laws of God, the good defenders – nobles and knights – and the faithful workmen. The worldly masters are also in charge of spiritual things. But how can the ideal of true poverty be lived by the upper classes?

A garden is akin to a city: In their perfection both are divine and their return is a celestial event. The celestial garden is paradise, anticipated in the »hortus deliciarum«, the monastery garden. The heavenly city, on the other hand, is the cathedral – heavenly Jerusalem.

Joachim of Fiore (1130–1202). The Third Era, 1180

Joachim is convinced that there are three statuses, three eras: »After the era of the Father, the First Era of patriarchs, kings, and slaves, of power and fear, which we know from the Old Testament, there followed the Second Era, the era of the Son and of love and mercy in the New Testament. This era, however, will end with the year 1260. That is the dawn of the New Era, and this will be the Third Era, the era of enlightenment and freedom, of friends and mystics, which will last a thousand years until the end of time.« This Third Era will be the interim between our world and the end of all time. Joachim believes in the historical fulfillment of the »evangelium aeternum« and prepares the way for Christian spiritualization. Thus hope springs up for a world that keeps unfolding toward the good.

Yet Joachim also has a vision of a city. In his city believers await the Third Era. They will experience a mystical democracy without overlords and without a Church – an era of spiritual perfection and love, where there are no poor people or rich people.

From a bird's-eye view we see a fine panorama of Joachim's city: It is a cross with a kind of predella. Thus the city is dedicated to Christ from the outset. In the middle is a central building, and the four oratories or houses form something like a Romanesque cross. The predella takes up

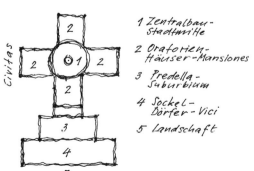

1 Zentralbau-Stadtmitte
2 Oratorien-Häuser-Mansiones
3 Predella-Suburbium
4 Sockel-Dörfer-Vici
5 Landschaft

the *suburbium,* and the base with the villages provides a connection to the surrounding landscape.

But we do not meet only priests and monks here: As in the heavenly Jerusalem all kinds of people – families, craftspeople, farmers – live here in an atmosphere of mutual assistance and respect.

»We live in small communities«, explains Joachim. Not without pride he sees this city as an »ark in the ocean of traditional Christendom«.

The inhabitants of this city live like the early Christians: »They share everything«, including food and clothing. All inhabitants are obliged to work, but the work is not toil.

»Among these Christians no idle folk shall be found. Those who do not work according to their capacity, however, shall be accused by the master and rebuked by everyone«, Joachim explains one of the strict rules.

Bloch 1973; Seibt 2001.

Joachim of Fiore, the Calabrian mystic, first formulated the doctrine of Christ's thousand-year reign on earth, the »Millennium«. Joachim's influence on his contemporaries, on subsequent religious movements, and on utopians will no doubt continue to be controversial. Yet presumably Thomas Müntzer, the Hussites, Albigensians, and Anabaptists were influenced by his teachings. Again and again we shall be struck by the fact that purely literary manifestations have had a considerable influence on later, quite concrete concepts.

At any rate Ernst Bloch calls Joachim's notions the »most momentous social utopia of the Middle Ages« and believes they had a »definite influence on Thomas More«.

The social communism we encounter here is a common theme in utopias through the centuries and is still present now.

The idea of the three eras became a firm component of European social mythology and philosophy of history, for example, in the works of Lessing, Hegel, and Dostoyevski. The idea of the Third Era is a philosophical idea that goes far beyond reality, but then inevitably includes political elements.

We meet the idea again in National Socialist thinking. Adolf Hitler founded the »Third Reich«. The first Reich (Empire) was the Holy Roman Empire, while the second was Bismarck's empire. Joachim was never alluded to, but Hitler's reference to the two preceding secular empires and the claim that his was the »Third Empire« has something magical and mythical abut it. And like Joachim, Hitler spoke with almost mystic enthusiasm of the »Thousand-Year Empire« that had already arrived but that would actually last more than a thousand years – an eternity as it were.

Saint Thomas Aquinas (1225–1274). The wise *Government of Princes* (*De regimine principum,* 1266)

What shall a man do to become happy in the city? We are surprised that Thomas not only makes faith a condition for this happiness, but rather names two fundamental stipulations: ethical principles and material security.

»Each person shall act in accordance with virtue and take care that material goods are available.« And thus Thomas also sees the conditions for the city quite pragmatically. It shall have abundance in two ways: It must be located in a fertile region and make sensible use of trade. Yet the moral dangers inherent in trade must not be overlooked.

Among the doctors of the Church, Thomas is the great realist. For him the general cannot be obtained directly, but rather only by way of abstraction from the insights of experience. Thomas's teachings are founded on natural reason. Natural law can be realized by practical reason, and it is from this perspective that the state, authority, and society should be seen.

12, 13. Gustav Doré, illustrations of Dante's Paradise, 1321, 1870.

4. Renaissance, c. 1300–1650

4.1. Italy

Dante Alighieri (1265–1321). The paradise (Il paradiso, *La divina commedia*, 1321), interpreted by Gustave Doré (1832–1883)

We've left behind the Inferno und Purgatory, to which Dante and Virgil have accompanied us. Beatrice is our new guide to Paradise. Like the Inferno it is built of gigantic circles and rings, though not characterized by torment and punishment, but by the bliss of love, the grace of angels, the sanctity of virtues. Here is Dante speaking to us:

> »*Soon as its final word the blessed flame*
> *Had rais'd for utterance, straight the holy mill*
> *Began to wheel, nor yet had once revolv'd,*
> *Or ere another, circling, compass'd it,*
> *Motion to motion, song to song, conjoining,*
> *Song, that as much our muses doth excel,*
> *Our Sirens with their tuneful pipes, as ray*
> *Of primal splendour doth its faint reflex.*
> *As when, if Juno bid her handmaid forth,*
> *Two arches parallel, and trick'd alike*
> *Span the thin cloud, the outer taking birth*
> *From that within (in manner of that voice*
> *Whom love did melt away, as sun the mist),*
> *And they who gaze, presageful call to mind*
> *The compact, made with Noah, of the world*
> *No more to be o'erflow'd; about us thus*
> *Of sempiternal roses, bending, wreath'd*
> *Those garlands twain, and to the innermost*
> *E'en thus th'external answered.*«
> (Canto XII)

And, continuing our journey, we encounter a mighty rose: It is Paradise and Heaven and is at the same time the terraced arena of the saints, the angels, the transfigured, children and women. We meet Eve, Mary, Rachel, Sarah, Rebecca, and Dante's companion Beatrice.

> »*In fashion, as a snow-white rose, lay then*
> *Before my view the saintly multitude*
> *Which in his own blood Christ espous'd.*«
> (Canto XXXI)

It is more than Paradise, it is the cosmos we cross: The seven rings are the seven planets, the crystal sky no longer has any stars, no shapes or spirits; divine peace now prevails in the movement of the concentric, rotating circles in which the hierarchies of angels soar, each of them responsible for a circle that lies below it.

Beyond the nine heavens, in the empyreum, beyond all that can be known, we enter the truth, which is hardly veiled at this point. Radiant light unites everything.

In the center of the universe soars Earth, and above it are seven transparent spheres with the planets, the Moon, and the Sun.

We travel through the rings and the closer we get to the center, the more the world resembles Paradise.

Dante 1935.

We've seen the city as a circle or composed of rings earlier, in Atlantis, and we shall encounter it many more times. Yet Dante goes one step further: The Inferno and Paradise, too, consist of huge, three-dimensional rings, and in the final analysis the entire cosmos follows this divine design.

14. Ambrogio Lorenzetti, Good city government, Siena, 1337. Council hall of the Palazzo Pubblico.
15. Leon Battista Alberti, *De re aedificatoria*, column as monument, 1452. Building of a tower, plate X, figs. 1, 2.

Ambrogio Lorenzetti (1285, 1290?–1348). Good city government (*L'allegoria del buono e del cattivo governo*, 1337)

The people has just successfully defended its freedom and independence and preserved its democratic basis – they are certain of a benevolent city government.

Inside the city walls are the well-built houses, painted in many colors, and having high windows. The dark background of the windows seems strange to us, as though they were merely empty openings in the walls, without a room behind them. The happy inhabitants of the city walk about in the squares. They are at work, and work is not a hardship. They are free and their supervisors are intelligent managers. We see them plying their trade, buying and selling, loading their mules or driving their sheep and rams before them. Construction workers are busy finishing building a house between tall towers. The women, holding hands, dance a merry round dance – or are they playing a lively game to the rhythm of a tambourine?

Tod / Wheeler 1978; Vercelloni 1994; Eaton 2001.

The belief in the benevolent ruler, whether he governs a state or a city, is one of the permanent utopias we find in all periods. As a matter of fact, very frequently the Italian city-states may have turned this ideal – as shown in the frescoes by Ambrogio Lorenzetti in the council hall of the Palazzo Pubblico in Siena – into a reality.

Leon Battista Alberti (1404–1472). The practical city (*De re aedificatoria*, 1452)

Alberti's city fulfills a very pragmatic dream: »*Of the disadvantages of a city not one is present. And of all the things that are desirable for the necessities of life none shall be lacking.*«

Alberti at first explains to us the location of his ideal city, and clearly we can hear echoes of the theses of Vitruvius: The city is built exactly according to the directions of the winds and takes the climate into account: »*In particular the air we breathe will contribute wonderfully to our health if it is as clean as possible. And it goes without saying that air is healthiest when it is most unspoilt. Incidentally, I prefer a region which it is possible to access in many and varied ways, allowing one to bring in all that is necessary by ship, draft animals, and wagons both in summer and winter as easily as possible. Also the region itself should be neither damp as a result of too great an abundance of water nor too dry, but favorably tempered.*«

The city is round in circumference, which makes it most spacious. True, we are astonished that the population is divided into classes: The scholars and the wealthy, the soldiers and leading employees and the subordinates live in very different homes. However all the houses are very harmonious, so that one could »*neither add or subtract anything without making them less pleasing*«.

The streets curve gently. As a result the façades produce a more pleasing effect, and moreover there are defense advantages in street battles.

In designing buildings, three things are of utmost importance: functionality, durability, and beauty. We must distinguish between the different kinds of buildings: »*Some are public, others private, some holy, others profane, some are purely functional, others serve to ornament the city.*«

Alberti portrays life in the ideal city as very idyllic and peaceful: »*Here you can pursue the most stimulating studies, here you will have children and a loving family, here you will spend days of*

16. Leon Battista Alberti, *De re aedificatoria*, view of a landscape with cisterns, 1553. Illustration from the French edition.

work and leisure, here all the threads of your life come together. That is why I am of the opinion that in human life, beside hard work, there is nothing to which one should devote greater care, effort, and diligence than to living happily in a beautiful home with one's family. And who could claim to have a good life if he pays no heed to all I have said?«

Alberti 1485, 1553, 1912, 1975; Borsi 1975; *Stadt und Utopie* 1982; Vercelloni 1994; Rykwert 1994.

Once more the work of the architect is viewed with great expectations. What Alberti describes is almost identical with our present-day concept of »quality of life« and he portrays the kind of family harmony that has long since become very rare. The architect is seen as a great demiurge who can create both of these by virtue of the perfection of his work. We have long since stopped believing that. One thing that is noteworthy is the motivation for the winding streets: As is often the case with architecture, both aesthetic and functional arguments are cited.

17. Antonio Averlino, known as Filarete, Sforzinda, House of Vice and Virtue, 1461. Exterior, section.
18. Antonio Averlino, known as Filarete, Sforzinda, 1461. Temple.
19. Antonio Averlino, known as Filarete, Sforzinda, 1461. Floor plan.

Antonio Averlino, (Filarete, 1400–1469). Sforzinda (*Trattato di architettura*, 1461–1464)

We begin with a stroll through a pleasant landscape, for the city of Sforzinda is situated in a »*lovely, fertile valley*« with a river winding through it. The surrounding hills shelter the city from the winds.

The ground plan of the city is characterized by the great archetypes, the circle and the square: for the walls are formed from two squares turned toward each other in such a way as to form a star surrounded by a circle. Each side of the square is 3,500 m long. The center forms a square with the most important public buildings, pleasingly arranged: here, a magnificent church, next to it administrative buildings and schools. The Palazzo del Capitano and the Palazzo del Podestà are no longer surrounded by ramparts, but are placed among the houses of the citizens. Especially surprising is the fact that Filarete has borrowed features from Venice: the piazza and the markets and every other major street have navigable canals and there are colonnades along them.

From the square, sixteen major streets radiate outward. Eight of them go to the city gates, which are located in recessed corners. The intersections of the streets are enlarged into small squares, some of which feature a simple church or are used as marketplaces. Round towers mark the projecting corners of the city wall. Halfway down the major streets there is always an impressive building used for public functions. A fine central building is flanked by four minaret-like towers and has a touch of the Orient about it.

In the middle of Sforzinda is the House of Vice and Virtue, accessible to the public. The lower floors belong to vice, and thus we find a bordello, the apartments of the prostitutes, baths, but also a restaurant and a police station here. The seven upper floors, on the other hand, are devoted to the virtues: libraries, a theater, workrooms, and science rooms serve primarily the education of youth.

The city also has a labyrinth, a hospital, and the Casa di Sapienza, the House of Wisdom. To promote arts and crafts, a sufficient number of studios are available. This careful infrastructure is completed by the mint, the bank, and the prisons.

We are particularly interested in a long row of identical houses: This is the housing of the simple townspeople. Their houses are also arranged along a system of canals, and each has a little garden and its own well.

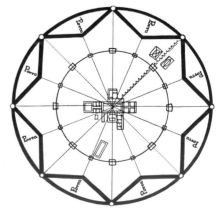

However, the citizens no longer live under the aspect of the »bonum commune«, but rather are subordinates, dependent on the power of the prince in whose honor and glory the city was built.

Tod/Wheeler 1978; Schumpp 1971; Cigola 1999; Eaton 2001.

Through the ages, architecture and city planning have been dependent on the favor and mercy, the money and power of the rulers. Even utopias need the princes' goodwill. Filarete dedicates his treatise to Lodovico Sforza, after whom the city is also named. Filarete became better known through his *Trattato di architettura* (1461–64), in which he published Sforzinda, than through his buildings, such as the Ospedale Maggiore in Milan.

Francesco di Giorgio Martini (1439–1501) and others. Model cities, c. 1475, 1500, 1530, 1580, 1590

»Yes, weapons are changing – and consequently so is defense – and therefore cities as well.« Thus Francesco, too, derives the forms of his cities primarily from matters related to fortification. »But that doesn't mean a city can't still be a work of art«, states Francesco.

At the outset, he explains the fundamental principles of his planning: »*A new city, in which everything still needs to be created, must, I believe, take in hand and decide almost the entire architecture, including details like temples and walls. As for the sanctuaries, they must be erected around the marketplace, and the entire town must be planned in a circular form up to the hills, for the sake of security and cleanliness. As for the design of private buildings, they should from the outset be built in such a way that the entire city forms one single wall and the residential houses, having the same height and same design, appear like a fortress on the street side. It is by no means an unpleasing picture for the eye when the entire town looks like a single house, and as far as its security is concerned, guarding such a city would become far easier.*«

Admittedly we find it quite impossible to inspect the host of Francesco's cities in detail, and for the time being we shall content ourselves with one. We've selected the one that represents a kind of architecturally geometrical archetype and whose basic plan has a very strict central structure – an octagon derived from a square. The corners of the city wall are marked by eight round towers, but four city gates are sufficient.

»The gates need to be defended, and that is why four are sufficient, and they lead to the four major streets that run into the central square«, explains Francesco. »I will make do without a central building: The octagonal square belongs to the townspeople for their markets and festivals. And the public buildings are placed here. The buildings have arcades and are magnificently ornamented.«

The cathedral and the town hall are here, and the stock exchange across from them. Clean industry can be located here as well, while polluting industry is moved to the outskirts of town. The baths and theaters, on the other hand, are spread out all over town, in smaller squares created at street intersections.

We would be glad to get to know the other towns as well. From a bird's-eye view it is at least approximately possible. Most cities over which we now fly are built on an octagon. Francesco shows us two possible street configurations: They run radially from a central square to the town wall or are arranged in a grid, a system already familiar to the Greeks. As far as possible, Francesco has diverted a river through the town and has added outworks to the walls. This way the octagon gets a longer axis in one dimension.

»We should view a completely different type of town«, advises Francesco: »I mean the mountain towns. The peak is crowned by a castle or church, and I have tried different systems of configuring the streets.«

And now Francesco has another surprise in store: We are flying toward the sea and can already see a sprawling harbor town. The massive fortification looks as though it were broken open, a spacious square, surrounded by monumental buildings, pushes forward toward the sea. Like powerful arms the breakwaters hug the harbor basin. Watchtowers or lighthouse towers stand in forward positions in the sea.

Not satisfied with Francesco's buildings alone, we are interested in several other Italian architects. But here too we can get only a few impressions during a flyby.

Baldassare Peruzzi (1481–1536) prefers the form of a decagon. He is hardly bothered by the fact that the streets do not correspond with the corner bastions. He does not leave the center empty, but places the castle with its corner towers on the large square.

So does Fra Giocondo (1433–1515): in the center there is a domed building. Fra Giocondo builds a double ring of walls around the city, but how will the gabled houses at the outer ring of wall protect themselves?

For Antonio di Sangallo (1482–1546) the military is important. The barracks are orientated toward a large central square, which he left empty in the version shown here.

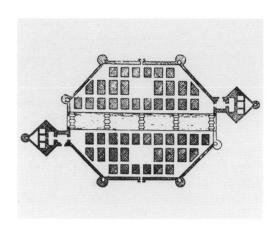 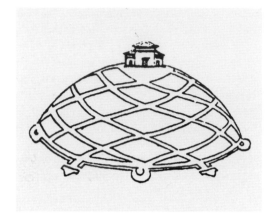 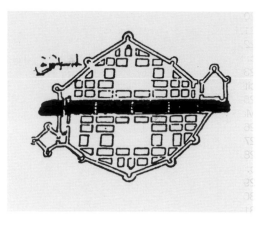

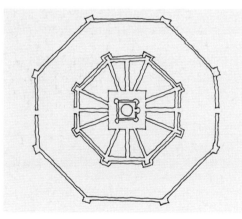  

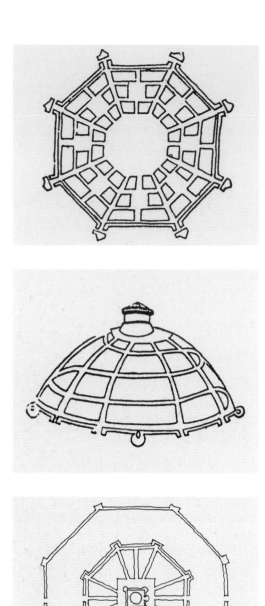 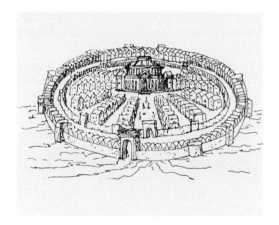 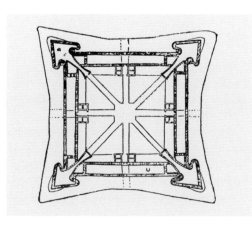

 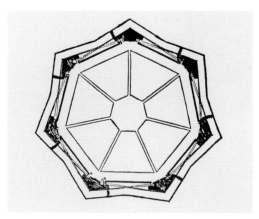

Buonaiuto Lorini (1543–1626) chooses a nonagon as a basic geometrical figure, while the center of the city is based on the hexagon. The result is that the city plan is peculiarly confusing. The church is given a dominant position.

Giovanni Battista Bartolomeo Belucci, called San Marino (1506–1554), tries a heptagon, but finds it easier to cope with a square.

We could go on flying for hours, but the basic types with which we have familiarized ourselves would soon be repeated.

Martini 1475; Münter 1957.

The wide range of possible variations proves that fortification determines the shape of the city only in part. Above all, we find the duality of concentric city and grid city interesting. We shall visit one of the most important implementations, Palmanova, in chapter 4.1.19.

Piero della Francesca (1410/20–1492). The ideal city space, 1480
Piero's students. The city of perspective, 1490

»This is the precise vantage point for seeing my city in its full beauty.« With these words Piero takes us to a very specific point in the city's beautiful, geometric marble pavement. »The city is not a closed spatial configuration, but an open space, and perspective is my method of bringing the city into the infinity of the landscape.«

We are now standing in an open hall. The roof is supported by four columns, the base is classically profiled, unlike the capitals, which show Egyptian influences. On the sides, corresponding to the columns, there are similarly designed wall pilasters, and the space between them is spanned by a completely plain round arch.

»Now look directly into the axis of the square!« Our eyes follow the friezes on the ground and are thus directed past the splendid façades of the palazzo straight at the sea, where two ships are waiting with their sails hoisted. Past these, we see the mountains, our gaze sweeps along the bottom of the valley for a short distance and ends in infinity. Not a single person can be seen in the square with its classic Renaissance façades. There is no a sign of life, only a little tree in the background peeking over the wall. It is early morning, and the city has not awakened yet.

With Piero's students we continue our tour of magnificent Renaissance cities. One hundred and fifty years after Lorenzetti the city is not a lively conglomeration, full of nooks and crannies, but a grandiose stage setting, rich in perspective, though to be sure the people are absent. But Piero or his student has fulfilled the great dream of the Renaissance. The pure central building, a harmoniously beautiful round temple, stands out self-assured against a backdrop of houses: The heritage and perfection of antiquity have finally been successfully recreated.

We continue our journey and come to a square that is no less magnificent. Here the architect has as it were conjured up the architectural history of his country, placing three buildings, like models, at the back of the stage without a visual relationship among them: the dark round building with the three arcades is reminiscent of the Roman Colosseum; in the middle there is a triumphal arch with three gates, and the hexagonal central building could be a Christian baptistry. The incredible spaciousness of the square with its flights of stairs, walls, and solitary columns underlines the isolation and solitude of the three quotations even more.

Tod / Wheeler 1978; Vercelloni 1994.

The wonderful architectural ideas of Renaissance painting in their fantastic dimensions could be implemented only rarely – and actually not until the Baroque period.

Two other Italians render the atmosphere of the huge, empty, almost eerie squares almost 450 years later: Giorgio de Chirico and Carlo Carrà.

Nor did Renaissance architects succeed in fulfilling the dream of the monumental round building modeled on the pantheon: The ideas of Bramante and Michelangelo for St. Peter fell victim to pragmatic considerations.

Andrea Palladio (1508–1580), Vincenzo Scamozzi (1552–1616), Sebastiano Serlio (1475–1554), Josef Furttenbach the Elder (1591–1667). The theater cities

Really, the Italian town through which we are walking with Andrea Palladio is very charming, and the people we meet are cheerful. This is probably Vicenza, and the five streets along which we stroll have beautiful, classic façades.

But no less magnificent in terms of its architecture is the city through which we are guided by Sebastiano Serlio. On our left are the rather simple, three-storied houses of the townspeople, on the right are stately palazzi with arcades and columned halls, but both sides, in a handsome perspective, move in the direction of the triumphal arch.

Serlio's German colleague, Josef Furttenbach, is also an expert in urban development: The building on the right side of the square is more a temple than a house, and diagonally across from it, on a base with many steps, are five-arched arcades. And with a three-gate, two-story portico Furttenbach surpasses his Italian colleagues.

The aristocratic men and women we encounter have just come out of the temples and palazzi into an alley that turns into a square and are now ready to join our stroll as we enjoy the city.

Palladio 1979; *Teatro* 2001.

There is a wonderful overlap between utopia and reality: Both levels share the illusion of theater. Palladio and Serlio actually brought their »cities« into concrete existence. For the stage sets are three-dimensional events in which people move in social constellations: In other words, it actually is a real city and at the same time the most extreme illusion.

Serlio created a type of stage for each category of play: the scena tragica, scena comica, and scena seria. Furttenbach followed this principle, at least in the pictures engraved by Jacob Custos. Incidentally: we shall experience the same confusion between illusion and reality four hundred years later: in the world of film.

35. Andrea Palladio, Teatro Olimpico, Vicenza, 1580.
36. Sebastiano Serlio, tragic stage setting, 1545.
37. Josef Furttenbach, scaena comica, 1628. Engraving by Jacob Custos.

38. Francesco Colonna (?), *Hypnerotomachia Poliphili*, 1499. Pyramid.
39. Francesco Colonna (?), *Hypnerotomachia Poliphili*, 1499. Mobile fountain.

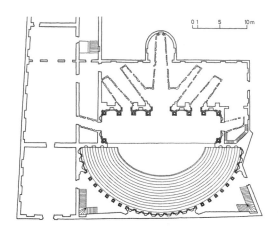

Francesco Colonna, 1433/34–1527?). The *Hypnerotomachia Poliphili*, 1499

We are able to accompany a young man, Poliphilo, on his adventurous journey in search of his beloved, the lovely Polia. Traveling on land and sea we come alternatively to a *locus amoenus* or a *locus terribilis*, and then to a deserted place where there are the remains of an ancient civilization. Now we walk through an ancient portal. It leads through a labyrinthine pyramid, crowned by a pyramid, into the »Realm of Free Will«. We enter the splendid palace of the king and are amazed to see a mobile fountain made of exquisite materials.

We resist many temptations and endure great terrors. Finally we have reached the island of Cithera, and Poliphilo is reunited with Polia. We are now at the center of the island, by the fountain of Venus, a symbol of the womb and of yearning, passionate love.

Francesco Colonna now concludes the narrative: »*Matter is full of longing for form, just as the feminine longs for the masculine and the ugly for the beautiful.*«

What we are interested in is the form of the island. Francesco is glad to tell us. Indeed, he shows us a plan with whose help he can give us exact information about the size of the individual zones. The island is round and has a diameter of a thousand *partes*. It is divided into a number of concentric segments, through which we now travel with great interest.

Coming from the center, we walk through segments IV, III, II, and I, having XV, XX, XXV, and XXX *partes*. A broad ring road XII is connected to the river, and after crossing the bridges we reach a beautiful covered walk and then come to the outer rings 3, 2, and 1, having XXXVIII, XLVIII, and LVIII *partes*. This ring consists only of meadows and greenery, and an orange grove. The outer ring is the largest, and here we find the theater, having XXV *partes*, a graveled walk of XIIII, and a forest of XX *partes*, as well as a myrtle grove and the grove of Diana. Francesco is very precise, and thus he even gives additional measurements: Half a third (a sixth) has CLXVI (166) *partes*, while a third has CCCXXXIII (333) *partes*. Finally – we have walked through the entire city starting from the center – we reach the shore of the island and have a view of the sea, over the harbor.

Now we clearly realize that the giant concentric steps gradually rise as one moves from the sea toward the middle, and that the built-up zones of houses and the plantings of trees (cypresses which are of the same height) alternate.

Yet the geometry and order of the city, and of the island, is not the most important thing about it: Francesco does not forget to assure us that all the inhabitants live in happiness and peace.

Colonna 1997, 1999; Vercelloni 1994.

40. Francesco Colonna (?), *Hypnerotomachia Poliphili*, Cythera, Island of Love, 1499.
Inner rings (approximate circumference given for each): I XXX (30) *partes,* II XXV (25) *partes,* III XX (20) *partes,* IV XV (15) *partes.*
XII Ring street: 1 River, 2 Bridges, 3 Covered walkway with columns.
Outer rings: 4 First ring, meadows, I VIII (58) *partes,* 5 Second ring, XLVIII (48) *partes,* 6 Third ring, XXXVIII (38) *partes,* 7 Orange grove, 8 Theater, XXV (25) *partes,* 9 Graveled walk, XXIII (23) *partes,* 10 Forest, XX (20) *partes,* 11 Grove of Diana, 12 Myrtle grove, 13 Seashore, 14 Third, CCCXXXIII (333) *partes,* 15 Half a third (sixth), CLXVI (166) *partes.*

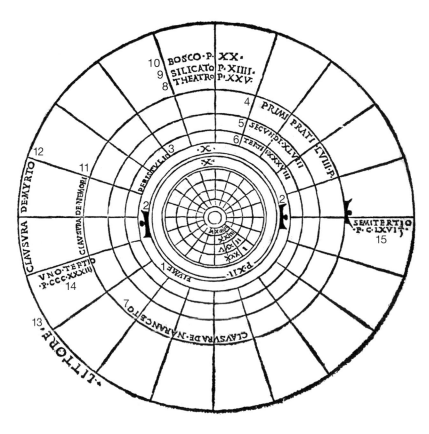

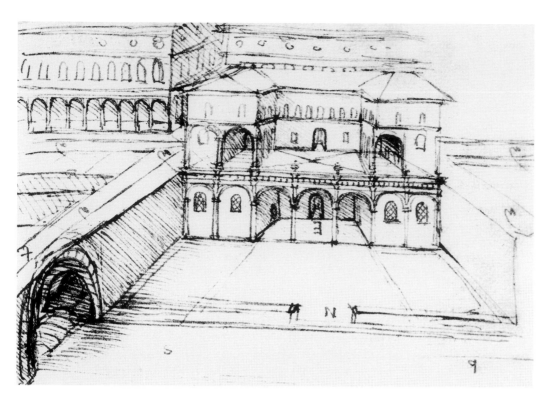

41. Leonardo da Vinci, city on several levels, (Milan?), 1487–90.
42. Leonardo da Vinci, city regulation, (Florence?), 1506.

The Hypnerotomachia was one of the most popular books of its time. It is not certain whether Francesco Colonna is the author. The combination of adventure novel, love story, and urban utopia is no doubt a very old literary genre that still has fascination for its audience today – though now the medium is the film.

Leonardo da Vinci (1452–1519). A city on several levels, 1485, the water city, c. 1500, Fiorence, 1503

After the devastating pestilence of 1485 Leonardo improved the city of Milan. He built a canal through the town fed by a big river outside town. The canal considerably improved the city's hygiene.

Leonardo's city has become three-dimensional: Under the houses and streets there is a system of canals, mostly invisible to us, and a system of tunnels for ships and wagons. Above ground, however, we can walk quite comfortably. But these pedestrian promenades are at times divided one more time – vertically: The upper levels are only for patricians, while the lower levels are intended for plebeians. Leonardo also had in mind the many feuds and wars, and the fact that the new weapons are far more destructive. That is why he surrounded the city with very strong, polygonal walls.

The next city visit takes us to Vigevano in northern Italy. »Why should only Venice be a city on the water?« asks Leonardo and replies: »Any city can actually be a water city is there is a river nearby.« And Leonardo further developed the model of the canal of Milan.

Initially, we follow the course of a river across meadows and fields and come to a city wall. There we see something astonishing: The river divides, comblike, into parallel waterways that now run through town as a system of canals. The system creates completely new transportation routes for people and merchandise: An elementary problem faced by every city to this day is addressed here and resolved. After leaving the city the canals join together into a river again.

The next town, too, is characterized by water – a completely redesigned Florence. The city plan is now an asymmetrical decagon, and the river bed is made to run through the middle, straight and rigid. We no longer recognize the Arno River: Nature has been domesticated to adapt it to human needs and geometry. Leonardo, the universal genius, is also an expert in physics, hydraulics, and mechanics. That is why he was capable of implementing this ingenious engineering construction. Part of that, as a matter of course, was the appropriate fortification of the city, for military conflicts were on the rise.

Tod / Wheeler 1978; *Stadt und Utopie* 1982; Vercelloni 1994; Eaton 2001.

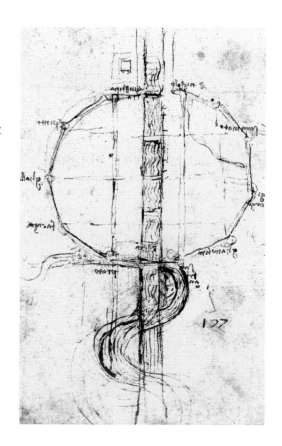

It should come as no surprise that this great universal genius is also interested in urban planning. Leonardo was aware of the importance of water, and by designing a city built on several levels he was five hundred years ahead of his time.

Antonio Francesco Doni (1513–1574). The wise and insane world (*Mondo savio e pazzo*, 1553)

Francesco Doni guides us across the mountains into a pleasant, sunny plain. Soon the city lies before us and we realize it has a circular layout.

Doni enthuses about the size of the city and claims that the temple in the center has 100 gates from which the streets radiate, leading to the 100 gates in the city wall. To be sure, as we approach we wonder whether Doni has been exaggerating, for we can make out only 24 rather modest city gates, each directly turning into a wide street that leads to one of the 24 portals of a huge round building – the temple of wisdom, topped by a cupola on a drum.

»The cupola«, claims Doni, »is at least four times as large as that of the cathedral of Florence.« But by making this statement, Doni has probably let himself be carried away into yet another exaggeration.

By the temple, we are fortunate to make the rare acquaintance of two gentlemen with surprising names: Savio, that is, the wise man, and Pazzo, the crazy man. And we are able to listen to their interesting dialogue for a while:

Pazzo: *»Are there other cities of this type in the new world?«*

Savio: *»Each province has such a city – Lombardy, Tuscany, Romagna, Friuli.«*

Pazzo: *»And the rest of the land? What is it used for?«*

Savio: *»It is fertile according to its nature, like any other terrain, and there is no need to plant anything else that is not suitable in addition to the wheat, hay, and wood.«*

Pazzo: *»And how is the city itself organized?«*

Savio: *»We have at least two crafts or artisans on each street. For example, on one side are the tailors, on the other the cloth merchants. Or on another are the physicians, on yet another are the shoemakers and leatherworkers, or the bakers and across the street from them the millers or the women who spin and weave.«*

Pazzo: *»But what about food?«*

Savio: *»There are two or three streets that have inns, and what one cooks, is also cooked by the others. And they give the townspeople enough to eat. And it's the same with all commodities. Once everybody has had enough to eat, the doors are closed. Every street has a priest; the oldest is the head priest, he and the others are equal. The clothing is completely identical, but the colors vary: Up to the age of ten, you wear white, up to 20 you wear green, purple from 20 to 30, red from 30 to 40, and black the rest of your life.«*

Pazzo: *»I like this equality. But what if someone falls ill?«*

Savio: *»They go to the hospital street, where they are examined and cared for by the doctors. They have experience and use all their knowledge for their good deeds.«*

Pazzo: *»Yes, those who are rich go to the hospital.«*

Savio: *»Nonsense! Here one citizen is as wealthy as the next one. People all eat, dress, and live alike.«*

Pazzo: *»And where do they go to give birth?«*

Savio: *»One or two streets are for women. Birth is a community affair, for, you see, no one knows who fathered the child, and after the birth it is raised by the community. When young persons are old enough, they are sent to university or taught a craft, depending on what nature has endowed them with.«*

Pazzo: *»Blessings upon such a country, where a woman feels no mortal pain for her husband, or children for their parents, where one never has to weep. And what is it like when people die?«*

Savio: *»Then they are buried, simply and without any pomp.«*

We would have been glad to go on listening to the conversation, but we felt the urge to have a closer look at this completely organized city. Again, we talk to Francesco Doni. But first he explains his systems of viewing the world. Simply put, there is *il mondo piccolo* (the small world) – *grande* (the great world) – *massimo* (the greatest) – *misto* (the mixed) – *immaginato* (the imagined) – *risibile* (the ridiculous), and *il mondo dei pazzi* (the world of the insane). And the infernos are categorized as follows: *il disperato* (the desperate) – *lo smarrito* (the lost) – *il pazzo* (the insane) – *l'ardito* (the bold) – *il savio* (the wise), and *l'ostinato* (the obstinate).

43. Antonio Francesco Doni, ideal city, 1553.

These categories are quite interesting, but we doubt whether they can really be used to explain the nature of the world and of human beings. But let's move on to daily life in Doni's world.

»Our communal life«, says Doni soberly, »needs no great ideologies, we look at our life together purely from the practical side.«

What is the story of the gigantic temple and the hundred priests who are active here? »The cult is very simple: Every week there is a festival. We worship together, and under the cupola there are a hundred kinds of music. We thank God for his gifts and we all embrace each other.«

We continue our stroll through the town. The streets are bordered by simple row houses, each with a plain gable. The people who live here have completely identical houses and, as we learned earlier, they share everything: all goods and possessions, bet also women. And this ensures that there will be no quarrels.

Doni 1553; Curcio 1941; Firpo 1957; Manguel 1981; Vercelloni 1994; Rahmsdorf 1999; Eaton 2001.

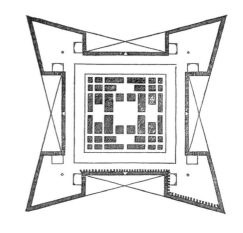

Francesco Doni translated Thomas More's *Utopia*, and thus his world is influenced by More's social ideas. The star-shaped, radial city has, in the meantime, become a topos, and the star principle is part and parcel of the regular inventory of city planners from the 18th to the 20th century.

Pietro Cataneo (?–1569). The fortress cities, 1554

»What is the ideal city?« asks Pietro and replies: »A city is ideal if it is capable of defending itself, if it can't be occupied, plundered, and burned down. But that means the city has to be a regular polygon, a quadrangle, pentagon, hexagon, or decagon, and the bastions and outworks are their quoins.« Yes, but how about the aesthetics of Renaissance geometry? we interject. »Nonsense, this aesthetics is created by cannons!«

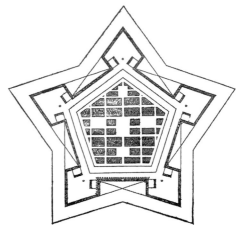

And Cataneo explains a few examples and claims that the architect must first be well versed in ballistics and in the »art« of the siege. »The purpose of the system of bulwarks, bastions, and ravelins is our ability to sweep the entire approaches, without dead angles, with our artillery.« Then why is there not an optimal fortification system, why this variety, symmetry, order?

»Well, maybe it's because architects enjoy the beauty of geometry and take pleasure in the variety of forms.«

Cataneo 1554; Münter 1957; Kruft 1989; Vercelloni 1994.

As is often the case in architecture, there is no clear separation between functional and formal aspects. Cataneo presents a rich geometry: He believes a square, pentagon, hexagon, and decagon seem equally suitable; the layout of the cities inside the walls are consistently right-angled, with all the problems associated with spandrels; a large public square and four small ones are considered the standard.

Daniele Barbaro (1513–1570). Emulating Vitruvius, 1560

For Barbaro, Vitruvius is the undisputed and unsurpassed master or architecture and of city planning, and he feels his sole duty is to interpret and illustrate Vitruvius.

This is why his city seems very familiar, for we have already become acquainted with every detail of Vitruvius's cities. The octagonal layout, the large square in the center with its public buildings, the right-angled streets are well known to us.

»I think my colleagues often exaggerate the fortification of cities. It is my belief that the strong walls and eight corner towers offer enough protection. I, on the other hand, included only two gates in my plan.«

We barely have time to acquaint ourselves with these two very arbitrary entrances to the city. No sooner have we found them than we reach the ring street.

Barbaro 1557; Vercelloni 1994.

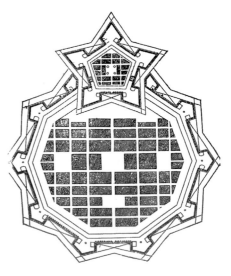

Daniele Barbaro is an expert on Vitruvius and his interpreter, universally educated and a rational thinker. He sees no need for a comprehensive, complicated fortification of his city and justifies the modesty of his system.

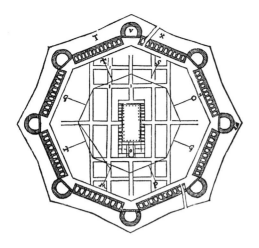

Giacomo Castriotto (1510–1563) and Girolamo Maggi (1523–1572). Geometric fortification, 1564

If we look at the little town from a bird's-eye view, its geometry is familiar to us: The two squares, turned forty-five degrees, are something we encountered earlier in Filarete.

»It goes without saying«, comment the two experts in building fortresses, »that our town must be easily defendable, and moats and a wall with bastions form an octagonal star. However, the core of the town is more in the shape of a circle.«

A bridge leads across the moat to the small, outer town gate, and after we cross the bastion, we enter the city through the inner gate. The streets are arranged radially, but we are very surprised that the houses themselves follow no geometry of any kind. Irregularly, almost romantically, as in a medieval town, they fill in the segments. Only in the center is the geometry resumed once more: there is a little circular temple in the middle of the square.

Vercelloni 1994; Münter 1957.

The primary geometric vocabulary of the Renaissance, archetypes, are used here: Two squares are turned into the shape of octagons and form triangular bastions. The town has two ring streets and eight radial streets orientated toward the central building in the middle of town.

Bartolomeo del Bene (1514–?). The true society (Civitas veri), the philosophical city, 1565, 1609

»We're constantly in search of the ›Civitas veri‹, the true, the ideal Christian society. But without a great philosophical idea we won't find it«, explains Bartolomeo del Bene. Thus the philosopher actually leads us into a city of ideas, but one that has assumed a physical shape.

Again the plan of the city is determined by the great round: A solid structure of stone, a wall with towers protects the town.

Strangely enough, it is divided into five sectors – a complex geometry – and has five gates. These are meant to symbolize the five senses of man: *porta della vista*, *dell'odorato*, *del gusto*, *del tatto*, *dell'udire*, the portals of vision, smell, taste, touch, and hearing.

Each gate is the entrance to a row of seven courtyards leading into a central square. Between the five rays of the courtyard systems, there seem to be green spaces. Clouds or mists billow from nozzles and float above the segments. Water gushes over ledges. As we make our way through the courtyards, we are instructed about the virtues and vices with which good Christians have to come to terms. There are three great zones: politics and morality, intelligence and spirit, vice and sin.

44. Pietro Cataneo, square city plan, 1554.
45. Pietro Cataneo, pentagonal city plan, 1554.
46. Pietro Cataneo, hexagonal city plan, 1554.
47. Pietro Cataneo, decagonal city plan with advance fortress, 1554.

48. Daniele Barbaro, fortified city, 1557.
49. Giacomo Castriotto, Girolamo Maggi, geometric city, 1564.
50. Bartolomeo del Bene, Civitas veri, 1565, 1609.

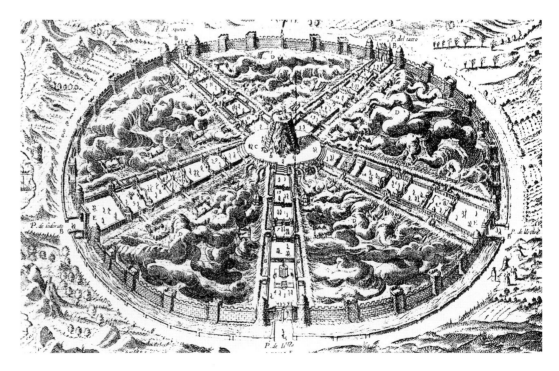

The journey begins by the Palace of Strength and takes us to the Palaces of Moderation and Excess. Then we arrive at the Temples of Glory and Generosity, and finally at the Labyrinth of Vices.

The Basilica of Magnanimity and Modesty is a dignified structure, and so is the House of Courtesy. It doesn't take long for the contrast to appear: Arrogance, falseness, and injustice are present in the form of buildings. The Edifices of Heroism, Abstinence, and Justice, however, represent the goal of a virtuous life. In the Civitas veri, the City of Truth, the entire moral cosmos is present.

After all these joys, perils, and purifications, we arrive at the longed-for goal in the center of the city, a steep hill whose top we reach by climbing a staircase with many steps. We come to a large plateau and stand directly in front of the temple. Now we are expected to offer a sacrifice to the divine on altars and in the temple.

Bartolomeo del Bene 1609; Vercelloni 1994.

Long before the Enlightenment, morality begins to separate from religion, to become independent. True, ostensibly the focus of discussion is still the Christian society, but the ethical categories that are cited no longer have a need for this society, und the temple for »the divine« has no Christian symbols.

This separation between religion and morality, for example in »ethics courses«, is a notable problem for our time.

Ludovico Agostini (1536–1609). The imaginary republic (*La republica immaginaria*, 1583–1590)

Ludovico Agostini has invited two more companions to join us on our tour – Signori Finito and Infinito. They are the ideologues and planners who are responsible for the city-state.

First of all, we have endless admiration for the town's wonderful site by the Tyrrhenian Sea. It has not been selected for romantic reasons alone, however: The location was picked after careful consideration.

»A city's health is the first and most important requirement«, say our guides. »Pleasant temperatures in all seasons, good quality air, very pure water from springs and fountains, delectable fruit in all seasons, and, last but not least, good wines are the prerequisites.« We were able to see these qualities with our own eyes during our walks. But our guides expect even more benefits from the healthy locale:

»This air has produced moderate people, erudite in all the sciences. They are no one's enemies, but rather the friends of all people, yet strong in battle. And they are unique examples of piety and justice.«

In the meantime we have gained a fine impression of a most civilized, well organized, and geometrically laid out city. Pure chance confirms our impression of how absolutely clean the city is: We see how the streets are suddenly flooded with water and all dirt is washed away. This process is repeated every eight to ten days.

The houses in the wide streets have at least two uniform, simply designed façades on the street side, and there is a courtyard and a small garden next to each house. We are amazed how extensive, though not general, is the similarity between the façades, and our companions explain why this is so.

»Until recently the poor lived in wretched lodgings among the scum of the city, in cramped quarters and in stench, segregated from the nobility. That's a thing of the past. The houses are all erected at public expense, with basements and a system of canals. Those who want a finer or larger house can have one built by the town architect if they pay the additional cost. But larger houses are provided not because of a whim or love of luxury, but when families have a need for more space.«

The house cannot be enlarged laterally or frontally – any addition can be carried out only in the back, perhaps even all the way to the next street. And the uniform height of buildings must be observed at all events.

During our walk, we do see people who might belong to very different social classes. How does that affect their housing? The answers of Finito and Infinito surprise us: »All the people live together, but the plebeians, the simple folk, live on the ground floor, and the nobility and the wealthy live on the top floors.«

51. Bartolomeo Ammannati, large residence for priests, 1584.
52. Giorgio Vasari the Younger, collective ideal city, 1598.

This makes us curious about general living conditions in the city republic, and we learn some things that seem strange, and others that are disturbing. »All citizens have a very disciplined daily schedule«, explain our guides. »It is the same for all, and is marked by the firing of cannons.«

No one sleeps more than seven hours, and never in the daytime. At six o'clock, the signal for waking up is given. Everyone gathers, hears holy Mass and the sermon, and receives the blessing. Work begins. Exactly one hour is reserved for the communal noon meal. The cuisine is excellent, for all food is examined for ripeness and freshness by public inspectors. It goes without saying that this is also done in the markets. During the day, there is no one about in the city unless he has special errands. But after work, too, the fathers – models in their families   must avoid the public houses. Young people do not get to drink wine until they have reached their intellectual maturity. – Banquets are permitted only on especially important occasions. Playing cards, dancing, and drunkenness are vices that are frowned upon.

»We have three sources of wealth: agriculture, trade, and industry. That guarantees prosperity. There are no poor people, and one reason for that is that all vices are frowned upon.«
Curcio 1941; Firpo 1957.

Agostini does not locate his town on a legendary island but places it in a specific place and wants it to be seen as a reproducible model. Agostini's hygienic and architectural measures are fascinating for the 16th century, but he echoes the familiar authoritarian, dictatorial daily schedules that we know from earlier projects and that we will encounter time and again.

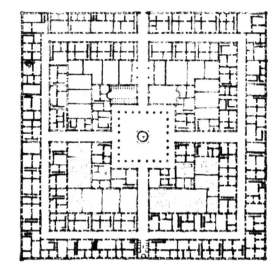

Bartolomeo Ammannati (1511–1592). A large residence for priests, 1584

»What does this have to do with the city? Why, it's only a gigantic residential building«, you may object. »We can't actually draw a clear boundary between the house and the city: Both follow the same structures, laws, and systems«, Ammannati states when we visit him.

»Just look around! This huge house is really laid out like a city: The outer diameter is a large square, and there is a single entrance. Inside there is a square created at a large intersection of streets. It is connected with another square with open arcades and a fountain in the middle of the square. From the square's access street we reach the two church buildings, whose entrances are off the square. The innermost group of buildings includes representative buildings, the next quarter is occupied primarily by landscaped courtyards, then there is another block of buildings accessible from the square, and finally the last square ring zone has many apartments similar to two-level maisonettes. The apartments are not particularly large; both levels are connected by a narrow flight of stairs, and the rooms have rather small windows toward the outside.

»On the square and in the gardens we have sufficient light«, Ammannati says with satisfaction, »and above all we want to build as economically as possible, which is why we've standardized the apartments.«
Ammanati 1970; Vercelloni 1994.

Ammannati's design may be regarded as a precursor of urban superblocks, particularly those built in the period between the world wars. Standardization, too, is a forerunner of 20th-century urban planning. The landscaped inner courtyards are noteworthy. No vehicles and probably no horseback riders have access to them. It is not quite clear why such a huge number of clerics should need living quarters together outside a monastery.

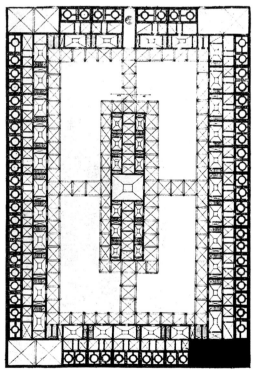

Giorgio Vasari the Younger (1562–1625). The collective ideal city, 1598

We visit a city designed by Vasari, but only very briefly, for we have already seen too many similar places, although Vasari has taken pains in designing the squares. What we are interested in is a gigantic block of houses that almost bursts the city apart. As with Ammannati, we might ask what the demarcation between a house and the city is. Vasari defends his concept: »It is true that my city is not a square but a rectangle, but it is laid out in a more systematical, more well-ordered way than Ammannati's city. The rooms and apartments are also standardized – but a few designs are sufficient for me. That means not only that construction moves forward rapidly but that prices are low. Moreover it is quite logical that in my city, where all people really are equal, everybody lives in the same kind of apartments.«

When we walk through the complex, we do have the impression that this is collective housing. On the ground floor we are able to view 42 apartments for the clergy, the same number being available on the top floor for curates – in other words, equality does not seem so easy to implement after all.

Vasari is lavish in his use of open spaces: Four large courtyards, generously supplied with arcades, form the rectangular square. In the interior there is another block, surrounded by arcades. This is where the rooms for community meetings are. We are surprised that here, too, there is only one small entrance – no doubt easy to keep a watch on, so that peace in the house is absolutely guaranteed.

Stefanelli 1970; Vercelloni 1994.

Just as in Ammannati's design, the plain, almost mass-produced apartments are also intended for priests. What is noteworthy is the modular, standardized system of courtyard arcades, which are reminiscent of industrial grids.

53. Francesco de Marchi, military architecture, fortified city, 1570, 1599.
54. Francesco de Marchi, military architecture, fortified city, 1570, 1599.
55. Francesco de Marchi, military architecture, fortified city with harbor, 1570, 1599.

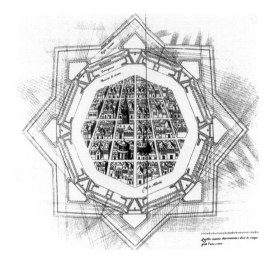

Francesco de Marchi (1504–1576). Military architecture (*Della architectura militare libri tre*, 1570)

Only a few years after Castriotto and Maggi, Francesco designs his ideal city, though according to a long-familiar geometry: Again, the basic form is created by squares turned toward each other. These provide the basic form and constitute the fortification. But Francesco rejects the total dictate of fortification for the city and declares: »It is not appropriate for all cities to be made into fortresses, nor that the cities themselves should all be fortified.« Then why does Francesco again design an enormously fortified city with a small core? And why does Francesco leave the entire surrounding countryside free of villages, houses, even trees? Simply so that attackers find no protection and villages do not suffer when the city is besieged.

Curiously enough, in Francesco's design the core of the city is squeezed into an octagon, and some of the houses are strangely indented. »I built a grid-based town with streets that intersect regularly. It's a sensible plan known even in ancient Greece.«

Pretty, two-story gabled houses predominate, though between them there are also irregular houses full of nooks and crannies. The church, with its massive, Gothic-style tower, does not provide a true center, and in another area there is a second church, perhaps for the civic hospital, while in the area next to it there is a round church.

If we calculate that each of the town's 28 sections has about ten houses in it and that ten people live in each house, that's a sum total of a maximum of 2,800 inhabitants for the little town. There are no open areas or landscaping, but, as In all fortified towns, people can promenade on the landscaped ramparts.

A hundred years earlier, in the work of Antonio Filarete and 30 years before him in Maggi and Castriotto, we encountered this form: A square superimposed on another and turned 45 degrees produces an eight-point star. The development looks ordered and accidental at the same time and reminds us of a set of building blocks. Here we also clearly see that the switch from an octagon to a rectangle is accompanied by a number of problems.

Francesco wants to show us two more towns, and demonstrates the rich repertory of his models.

The next town over which we fly is built in a hexagon shape, and the town center, except for the central square, follows this geometry. Between the buildings and the ramparts, ample green spaces have been created.

The next town is located on the seashore, and from a bird's-eye perspective the impression is that the geometric shape has been torn open and the sea is, as it were, streaming into the town: A huge round basin forms the harbor, whose entrance is guarded by towers.

Marchi 1599, 1810; Vercelloni 1994.

We are familiar with the geometric vocabulary: Hexagons and octagons predominate, while pentagons or decagons rarely occur. The fortifications, too, show only minor modifications: It is not the society, but the weapon that determines a town's layout – overlaid with the aesthetics of geometry.

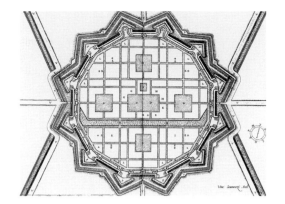

Vincenzo Scamozzi (1552–1616). The geometric city, 1615, and Palmanova, 1593

Our first visit is to a town that was conceived by Scamozzi around 1615. From the air we see that the town's geometric base is a dodecagon, and that it thus approaches the form of the circle. Naturally Vincenzo Scamozzi has to admit that the form of his town is dictated by its fortification. But he qualifies this:

»Even if in building a fortress the functions are predominant, architecture is still an art. Beauty, order, geometry must be given their due.«

Admittedly we must note that Scamozzi's system is not really new: We visited similar towns by Francesco di Giorgio Martini, by Pietro Cataneo, and other architects decades earlier. As in Scamozzi's designs, the hexagon and octagon were the basic figures. In subdividing the buildings in the interior of the town, the architects have taken a number of different paths: Streets run in the shape of stars or at right angles. Scamozzi chooses right angles here.

There are only four small entrance gates. We enter town by the eastern gate after crossing a bridge over a watercourse. A canal eccentrically flows through the town. It is fed by the four arms of a river that we have already seen from the air. These also feed the town moat.

»A watercourse in town offers a number of advantages. It makes it possible to transport people and merchandise, provides pleasant air and a lovely view. Thus we use both art and technology to good effect«, Scamozzi praises this aspect of city planning.

Now we stroll through the town's strictly right-angled streets, discovering smaller squares in the process. In the center there is a larger quadrangle with throngs of busy people. This is where the public buildings are located as well.

Not satisfied with this visit, Scamozzi guides us to the next town. And again, like an eagle in flight, we approach the town from above and are able to take in its remarkable geometry: Here, six radial streets issue like rays from the piazza. They cut through the four rings of buildings and surprisingly arrive at a nine-cornered town wall. Only three gates lead into town. The wall has nine bastions and after the moat there are nine outworks.

Coming from the direction of Udine we now approach the town.

Scamozzi 1615; Tod / Wheeler 1978; *Stadt und Utopie* 1982; Vercelloni 1994; Eaton 2001.

But what a surprise! We have taken a leap back into the real world: We are in Palman(u)ova, not far from Venice – this town was actually built and exists in the present day: »Yes, the idea for this town is also mine, of course«, the architect tells us, »but it was implemented by military archi-

56. Vincenzo Scamozzi, ideal city, 1615.
57. Plan of Palmanova, Civitates orbis terrarum, Cologne, Germany, 1593.

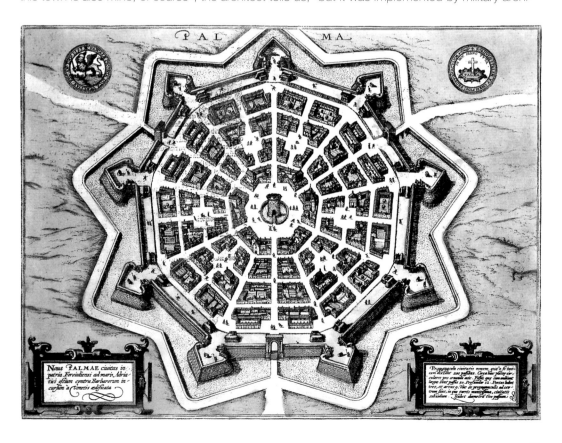

tects. I think Giulio Savorgnano was the site supervisor. He improved some things and spoiled others.«

There is a bridge across the wide moat. The town has only three gates. The street we are on leads to a hexagonal piazza where the public buildings are situated: a church and the town hall.

In the middle of the piazza there is a round tower – no, not in the real world, for we have jumped back into utopia for a short timei, and in other ways as well many things have been built differently.

Only our imagination allows us to visualize the beautiful squares at street intersections. Now we are crossing the inner ring of streets. The design of the houses is quite varied. We are astonished that the geometric system makes it so difficult to get one's bearings, so that we barely notice we are suddenly back at our point of departure. What a shame that the idea of a canalized river through town could not be implemented here. Deeply impressed by the strange and confusing overlapping of utopia and reality, of imagination and reality, we leave the town and its master architect.

The town of Grammichele, built in 1693, probably also goes back to the Palmanova model.

Tommaso Campanella (1568–1639). The sun city (*La città del sole*, 1602)

Again we land on an island. It is called Taprobana. Again, the city planner, Tommaso Campanella, explains the basic layout to us. »*In a vast plain there rises a huge hill, and the largest part of the town is built on its slopes. The town's many rings extend a considerable distance from the foot of the hill. The hill is so big that the circumference of the town is seven miles. It is divided into seven giant circles or rings named after the seven planets. One gets from one ring to another by means of four paved streets and through four gates facing in the four cardinal directions.*«

We enter through the north gate in the first ring, amazed by the clever mechanism that raises and lowers the gate. Now we are looking at magnificent palaces, all connected by the walls of the second ring. We walk into one of the lower chambers and walk up a marble staircase leading to the inner circular galleries from which we can reach the splendidly furnished upper floors. There are more stairs and galleries giving access to the rest of the town.

»*The town walls are ornamented outside and inside with wonderful paintings that vividly depict all the sciences.*«

In the lower rooms of the houses are the workshops and kitchens, pantries and storerooms, armories and laundries. The water flows down gutters into the sewer canals.

We inquire as to the function of a representative building that obviously contains a hall. »It's a swimming pool«, says Campanella, »and another one was built outside the walls. For every citizen must learn how to swim.«

There are fine palaces for everyone, and now we've arrived at the top of the town hill. From here, there is a view far across the plain to the sea. A magnificent temple in the center crowns the town and outshines the houses. That is where the Scriptures are interpreted. The most important science is astrology, and it is to astrology that this temple is dedicated.

»The towns people observe the stars and their movements«, continues Campanella, »and they read everything about the power of the constellations and their effects on human lives.« Full of enthusiasm, Campanella describes the temple: »*The temple has a characteristic, completely round shape. It is not surrounded by walls but rests on strong, beautifully made columns. The large cupola, which is vaulted with fabulous skill, has an even taller turret in the middle. In this there is an opening to which the altar ascends; it is the only altar, and is surrounded by columns. On the altar there is nothing but a large globe on which the firmament is depicted and another globe on which the Earth is painted. In the vault of the large cupola one can see all the stars of the firmament.*«

Along the walls of the temple, curtains are lowered when there is an address so that the voice of the priest can be heard more easily. Now that we have admired the town's beauty, we are interested in the life of its citizens. Campanella is glad to describe it. »A just social order is easily maintained, for there is no private property. But the work of all citizens aims at the welfare of the entire community.«

And Campanella adds: »*Everything the inhabitants have is communal property. But the distribution of property is handled by the authorities. The concept of private property comes from the fact that people have their own housing and their own children and wives, This is the origin of egoism. For in order to procure wealth and dignity for our son, we all rob the community. When we give up egoism, all that is left is love for the community.*«

How can that be? we want to know. For then nobody will want to work. Everybody will expect the others to work, and he will profit.

58. Tommaso Campanella, 1602. Attempt at a reconstruction by A. Schwarikow, 1935.
59. Tommaso Campanella, *La città del sole*, 1602, 1623. Attempt at a reconstruction by J. Hruza, 1965.

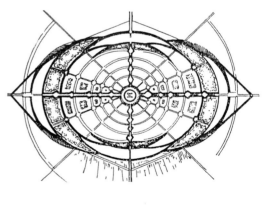

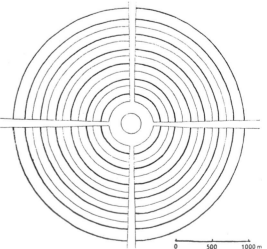

»That is not the case at all«, Campanella reassures us, »for all the townspeople are filled by love for their community and for their native country.« Children are taught everything that is worth knowing, but in addition to this they become familiar with manual skills and with work in the workshops. Physical training is also not neglected, since in the case of war each person must be ready to fight for his community.

The wonderfully painted city walls we saw earlier are the best and most graphic textbook. Girls and boys receive the same education, of course.

Later Campanella emphasizes the commonalities in all aspects of daily life: *»Instruction in the mechanical arts and in the speculative sciences is also offered to both men and women.«*

We do observe, however, that there are very clear differences between men and women as far as the practice of a large number of different activities: Strenuous work, such as plowing, harvesting, threshing is done by men, while milking, gathering herbs, weaving, spinning, cutting hair is women's work. And music is reserved for women alone, as is cooking.

The highest master is the priest, the metaphysicus, and at his side are three dignitaries – »Power«, »Wisdom«, and »Love«. »Power« is responsible for war and peace, »Wisdom« is in charge of the arts and sciences, the authorities and schools, and it is Wisdom that has ornamented the entire town with paintings. »Love« is in care of procreation, for men and women must we united in such a way that they produce the best offspring. »Love« is also in charge of everything that has to do with health: medicine, sowing and reaping, cattle breeding, nutrition and food, clothing, and copulation.

»They share housing, bedrooms, beds, and other necessities of life. But every six months the authorities determine who should live in this ring or the other, and who should sleep in the first or the second bedroom.«

We are honored to be invited to the noon meal by the community. We enter the big, brightly lit dining hall. There are first and second tables, the women sit here, the men over there. There is complete silence, but a pleasant-sounding voice reads something edifying from a book. It is delightful to see the boys and girls waiting on tables: They hand people napkins, dishes with delicious foods, and dessert. We observe that larger dishes are being carried in. »Certainly«, says Campanella, »these are for the dignitaries and are better prepared. But they share them with well-behaved children – as a special honor.«

That's why it seems to us that everyone is not perfectly equal after all. However, everyone benefits from the wholesome and careful preparation of the dishes: *»It is the job of the physicians to tell the cooks what kinds of dishes they are to prepare each day, which ones are for the old men, which for young ones, and which ones are intended for the sick. Venerable old men supervise the entire kitchen and the cooking.«*

We'd like to find out more about procreation. Campanella explains how healthy offspring is produced. No woman is mated with a man before reaching the age of nineteen. And no man may father children before reaching the age of 21. Before that age he may have intercourse only with barren or pregnant women so that he will not be forced to seek unnatural alternatives. Older women and officials look after the erotic pleasure of those whose desire is too stormy and who are too troubled by it. They secretly approach the officials, or else the officials notice their desire in the sports arenas. Sodomy – which is what homosexuality is called here – is severely punished and the perpetrator *»must wear his shoes tied around his neck as punishment for two days, as a sign that he turned order upside down and put his foot on his head.«* If he relapses, he risks the death penalty.

»Since all men and women are completely naked in the sports arena during exercise, like the Spartans of old, the officials recognize who is capable of procreation and who is unsuitable for intercourse. Tall and beautiful women are mated only with tall and capable men, plump women with skinny men and slim women with corpulent men, so that their differences are successfully evened out. For procreation is regulated for the good of the state and not the benefit of the individual. Those who abstain from intercourse up to the age of 21, however, are celebrated in public gatherings by honors and songs.«

Intercourse is a dignified matter. The children prepare the separate bedrooms, the couple takes a bath, they eat and pray to God. The women gaze upon sculptures that portray handsome men. They look up to heaven and pray to God to give them fine descendants. Only after physicians and astrologers have determined the right time and at their direction do the attendants open the doors and allow intercourse. What happens, though, if a woman is barren? we'd like to know. *»If one of the women is not impregnated by a man, she is mated with another man. If she then still remains barren, she becomes common property.«*

In the sun state we find no prisons or torture, though there are severe punishments – including capital punishment, for example, for »vain« women. Spies report all offenses to the state. The punishments for offenses are cruel: Banishment, whipping, being deprived of communal meals, being forbidden to go to church, or to talk with women, threaten wrongdoers, and therefore we are sceptical whether the government is truly benevolent, and much that we have observed does not seem to tally with the kind of ideal state we imagine. Admittedly – unlike in Utopia – we find no slaves or mercenaries, and Campanella is convinced: »*In the sun state everyone is well governed.*«

We're also interested in religion and discover that there is a large number of priests, These are ordained officials. The citizens confess to the priests in secret, and they in turn confess the sins of the entire people publicly to God and pronounce the people free of sins.

An unusual phenomenon is that there are voluntary human sacrifices: The person is pulled up into a tower on a board that has four rings. There, in isolation, he or she remains with barely enough food until the people is atoned for, and then becomes a priest.

Christ is honored by the people, and so we were surprised that the sun and stars are also venerated like living creatures, even though no one prays to them.

Two questions that would have been of supreme interest to us did remain unanswered for the moment. Number one: The sun state's inhabitants have boats that are moved, not by sails or rowers, but by a clever mechanism – but what kind of mechanism? Two: We heard the assertion that they have already invented the art of flying – but how did they manage that?

Before taking our leave, we call Campanella once more, and he finally explains how the flying machines work: »*Over their tail they have a large fan ending in a rod; a weight suspended from this creates balance, so that a boy is able to raise and push it down with one hand. Large wings are attached at the tip. The whole is supported by an axle that is easily moved by means of two shafts.*«

And here is how the ships function: »*They move a different kind of boat with two wheels that turn with the aid of hawsers running over a big wheel installed on the fo'c'sle, and diagonally over the stern wheels. They move the big wheel easily; it in turn pulls the small ones installed under the surface of the water, similar to the tools with which the women of Calabria and France wind, prepare, or spin yarn.*«

Campanella 1643, 1863; *Der utopische Staat* 1960; Mohl 1960; Servier 1971; Trousson 1975; Tod/Wheeler 1978; Manguel 1986; Wuckel 1986; *Mosca* 1991; Brentjes 1993; Rahmsdorf 1999; *Visionen und Utopien* 2002; Seibt 2001.

Campanella's ideal state has undoubtedly been influenced by Plato and many other models. Once again, the community of property is offered as the most important method for solving economic and societal problems and for constituting an ideal society. The careful supervision and planning of sexual relations is yet another shocking aspect of eugenic methods.

Ships driven by wheels in the sun state are no fantasies. Andreas Johannes Laskaris invented a paddle wheeler for Charles the Fifth that was successfully tested in 1543 in the harbor of Barcelona. In 1575 the Dutch devised a floating fortress whose paddle wheels were moved by human energy.

4.2. England

Thomas More (1478–1535). *Utopia (De optimo reip. statu, deque nova insula Utopia, libellus vere aureus, nec minus salutaris quàm festivus, clarissimi disertissimíque viri Thomae Mori inclytae civitatis Londinensis civis & vicecomitis*, 1516)

We reach Utopia by sailing ship. The island has the shape of a waxing moon. Thomas receives us warmheartedly together with his friend Raphael Hythlodaeus. Our questions for Thomas prove to be superfluous, for he himself begins a witty dialogue with Raphael As we listen, we learn all about the island and its inhabitants. At first Raphael speaks about the geography of Utopia:

»*The island has 54 towns, all spacious and splendid. They are all laid out in the same way and look the same. The closest towns are 24 miles from each other; on the other hand, none is so isolated that one could not walk from it to another in one day. Amaurotum is considered to be the first and leading town. No town tries to enlarge its territory, for each considers itself the cultivator rather than the owner of the land.*«

60. Thomas Morus, Utopiae insulae tabula, 1517.

Farming, Raphael tells us, is well organized. »In the country we have farmsteads that are systematically distributed over the entire arable land and are equipped with agricultural tools. They are inhabited by townspeople who take turns moving out of town to live there. From each household, twenty move back to town every year – the people who have spent two years in the country.«

Thomas and Raphael now take us to Amaurotum, the most important town in Utopia. It is »located on the gentle slope of a hill. The town's layout is almost square. A high and broad wall with many towers and outworks surrounds the town. The streets are planned efficiently, so that they are favorable for traffic and protected from winds. In the middle of town is the marketplace with storehouses for goods intended for daily use. In the storehouses the goods manufactured by all the families are collected. The head of the family asks for what the family needs, but there is no need to pay. All goods belong to all people, and there is no private property.«

Next to the storehouses are food markets for vegetables, fruit, bread, fish, and meat. The meat is slaughtered, dressed, and soaked by slaves outside the town. The townspeople do not want to get used to slaughtering animals, because this reduces pity and causes air pollution.

»The Utopians themselves need no money and despise gold and silver from which it is minted: Chamber pots and chains and similar inferior objects are manufactured from these metals. The houses are by no means unsightly. There is a clear view of the long row of houses, which are connected together for blocks, from the row of houses across the street. The latter is twenty feet wide. At the rear of the row houses, a large garden enclosed on all sides extends the whole length of the block. There is not a single house that does not have a back door leading to the garden. The double front doors, which can be opened by the light pressure of your hand and which then close again automatically, let in all comers. Thus there is no private space. For people even change their houses every ten years, by lottery. Today every house is an impressive three-story building. The outside walls are made of granite or brick. Inside they are plastered with stucco. The roofs are flat and are roofed with artificial stones.«

While we are admiring the solid houses – none shows signs of dilapidation, for when there is the least damage, they are repaired – there is the sound of brass trumpets. At once the inhabitants of the residential district gather – except for the sick – in the spacious dining halls. We are glad to follow the townspeople as they walk to their meal, and together we eat the ample, delicious food that is prepared for everybody in a community kitchen. The men sit by the wall, the women in the outside seats, so that in case of sudden nausea (as sometimes happens wth pregnant women) they can get up without bothering other diners and join the nursing mothers, who are sitting in a special dining room set aside for them.

The townspeople are by no means averse to everyday pleasures during meals: No dinner is without music, all kinds of tidbits are available for dessert, incense is lit, perfume is sprayed, indeed everything is done to put the guests in a pleasant mood. No kind of entertainment is inadmissible as long as it causes no harm.

It is customary to listen to public lectures daily early in the morning. After dinner, people spend an hour playing games or with music – in summer in the gardens, in winter in the public halls. There is one occupation all men and women practice together: agriculture. In addition, everyone also learns a special craft – not only men, but women as well.

Only six hours of the day are set aside for work: three before and three after the noon meal. This number of working hours is sufficient, because there are no idlers, parasites, or unproductive people, and only few citizens are released from work. Nevertheless people all have what they need to live.

Useless, slovenly idleness is avoided, and, as our companions explain: »*There is no excuse for idleness; there are no taverns or bars, no houses of pleasure or opportunities for dissipation, no hiding places or quiet nooks and crannies – life must take place directly in front of everybody.*«

Moreover, life is filled with reading, learning, discussions, walks, and party games. Utopians find pleasure not in foolish games of chance, in cruel hunting, in precious jewels and expensive clothes. Rather, people discover real pleasure in a life spent virtuously, imbued with beauty, strength, and agility, but also in health, food and drink, and even in emptying their bowels or fathering a child.

The size of families is regulated: None consists of less than ten and more than sixteen adults. This number is maintained by incorporating surplus children in families that have few children. Women are under the control of men, and children are under the control of parents.

Marriage laws are extremely strict. Women do not marry before the age of eighteen, nor men before the age of twenty-two. There is severe punishment for premarital sex. Before marriage the man and woman are brought face to face completely naked, for, so the argument goes, even when you buy a horse you remove the saddle and blankets.

It goes without saying that adultery, too, is punished very severely. When both spouses agree, however, separation is possible.

We learn quite a lot about war from the Utopians and we are happy that they abhor war as »*something that is simply bestial.*« Admittedly, when we find out more about the way they wage war, and how they treat mercenaries and enemies, we tend to lose some of our sympathies with the Utopians again.

We are also very surprised that the noble nation of Utopians keeps slaves. It is true that these come from foreign cities and have committed crimes there, but day laborers from another nation also voluntarily agree to become slaves. Yet we are somewhat placated when we learn about the great religious tolerance of the Utopians.

People of different faiths and of different sects share a single house of worship. This building is extremely beautiful and ornate, and is very spacious. However, we felt it was strange, in spite of the Utopians' positive lifestyle, that the interior is rather dark. The reason for this, explains a priestess (for widows are admitted to the priesthood as well), is that excessively bright lighting is distracting, while twilight promotes composure and devotion.

Since we are aware of a number of problems with Catholic priests (and Thomas is a Catholic, of course), we are interested in the situation of priests in Utopia.

»There are only few priests, but they are exceptionally devout. They are elected by secret popular ballot and ordained by their fellow clerics. Children and young people are taught by priests. The priests are married to the most carefully chosen daughters of the land, and it goes without saying – as we just mentioned – that women are not excluded from the priesthood.«

Utopians have complete religious freedom, and thus we find many kinds of religion. Some venerate the Sun and the Moon, others an unknown, eternal, infinite, incomprehensible divine being, a force present in the entire universe, which they call Father or Mythras. Many Utopians have been converted to Christianity. Their attitude toward death is extremely strange. Though nursing is of a very high level, incurably ill patients are killed at their own request: They are deprived of food or put to sleep. But the bodies of people who have killed themselves without the priests' or the senate's approval are ignominiously thrown into a swamp.

Once again Raphael goes into the nature of this community: »*In fact, wherever private property still exists, where everyone measures everything according to the value of money, it will scarcely ever be possible to pursue just or successful policies unless you believe that justice is served where the best things are always awarded to the worst people, or that there is happiness where everything is distributed to very few people. ...*«

Yet Thomas has serious reservations, which we definitely share with him: »*It seems to me that in a place where everything is common property it is impossible to live a tolerable life. For how could the amount of goods that is available be sufficient if everybody avoids work, since no compulsion forces him to earn his living, and relying on the hard work of others makes him lazy?«*

»*It just seems like that to you*«, answers Raphael. »*Once you see their customs and institutions, you will concede that you've never seen such a well-ordered state anywhere else.*«

Thus Utopia is the only state »*that is fully justified in calling itself a ›commonwealth‹. For when there is talk of common welfare elsewhere, people ordinarily have only their personal welfare in mind; here in Utopia, on the other hand, where there is no private property, people are seriously interested only in the interest of the community at large.*«

More 1524, 1563; *Utopische Staat* 1960; Mohl 1960; Servier 1971; Trousson 1975; Morus 1983; Berghahn 1983; Wuckel 1986; Kruft 1989; Brentjes 1993; Rahmsdorf 1999; Seibt 2001; Bloch 2002 Eaton 2002; *Visionen und Utopien* 2002.

What ideas and motivation on the author's part form the basis of More's Utopia? A critique of his own time, of social ills was doubtless the most important impetus for his blueprint of an ideal state. Yet existing realities may also have had an influence on More. Undoubtedly he was familiar with the reports of sailors about the empire of the Incas. The state was an early 15th-century fabrication, as it were, and we may recognize a series of very authoritarian Inca institutions in More's work – for example, the fact that all citizens are obliged to work, that they abstain from luxuries, that the economy is under state control, goods are distributed to families from public warehouses according to their needs, and so on.

Amerigo Vespucci's journey was a reality, and he gives an account – not necessarily authentic – of the inhabitants of the New World: It is only there that people live naturally, but they are »epicures rather than stoics«. They live »without the curse of money, without laws, and without unjust judges«. Thomas More's state is an authoritarian one, and even the many »democratic« institutions do not change this fact; some Utopian moves toward collectivization are totalitarian in character. The fact that Utopians keep slaves and employ impoverished guest workers, the strict marriage laws, euthanasia by starvation, and many other measures are the reason that we can in no way regard Utopia as an ideal state today, although many aspects of the system have actually been implemented since the book was written.

Nevertheless, after Plato, Thomas More's story is the second milestone in the history of utopias – and has given its name to similar visions during the centuries that followed.

Simon Stevin (1548–1620). The standardized city, 1594

»Why does every house have to look different? And why do they all have to be full of decorations? People are alike, therefore we can have houses that are alike, constructed from the same building materials.« This is Simon Stevin's justification for his grid city, though it does have a few positive qualities.

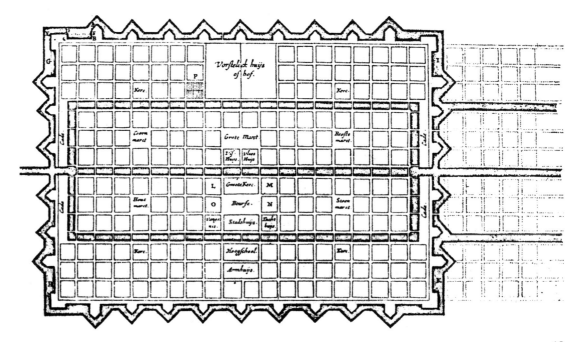

62. Simon Stevin, standardized city, 1594.

A straight watercourse, more of a canal, is connected with the zigzag moats by the town wall, and the outer canal divides into three in the town. The town is thus divided into three zones, each with three rows of houses. The houses are exact squares and are all standardized, as are the roofs, windows, and doors, of course.

We find the public institutions arranged astonishingly systematically along the middle diagonal axis. Directly by the river is the big church, orientated towards the square. Then come the town hall, the university, and the poorhouse. On the other side of the river are the two community centers, then the big market, and, not far from the town wall, the vorstellickhuijs (prince's house) with a courtyard. The grid includes another four square areas for the markets and four for smaller churches.

»I also planned for the expansion of the town«, explains Stevin, »and the town's grid system can definitely continue growing even beyond the walls, along the canals.«

There is also a stock market, for the mathematician and engineer Simon Stevin has long since moved away from idealistic communism and counts on an organic, mercantile financial system and a powerful military.

Vercelloni 1994.

We realize that 400 years ago, long before the industrial revolution, standardization, perhaps even prefabrication, was practiced, and with surprising rigidity.

Francis Bacon (1561–1626). Bensalem – the new Atlantis (*Nova Atlantis*, 1626)

We are shipwrecked on the island of Bensalem, a place we have never heard of before. We are warmly welcomed by the indigenous people, and are able to stay for six weeks. We are put up in a beautiful, spacious strangers' house, built of red brick, with glass windows, cheerfully furnished and clean. We find a very similar, Christian society as the one back in our home country, but the island is a huge field for experimentation whose goal is to »*discover the causes and motions as well as the hidden forces of nature, and to expand the frontiers of human power as far as possible.*«

The island state was founded 1,900 years ago by King Solamona, who has ruled it benevolently ever since. He created the »College of the Works of Six Days«, the House of Solomon, and it is now dedicated to the study and contemplation of the works and creatures of God. This House of Solomon is the university, and it is the actual center of the town. The scientists are part of a kind of order and are priests at the same time. Their rank is higher than even that of kings. And the elite that resides in the House of Solomon forms an exclusive and elitist community, secluded and sufficient unto itself.

It took several days to get to know all the magnificent and wonderful institutions on the island, and we can only give a short report about our most important impressions. For many of the facilities, we have to descend deep into caves, up to 600 fathoms (about 1,200 m) down. This is where the institutes and laboratories that do not need light are housed. To visit other institutions we climb up into hollowed-out mountains, up to three miles (roughly 5,000 m) high. Occasionally these are topped by towers half a mile high. These house complex, varied laboratories that conduct scientific experiments on substances, materials, metals, earths, apparatus, and machines. Back in the daylight, we now pass large lakes.

»They are salt-water or sweet, and we raise fish, birds, and water animals of all kinds«, explains our guide. »In artificial fountains, cataracts, and wells, dead and living matter is observed.« Now we enter widely spanned, brightly lit halls. These contain the medicinal baths. Water and air are suitably enriched and the most varied illnesses are cured here.

Why are so many animals locked up in cages and enclosures? Our guide fills us with amazement: »Here the animals wait for all kinds of different experiments. We cause them to fall ill and put them in suspended animation. We make them bigger and smaller, fertile and infertile, poisoned and amputated, discolored and malformed. All these are things that the animals must endure for the benefit of human beings.«

Our next stop seems much friendlier: Here there is a winepress, beer is brewed, bread is baked, and in the kitchens rare and unusual foods are prepared. In addition there are dietary foods, healing dishes, and immediately adjacent to the kitchens, there is the big department for remedies of every kind, including many that are chemically treated or produced.

Once again we come to big halls containing equipment and machines for many different types of materials and goods: paper and linen, silk, and other textiles. Our tour continues as we view the optics workshops with beautiful lighting effects and telescopes, then the acoustics workshops with sound experiments, and finally the olfactory rooms with rare perfumes.

It is impossible to see everything in one day. The next morning we go on to look at the mechanics' workshops, with machines, propellers, mechanisms, engines of war, with automats and mathematical instruments.

Now we arrive at the seashore, and here it is possible to experiment on an even larger scale than by the lakes. At the seashore artificial birds and underwater boats are launched. And finally, as a conclusion to our inquiries, we arrive at the house of illusions, with sleight of hand and artifices, with lighting effects and magic surprises.

Deeply impressed by this wealth of ideas and inventions, we return to our quarters. In this way we have learned a great deal about the priest scholars and their work. About the other people in this country, however, we can discover hardly anything except that they live in exemplary Christian chastity and that the Christian commandment of brotherliness determines how they live. There are no houses of pleasure, no bordellos, and no prostitutes. Married men are punished more severely for offences than bachelors. Couples selected for marriage are not allowed to look at each other naked. This is done by a male and female friend during segregated swimming in the two pools »Adam« and »Eve.«

During our stroll through town we now come upon a large square and are surprised by a merry, strange festival here – though today is not listed as a religious feast day in the calendar, or is it? Our guide explains: »When a married couple has 30 living descendants, with the youngest over three years old, there is a big celebration and they are all honored by the city. Problems are discussed, quarrels are settled, advice and help are offered. Those who lead a depraved life are criticized. But weddings and life problems are also discussed.«

For us it was a special honor and pleasure that we were given an audience with the venerable Father of the House of Solomon. His appearance, clothing, and language were dignified and measured. The throne and the room in which it is placed without a pedestal showed exquisite taste. In a detailed conversation the »Father« explains all the amazing institutions on the island, and we express our gratitude and respect.

Our stay had reached its end. When the winds turned favorable, we left the island with many good wishes, still full of amazing impressions.

Bacon 1626; *Der utopische Staat* 1960; Mohl 1960; Berghahn 1983; Vercelloni 1994.

Bacon's description remained unfinished. We do not know what concepts he was planning to discuss in the second part of his essay. The magnificent institutions portrayed by Bacon would be possible only if a country achieved a considerable potential for power, more or less like that propagated by Machiavelli. In another work Bacon comes to terms with idols – flaws in human reasoning. He mentions four of them:

1. Human delusion about themselves and about the nature of the human race (*idola tribus*).

2. Delusions about the nature of the world, or, more precisely and expressed in modern terms, the environment (*idola specus*).

3. The delusions of the market. They are a consequence of the limited vocabulary of colloquial language, of the masses' unthinking clichés (*idola fori*).

4. Delusions that result from different systems of philosophy and religion (*idola theatri*).

Thus, for the first time, Bacon pointed out the risk to humankind as it teeters in a gulf between reality and consciousness without being aware of its delusions. However, there is a delusion contained in Bacon's utopian fragment itself – the assumption that a future human society can be organized exclusively according to scientific insights.

Richard Newcourt (1602–1679). A rebuilt London, 1666

It was an unimaginable catastrophe: In 1666 four-fifths of the city of London were destroyed by fire. But Richard Newcourt jettisoned the chaos of the medieval wooden houses and built a modern London out of stone – and how could that be anything but a consistent grid city?

We enter through one of the middle gates of the three times three town gates – the fourth side of the rectangle is located directly on the Thames River – and, passing the rectangular blocks of buildings, reach a large square. Each of the blocks has a small courtyard in its center, and as we walk further, we discover four more squares. But we cannot ascertain where the public buildings,

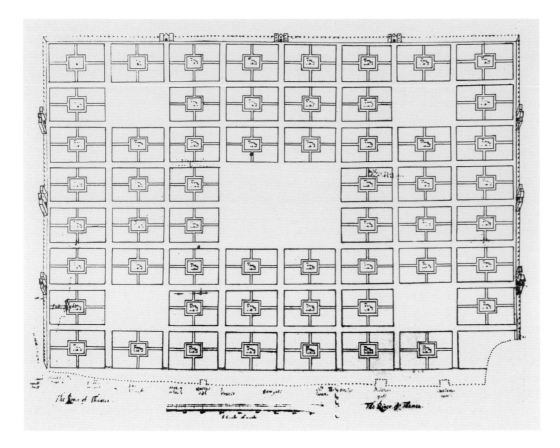

the buildings for the community, are located. Mr. Newcourt tells us how much trouble he had pushing through such an ideal model with the existing distribution of property and antiquated infrastructures. »But«, adds Mr. Newcourt, »we do have fantastic opportunities for implementing such concepts radically and single-mindedly: in the New World, in America.«

Vercelloni 1994.

Defense is no longer a necessity, and thus the polygonal or round city layout becomes superfluous. Rather, a completely logical, indeed monotonous, plan is proposed: We've been familiar with the grid city since antiquity, and it still plays an important role today. In his arrangement of the five squares Newcourt adapts earlier typologies.

Samuel Gott (1613–1671) with John Milton (1608–1674)? Nova Solyma (*Novae Solymae. Libri sex*, 1648)

Nova Solyma is a wonderful city on top of a mountain. A four-foot-thick wall surrounds it protectively. Twelve solidly built gates afford entrance as well as protection, and above each gate there is a strong tower for guarding and protecting the city. The names and tribal symbols of the twelve prophets are engraved in the gates. We travelers enter the city through the gate of Judah and find ourselves on a lovely street; on both sides of it, in individual blocks, are houses built of stone, all of which have the same frontal view. While nothing remains of the old Solyma, the city has been renewed in the same location, on an even larger scale.

Now we have reached the big marketplace. Here is the commodity exchange with passages leading to a colonnaded courtyard with columns of fine marble. In small shops, all kinds of pretty and useful objects are for sale, and in the upper gallery there is a bazaar exclusively for women. The schools and universities are located on the edge of town. Their main task is religious education. Young people are trained to be tough and persevering, Lies and shamelessness are severely frowned upon. We are very impressed with the education of the boys: With love of God and of their native land as a foundation, they are taught philosophy, economics, theology, medicine, and law, depending on their age.

We are most disappointed to learn, however, that in this community, which appears to be so ideal, girls enjoy this careful education only in part.

In addition to education, the community also highly values a sound family; both are necessary to produce good citizens. Then they can responsibly participate in the yearly elections. It's true that the different social classes are strictly separated from each other. And there's something else that disconcerts us: Jews have had to convert to Christianity in order to live in this city.

Gott 1648; Trousson 1975; Manguel 1981.

The layout of the city is reminiscent of the apocalyptic Jerusalem with twelve angels above the twelve city gates – the Lamb in the center is replaced by the stock exchange. What was the city supposed to look like? A square with three gates on each side, as in the medieval depictions? A hexagon? A dodecagon? Samuel Gott's original tract was divided into six chapters:

1. De Puerititia (about boyhood), 2. De Creatione Mundi (about the creation of the world), 3. De Juventute (about youth), 4. De Peccato (about sin), 5. De Virile Aetate (about manhood), 6. De Redemptione Hominis (about the resurrection of humankind).

After some doubts as to Samuel Gott's authorship, the matter seems to have been settled, and John Milton's participation in the work, if any, is probably only marginal.

4.3. Germany

Johann Eberlin von Günzburg (1465–1533). Wolfaria (*New Statuten die Psitacus gebracht hat uss dem Land Wolfaria welche beträffendt Reformierung geystlichen stand ... . Der X Bundtgnosz and Ein newe Ordnüng weltlichs standts des Psitacus anzeigt hat in Wolfaria beschriben. Der XI Bundtgnosz*, 1521)

It's a wonderful city Eberlin von Günzburg leads us through, for here, he assures us, »there are all those things for the inhabitants that the nobles have gradually stolen from the peasants.«

It's a pretty town, and we admire the cleanliness of the streets, the lovely colors of the houses, the majestic church.

But something that is even more admirable is probably the virtuousness of the inhabitants – or rather, their compliance with the laws and regulations, which Johann Eberlin is only too happy to explain to us:

»*There is to be no honorable work but farming. All nobles shall live on agriculture. Every town has ten bailiwicks under it and a count as its head. No one has power to do anything without the aid and advice of those who have been set and ordered to do this by the community of citizens.*«

We are primarily interested in how the lofty morals of the townspeople can be maintained, and we are horrified by the severe punishments, for every publicly known adulterer (but what about secret adulterers?) is to be killed, every drunkard to be drowned, and everyone who has committed perjury is to be caned. Every murderer is murdered, while a thief works as a servant for a year, doing menial work for the community and wearing chains on both feet.

What entertainment can be found in the town? »*Board games for diversion are allowed at proper times, but [betting is] not to exceed one kreuzer and not in a place where the players can be openly seen. All young people are forbidden to play cards and dice games for money. Every week there is a day when one may dance at a public place for three hours after noon, men and women. Every month there is a special delightful public entertainment. None shall last longer than half a day or be too costly.*«

One more thing interests us: How did Johann Eberlin achieve the fine order in the little town? Here are a number of town regulations:

»In all towns all craftspeople have special streets. No excessively expensive house is built except for public buildings, such as the town hall, large shops, bathhouse, school, houses of entertainment, etc. All men and young boys, and all women and young girls have special bathhouses. In every bathhouse there is a sweat room and a water bath. All children are sent to school at the age of three until they are eight years old. Schools are paid for from community coffers. When a child is eight years old, it is apprenticed to a craftsman or it may be allowed to continue its studies. In school children learn German and Latin, the art of measuring and calculating, astronomy, and playing a stringed instrument.«

Eberlin 1525; Dirx 1982.

The Franciscan Father Johann Eberlin was relieved of his office as a preacher in Günzburg – he had too positive a view of Martin Luther's reform proposals. We clearly sense – and this includes his cri-

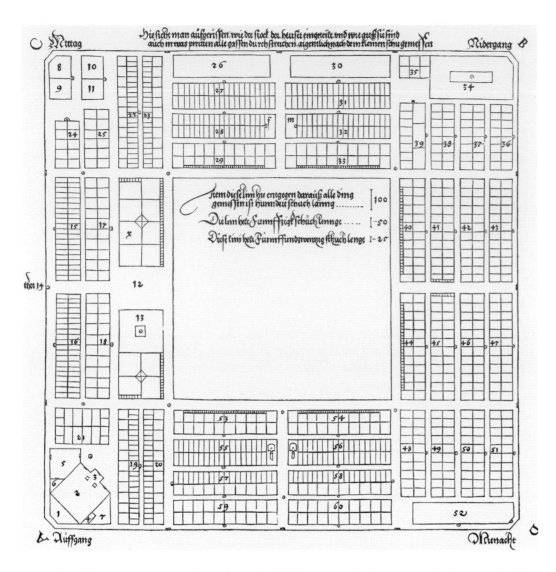

tique of the Church and clergy – that Johann Eberlin is not proclaiming any utopias here. Rather, in his »Wolfaria«, as he calls the rules, he ventures to tackle long overdue reforms – against a background of peasant wars, rebellions, and strikes.

Albrecht Dürer (1471–1528). The ideal town (*Etliche Unterricht zu Befestigung der Stett, Schloss und Flecken*, 1527) and the round fortress, 1528

A plain wall, its corners beveled, surrounds the town. As we enter by the only gate we walk past two perfectly straight rows of houses and come into a spacious square. From here we can see that only a small number of buildings and a few squares detract from the perfect grid geometry. There are very narrow and somewhat wider houses, but they are almost equally deep.

The craftspeople's workshops are very cleverly placed. For example, the smithy is right next to the foundries, and the wine shops are also well positioned.

All those we meet have their specific moral task, for, as Albrecht Dürer informs us, »*no useless persons may live there. Rather, the inhabitants are capable, devout, wise men, honorable and experienced in the arts, good artisans.*«

Although Master Dürer knows that we are interested only in towns, he invites us to visit a marine fortress, and we agree with pleasure. Our approach by ship is extremely beautiful. A round area with a wide staircase projects into the sea, and we walk out into the monumental, circular structure. Master Dürer shows us a plan and explains how he proceeded during construction: »*First one builds the interior round floor B with all its upper story, seventy feet high, then storeroom D built 50 feet high, ditto the upright storerooms that extend as far as the cliff and into the water. At the top they are built like the bastion described earlier, completely freestanding at all its battlements. The road should be on high ground.*«

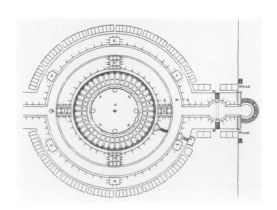

A tour over the bastions and over the moats shows us that here, too, there has been a synthesis between large, gestural form and defence.

Dürer 1527; *Stadt und Utopie* 1982; Kruft 1989; Vercelloni 1994; Eaton 2001.

The town's layout is reminiscent of Tenochtitlán in Mexico, whose plan the conqueror Cortès laid at the feet of Emperor Charles the Fifth, and it is possible that Dürer knew about this plan. Only ten years after More's *Utopia*, the sensitive, devout painter surprises us by the way he distances himself from romanticism and enthusiasm as he sketches the new city. It is characterized by an inexorably approaching rationality, which will be raised to excessive aesthetic heights once more in the star patterns of the Italian and French fortress towns. A look, particularly at American towns founded during the last 500 years, shows us to what extent Dürer's ideal plan was actually implemented.

Dürer surprises us with a little-known circular layout. While this is not a city but a marine fortress, its ring system is a thoroughly urban concept.

Caspar Stiblin (Stüblin, Stiblinus, 1526–1563). The blissful republic on the island of Macaria (*Ejusdem de Eudaemonensium republica commentarioulus*, 1555)

A modest harbor receives our ship and at once we find ourselves in a most charming landscape. Gentle hills, little groves, flowering meadows delight us, and among them are simple small houses, a little church, a mill.

We also really like the little town of Macaria.

»A round city always has many advantages«, explains Caspar Stiblin. »It is easy to defend and pretty to look at.«

The town is protected by three ring walls and moats. A bridge leads across the moat to one of the four town gates. We pass two more fortification rings and another gate, then the street takes us into the center past pretty, two-story houses. In small squares there are fountains, and we can also look inside the rooms where artisans do their work. In the center the symbols of the two rul-

66. Caspar Stiblin, Macariae et Eudaemonis Tabella, 1555.

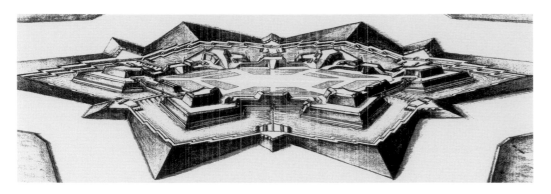

67. Daniel Speckle, fortified city, 1589.
68. Daniel Speckle, plan of the fortification of a city, 1639. 1 church, 2 churchyard, priests' dwellings at the side, 3 municipal hall, quarters for the prince, 4 town hall, 5 long alleyways and transverse alleys with citizens' dwellings, craftsmen and soldiers on the periphery, 6 weighmaster's building, trading house, inn, soldiers' quarters, hospital, stables, arsenal, 7 warehouse, granaries and fruit stores.

ing powers stand peacefully side by side: a majestic church with a tower, and next to it the town hall with a turret.

All the townspeople are by no means equal. There are plebeians and patricians. But all the people, be they simple citizens or highly placed, work for the good of the community.

Of course there is also severe punishment for such offences as drunkenness, and those who blaspheme have their tongues cut off.

The citizens do not have to work a great deal, they are content with very little. Their children do not receive a rich inheritance, but a strict education.

»*Some are highly respected and recipients of many honors, others are lowly and modest, but without hatred toward those in power, who in turn do not despise them – far from it – but give them protection.*«

They all wear similar simple clothing, with only slight differences related to gender and social rank, depending on whether the person is a senator, patrician, married woman, or young girl.

»*True nobility is not achieved by ancestors or snobbery, but only through honorable deeds.*«
However, the preservation of morality does seem to be linked to a few restrictions of freedom:

»*Believing that people tend by nature to be vile rather than virtuous, the authorities forbid travel abroad and allow it only in emergencies or when urgent business requires it, so that the citizens are not contaminated by the customs of other nations.*«

Stiblin 1555; Servier 1971; Manguel 1981; Rahmsdorf 1999; Seibt 2001.

We are reminded of certain aspects of the Platonic state. The city is a closed system, the burghers may not leave it so that they will not become corrupt. But the townspeople do not know war, hunger, or unemployment.

Daniel Speckle (1536–1589). A fortified town, 1589

»It's not just the Italians – we Germans, too, know how to build fortified cities!« explains Daniel Speckle with some degree of pride. »And that is necessary, of course, so that we can resist the Turks!« And Speckle explains the nature of the fortification.

Admittedly, at first we have the impression of walking through one of those Italian towns that we visited a good 30 years ago. But soon we notice a few innovations. True, Speckle has again chosen the octagon as the basic form, but the four massive outworks fill it out to something that is nearly a square. As usual, eight main streets, and an additional four side streets, run from the octagonal square in the center. Here are the simple but well-kept middle-class residential houses and, more toward the edge of town, the soldiers' quarters and the artisans' workshops. Four sectors are reserved for special functions. First and foremost, here is the church with a pretty but simple façade facing the square. Just behind it is the churchyard, with the housing for the priests off to the side.

The governor's building with its two courtyards is considerably larger, since it has the task of providing accommodation for the prince during his visits.

Opposite the church is the large store with the public weights building and the inn. »In the rear wing«, explains Speckle, »there is room for everything that might cause bad smells: the hospital, the stables, the mercenaries' quarters.«

The fourth sector, finally, is filled by the town hall. In the two exterior rings, almost by the fortress walls, are the storehouses, granaries, and fruit storerooms.

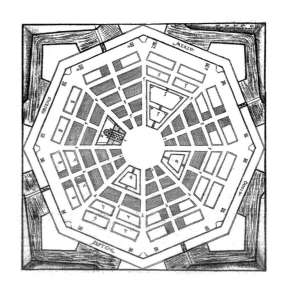

»My town is not only safe and beautiful, but also pleasant. For we all share a common property and work hard. Also there are no vagabonds in my city.«
Speckle 1589, 1589, 1608, 1639; Vercelloni 1994; Neumeyer 2002.

In the Italian fortress towns we find the square only as an exception, while it is often found in German ideal towns. The Italians would no doubt question how well the latter fortifications work.

Heinrich Schickhardt (1558–1635). Freudenstadt, 1599–1604

When we approach the town, we are surprised that it is surrounded by a moat and two walls with corner towers, for compared to the Italian towns the quality of its fortification is not very convincing. We enter Freudenstadt by one of the four bridges through a modest town gate. The street leads directly toward the ducal palace of Frederick the First of Württemberg, though not toward its portal, but toward one corner of the building with one of the stairwells: The square building lies rotated by 45° on the spacious marketplace, which we reach after going past the five streets and five rows of houses. The moat with its two bridges seems more of a symbol rather than a protective measure. After arriving in the town square we become aware that it is a symmetrical square, broken up by pergolas. Its corners, however, do not open into streets (something we are familiar with from Dürer's ideal town), but rather are closed off by strange angled buildings: Here are the school, covered market, town hall, and – what is particularly remarkable – the church.

The Protestant pastor Andreas Veringer speaks about the »God's level square«, but not very convincingly: Rather, we suspect that the function and symbol of the church were subjected to the geometric system of the architect, and this conviction is confirmed when we enter the space. The nave gives us an odd sense of space. »So as to ensure order«, Master Schickhardt points out, »I naturally erected two church towers.«

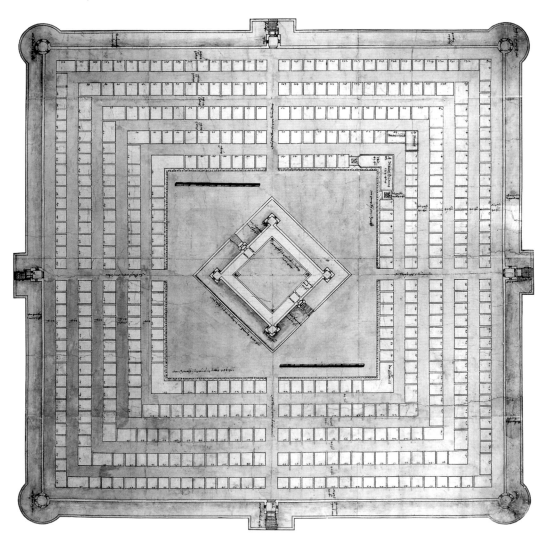

69. Heinrich Schickhardt, plan of Freudenstadt, 1604.

The town square is defined by the remarkable uniformity of the buildings that seems to be made less monotonous by using beautiful arcades. We might think of another, albeit more magnificent, model: the Place Royale in Paris.

»The fact that the citizens are equal«, says Mr. Schickhardt, »must also be expressed in the similarity of the buildings. In addition to the four corner buildings, somewhat larger houses are found only at the corners of the rows of houses.«

We tell Schickhardt we're also interested in the dimensions. He gives us a precise answer: »The inside of the marketplace measures 786 feet, while the outside of the town measures 1798 feet. Each house is 50 feet wide,* and we've built a total of 490 farmsteads.«

With astonishment we learn that here in the Black Forest the town is inhabited by Protestants – Lutherans, Calvinists, and Huguenots. They were banished from a Catholic France, but also from Carinthia and Styria, and Duke Frederick the First built this town especially for them.
Kruft 1989; Rahmsdorf 1999; Eaton 2001.

But now we become aware that we have left Utopia: Freudenstadt was actually built – only the castle in the center was never erected, and we also look in vain for the logical, rigid arrangement of the rows of houses and two of the angular buildings. The arcades were erected, and the town square is now filled in by the city hall, a council building, and a green space. Thus the ideal plan remained a utopia after all.

The public buildings – the town hall, covered market, school – were destroyed by a fire back in 1632. In 1945, a large part of the town was laid waste by bomb raids. From 1947 to 1950 it was rebuilt.

The archivist of the Danish King Christian IV (1577–1648). Glückstadt, 1616, 1756

Our flight brings us a surprise: It's as though a hexagonal Italian Renaissance town had been broken in half and joined to a completely irregular town. From the rectangular town square seven radial streets go only in an eastern direction. On the western side the »Fleth« (a river port) is the connecting seam to the irregular part, through which the Rhin River flows. The irregular ribbon of the fortification ties together the dissimilar parts of town.

Our walk leads us through a very beautiful town. On the main square are the town hall, the main police station, and the Lutheran church; close by is the Reformed church, while the Catholic church is far away and, naturally, there is a small synagogue in Judenstraße (Jews' Street).

»Yes«, says our guide, »as you see, the town is open to all faiths, and though there are occasional conflicts, tolerance is important for us.«

70. Plan of the fortress Glückstadt, Schleswig-Holstein, Germany, 1616, 1756. 1 Round Bastion 2 On the Sortie (Auf der Sortie), 3 laundry, 4 High Bastion, 5 High Cat (Hohe Katze), 6 large powder magazine, 7 Behind the Justice, 8 By the Bear (Bey dem Bähren), 9 by the small powder magazine, 10 Rantzem Bastion, 11 By the Sheepfold, 12 Come Back (Kehr-Wieder), 13 Take Care (Sieh-dich-vor), 14 house of provisions, 15 sailors' guardhouse, 16 materials yard, 17 peat stable, 18 new corps de garde, 19 marine budget storehouse, 20 guardhouse by the Take Care, 21 New Gate guardhouses, 22 guardhouse By the Bear, 23 Cremper Gate guardhouses, 24 jail, 25 wall master's residence, 26 guardhouse by the Dyke Gate, 27 laboratory, 28 armory and smithy, 29 main police station, 30 foundry house, 31 coach house, 32 powder magazines, 33 battery gunpowder stores, 34 town hall, 35 prison and workhouse, 36 Lutheran church, 37 Catholic church, 38 Reformed church, 39 Jewish synagogue.

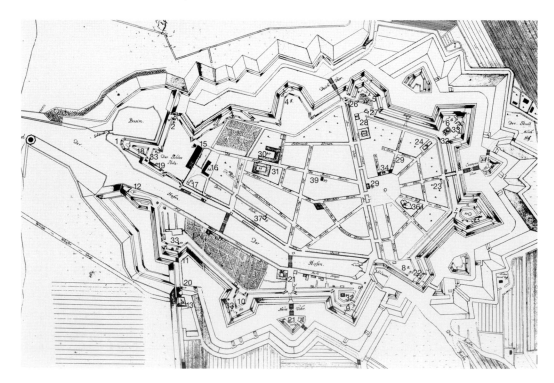

Nevertheless, of course, the Jewish cemetery is far distant from the Christian one. Both are outside the walls.

The castle is a very plain building with a spacious square in front of it, at the western end of town. The bastions and ravelins are amply equipped with guards, powder magazines, and storage depots.

We conclude our tour with a visit to the beautiful parks and the harbor on the Rhin River. Glückstadt 1984.

A town – this one in the North – that turns the ideal plan of Italian fortress towns into a reality – but only halfway, for the topography and older settlements determined the bizarre layout. The town was intended to be a stronghold against the commercial power on the Rhin.

Robert Fludd (1574–1637). Ideal fortress town, 1617

In Robert Fludd we meet a highly educated, rounded personality. The man who is to be our guide through the town is not only a physician, philosopher, designer, but is also familiar with mathematics, alchemy, the occult, and harmony, and has traveled to many countries.

His town is hard and severe and mightily fortified. The extensive fortifications are at least five times bigger than the inhabitable center itself.

»A city is complete only when it is fortified absolutely securely« says Robert Fludd. »I chose the form of a hexagon, and with the addition of the large-scale bastions we have a lovely twelve-cornered star.«

Fludd is not content with one moat. He considers it necessary to have two, but we do not know how this vast quantity of water can be brought in. There is only a temporary bridge as we cross the first, uncommonly wide moat. The small bastions are connected with the first town gates by wooden bridges. Then, crossing another wooden bridge, we reach a second moat and fortification. Only then do we enter the actual town through the next town gate. The town is divided precisely into six segments. From the six inner bastions, six radial streets lead to the inner ring of streets and finally to a central square.

But these magnificent installations were only possible by acquiring the kind of power advocated by Machiavelli: the prince as an absolute ruler, whose universal exercise of power serves to safeguard the public interest.

Robert Fludd is by no means interested merely in the fortification of the town. Rather, what matters to him is knowledge and wisdom, which can prosper only in a good city. Therefore Fludd has built a special house, a kind of temple of knowledge.

The scholars who live in »Solomon's House« form an exclusive and elitist community, secluded and self-sufficient and completely devoted to science, like a monastery.

As for the other people in this state, we are able to learn hardly anything about them, except that they live in exemplary Christian chastity and that the Christian commandment of brotherliness defines their lives.

Fludd 1617; Manguel 1981; Vercelloni 1994; Eaton 2001.

The fortress town depicted by Robert Fludd in his large engraving probably represents the most extreme discrepancy between a fortification and a residential town. We find no entrance, no bridge leading to the ravelins.

Johann Valentin Andreae (1586–1654). Christianopolis (*Reipublicae Christianopolitanae descriptio*, 1619)

Before we are allowed to enter Christianopolis, we have to submit to a threefold test: Are we quacks, beggars, or showmen? Do we have a good moral character and temperament? Are we sufficiently advanced in the contemplation and knowledge of heaven and earth, nature and art, language and science?

Found worthy, and especially welcome since we are Protestants, we enter the town. It forms an exact square, each of whose sides is 700 feet (210 m) long, *»amply fortified with four strong bastions and a wall. It is located exactly according to the four winds of the world.«* There are four rows of buildings with a public street and a splendid wide market. In the middle there is a round

71. Robert Fludd (?), ideal fortress town, 1617.

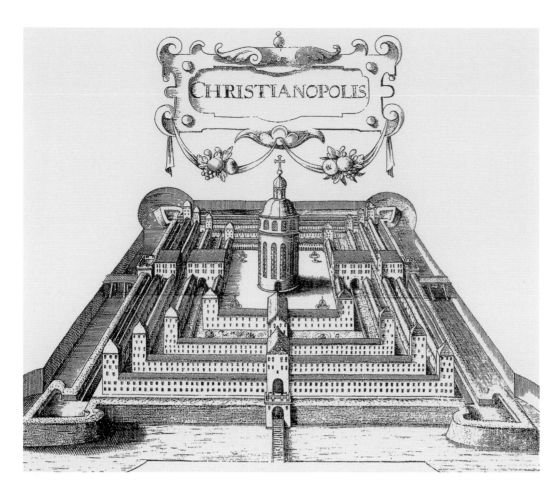

building whose diameter is 100 feet (30 m). We enter a room with a high ceiling, a small round church. A narrow staircase goes up to the top floor. Here, in the council hall, the city administration, which numbers 400 community members, holds its meetings: Ecclesiastical and worldly power are united in one tower – the idea is a new synthesis of the influential powers. The rest of the buildings are three stories high and made of fired bricks, »*all built the same way and clean, without any filth. The commonest have three rooms – a living room, bedroom, and kitchen.*«

The outer blocks of houses are intended for the trades and farming. In the middle blocks there are 88 houses with 264 apartments for 400 inhabitants. The houses have lovely arcades on the street side. In the rear, each house has a small garden.

We are very impressed by the technical installations: Each house has running water, and together with the sewer system this prevents all epidemics and many diseases. The houses are constructed alike by the state for all the citizens. As we wander through the town, we are surprised to see that it is organized according to individual functions, but more so than medieval cities, which are merely divided into districts for various craftspeople. The trades are organized according to the material the craftspeople work with: metal, stone, wood, and textiles each have their own area.

The town is roughly divided into three districts: one for food, one for training and education, and one for reflection. Additional areas are dedicated to farming and workshops. Thus material life is safeguarded and the people have enough leisure to dedicate themselves to philosophy and theology.

In the inner district we find the »college« for science, education, and administration. In science, arithmetic is the specialty of the scholars. And Master Andreae reminds us of the many aspects of this discipline, which is at once rational and metaphysical: »*Every day in arithmetic we find something we marvel at, something that sharpens our intelligence and reduces the amount of work. Numbers are revealed by God. The divine dimensions show us how God, in ineffable harmony, holds everything together, moves everything powerfully and wisely.*«

Thus, the city itself is laid out according to the figures and measurements described in Revelations. »The holy city of Jerusalem comes down out of heaven from God. And the angel with the measuring rod of gold measured the city, its length and breadth.«

Andreae now takes us into the extensive scientific institutions and the science museum. Especially interesting is the precision workshop for manufacturing mathematical instruments. The large library is open to everyone, and the citizens themselves are invited to write books about a diverse number of topics. Many of these books are acquired by the library.

Yet the arts are not neglected either. In the painters' academies the young men endeavor to create a noble and pure art, and therefore we will look in vain for the lascivious nudity of the goddesses of antiquity. The artists are very productive, and thus we are not at all surprised that all rooms are most richly ornamented with fine paintings, an important contribution to human education. It is no wonder that we find a beautiful artists' studio, or that the entire city is decorated with splendid paintings on historical themes.

Education – in a strictly Christian sense, of course – is considered very important, and it is the responsibility of the community. We are also not surprised that the schools are very spacious, beautiful, and well lit. They too are decorated with countless pictures. Once children are six years old, the parents send them to be educated in boarding schools. In eight large halls, the individual disciplines are taught. Spacious and well-equipped studios and laboratories are dedicated to the arts and natural sciences. Moral education is given priority over accumulation of knowledge. In later life people become members of one of three classes – professions dealing with nutrition, teaching, or dedicated to contemplation. However, craftspeople are also scholars, and conversely scholars have mastered a skilled trade.

In this Christian, Protestant republic – and in this it resembles early Christianity – there is no private property, for all persons receive everything they need from the community. »*No one has more wealth than another.*« They also do not have to work more than a few hours a day. »*Nobody has money*«, Andreae informs us, »*and besides it has no value for private purposes. And it is precisely in this respect that the inhabitants may be regarded as fortunate: No one surpasses another by the wealth he owns, because competence and intelligence are more in demand, and morality and piety enjoy the highest esteem.*«

Indeed, in our walks through the town we have seen no sad, distressed faces, people are friendly toward each other and toward strangers. And Andreae again reminds us of the root causes of this mentality: »*Yes, these are cheerful people, and skilled in everything they have to do in this world. They share whatever gifts of God they have with the community and keep almost nothing for themselves.*«

Meals are eaten in the families, and food is handed out from the general supply and distributed weekly. The citizens do not want collective meals because those are inevitably accompanied by immoderate eating and drinking and noise.

Everywhere we encounter expressions of Christian virtue: Work is held in high regard though it is not done for profit, and three times a day people worship, giving thanks to God. »*We strive for marital chastity and value it especially, so that no one will be consumed and weakened by lust. Procreation has inherent dignity, while the ardor of sensual desire must be condemned.*«

In everything, however, the goal is to do good and please God.

Now Andreae invites us for a walk outside the city walls, and we are struck by the clever division of economic facilities: In the east there is agriculture, in the south they breed cattle, and the mills are located by the water. All the workshops that need fire, such as smelting plants and forges, are located in the west, and finally storehouses and butcher shops are located on the north side.

No sooner have we left the work area than we are walking through lovely gardens that not only provide decoration and enjoyment, but also supply the inhabitants with fresh fruit and vegetables. These cultivated gardens merge directly into the natural landscape.

Master Andreae talks to us about the basic philosophy of his city: »*Intelligence, knowledge, and work are not opposites, but we have to make sure there is a mediating moderation. Human beings have three spheres of duty, and we observe them unquestioningly. There is our duty toward God, toward the state, and toward science and the economy.*« He continues: »*If matter is not analyzed by experiments, and gaps in human knowledge are not closed with the help of appropriate instruments, human beings are worthless.*«

Andreae 1619; Mohl 1960; Tod/Wheeler 1978; Manguel 1981; Berneri 1950, 1971; Kraft 1989; Vercelloni 1994; Rahmsdorf 1999; Eaton 2001; *Visionen und Utopien* 2002/03; Seibt 2001.

The influences of Tommaso Campanella, of the Rosicrucians, and the intellectual trends of his time cannot be overlooked in Andreae's philosophy. However, the accusation that his work was plagiarism is surely unjustified.

We might regard the structuring of Christianopolis according to individual functions as an early model of a modern idea of the city – urban functionalism as expressed in the ideas of the 1930s. Lewis Mumford (1922) correctly evaluated this protofunctionalism: »When planning the industrial zones of Christianopolis, these seventeenth-century utopians anticipated the best practice that has been worked out today, after a century of uncontrolled building. The division of the city into zones, the distinction between heavy and light industry, the clustering of similar industrial plants, the planning of an agricultural zone adjacent to the city – in all these aspects, our garden cities are merely belated reproductions of Christianopolis.«

Joseph Furttenbach the Elder (1591–1667). The oval city, 1650

»All buildings in the city must be in a meaningful and ordered relationship to each other«, Furttenbach announces his principle. »But of course the city's fortification must also be perfect.«

For his city, Furttenbach has chosen a roughly oval layout. The moats are not too wide, the walls are strong, interrupted by eighteen bastions. Six ravelins are in the foreground, and we reach the city by these without having to pass the soldiers first. »I've lined up the most important city functions along the longitudinal axis. The armory is in the center, for it is the most important in times of war.«

The church, which is adjacent on the west side, then has to be smaller, of course. It is flanked by the town hall and the Latin school. When we walk further west from the church axis, we can first visit the wine tavern and the manor house or refresh ourselves in the baths. Between these and in the remaining parts of town, pretty, simple residential houses have been built in a somewhat uniform style.

Toward the east a huge freight depot has been built and further still, almost by the town wall, is the workhouse and, on the other side, the hospital, while between them there is another church. Thus we have found little that is romantic, but also nothing superfluous, and everything seems to have been carefully planned.

Furttenbach 1650; Vercelloni 1994.

Furttenbach's plan definitely deviates from the mostly central plans of the ideal towns. It has a clear, linear organization and might be regarded as a precursor of the linear city idea; the central axis is very clearly delineated, and the layout of the buildings certainly follows functional guidelines.

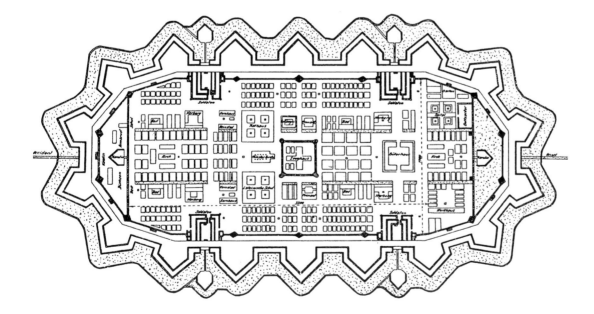

73. Joseph Furttenbach, ideal city, 1650.

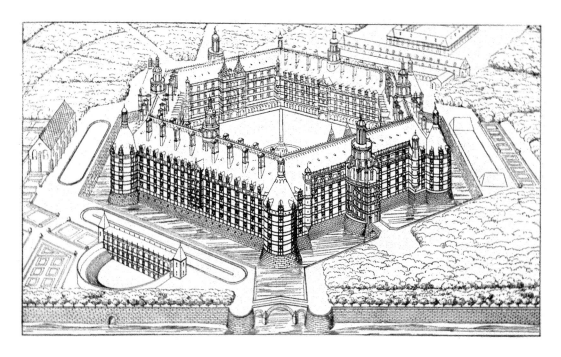

4.4. France, Netherlands

François Rabelais (c. 1494?–1553). The Abbey of Thélème (*Les horribles et épouvantables faits et prouesses du très renommé Pantagruel Roi des Dipsodes, fils du Grand Géant Gargantua. Composés nouvellement par maître Alcofrybas Nasie*, 1532; *La vie très horrifique du grand Gargantua, père de Pantagruel*, 1534/35)

What a monstrous creature our guide Pantagruel is! In spite of the excessive size of his body and its volume, he emerged at birth from his mother's left ear. Nevertheless he grows up to be a respected man, and Rabelais has already told us a few of his amazing adventures.

Now Pantagruel is under an obligation to a pious monk and wants to give him an abbey. But the monk wants to set it up entirely as he wishes and Pantagruel is ready to listen: »The monastery shall have no walls and shall admit only handsome and well-proportioned men and women, and they shall come in pairs, the men at twelve to eighteen years of age, the women at ten to fifteen.«

With Rabelais and Gargantua we now visit the abbey. Thélème is well planned: a large, hexagonal building whose sides are more than 200 m long, and which has a massive round tower at each corner. The Loire River flows past it on the north side. The fortress town has six floors and is architectonically sound and beautifully furnished. The ceilings are amply stuccoed, and on the second floor we admire the wide span of a vault. The roof is covered with slate and lead and there are gutters. On the roof ridges there are small figures of animals and men. The castle has not less than 9,332 chambers, each of which has side rooms. In the middle, between the towers, there is a large spiral staircase.

Now we enter the courtyard through a magnificent gate. In the middle of the courtyard there is an alabaster fountain adorned by the three Graces, and from their breasts, ears, mouths, eyes, and other orifices water bubbles forth merrily. The courtyard is broken up by lovely arcades. The columns are made of chalcedony and porphyry.

During our visit inside the town-castle we admire the splendid women's quarters, three-story baths, theaters, halls for ball games, and game preserves. Finally we stroll through the beautiful gardens. The chambers provide every kind of luxury: papered walls, large glass mirrors, carpets, embroideries are symbols of wealth and exquisite taste. In front of the halls of the women's quarters are the perfumers, through whose hands the men pass when they visit the women.

We are not surprised when we encounter men and women dressed in costly garments as they walk with dignity, accompanied by many servants. The men carry daggers and rapiers, and a white feather flutters from their black velvet caps. They coordinate their clothing with that of the women, for everything is done according to their will.

The Thélèmites pass their time in pleasurable activities: playing and jumping, racing and swimming, dancing and wrestling – and especially horseback riding. *»Their entire life is not lived according to rules or statutes, but according to their own free choice. They get up from bed when* *they please, they drink, eat, work, sleep when they feel like it. In their rule there is only one pro-viso: Do What You Will.*«

Rabelais 1540, 1548, 1913; Servier 1971; Berneri 1950, 1971.

Rabelais portrays the model of a life of luxury, of optimum life quality current in his time. Of course this lifestyle can be the privilege of only a small upper class, and so it is simply a slightly hypertrophied aristocratic lifestyle of his period – in other words, basically not a utopia. And Rabelais also leaves us in the dark as to what economic foundation this elitist hedonism might have: What do these people with their many servants live on, unless it's on the slave labor of a large underclass?

The story about Thélème is part of the abstruse novel *Gargantua and Pantagruel*, which appeared in 1540 and was translated into a deliberately antiquated German by Gottlieb Regis in 1913. The fact that the structural data are contradictory is probably part of the novel's boundless exaggerations.

Jacques Cartier (1491–1557). The city of Hochelaga in New France, 1556

We've been driving along the St. Lawrence River and are now at our destination. The road leads through a hilly landscape with sparse vegetation. Mont Real is on the left, and now we recognize the town's enclosure: Skillfully placed conical palisades, erected in a precise circle, form a sturdy wooden defense wall. The battlements can be reached with wooden ladders.

At the only entrance gate our delegation is warmly welcomed by a group of Indians. Other natives, scantily dressed, stand in the background looking on with astonishment.

Now we walk through the town gate directly toward the rectangular central square. Here King Agouhana has his residence. In the beautiful courtyard, a perpetual, magical fire is burning. In a few of the other houses, too, we can see flickering flames: However, these are the community kitchens for the whole town.

We are happy to get an overall view of the town, and between the houses and the palisades, the battlement invites us for a walk. We reach it by climbing a ladder from the circular road.
We see that generally six or ten rooms are combined into a block.

Ramusio 1556; Vercelloni 1994; Eaton 2001.

The town actually did exist. Fifty years later a larger settlement was built in its place. After this settlement was destroyed by the Iroquois, Ville-Marie de Montreal, modern-day Montreal in Canada, was founded in 1642.

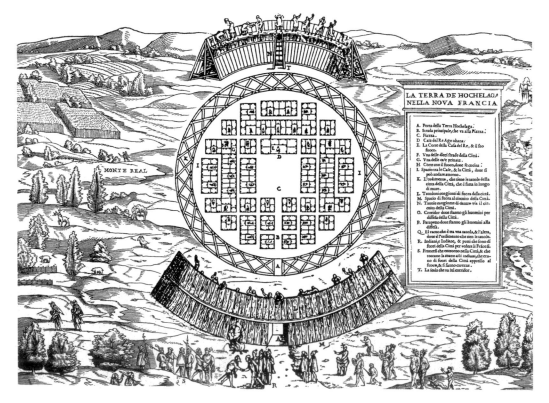

75. Jacques Cartier and Giovanni Battista Ramusio, la terra di Hochelaga, 1556. A Gate of Hochelaga, B main street leading to the square, C square, D house of King Agouhana, E courtyard of the king's house and its fire, F one of the town's ten streets, G one of the private houses, H courtyard with fire for cooking, I space between houses and town, where one can walk around it, K construction holding the slabs of the town's circular walls, L slabs connected to the town's exterior, M exterior space – the passage around the town, N slabs connecting the inner streets with the circular passage around the town, O corridor where the men stand as they defend the town, P parapet where the men stand as they defend the town, Q empty space between two slabs and the construction that holds the slabs in place, R Indian men, women, and children outside the town come to see the Frenchmen, S Frenchmen standing near the town, shaking hands with the Indians who were outside the town, by the fire and showed their friendship, T the ladder leading to the corridor.

E

Jacques Perret. The citadel towns, 1601

»The town«, Perret explains, »does not take its form only from the conditions of the fortification. Rather, I extended the old polygon forms somewhat. The city is actually a 24-cornered shape – in other words, it is almost a circle, and the circle, as you know, is a wonderful ideal form.«

Perret's aesthetic remarks are hardly convincing, for the town is surrounded by impressive moats, walls, and ramparts, and there are only four small town gates.

As we ride around the town between the two exterior town walls, we are struck by the fact that the circle is suddenly interrupted by an additional system of walls, although the moat and ramparts are built around it. »Here is the head of the citadel, a special defense system as an out-work«, explains Perret. In the center stands a well-fortified block of buildings with many towers. The fortification around it is orientated toward the hexagon.

Now it is time to ride into town. Immediately, we are struck by the straight radial streets, eight in number, formed by linear buildings. In the segments of blocks of houses no spandrels are formed. All the buildings are conceived as being strictly right-angled and are quite impressive. The town is not densely built-up – there is even room left over for four beautiful gardens.

What amazes us most is the royal palace, which we've already glimpsed from a distance, for the building rises to a height of at least ten floors above the square base. And although we are now at the beginning of the 17th century, Perret is not afraid to allude formally to the Gothic period.

Very similar in its exterior fortification, but with the buildings inside organized in a grid pattern, here is the town of scientism. »What we have here is another citadel town«, explains Mr. Perret. »My friend Thomas de Leu, a fine sculptor, designed it, and I was glad to include the plan in my book.«

But how are these towns different from the many Italian ones we've already looked at? we ask Jacques Perret skeptically.

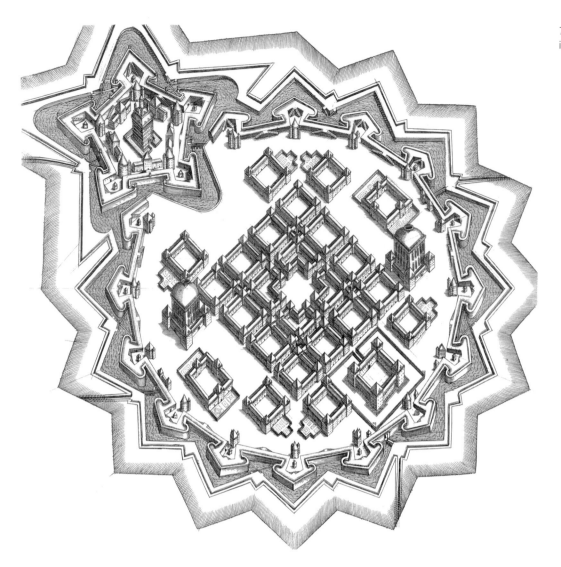

»One can hardly recognize the geometry from the outside, and the basis is very diverse, always a different figure – for example, there's even a sixteen-cornered plan, that is, a quadruple square. And above all, I always made sure the towns had a large number of towers.«

Now we really do notice that there is a turret on each of the bastions. And the massive outwork on the pentagon figure has a huge tower in the middle, which is in turn surrounded by no less than ten smaller turrets.

To say nothing of what we see when we enter the town itself: There are massive towers both on the east and west side. Fitted in between them is a grid city consisting of 22 blocks of buildings, each of them again with a turret at every corner, and with a spacious courtyard. In the center the open spaces become a large square.

Perret 1601; *Stadt und Utopie* 1982; Vercelloni 1994.

Because the layout of his towns is formally so varied, Perret convincingly argues that defense technology is not the only factor that functionally determines the city layout. In addition to the familiar hexagonal, dodecagonal, and 24-sided figures, quadrilaterals, pentagons, heptagons, and decagons also appear.

Anonymous (Joachim du Moulin?, Jean de Moncy?). *Histoire du grand et admirable Royaume d'Antangil incogneu jusques a present à tous historiens et cosmographes … Le tout compris en cinq livres,* **1616**

The year is 1598, and we are in Baudan, an island near Java. We've met an Italian merchant, and he reveals the wonderful kingdom of Antangil to us. Antagil was founded at the end of a long war, and a wise, unconventional king put an end to the time of troubles with a benevolent hand. The king has unique advisers to help him. They are mathematicians and geometricians, for these disciplines alone can provide order. The kingdom is divided into 120 equal provinces, and the land has been fairly distributed among the families. The island's capital is in the center, and the inhabitants are divided into groups of ten persons each. They select a leader, and ten such groups form a new community.

The town's assets belong to the entire people, and it is the people who make decisions regarding all public matters, including taxes.

Trousson 1975; Berneri 1950, 1971; Manguel 1981.

Many of More's ideas have been taken up again here, but the author is carried away by the exact working out of the constitution and organizational matters. Close to fifteen chapters are devoted to the organization of the police.

Hans Vredeman de Vries (1527–1606). A town in the Netherlands, 1596

The master gives us a tour of the most beautiful squares in town, and we experience its elegant, courtly, and artistic life.

We've walked down a long arcade and are now on a square dominated by a late-Gothic secular tower. The three-story arcades, however, suggest that the Renaissance has long since dawned in Italy and inspired the architect. This becomes quite clear to us when we enter the columned hall, which is open on all sides. It is true that the arches are still ribbed, but the slender Tuscan-style marble columns on high bases, the archivolts, decorated with rosettes, and the rich ornamentation of the arches announce the new era. From the broad basin of a bubbling fountain water overflows into a smaller one.

Now we have the delightful pleasure of hearing a concert performed by four men and one woman. Flutes, a cello, chamber organ, and violin are played by a virtuoso quintet. The pairs of lovers reclining and strolling here do not seem to be paying much attention.

The towns of Vredeman de Vries – and those of his Dutch fellow painters – are by no means utopias. Rather, they are ideal montages from existing towns. In a wonderful way, the formal vocabulary of the Middle Ages is overlaid with the elegance and openness of the Italian Renaissance.

78. Hans Vredeman de Vries, palace architecture with musicians, 1596.

Adrian Antonisz. Wilhelmostadum, 1647 (Willemstadt)

»It isn't Venice, and yet we've wrested the town away from the sea«, the great fortress engineer
Adrian Antonisz tells us.

We approach the little town by ship and are surprised by the fine access directly from the sea
into a small inland port. »The fortification system won't be new to you«, says the architect, »although the somewhat irregular heptagon form occurs very seldom. Yet it is a logical consequence
of the town's connection with the sea.«

We enter a small square, open to the sea, which also serves as a marketplace. From here the
street leads directly to the center of town. Something that shocks us is the lavish way all the
houses are furnished. These are small gabled houses with gardens that have a profusion of
plants. In other words, we find not a trace of urban crowding behind the town walls. The settlement – for this is hardly a town – feels like a garden city, and many of the cottages look out on the
canals that flow through town. Again, two areas have been left open: one for the market, directly
near the harbor where we arrived, the other for a small central church with a cupola.

The cozy houses, clean streets, and carefully tended gardens of this town make for a wonderful atmosphere.

Vercelloni 1994.

What we have here is a very early and no doubt utopian form of a garden city. The probably low
number of inhabitants is in stark contrast with the immensely costly fortifications.

5. Baroque, Rococo, c. 1630–1760

5.1. France, Spain

The Jesuits in Paraguay, 1588–1768

Since time immemorial we have learned, especially in the works of Augustine, that we are not destined to have the kingdom of God, the ideal city in all its perfection, here in this world of ours.

»My kingdom is not of this world«, it says in the Gospels. Yes, but is the kingdom of Christ not in this world? Can't we create kingdoms that at least come close to the kingdom of Christ, the kingdom of God? Are those really only utopias?

Again we take a leap into reality – and go on a journey to Paraguay.

Gothein 1883; Schempp 1969; Vercelloni 1994; Hartmann 1994; Eaton 2001.

A venerable Jesuit father, Rocco Gonzales, welcomes us in a »city« of a very different kind. »*The Indios, from the Guarani tribe*«, the father tells us, »*are originally a wild, impetuous, and godless people, often depraved and bestially brutal. We bring them the true faith and true salvation and thus the only true happiness. We want to educate (›reducere‹) people ›ad Ecclesiam et vitam civilem‹, for the Church and for a civilized life, which is why we call the towns ›reductions‹.*«

We learn a few things about how the »reductions« developed. The royal Spanish decree of 1609 stressed that the people may be »subjected only by the sword of the Word« – and this requirement is in stark contrast with the cruel Spanish conquests. The first 200 Guarani families made up the first reduction, called Loretto. The second, Sanct Ignatius, followed soon.

Not that there were no grid towns in earlier times, but we do find the rigidity of this geometry rather shocking: A »pueblo«, or village, consists of not less than 128 completely identical, unadorned houses. Each is inhabited by about ten families, which means a total of over 1,000 families in each pueblo. Thus something like 100,000 Indians live in the 31 pueblos. And then many hundreds of Jesuits are no doubt necessary to control them? »Not at all«, Father Rocco explains. »There have never been more than 150 brothers in the entire region.«

The village is situated at a healthy, fertile altitude, near a river. At the entrance to the village there is a crucifix. From there, a straight road leads to the middle of the village. A somewhat eccentric large square, about 130 m squared, has been left open and planted with four trees that provide shade. A church and communal buildings, the fathers' theological college building and asylum together with the hospital and school are aligned here.

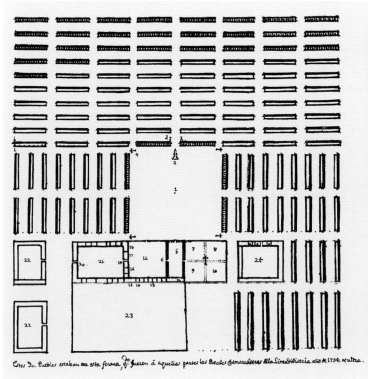

80. Pueblo of the Guarani Indios (reduction), Paraguay, 16th century.

In contrast with the simple houses the church has been built with great splendor, using beautiful stone and rich sculptures and paintings done by the inhabitants. In the three- or five-nave churches there is a lofty high altar. Men and women enter the sanctuary separately.

And the father assures us that the villagers develop an ardent faith of their own accord, like to receive the sacraments, and fervently worship the Virgin Mary. However, none of them has been ordained as a priest.

Holy Masses are very solemn and accompany daily life – which begins early in the morning for everybody before they walk singing to the fields together.

On Sundays and holidays there is church music, provided chiefly by a group of 40 musicians. There are also religious dances, but only for boys: pantomime, stage plays, and nativity plays. But outside church, games and dances are frowned upon.

Easter, after a strict period of fasting, is celebrated with special fervor, as is Corpus Christi. On the day of the church's patron saint, there is a kind of kermis: During a feast with wine and music, people celebrate the patron saint. Admittedly, women have to stay in the houses, and cards and dice games are forbidden.

The simple huts of the Indians, made of canes and clay, mostly one-story buildings, have long been replaced by wood and stone structures and roofed with tiles. A canopy, a kind of wooden veranda 2 or 3 m deep along the entire front of the house, gives protection from sun and rain. Furnishings are extremely modest: People sleep in hammocks.

»The villagers work hard in the fields. For two days of the week, each person cultivates his own field for his own family. But everyone has also learned a craft and specialized in some kind of work.« The working day is only six hours long, or eight hours maximum.

Father Rocco shows us the craftsmen's workshops, and we are very astonished that objects are manufactured serially. »The workers' diligence creates more than we need ourselves, and thus products can be sold or sent out, and we are able to pay the required tributes to the king«, Father Rocco explains about the villages' economic basis. And the rich spectrum of exported goods is impressive indeed: Corn and cotton, hides and sugarcane, tea and tropical fruit, and above all meat, which is also the most important food of the inhabitants.

The Guarani work with much enthusiasm and diligence. They work individually and yet are joined together in teams. Their technical skills are well developed. There are also a few real »factories«: These are quarries and brickworks, tanneries and water mills. Most of the work is done in public workshops: baking and cooking, slaughtering and tanning, throwing pots and wood turning. Art and crafts are not neglected: There are skilled sculptors, painters, lute and harp makers, and cabinetmakers and goldsmiths develop amazing facility.

The women gather cotton and spin, but only in their homes. It is clear that the Fathers are strict. »They must not be given the opportunity to sin. Every house has well-defined boundaries, and there is no access from one to the other. Nevertheless people are happy, for they lead virtuous lives. Above all they live like the early Christians: Everything belongs to everyone.«

In addition to praising the diligence and skill of the people, Father Rocco sees much that is blameworthy: »We value the good qualities of the population, but we constantly need to struggle with four shortcomings: lack of prudence, laziness, lack of efficiency at work, and gluttony.«

There is no private property, except for plows, axes, and table knives and hammocks – precious possessions that couples are given when they marry. Houses are not inherited, but revert to the community after death. A woman's jewelry must not exceed the value of two ounces of gold.

What is the relationship of the sexes like? »There are no problems in that respect, for at seventeen every man is urged to marry a fifteen-year-old girl, and so there is no desire for premarital dissipation. When a couple marries, they receive a house, a yoke of draft oxen, a sufficiently large field, and all necessary implements.«

What happens to the girls who do not marry? »They are provided for: They move to the women's house to join the widows, childless women, and orphans. There they work for the community, but the community also looks after them. And the same is true of the handicapped and those who are old and infirm.«

Children live with their parents, and families eat their meals together. The children are asked to do chores. In school they learn to read and write, and practice music and dancing.

Our next question addresses some objections that have occurred to us: People are trained to be dependent, the Jesuit order is authoritarian, and, what is worst, makes a lot of money on the surplus. »We look at this differently, of course. The Guarani are a very simple people. We give them the religious foundation and teach them virtue without vices or passion, even here on earth. We try to give

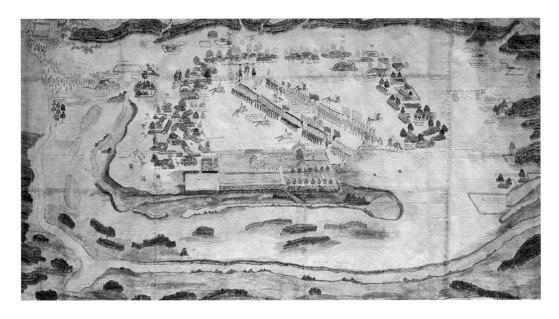

them fatherly guidance. – We certainly don't get rich in the process – everything we sell is plowed
back into the reductions.«

Now the friendly father recommends that we make sure to visit the reduction of San Javier de
Mocobies. We certainly do find two interesting aspects there:

For one thing, we are surprised that the houses are arranged quite loosely, scattered like the
buildings in a nucleated village. For another, we enjoy a festival that is just reaching its peak: Riders
have just lined up, and we are waiting for games and attractions.

We leave the country deeply impressed. Returning many years later, we are told a sad story: As
the years went by there have been many difficulties from the outside: In 1693 a critical episcopal visi-
tation is sent from Madrid, there are recurrent enemy raids.

But during the period from 1735 to 1750 there was a particularly peaceful, fruitful development.
The successes do not go unnoticed. Envy and jealousy, slander and greed on the part of the colo-
nial masters increasingly produce conflicts. Polemical, spiteful writings are disseminated. In 1767
Charles III expels the Jesuits from the Spanish colonies. Five years later Rome prohibits the reductions, which are destroyed.

The Indians are left helpless, bereaved, and desperate. The official administrator is unable to stop
the decline, and in 1848 the total decline of the reductions is sealed.

Not many years before the founding of the first reductions, in 1602, Tommaso Campanella wrote
his State of the Sun, and the Jesuits came very close to this ideal, but they probably also dreamed
of a theocracy on earth. Did the great idea fail – from the outside or the inside? Is a »state within the
state« even possible – and if so, how far can it go in its autonomy, in its sovereignty, in its totality?
And don't such grandiose experiments have to expect, if not failure, then at least time restrictions
right from their inception? Rarely has there been so fragile a boundary between a success story and
a chronicle of failure.

The following were the most important reductions: La Santissima Trinidad de Parana – Jesus
de Tavarangne – San Ignacio Guazu – San Cosme Damian – Santa Maria de Fé – Santa Rosa de
Lima – Santiago.

They still arouse our interest: As recently as 1940, Fritz Hochwälder wrote the noted drama *The
Holy Experiment* (*Das Heilige Experiment*).

Cardinal Richelieu (1585–1642) and architect Jacques Lemercier (1585–1654). Richelieu, 1631

In vain do we ask the Cardinal to accompany us through Richelieu: We do not find him in the
town, nor has he ever seen it. For the minister of Louis XIII is content if the fame of the huge
building project has spread through all of Europe: the founding of a city as the prestige of a distinguished man, as an absolutistic presence, as a reflection of societal processes.

Through the vast park, we walk toward the castle, a bold imitation of Versailles. After we cross
the cour d'honneur, the road branches off to the left of the castle and goes toward the town.

82. Jacques Lemercier, city plan of Richelieu (modi-fied), 1631.
83. Anonymous, Cyrano de Bergerac rises into the air, 1642, 1913.

A round square is formed by plants on one side and a house segment on the other side. We enter through it, and a symmetrical square, from which radiates the Grande Rue, lies before us. On the left is the church, and demonstratively across from it is the covered market.

A long row of identical two-story façades, collectivistically strung together, lines the Grande Rue. But many houses are not inhabited: People are hesitant to move to the artificial town, and the aristocrats, compelled to buy houses by Richelieu, stay away, like the Cardinal himself.

The Grande Rue is the axis – the backbone of the body of state. It connects the market / church square – the Place Cardinale – with the academy square – the Place Royale. These are the poles of power that are manifested in developing a town.

We look in vain for a center; the town is not built for people, but in its totality is a document of absolutist power.

Batifoll 1937; Boudon 1978; Kruft 1989.

Again we leap from Utopia into reality: Richelieu was actually built, and we recognize the Grande Rue of the plan as well as the parallel streets – but the reality has transformed the original concept beyond recognition.

Savinien de Cyrano de Bergerac (1619–1655). On the moon (*L'autre monde ou les états et empires de la lune,* 1642/55)

The first flying machine Cyrano demonstrates to us at first seems as ingenious as it is simple. A large number of little bottles full of dew are attached all around one's body, and the heat of the sun that attracts them immediately lifts the person up, so that he is soon above the highest clouds, but lands again after some time in an unfamiliar region.

After this test flight, Cyrano had to improve his system, and one day the machine is ready: We climb into an apparatus equipped with three rows of some kind of rockets. The first row is ignited at once, so that very soon we are above the clouds. More are then ignited at short intervals. Thus we land on the Moon without further incidents, and our conjecture that conditions there may be very terrestrial is soon confirmed. Four large rivers subdivide this »Earth« and form a lake. Huge trees loom in the sky, marvelous fragrant flowers grace the meadows – we are soon convinced that we've found paradise.

Our welcome by the inhabitants is at first not very friendly: They think we are animals and put us in a cage. But we soon manage to convince the king and his court that we are human beings. And straightway we learn the strangest things, such as the fact that people here run around very quickly on all fours, or that people nourish themselves only through their nose by smelling the foods.

Above all, however, we are interested in architecture, and there is enough here to fill one with wonder. A friendly young man who has joined us enlightens us: »*Our towns, dear friend, are of two kinds – mobile and stationary. »An architect builds every palace out of a very light wood. Under it he installs four wheels. Inside one of the walls he places a large number of big bellows whose pipes go in a horizontal line through the top floor from one gable to the other. If one wants to tow the towns somewhere, each person unfolds a large number of big sails on one side of his house in front of the bellows.*« And he has hardly finished speaking when a mobile house sails past us like a proud ship on the sea.

In the stationary towns, the houses resemble towers, but are made of wood. In the middle a large strong screw, on which it is possible to move the houses vertically, goes from the cellar to the roof. The ground is excavated to the same depth as the building is high. When the frost begins, the houses are lowered into the ground by means of the screw and are covered with big furs. When the balmy breezes of spring blow again, the house is screwed back up. The night is illuminated by countless glowworms or by rays of sunlight that are gathered during the day and from which the heat is cleaned. They are then enclosed in transparent globes and illuminate the night.

Here on the Moon we now discover a wonderful way of making »books«: Our guide opens a little box that contains something like a clockwork, but one needs one's ears to read it, that is, to hear it. One turns on the little machine, switches it to the chapter one would like to hear, and at once one hears music and speech. The inhabitants carry these »books« with them constantly or attach them to their ear and thus listen to the voices of great men.

Now that we've been accepted by the king and the inhabitants, our conversations with them teach us quite a lot about the religion, philosophy, and lives of the inhabitants of the Moon.

Soon, however, we felt impelled to continue our journey in order to get to know the kingdoms of the Sun now that we had seen the countries of the Moon.

Cyrano 1656, 1910, 1913, 1977; Krauss 1964; Baumer 1967; Swoboda 1969; Trousson 1975.

The device for flying to the Moon probably seems incredibly naïve – but is still far ahead of its time. When water boils as a result of the heat of the sun and the bottles have a jet in the cork down below, the author would seem to anticipate the principle of rockets.

No less astonishing is the anticipation of our walkmen in the »listening books«, which can even be attached to the ear – like modern-day earplugs. The concept of listening books, that is, literature on CDs, has become extremely relevant again in recent times.

André Lenôtre (1613–1700), Charles le Brun (1619–1690) and others. The ideal park of Versailles, 1662–70

»*L'état, c'est moi*«, proclaims Louis XIV. But that's not enough. Not only the people, but nature too is dominated by the »Sun King«: the plants – trees, shrubs, flowers – the water, the earth are subjected to the ruler's absolute will. The obvious symbol for this is a huge garden, in which world, power, and rule are represented.

As we fly over it, we are fascinated by the magnificence of the park, the geometric system, the occupation of space: All these are also elementary components of a town.

The huge palace becomes a modest set piece, but is nevertheless the core of world domination, and inside it, in turn, is the king's bedroom.

The arms of the roads reach south in the direction of Paris, while in the north the axis runs through the garden for ten km to its goal, an elegant little castle. The endless road is interrupted by five breaks – squares, ponds, fountains, places from which the transverse axes open up more infinite vistas.

»We began creating the park before the palace was built«, Lenôtre tells us, »for by the time the palace was completed, the park was already supposed to be green and full of flowers, and this was the king's special desire.«

Still we are astonished that the trees – all strictly geometrically trained – are all so tall. »These didn't grow here. We've developed methods of transferring huge trees. But I must admit that many didn't survive being transplanted.«

It is not only the trees, shrubs, and flowers that have been domesticated, but the water as well. It falls in wide cascades over stone walls, flows in straight brooks and canals, rises to a height of up to 30 m, entertains the courtiers in amusing games. We're amazed at the abundance of water!

84. Anonymous, Cyrano de Bergerac, residential building moved by air, 1642.
85. Anonymous, Cyrano de Bergerac, residential building that can be lowered, 1642.

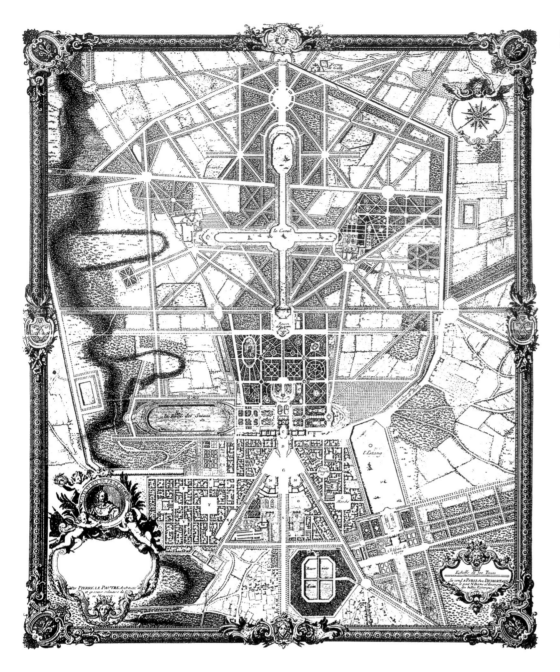

86. André le Nôtre et al., plan for the park of Versailles. Engraving by F. Blondel, 1662.

»The king and his guests can admire this miracle only when they stroll here, and they have no idea of the enormously extravagant project created by the water engineers – and there still was not enough water.«

For the vast amounts of water, canals and drainage ditches, collecting pools and ponds were excavated. Windmills and bucket wheels pump the water into reservoirs. Water was brought over distances of more than 30 km – all of it not sufficient. »We had a magnificent idea«, continues Lenôtre, obviously embarrassed. »We began to divert the Eure River, and tens of thousands of soldiers were hard at work on this! But they had to go to war again – the project failed!« As a result, water has to be collected for a whole week in order for people to enjoy the glory for a few hours.

We interrupt to say that it was lucky they found such a large, level area for this Garden of Eden. »That wasn't the case at all«, Lenôtre informs us. »It was pretty hilly and marshy: We redesigned the topography. The king recreated the landscape.«

All this was done without machines. Just to move the earth alone, 800 horses and 36,000 men worked continually – there were hundreds of deaths as a result of accidents, exhaustion, disease. It is difficult for us to return from our distress about power and violence to the contemplation of art: to the opulent mythology in the sculptures, to the basins and fountains, to the ships on the »Grand Canal« and finally to the Petit and Grand Trianon and the romantic Hameau.

The park of Versailles had been created, but the visions of the king went far beyond this: The net of power, three times as large, was intended to dominate the surrounding country.

Denis Vairasse D'Alais (1637–1683/1700) and Captain Siden. The Sevarambi (*Histoire des Sevarambes, peuples qui habitent une partie du troisième continent, communément appellé la Terre Australe*, 1675/78)

»The stories I'm telling you are no fantasies or utopias, but true occurrences«, Denis Vairasse begins. »Captain Siden told them to me, and I believe him – he was shipwrecked and landed on the island of the Sevarambi, and he will now accompany us there.«

The island lies between two large rivers and was created out of a peninsula by digging away the land connection.

At first we visit the town of Sporounde. It is regular and ordered, laid out in the form of a square. The center of the town consists of 76 big, rectangular buildings, four stories high. Each is inhabited by about 1,000 persons. Denis Vairasse praises the advantages of the town, of which we can convince ourselves at once: »The town is as splendid as it is tasteful. Its buildings are magnificent, the streets are straight, wide, and comfortable, since special sidewalks have been constructed for pedestrians.«

In the center of town, there is a large, regular marketplace. »In the market, buyers and sellers are busy trading. Round about the market, in shops and vaults, artists and craftspeople display their wares.«

The grounds of the palace are more imposing through their art than their size, more through elegance than splendor.

In the middle is a rectangular palace built of white and black marble, the gate is decorated with splendid metal sculptures. We wander through the individual courtyards, also built of marble, and arrive in the first hall, richly furnished with paintings and gold ornaments. But the two subsequent halls surpass it in splendor, and in the last is the throne of the ruler, Sevarias, about whom we are yet to hear much praise.

Naturally the Temple of the Sun is also built with much care and beauty. Now, as chance will have it, a great festival is being celebrated in the temple as we arrive, and we are invited to participate. We are told the reason for the festival: Four times a year, a general marriage ceremony takes place.

Young people, festively dressed and adorned, enter the temple to the sound of trumpets, flutes, and shawms, followed by dignified men in sumptuous garments – the priests. We too are allowed to enter the temple, whose interior is also furnished with precious materials and rich decorations.

Now the curtain that has concealed the main section is lifted, revealing the magnificent altar. In front of it on the right, on a pedestal, is a huge crystal globe that transforms the light wonderfully and itself emits light, so that almost the entire temple is festively illuminated.

On the left, also on a pedestal, is the bust of a woman with many breasts, no doubt a recollection of Artemis, surrounded by small children, some suckling her breasts.

There is the sound of music, the priests take up their position, and young women and men line up facing each other and express their intention to marry. Now the first girl steps forward, goes to the row of young men, and chooses one – he agrees to marry her. The others follow suit.

Eight young girls are left over. Three of them each pick one of the councilors between the age of forty and fifty, the other five return home weeping with shame. The couples make their vows on a holy book.

On the morning of the next day, there is more music by the temple, we hurry there. Again we see the couples, holding up branches with the bridal wreaths, and a bloody scarf wound around them: The bride was a virgin.

We go on to the amusement center, a large round building with high vaulted ceilings and big windows. Along the walls rows of comfortable benches invite people to rest and look on. We observe all kinds of different diversions: dancing and fencing, comedy and music, games, wrestling, and athletics. »Some days«, says Captain Siden, »things get dangerous – there are wild animals.«

Vairasse and the captain want to show us another town as well, however – Sevarinde. It is also located on an island in a river and is surrounded by strong walls. Outside there is fertile farmland. Like architects, farmers are held in high esteem. The concept of this town is similar to that of Sporounde, but here 267 rectangular buildings have been erected for the inhabitants. Each has four floors and four big gates. Gleaming marble has been used lavishly. The beautiful inner courtyards are landscaped, like the rest of the town, which is embedded among trees, flowers, shrubbery, and lawns and has many fountains and sculptures. On the flat roofs of the houses, too, there is a profusion of flowers and plants in earthenware containers.

Particularly charming are the galleries, wide canopies on iron columns that protect you from rain and sun. In very hot weather additional sails are stretched over the entire street.

We were able to view one of the bright, friendly apartments, and it goes without saying that running water is installed in the bathroom and kitchen.

»The Sevarambi are a happy people«, assert our guides. What is the source of the Sevarambi's happiness and prosperity? »All that is necessary is to eliminate the three main evils of humanity«, Mr. Vairasse informs us. *First, there is the arrogance of the aristocracy. They actually imagine that they exist in order to order other people around, without considering that Mother Nature created us all to be equal and saw no difference between burghers and noblemen, that she made all of us subject to the same weaknesses ... and that the finest advantage one person has over another is virtue.*«

The second evil is miserliness and greed. These tempt us to accumulate wealth and possessions – but this always happens at the expense of the poor. *»In our town all property belongs to everyone. That is, it belongs to the state, which takes care of distributing it fairly, depending on each person's needs.«*

Private property – except for personal possessions – has been abolished.

The third evil, finally, is idleness, especially that of the rich. *»Here, every healthy citizen is obliged to work eight hours a day, no more and no less.«*

Is it enough, though, to root out the evils? In the final analysis, what makes the citizens happy? It is the following: physical health, mental serenity, the freedom of a good education, the practice of virtue, the companionship of honest people, good food, fine clothes, and comfortable houses. And all these are things a citizen of this town is able to enjoy.

We'd love to hear more about the lives of the Severambi, and Captain Siden, who's been living here for sixteen years, is glad to inform us.

»We owe it all to Sevarias, the benevolent and ingenious ruler, who is a descendant of the Sun. We have no poor, no one lacks the daily necessities, we pay no taxes, and there is no crime, no capital punishment.«

Children are placed in the care of the state at the age of seven and are dedicated to the Sun divinity. After four years of school they go to the country. Here they do four hours of farm work and spend the rest of the day in school. Boys and girls are always separated. At nineteen the men, and at sixteen the girls, meet each other during dances, hunts, festivals, and ceremonies, and get married soon thereafter.

If a woman does not find a husband, the authorities provide her with one. However, if she is weak or frail, she is sent away. During the first three years of partnership, couples are allowed to have intercourse every third night, then every other night up to the age of 28, and as often as they please after that. If the women are infertile after five years or if they remain unmarried, they become slaves and public sexual partners. They earn their living as nurses and educators. Every man has a wife, but higher officials live with several wives, and the head of state is entitled to no less than twelve wives.

We did find this partnership system and the enormous obligations of individuals worthy of severe criticism, but were assured that the Severambi enjoy utmost happiness.

We've heard a loud bell signal several times and ask what it means. »The citizens love an ordered life, and so there is always a bell at the beginning of work and at the beginning of meals. By the way, the day is nicely divided into three parts: a third each for work, for pleasure, and for rest.«

We follow the noon bell signal and go to the big communal dining hall. There are three daily meals. Two are eaten communally, while the evening meal is taken with one's family.

Now Captain Siden tells us one more incident from his arrival on the island. »We were 30 men and only seven women, and so we had difficulty regulating the meetings with the women in an appropriate way. Thus we were forced to share the women as follows: Officers got a woman for the whole week, noncommissioned officers were allowed to sleep with a woman twice a week, while ordinary men were allowed to do so only once. One night, however, we were brought into a big hall and were quite surprised to find a large number of beautiful women there. They are slaves, as we were told, and they were available to guests two days a week. Admittedly we had to be examined by the doctor for the Neapolitan disease before we raffled off the women as bed partners among ourselves. However, we were not allowed to switch partners so that the fathers of the children from these unions could later be identified.«

Though prostitution is not a new phenomenon, we did find the way it is practiced here somewhat disconcerting.

Now we were taken to the next town, Arkropofinde. Over the wide river there are arched stone bridges. Again, many houses have roof terraces, the corners are ornamented with turrets, and a lovely landscape surrounds the town.

As we reach the bridge, something very strange happens: A man falls into the river – but wasn't he pushed? And then another man jumps in, and a bitter struggle ensues. However, five rowboats arrive, separate the fighters, and bring them ashore. What's happened? From one of the onlookers we learn the wicked but scurrilous story: A draughtsman has stolen a sketch from a mathematician and will return it only if he throws his enemy into the water. And sure enough, the mathematician throws him from the bridge – but then he throws the draughtsman right after him! We must admit we have no idea how to reconcile these nasty events with the happiness of the Severambi!

Be that as it may – we continue our journey and learn about even more surprising institutions in the town of the Severambi, but can only mention a few of them.

In a pleasant valley we see a number of large sleigh gondolas. Each has room for 20 persons. They hang from thick ropes that come down from the mountains and are securely attached at the top of the mountain. We get into one of the gondolas. After a whistle we become aware that a rope that goes to the summit is pulling the gondolas upward. Halfway up we meet a similar gondola going down toward the valley: It is the counterweight that pulls us up, and so we soon arrive at the summit.

Another technological miracle is no less amazing. The cables in one mountain have been connected with tunnels, so that we can traverse the mountain underneath in a short time.

We're sure there are many more wonderful things to see and experience, but we're glad we can think over all our adventures during our return journey and reap the benefits of what we have learned for our own country.

Vairasse 1675, 1679, 1689, 1702, 1711; Roberts / Veiras 1707; Kirchenheim 1892; Mohl 1960; Krauss 1964; Servier 1971; Swoboda 1972; Berneri 1950, 1991; Berghahn 1983; Brentjes 1993; Rahmsdorf 1999.

Once again, a narrative that touches on the subject of the benevolent dictator, but the tremendously rigorous regulations that govern people's lives make us question this benevolence. Instead many things remind us of the real dictatorships of history, particularly during the last century.

Of course, the fact that guests or business associates are provided with the services of prostitutes is a phenomenon that is still common today.

The marriage ceremonial of the Severambi is far removed from Christian rituals and is more reminiscent of the symbols and ceremonies of Freemasons. It is remarkable that the choice is up to the women. Obviously there is a surplus of women, so that often some are left over – in other words, everything is not organized in the best possible way.

Gabriel de Foigny (1630–1692). The adventures of Jacques Sadeur (*Les aventures de Jacques Sadeur dans la découverte et le voyage de la terre Australe,* 1676) and the unknown continent of Australia (*La terre Australe inconnue,* 1693)

Gabriel de Foigny and Jacques Sadeur guide us through this strange land in which no mountain is to be seen far and wide, or forests, or swamps and deserts: the natives have leveled everything. The country is well organized, and Mr. Sadeur describes the structure and organization with mathematical accuracy:

»In this odd country there are 15,000 seizains. Each seizain consists of sixteen residential districts, not counting the Hab and the four hebs; in each residential district there are 25 houses, and every house has four apartments of four persons each; thus each seizain has 400 houses and 6,400 persons. Multiplied by the 15,000 seizains, this means a total of roughly 96 million inhabitants for the entire Australian country, not counting the young people and teachers in the hebs, which must have at least 800 inhabitants; and since there are 60,000 hebs in the 15,000 seizains, the total number of young people and their teachers is roughly 48 million.«

Now we come to a splendid building that struck us even from afar because of its wonderful reflections. It is the great house of the seizain referred to as the Hab, which means the Sublime House. It is built only out of transparent glass stones, like our finest crystals, only these stones are

88. Anonymous, the town of Arkropofinde, scenes of struggle near a bridge, 1675. Engraving, 1783.

animated with an amazing number of delicate living figures in every color that represent in their infinite variety now human shapes, now fields in all their beauty, now suns and other figures, so vividly that one cannot admire them enough. The entire building is constructed without sleight of hand, except for the strangely polished stone that surrounds it completely, and big tables of a red brighter than our scarlet. The building has four rather large entrances at the end of four wide roads that lead up to it: Everywhere there is an abundance of highly unusual inventions. We climb over a thousand steps to the top. Here there is a kind of platform that has room for easily 40 people.

»*No one lives there continually, but all the residential districts take turns to supply the tables with enough food for twelve persons as refreshment for the passersby.*«

As for the ordinary houses, which they call *hiebs,* meaning residences of the people, there are 25 in each residential district in an area of 80 yards. Like the *hebs*, they are divided by two large walls that form for separate sections, each of which represents an apartment. Each section is inhabited by four persons, called *cle*, meaning brothers. These buildings contain nothing but four benches, on which they sleep, and a few similar furnishings that serve the same purpose. Monsieur Sadeur introduces us to the Australians. They are well born and free, and so need neither a government nor a religion – or rather: They speak of no religion, and of course they have no private property. They cannot tell the difference between mine and yours, and there is complete frankness among all the people. Their language and all the objects they use are completely equal. They know no clothing and walk about in a natural state of nudity. They eat only fruit and plants.

All the people are androgynous and know no sexual relations. But Monsieur Sadeur, who had lived in this country for many years, was unable to explain how they get children. However, he is sure they do not beget children through sexual union, although they love each other very much. The mother nurses the children for two years, at which time she leaves. The children's further education is done by teachers, and they go to school until they are 35 years old.

Now we have the opportunity to visit one of the school buildings. »*The house called a* heb *(which means house of education) is divided into four parts. It is built from the same stone with which the* Hab *is paved, except for the roof, which consists of transparent stone and lets in light. This beautiful building is divided into four areas by four partitions. Each area is assigned to the young people of the residential district of which it is a part.*«

The young people are divided into five groups corresponding to the five learning phases that they go through during their studies up to the age of 35. The daily schedule is the same for all inhabitants and is clearly structured. In the morning food is distributed, as much as everyone needs. The day is divided into three phases: The inhabitants spend one-third of each day in meditation, during which they do not speak at all. A third is spent in school or in studying the sciences and working in the garden, and during the last third of the day they produce new inventions or manufacture weapons. Our question to Mr. Sadeur as to when they sleep and eat remains unanswered.

On the other hand, we discover another fact about this apparently so peaceable nation: When they are forced to wage war, they are extremely cruel. The enemy is completely destroyed and the enemy's country is razed to the ground.

Nevertheless Mr. Sadeur persists in his admiration for the people. »*In their ordinary lives they have reached a pinnacle of virtue that we could not reach with the utmost effort of our noblest ideas.*«

Aventures 1543, 1676, 1705; Mohl 1960; Trousson 1975; Tod/Wheeler 1978; Berneri 1950, 1971; Brentjes 1993.

Gabriel de Foigny's description of the Australians is closely linked with his life, and the meaning of the scurrilous and entertaining story is a result of de Foigny's outrageous biography: A Catholic priest and preacher who behaved scandalously in France, an impoverished Protestant in Geneva, banished because of his affairs with women, drunkenness, and »popish idolatry« – in the end the fact that he wrote the La Terre Australe inconnu provoked the indignation of the Protestant commissions. De Foigny lands in jail, is released on bail, and returns to France with a servant girl he has seduced and his illegitimate children. He becomes a Catholic again and dies – in the monastery.

The motif of leveling the mountains appears a few times in progressive-aggressive concepts around 1970: such as, for example, the idea of leveling the Alps.

89. François Fénélon, plan of the journeys of
Telemachus, 1699.
90. François Fénélon, Adventures of Telemachus,
Arrival in Salante, 1699.

François de Salignac de la Mothe-Fénélon (1651–1715). The adventures of Telemachus (*Les aventures de Télémaque*, 1699)

Telemachus, the son of Ulysses, is shipwrecked and lands safely with his friend Mentor on the island of the goddess Calypso. She welcomes him warmly and her goodwill toward him is assured.
However, the rest of Telemachus's journey is characterized by frightening adventures and dangers.

Telemachus shows us a town that has impressed him deeply. He takes us to Salante, a blossoming land, to a happy people. But how is that possible? The king of this realm rules not by
virtue of tradition and the power of his rulership, but from his wisdom and insight. Mentor, separated from Telemachus, is the king's adviser, and the king follows his wise suggestions. Thus the
nation is divided into seven classes, who are distinguished by their clothing. The administration
works according to simple rational principles. It gets its bearings from statistics, and problems are
discussed in surveys. Agriculture is promoted. Crafts and trade are intelligently directed.

»Naturally not everything runs automatically«, says Mentor. »No doubt it is necessary to supervise merchants and commercial companies, and people who go bankrupt can expect to be punished severely.«

We can understand that quite well, and yet we feel some measures restrict some of the freedoms of the citizens: All luxuries are prohibited by law, and there are strict laws governing food,
clothing, and entertainment. Superfluous goods may not be produced and imports from abroad
are forbidden. Rigorous simplicity characterizes everyday life. Gold is forged into plowshares, and
wars are unknown.

And education? What principles is it based on? »Principles such as living simply, of course, an
ethical family life, and education for community living. And in this context the noble arts flourish in
the academies. In all this our wise and benevolent prince helps us, and his throne rests upon the
love of the subjects.«

Telemachus leaves the town again, and after further dangerous adventures, and a 22-month
journey, is able to embrace his father Ulysses once again.

Fénélon 179; Freyer 1936; Servier 1971; Swoboda 1972; Trousson 1975; Brentjes 1993.

Fénélon's work had a tremendous influence in his own era and far beyond it. The ideal of the noble,
wise, benevolent prince was beautifully expressed here, though in a utopian way, and the enlightened
absolutist ruler has been sketched as a model, a counterfigure to Louis XIV.

Jean-Baptiste Alexandre Le Blond (1679–1719). St. Petersburg, 1717
Johann Baptist Homann (1664–1724). St. Petersburg

»A magnificent deed«, the architect Le Blond exclaims enthusiastically. »Tsar Peter the Great has made St. Petersburg the capital of his empire, and I have become his court architect!« But Le Blond was not satisfied with the architecture of the splendid Peterhof Palace. »I founded my new city on the island west of the city, but I also included parts of St. Petersburg Island and Admiral Island.«

As we fly over it, we are astounded at how successful Le Blond was in shaping the irregular islands into an oval, the city fortress. »Fortification and the beauty of geometry must be made into a single whole«, says Le Blond.

However, we believe this involved quite a few problems. The river delta represents a serious topographical handicap. That, and the oval form of the powerful fortification, can be managed quite well, and the beautiful fort stands well fortified in the middle of the river.

Let us now tour the city. When we've finally found a city gate, the city seems to have an entirely different geometry: Avenues and boulevards, straight axes and squares of various sizes form a pleasing geometric system, the public squares and representative buildings are beautifully integrated, and we cannot help thinking of Paris and Versailles. Three large symmetrical squares, landscaped in geometric patterns, provide accents and structures. There are also squares that have monuments and obelisks, but no plants or grass: This is where festivals and gatherings take place. Yet when we approach the city walls and riverbanks, it becomes clear that the geometry doesn't always work: rectangles and squares are abruptly cut off, acute-angled floor plans result, and the streets along the banks are very narrow. Still, we are fascinated by the solidity, order, and beauty of the new city, which can surely compete effortlessly with Moscow.

We return to visit St. Petersburg once more, and Master Johann Baptist Homann explains his city to us: »We have to build cheaply. We left the old parts of the city as they were. And on Vassili Ostrov Island, Prince Menzikoff Island, we created a fairly regular city for thousands of people.« With incredible strictness the grid has been mercilessly laid over the island. The main street and side streets are ordered systematically. A large green zone and two squares with trees and galleries break up the stringency of the plan.

Vercelloni 1994; *Traum* 2003.

Ambitious, eager to build, undecided – that's Tsar Peter the Great when it comes to the urban fame of the new capital. Le Blond's plan was a utopia from the outset, though not the planning of it as Homann described it: The layout of the streets was begun and, in the eastern part of the island, implemented by 1720. We can still identify it today. The plan for Vassili Island has remained a utopia.

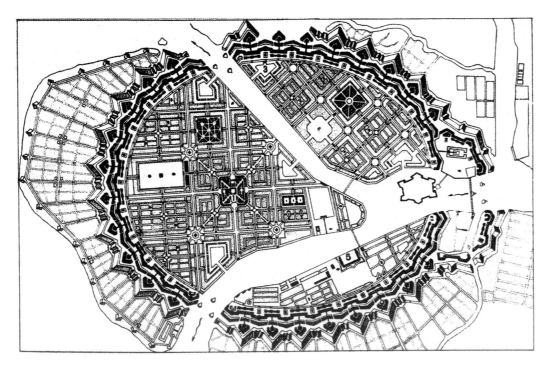

91. Jean-Baptiste Alexandre Le Blond, plan for St. Petersburg, 1717.

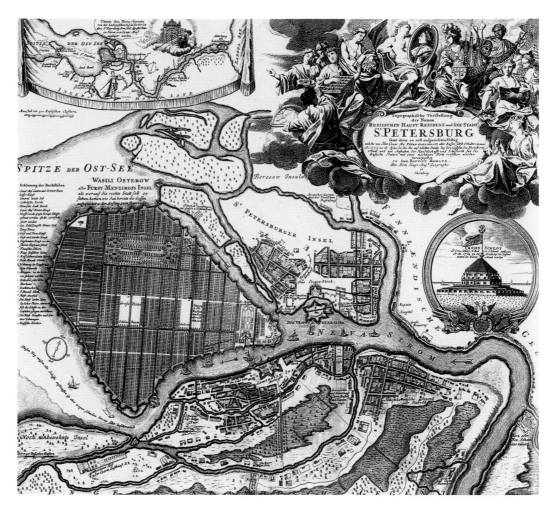

French and North European fortress builders. Fortress towns, c. 1700–20

A »Friendly Competition of French, Dutch, and German Military Architecture« erupted around 1700. But is this really only about impregnable fortified towns? Do not these magnificent formations also keep alive the ideal geometry of Renaissance theoreticians?

Without doubt, in the dispute among nations, Sébastien le Prestre de Vauban (1633–1707, *De l'Attaque et de la Défense des places*) is the great master of military architecture. Yet when we look down at the town of Neu-Breisach from a bird's-eye view, it feels more like a precious piece of jewelry, a radiant brooch, than like a warlike city, and we have trouble counting the points of the jewel: The plan is based on an octagon, and thus there must be sixteen bastions. The two watercourses follow the points of the octagon. What an immense fortification was required compared to the town's small area!

Sturm 1718; Parent 1982.

But beautiful as the pattern is, what mattered were quite different purposes – hard, functional necessities, effective protection for the town.

Let's look at the reality: As early as 1648 the town becomes a French fortress. In 1700 it is incorporated into Austria and a few years later the fortification is built, though not in the form drafted by Vauban. The fortifications were razed in 1743, and the town was almost completely destroyed by bombing in 1945.

Vauban was the great master architect of fortifications – and thus he is far removed from utopia. His life work is substantial – we can examine much of it today. His career shows him to be not only a master builder of fortifications, but also a town planner and architect. Mont-Louis in the Pyrenees, Mont Dauphin, Queyras Castle on the border of Savoie, and especially Lille and Maubeuge are, beside Neu-Breisach, his most important works. Fort Carré in Antibes, Alpes Maritimes, is still well preserved.

But he was not only a planner and builder. As marshal of France he successfully led more than fifty battles.

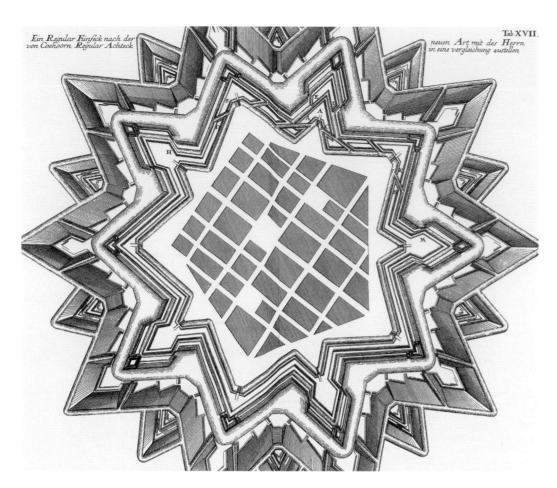

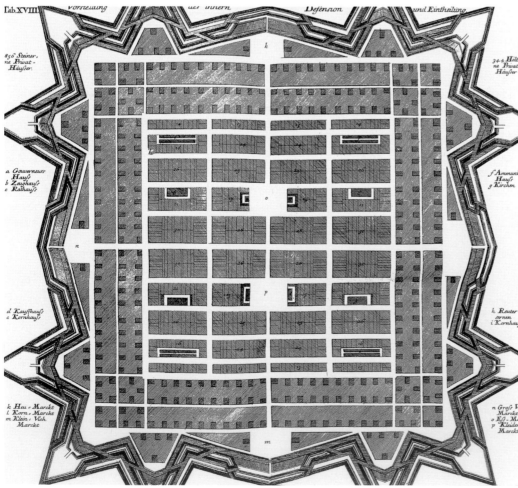

94. Meister Coehoom, pentagonal urban fortification. After Sturm, 1718.
95. L. C. Sturm and G. Rimpler, ideal city. After Sturm, 1718.

No less costly, indeed even more lavish in the way the defense was fractured and complicated is the conception of the Dutch Master Coehoorn. He bases it on a pentagon, a polygon rarely found in city layouts, and does not fail to include a watercourse.

We approach the town from the open country, and the effect of the salient angles of the bastions with their very sloping walls, the better to ward off cannonballs, is quite aggressive. It isn't easy to find the small city gates and it takes a bit of effort to enter the town – whose area is no doubt considerably smaller than the entire fortification.

The planner goes from a pentagon to a rectangle, creating quite a few peculiar floor plans with acute angles. Of the grid area, three public places have been left blank.

Finally we come to the German fortress town of L. C. Sturm and G. Rimpler.

They have chosen the square – like Dürer and Speckle before them – and find a good relationship between the area of the fortress and the town. As we walk toward the town, the fortifications no longer feel as monumental and the road past the bastions and outworks is short and pleasant. The planners have chosen precise rectangles for all the ground plans. In the outer rectangle they place 856 stone houses, and between the lots and the fortification there are four markets for hay, grain, and small and large animals.

Crowded in the inner square are 344 wooden houses, and between them are churches, barracks, granaries, and stores. The houses of the governor and the town hall, of course, have a privileged location, but appear relatively modest. A kind of center is formed by the food market and clothing market.

Sturm 1718, Parent 1982.

Compared to Italy in particular, the North has developed a very distinctive style of fortification architecture, and in the compendium of L. C. Sturm the geometric types are represented: the octagon, approximating a circle, the pentagon, and the square.

Thus here, too, it is difficult to believe that formal aspects had only a secondary significance. Even today, we are still fascinated by the combination of functionality and the aesthetics of ground plans: a very relevant contemporary issue.

Of all the fortresses that were actually built and are still preserved, in addition to Neu-Breisach and Palma Nova – which we have already visited – Rocroi in France is of interest.

5.2. England, America

Gerrard Winstanley (1609–1676). *The law of freedom in a platform,* 1652, and the Diggers, 1648–50

It was an unheard-of act of audacity: simply to occupy a hill on the outskirts of town and then to dig and plant there. But Winstanley is able to justify this revolutionary action: »*We justify our act of digging upon that Hill to make the Earth a Common Treasury. First, because the Earth was made by Almighty God to be a Common Treasury of Livelihood to the whole of mankind in all its branches, without respect of persons.*«

Winstanley is successful: »After an unending multitude of setbacks, prohibitions, spitefulness, and destructions I have finally managed to turn my ›law of freedom‹ into a reality.« Winstanley has reached the goal of his life, the reforms have been implemented, and the small group of Diggers has become a powerful reform movement.

Now »*no man shall have any more land than he can labor himself or have others to labor with him in love, working together, and eating bread together, as one of the tribes or families of Israel, neither giving nor taking hire, and all persecutions come to an end.*«

The community to which Winstanley introduces us lives very modestly. The housing is very simple, and people are plainly dressed.

Winstanley portrays the moral principles of his community: »Never shall a person rule over, or lecture another, for every person contains the perfect individual within him and God is in every person, so that there is no need for rule. And God himself and he alone is the spirit of justice and reason. But people have turned away from God and turned toward the serpent, the Evil One: Therefore they are ruled by greed, selfishness, arrogance, pride, envy, hypocrisy, and impurity.«

All people, rich and poor alike, cultivate the land together, not as tenants or leaseholders, but as members of the same family. Humanity is freed from slavery and all people can find what the

»Diggers« have found: »*Peace in our hearts and a peaceful joy in our work, filled with sweet satisfaction.*«

Competition among human beings, in Winstanley's view, comes from the Fall of Adam and is not a true characteristic of human nature. Seen this way trade, too, is superfluous, because it accumulates capital and makes it possible for traders to acquire land. That is why we now tour the big warehouses, where agricultural produce, raw materials, and finished products are stored and directly distributed to the population.

Admittedly every able-bodied person is obliged by law to be involved in society, to share work in cooperative and manufacturing organizations, but no person is allowed to be another's employer.

In the new society school attendance is compulsory. Children are educated to believe in community and justice, and learn practical skills such as crafts, science, art, and languages. They learn at an early age to be productive members of society. Fathers care for children until they reach the age of reason, and will not tolerate idleness.

In the new society, officials are elected every year, and only those can be candidates who have an outstanding character, promote freedom, and have a peaceful spirit.

Parliament, too, is elected every year and is the highest court of justice in the land. It has abolished the old laws of the king, and the new laws serve the peace and freedom of the whole country.

To us, this polity of peace and freedom seems to be highly humane and tolerant. How is order maintained? From Winstanley we hear about some measures that astonish us, indeed disturb us greatly: When children are idle, the father whips those who refuse to obey, »*for the rod is there to bring those who lack judgment to reason and moderation*«.

Winstanley has not abolished private property: House, household goods, food, wife, and child belong to everyone personally, but the public storehouses belong to the whole community, and there is neither money nor wages. Each person gives according to his abilities and receives according to his needs.

In the town there are peacemakers who resolve conflicts. But there are also overseers who make sure people fully do their duty, and there are disciplinarians who watch over the prisoners and reduce the portions of the rebellious or whip them. And finally there are the executioners who behead, hang, or shoot wrongdoers.

Winstanley is not too particular where capital punishment is concerned: Those who administer law in return for money, who are caught escaping from prison, or men who rape a woman – are sentenced to death.

In conclusion Winstanley tells us about his spiritual basis: »There are three ages according to the Holy Trinity. God the Father is present in the Old Testament, God the Son fulfills the New Testament. But the age of the Holy Spirit is yet to come and will make all other systems of rule superfluous.«

Winstanley 1654; Berens 1906; Tod/Wheeler 1978; Berneri 1950, 1971; Seibt 2001.

The social abuses in 17th century England brought reformers, revolutionaries, and idealists on the scene.

Around 1648 Gerrard Winstanley founded the »True Levellers or Diggers.« They wanted to reconquer the land for the peasants and create completely new laws. A group of 20 men dug up a public square and sowed carrots and beans.

In 1649 Winstanley together with twelve friends occupied and cultivated some fallow land.
Thus the communities of the »Diggers« were actually founded, but just a year later they fell victim to animosity, destruction, and prohibitions. If we disregard the radicalism of agrarian communism, then Winstanley may be interpreted as the precursor of modern social democracy.

The »Diggers« want absolute freedom. But that means access to all sources, the right of each individual to cultivate the soil. Now, however, the poor of the land are not allowed to dig, plant, and live as comfortably as the landlords.

The Diggers are convinced that the poor have the right to cultivate all waste, deserted plots of land, in England and in the rest of the world. These will be taken by the people in all fairness, because the Earth is the common treasure of all humankind.

We encounter the name »Diggers« again in the revolutionary scene of the 1960s – for example, in anarchistic guerilla and street theater groups in San Francisco.

James HarrIngton (1611–1677). *The Commonwealth of Oceana*, 1656

»Winstanley was not on the right path with his idea of commonly owned land«, Harrington criticizes his fellow countryman. »The basis for a stable government is a small-scale democracy with private land ownership. But no one may own land worth over 2,000 pounds, and only landowners may participate in the government.«

Harrington thinks of the farming culture of someone like Aristoteles. »Of course we have a parliament«, says Harrington, »it is a two-chamber system. One chamber debates, the other makes decisions. Strict regulations exist regarding members of parliament. They must be male, at least 30 years old, they must have done their national service, must be married, and be able to prove they have land, property, and money worth at least 100 pounds.«

Family structures are no less rigorous: »We prevent the splintering and division of landed property; only the oldest brother is to get the whole inheritance«, explains Harrington. But what happens to the younger brothers? »The clergy and the independent professions offer them adequate opportunities for development«, is Harrington's view.

In other words, the farmers' land is not divided. In contrast, the giant latifundia have been divided into easily farmed areas and handed over to the farmers. Harrington has reached another goal as well: »We've founded a national church. That is the basic condition for our independence. And we've also won the freedom of science from all patronage: It goes hand in hand with civil, personal freedom.«

Large families are Harrington's very special concern, and he tries to promote them: Families with ten children or more pay no taxes. Families with five children pay only half their taxes, while childless families and unmarried people over 25 pay double taxes.

Now Harrington begins to explain the various election systems, and for a while we try to listen. Soon, though, we must confess, our patience wears thin and we can hardly follow the methods and processes he has thought up, though we don't deny that Harrington has reached an optimal democracy. The ideal constitution for Harrington is an absolutely rational structure. However, what astonishes us is the relatively short term for which government bodies are elected. We believe this makes long-term planning very difficult.

Harrington 1656, 1700, 1924; Kirchenheim 1892: Mohl 1960; Manguel 1981; Berneri 1950, 1971; Berghahn 1983.

Harrington tries to combine the sovereignty of the people and effective government. A hundred years later, Harrington's political ideas undoubtedly influenced the American constitution. And his law of farm inheritance was emulated much later by Hitler's hereditary farm law. With his *The Commonwealth of Oceana* Harrington probably conceived one of the first reform programs for England.

Many of the often hypertrophied election systems, democratic processes, and term limits described by Harrington have long ago become a reality in modern democracies.

Robert Mountgomery. The garden city Azilia in Georgia, USA, 1717

Sir Robert Mountgomery is the margrave of Azilia, and he designed and founded his own city, as it were. »A new city must have many advantages: Of course it must be fortified, but within its walls there must also be fields and meadows. And geometry is definitely the appropriate form for it«, comments the margrave.

Thus we're looking at an entirely new ideal. The dream of the city – the New Jerusalem – and the dream of the garden – Paradise – are to be united here.

Again, we should approach the city by air in order to grasp its impressive geometry: Everything down to the last detail is based on the square. If we come from the land side, however, we have trouble finding the access to the city, for an endlessly long wall, which forms a giant square, with countless bastions, protects the city, but not as martially as proposed by the Italians and French. The effect of the series of wall projections behind which the meadows are spread out is almost ornamental. When we walk through the next enclosure, we are not in the city yet by any means, but rather in a fertile garden landscape (though one that has perfectly straight boundaries) with fields and meadows, and small farmhouses scattered here and there. The lovely greenery does not leave us even after we enter the city – or rather, the city garden. For the countless square blocks are all little enclosed gardens, each with a house in the middle. The gardens themselves allow inhabitants to grow a modest amount for their own needs.

A Plan representing the Form of Setling the Districts, or County Divisions in the Margravate of Azilia.

But that's not enough. Following the model of many ideal urban plans, the town's geometry demands four additional large square fields where all kinds of domestic animals roam freely, a pretty, natural idyll behind fortress walls. But when we come to the fifth, central, square, we do find larger houses clustered close together. They form a courtyard in which stands the margrave's rather modest castle.

Moholy-Nagy 1968; Vercelloni 1994.

While in the Renaissance cities were occupied by fortifications, an ecological concept, as it were, now totally supersedes the martial elements. Urban »nature« is now given priority. In comparison the fortifications seem tiny. We'll have to wait more than a hundred years until Ebenezer Howard conceives his ideal garden city – and implements it.

Jonathan Swift (1667–1745). Lilliput, Brobdingnag, and Laputa (*Gulliver's travels*, 1726)

Lemuel Gulliver first tells us about his journey and his adventures. He was shipwrecked, but swam ashore in Lilliput and was captured – but by a people whose physical size is scarcely one-twelfth of his own! Released again thanks to the emperor's favor, he learns about the strange people of Lilliput and acquaints us with some of their customs.

We are chiefly interested in the cities and architectures of the Lilliputians. Thus Gulliver takes us to Mildendo, the capital. Naturally, the size of all the houses and installations corresponds in size to the tiny people and we are extremely careful not to destroy anything with our heavy footsteps. The population has been prepared for our visit.

The city wall is 500 feet long, two and a half feet high, and more than eleven inches thick, and we are quite astonished to see a coach galloping along on the wall. Every ten feet, the strictly square wall is interrupted by strong towers. We climb into the city across the west gate and walk along one of the main streets. There are no people, for the inhabitants have been warned and remain in their houses, but they observe the visitors from the rooftops and skylights. The two main streets, five feet wide, divide the town into four quarters. The lanes and passages, which we could not use, of course, are between twelve and eighteen inches wide. The houses have from three to five stories as the case may be, and Gulliver has heard that roughly 500,000 people live here.

Now we have reached the emperor's palace and look down at the rooftops. A two-foot wall surrounds the courtyard of the palace. It is 20 feet away from the other buildings. We've obtained permission to step over the wall and now stand in front of the palace, a 40-foot rectangle. By means of an ingenious device we get into the courtyard as well and, lying on the ground, are able to admire the splendor of the palace interior through open windows.

After our tours of Mildendo, we return to the open countryside, and Gulliver tells us a little about the many curiosities he has encountered here. The education of children is by no means left to the parents. Rather, at the age of 20 months, the public kindergartens assume the children's early education. »*Skilled teachers*«, Gulliver tells us, »*educate the children until they attain those life circumstances for which they are suited because of their parents' status and their own abilities and inclinations. The schools for boys employ famous and learned professors. The students are constantly occupied, except during meals and sleep and a two-hour break used for physical exercise. Parents are allowed to see their sons only twice a year; the visit lasts only an hour. They are allowed to kiss their children upon arriving and leaving. In the girls' schools, young upper-class girls are raised much like the boys.*«

Lemuel Gulliver is fated to live an active, restless life, and so we are not surprised when he sets off for further adventures, on which we again accompany him.

They are no less strange, for suddenly we arrive on the island of Brobdingnag, and are seized by both horror and amazement when we find that it is inhabited by people who are as tall as a medium-sized church tower. We are regarded as little animals, as curiosities, as novelties and toys, though we're treated fairly well.

The capital is laid out reasonably well. Here, 600,000 inhabitants live in 80,000 houses. Obviously the houses have huge dimensions. The beautiful church tower is higher than all of them – it is more than 3,000 feet (1,000 m) high.

We particularly like the king's kitchen. It is a magnificent, mighty structure with a tall vaulted ceiling.

We have long since won the king's goodwill. We entertain him with many skills, especially making music, and so are assured of his favor. Nevertheless we leave the country again after a few months, richer in experience.

Swift scurrilously brings to life myths and fairy tales, transferring them into his present. Yet we can discern metaphors for dominating and being dominated – primeval fears.

Gulliver's thirst for travel is unabated, yet we follow him, or rather his stories, only to Laputa, for here a few unusual features interest us.

Gulliver explores the island where he has been cast up. Suddenly the sun seems to grow dark – a huge dark body appears in the sky, approaches the island – and Gulliver realizes this is a flying island with a sizeable little town on it. His joy is great when he is hoisted aloft on a comfortable chair. Of the curiosities, thinks Gulliver, one will be of particular interest to us: An ingenious architect has invented a new method of building houses: he starts with the roof and builds down from the top to the foundations, the way bees and spiders do.

Swift 1726, 2004; Wuckel 1980.

Flying islands, UFOs, drifting islands and cities fill science fiction stories, but also the fantasies of architects.

Without doubt Lilliput has indeed been turned into a reality – but it is called Minimundus or something similar. Miniature copies of cities and their architectures delight young and old visitors alike and are at the same time lessons in the history of architecture.

98. Jonathan Swift, Gulliver in Laputa, flying city, 1726. Illustration by Grandville, 1838.
99. Jonathan Swift, Gulliver in Laputa, the building of a house, 1726. Illustration by Grandville, 1838.

Arthur Bedford (1688–1754?). The camp town of the Israelites (*The scripture chronology demonstrated by astronimical calculations*, 1730)

Again, here is a town characterized by well-ordered geometry. We see, though, that it is not a city with well-placed masonry houses but a camp, the tent city of a nomadic people.

The location and shape of the camp result from astronomical calculations. The center is, so to speak, the modification of the temple of Solomon into a tent sanctuary. It is protected, standing in a small sacred space. Outside, however, a large rectangular courtyard with gardens and enclosures for animals creates the appropriate environment. The tents where people live are arranged in almost military formation. A large rectangular field is provided for each of the twelve tribes of Israel.

Rosenau 1979; Vercelloni 1994.

Urban structure according to »tribes« is by no means a thing of the past: World cities today are layered – socially, by religion, according to ethnicity.

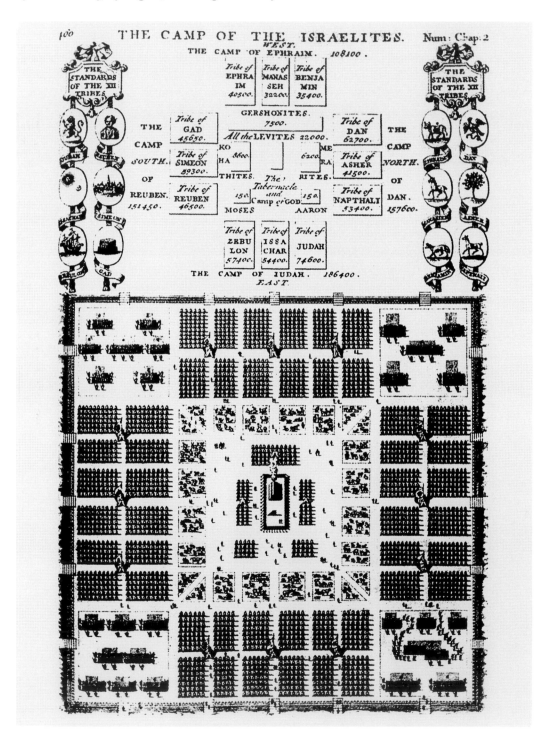

100. Arthur Bedford, camp town of the Israelites, 1730.

101. Athanasius Kircher, Mundus subterraneus,
de lapidibus, plan for a tower city, 1664.
102. Athanasius Kircher, Renaissance city (Babylon),
1679.

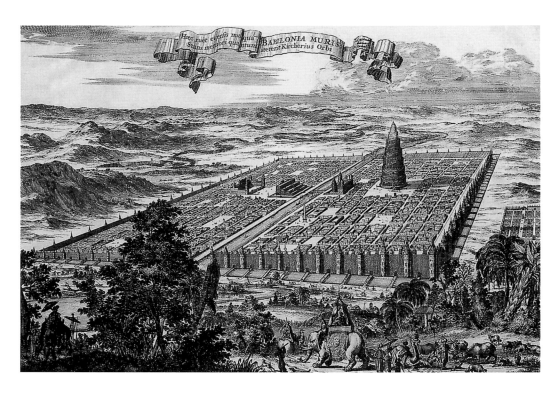

5.3. Germany, Austria, Netherlands

Athanasius Kircher (1602–1680). The tower city, 1664, the city tower, 1679, and Babylon, 1679

Athanasius Kircher reveals a strange world to us: Studies for the Mundus Subterraneus, or subterranean world, are prompted by volcanoes, which are portals to the underground world, but
without any mythology. Rather, Kircher approaches geology, geomancy, and all related disciplines
with the scientific precision of his time. In Book VIII, De Lapidibus, about stones, Kircher portrays
an imaginary city, quite unusual for the period. Cylindrical and cubical houses, mostly with cone-
shaped roofs, are clustered close to each other, like a construction kit, as though there were no
streets. Windows of various sizes are unconventionally cut into the cubes. Now we're off with
Athanasius far into the landscape. »There, you see«, says Athanasius Kircher proudly, »my tower
city reaches the sky. It is the Tower of Babel, it disappears in the clouds: We could call it a skyscraper.« And we are truly impressed with the power and monumentality of the building. At a
height of 300 m and a lower diameter of 180 m we certainly did not overestimate its size.

Athanasius Kircher does not tell us what is happening deep in the core of the building, but he
does refer to the fact that even wagons can reach the topmost platform: The wide spiral ramps
wind around the tower. When we get closer, however, we see that the tower is the center of a
town. It feels like being in a German Renaissance town. A high wall with not less than a hundred
turrets, with a watercourse flowing past it, seems to protect the town – two areas of the wall remain open, and here the river, straight as an arrow and domesticated, flows through the town.
The main square is dominated by the mighty tower on one bank and by a massive terraced
house on the other. »Those are the famous hanging gardens of Queen Semiramis«, explains
Master Kircher. »I visualize them as a giant terraced house.«

The tour of the city takes us across spacious squares, past castles, obelisks, and monuments.
These pleasantly break up the strictly right-angled grid of residential buildings.

Kircher 1664; Thomsen 1994.

We'll encounter collage towns more often, and more expertly designed, in the work of such planners
as John Soane, Charles R. Cockerell, or Erastus Salisbury Field. But present-day towns are also correctly described as collage towns, characterized by patchwork architecture.

The tower city is modeled on the Tower of Babel, and several similar towers are supposed to exist
in the landscape. But obviously they have been stripped of their magic symbolism. In his blueprint for
Babylon Kircher amusingly imagines the Tower of Babel and the gardens of Semiramis as an ideal
city of the German Renaissance/Baroque era.

Georg Andreas Böckler (1644–1698). The Huguenot town, 1686

Once again the square is the basic geometric figure for the town. We enter through one of the four gates and catch sight of a lovely fountain standing in the center. We pass by simple house façades. The houses have one, two, or three stories and steep roofs; the attic has mostly been converted. Entering one of the gates, we find ourselves in a quiet courtyard surrounded by houses.

A large marketplace forms the center of the town, but we look in vain for a church. »Huguenots carry their Christianity inside far too much to build houses of worship«, asserts Andreas Böckler. But we can't help suspecting that he did not wish that the rigid schematism of the architecture should be disturbed by a church building.

The people we encounter tell us that they all try to fill their lives with lofty moral and religious values, but they also want to make sure that their faith is disseminated – the faith because of which they were banished from France.

Kruft 1989; Vercelloni 1994.

The Puritan faith on principle forbade any kind of rich ornamentation of buildings. On the other hand, mass production of houses was a natural. Still, there are small »confusions«: When the corners of buildings are indented, small squares are created.

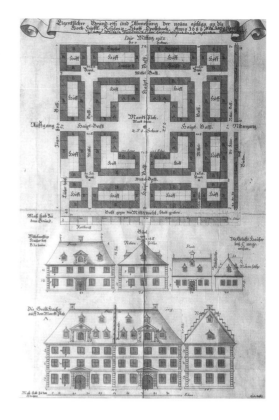

Margrave Karl Wilhelm von Baden-Durlach and Friedrich Weinbrenner (1766–1826). Karlsruhe, 1715–1800

Again we fly over a city and, even from a great height, recognize the precise circle in whose center the castle is located. But no infinite axis radiates from it. Rather, in the center, the 32 streets meet virtually. One-fourth of them, going beyond the ring, have a direct reference to the castle, and these are the town's streets. The others cut through the forests.

»I was not planning a Versailles here«, the margrave tells us. »I preferred strict geometric unity and order, even though the radial roads extend far into the landscape, the meadows, and fields.«

As we approached from the air, we had already discovered an additional figure: A square is inscribed in the circle, and we cannot help thinking of Vitruvius's and Leonardo's human being inscribed in the circle and square.

Karlsruhe, too, was actually built – and yet it remained a utopia. Only with difficulty are the south roads able to create some kind of order; the north roads have remained rudimentary; only in the east do they reach far into former hunting grounds.

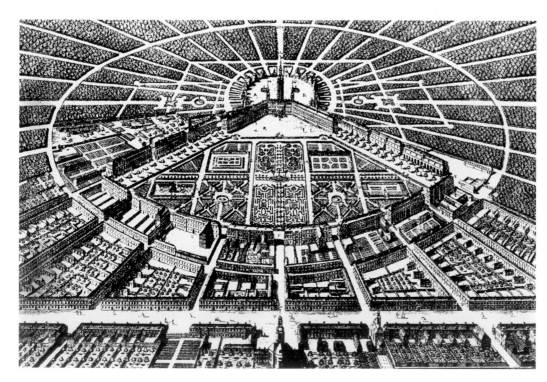

103. Friedrich Weinbrenner, plan of Karlsruhe, castle and park, 1715–1770. Engraving by Christian Thran.
104. Georg Andreas Böckler, the Huguenot town of Onoltzbach near Ansbach, Germany, 1686.

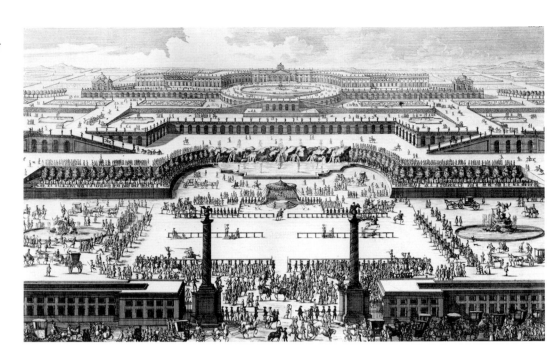

Johann Bernhard Fischer von Erlach (1656–1723). The Habsburg dream – Schönbrunn, 1690?

Yes indeed, Schönbrunn, too, is actually a town – far from the gates of the city of Vienna, located among gently rolling hills.

Today we have a wonderful opportunity. We've been invited to a prestigious festival, a baroque display of magnificence. On the large square in front of the entrance, the throng jostles for room, and congested rows of splendid carriages, drawn by up to six horses each, wait to be admitted into the first big courtyard. In our coach we drive inside between triumphal columns whose spiral reliefs tell a story. The adjacent residential and housekeeping buildings on both sides are plain in style. They close off the square we are entering now. The two big basins with groups of sculptures leave enough room for a drama unrolling at the moment:: a magnificent parade of riders with a horse ballet, a parade of carriages, and peaceful simulations of martial games. In the middle an oval tent has been erected. People are waiting for the empress, who will graciously watch the spectacle.

But as for us, we drive on as Master Fischer explains his concept: «A gently sloping hill is the gigantic building site, and the cascades I built are not merely waterworks, they are cascades of stone and squares, so to speak, tumbling down over the hill in huge terraces.« The first of these cascades of terrain is dedicated to domesticated nature: In geometric order the trees of the avenue stand on the terrace, with strolling people among them. A large quadrant unifies an artificial landscape of rocks over which a dozen brooks splash into a big basin.

In the meantime, we've reached the next level by a ramp terrace. Simple arcades enclose this level. One of the side ramps for carriages takes us to the next terrace, whose charm comes from two basins with fountains and which is completed by balustrades with dozens of figures. The next level is particularly attractive, for there are flower beds, and the terrace is again closed off with arcades. The last ramp takes us to the grand finale of this superb production, an oval area with a large water basin on which one of the *naufragies*, or water games, is being practiced just then.

»The actual castle, the residence, is the conclusion of these spectacular shows for me«, comments Fischer von Erlach, »one's eyes roam far over the landscape and rule it in the true sense of the word. The 75 axes are like the outspread arms of a ruler, and I believe that I have designed something that is at least as fine as St. Peter's Square in Rome and the Escorial in Spain.«

The occupation of nature is not over yet: On both sides and toward the back, there are extensive gardens.

The Austrian monarchy still seems to be at its peak. The Turks have been vanquished for the second time, the plague is over, the country encompasses vast lands. Still, the ruler's ambition has overreached itself: The goal is to surpass Versailles by far. Yet what is created is a comparatively modest building – Nicola Pacassi completed Schönbrunn and left his considerably plainer mark on it.

Johann Daniel Herz (1693–1754). A Baroque Jerusalem, 1730

Into what period is the artist really taking us? Surely, from this hill, we are looking down upon a medieval town with a moat, walls, and towers? Coming closer we see that it is a Renaissance town, but without geometrical order, more imaginative, baroque, put together like a collage. Why this tumult in the streets, on the squares, though? We can't believe our eyes – what period are we in? There, Christ is being tortured, condemned to death, and led out the town gate – Golgotha rises on the horizon.

»Everything is different«, the artist explains. »We're beyond all time – for actually we're in the New Jerusalem, in which Christ's sufferings will become present once more.«

Stadt und Utopie 1982.

Once more, Jerusalem represents the city as such. The artists spans a wonderful arc in time: The Jewish Jerusalem, then the city of Christ's sufferings, but also Rome, and then the Renaissance – but all of them drawn in the Baroque era.

Johann Gottfried Schnabel (1692–1751/58). Felsenburg island (*Wunderliche Fata einiger Seefahrer, absonderlich Alberti Julii, eines gebohrnen Sachsen*, 1646)

It was not at all easy to find Felsenburg island. In many places sandbanks and cliffs prevented our landing. But now we're pleased that we can roam over this island of happy people. We're on Tristan da Cunha in the South Atlantic, and the year is 1726.

A young student, Eberhard Julius, is our guide. He has good reason for coming to the island: His grandfather, Albert Julius, or Julio, discovered the island one day, in the year 1646 – and now father and son embrace full of emotion.

Now we learn the thrilling story that took place in 1646 from Albert: The ship ran aground on a sandbank, but four people escaped death by drowning: beside Albert, they are the Dutchman Franz Karl von Leuven and his charming wife Concordia, and the evil Captain Lemelie. He throws good Mr. Leuven off a cliff, but Concordia rejects the murderer, and Albert approaches her only chastely – until Concordia in turn falls in love with him. Lemelie, on the other hand, is accidentally killed by Albert – now he and Concordia live in peace and she bears him nine children in eighteen years – soon there are grandchildren as well. News of the island's beauty reach Europe. Teachers, craftspeople, priests arrive on the island, so that all the children find partners. Gradually, the population of the island grows to 300.

But now it is time to take a closer look at the island. From the fortress hill high above we recognize that the island is roughly rectangular. Three rivers run through it. They are fed by the »Big

Lake« and flow into the ocean. On the edges of the island there are dense forests. The individual districts of the island are called »space.« In »Stephan's Space« we find fifteen residential units, and stables and barns next to them. Albert's Space is divided by two avenues both leading to the church. This is just being built but promises to be an imposing structure. We cross a bridge and are now in »Simon's Space«, and after visiting the zoo we rest by the Little Lake. There are thirteen houses here. We are glad to be invited by one of the homeowners, since we are now able to admire the solid and neat construction from the inside as well.

The towns are very carefully laid out. If they are not on a riverbank, they have canals running through them. Well-tended gardens break up the town, and vineyards crown it like garlands. All the houses are solid, well taken care of, orderly, and characterized by simplicity and thrift.

Enough for one day! The next morning we have time to roam through Robert's and Christoph's Space, and finally Johannes's and Stephanie's Space.

The highlight of the day, though, is the invitation to visit the Albert Fortress, erected on a rock. The main building is flanked by four towers. The interior is solidly structured, but there is none of the luxury that is customary in other castles.

What would be the beauty of a town, or an island, if the people themselves were not contented? They go about their work with great joy, and their Protestant faith gives them confidence and hope. On a holiday, we realize how deeply they are connected to their community: The entire population is united in devout prayers.

Schnabel 1828, 1969; Manguel 1981; Berghahn 1983; Glaser 1996.

This is one of many island worlds, but from the initial shipwreck robinsonade Schnabel develops the idea of an ideal community based on Protestant Christianity. Of course, Schnabel does not fail to start by first telling the dreadful and moving story of Concordia and Albert. In the »pure nature« of the island, human beings are restored to reason.

107. Johann Gottfried Schnabel, Felsenburg island, 1646, 1726.

Johann Friedrich Bachstrom (1688–1742). The land of the Inquiranians (*Das Bey zwey hundert Jahren lang unbekannte nunmehro aber entdeckte vortreffliche Land der Inquiraner*, 1736)

The land is so wonderful that we think the goddess Calypso could have her residence here! At the same time the country and the town seem to us to be very sensibly built and administered. How many people live here and what is the organization of the town? we'd like to know. »There are 200 families here – a total of 660 people«, Master Bachstrom informs us. »They live in 400 huts in four districts.«

Now we can also easily discern how the town is built. It is placed on the intersection of four large streets. This intersection forms the boundaries of the four districts. Along the big streets the houses are lined up in beautiful order. They are built in a simple yet classic style. Master Bachstrom tells us his architectonic credo: »For in architecture one must observe three things. First, a building should be very solid and safe in every way; second, it should be conveniently and advantageously set up for the business that will be transacted there. And then, third, it should be ornamented to the extent that the first two intentions permit this. These days, people generally put the cart before the horse and think of nothing but splendor, decoration, and appearance: The so-called orders of columns with which most books on architecture begin and end are pure decoration and a silly, unnecessary notion from antiquity.«

Now we are able to visit one of the houses. Its entrance is on the main street, but there is another building behind it, for children, but also for cattle, tools, and supplies. There is also a little garden, from which an exit leads to a side street.

We stroll through the various districts and are struck by the fact that people look slightly different in each. »That's easy to understand«, Master Bachstrom explains, »a different professional group lives in each district. There are the fishermen, sailors, and shipbuilders, next, the farmers and gardeners, then the cattle breeders and stable builders and carpenters, and finally the tailors and furriers. There are big workshops as well, for example, for cabinetmakers and blacksmiths.« We are struck by the very simple cut of the clothes, and their different colors.

»There is no luxury, clothing is like that of soldiers«, Master Bachstrom informs us, »but in each district a different color is worn merely to distinguish the individual occupations. The chairman, the heads, and the supervisors can be recognized by the color of their clothes.«

The trades seem to be doing well, for we see how cleverly the people make salt, look at the fine fruit, the abundant fish and game market, the spinners of hemp and flax. Finally we sample wine, honey, and bread, and we are full of praise. »The credit is not entirely ours. We have a wonderful climate here.« But how is it possible that everything functions so seamlessly? »There is no idleness – that is the worst vice. All inhabitants, including unmarried women, are obliged to work. The young help too. But those who are sick are nursed carefully. There is no wastefulness, for every household is allotted what it needs depending on the number of persons. The four working companies each have a head, that is, the district elder, and a supervisor. He is appointed by the chairman, who is the most respected in the district; he is both the physician and apothecary.« And what do the women do? »They're at home with the children, provide food and drink, and keep house.«

Finally we'd like to know how the »Inquiranians« got their name. »Aha – now you're getting to the heart of the matter! Most of us fled the Spanish Inquisition because we did not want to be forced to accept the Catholic faith. But many exiles have gathered here: Mohammedans and Jews, Greek Christians, the church of Geneva, believers of the Augsburg confession, but also Roman Catholics – a small minority, mind you – who, being heretics, were galley slaves.«

And how have they all created this harmonious coexistence? »Well, in the beginning things went quite well. We founded religious guilds for each faith, you see. And we swore to each other to live side by side in unity, peace, calm, happiness and bliss. There was to be no religious fanaticism. But soon it was the same old story again: jealousy, envy, arguments, lack of understanding. There were even fights.«

Let's admit that when we heard this, we were a little disappointed by this peaceful island! Bachstrom 1736.

Johann Friedrich Bachstrom took generous helpings from the fund of ideal towns and communities. We've visited a kind of emigrant town several times.

What is new, however, is the idea that many different faiths can live side by side within a confined space. However, in the long run, Bachstrom does not see only ideal traits in this model.

Ludvig Holberg (1684–1754) and Niels Klim. The underworld – Potu (*Nicolai Klimii iter subterraneum, novam telluris theoriam ad historiam quintae monarchiae exhibens*, 1741)

Through an endlessly deep cave in the town of Bergen in Norway we reach the planet Nazar in the interior of the Earth and its capital, which, as we learn, is called Potu – and that is obviously Utop pronounced backwards.

Lovely landscapes with hills, waters, and trees delight us. But we are both amazed and frightened: Suddenly one of the trees walks toward us and as we approach we see that it has not only legs, but also a face, though we cannot recognize its gender. These beings all have the same rights, and there is neither favoritism nor corruption, yet by the number of branches one can tell differences in rank. A widow with seven branches holds one of the foremost offices in the state.

Now we visit the neighboring country and are struck by how incredibly healthy, cheerful, and young people look. Actually, they have no worries and no illnesses, but we find contact with them difficult, for they are insensitive and boring.

The next land we tour is dominated entirely by women, while the men do the cooking. In the middle of the country the queen has had a magnificent building erected: It is the men's harem, and no less than 300 handsome youths and men are being kept here for the pleasure of the ruler.

But there are more strange phenomena to come as we travel to the next country. Our amazement is even greater, for now a one-legged creature comes hopping toward us – it is fused with a sort of double bass and plays its own body with the bow. Lawyers scratch their bellies here, the judge plays a solemn grave movement, and the court usher finally takes away the criminal's bow, which is the equivalent of a death sentence.

After all these surprises in the strange country it is no longer so unusual to meet a group of apes with luxuriant heads of hair, wearing flowing capes. The stories of these beings are no less unusual: In their country, peasants are completely free and are the most important members of society, and women are completely on a par with men.

It seems almost a miracle to us, however, when we see a ship crossing the sea without sails or rowers, yet moving with incredible speed.

Finally we witness our traveling companion Niels Klim being greatly honored in the next country because of his intelligence – he is crowned emperor. But errors and cruelties during his reign cause him to be banished. During the escape he falls through a cave – and we along with him – and we land back in Bergen again.

Holberg 1741, 1753, 1828, 1848; Kirchenheim 1892; Manguel 1981; Wuckel 1986.

Here, people are so close to nature that they become part of it, which means an end to worry and disease: an idea with which we're very familiar today – think of those who advocate going back to nature. But man, music, and nature also enter into complete synthesis in this utopia.

5.4. Italy

Bernardo (Antonio) Vittone (1705–1770). The sea city, 1732

An eagle's-eye view of the town shows a total geometry of archetypes: Square, cross, and circle determine the plan. The perfect circle with its small bastions is interrupted in one place: Like the pincers of a crab, two arms jut into the sea, forming an elliptical harbor basin. A representative building creates a hinge, and hexagonal towers form the portal of the harbor entrance. A lighthouse is in the foreground.

»Geometry and mathematics are the great regulators in architecture and in city planning«, the young architect Vittone explains. »I used the whole wealth of forms harmonically and functionally. I brought especially the circle and square, but also the pentagon, triangle, and ellipse into harmonic unison.«

The town is situated in the middle of the sea, and we approach it by sea. Cruciform, navigable canals divide the town, while bridges connect it. On the big round square in the center, water is present once again in the form of fountains. The architect has devoted special care to the four central districts. Each of them contains a monumental structure – a church and a big square, placed on a diagonal axis. Adjacent on the left and right are hexagonal open spaces. Behind the

108. Ludvig Holberg, citizen in Potu, 1655, 1741.
109. Ludvig Holberg, music man in Potu, 1655, 1741.

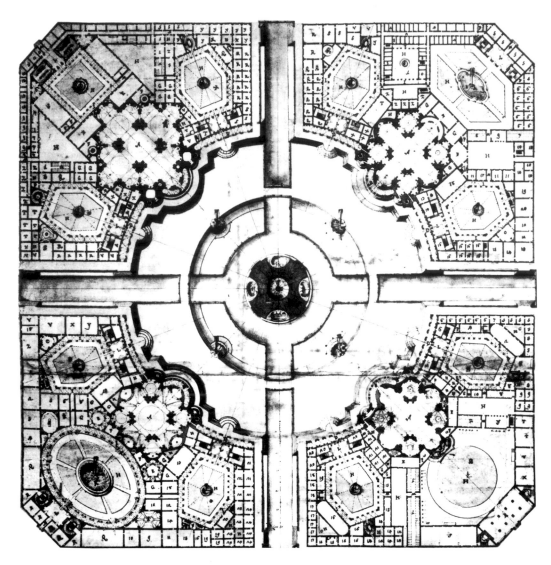

110, 111. Bernardo Vittone, ideal city in the sea, 1732.

church buildings the architect has devised various forms for public squares. »I assigned a typical geometric form to each of the public spaces behind the churches«, says the architect. »The square, hexagon, ellipse, and circle give each space its distinctive character.« But why four churches – and four identical churches into the bargain? we wonder. »The churches aren't identical at all! If you go inside, you'll see that each space is different.«

We really are surprised by the interesting spatial variations, but also by the fact that all the plans resemble that of St. Peter's Basilica with its central building, Bramante as well as Michelangelo. »It is legitimate to develop further the great masters' ideas about space, even on a smaller scale«, asserts Vittone. »The churches are coordinated with the functions of adjacent buildings: the university, the bishop's seat and the residence of the governor, the curia and the court of justice, and the riding academy.«

We haven't seen the entire bold plan, and leave the center of town to continue our tour.

»In the south there is an island, and at its tip, corresponding to the harbor towers, I built another fort, choosing a pentagon form. But follow me northward now. That is where the citadel is – really on land, but still surrounded by water. A bridge connects it with the island town.«

The master has chosen the decagon form here, and streets radiate from a public square. We wander through a seemingly perfect large town that arises from the accumulation of buildings and styles. It is an architectonic paradise as it were, in which the eye partakes of the perfection of architecture with tremendous pleasure.

Portoghesi 1966; Vercelloni 1994.

The vocabulary of Bernardo Vittone's use of forms is extremely rich. The great yearning of Renaissance urban planners flares up once more: the central structure, the central town architects so rarely had a chance to design. Once was not enough: There are as many as four other ideal plans in the style of Bramante and Michelangelo.

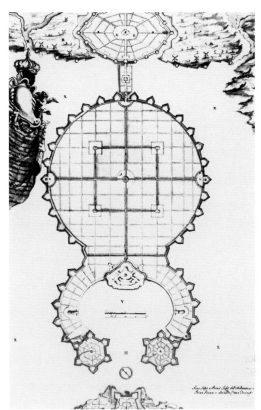

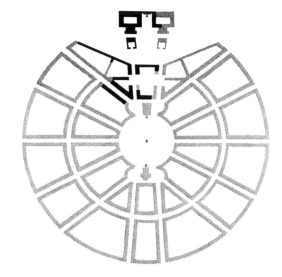

Luigi Vanvitelli (1700–1773). San Leucio I near Caserta, 1752–1756
Francesco Collecini (1723–1798) and Ferdinand IV. San Leucio II. Ferdinandopoli, 1798

»While it was not the intention of my client, Charles of Bourbon, to overshadow Versailles, for how would that even be possible«, we are told by Vanvitelli, »the splendid royal palace and its garden naturally did inspire him.«

Indeed, we do find numerous quotations from the magnificent French building. The castle with its five floors, corner towers, and a central cupola is very impressive. There is an oval area in front of the castle whose sides are formed by two-story buildings for the sentries, buildings for the servants' quarters, stables, and outbuildings. Adjacent to the oval is »New Town.« These are self-contained building units on the wide radial streets with spacious courtyards, all of them two stories high.

»On one side the castle is orientated toward the new town, while on the other side it faces the park and the countryside«, Vanvitelli explains the principle with which we are already familiar from Versailles. In the well-tended garden we find everything that is in keeping with aristocratic standards: riding arenas and a theater, terraces with a view of flower beds, many fountains, and ancient statues.

Now we meet Vanvitelli's former colleague, the architect Francesco Collecini. »With my new San Leucio client, King Ferdinand IV, we developed a completely new concept – for a new epoch seems to be dawning. From now on it will no longer be hunting and agriculture that determine the future, but production, machines.«

The circle has consistently been used in the city, and the center of »Ferdinandopoli« is now a circular public space from which, even more consistently, streets radiate like rays, crossing a tangential street in the process. Toward the north, in a square-like widening, is the cathedral, which has an elegant façade. It is orientated toward the palace, its magnificent antithesis, which with its paired buildings takes up a wide notch in the circular city.

Collecini very skillfully expanded the existing »casino« toward the rear and mirrored the entire group of buildings. In this way he created quite an impressive castle. From the central second-floor window we see the majestic statue of a Roman emperor: It is the ruler who commissioned the palace, Ferdinand IV. We tour the wing of the *cour d'honneur* and now understand Collecini's words. There are no salons, no palatial rooms, no halls built merely for representative purposes. Instead, looms and spinning machines rattle in the large rooms. All workers, both men and

112. Francesco Collecini, San Leucio II, Ferdinandopoli, 1798. Reconstruction by Eugenio Battisti, 1974 .
113. Luigi Vanvitelli, Caserta, San Leucio I. Engraving, 1756.

women, are housed in the simple, uniformly two-story row houses of the town. In the rear, each house has a small garden.

We are very fortunate to get an audience with Ferdinand IV, the king of both Sicilies. He is not only the founder of the new town, but has also given it its regulations and laws, which he proudly explains to us.

»I founded the new town of San Leucio near my palace. Here the air is excellent and the food is wholesome. That is why the eighteen families who moved in, and later fourteen more, were extremely fruitful: Within a few years the community has grown to over 200 persons.«

Asked what the basic moral principles of the population are, the king answers: »That's very simple: Our life is based on the love of God and our fellow men, supported by prayers. None may be injured as to their person, their good name, or their property.« The king now hands us a booklet, a kind of catechism codifying all the regulations of spiritual and worldly life. Special attention is given to the exact times of school attendance.

As we arrived, we were struck by the simplicity of the castle. »I, too, observe the prohibition against ostentatious wealth. And since all citizens are equal, they all wear the same simple clothing.«

During our visit to the workrooms we particularly noticed the incredible enthusiasm, the quiet hard work. »All of them are constantly encouraged in this, they get used to being busy. There is no idleness, for it is the father of all vices. And of course there is no gambling, no lowlife pubs. I try to motivate people by means of competitions, there are prizes for the finest work.«

Working as hard as they do, how do people find a marriage partner? »Girls must be over sixteen years old, the men over twenty, but are not allowed to marry until they have the certificate from the foreman. At that time they get a new house with a workshop. Every year at Pentecost those who are eager to marry gather. Young men and girls who like each other exchange their little bouquets of flowers and marry soon thereafter. It is true that there is no dowry, no marriage portion, and children may inherit only from their parents and spouses from each other. If a person dies without heirs, the property goes to the relief fund of the orphanage, to the funds for brothers, widows, old people, and the sick.« We cannot help expressing our admiration for the extensive social welfare.

After we take leave of the king and thank him for the interesting information, we have a little time for a last walk, when we see that care has been taken to provide all necessities of life: a church, a theater, schools, and a home for craftsmen. In the so-called »trattoria« everyday needs are taken care of. The hospital is located in a healthy, quiet spot, and here all citizens are inoculated for smallpox.

San Leucio 1791; Kruft 1989.

What part of this project was actually implemented? So little that in the end Vanvitelli's and Collecini's plans remained a utopia after all. Of San Leucio I and II, only the central square and the belvedere with the expansion behind it, a few rows of living quarters and the town gate were built.

It is probably difficult to check whether the account about yet another »benevolent ruler« was historically correct, for in the report about the town, Ferdinand IV is actually given as the author.

Franciscus Contini (c. 1650/1670). Emperor Hadrian's Rome, 1668, c. 130

Franciscus Contini takes us far back in history, the time of Emperor Hadrian (76–138). We owe the Pantheon, the Castel Sant' Angelo, and his own magnificent villa to this ruler, who was eager to build, and obviously totally rebuilt Rome. We are quite familiar with monuments like the Cestius pyramid, near which our tour begins.

Without Contini's help we would be hopelessly lost in the cramped tangle of streets, lanes, and squares.

Contini mentions the names of many of the streets and buildings, though they have little meaning for us. We do recall a few, however. Starting with the pyramid, we see arcades that point in the direction of Ostia. We notice the many potteries and storehouses. After passing under the aqueduct of Antony, we reach two large adjacent squares: On the public main street is Victory Square with the city's highest building – a six-story stepped building with a temple on the topmost platform. Next to it is the square of Antonius, where a large complex of buildings surrounds a courtyard. »It is worth your while to take many detours from the main streets, for

there are very beautiful inner courtyards, many with arcades, and some with fountains«, Contini
informs us. We're glad to take his advice, and are even more surprised to see numerous small
and large domed buildings, though none reach the dimension of the Pantheon. »These are temples dedicated to individual deities: to Mars, Minerva, Diana, but also to the Egyptian goddess
Isis.«

Later, walking through the city, our first stop is the thermal baths, which seem rather modest to
us. »I'd like to draw your attention to two important building forms: Here, next to one another, are
the triumphal arches of Augustus and Trajan, and not far from these are two arches that are related to the aqueduct. Now you can also see that the Cestius pyramid is not the only one in the
city. Two more are close by – also mausoleums.«

Now we are near the city wall with its closely set towers. Confused and fascinated at the same
time, we are under the impression that we have seen the largest part of Rome. »Far from it«,
Contini points out. »We've hardly walked through a tenth of it!«

Thus, on the next day, we meet with Contini again. To our surprise he's arranged a flight in one of the clever flying machines available to prominent visitors to the city since the time of Leonardo. We enjoy a view of the city from the air.

It is impossible to describe all the wealth before our eyes. The main arteries and, soon, the Tiber River help us get our bearings. We note a few of the most important splendid buildings: the hippodrome of Aurelius and the temple of Minerva Medica, the thermal baths of Diocletian and the forum of Sallust, the Basilica Ulpia and the forum of Trajan with the column of Trajan, the hippodrome of Hadrian and the Circus Maximus. The high points are unforgettable: the Pantheon, the Flavian amphitheater we now call the Colosseum, and the mausoleum of Hadrian, now referred to as the Castel Sant' Angelo.

Exhausted and overwhelmed, we sit down near the big water arena, and are just in time to see a naumarchy, a gigantic water battle spectacle.

The fascinating thing about Contini's Rome is the total uncertainty we experienced: Which was reality and which was fiction? Naturally many of the prominent monumental buildings do exist – some to this very day – but they are interspersed with the products of Contini's fertile imagination, and this alternation between different levels of reality is reminiscent of modern dramatic practices.

Besides Contini's Rome we shall visit a few other imaginary cities that have been created by the agglomeration of very real buildings. It seems as though there were no blueprint underlying these cities, und in this they are surprisingly similar to the proliferation of modern cities. The »collage city« is a very topical issue. Our next tour takes us back to Rome, as envisioned by Piranesi.

Giambattista Piranesi (1720–78). The *Carceri*, 1745, fantastical Rome, 1762, and the landing place, 1750

Is it reality, is it only a dream into which Piranesi has led us? Is this fantastical, strangely beautiful world built architecture? In the *Carceri*, the cellars, the dungeons (though filled with light), our eyes look for order, for comprehensible three-dimensionality, for systems and structures – in vain, for hardly have we discovered a classic principle than it changes, floats away. In vain we look for orientation. Overlaps, superimposition, fusion, confusions, the bold staircases, the daring vaults: an expressive phantasmagoria, alarming, overwhelming – yet fascinating.

Now we leave the dreamlike chiaroscuro of the *Carceri* and step outside into the glorious southern sunshine – and suddenly find ourselves in ancient Rome. We stroll along the Via Appia, and on to the Via Ardeatina. At first it looks like a junkshop of antiquity: Shattered columns, toppled torsos, dignified busts, animal figures, vases, tombstones line the street. But we look beyond this and see the maginificent buildings, piled on top of each other into architectural moun-

115. *Idea delle antiche vie Appia e Ardeatina*, 1755.

tain ranges. We can barely make out how to reach all this grandeur, what roads or streets we need to take to the monuments, or whether, crowded together as they are, they leave enough room for us to sit down.

Piranesi, however, sees Rome not as a wounded city, quite the contrary: »I've resurrected Rome, rebuilt in all its glory and diversity, in its beauty and power«, Piranesi declares proudly. »I have far surpassed Rome«, he says. »I imagined a city to come, the city people had longed for even in antiquity. I haven't reconstructed that Rome, but completed it out of my own imagination.«

Along the Via Appia we go on directly to Rome. We visit the Field of Mars, and now the chaos seems to be completed. What boldness: Buildings that no longer exist, have not been clearly archeologically defined, have simply been added, created by Piranesi's imagination! We admire the sublime perfection of the classical composition, the power of the monuments, the beauty, order, and symmetry of the individual buildings – but as for the overall picture of this part of the city as put together by Piranesi: We find scarcely any order indicating urban planning, there seems to be a chaos of axes, streets, and perspectives, unimaginable confusion, and incredible density and narrowness.

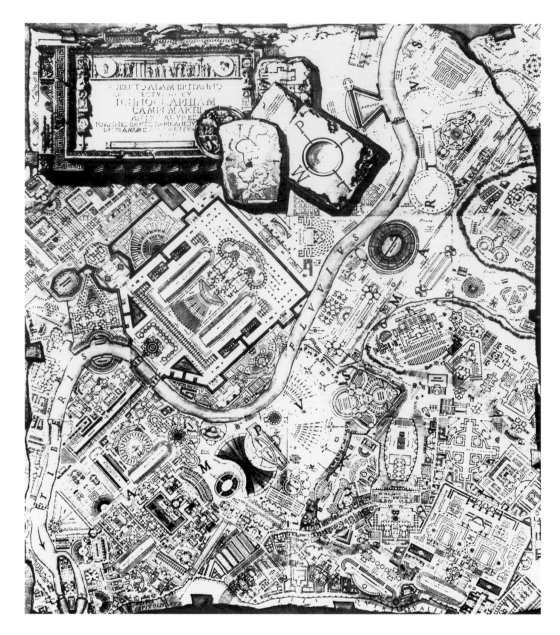

117, 118. Giambattista Piranesi, the field of Mars, Rome, 1762.
119. Giambattista Piranesi, fantasy landing place, c. 1750.

Our subsequent tour of the landing place is no less stimulating, while also confusing. We are happy to have Piranesi as our guide, for we are barely able to find our way through the seemingly compressed architecture: Convex and concave, with colossal orders, the façades form a curving street and change directly into a triumphal arch, which in turn seems to be propped up on a temple façade. Triumphal columns, a mausoleum, temple-like pavilions, the columns of rostra and an enormous number of sculptures accompany us as clouds of smoke rise into the sky. We pass a gigantic archway, and a monumental flight of steps goes down to a small harbor. And here, a rowboat with rowers awaits us: Piranesi invites us for a ride on the river, and an outdoors sightseeing tour from the water side concludes our truly fantastic walk.

Tafuri 1976, 1999; *Inventionen* 1981; Vercelloni 1994; *Nouvelles* 2001.

Two thousand years after Rome and two hundred years after Piranesi, we may often find a similar, arbitrary-looking collage in the big cities: The concept »collage urbanism« characterizes an aspect of our cities. What Piranesi claims is reconstruction is actually a fantastical invention with a few fixed points in reality. Thus, for instance, the Pantheon is a reality, of course, while the buildings that surround the temple are chiefly products of Piranesi's »intervenzioni«.

Were any of Piranesi's fantasies ever implemented? Certainly! Two hundred years later, the architects of »deconstructivism« will, among other things, orient themselves by them. But that's not all: Wherever we encounter confusing beauty, fascinating chaos, unreal monumentality, the name of Piranesi is invoked!

6. Enlightenment, Classicism, c. 1750–1850

6.1. France

Voltaire (1694–1778). *Candide*, 1759

Born in Westphalia, Candide arrives in the country of Eldorado after adventurous journeys through Bulgaria, Portugal, Spain, Argentina, and Paraguay. Together with his companion Cacambo we experience the splendor and wealth of this country. Even in the first village we notice that the village boys, dressed in brocade jackets, are throwing rocks at a target, but oddly the rocks are round, yellow, red, and green, and have an unusual glitter – and when we pick up a few, we realize they are emeralds, rubies, and pieces of gold.

Here is the first house of the village – a splendid palace – but it is the village inn. We hear music, a delicious smell fills our nostrils, we enter and at once the waitress, dressed in gold fabrics, serves us a sumptuous meal. »In this country everything must be for the best!« exclaims Candide full of joyous enthusiasm.

Now we make our way into town, and here too we cannot get over our astonishment. For the buildings seem to rise to the very clouds. The town's marketplace is decorated with a thousand columns. Crystal-clear fountains adorn the square, fountains spouting rose water and others spouting sugarcane liqueur. The jets of liquid pour without interruption into large basins embellished with a kind of precious stones, and from them emanates a fragrance resembling cloves or cinnamon. – We'd like to see the palace of justice but are told there is none, since there are never any lawsuits, and there are no prisons either. What surprises and delights us most, however, is the Palace of Sciences, in which we see a 2,000-meter long gallery full of mathematical and physical instruments.

It's a great pleasure for us to visit the house of a scholar, who lives very modestly: The doors are made of silver, the rooms are paneled with gold, and the anteroom is inlaid with rubies and emeralds. We ask many questions and receive intelligent information about the government, fine arts, women. We are particularly interested in religion. »We have the religion of the whole world, we worship God from morning till night. We do not know prayers. God gives all of us what we need. And everyone here is a priest: The king and every inhabitant sing a song of praise to God every morning.«

We take our leave of the wise man, and a swift carriage drawn by six wethers brings us to the king, who welcomes us warmly with a banquet. Once more Candide and Cacambo come to the conclusion: »If there is any place where everything is superbly arranged, that place is Eldorado and nowhere else in the world.«

Voltaire 1964; Krauss 1964.

Eldorado pais, the legendary, golden land in the northern part of South America, was given a new definition by Voltaire. He placed it, »superbly arranged«, in Cayenne (Guiana). The boundless, extravagant affluence, as the Europeans see it, becomes completely relative, and wealth needs to be redefined. Here, »buildings that rise to the very clouds« – in other words, skyscrapers – are indications of a wonderful city.

Louis-Sébastien Mercier (1740–1814). The year 2440 – A dream to surpasss all dreams, 1799, *2440* (*L'an deux mille quatre cent quarante. Rêve s'il en fut jamais*, 1771)

We are in one of the loveliest and most famous cities: in Paris. How much it has changed, though, over the past nearly 700 years! The atrocious chaos of the city, the misery of the people, the despotism of the aristocracy, the cynicism of the wealthy, the hunger and crime: All that lies behind us in the remote past.

Now the entire people are a single big family and there are no class differences. Thus there are also no idlers – something that could easily be achieved by abolishing the aristocracy. Admittedly it is necessary to have foremen supervise the work. But diligence and a self-evident morality never allow work to become a burden. The women have a better life than in former times, we are told: They can marry according to inclination and love, and simply separate again as well. They have the same rights as men, but are supposed to do work that is in accordance with their nature: as mothers and housewives.

Magnificent tree-lined avenues, which are perfectly straight, cross the city and are carefully watched; the houses are spacious and clean. From a landscaped roof terrace on the bank of the Seine we gaze far over the city center and can recognize the large-scale squares with their majestic monuments. Especially the square in front of the Louvre is the preferred place for splendid festivals. Opposite the Louvre we can make out the town hall.

After looking at this panorama, we continue our stroll through the well-maintained streets. The elegant carriages of the aristocracy have vanished from the streets. There are simple horse-drawn wagons, however, which follow strict traffic regulations. The people are simply and wholesomely, yet tastefully dressed, and their houses are similarly furnished. Now we round a street corner and discover a beautiful, spacious square where there is a rotunda-like temple crowned with a magnificent cupola supported only by a series of columns. There are four great gates, over each of which an inscription proclaims »Temple of God«. In the interior, a solemn, majestic room welcomes us. The altar is in the middle. Like the room, it is completely unadorned. No pictures or statues distract one from contemplation. Now we become aware that the cupola is made of glass and the sky is brought directly into the interior. In the meantime the room has filled with peaceful, collected people, and soon reverent hymns and prayers are heard.

We leave the temple. The walk has made us hungry, and our guide wants to take us to an inn. Surely not the distinguished, princely building we are just entering? »Oh yes, the ruling prince is really kind, he always pays for three tables in the house: one for himself and his family, the second for strangers, and the third for the needy, the elderly and convalescents, for pregnant women and orphans.«

We sit down to eat. There is healthy and light food, a hearty soup, vegetables, a little game and fruit, everything very simply prepared but appetizing.

As we continue our walk, we ask to see the royal library, which is no doubt accessible to all citizens. We expect immensely long halls. But we find only small rooms with few books. Has a fire destroyed it all? »True, but we set the fire ourselves. And we preserved only a minimum of books, the really valuable ones, for we need no collections of the most extreme excesses and the most foolish illusions.« This course of events, we must confess, seemed exceedingly strange: All superfluous books were piled up in a pyramid and burned, and a commission decided which books are truly valuable and worth reading.

Meanwhile dusk had fallen, and we were delighted to follow an invitation to the theater. The hall is built in the form of a semicircle. Every visitor has a comfortable seat with a good view. The women are modestly and simply dressed. The play paid homage to the virtues and was very skillfully performed.

The next day brings us another big surprise: We are taken into a hall, in which, on a white wall, living images suddenly appear. At the same time we hear music, though there is no musician in sight. It comes from the phonograph.

Our next question concerns the education of children. »We've shaken off that medieval religious junk. The monasteries have been abolished, and almost all the monks and nuns have married. Religion has been replaced by morality. Only the principles of the Enlightenment and of the sciences are in force. Certainly those who offend against them must wear a mask in public until they come to their senses. Teaching has been freed of all pedantry. Every citizen writes down his important thoughts in a book, which is given to his descendants as a memento.« And what are the most important subjects in your schools? is our question. »We no longer teach Greek and Latin. Why teach dead languages? We have enough good translations of the classics. History is rarely taught, for it is the disgrace of humanity, and every page is a tissue of crime and folly. We have much too much scorn for metaphysics. But we emphasize mathematics and physics. They are the key to nature.«

Have writers been abolished, too? »By no means, but if an author writes a bad book, he must wear a mask as well.« Doesn't censorship make sure there is quality writing? »We haven't had any for a long time. Freedom of the press is the true criterion of civic freedom.« However, we do feel it is a kind of censorship if someone decides which books are good or bad.

And what new type of state have you devised? we want to know. »It's new – yet old«, explains Mercier. »We have a king, but without pomp and splendor. Versailles, you see, fell into ruin long ago. The king lives in the middle of town and has a senate to advise him.«

There is only one class now – the middle class. Admittedly it is not possible to do away with poverty entirely, but each person does have a livelihood guaranteed by the state. Taxes are paid as voluntary gifts, about one-fiftieth of a person's income. At the big intersections of streets there are boxes on wheels, where the taxes are thrown in through a slit. The word credit, used to conceal assiduous cheating, is unknown here. »Thanks to our good economic situation and the new morality, we've managed to raise the wellbeing of every citizen, and we live in universal peace.« »This peace«, says our guide, »makes us all brothers. *The Indians and Chinese are our fellow citizens as soon as they set foot on our soil. We accustom our children to regard the whole world as one family gathered in the presence of the Father of us all.*«

And this universal and global peace has had worldwide effects: Japan has opened to the world, Italy has been unified, Australia has been settled, in Russia serfdom has been abolished, and America has become an autonomous and independent state.

Mercier 1771, 1772, 1786, 1989; Tod / Wheeler 1978; Manguel 1981; Schwarz 1982, 1985; Wuckel 1986; Brentjes 1993.

The supervision of work – even if we no longer use such harsh words today – is now, in one form or another, a matter of course, if only as »quality control«. The fact that women are no longer only mothers and housewives was a utopia that went too far for Mercier, however.

Mercier's anticipation of the cinema or television and telephone is amazing. But his imagination was not sufficiently fertile to envision new means of transportation instead of horse-drawn wagons. The authoritarian character of the system is probably expressed most painfully in the burning of books and can hardly be reconciled with the author's great love for peace.

Louis-Antoine de Bougainville (1729–1811). A voyage round the world (*Voyage autour du monde*, 1771)
Denis Diderot (1713–1784). The other Bougainville journey to Tahiti (*Supplément au voyage de Bougainville*, 1772)

A long, interesting ocean journey is behind us – finally we drop anchor near an island.

The land that welcomes us is magnificent, richly fertile, and beautiful: We've arrived in Tahiti, the New Cythera. Pirogues – dugout canoes – swarm around our ship. As a symbol of peace, the naked rowers have banana branches in their hands. Soon the first women appear. They are unbelievably beautiful and completely naked, for the men who accompany them have just removed their loincloths. Now we travel farther into the island's interior and find the most fertile soil in the world. We think we've landed in paradise, inhabited by friendly, peaceful, and beautiful people. Gradually we learn about the social order here. It is a mild form of patriarchy. The tribes follow a chief, who, however, consults a council in all his decisions. The high priestess represents the power of women in this society.

The fertility and thus the wealth of the country facilitates an ideal sharing of goods by the community. That certainly doesn't mean there is total equality. Thus we are somewhat confused when we discover that meat and fish are reserved for the table of the dignitaries, while the common people live on fruit and vegetables.

However, we are deeply impressed by how much trust and openness in the true sense of the word there is here: The houses are open day and night. The hospitality of the inhabitants is quite surprising and we experience an extremely remarkable aspect of their friendliness. During one of our visits we were welcomed, and the house filled with men and women. There was music, the floor had been covered with flowers and leaves. Venus is the goddess of hospitality – and a lovely young woman was brought to us.

We now learn that polygamy is generally practiced, at least by the dignitaries. Sweet idleness is the prerogative of the women, and they are able to choose the most pleasant activities. Yet they are completely subordinated to their men but in no way obligated to be faithful to them. Thus we get to know a great freedom of the sexes with its many shadow sides.

A few years later, with Denis Diderot, we listen in part of a conversation that refers to Bougainville's journey – a postscript to his journey, as it were. After Mr. A has talked to Mr. B, the ship's chaplain begins a conversation with Oru, an inhabitant of Tahiti. Oru asks the chaplain some very astonishing questions, which the latter tries to answer by drawing on the Christian moral code: »Does your creator have hands, feet, a head? Where does he live? Where can people see him? He forbids you to sleep with a girl? Then why did he create two genders? A man may only belong to one woman and vice versa? For his entire life? Why is the freedom of men and women violated this way? In your coutry, does a woman who has sworn to be faithful never give herself to anyone else? Why is she scorned in that case? Why are you disturbed if the woman is involved with the children of these men, or a man is involved with a man? Why is it supposed to be a crime for a father to sleep with a daughter, the mother with her son, the sister with her brother? Why does that supposedly go against nature? You are a monk, you have voluntarily condemned yourself not to be a man? And you always observe the commandment of infertility?« It was not easy for the chaplain to answer all the questions based on the essence of »nature«. And Oru responds to the chaplain's embarrassed arguments: »*We are true innocents and we are happy, for we obey the pure instinct of nature.*« Finally, the chaplain fulfills Oru's urgent request to make the people richer by one person – after refusing three times, he sleeps with the youngest daughter.

Bougainville 1772; Hinterhäuser 1957; Berneri 1950, 1971; Glaser 1996.

»Noble savages« increasingly become a societal ideal. Human beings who are still directly connected to nature, free from property and authoritarian rule, are not yet inhabited by evil. We learn a variation of Rousseau's »back to nature« – it is not a historical reconstruction of nature, but rather a geographic and ethnographic rediscovery of a supposedly ideal world – and this world is usually found on an island.

Etienne-Gabriel Morelly (c. 1715–?). Shipwreck of the floating islands (*Naufrages des îles flottantes, ou les basiliade de Bilpai*, 1753) and the Code of Nature (*Code de la nature*, 1755)

Again a shipwreck casts us up on an island and Mr. Morelly is our guide through the strange isle. A luxuriant nature welcomes us. Branches groan from the weight of the delicious fruit, the creeks run gold and pearls, and beautiful ponds and lakes lie among fertile fields.

Interspersed between these are cities and villages full of happy people. But the happy people do not belong only to particular classes. All people are blessed with good fortune. How is that possible? The origin of all evil is personal property – and that has been abolished forever. Morelly expressed his theses very clearly in his *Code de la Nature*. Here are the immutable basic principles:

»*I. Nothing in society may be the private property or possession of a single individual. The only exceptions from this are articles intended for daily use, that is, objects each individual requires for his needs, his pleasure, or his daily work.*

II. Every citizen belongs to the state and is supported and employed at the cost and for the best of the community as a whole.

III. Every citizen is under an obligation to contribute to general welfare according to his abilities, his talents, and his age. Accordingly his duties are regulated by economic law.«

Citizens receive everything they need, and products are kept In public storehouses. Therefore citizens do not have to and are not allowed to buy, sell, or exchange anything among themselves. All citizens must devote themselves to agriculture from age 20 to 25, but are married as early as age fifteen or eighteen.

All men are under the obligation to marry. Only those who are over 40 may live a celibate life. The first marriage may not be dissolved for ten years. People who are divorced may only marry women who've already been married and are older than they themselves and their divorced wife.

Every mother must nurse her child herself. Beginning with their fifth year, children begin their public schooling, separated by gender. They are taught by fathers and mothers who take turns every five days. The children are not drilled to memorize facts: Rather, playfulness, physical activities, and common sense are given priority. When obedience is required, there must be a rational basis for it, and every command must be justified.

At ten years of age children are apprenticed with masters of trades and crafts who teach them not only skills, but also manners and morality.

Particularly talented persons are selected to pursue science and the arts.

Clothing is simple and uniform: Ten- to thirty-year-olds are given a uniform – a different one for different occupations – and after reaching the age of 30 people may dress as they please. The state pays for an everyday outfit and formal dress.

False shame no longer exists, and the sexes are joined In natural tenderness, including mothers and sons, and fathers and daughters.

The population is very well structured. It is divided into families, clans, towns, and provinces. Now we have a chance to tour one of the towns. Its plan is simple – a radial layout. »Around a regularly laid-out square there are identical, pleasing buildings that contain the public storehouses

120. Etienne-Gabriel Morelly, ideal city after *Code de la Nature*, 1755. Reconstruction after Hruza, 1965.

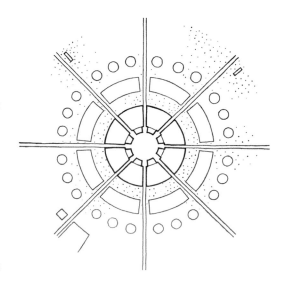

and assembly halls. Adjacent to the rear of the buildings are individual districts, which are very regularly laid out according to a uniform, radial plan. In a subsequent zone are the workshops, while the next contains housing for the agricultural workers. Lastly, the outermost ring houses people in special circumstances: The sick, the senile, but also otherwise disabled people incapable of working are confined here. And not far from these nursing homes are the prisons.« We find this layout quite sensible and clear, though we do wonder why the cemetery is located next to the prison and what the barred cells are for. »Criminals who are condemned to civic death«, we are told, »are forever banished from society. They are put in the cells – and those are at the same time their tomb.«

Morelly now describes the country's organization: »*Groups of approximately 1,000 people each representing all professions and trades receive as much land as is needed to feed them. They agree to share everything, and so that no disorder should reign in this community and so that everyone can make a contribution without revulsion, boredom, or fatigue to the production of objects needed for life, they agree on the following arrangement:*

All of them together cultivate the fields, bring in the harvest, and store the fruits in a communal storehouse. In the time between these farm chores each person works on his own particular occupation. This way there is a sufficient number of workers to process raw materials and manufacture all commodities required for everyday needs. The workers, who are supplied by the community with raw materials, tools, and the means of subsistence, are merely responsible for producing the articles in question in sufficient quantities and for distributing them so that no member of the community lacks any of these things.«

And Morelly once again emphasizes his conviction: »*Human beings are good by nature, but their environment entices them to do evil. But one day the concepts* good *and* evil *will be abolished in society.*«

Morelly has already shared many of his thoughts and reflections. Nevertheless we intend to take a look at his *Code de la Nature*, in which he explains »le véritable esprit de ses loix«, the true spirit of the laws of nature, and we are profoundly impressed with the lofty moral view.

Morelly exposes the errors of ancient and modern moralists, he cites the true foundations of a community and speaks of natural honesty and of the prevention of corruption. He bemoans the flaws of education and false morality, and complains that the laws of nature have become unusable. Morelly looks into human inertia and corruption and into the flaws of politicians and laws, and claims that the spirit of Christianity brings human beings closer to the law of nature, while the monastic spirit is opposed to the law of nature.

There is a connection between physical order and morality, and charity is the first moral idea. The basic motive for every human action is that of complete societal harmony. »We must find a situation«, Morelly concludes, »in which human beings are as happy and charitable as they can possibly be in this life.«

In an appendix Morelly systematically summarizes the individual laws once more according to their intentions.

Morelly 1755, 1910; Kirchenheim 1892; Ramm 1955; Mohl 1960; Tod/Wheeler 1978; Berneri 1950, 1971; Brentjes 1993; Seibt 2001.

Probably there has never been a serious attempt to establish what human beings actually need – and who would be qualified to do such a thing? The question of »everyday necessities« continues to be controversial to this day, since it keeps foundering as it encounters human individuality.

As in so many utopias, humanity and cruelty often seem to be next-door neighbors. Morelly's ideas about education sound incredibly modern to us, but the fact that criminals are seemingly buried alive is hard to understand, and the rigorous marriage regulations are more than strange.

The leap from »utopia« into »reality« is also performed when thoughts, ideas, concepts are handed down to the future, when the thinking of generations to come – both theoreticians and pragmatists – is influenced. Morelly was in contact with Babeuf, and the latter referred to Morelly as the man who »instigated the conspiracy of equals«. Thus, like many others, he indirectly contributed to the development of socialist thought.

Morelly's 1755 *Code de la Nature* is a typical product of the Enlightenment and had a tremendous literary and political effect, far beyond his contemporaries.

Nicolas-Edme Rétif (Restif) de la Bretonne (1734–1806). A journey in time from 1790 to 2000, 1790 (*La decouverte australe par un homme volant, ou le dédale français*, 1776)

We don gigantic wings that reach from the neck to the legs and are tied to our arms with string. A small parachute is attached above our heads. We take off from the top of a cliff and after a few wingbeats we are lifted in the air and fly over the landscape. The pleasure of flight lasts too short a time. We land in a lovely landscape. »We're in Megapatagonia«, Rétif informs us, »and you will be surprised by the intelligence of the people here.«

We reach the first simple, attractive houses and are amazed at the cheerful demeanor of the people at work. »Is work a burden for us, you ask?« a young man answers our question. »No, not in the least. It's part of our completely normal life – and continues to give us pleasure. Incidentally, we work only four, or six hours at most, a day.« Mind you – idleness and uselessness are shameful vices and may result in incorrigible individuals being banished from the main island.

Are there no conflicts, no crimes, no courts of law? – »Of course there are conflicts, but we resolve those by talking, in community – but without fighting – which is why we need no courts of law. And crimes are caused by greed, and here everything belongs to everybody, so there is no envy.« Admittedly they're unable to explain to us why there are such rigorous punishments for certain offenses: whipping and banishment to rocks and islands, capital punishment, public humiliations. When a man is banished, he is given a wife of the lowest sort, ugly and repulsive. Not very convincing is the fact that on the other side there are many honors and bonuses for good deeds, inventions, and services to the fatherland. And the equality of all citizens is by no means consistently expressed in everyday life, for there is clearly a hierarchy according to age: In principle all younger people are subordinated to their seniors. While autocracy is forbidden, the »pope«, a venerable and wise old man, is paid solemn homage.

What about the situation of women? »They enjoy exactly the same respect as men, without class differences. They are also honored in accordance with their age.«

And again it is hard to give credence to this equality, for the honoring of women is dependent on the dignity of a woman's husband, and when the latter is 40 years old, his wife is given the title of matron. When he reaches 70 years of age, the wife becomes an (assistant) priestess – and is then responsible for cleaning the temple, for keeping things clean and tidy. For Rétif this is the basis of the ideal community: »All of the property of our brothers and fellow citizens is held in common, and the work is also distributed among all people. All work is considered to be equally honorable.« All purchases are at the expense of the community. Salaries for work are paid in accordance with people's true needs. A man who has six children receives twice as much as one who has three.

During our tour we are struck by the clothing of the citizens. It is almost identical for all people and extremely simple. If women want something pretty they need permission to get it.

Now we rest from our walk and our amazement, and sit drinking a glass of wine with Rétif and a few Australians. That's when Rétif takes a letter from his pocket and gives it to us to read. We are amazed at the report of an ape to his horde: »Oh yes, human beings do have more reason, but how do they use it? To make people unhappy! For only few are wealthy and many are poor – and the wealthy make the poor bear the burden of work – until they become criminals. But even these wealthy people are not happy: eternally chasing after money, constantly anxious… *You see, this is what human beings are really like, these creatures we apes consider to be happy and admire for being perfect!*«

Réstif de la Bretonne 1776, 1781; Krauss 1964; Mohl 1969; Manguel 1981.

Again and again we encounter the antagonisms in an »ideal« society, and in Rétif de la Bretonne's work they are particularly glaring: Equality and hierarchy, emancipation and subordination, human perfection and cruelty confront each other in unresolved contradiction. Nor has the author resolved the problem of how people's »real« needs can be determined. The superiority of an ape to human beings is the topic of Franz Kafka's *Report to an Academy*.

Louis Abel Beffroy de Reigny (Cousin Jacques, 1757–1811). On the moon (*Les lunes de cousin Jacques*, 1787)

When we arrive on the Moon, we immediately hear the advantages of the country and its population praised exorbitantly: peaceable and hard-working, educated and happy. »And what do you think is the source of these qualities? There are a few simple causes: All the citizens are equal, regardless of whether they are nobles or peasants, and the rulers' sole concern is the happiness of their subjects. This is made possible only by an outstanding education – there is our secret.«

As we drive to the capital, Lunol, we are at first struck by the streets and the carriages. The latter are light and comfortable and have a much smaller wheelbase than in our country, without detracting from the safety of the carriage. Although the streets are much narrower, pedestrians are not endangered. »The interests of people in the city come first and must not be violated.« The carriages have springs, and spirited horses are immediately slowed down by this arrangement. The narrow roads have another advantage: Enormous areas are left free for agriculture.

As we arrive in Lunol, we note that it is a very pleasant town, clean and quiet. The people are considerate and friendly. We observe with surprise that the people – all dressed in very simple clothing – wear little colored ribbons in their buttonholes. What does this mean? »Though we're all equal, you see, there are certain distinctions, for example differences of occupation and class. Those are shown by the modest bits of colored ribbon. That way no one's clothing needs to be extravagant.«

Lunol is an extremely stimulating and interesting city of 650,000 inhabitants. The city plan is well ordered: The streets run in straight lines from one city gate to another. The church towers and fortification towers are built in very varied styles. Some are shaped like pyramids, others dome-shaped. The ground plans are square or round, sometimes triangular, the walls are often very massive, but broken up by many openings. In the city the streets are broad, passersby are protected from vehicles by curbstones connected with chains. To make their safety complete, a watchman warns all those using the city streets with a bell. This way traffic jams, any sort of danger, even accidents, are impossible. Something that is very beautiful is the way building heights change: Next to tall houses, there are medium-size or one-story buildings. Naturally the ruler's palace stands out even from afar, and the style of public buildings is also somewhat more ambitious. Residential houses, on the other hand, may have no more than four stories. They are built on wide streets, and because the air is good, the health of the inhabitants is ensured.

A sign invites us to stop: »Restaurant Chez Frère Martin«, it says. In the restaurant, we notice that everyone, including the owner and the staff, is addressed as nephew, cousin, and son – and the ruler of the country himself is referred to as »Papa«.

After an excellent meal, to conclude our tour, we drive outside the town again and see that directly outside city limits, a lovely landscape spreads green before us disturbed by no suburbs – a little paradise for the townspeople.

Beffroy de Reigny 1801.

Naturally people hesitate for a long time as they toy with the idea of abolishing the aristocracy and royal rule – they fear they might not go unpunished. This is why unusual syntheses of equality and supremacy are expressed: People are distinguished with bits of colored ribbon at least. But strictly speaking this problem was not solved in the centuries that followed either, least of all in communist societies.

Donatien Alphonse François Marquis de Sade (1740–1814). Tamoé (*Aline et Valcour*, 1783/1790)

We're glad that the Marquis de Sade is available to accompany us on an ocean journey during the brief period he spends outside prisons and insane asylums.

We find a good landing place for our ship and drop anchor before a fine red sandy beach: We're on the island of Tamoé. The capital is near the ocean, a town surprisingly regular and beautiful. »*It is laid out in a circle, all its streets are straight as an arrow, but each is more a promenade than a passage. They have trees on both sides, and there are sidewalks along the houses. The middle of the street consists of fine sand where walking is pleasant. All the houses are identically designed, not one is taller or bigger than the others; all have a ground floor, a second floor, and an Italian-style terrace above. All the façades are regularly painted pink or green in symmetrical order, so that each of these streets creates a neat impression.*«

The main thing that interests us is how people live in this pleasant city, on this lovely island. »They live happy and contented, in harmony and peace«, the marquis assures us, »and they owe this primarily to the wise Zamé, a benevolent ruler, and his intelligent laws, which admittedly must be strictly observed.«

Now the marquis describes the ruler's most important principles, but we realize we're familiar with most of them from our earlier travels: There is no private property, people live in a socialist idyll based on an agrarian economy. Class differences have been abolished, luxury has been done away with, children are educated by the state. Arrogance, greed, and miserliness have vanished.

Some of the measures introduced here are new to us, however, and during a meeting with Zamé we find out more about them: »*By introducing divorce, I eradicated almost all the vices of immoderation; there would be no more vices of this kind if I had tolerated incest and homosexuality.*« Zamé explains that he considers these vices to be only relatively harmful, with regard to his administrative plan, since they impair equality. »*Homosexuality creates a separate class of people who are self-sufficient and inevitably destroy the balance. But it must by no means be punished.*« And Zamé is convinced that as few laws as possible should be passed. Then there would also be fewer violations.

Now we also learn the lamentable story of an unfulfilled love between Aline and Valcour: Desire, lack of control, intrigue, incest prevent their being united – Aline takes her own life. Furthermore, the marquis embroils us in a long discourse, trying to explain the nature of vice and virtue, to explain the reason for »perversité naturelle«, cruelty and dissipation.

Yet all of the marquis's eloquence fails to show us the antithesis, to abduct us to the kingdom of Butua, to the land of the good ogres.

The marquis dismisses us by stating his conviction: »I am quite sure that after the impending revolution these circumstances will prevail not only in Tamoé but in all of France, indeed all over the world.«

Sade 1790; Favre 1967; Manguel 1981; Delon/Seth 2004.

In De Sade's little-known story of Aline et Valcour the priciples are played off against each other: Butua as the island of the ogres, Tamoé as an ideal society, yet on both islands, at the time of the French revolution, we experience a new libertinism, which only distantly resembles de Sade's great novels. De Sade speaks prophetically about the »coming revolution«, though actually he did not write this novel until after the revolution.

Claude-Nicolas Ledoux (1736–1806). The saline de Chaux, 1779, 1789, 1801

Through a massive portico of columns leading into a symbolic stone cavern we enter the massive round of the imposing complex. One building in the entrance axis almost forces one to look at it: The director's house emanates the kind of power that will marginalize the old powers in the following century. The head of the plant, Claude-Nicolas Ledoux, receives us in person and speaks about his work with pathos and complacency. »*The form is as pure as that described by the sun in its course. Everything is suitable to shelter us, to protect sleep and forgetfulness.*« Ledoux goes on to say that the façade of his residence, but also of the entire plant »*en impose, inspire le respect; elle étonne, remue nos sens*«, »*it impresses us, fills us with respect, astonishes us, and moves our senses.*«

In vain we look for a church in the large circle: only when we step into the staircase of the administrative building do we catch sight of the chapel. It is incorporated in this seat of administrative power to crown the structure.

Adjacent to the house of the director, like outspread arms, and dividing the circle, are the factories. Salt, long since a state monopoly, is produced here.

The houses of the workers are orientated towards the factory, and especially towards the director. The center of town, once reserved for the temple, the church, the castle, is now occupied by the boss. He overlooks the entire plant – and the »surveillance«, supervision, like that found in prisons, is represented both symbolically and in factual fact.

Once we walk over to the workers' houses, we are welcomed first by a spacious lobby, suggesting generosity. In three corner rooms off the lobby are the communal hearths. In the center is the fireplace. Thus it makes sense that in the evening we find all the inhabitants in the entrance hall eating their simple meal.

When we enter one of the so-called »apartments«, we are deeply disturbed by the way the architect of the »revolution« and humanist houses the workers: The whole family of four or five lives in a single, poorly lit room. The primitive bedsteads stand in the corners. The rest of the room is sparsely furnished, and the little gardens that belong to the families, placed in the rear of the

121. Claude-Nicolas Ledoux, saline de Chaux, 1779.
122. Claude-Nicolas Ledoux, saline de Chaux, market, 1779.

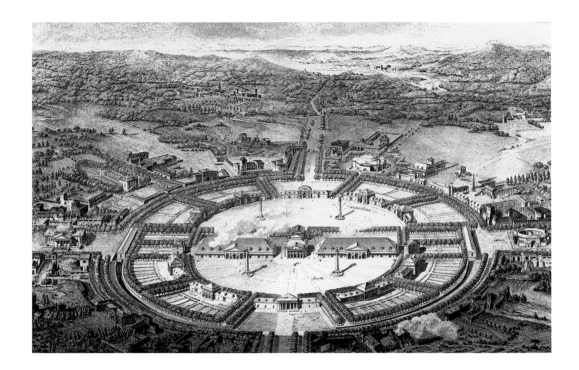

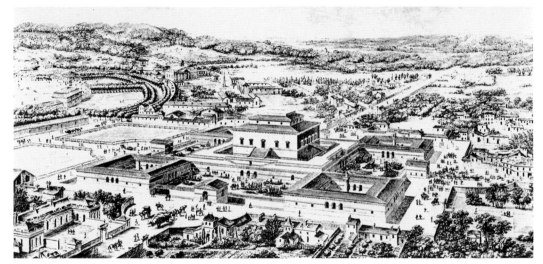

buildings, are used to raise food rather than ornamental plants. However, for Ledoux the big rooms, their solid construction, the fact that they are situated in the country represent progress when compared to thousands of working-class housing units during this period of looming social changes.

Admittedly we are also struck by the fact that the town has no law courts or prisons. This society has come of age, has become peaceful and freed itself from police, punishment, and bureaucracy. The »Pacifère« represents peace, and there is also a special temple dedicated to women. Ledoux designs highly stylized architecture and, notwithstanding our criticism, he says: »*J'ai placé tous les genres d'édifices que réclame l'ordre social*« – »*I included all the types of buildings demanded by the social order.*« But he assigns tremendous importance not only to the architect, but also to architecture: »*L'architecture, par ses attractions, est la souveraine du monde.*« – »*Architecture, thanks to its attractions, rules the world.*«

Outside the large circular ring, part of a transition to the countryside, are the parish church and the town hall, the public baths and a barrack. We have time to visit the covered market. The market has a completely autonomous geometric form: Around a tall central two-story building four low buildings are grouped in a courtyard. All are strictly placed in a square. The little houses in the vicinity look very middle-class, at times even romantically ornate, in contrast to what we are going to see immediately thereafter.

We now turn to the environment, the lovely forest between Arc and Senans, with the Loue River flowing through it. Here we find the most remarkable buildings in clear geometric forms. The field guard lives in a spherical house, the hoopmaker in a ring-shaped house, Water flows through

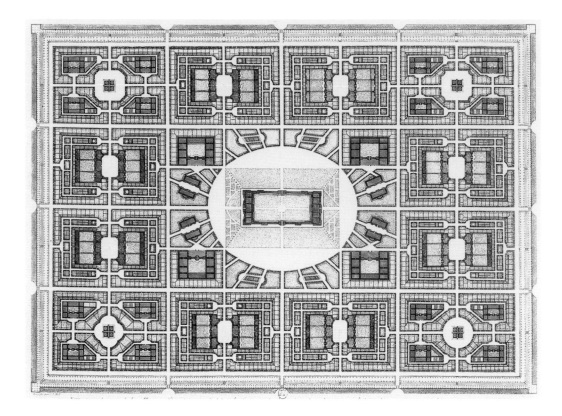

the house of the fountain attendant, and the mechanic has a pretty, rationally square villa, all of them purposefully scattered in the beautiful landscape. We are especially interested in the »maison du plaisir«, laid out in the shape of a phallus. Here, Ledoux explains, men are meant to gather experience with women and become mature enough to marry. Ledoux takes his leave of us with a poetic eulogy: »*Let us see the present in a brighter light, but let us scatter flowers for the future. In youth, in the spring of my days, I see thousands joining my delight, see them building for immortality. I am founding a city for a people that loves to work.*«

Ledoux 1789; Christ 1961; Revohnt, A. 1970; Schumpp 1971; Vogt 1974; Stoloff 1983; Gallet 1983; Vidler 1988; Kruft 1989; Vercelloni 1994; Eaton 2001; *Nouvelles* 2001.

Two hundred years later we revisit Chaux – now in reality: impending demolition by speculators was prevented, the plant has been beautifully restored and turned into a cultural center.

But what a difference from Ledoux's ideal plan: Instead of the bold gesture of the circle, there is only a semicircle, and outside the complex not a single house was built. The saltworks was a reality, but on paper Ledoux transposed it into a dreamlike utopia and transformed himself, the royalist, into a revolutionary. And the more than modest housing of the families was a reality as well.

Ledoux – and with him the »architects of the revolution« – have been given a completely different concrete existence as well: With Edgar Kaufmann's 1933 book *Von Ledoux bis Le Corbusier* he was introduced for the first time to less interested readers, while since the 1960s he has exerted an enormous influence on modern architecture – to the very limits of eclecticism.

Jean Jacques Moll. Napoléonville, 1809

The artist takes us to Brittany. Here, at the behest of Napoleon, he has designed a town for 100,000 citizens. It goes without saying that the town bears the name of the famous dictator. »A city, a blueprint for a city, must be something flexible, like life in general«, explains Mr. Moll, »and that is why I drafted not one, but six plans, then one has a choice, and what is more the blueprints are also suitable for other countries, other places, and they can be combined as one wishes.«

The geometry and symmetries dominate the city plan, though the basic figure is neither a circle nor a square, but a rectangle with a large elliptical open space in the center. Here, surrounded by a park, there is a big rectangular building for the community. Additional buildings for the general public are adjacent to the oval. The rest of the site is divided into sixteen fields, and in each of

124. John Soane (drawing by J. M. Gandy), Triumphal Bridge, 1776.

them two or four groups of houses are immediately connected with small gardens. »The city combines all the comforts and progress that anyone could wish for«, Mr. Moll repeats the basic principle that is also stated at the head of his meticulous plan – a plan that is precisely supplemented by 24 additional plans.

Oechslin 1983; Eaton 2001.

Jean Jacques Moll manages with just six absolutely standardized building ground plans. The plan gives no information about the size of the houses. If 100,000 citizens are to be housed here, we should, according to the plan, reckon with at least three-story buildings.

6.2. England, Italy

Thomas Spence (1750–1814). Spensonia, 1795

One hundred years ago, the crew of a boat was cast up on this island during a journey from England to America. The island's main source of livelihood is agriculture, but the land belongs to all the inhabitants jointly. Everyone is equal not only in owning the land, but also all have the right to vote by secret ballot and are allowed to bear arms: The entire people is armed.

We now have the opportunity to watch a military exercise by the people's militia and are impressed by how fit the men are and by how cheerfully and boisterously they compete in sports events and engage in leisure activities.

We are able to take a look at one of the housing units and note that they are neat and clean. *»So far distant from the inflated pomp and ghastly solemnity of the palaces of the great and the confined miserable depression of the hovels of the wretched, that seem the habitations of the rational beings.«*

We leave the town and admire the well-tended meadows and fields, the luxuriant orchards and vegetable gardens, the fine cattle. And so we could certainly agree with our host as he proudly reports*: »If ever there be a millenium or heaven upon earth, it can only exist under the benign ›System of Spensonia‹.«*

In Spensonia women have obtained their rights and are idependent of their men, including professionally independent. Women have won their rights themselves. It goes without saying that they also have the right to vote – but when we listen more attentively we notice they only have the right to vote but not to run for office. »In consideration of the delicacy of their sex, they are exempted from and are ineligible to all public employments«, we are told.

Heuermann 1984.

Like so many utopias this one, too, is produced by the negative experiences of the past and intends to demonstrate the positive, and indeed the ideal aspects of the future. The following topic is also discussed at great length: the absolute advantages of communal ownership, especially the ownership of land – but soon of production plants as well. Thus, in a certain sense, Thomas Spence went far beyond literary utopia: His journalistic, public, and political work is a significant step into the real world.

John Soane (1753–1837). The Triumphal Bridge, 1776, and the City of Old Age, 1820

The bridge is a town – the town is a bridge. John Soane convincingly argues: »Rivers separate the parts of town, and bridges should connect them – but there is no life on them, apart from a few exceptions. I've made the bridge into a splendid part of town!«

We come from the mother town and gaze at the seven arches that span the river. As we continue our walk, we scarcely notice we are now on a bridge, for it is so artistically designed. Thousands of columns, or so it seems, take away all the heaviness of the structures, give them elegance and transparency.

We walk along the lovely covered walk with a view of the river. But that's not enough: When we stroll through the splendid columned halls, our eyes move to a series of monumental structures along our route: We've already left the bridgehead behind us. Now we are looking at a rotunda with classical column orders and a sculpture gallery on the architrave. »The interior is also the exterior: The courtyard of the rotunda has the same rows of columns. And the connection to the next dome-roofed rotunda makes a lovely square«, John Soane explains.

125. John Soane, Vision of Old Age, 1820. Drawing by J. M. Gandy.

However, the sequence is not yet done: An additional section of columns leads to yet another open rotunda. Now we go on to see a wonderful hilly landscape. What a surprise as we approach! We seem to be in a museum containing life-size models. »Soon, I will be 70, and I have made a dream of mine come true: I've created a landscape of the most beautiful edifices.«

It is easy for us to see the origin of the master's ideal of beauty: It goes without saying that it is based on Roman and Greek architecture, differently shaped temples, triumphal arches, columned halls, arcades, as well as cupolas. And all of them are placed in the landscape from which they are strangely disconnected.

We know some inhabited bridges: the Rialto in Venice, the Ponte Vecchio in Florence are familiar to us. The idea is very topical: In 1998, for instance, there was a contest in London for a »habitated bridge.« As for the city of Soane's old age, today we would refer to it as »collage architecture«. It is a principle that plays a very important role in present-day discussions about urban planning. Great »harmonious« townscapes are no longer possible.

John Soane has his emulators: Charles R. Cockerell and Erastus Salisbury Field.

Charles R. Cockerell (1788–1863). *The Professor's Dream*, 1848

»At first glance it may seem strange that I want to put together a town consisting only of magnificent buildings«, Cockerell qualifies his vision somewhat. »But the thing that is unprecedented about this is that we add another dimension to space and time.«

People have always dreamed of time travel, not only forward into the future, but also into the past. In the medium of architecture, however, we apparently experience many pasts. Architecture is a journey through the entire human history.

How else could we imagine the dream of a professor of architecture than as a town crammed with the most important buildings in the history of architecture? Cockerell's vision includes the history of the Egyptians and goes up to the 19th century. We discover how abstruse is the idea that a city is supposed to be a collection of all that is magnificent.

Erastus Salisbury Field (1805–1900). *The Historical Monument of the American Republic*, 1876

What does this colossal collection of even more colossal towers have to do with the American republic? we want to know. »Each individual tower is no doubt a symbol of power«, argues Mr. Field, »and this power is legitimate because it is democratic. But over and above that the towers are sublime and beautiful.«

What we suspect is that here two dreams that architects have had since time immemorial, millennia-old archetypes, have materialized: to build a round temple – a rotunda – and a very, very high tower.

This town, which is actually functionless, is imposing, and we stroll through it feeling both troubled and awestruck. We've heard that in New York and Chicago the first high-rises are already being built, still pretty modest at ten or twelve floors, but naturally already equipped with elevators. Of course, these high-rises – soon we can call them »skyscrapers« – will be surpassed by Mr. Field's buildings, which will be a good 60 m higher. »Now take a closer look at the outside walls of the towers, and you will get a further answer as to what is American about them: Artistic reliefs represent the history of the nation.«

Tod / Wheeler 1978; *Stadt und Utopie* 1982; Eaton 2001.

Mr. Field frequently borrows from the fund of history, and Greek and Roman antiquity supply most of the material, but ancient Egypt also provides a few contributions.

We encountered the principle of the »collage city« earlier in the work of John Soane. But the dense agglomeration of beauty and ideal architecture might also become oppressive and alarming.

126. Charles R. Cockerell, *The Professor's Dream*, 1848.
127. Erastus Salisbury Field, *The Historical Monument of the American Republic*, 1876.

John Claudius Loudon (1783–1843). The green belts of London, 1829

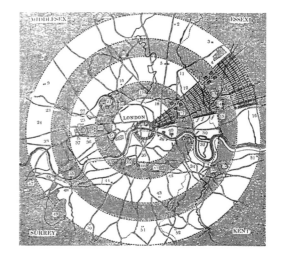

We'd have to have a very swift carriage to experience the new, greener, London, but John Claudius Loudon first explains his basic idea: »I've provided London with concentric green zones. They're about a mile wide, then there's a mile of dense development, followed by another zone of gardens and parks. No citizen of a town will then be more than a mile away from a green zone in which he can go for walks or horseback rides or relax and enjoy himself in every imaginable way.«

We actually do discover dense urban development right next to the loveliest parks and landscaped gardens. Admittedly they are not as clearly geometrically defined as Mr. Loudon indicated in his plan.

»That is most desirable«, claims Mr. Loudon. »The topography of the terrain, the course of the streets, the irregular form of the public buildings create an irregular line that is not only more pleasing, but also more economical.«

Vercelloni 1994.

Even in the fantastic description of Atlantis mention is made of alternating rings, and the subject later appears time and again. The fortified town, too, suggested the importance of this design by the form of the fortifications. Ebenezer Howard with his circular garden city brings it to perfection (cf. chap. 10.1).

Giovanni Giacomo Casanova (1725–1798). The Megamicres, 1780, *1533 (Icosaméron ou Histoire d'Edouard et Elisabeth, qui passèrent quatre vingts un ans chez les Mégamicres habitants aborigènes du Protocosme dans l'intérieur de nôtre globe,* 1788)

Casanova accompanies us to the interior of our planet, and there we meet a brother and sister, Edward and Elizabeth, who after a shipwreck in 1533 arrived adventurously in the interior of the Earth in a watertight chest. Here, to our amazement, we find a paradise people only dream of, though it has a number of flaws. This troglodytic world is inhabited by »Megamicres«, the »Big-Little Ones«, and – something that is especially surprising – they only have one gender, and are all both male and female, just like the original human beings described by Plato in the *Symposium*, before they were split in two. We have the same impression as Edward and Elizabeth when they first met the strange creatures: »*At first glance we had thought they were female, judging by the shape of their breasts. For these began just below the neck, bulged out as they do in us humans down close to the stomach and each had a green wart in the middle; yet upon closer inspection we believed them to be male. Later we discovered that they are neither one nor the other, for in a world which has no idea that humanity must be divided into two sexes one can also be neither one nor the other. We have called these creatures androgynes, partly in order to give them a name that describes them in a certain way, and partly in order to come close, in our English translation, to the generic term by which they call themselves and which is a combination of the vowels a, o, i, e. They also call themselves e a i e, the sound of which suggested the name Megamicres to us – a word that alludes to the greatness of their spirit and their short physical stature.*«

These people are no more than a cubit tall (about 60 cm). They are completely naked, and their bodies have different colors. The red people have the highest rank, and the multicolored ones are the most numerous. They live chiefly on their own milk and therefore need no teeth. Very soon we realize that night does not fall here: A central sun shines forever over the kingdom, and the Megamicres also need no sleep.

Our reception by the Megamicres, but especially by Edward and Elizabeth, who've been living here for quite some time, is extraordinarily hospitable, and we get many explanations. Our first walk shows us much that is remarkable, even apart from the strange inhabitants.

The layout of the Megamicres' towns is very regular. They have fine, wide, very straight streets roofed over by carpets. On both sides, the streets have pretty shops. The cathedral is an unusual building: It is completely spherical, and the floor is formed by different-colored types of wood. In the middle of the room hangs a sphere that emits intense light. Another 500 lamps plunge the room into radiant brightness and illuminate the pictures of the 500 towns of the realm.

The state is divided into 80 rectangular kingdoms, each having ten republics. They have the same size and each consists of 216 large and small triangular fiefs.

128. John Claudius Loudon, the green belts of London, 1829.

We find it impossible to imagine how the androgynous creatures reproduce. Edward and Elizabeth have long since learned about the strange process. After a solemn ceremony in the temple, lovers go to their room and, notwithstanding their androgynous nature, a kind of union takes place. Straightway they produce two eggs that have grown in their breast and are expelled from a cavity between their gullet and their windpipe. In a solution of nutrients the creatures develop and are raised in a cage.

Elizabeth tells us that she was impregnated by her brother and that the Megamicres believed her swelling belly was a sign of a deadly disease. They were quite bewildered by the birth of two children. But it didn't stop there: A throng of children and grandchildren populated, indeed, came to rule over the realm very soon.

Edward and Elizabeth introduce a large number of very unusual institutions and customs to us. Thus, for instance, the Megamicres have horseless carriages driven by a kind of motor. They also have a kind of winged horses with which they rise in the air. Their language is actually music, a melodious chant. They have no diseases and do not age, but quietly depart from life after 48 earthly years. However, since they know neither sleep nor illness, their lifespan is scarcely shorter than ours.

We are given the unique opportunity to visit the capital, Poliarkopoli, distinguished by its particular beauty and size. We are amazed how accurately Casanova is able to cite the precise dimensions of the town, which we can repeat only approximately here.

A ramp, 50 m wide, accompanied by marble steps, leads into the city, which lies in the landscape in a depression approximately 10 m deep. Its walls go up to the level land. No less than 96 gates lead into the city, which, along the periphery, has 4,800 rectangular houses, eight times 12 m large, that are made available free of charge to the poor. Round about the town there is an esplanade, about 100 m wide, along a canal, which is 20 m wide. A 24-sided polygon forms the basic geometric figure for both. On each of its corners there is a stone bridge, 20 m wide, with walkways for pedestrians on both sides and a 12-meter-wide roadway in the middle. On the other side of the canal there is a quay that is about 50 m wide, a circle whose circumference is no less than 15,000 m long. 96 rows of houses line the circle, each 120 m long. They form the boundaries of the individual city districts, separated by 96 streets that are 40 m wide. Each about 800 m long, they run directly to the center. In the middle of the street is a 15-meter-wide avenue planted with tall trees. The streets end in square public spaces about 80 m square, bordered by pretty arcades. In the middle of the squares splash fountains topped by a statue of the royal couple. In each of the 96 districts of the town live 10,000 infertile Megamicre couples, working in all professions. From the 96 squares a 30-meter-wide staircase leads further into the town center proper. At the foot of the staircase is a ring-shaped park, a good 700 m wide. In the middle of this huge park there are 24 temples, each with a ground plan of 70 by 80 m. They belong to the aristocrats, the wealthy, the clergy. At the edge of the park, toward the city center, are 48 cubical palaces 60 by 60 m large, inhabited by 250,000 couples.

Once more we cross a canal and finally reach the royal palace, built with great skill.

Edward and Elizabeth tell us of their first visit with the king. They had to submit to a lengthy interrogation. He listened with interest and satisfaction, and they were graciously dismissed. What is more, Edward and Elizabeth gain the king's favor to such an extent that he gives them a palace.

Deeply impressed, we leave this realm of peace, of piety beyond conventional religion, where polarization of the sexes has been abolished, where people know no hatred or envy.

Many years later, in 1614, we meet Edward and Elizabeth, who, 81 years later, have returned to Earth thanks to an explosion. They give us an account of the most important events they have witnessed.

They have shared a large number of useful institutions, inventions, methods, and practices with the Megamicres: a new method of writing, a paper mill, a printing shop, gunpowder, bells, healing essences, and much more. Their descendants – children and grandchildren – become a powerful race, numbering about 40 persons. They have survived many dangers and adventures, but also been able to do many useful things for the country's strange people.

Casanova 1780, 1788, 1800.

Giovanni Giacomo Casanova, unjustly known only because of his erotic *Memoirs*, saw himself as a great writer and wanted to prove this fact primarily with his *Edouard et Elisabeth*. In more than 1,000 pages, usually printed in three volumes, he develops not only a novel, but also a very personal cosmos, though his book also owes a great deal to the new era of Enlightenment. Over and above all the grotesquerie, he paints the picture of an ideal society.

7. Early socialists, philanthropists, c. 1780–1860

7.1. America, England

Nikolaus Ludwig Count of Zinzendorff and Pottendorf (1700–1760) and August Gottlieb Spangenberg (1704–1792). Herrnhut (Oberlausitz, Germany) and Bethlehem, Pennsylvania, USA, 1766

»We are building a completely new, action-based Christianity whose source is the Holy Scripture alone, and which we want to live truthfully in a new community!«

With great ideals, Count Zinzendorf wants to renew Christian life. Doctrine and ministry are the prerequisites for this. The Count rapturously expounds the theological basis of the community: »We worship the crucified Christ. His wounds and his blood are holy to us, and we must always have his sorrows before our eyes and in our hearts.«

Zinzendorf's ideas become reality: In 1717/18 he founds the »Herrnhut Unity of Brethren«, a colony of crafts and faith, at his country estate of Herrnhut (Oberlausitz). Ten years later he is consecrated as a bishop.

Then the brethren of Herrnhut succeed in making the leap to America. Bethlehem in Pennsylvania is the first community they found, in 1741, and we get a chance to visit.

A new Protestant religious community is created, borne by lofty ideals: The teachings of the Holy Scripture are supported by Zinzendorf's »mottoes«, pious daily maxims. A shared pietistic way of life is formulated.

We encounter a close friend of the Count, August Gottlieb Spangenberg. »It was Count Zinzendorf who summoned and inspired me to found this settlement. Our model is the settlement he developed in Herrnhut beginning in 1722, and an enthusiastic religious movement grew from these beginnings. Above all, they welcomed the Bohemians and Moravians who had fled for religious reasons.«

The settlement gives the impression of being well cared-for and clean. Its layout is loosely geometrical. The communal houses are three stories high, while the residential buildings have only one or two stories. The buildings that house the workshops are located outside the square. Water is piped into the houses directly through a simple supply system. The style of the well-looked-after buildings is baroque. They are surrounded by gardens, meadows, and fruit trees.

But where are the fields? »We started four farms not far from the settlement. But that's not all: There are 500 Indians living 40 km from here – that goes back to one of Count Zinzendorf's ideas.« Farming flourishes here, and it is supplemented by the trades. The craftsmen come chiefly from Germany, and the factories have developed gradually. We visit one of the warehouses and wonder at the variety of goods, almost all of which are manufactured here: textiles and leatherwork, ceramics, hardware, brewery products, and much more.

Their success, to be sure, is also the result of hard work: »Worship«, in other words, work for the community, takes up to sixteen hours. The yield is brought to a central collection point and all members receive everything that is essential. Money has completely lost its meaning.

And what is their attitude towards marriage and the family? »That is strictly regulated, but there is no celibacy. Every year Count Zinzendorf gets a list of marriageable persons, though there are too few girls among them, and so the Count sends additional girls from Germany and then personally selects the couples – without previously knowing them.«

The mass wedding that is celebrated then by no means concludes the selective breeding: The couples live separately, and the time and place of copulation are determined by the community. Nevertheless there is quite a large number of children, but the children stay with the mother for only one year and are then handed over to the community to be educated.

Schumpp 1971.

Bethlehem thrives, is modified, grows. In 1904, the Bethlehem Steel Corporation is founded. It is soon the second largest American steel industry corporation, and Bethlehem has something like 100,000 inhabitants. It has continued to be the headquarters of the still extant Unity of Brethren, and thus we have the astonishing phenomenon of a utopia developing into a real, rational, and modern city.

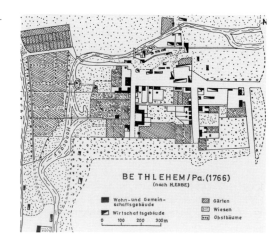

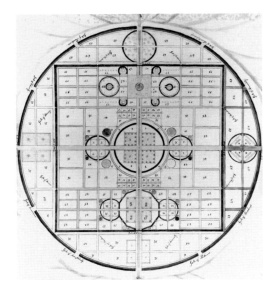

Ann Lee (1736–1784). New Lebanon, 1774, 1787, 1803, 1810 – Shaker
James Whittaker (1751–1787). Hancock, 1780–1960

»*The Fall of Man in the Bible*«, preaches Mother Ann, »*can be expiated only by leading a completely pure life.*«

And heaven is reserved only for these truly pure persons. She herself, meanwhile, is the bride and mother of Christ, and her vision has told her that Christ will return. With the founding of her community, the Shakers, God's »Millennium« on earth has already begun.

And now, many centuries later, we visit another »Holy City« on earth. This is the vision of Mt. Lebanon. The circle and square, the divine and the worldly, have formed a synthesis. As in the apocalyptic Jerusalem vision of St. John there are twelve gates, outer and inner ones. They are consecrated to the twelve virtues that open the gates for us. Now we enter a city that is once more characterized by circles and right angles. What an inexhaustible abundance of holiness, virtue, and beauty there is in this city! We are glad that Polly Ann Reed is our guide in this cosmos of faith.

The middle is formed by four temples with twelve pillars. The Living God and Holy, Eternal Wisdom are present here. On both sides are the courtyards where the saints receive messages from God.

Now we come to the dwelling places of the angels: In each large, elegant house they represent destruction, order, strength, wisdom, and justice respectively

We enjoy the fresh water of the fountains whose water bubbles in many different colors. The fountains are dedicated to the eternal values of love, strength, wisdom, charity, consolation. The enchanted orchards and flower gardens belong to the eternal Father, the eternal Mother, the eternal Savior, eternal Wisdom – they belong to the saints and the angels.

Now we see a tall square tower. The closer we come to it, the clearer are the lovely sounds we hear: The angels and the Holy Spirit are the creators of music.

We could go on enjoying this heavenly city for a long time, this cosmos of holiness, but we end our tour near the dwelling of the true son and daughter of the king and queen of the New Creation: Christ and the Mother have a majestic throne and reside in the temple, surrounded by wonderful gardens.

Schempp 1969; Hayden 1976; Tod/Wheeler 1978; Schiffer 1979; Schwarz 1982; Kruft 1989; Vercelloni 1994; *Shaker-Architektur* 1996.

This is a complex utopia, characterized by noble piousness. However, what a wealth of solid realities have sprung from it!

Only the spirit of »Mother Ann« accompanies us to New Lebanon in New York state. She herself, who arrived in America in 1774 with great ideals, did not live to see this place – a village, yet a polity like a city – and also never saw the communities founded in Pleasant Hill (Kentucky), Hancock (Massachusetts), and in twenty other localities from Maine to Indiana and Florida.

Full of admiration we come to the very simple wooden houses loosely scattered through the landscape, surrounded by fields.

Something like 70 homes were gradually constructed by the community, all solidly and carefully built, using wood, bricks, and stone. We visit one of the houses and begin in the basement. Here, provisions are carefully stacked and the kitchen is in the next room. Other houses have their kitchens on the ground floor. We walk up the marvelously made staircase and come to the meeting room, which is completely without supporting pillars. Women and men have separate entrances.

We don't have long to wait – already the room begins to fill in complete silence, people sit down on the benches surrounding the room, with men and women sitting separately, as is to be expected. The village elder gives a sign, many persons rise, stand in a circle, and an unbelievable drama unfolds: Their movements violent yet disciplined, people begin to »shake«: The »Shakers« have the hour of dance, which is more than a sport or amusement and is reminiscent of the ritual dances of primitive peoples.

After this impressive performance, which we were allowed to witness only as a special favor, we are able to view the other rooms.

On the top floor are the »rooms for rest.« Separated by gender, four to six persons sleep in one room. Individual persons change rooms frequently, for the community is supposed to include everyone and there are to be no cliques. Everyone loves each other.

The interior of the houses, simple and distinctly functional in all its details, has a fascinating beauty. We feel the loving, careful work that went into the construction and the built-in furniture,

130. Polly Ann Reed, Holy City, vision from Mt. Lebanon, 1843.
131. Anonymous, Shaker meeting for worship, introductory dance, c. 1780.

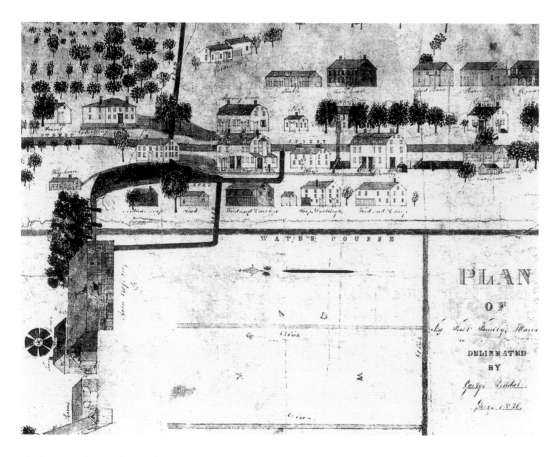

132. Anonymous, plan of a Shaker village, c. 1800.
133. Shaker settlement, Hancock, Massachusetts, USA. Contemporary drawing, after 1820.
134. Shaker settlement, Hancock, Massachusetts, USA, after 1780.
135. Shaker settlement, Enfield, Connecticut, USA, 1836.

chairs, wooden stairs, tools: nothing that was not touched by a kind of holy creative will that moves all the »Believers in Christ's Second Appearing«. These noble forms make the almost Spartan simplicity and modesty very appealing.

Now someone draws our attention to the special forms of the buildings. These are naturally the depots, stables, storerooms, but particularly the workshops that produce all manner of goods: hats, shoes, saddles, mittens. There are spinning mills, dyeing works, weaving mills.

But we also visit two special types of homes: The boys and girls and their educators live separately in little cottages. And the four oldest ones – two women and two men – have left the association some time ago and formed a kind of spiritual group – each of them has his or her own home. Life itself is simple, and everyone owns only what he or she needs.

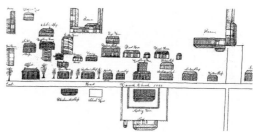

In fact, all of life takes place under the sign of God and of absolute morality. To be sure it is built on the total prohibition of any kind of sexuality, and thus no children are born here either. In all they do, men and women are strictly separated, and there is severe punishment for sexual contact. The »families« comprise between twelve and a hundred persons, but these are only ideal communities of mutual assistance and love, not families in the sense of groups that live together permanently.

And here is something wonderful: Indians, blacks, Jews, and other ethnic groups were also welcomed fraternally, often only temporarily – a miracle in America at the time. The days are filled with unending industriousness – the kind of hard work that has created considerable wealth. All the workers get up and go to bed at the same time.

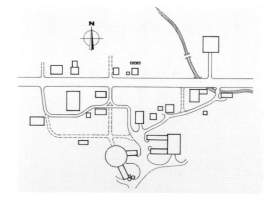

All the men are dressed alike, and so are the women. The meals are eaten together, three times a day. We've been invited to the simple meal, and are about to enter the hall as we chat with each other – when we are struck by the complete silence: Speaking during meals is strictly prohibited – people are supposed to concentrate completely on God's gifts. Men and women sit in the hall together, but on opposite sides.

When we visit the workshops, we cannot help being amazed: The functionality and at the same time the beauty of the tools seem like an early version of modern design. We're particularly amazed at the sight of a buzz saw, and not without pleasure we are told that it was invented in 1810 by a woman, Sister Tabitha Babbitt.

Men's and women's work is only functionally separate, but otherwise everyone has equal rights. No one dominates another. Thus all of life is oriented towards pleasing God. Joy is considered to be one of the highest values. Twenty years later, the Shaker congregations comprised about 5,000 members.

We are able to visit a second settlement. Pleasant Hill in Kentucky was settled as of 1805. The basic principles of the settlement are very similar, but we learn more details about the life and spirit of the Shaker community. The inhabitants are convinced that their settlement was organized according to a divine plan. A few members of the congregation were called to be »tools«, or »mediums«, and received divine inspiration, messages from the »spiritual world«, that is, from the world that according to Shaker belief is clearly demarcated from the physical world. Beside the impressive dances there are further aspects of religious life, which our friend told us about – for we had absolutely no access to them.

In the houses, parlors have been set up. They offer an opportunity to have personal talks, that is, a kind of confession. On a larger scale, there are »house evenings«: Brothers and sisters gather to talk, though they are seated separately.

How do we see these realities from today's perspective? It is amazing that the »spiritual city« was by no means reserved for the Middle Ages, or solely for the Orient, but that as late as the 19th century »divine plans« were realized in America. But the heyday of the congregation did not last very long: The small crafts enterprises were no longer a match for beginning industrialization.

Pleasant Hill is part of reality in another sense as well: The settlement became a museum in 1960 and is open to the public today. One place is still inhabited today: Sabbathday Lake, founded in 1795 and significantly changed in 1883.

Now we meet James Whittaker, who takes us to visit the Shakers in Hancock. Again we follow a powerful, charismatic man who continues to uphold the great expectations of Ann Lee's Shakers: We can experience the New Jerusalem already on this earth, where human beings are entangled in sin. The conditions for this are virginity, lack of possessions, and separation from the world. While here on earth, we must make the reflection of perfection visible in architecture, in the world of objects. That means simplicity, lack of ornamentation, usefulness.

And again we leave utopia; for Hancock in Massachusetts was an amazing realization of a Shaker vision – and still exists today, though only as a museum. Let us take a look back at this reality. The basic principles are already familiar to us from New Lebanon and Pleasant Hill: Individual »families« comprising about 50 persons, where women and men are strictly separated, live in a large residential building. Gatherings take place in the big meetinghouse. Such were the cornerstones of a modest social life. Everyday life, too, was very similar to that in other communities: food and clothing, music and books, language and movement were fixed, codified. »Private« human relationships were reduced. Only in the ecstatic »Shaker« dances people could emotionality unfold, but in the service of God.

Agriculture and crafts filled their daily lives completely, and there was a strict prohibition against ornamenting houses, furniture, or everyday objects: one hundred and twenty years before Adolf Loos they freed themselves from ornamentation – on religious and moral grounds – and perhaps the goods manufactured by the Shakers were a model for early functionalism, for the Shakers' formulation of their guidelines were equally consistent: *»Believers may in no case manufacture objects that are unnecessarily worked and would tend to nurture human pride and vanity.«*

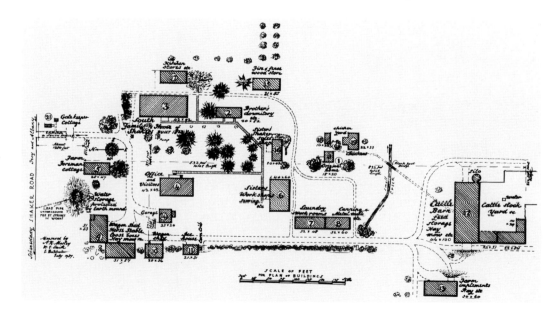

136. Shaker settlement, Watervliet, N.Y., USA.
1 original home, 2 brothers' dormitory, 3 south family home, 4 office and visitors, 5 farmer cottage, 6 sisters' workshops, sewing, etc., 7 laundry, workrooms, 8 canning tower, metal work, etc., 9 wagon shed, horse stable, hay shed, 10 wagon shed, 11 corn house, corn crib, 12 cattle barn, feed storage, haymow, etc., 13 farm implements, hay, etc., 14 garage, 15 wood store, 16 sisters' Shaker sales shop, 17 kitchen, stores, etc., 18 chicken yard, 19 chickens, 20 water storage protected by earth mound, 21 settlement gatekeeper.

And the Shakers' lofty moral motivation becomes even clearer in another statement, which attacks even the beautiful for the sake of morality. »*The beautiful is absurd and abnormal. Divine human beings have no right to waste money for something they would call beauty while they are people living in misery.*«

A visit to Hancock convincingly illustrates the moral and visual world of the Shakers: Different than those on the simple plans, yet improvised and seemingly without a center, in spite of the strict right angles of their design, a few houses are still standing: the »brick dwelling house« for about 100 inhabitants, a second residential building, the »meeting house« that was also used as a church, the »Brethren's workshop«, and finally the »machine shop« and the laundry.

Particularly striking, however, is an almost monumental rotunda that has sacred solemnity. Actually, however, it is the central barn, conceived strictly functionally. Hay is stored in the middle; then follow three concentric zones, with separate access, for manure, the cattle, and for farm vehicles.

Two more villages have been recommended to us: Watervliet near Albany, N.Y and Enfield in Connecticut, the end of our journey.

William Godwin (1756–1836). Political justice (*An enquiry concerning political justice and its influence on general virtue and happiness*, 1793)

Not only church authority but every kind of authority is now abolished. Godwin has established a network of independent parishes without any authority. He has secularized the radical part of the deviant traditions and changed the goal in life from a heavenly kingdom to a realization of heaven on earth.

Godwin has implemented all his reforms and now the best social sphere presents itself for mutual aid. The solution is the decentralization and simplification of society. The state has been broken up into local administrative units based on the parishes, and the work load has been distributed as fairly as possible. The need for violence in past societies did not come from human nature, but from the institutions of a corrupt nation. The abuses have now been done away with, and the nation is ruled by justice and wisdom. The difference between society and individual interests has disappeared long since.

Godwin's optimism has proved him right, and he proudly claims: »The morality of each individual and thus of all society has been extended and strengthened. As a result, politicians are now superfluous. Likewise, the mental enslavement by laws and private property that has prevailed until now is at an end. The road is free for the new man: Emotion rules over matter, mental perfection takes on physical form, and thus we can now control disease and old age.« Godwin expects salvation to come from a just distribution of goods: »Justice appeals to all people, regardless of how much they have contributed to the good of the nation. It has distributed the joint proceeds from agriculture in such a way that each person can consume his share. This set of circumstances is the true essence of justice.«

Godwin 1793; Ramm 1955; Tod / Wheeler 1978.

Godwin founded a type of philosophical anarchism. Once again he takes up the idea of community of property. In conjunction with high moral standards and mental perfection, he believes, we could even attain immortality.

John Humphrey Noyes (1811–1879). The perfectionists of the Oneida community in Putney, Vermont, USA, 1846–1880

»God, in his absolute perfection, is male and female alike«, preaches John Humphrey Noyes. »We believe that we shall become perfect only if we fully accept Christ into our hearts. Under God's guidance we can reach perfection. And then we can await Christ's second coming.«

To us this perfectionism really seems utopian. But Mr. Noyes by no means takes us to Utopia, but to a solid, successful community with a Christian basis: Again we are in reality.

The first settlement was founded in Putney, Vermont. John Humphrey Noyes had already developed his theories. He sees himself as God's agent on earth. But a hostile environment forced him to move – we are now in the little town of Oneida, N.Y., the year is 1860, and the community has been flourishing for a good ten years.

137. John Humphrey Noyes, Oneida community, Putney, Vermont, USA, industrial buildings, 1850. View of the workshops.

John Humphrey Noyes gives us a tour of the place. The center of the settlement is quite attractive: The showy three-story central brick building consists of a middle section and two wings, like a palace. On the ground floor are the dining hall for joint meals and the rooms for cultural activities. Then there are the library, museum, church, theater, and the printing shop. On the top floors we visit the living rooms and dormitories. In all the rooms we are surprised to find central heating. Grouped around the faux Gothic-style central building are the schools, workshops, barns, and stables. A sauna, lovely gardens that merge into open country are not far from the simple residential houses. Admittedly we are not too enthusiastic about the conglomeration of seemingly unplanned factory buildings.

But the economic success is certainly surprising: In addition to the »Perfectionists« – over 100 members – close to 200 paid workers from outside also work here. Life is simple, if not Spartan: We meet women, simply dressed, wearing trousers, their hair cut short.

We've been invited to a meal with the entire community. After all we have seen, we are not surprised that there is only vegetarian food. We don't have to add that alcohol and tobacco are forbidden.

Monogamous marriage is regarded as religious and social tyranny. By practicing birth control and yoga they separate pleasure from reproduction and follow a program of family planning where all members of the community vote in a special committee on reproductive issues.

Couples are selected for reproduction on the basis of their mental and physical qualities and there are then no limits imposed on their sexual activity. The community's master, J. H. Noyes, has approximately ten children. He reserves the right to introduce the thirteen-year-old girls to the mysteries of sexuality.

The community is trying to produce particularly high-quality descendants. In the first years after founding the community, free love – »complex marriage« – was practiced. Each of the men was allowed to have intercourse with each of the women, and vice versa, though with the consent of both partners and under the control of a third person. The members believe this custom is legitimized by the Bible. But the practice was given up in 1879. Members have conventional marriages again. They practice »male continence« as a birth control method: Ejaculation is held back or coitus interruptus is practiced. As a result, only 40 children were engendered by 150 persons. The children belong to the entire community and are raised in children's houses.

In Abigail Merwin, Noyes at first finds an enthusiastic follower, but she leaves him, and Noyes celebrates a spiritual wedding with Harriet Holton: Her wealth, together with a legacy from his father, creates many opportunities for Noyes.

All decisions are made at plenary community meetings and here, too, all property is communal. The community has become a great economic success, for they have gradually made the transition from crafts and farming to industrial production. Thus the community provides a small sensation as hundreds of curious visitors flock there every week, often smiling at the members, particularly because of their clothes and hairstyles.

It doesn't take long for hostility to develop as well: A lawsuit is brought against Noyes for raping minors. He flees to Canada, where, in 1879, he dies.

In 1881 the community in its original form is dissolved, but industrial production develops successfully – of course there is no communal property, and the families have long since become respectably bourgeois. The rudiments of the Perfectionists survive until 1949. Today, Oneida is a modern industrial city.

Schempp 1969; Schwarz 1982.

Changing and very different conceptions of love, marriage, family, and reproduction cannot be discussed in detail in this study. But we cannot help comparing the Oneida community with that described in chapter 21.23, Otto Mühl's commune: He too reserved for himself a kind of »jus primae noctis« for girls who joined the commune. His authoritarian attitude may have resembled that of J. H. Noyes, and another parallel is his contact with very young girls. Over and above this, the Oneida »breeding methods« anticipate fascism.

Johann Georg Rapp (1757–1847). Harmony, 1805, and New Harmony, USA, 1815

Johann Georg Rapp, a sober and intelligent man from Württemberg, is convinced that the new age, the millennium, will dawn soon and that the second coming of Christ is imminent. But he transforms this utopia into a reality we visit with a sense of wonder.

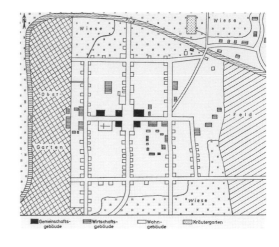

Johann Georg Rapp welcomes us in Harmony, not far from Pittsburgh. He came here together with like-minded companions in 1803. Once again, we have people living in an ideal community where property is shared. They have renounced sexuality and thus descendants, but children are adopted. Each of the original families has its own little house, and the family eats its meals together. Rapp's agrarian commune is extremely successful. The members enjoy a certain prosperity and accept the authoritarian control.

As we walk through Harmony, we see that the name seems to be appropriate. The place is situated at a bend in the river. The center is an open square with the public buildings at its corners – a community center, an inn, a store, and the house of »Father Rapp.« The church is somewhat off to the side. The four streets radiate from the square, with residential buildings on both sides. The farm buildings and workshops are placed where they are needed. Fields, meadows, and an orchard surround the little town.

Ten years later Rapp sells the land and property to the community of Robert Owen, whom we shall visit later, and moves further down the Wabash River valley, where he founds »New Harmony.« Again he meets with success, and soon close to 1,000 people are living here in substantial houses, attaining considerable prosperity.

However, Rapp moves away from here as well, only to found »Economy« north of Pittsburgh. He again uses his recipe for success, and even after his death in 1847 the Harmonists were able to remain successful running coal mines, railroads, and oil wells. However, the end of the century also means the gradual decline of the Harmonists.

Schempp 1969; Seibt 2001.

The new communities, mostly very idealistic in character, show a wide spectrum of success: From complete flops to wealth the arch spans a vast distance even when the ideological points of departure and theories are identical or similar. The »Rappists« were extremely successful, and people praised the industriousness of the »German« Johann Rapp.

Joseph Smith (1805–1844). Utah, the state of the Mormons, since 1830

Joseph Smith, the founder of the Mormons (Church of Jesus Christ of Latter-Day Saints), is impelled by lofty ideals. »It was a miracle from heaven«, he tells us with enthusiasm. »I received divine guidance from the Angel Moroni, who instructed me to travel to the hill Cumorah in New York state and to dig there. I unearthed two golden tablets with curious writing on them. It was reformed Egyptian, and yet I was able to translate them easily: It was the Book of ›Mormon‹, which tells the story of the settlement of America by one of the lost tribes of Israel.«

The year is 1827. What a strange, abstruse story – told by a simple man with little education. But he continues weaving his web of visions: »The second coming of Christ is near. It will take place in America – we expect him in the city of Zion.«

Here is what Joseph Smith read word for word: »America is the land of promise; a land which I have prepared for you, yea, a land which is choice above all other lands.«

This is devoid of all reality, isn't it? By no means: Joseph Smith is a very active visionary and, in 1830, founds an enormous religious movement that is still in existence –the Mormons, the Church of Jesus Christ of Latter-Day Saints.

138. Johann Georg Rapp, the settlement of Harmony, Butler Co., Pennsylvania, USA, 1805.

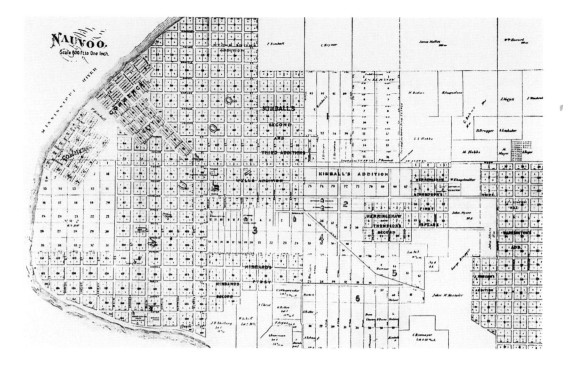

To be sure Joseph Smith does not show us around the biblical Zion (that city is not founded until later), but the very real town of Nauvoo, on the east bank of the Mississippi. Yet in the final analysis every Mormon village is a realization of the divine city of Zion. But where will Christ actually appear? »We have many troubles behind us. We've had to bear hostility, hatred, murder, being driven out again and again, seeing our work destroyed, until, in 1839, we were finally able to settle here.«

The ground plan of the city, a rigidly geometrical grid, has been prescribed in the Book of Mormon. »Our cities are sacred yet rational at the same time, for they obey a simple geometry.« Now we stroll through the extremely attractive city. It is situated above the fluvial plain and follows a moderate topography. The clayey soil provides fine building material, supplemented by wood and stone.

As we look down the streets past the precise squares of the properties, our eyes can find hardly a single resting place. But on the plots themselves the cottages, which stand close to the streets, are scattered loosely and surrounded by gardens and fields.

Faith in Christ is the community's foundation. But Joseph Smith considers the traditional form of marriage to be outdated and advocates polygamy – he himself has 27 wives. The envy of the neighbors does not fail to materialize. It is primarily the polygamy practiced by the Mormons that becomes a stumbling block. Joseph Smith is murdered and it is now impossible for the community to remain in Nauvoo.

After Joseph Smith's tragic death, Brigham Young assumes the ongoing leadership of the sizeable group. A huge migration now begins, comprising 15,000 persons and 30,000 head of cattle. The place chosen by God is not found until one and a half years later – »Great Salt Lake City«, the big Mormon city, is founded in Utah. A series of settlements conquers Utah and makes it a Mormon state, which it still is to this day.

Even more colossal is the grid of the city, which is also conditioned by the luxuriant growth. Brigham Young is our guide now, and he dispels our misgivings: »Here too the dominant element is the great, clear geometry of the grid«, emphasizes Brigham Young.

»But the city is not monotonous. Just take a look: There's a garden by every house. Vegetables grow here, and flowers bloom, and the people live in peace and quiet.«

We now approach a gentle slope. Here is the temple, made entirely of white limestone. »The blueprint was sent by God. We built this temple with great care. It is solidly constructed, for it must be worthy of a great event: the second coming of Christ.« From here we have a fine view of the huge chessboard.

The spread of the Mormons in America and soon in Europe as well is unprecedented. Therefore we feel justified in visiting a few more »villages«.

Escalante is settled by the first families in 1876, and its plan, like that of all Mormon towns and villages, follows the strict grid system. The town is divided into eighteen blocks of five acres (two hectares) each. Each of these is divided into four 1 1/4 acre blocks (1/2 hectare), and each family receives a plot this size. From the original eighteen blocks the town has grown to 50 blocks, and more than 1,000 persons live here. The fact that construction is immediately begun on the first meeting-house (VIII) and that the building is also used for church services attests to the inhabitants' great public spirit. The grade school is completed one year later, followed by a high school and college. The first houses, crude log cabins, are soon replaced by brick buildings, one-story gabled houses. Only the school and the community center have two stories. Are we justified in including the Mormon villages, which, especially in the beginning, were purely agrarian in nature, among the towns, since they often had hardly more than 1,000 inhabitants? Basically a Mormon village is a structured social intervention that goes far beyond the rational village: And actually it was seen as a town called Zion, and the Savior, when he came, was to have a place to stay wherever he chose to visit. The group solidarity of the villages goes far beyond that of similar settlements and is characterized by faith and love.

The village of Ephraim is at least double the size of Escalante. It is 20 years older and a little more isolated. Here we also encounter unusual languages: A majority of the inhabitants comes from Scandinavia, especially from Denmark. For protection from the Indians they have built a kind of fort: The walls are seven feet (2.5 m) high and enclose an area of one and a half acres.

All the houses are located inside the walls, and we are reminded of a medieval town. The community house in the center is constructed from strong cedar logs. They stand a few feet apart, and the interstices are filled with clay. The roof is made of logs, willows, and clay.

However, the township was considerably expanded to seventeen acres. The walls are now fourteen feet (5 m) high.

We would have liked to visit the township of America Fork with its 3,000 inhabitants as well, and also villages in Canada, directly by the border, such as Cardston, Stirling, Orton. However, we've been assured that they are all constructed pretty much according to the same plan.

Smith 1927; Lowry 1952; Vercelloni 1994.

The Mormon towns are primarily characterized by one thing: In contrast to most realizations of utopian or idealistic town concepts, almost all of them have been preserved to this day. Of course, there have been many structural changes, chiefly from an agrarian to an industrial economy; of the social and religious concepts, many have been lost.

Robert Owen (1771–1858). The Village of Unity, 1817, New Lanark, 1815, and New Harmony, 1825

We pay our first visit to the Village of Unity and Mutual Co-operation (1817). The strictly square urban plan is embedded among gardens and undeveloped countryside. None of the buildings are more than two floors high.

The small community, numbering roughly 1,200 persons, is visible at a glance. It is completely self-sufficient, and the inhabitants are employed both in agriculture and at the factory, enjoying the full proceeds of their work.

Robert Owen explains the plan of the village to us: The center is a large rectangular square. Thus, Owen believes, »*the great advantages inherent in this form can be combined with the community's domestic arrangements. Private residences – bedrooms and day rooms – have been placed on the four sides of this rectangle. Three sides of the square are reserved for married couples' housing. The fourth side is occupied by communal dormitories, in which all surplus children (those over and above the permissible three children per family) are housed and, if necessary, children who are over three years old as well. In the center of this fourth side are rooms for the dormitory supervisors. At one end is the infirmary, at the other a kind of hotel for strangers. In the center of the first two sides are the apartments of the head supervisors, ministers of education and the arts, teachers, and physicians, and in the center of the third side are storehouses and storerooms for various goods, an inn, a clinic, etc. Along a line running through the central point of the rectangle, the church and places of cultural interest, schools, kitchen and community dining hall have been erected, and sufficient room has been left for light, air, and ease of access.*«

Mr. Owen takes us into one of the family apartments. The generous amount of space is surprising: Every unit has four rooms, though we vainly look for a kitchen, because it has become superfluous thanks to the communal kitchen. Cleverly devised mechanisms, a kind of air conditioning, make it possible to heat, cool, or air the rooms.

141. Plan of Escalante, Mormon city, settled in 1876. Status in 1950.
142. Plan of Ephraim, Mormon village, c. 1800. Status in 1925.

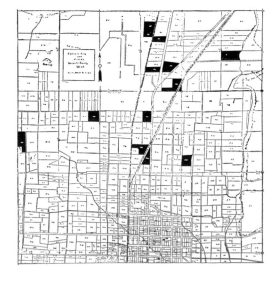

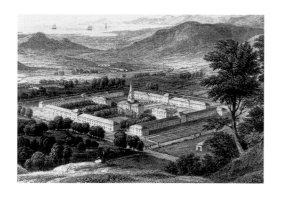

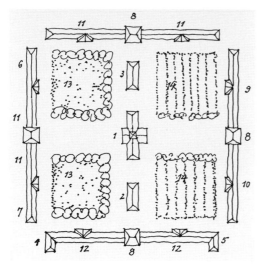

From the apartments we can look directly into the big courtyard. In the four small squares there are fine trees, and the lawns are used for sports and recreation.

Mr. Owen gives us an interesting insight into the children's everyday lives. All children over three years of age attend school, eat in the dining halls, and sleep in the dormitories. Before they leave school, they have learned everything that is important for them to know. The older children are encouraged to help in the gardens or with industrial work for part of the day, according to their abilities.

All the men do farm or industrial work, or are employed in another useful sector of the community. Robert Owen tries to give us a brief explanation of the basic tenets of his ingenious reforms: Education is the beginning of being human. Its primary focus is practical love for one's fellow human beings. Workers have a share in the proceeds of their work, wages are gradually raised, production is well organized, and finally private property has disappeared, including men's ownership of women.

The goal is not individuals earning money, but the well-being of all people. Now we go for a walk outside town and are suddenly in a wholly different idyll: Large gardens invite us to stroll around and do physical work. But next to them there are also large areas of land used for farming and the necessary buildings: stables, farm buildings, workshops are placed in harmonious clusters. Thus, complete harmony between town and country is reestablished.

We go on to visit New Lanark in England.

Now, however, we have abruptly left utopia – we are in New Lanark, in an almost idyllic village landscape – and yet this is a large manufacturing plant that Owen, at the young age of 29, took over from his father-in-law in 1800. »It is here in New Lanark that I realized my ideas, my dreams. I think that everybody here lives a happy and peaceful life.«

Owen has transformed the factory into a cooperative and has implemented a type of a planned-economy model. Little New Lanark becomes a much admired model town. We compare life here with the horrifying conditions in English working-class districts during the early industrial revolution – and we feel deep respect for the amazing achievement of the idealistic philanthropist.

The River Clyde, with a small wooded island, is the source of energy, so to speak. It drives the watermills for the factory, a cotton and silk spinning mill. The factory halls with their mechanical looms are well lit and clean. They have several stories, and are equipped with central heating and elevators. »I managed – and this is only a first step – to reduce working hours from sixteen and often eighteen hours to twelve hours, including a one-and-a-half-hour break. I was especially concerned about the children: Instead of working up to ten hours a day as before, they now work only a maximum of six hours. Admittedly, that's still too much. But I raised the age from seven years to twelve and made school attendance compulsory – we do not employ illiterates here.«

143. Robert Owen, Village of Unity and Mutual Co-operation, 1817, 1823.
144. Robert Owen, plan of the Village of Unity and Mutual Co-operation, 1817. 1 church, 2 kitchen, dining house, 3 school, 4 sickbay, 5 guests, hotel, 6 arts management, 7 doctors, 8 supervisors, 9 warehouse, store, 10 guesthouse, 11 dwellings, 12 dwellings, 13 recreational space, 14 agricultural area.
145. Robert Owen, New Lanark, c. 1825.

It goes without saying that the kindergartens and schools are orderly and well lit. Owen implements his educational goals, which he had already expressed in the Village of Unity. One of the goals is complete nonviolence, and thus it gradually becomes possible to reduce the crime rate of the grown-ups.

Now we pass a building on which a sign proclaims »Institute for Character Building« in large letters and we ask what that is supposed to mean. This »New Institute« is the stronghold of Owen's moral ambitions: The festivals and community celebrations, too, are more than pleasure; they contribute to the struggle against alcoholism and prostitution. »Knowledge alone is not the only thing that matters. It is useless unless it is accompanied by morality and character. These are taught in school, but in addition we've also established this house for everyone.«

The inhabitants of New Lanark are asked to attend regular gatherings. There are special meeting rooms where the problems of self-government and self-control are discussed, elections take place, and matters of concern are brought to everyone's attention. Of course such meetings are not always without conflict, but Owen is the great, wise father and tries to act as a mediator, no doubt at times in an authoritarian manner.

Now we have a look at the large multipurpose room (fig. 146). In the lovely, bright hall it is wonderful to see the young girls dancing gracefully, instructed by teachers, assisted by the mothers. On the walls are big colorful panels with pictures of all kinds of animals, for education by means of images is considered to be more valuable than book learning. First and foremost, however, the whole personality is to be molded, which is why it is important that the children should feel joyful and happy, but also that they should engage in conversation with the grown-ups.

Now we stroll past the residential buildings. They are from three to five stories high. All were properly renovated, though they had often been half dilapidated, and new buildings were added. We are able to visit one of the apartments. The rooms are light and spacious and, to our amazement, have central heating. We already know why the new apartments lack kitchens. »The people, especially the women, do not have to do housework, cooking: The communal kitchens provide abundant and tasty food.«

Nevertheless, there is still demand for many everyday items, but this need is met by the cooperative stores: Fair prices and good quality are prerequisites.

There are no private businesses, only these communal stores with quality food, which, however, is 25 percent cheaper than in regular stores – and there is good whisky instead of rotgut.

Robert Owen has been accused of being hostile toward religion, indeed toward faith. Why is that? »I have preached not against religion but in favor of reason, and particularly in favor of tolerance. I've built a church, but it is open to all religions, not only the official Church of Scotland.«

But how was it possible to finance all these institutions? »New machines, better quality, rationalization, organization are the key concepts«, says Owen optimistically.

Was that sufficient for the »miracle of New Lanark«, though? »Not quite. I admit that I had to subsidize many things from my own pocket.«

Once again we realize that the »miracle« is completely dependent on Owen, who is both charismatic and wealthy. But even so, a great philanthropic dream has been fulfilled.

The schools are a very important focus, but they are not only about the imparting of knowledge but equally about the formation of character, about music and dance. Of course, inevitably, the boys also learn military drill. Yet there is no punishment, no tyranny, and the children develop the necessary sense for the community. But primarily they learn that every action can be expected to have inevitable consequences.

»This form of life is an invention that will augment the physical and mental energy of the entire community many times and lead to enormous expansion without inflicting an injustice on anyone«, Robert Owen is convinced.

And once more Owen refers to the advantages enjoyed by the workers: »Daily working hours were reduced. Every week a certain amount is deducted from the workers' wages, money that is available if they become ill or retire. When a worker is unable to work, his wages are paid for an additional three months. It is true that the wages are somewhat lower than in other factories, but on the other hand the social benefits are incomparably larger.«

Not without pride Mr. Owen speaks of his achievements: *»I've succeeded in transforming a lazy, dirty, dissolute, alcoholic people, and by their own conviction they now live a well-ordered, regular, and respectable life.*

»Up till now the means of governing human beings in the world have been violence and threats, pain and fear, ignorance and superstition. I want to put into action the moral idea of love

146. Robert Owen, dance class in New Lanark.

and goodness, which shall bring all people freedom from want, beauty, knowledge, and truth. I want to help people to live their lives according to these principles. It will work – in Scotland, in England and Ireland, in continental Europe, all over the world!«

But doesn't that optimistic statement again plunge us into the realm of utopia? To be sure, Owen is no Luddite and no nature freak. He realizes that the process of industrialization is not reversible, but he also knows the key concepts:

»*The combination of true philanthropy and sympathetic discipline brings with it trust and, in the end, good results.*«

A beautiful maxim is quoted under Owen's programmatic portrait: »*People's character is formed **for** them, not **by** them.*«

If a person's life develops positively, his / her character, too, will change. The ultimate goal is human happiness, attained by »*the only religion, the religion of that which is human.*«

Robert Owen actually proved it to us: His company by no means remained a utopia, and he realized his ideas in New Lanark. His work became a model and inspiration for many similar movements. Owen was an experienced entrepreneur, and his cotton spinning mills in New Lanark flourished for a quarter-century, so that he was able to implement his philanthropic reforms. In 1825 he ventures a move to America – where we plan to visit him shortly.

But his success in England did not last long: Owen was unable to weather the economic crises after the Napoleonic Wars: Production decreased, wages were cut back, poverty and unemployment loomed. In 1829 Owen left New Lanark for good.

Today, New Lanark has been partly turned into a museum. Of course, as we stroll through this site of pilgrimage for all historians interested in social reform, we can see that the place has hardly anything in common with the ideal plan of the Village of Unity.

Owen did not get discouraged and in his idealistic optimism and his critical view of his time made programmatic pronouncements like the following: »*That is why the best government is one that actually produces the greatest happiness for the greatest number of people – rulers and subjects alike.*«

And, becoming more specific while still curbing his social criticism – since Owen was after all trying to win over those in power – the passionate reformer states: »*The next move for national reformers ought to be to abolish or change those laws that leave the lower classes in ignorance and train them to be immoderate, which results in idleness, addiction to gambling, poverty, disease, and crime. The production and consumption of alcohol are now encouraged by law; thousands of concessions are distributed every year to the owners of liquor stores and superfluous taverns.*«

Passionately, he supports the cause of the growing number of poor, though without making any concrete proposals: »*The next measure for the general improvement of the British population should be a revision of laws concerning the poor. For no matter how pure and benevolent the motives of those who passed these laws are, the direct and certain effect of these laws is that the poor, and through them the state itself, are badly harmed.*«

Owen's models were the classical education of the ancient Greeks, and the noble savages of the Enlightenment. Thus he praises the original inhabitants of America and at the same time chastises the escalating greed of the Americans:

»*And in America, where once the noble native tribes fearlessly roamed through their pathless forests, evincing that bold, astute, sublime, and sincere character that found it difficult to understand why a sensible person could wish to own more than he was able to consume – on that same soil and in that same climate, characters are now developed amid such opposite customs and laws that all the physical and mental abilities of an individual are exerted in order to acquire ten thousand times more, if possible, than any single person can consume.*«

Let's make a sudden leap into a fascinating utopia: »New Harmony«, planned by Thomas Stedman Whitwell in 1824/25 for Robert Owen. Having seen the Village of Unity, we are already familiar with much that we observe here.

A huge square causes us to suspect at first glance that we are looking at a feudal castle. But as we come closer we see that countless small gabled houses are strung together, only the corners have been emphasized and in the interior of the spacious landscaped courtyard a few towers emphasize the importance of communal buildings and technical equipment.

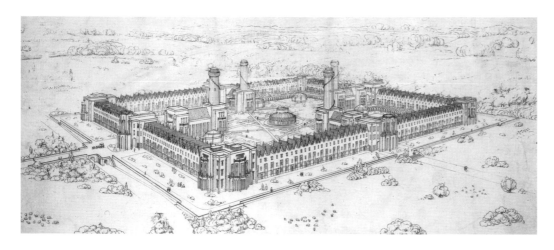

147. Stedman Whitwell, New Harmony after Owen, c. 1825.

After going up a wide staircase we are on the base plateau. One building projects markedly from the row of houses: a kind of book palace containing a library, reading rooms, and the printing shop. We enter the vast interior courtyard, and from here we visit the extensive dining halls; the children's dining rooms, however, are separate, along the sides of the anterooms. The kitchen is located on the lowest floor but is connected to the halls by service elevators. Its counterpart on the opposite side is the proud forum for lectures, exhibitions, discussions, etc. There is an adjacent lab with a small lending library. In the diagonal axis the dominant buildings are occupied by ballrooms and music rooms and by the baths. The intersection of the two axes is marked by an opulent domed building: The conservatory is placed in the middle of the botanically designed gardens, which are bordered by elegant arcades.

The dominant corner buildings emphasize the important role of education: This is where the schools for all ages are located. It is surprising that the breweries, bakeries, and laundries are grouped around the base of the towers.

And the towers, we ask Owen and Whitwell, who have joined us in the meantime, are they merely symbols? »Not at all«, the architect informs us. »On the top floor, there are observatories. Gas-lit clocks show the exact time, and at the top huge gas spotlights shine down into the yard and turn night into day. That's not all, though – follow me down below the ground.«

We climb down into the extensive basement rooms and are again surprised by a subterranean town: Here goods are transported along tracks and conveyor belts run in all directions. This is where the big kitchens are located, and heating and ventilation equipment and water heaters ensure the well-being of the residents – and in the middle of the towers are the flues for this technology.

Here, too, special care has been devoted to the education buildings, and the importance of early childhood education is clearly recognized: The three- to eight-year-olds learn by playing in the kindergarten and are meant to learn to develop independent thinking at an early age, though not exclusively in the bosom of the family. Schools also are interested in raising the children to be people who think for themselves. Above all, however, girls and boys receive a completely equal education in coeducational classes. The idea of equality must find expression in an ideal, communist society, as it were.

Owen now proclaims the three evils that beset humankind: private property, the absurd, irrational religious systems, and the conventional forms of marriage.

What about Owen's own democratic views? we ask ourselves. *»Democracy and common property cannot function without firm leadership. That is why I am forced to make all decisions myself and on my own, and I have reserved the right of veto in all areas.«*

Let us now return to reality once more as we visit the real New Harmony in Indiana, USA (1825). Owen meets the »Rappists«, a pious, celibate sect of the Pentecostal Church, founded by the German Georg Rapp, but now in its final throes: Mismanagement and malaria force Rapp to sell (cf. chap. 7.1). Robert Owen buys the land and little town for $ 150,000 to house 1,000 persons. In 1825/26 Owen founds the »New Harmony Community of Equality«.

We now walk towards Harmony. It is a small place, quite rural, at the foot of a hill with gardens and parks, with a pointed church steeple, lanes, and pastures. The Wabash River snakes in a wide curve through the landscape. There are orchards on the hills, and terraced vineyards. In the plain the waving grain crop gleams yellow, and healthy cattle graze in the pastures.

148. New Harmony, after W. Liebknecht, 1892.

We stroll through the real town of Harmony: The streets with their low houses cross at exact right angles, and in the center of town a large square has been left open, bordered by taller, public buildings, such as a school, church, and administration building. But of course New Harmony was not built according to the beautiful, visionary plan of Whitwell.

Even more than in New Lanark, Owen devotes his whole personality, his eloquent charisma to the community. »We are members of a big family with the same lifestyle, we live in a community of work and zest for life. Because property is communal, there is no hatred or envy. We are the first true human community in the entire world!«

And Owen again propagates the three great freedoms as the foundation of the community: freedom from private ownership, freedom from irrational religious systems, and freedom from forced marriage where women are the slaves of men. Indeed, the first years are characterized by amazing successes and by great idealism. The houses are repaired, hundreds of people apply for admission, work assignments are made, and rules are established. And again Owen pays special attention to the school, to new, free education.

Thus we are actually walking through a place of »new harmonies«, through a peaceful, respectable little town. On one building there is a surprising inscription: »Hall of Women.« »Here women are not the same as men, but have equal rights, which is why they have their own assembly rooms.«

In 1826 Owen returns to England. Production in New Harmony is sluggish, internal strife shakes the community, and William Maclure and Feiba Pevey split off to found their own commune with 150 of the conservative members of New Harmony. In »Macluria«, as the community calls itself, the education of children is the most important concern.

New Harmony was now decimated, and lack of farming and manufacturing skills gradually became noticeable. In the end, New Harmony failed, and in 1828 Owen sold the property. But Owen's charisma and charm have lasted to this day.

New Harmony, in the early phase of its success, motivated others to found additional settlements, such as those in Wanborough, Illinois, in Bloomington, Indiana, and in a few other states. None of them was destined to last long.

Owen now devotes all his time to his theoretical writings, agitation, fighting for justice on behalf of working people. Lectures, petitions, interventions, calls to action, meetings fill the latter part of his life, and his involvement fluctuates between sectarian faith and the productive activation of working-class movements.

Owen's great philanthropic Idealism seems unbroken. He publishes his »Declaration of Mental Independence«: »*We must liberate ourselves from the monstrous viciousness of private and individual property, from the absurd and irrational systems of religion and marriage, which are both rooted in individual property. New Harmony marks the beginning of the new millennium.*«

Owen 1813/14, 1832, 1857/58; Whitwell 1830; Noyes 1870; Wagner 1942; Ramm 1956; Hasselmann 1958; Armytage 1961; Harrison 1969; Servier 1971; Schumpp 1971; Benevolo 1971; Bollerey 1991; Tod/Wheeler 1978; Manguel 1981; Brentjes 1993; Vercelloni 1994; Dilas 1994; *Utopie* 1969; *Impossible Worlds* 2000; Seibt 2001; Eaton 2001; Liebknecht 1892.

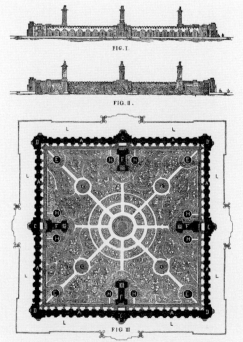

Amazing as Robert Owen's magnificent initiatives were, we do have one question: What was the nature of the freedom in Owen's settlements and factories? Did it not depend on the kindness of his heart? Factory work, housing, education, cooperative, culture: In the cosmos of New Lanark and New Harmony, which functioned smoothly for a time, all bonuses, all social achievements were dependent on the great philanthropist – run, indeed dictated by him. He is thus the precursor of the large, omnipotent industrial magnates and their settlements, companies such as Krupp, Olivetti, and many others.

How could people organize their own lives when these were completely enmeshed with the company? What real choices did they have?

Admittedly, Robert Owen did anticipate the modern city in three important respects: a perfect infrastructure, technological equipment, and social services.

Did Robert Owen fail? If we maintain that he did – and the end of New Lanark and New Harmony would prompt us to do so – then we overlook the enormous effect produced not only by Owen's writings and lectures, but also by the real, concrete evidence of his work.

Looking at things from this perspective we must concede that Robert Owen took an important step forward in developing socialism from a utopia into a science, from fantasy into reality, and questions about utopia and real life, success and failure appear in a very different light. It is also of interest that in 1892 Wilhelm Liebknecht honors Owen's work in an illustrated publication.

John Minter Morgan (1823–1886). The Christian Commonwealth, 1845

From a hill we have a fine view of the settlement. We're reminded of the beautiful drawing that Whitwell did for New Harmony. The uniform houses surround a large courtyard, and the corner buildings and four buildings at the entrances to the courtyard are somewhat higher than the rest of the two-story buildings (cf. chap. 7.1).

In the center, at the point where the broad streets intersect, looking like a small fortress, is the building for community institutions. However, in order to reach the church – built in the usual Gothic style – we must go outside the little town.

Eaton 2001.

Islands – and we have visited a number of them by now – are one way of imagining a community that has broken away from a hostile, flawed world. The other way of imagining such a community is not quite as radical: The huge interior courtyard is a piece of land that is entrusted to the community for its needs.

James Silk Buckingham (1786–1855). The model town Victoria, 1849

Our depressing tour of the British industrial towns and their wretched suburbs was no utopia. We experienced the »hard times« Charles Dickens had depicted in his novel.

Thus we are glad that the seafarer, journalist, and scholar James Silk Buckingham gives us a tour of his model town, a new Victoria.

»We must finally do something to relieve the desperate lot of the wretched people in our cities«, Mr. Buckingham passionately appeals to Parliament in London. He has visited the American reform communities, the Quakers and Rappists, and sees in them an incentive for Europe.

Seen from above, his town at first reminds us of the big rectangular towns planned by John Minter Morgan and Robert Owen. The strictly geometric structure, with intersecting main streets and added diagonals, is not particularly surprising. From the periphery to the center, there are seven rows of houses. We are interested to note that the residential buildings become lower toward the center. The explanation is understandable even if we do not agree: The better-off classes live closer to the center, and the further from the center, the »simpler« the population – yet all of them have healthy housing, for slums have been eliminated. Cholera, which claimed thousands of victims, has also been conquered.

The center densely occupied by representative public buildings with domed roofs, and a bell tower exceeds all of them in height, reaching the astounding height of 90 m. Yet the tower has another function as well: An electric sun lights the whole town at night. The residential buildings in individual blocks have two to three floors and are no doubt densely populated, for Mr. Buckingham speaks of 10,000 people living here.

We are struck by the fact that the houses have different, classical orders of columns. »That is not an architectural game«, explains Mr. Buckingham. »The order of columns is a way of indicating a person's social rank. Take a look, for instance, at the composite order here: This is where the capitalists live, while the workers in the outermost square have Gothic houses.« Now we suddenly notice the street signs. »Oh yes, the names are at the same time the program for our town: Justice and Strength, Hope and Peace form the cross, and the diagonals are called Faith and Concord and Love and Unity. People are to be constantly reminded of their virtues and of the fact that only a virtuous town can be good. And so I dedicated the seven streets to the virtues.«

In addition to his poetic ambitions, Mr. Buckingham is very well informed about the hygienic requirements of a town: »*The highest degree of order, symmetry, space, and health with the largest possible supply of air and light and with the most perfect sewer system, with comfort and convenience for all walks of life; a balanced adaptation to the putative number of people of various social classes and their circumstances.*«

Now we walk outside the town once more. Fountains play at the edge of town, at the four corner points, After crossing the unusually wide road for vehicles, we enter well-tended parks with a natural look, which we find very pleasant, for green space in the interior of the town tends to be sparse.

Part of the park is bordered by long arcades. In another section we find a remarkable group of houses with buildings that have a semicircular floor plan and a turret with an onion dome.

Buckingham 1849; Howard/Posener 1968; Rosenau 1974; Bollerey 1977; Manguel 1981.

149. John Minter Morgan, Christian Commonwealth. Drawing by G. Müller, USA, 1845.

150. James Silk Buckingham, Victoria, USA, 1849.
Plan of model town.
151. James Silk Buckingham, Victoria, USA, 1849.
Bird's-eye view.

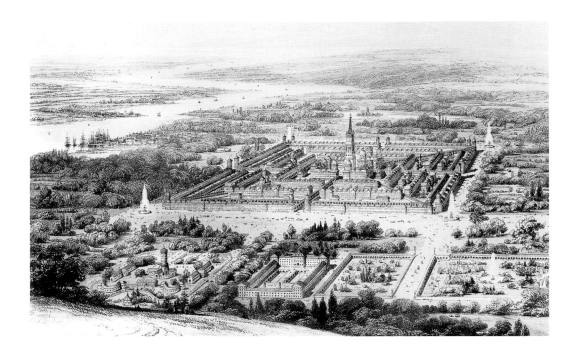

It is peculiar that in Victoria three urban concepts have been superimposed on each other as it were: First, there is the lofty moral and idealistic nonsectarian vision; second, the surprising way the architecture practically stigmatizes the inhabitants when every social class is characterized by a specific architectural style; and finally, the practical questions, though discussed by Vitruvius, Alberti, and others, anticipate functionalism. However, all three levels are also found in the modern town, in practical urban planning.

7.2. France, Russia, Germany

François Noël Gracchus Babeuf (1760–1797). The conspiracy of the equals, 1796

Babeuf's goals seem to be fairly simplistic, and yet they are revolutionary: A single tax is to be imposed on property and income, affecting all persons, including the aristocracy, of course.

Babeuf elucidates his elementary demands: »Each person is obliged to contribute to the needs of the general public in proportion to his share in these advantages.«

The possessions of the Church are not to be sold, but must be used as the basis of a national fund for the poor. Medical help, free drugs, a national education plan can be financed from this fund. Equal regard for all professions and an equal education for all people are indispensable. »Nature does not squander its gifts. It produces only nearly as much as is needed by all the living beings it has created. One group of people cannot enjoy abundance without others lacking the most essential goods.«

One more root of evil was eliminated: The selling of land was abolished, land that was fairly divided among all citizens.

Through his revolutionary reforms, Babeuf has reached his goal: »All people are happy, that is the aim of their social union. Everyone is always allotted adequate provisions. It was easy to lay the foundations of the new order, since the government was and still is republican.«

And Babeuf once more gives a succinct summary: »Prosperity for all. Schooling for all. Equality, freedom, and happiness for all.«

Babeuf's revolution extended to the citizens' concrete environment as well. The existing towns and villages have been razed to the ground. A thousand new towns are created. They have a two-mile circumference, and in the 15,000 new villages, 330,000 farms have been built.

Servier 1971; Höppner 1987; Ramm 1955.

The conspiracy of Babeuf, as it is called after its leader, marks the beginning, in 1796, of the history of modern socialism. With admirable patience, courage, and toughness, Babeuf fought for equality and justice, and his partial successes were interrupted by months and years in prison. Babeuf did not give up. In 1797, however, he was executed.

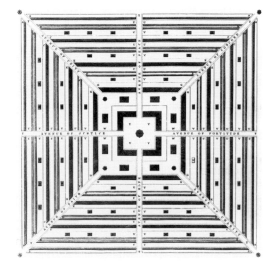

Success or failure? Events after the revolution, and the social movements, were much too complex to be able to judge in the long run. Marx und Engels explain the failure of the conspiracy as being caused by the »undeveloped form of the proletariat and a lack of material requirements for its liberation«.

Claude-Henri de Rouvroy, Comte de Saint-Simon (1760–1825). The ideal organization, 1820 (*Nouveau Christianisme*, 1825)

We arrive in a France that had the »bad luck« of losing, on the same day, the king's brother, the Duke of Angoulême, members of the royal family, the grand officers of the crown, all the secretaries of state, cardinals, archbishops, prefects, 10,000 of the richest landowners, and so on and so forth – and we realize with surprise that the loss of these 30,000 individuals has caused no political damage to the state.

Saint-Simon explains that France has been turned into a big factory, and politics has been completely incorporated into production. All class differences have vanished. Capital and means of production are owned by the state, there are only workers – in the broadest sense of the word: the term includes manufacturers, scientists, bankers, artists; the former, however, administer the country, there is government by the managers. Primarily, industrial leadership is now in charge of public administration and makes sure that profits from work are increased as much as possible. The principle of association has replaced competition, and the state is an association of working people.

And Saint-Simon argues: »*The (traditional) government always hurts industry if it interferes in its affairs; it even hurts it when it makes every effort to encourage it.*«

Here is how powers are divided according to Saint-Simon: »*Spiritual power is in the hands of the wise, temporal power is in the hands of the industrialists – that includes everyone who does useful work – the power to nominate the great leaders of humanity lies in the hands of all the people.*«

Three chambers determine political events, and for Saint Simon this is part of ideal organization. The legislative chamber and the examining or assessing chamber consist of scientists, engineers, and inventors, while the executive chamber consists of entrepreneurs, bankers, and industrialists. »*This is the path to a meritocracy, rule by deserving men*«, hopes Saint-Simon. »*Work is the source of all virtues, and the state has become the cooperative association of workers.*«

Saint-Simon has a low regard for the competence of the people. He asserts: »*Ordinary people themselves are passive and indifferent, and must be disregarded whenever this question is considered.*«

On the other hand, he gives women an enormously important role in society: »*Women are admitted everywhere. They may also be nominated to the science council.*« Salvation comes from science, but science must come to terms with practical life. Historical thinking must leave the realm of the empiric and find its way to the higher standpoint of scientific and causal interpretation. »*Science helps us on the path of social progress*«, Saint-Simon confidently claims. But he does not believe that we can eliminate the glaring social differences between the poor and the aristocratic parasites. Saint-Simon is himself an aristocrat, but has put aside his title. »*But we can raise the living conditions of the poor population to an acceptable level, and the people can become as wealthy as it wants to. To do so, however, the people's own efforts and talent are required.*«

Saint-Simon has not abolished property by any means, but each owner has made a commitment to use it in a beneficial way in the interest of the whole society, not only of one class. Every citizen is committed to work in a way that is beneficial to society. But not all citizens are alike: »*Each shall work according to his capacity, and his needs shall be met according to the work he has performed.*«

Saint-Simon has demonstrated »*that the French proletariat is capable of correctly administering property*«. To do so, of course, a prerequisite is that young people be appropriately educated. However, it must be stressed that »*for the proletarian class, training is infinitely more important than instruction*«.

Saint-Simon concisely sums up his idealistic vision: »*All my aspiration can be summed up in one idea – that all people should be guaranteed the freest development of their aptitudes.*« But all endeavors must be founded on the basis of Christianity. To be sure, what Saint-Simon has in mind is not traditional Catholicism. Rather, he believes in a »New Christianity«, a social religion. The commandment to love one's neighbor is, after all, the basis for all social action, but, Saint-

Simon is convinced, the commandment is ignored, even by those who call themselves Christians. And Saint-Simon judges the popes and Protestants harshly: They are not Christians but heretics. Saint-Simon has a great vision, however: »Christianity will reconstruct itself as a worldwide, single religion. The inhabitants of Asia and Africa will be converted, and the members of the European clergy will become good Christians. The true spirit of Christianity, that is, the most general teachings that can be deduced from the underlying principle of divine ethics will arise, and at once religious differences will vanish. Religion has the task of guiding society toward the great goal of improving the lot of the most impoverished class as rapidly as possible.«

Enfantin 1905; Saint-Simon 1832, 1857, 1859, 1979, 2003; Ramm 1956; Benevolo 1971; Servier 1971; Block 1973; Tod / Wheeler 1978; Berneri 1950, 1971; Höppner 1987.

Saint-Simon does not succeed in implementing his ideas, and he leaves us hardly any architectural ideas. In his old age, he still pins his hopes on Christianity: It could, he believes, hold together the social system by its doctrine of brotherliness and mutual love, and moderate signs of aggressive competition and rivalry. His proposals for the position of women mark the beginning of the powerful process of emancipation.

His theories are developed further and »Saint-Simonism« gradually becomes a movement with tremendous repercussions, posthumously building up Saint-Simon into one of the founders of socialism.

Saint Amand Bazard (1791–1832) has recognized the nature of class struggle, and wants to hand over all means of production to a bank that will be set up by the state. Capital and landed property are no longer to be subject to private inheritance.

His fellow traveler and competitor is Barthelemy Prosper Enfantin (1798–1864). He pleads for the total power of priests. He founds a small intentional community where people wear a distinctive costume, but in 1832 the group is dissolved by the police. Saint-Simonism thus ceases to exist. However, its theoretical influence on social development, down to Marx and Lenin, was considerable.

Louis Blanc (1811–1882). Production cooperatives, 1839

In this town we are immediately taken to a completely new kind of workplaces. In the most important branches of industry »social workshops« have been set up. They've already spread across the whole country. In these workshops everyone has the right to dispose of the product of his work. Louis Blanc explains his vision: »As of now the state is the sole proprietor of the means of production, but soon it will die off, once complete equality has been reached.«

Louis Blanc believes that a revolution is not necessary. He has made a peaceful compromise with the bourgeoisie.

The social workshops are controlled by the workers and make sure that their interests are protected. Louis Blanc rejects all luxury goods: »Every product must correspond to a use, and every use must correspond to a need.«

The goals of the early social movements are very similar: liberation of the worker, abolition of poverty, a humane existence. But the ways and means differ: Le Blanc believes in a compromise with the bourgeoisie.

Charles Fourier (1772–1837). The city of Guarantism, 1822, and the Phalanstery, 1830

First, we visit a very early urban settlement, and Charles Fourier submits an unusual thesis: »The town has gone through five periods. The first period was a muddled paradise, the second – a topsy-turvy wildness, while the third was an upside-down patriarchy. The period of barbarism came next, the fifth was civilization. Now we live in the sixth period, in the city of ›Guarantism‹. Two more periods up to perfection will follow: Sociantism and Harmonism.«

Fourier presents an incredible and almost confusing abundance of systematic and philosophical reflections, of moral and social structures, but we are interested primarily in the city. It is the city of Guarantism, where the society guarantees everyone the minimum absolutely necessary for existence.

»I believe«, Fourier tells us, »that we must return to the tried-and-true, optimal ring motif in urban planning. This town of the sixth period follows very exactly established construction laws and shows a strictly geometric order.«

As we approach the town we walk through huge parks more reminiscent of baroque gardens than of fields and woods, meadows and farms that are necessary for daily existence. We are now standing in front of one of the four temple-like façades of the public buildings that accentuate the outer ring of the town. On both sides, the eight streets lead to the center crowned by a delicate rotunda temple. The blocks of houses are up to seven stories high, with wide streets between them. All the buildings are very solidly built of stone, bricks, and wood.

»To subdivide the town I've created three zones, three rings. The first comprises the city center. The second contains the suburbs and the factories. The third comprises the area within which public meetings are banned, and the highways. The three zones are separated by green spaces with hedges, lawns, and flower beds, though these must not obstruct the view. Every house has a small courtyard and a garden, or at least a piece of developed land. All the houses are separated by an appropriate distance. They have a regular façade without many ornaments, though bare fire walls are not permitted.«

Fourier has developed the prototype of a very compact large apartment building that promotes collective contacts and makes possible efficient technical installations. He has drawn up the plan using exact dimensions and guidelines and has codified something like a set of building regulations. Still, aesthetic concerns are very important: »Guarantism is aimed at enabling us to have beauty and health. It might be quite likely that, as far as harmony is concerned, nature offers us a new path by way of the arts. It ought to choose the road of art, since that is the best way to satisfy all five senses at once. You'll see – architecture will be that new road.«

The monumental sculptures of animals and people that point the way from the town to the countryside are among Fourier's artistic contributions. One of his followers, Mr. André, has produced the beautiful drawings for the implementation of the statues.

We leave town by one of the wide roads, and the »town« to which Fourier now accompanies us fills us with amazement, as it has not the slightest bit in common with the guarantist town. Approaching the »Phalanstery«, as Fourier calls the complex, we initially think it is a gigantic baroque castle, a new Versailles: There is an enormous cour d'honneur, and the main section has a representative central projection. But our guide, Charles Fourier, tells us that this building houses an association, a cooperative that has 1,600 members. They are organized into sixteen »tribes« and 32 »choirs«, which means that each consists of 50 persons. They have 1,200 hectares of land.

If it had not been for the fact that Mr. Fourier is our guide, it would have been difficult for us to view this interesting institution, as no one else may enter the »palace«, for otherwise the order of domestic work and the quiet of the Phalanstery would be disturbed.

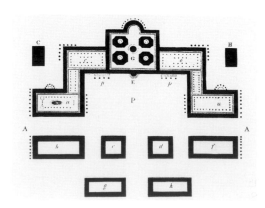

In the impressive complex we find the apartments in the center. They are all clean and comfortable, but are differentiated in size and elegance, for the Phalanstery is inhabited by wealthier and poorer people. However, the wealthy and the poor are not separated from each other. Fourier definitely supports class differences and rejects any kind of egalitarianism. And of course everyone can have adequate private property.

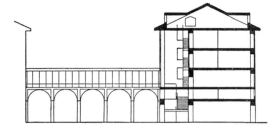

According to a very economical system heat, water, and light are provided in every part of the buildings. Adjacent to the residential wings there are large dining halls and kitchens, libraries, kindergartens, schools, sanitariums, auditoriums, rooms for arts and crafts, conference rooms, a perfect social infrastructure. Everything serves peaceable functions, including the town hall, of course, and the so-called »stock exchange«.

The latter is the room where the workers' individual and official programs and daily entertainment are discussed. This meeting is always set for the noon hour.

A temple-like church with a »Tower of Order« has also been built. The tower provides a clear point of reference. With an optical telegraph, messages can be transmitted for large distances, which is a purpose served by a large number of carrier pigeons as well. The observatory, Fourier assures us, has scientific aspirations, and in the ceremonial room solemn festivities take place. Fourier now invites us to a noon meal, and we enter the large dining hall, where the inhabitants have gathered. *»You will be able to see for yourselves how delicious our food is and that at a third of the price of a home-cooked meal we can eat three times as good and rich a meal. Indeed, we live three times as well at a third of the price while saving ourselves the preparation and the purchase of supplies. You will also discover that in the ›series‹, the individual teams of workers, no one is cheated and that the people, who are only too often made sly and boorish by ›civilization‹, radiate love of truth and politeness in the ›series‹.«*

The public »gastrosoph« provides impeccable and healthy dishes and hygiene, and, in a large part, created the delicious meal we just had. After our meal we continue our extensive tour of the »Phalanstery«.

In the wing buildings of the »castle« are the barns and stables, all the utility rooms, and the workshops. There are also large courtyards. All imaginable trades are represented here, everything that is the inhabitants' true need and that we would also find in a large city is produced here. *»One courtyard has been made into a ›winter garden‹, with green trees, fountains, pools, etc., while another is a winter yard with resinous plants.«*

The covered, heated, and ventilated arcades are on the second floor. Continuous communication among the residents, and among apartments and activity areas is thus ensured. Mr. Fourier is particularly proud of these covered gallery streets: *»People can walk very smoothly through the house, through workshops, halls, businesses, gyms for ball games, banqueting rooms and auditoriums without ever being exposed to wind and weather, heat or cold. It is strange that during the past 300 years of studying architecture people have not learned to design healthy and comfortable living spaces.«*

From the galleries, there is direct access to the second-floor apartments, and stairs lead up to those on the third and fourth floor. Here, the community's apartments are lined up systematically. We are surprised by the vertical allocation of apartments according to age. The old live on the ground floor, children are housed in the mezzanine, while the adults live on the top floors.
In one wing, all the noisy workshops are clustered together – the cabinetmaker's workshop, pressworks, smithy, but also the industry gathering rooms of the children, which are generally very noisy. By combining them in the same wing, it is possible to avoid noise, an annoying nuisance in our civilized cities.

The other wing contains an international hotel with bathrooms and guest rooms, so that the visitors do not detract from the domestic arrangements of the Phalanx. Now that we've inspected the interior of the buildings, Fourier takes us back outside. The big, impressive parade ground in front of the main façade is the public center of the Phalanstery. However, it does not serve a ruler's public demonstration of power, but rather the festivities that are frequently organized by the inhabitants.

Opposite the main building are the storerooms, studios, storehouses, and stables. They are grouped around a central courtyard for farm-related work.

»The structural system of geometry and order«, Fourier sums up, »is also a mirror of the human character. Every passion is characterized there, for human beings are in a harmonious relationship with passion. That does not mean that we do not address everyday details – the plans, diagrams, guidelines, time schedules, in short, a sensible system, help us do this.« Beauty, good taste, and perfection are relevant for everyday life as well. Factories assure that the residents have attractive clothing and pleasant homes.

Charles Fourier now goes into the details of the socioeconomic system: The fundamental basis is »le droit au travail – the right to work.« And Fourier elaborates: *»In the Phalanstery property has by no means been abolished. Rather, traditional wages have been abolished, but dividends are paid to the workers. For a society to function smoothly, it is absolutely necessary that there be a certain degree of inequality.«*

155. After Charles Fourier, Phalanstère, 1830. Section.

Everyone in the Phalanstery works in a »productive association«, does a minimum of work and receives a minimum salary in return, but there is no moral and social compulsion to work, nor is there drudgery. But those who do unpleasant or difficult work get higher pay, though everyone is entitled to a minimal living wage.

»Work is attractive for every worker. It is up to him to make it varied and satisfying. People work in small groups not exceeding seven persons. The activity can also be changed several times a day, often even after two hours. This creative and individual work is linked to the liberation of industrial and technological development. The large variety of benefits is provided in order to make the work attractive.

The communal office is the house for sales, distribution, and storage of agricultural products. When these are delivered, the producer receives one-third of the value as an advance. Thus he can buy food at the lowest prices, since there is no profit involved.

During our walk we come across an unusual scene: A parade of men and women moves through the streets with music and flags. Are they celebrating a holiday? »Not at all. They're walking to their workplace. You can see that happiness and high spirits characterize the entire day!«

Agriculture is still favored over industrial work, but the separation of work into industrial and agricultural production is gradually being phased out. Trade is being eliminated, for according to Fourier it is *»nothing but organized and legitimized robbery under a mask of legality«*. The people of the Phalanstery live in a harmonious collective and cooperative. *»Farming associations will alter the fate of the human race, for they take into account the instinct that is common to us all. The completely free choice of work, determined by instincts, is our human destination.«*

The personal needs of each individual must be implicitly respected, but Fourier has no great confidence in the conventional family and marriage. He has replaced these with free love, the »ménage«. He has completely redefined the position of women. *»Increasing the privileges of women is the general foundation of all social progress. All the rights and potentials that men have are also granted to women. Woman is no longer the man's subordinate but his equal and rival, for this is the role nature intended for her. Nature gave both sexes an equal talent for science and art. Women in a state of freedom will surpass men in all intellectual and physical activities.«* Mothers are not chained to their children. While children are nursed until they are two, they are then given into the care of the society. A maid takes care of children from the time they are toddlers, and later her work is taken over by teachers. Women are supposed to receive their »majority as lovers« at age eighteen. From then on they have the right to take lovers, and the lot of the children born of such unions is to be regulated by law.

Fourier's love of systems knows no limits here either: Women over eighteen are placed in three main categories:

1. The wives, who have only one husband for life.

2. The single ladies (*demoiselles*) or demimondaines (*demi-dames*), who can change owners provided they take them in succession, always one at a time, and that the changeover takes place in a regular manner.

3. The courtesans (*galantes*), whose statutes are even less strict.

The wives, in turn, are divided into three categories: constant wives, doubtful ones, and faithless ones.

And in the next, or seventh, period of development Fourier's system describes yet another differentiation:

a) The accepted male and female favorites, the lovers, who have no children together.

b) The male and female friends, progenitors, who have a child together.

c) The male and female spouses, who have at least two children.

Thus it can happen that a woman has three children with her husband, one child with her friend, but is not allowed to have a child with the favorites.

All these options are open to every person, male or female. However, a man who wishes to have children is not dependent on his wife's sterility. It is a symptom for a woman's equal rights that she can have contact with several men. And when, after four years of majority as a lover, she has not found a husband, she can live as she pleases.

»The source of hypocrisy and lies is marriage. It perpetuates the oppression of women. We have found other ways for the sexes to relate to each other.«

The entire Phalanstery is responsible for the welfare of the children. This statement seems to be in stark contradiction to a strange practice: The dirty jobs are done by the children, for this is in keeping with their predilection for dirt and messiness. The nine- to fifteen-year-old girls are organized in »small hordes«, while boys of the same ages are grouped in »small bands.« They are up by 3 a.m. cleaning the stables and repairing the roads. Other groups *produce and contribute to the proceeds while they believe they are just playing. They willingly teach themselves about farming, crafts, the arts, and science.*«

Thus the children cover the cost of their education and upkeep from as early as the age of three.

We can't deny that the position of children in the work process makes us somewhat uneasy. However, we feel reassured when we see with what care the children are educated in the beautiful classrooms.

We meet these truly happy people, for Fourier does not try to construct happiness from the objective side of industrial production, but from the subjective side. He realizes that the development of all the passions is the motivating force behind human happiness: *»Happiness arises when objective wealth is touched with the magic wand of fully unfolded passions. The human passions are not chained by reason, or by duties and prejudices. The new society is based on knowing about mutual attraction, which is the impetus given to us by nature.«*

Nature intends that we should satisfy our passion, but when satisfaction is prevented, the result is chaos. For we can find perfect harmony only in satisfaction, enjoyment, and fulfillment. True happiness can unfold only in a correctly constructed society, in a societal order that will make the state and its rule superfluous in the long run.

Admittedly we cannot completely identify with Fourier's praise of happiness and individuality, when we look at the strictly regulated daily schedule, which is by no means the same for all residents, but lists many pleasures for the rich, such as hunting, fishing, and entertainment, while the ordinary residents work in the forest, fields, and workshops. The only identical feature is the beginning and the end: Everyone gets up at half past three and goes to bed at ten o'clock.

Here is the schedule for the two social groups:

For the wealthy		For the less well-off	
3.30	Get up	3.30	Get up
4.00	Meet in morning hall, conversation about night experiences	4.00	Take care of animals
		5.00	Gardeners' meeting
4.30	First break, quality control	7.00	Breakfast
		7.30	Men's meeting
5.30	Hunting	9.30	Vegetable farmers
7.00	Fishing	11.00	Stable workers' meeting
8.00	Breakfast, newspaper	13.00	Lunch
9.00	Gardening, meeting under the tent	14.00	Forest workers' meeting
10.30	Pheasant-run	16.00	Factory workers' meeting
11.30	Library	18.00	Watering
13.00	Lunch	20.00	Planning meeting
14.30	Hothouses	20.30	Dinner
16.00	Exotic plants	21.00	Entertainment
17.00	Fish pond	22.00	Sleep
18.30	Sheep breeding		
20.00	Stock exchange		
20.30	Dinner		
21.30	Theater, entertainment		
22.30	Sleep		

Remarkable – the almost military discipline that governs petty everyday concerns represents an incomprehensible contrast with Fourier's visions: He imagines that one day the entire planet will be covered with two million phalansteries for four billion people. The omniarch will then reside in Constantinople, the capital of the world.

As Fourier bids us goodbye, he utters a strange maxim: *»Sensual pleasure is the only weapon God can use to master us and guide us back to his design: He governs the universe through miraculous power and not through violence.«*

Fourier 1835, 1841, 1843, 1845, 1966, 1972; Bebel 1888, 1921; Ramm 1955, 1956; Considerant 1921; Armitage 1961; Choay 1965, 2001; Schumpp 1971; Benevolo 1971; Servier 1971; Bollery 1977; Tod/Wheeler 1978; *Stadt und Utopie* 1982; Höppner 1987; Brentjes 1993; Vercelloni 1994; Eaton 2001.

And how were Fourier's visions implemented? First, a student of Fourier's, Mr. Baudet Dulary, tried his hand at it. The first community was founded in Condé-sur-Vesgre near Rambouillet in 1833. But Fourier's ideas were not realized as he had intended. He was furious and felt that the project was a caricature of his ideas. When the community very soon failed financially – only one building had been almost completed – he was neither surprised nor depressed.

Two more attempts in France, one in Brazil, and one in Algeria also failed.

Nevertheless Fourier's thought came into fashion all over the world: »Fourierism« developed thanks to lectures, books, newspapers, and his personal commitment.

There was considerable success in America: Not less than 41 small »Phalansteries« were founded. They had only little in common with Fourier's bold structural model.

In 1841, for instance, George Ripley founded Brook Farm in West Roxbury, Massachusetts. The main concern of Ripley and his comrades-in-arms was the school system. They built a »Phalanstery« that burned to the ground in 1846. Three years later the community was dissolved.

The Hopedale Community was created in 1841 in Mendon, Mass., initially with only 30 members from different states of the union.

Around 1820 a German, Joseph Bimeler, comes with 800 compatriots to Tuscorora County, Ohio. Frances Wright founds the Shelby Community in Tennessee. Her concern is the education and equal rights of Negro slaves – and of women.

The Blue Springs Community in Bloomington, Indiana, lasts only one year, 1826/27, and the Forrestville Community, also in Indiana, begins in 1825 with four families.

The Northampton Association, founded around 1853 by David Mach, might be regarded as a precursor of Fourierism.

The Wisconsin Phalanx began in 1844 with 20 settlers and grew to 180 inhabitants, who primarily did farming, but the community was dissolved as early as 1850.

The Northamerican Phalanx in Monmouth, Colorado and New Jersey lasted the longest – twelve years. It was founded in 1843 at the instigation of Considérant (cf. following chapter), and its 112 members were led by Albert Brisbane and Horace Greeley. The »social palace«, two three-story buildings, 42 m long and connected at right angles, no doubt came close to Fourier's architectural ideas. The big, well-lit rooms had substantial furniture, and the view was of gardens and fields. The inhabitants farmed and worked in the trades and could choose their own working hours. A big fire in 1854, however, meant the end of the community.

Considérant, Fourier's publicist and admirer, was destined to have considerable success, however. Our next visit will be to his particular Phalanx.

The problems of whether to accentuate farm work or industrial work are important during the following decades as well and appear in the Communist Manifesto of Marx and Engels. Engels's assessment of Fourier's ideas is ambivalent: »Fourier constructs a future for himself after correctly recognizing the past and the present.«

Victor Considérant (1808–1893). The North America Phalanx, 1837

Considérant deeply respects Fourier, and is thrilled by his ideas: »We no longer built houses for the bourgeoisie, or the aristocracy, but a palace where *human beings* can live. We built it with art, with harmony and foresight. There are impressive apartments and comfortable rooms, so that everybody can live here happily, according to his taste. We've also provided studios for all types of work, halls for all aspects of the trades and for entertainment.«

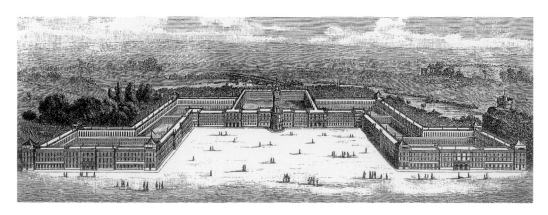

156. Victor Considérant, Phalanstère, in the manner of Fourier, 1837.

157. Victor Considérant, Phalanstère, in the manner of Fourier, 1840.

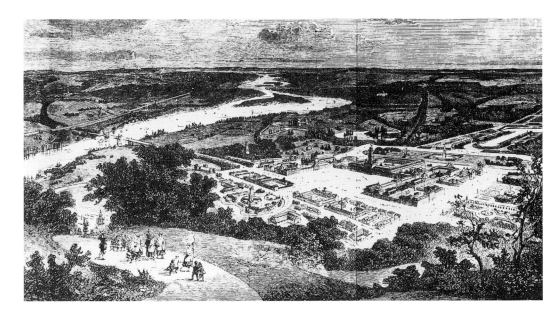

With enthusiasm Considérant describes the enormous complex of buildings, which vies with Versailles and which we are now approaching. *»A magnificent palace lies before us amid meadows, flower beds, and shady gardens, like a marble island floating in an ocean of green spaces. This is the regal residence of a population that has come back into its own. The extensive* cour d'honneur *is the gathering place of the legions of industry, the departure and arrival point of the active groups, and the square for parades, the communally sung great anthems, dramas, and maneuvers.«*

We already know the principle of the entire complex from Fourier. Here, too, there is a suggestion of Versailles: The middle section alone probably has no less than 50 window shafts. This section forms the main frontage of the large courtyard and has a central tower. In the rear there is a large enclosed courtyard, and at each flank three additional courtyards complete the monumental complex. The buildings throughout have from three to five floors. The corners and projections are barely emphasized.

Opposite the massive castle complex the buildings for industrial production are arranged in clusters, an then come the sheds for the harvest and the machine sheds and stables for the domestic animals that help mankind conquer the earth.

The noisy workshops and the »screaming« schools are located in an outer courtyard at the end of one of the wings. At the end of the other wing is the Caravansérail, a hotel for visiting strangers.

In the center of the palace are the rooms for the administration, the stock exchange, the banks, and the ballrooms and concert halls. They are close to the »Tower of Order«.

And Considérant has taken over Fourier's covered and glazed gallery streets as well, like so many other useful features. »The gallery street is surely one of the characteristic organs of social architecture. It is used for the main meals and for special gatherings. It is made completely of glass.«

Considérant has found architectonic solutions that meet both individual and societal needs for a total of 1,800 persons. The principle seems quite simple:

1. one house – separate from the others – per family,
2. a community center for gatherings of the families that make up the commune,
3. the farm and manufacturing buildings for self-reliance.

What impresses us particularly, though, are Considérant's artistic and aesthetic ambitions, which far exceed those of Fourier. He particularly loves the gardens and parks. The galleries and columns are filled with pictures and frescoes. Sculptures adorn the public spaces and the lodges. Shady gardens with curving paths, waterworks, and sculptures surround the buildings. Temples and altars invite people to worship.

One last surprise: We enter the large central courtyard and a flood of sound greets us. An orchestra with hundreds of instruments, choirs with a thousand voices make the walls shake. Hymns and poems are sung by the masses, accompanied by harmonious dance movements. The entire Phalanstery is involved in this multimedia performance.

Servier 1971; Bollerey 1977; Tod / Wheeler 1978; Brentjes 1993.

What do the realizations of Fourier's ideas look like? Again we cross the ocean to visit European ideas transferred to America.

158. Etienne Cabet, plan of Icaria, 1839.

»Charles Fourier is already dead«, regrets Considérant, *»But I brought his ideas to America, and Albert Brisbane, a capable newspaperman, helped me to spread them, and so I was able to found my North American Phalanx. Fourier's fundamental ideas of passion and community accompanied us; a harmonious daily life and attractive work were important for us; we practiced the equality of the sexes, though admittedly we did not consider the idea of dissolving marriage and the family to be practicable.«*

And Considérant sums up his premises concisely: *»Social reform without revolution, the creation of order, justice, and freedom, the organization of industry, and the nationalization of capital, work, and talent.«*

But in 1854 the buildings in New Jersey are destroyed by fire, and the land is sold. The Wisconsin Phalanx betrays the original ideals and fails. The land is sold in 1849.

Now we go on to Wisconsin: The Phalanx flourishes quite nicely, but it is individual, not collective wealth that grows.

Etienne Cabet (1788–1856). *Voyage en Icarie*, 1839

After an adventurous life Etienne Cabet accompanies us on his exciting *Voyage en Icarie*, on the journey to Icaria, and is pleased to tell us about all the innovations in this remarkable city. Icaria is located on an island, isolated from the world by mountains, rivers, and the ocean. Each of its 100 provinces is divided into ten municipalities, with its capital in the center. Each municipality consists of eight villages of four farms each. Railroads, streets, and canals link all parts of the island.

As we land in the island's river port, we are greeted by a monumental archway with the optimistic motto: *»The nation of Icaria is a brother nation to all the other nations of the earth.«*

We visit the capital Icaria, whose exterior outline has a circular plan, while the interior is laid out as a grid. A navigable river that forms an island runs through the city. On the island, on a large square, there is a public building, a palace with a magnificent, terrace-like garden. A colossal statue towers above every other building: It is Icarus, the city's founder.

The almost luxurious furnishings of the palace are astounding. A great deal of gold and silver is used. Crystals and jewels decorate the elevations. The windows have stained glass. On the roof there are gilt statues of outstanding men and women.

»The palace, the ›Great House of the People‹, is also a national monument and a symbol for the fact that now the nation is entitled to all the formerly princely splendor«, explains Mr. Cabet. Two rings give structure to the city. Each is a series of splendid squares, people's parks, and small people's palaces, 20 in the inner and 40 in the outer ring. The river, which divides the city, may be crossed by means of a cable railroad bridge.

Mr. Cabet reminds us of the Icarians' principles: *»In Paris and London I studied the advantages and disadvantages of cities and based on these insights I built a model city. It obeys the fundamental rule of the Icarians: First the necessary, then the useful, and finally the pleasant and graceful – principles the Icarians live by.«*

In Icaria we find wide, straight streets, and are surprised that many have four pairs of tracks installed on them. *»Most carriages are drawn by teams of six horses, and using the appropriate pairs of tracks there are no problems with oncoming traffic. Of course the carriages are there for all citizens; each has room for 40 persons. Private carriages are not allowed.«*

But how does traffic work in the streets without tracks if there are no private carriages? *»We have little carts drawn by strong dogs«*, Cabet replies. Icaria is a very hygienic city, wealthy and cultivated. The pedestrian areas are protected from thunderstorms and heat. Along the streets, there are up to three-meter-wide glass-roofed shelters, and the sidewalks are bordered by pillars. All the residential buildings are similar, four stories high, with a terraced roof, with gardens and drinking water. However, the façades are designed in different styles from one street to the next, and excessive monotony is thus avoided. Nowhere did we find a shack or a dilapidated house. The residential buildings were built on the basis of a contest in which all the citizens participated. The big interior courtyards are designed like parks. Family homes are vertical, including all four floors, in row houses, as it were. On every floor three rooms face the garden, two the street, and the windows have balconies.

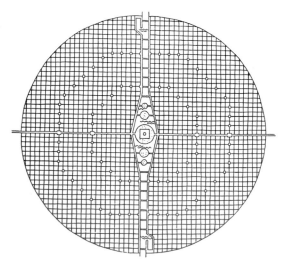

The ground floor houses apothecaries and workshops for each of the families. On the second floor there is a music salon. But we have our doubts how one family, no matter how many children it has, can sensibly use so many rooms and pay for them.

The city is divided into six districts, and each has the requisite public buildings – a school, church, and assembly rooms.

Icaria is quite »modern«. This is an industrial, centralist nation of workers with high scientific standards, a modern metropolis with technological equipment and up-to-date industrial production. We're particularly impressed with domestic technical conveniences: Water is piped into almost every room, and dirty water flows into a street canal. A modern solution has also been found for the toilets. Unfortunately, Mr. Cabet does not tell us what this is.

Garbage from homes and streets is neatly loaded by machines onto enclosed wagons and carted away.

The principle for all measures is clear: »Pedestrians must be safe and never be in danger of accidents caused by carriages or horses. And the city must be clean and orderly at all times.«

We can understand why pedestrian bridges and underpasses have been built along the streets that have heavy traffic. All the streets have gaslights giving lovely multicolored light through their stained glass cylinders.

Mr. Cabet now takes us to one of the national printing works. We discover that close to 5,000 people work here. The printing presses are on the ground floor, while the typecases are on the second floor.

What are the Icarians' working hours, we ask. »They're the same for everyone«, we are told, »six hours a day. In urgent exceptional cases people work for eight hours. And of course everyone is paid the same amount – whether he's a doctor or a locksmith.«

The huge bakery in six large halls a little outside the town is another surprise. Not a sign of people lugging sacks of flour or baskets of bread – everything is done mechanically, including transportation from floor to floor. And finally we visit the clock and watch workshop, no less impressive, and watch the incredible precision of the production process.

We have a clear sense that Icaria is a land of order and material abundance. But it is also a healthy city. The republic issues lists of wholesome and unhealthy foods. Clothing, which is produced in a factory and distributed to the families, also takes hygiene into consideration. There are only a few styles, but many colors and fabric designs. Mr. Cabet praises this wide choice: »Simplicity combined with grace, splendor and taste, especially for the female sex, characterizes our clothes. And both male and female clothing has a delightful fragrance.«

Mr. Cabet praises the beauty of city and countryside. »Outside the circular cities, farmland immediately begins – fertile fields and pastures, vineyards and flowering trees, and lovely groves, with picturesque villages in the middle of them.« The streets and squares of the city itself are richly ornamented with art and nature: carved columns and statues of animals, fountains and playgrounds, trees, shrubs, and flowers are tastefully arranged. Ponds and waterfalls delight the eye and improve the air quality. And everywhere there is the sound of music.

Artists are generously provided with public funding. Admittedly people make sure that virtue and chastity are preserved in the images. »*In the inner city there are no cemeteries, no dirty factories, no hospitals – all these institutions are located in a well ventilated spot near running water or in the countryside. The law assures that pedestrians must be safe. In one square you can find the ›necessaries‹, as elegant as they are comfortable, one for women, one for men, where one can enter modestly without offending against one's own or public decency.*«

There are no wild advertising posters, only well-designed announcements. There is also no retail trade, for because of their hard work Icarians receive all that is necessary for them to live on in sufficient quantities. And of course, vice has also been banished from the city, as are all the things that might contribute to it: In vain we look for bars and cafés, stock exchanges and gambling casinos, bordellos and barracks. Nor do we encounter drunkards, beggars, idlers, thieves, and adulterers.

»I wrote my *Voyage*«, Cabet tells us, »before the world became one great nation with community of property. But this community has not been created by violence and conspiracy, but by an exchange of views, discussion, propaganda, and conviction. It developed by virtue of public opinion.«

We are now invited to a splendid dance and wonder why many men dance with men and women with women. »That's quite normal«, we are told, »for women and men are allowed to dance with each other only as married couples.«

The Icarians are a community of total equality – and thus they all have the same daily schedule and the same menu.

But that's not all. They all have the same furniture in their apartments, wear the same clothes, have the same houses, the same education. What's the effect of this? Cabet gives us the logical answer: »All Icarians are also equal – happy and contented!«

What does the daily schedule look like? Cabet hands us one. It is the same for all Icarians and is quite startling: get up at 5:00 a.m.; at 6:00 a.m. the men take public transportation or walk to work; at 9:00 a.m. women and children appear; from 9:00 a.m. to 1:00 p.m. it's work in the factory or school. At 1:30 everyone leaves the factory and goes home to family, neighbors, the people's restaurant. From 2:00 to 3:00 p.m. everyone eats. From 3:00 to 9:00 p.m. everyone goes into the gardens, out on the streets, terraces, promenades, to the lecture halls and people's assemblies, or to the theater. Between 9:00 and 10:00 p.m. every family enjoys a small supper, consisting of fruit or sweets, at 10:00 p.m. everyone goes to bed, and from 10:00 p.m. to 5:00 a.m. the streets are empty.

But isn't such regimentation terrible? we risk a question. Cabet answers in the negative: »A timetable like that, and especially the curfew, if ordered by a tyrant would be unbearable harassment. But in Icaria the regulations are accepted by the entire population in the interest of health and well-ordered work, and I believe this is the most sensible and useful of laws.«

»In icaria, people have eliminated chance«, explains Mr. Cabet. And to our surprise this is true of the country's diet as well. The law dictates which foods are wholesome and which ones should be shunned. A council of experts has agreed on dietary lists. Dishes alternate, every day there's something different, and people can't complain the food is monotonous.

The »comité« even decides when and how long breakfast and lunch are to take, and what the menu will be.

But – we object – doesn't that mean the individual is treated like a child? »People are glad to observe an order they have created themselves«, explains Mr. Cabet.

There is only one family: the population of Icaria. »The republic where there is community of property is the sole owner, it alone organizes work and builds the workshops and storehouses, and makes sure the land is plowed, that houses are built, and that all items necessary for feeding, clothing, and housing every family are procured.« All citizens have the right to vote.

In Icaria we again encounter people who live in an ideal society with communal property. This system has developed slowly through mutual consent, convincing, and communication. In Icaria industry has an important role, and people have no intention to return exclusively to manual labor, for they hope »*with the help of machines and steam to increase productive power infinitely and to distribute equal wealth over the nation as a whole*«. Meanwhile, money has become superfluous. In the factory, everyone works under supervision, of course. Women work shorter hours to make up for time doing housework. Men begin work at 18 and finish at 60, women begin at 17 and finish at 50. But machines have made work very easy.

Marriage is seen as an absolutely moral institution. Children stay with their parents until they are five, after which they are raised by the community, the state. People's choice of a profession is determined by demand at any particular point.

Cabet is absolutely convinced that his citizens have the potential for happiness: »*Everything in combination makes work pleasant: Education, which teaches children to love work and value it, the cleanliness and comfort of the workshops, the singing that spurs on and cheers the masses of workers, the fact that all do the same work, the moderate working hours, and the respect paid to every kind of work in public opinion.*«

Cabet 1840, 1847, 1848, 1973; Ramm 1956; Mohl 1960; Benevolo 1971; Schwarz 1982.

Eventually Cabet risks the leap from utopia into reality: In 1848 he founds his Icaria in the New World, in Red River in Texas, his Icaria. Only 69 persons – initially without Cabet – cross the ocean, but once they arrive in America, they see they've been the victims of a gigantic fraud. Instead of the promised 400,000 hectares they find only 40,000. The properties are separated from each other, the soil is hardly fertile, the river far away. Then there are cases of yellow fever. Cabet arrives in December 1849 with 450 followers, and joins forces with other groups. Financial assistance arrives from France, and Cabet buys the town of Nauvoo in Illinois from the Quakers. Soon, 500 Icarians live there and the industry works well, the settlers are economically successful. But Cabet must give up his dictatorship, though he pushes through the prohibition of alcohol, tobacco, and extramarital sex.

At any rate, by 1849 the town has a communal dining hall, a school, a library, and a theater. Each of the families has its own apartment, while bachelors sleep two to a room.

The initial harmony is of fairly short duration. Two feuding factions develop. Conflicts escalate until there are strikes and street fights.

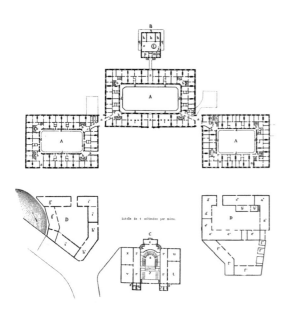

Cabet is driven out in 1856. He moves to St. Louis and dies soon thereafter. Of the settlers of Nauvoo, one group moves to Cheltenham in 1860. They manage to stay there for only six years. Another group moves to Corning. But eighteen years later, in 1878, there is another split: Near Icaria, New Icaria is founded. Icaria is transformed into Icaria Speranza and settles in California, but the settlers' »hope« was deceptive, for this community ends in 1886.

More and more, New Icaria deviates from its former communist principles and the ideal communion of goods. As early as 1896 this community, too, is dissolved. This marks the definitive ending of Cabet's dream.

The regimentation and enforced uniformity in this »ideal« Icaria terrify us. But are these not precisely the things that became a terrible reality in the dictatorships of the 20th century?

Even in democratic systems there is unavoidable regimentation: In every factory, the working hours are fixed, their control has become a matter of course, and every employee eats at least one meal at the same time as, and together with all the others.

Cabet's *Voyage to Icaria* became the most influential book of all early socialist literature. The »Icarian School« is said to have had close to 400,000 supporters around 1847; there was hardly a worker who did not know the novel, and the work was the source of undreamt-of new ideas. Control of food supplies, garbage removal, off-the-rack clothing, domestic utilities, urban art, cable railroads, two-level traffic, and many other things seem to be anticipated in the utopian Icaria, even though many institutions are very authoritarian in character.

Jean-Baptiste André Godin (1817–1888). Familistère, 1859–85 and up to 1968

Where shall we begin this tour of Utopia? With Godin? By no means: We'll start back in time with Fourier, as well as with Owen and Cabet.

And now, with Godin, much to our surprise, we immediately jump into reality – and into the past – and walk through Familistère near Guise in France. The community was active until 1939 and the buildings still stand. The utopian part is an imaginary Godin as our guide.

André Godin tells us that he was a workingman who enthusiastically believed in the ideas of Fourier. Now Godin himself has risen to the rank of entrepreneur and has founded an urban community: »Familistère« is still filled with Fourier's ideals, but Godin is a pragmatist and knows that industry is a reality we can no longer escape.

Recognizing the signs of the times, Godin has shifted his focus from farming to industry as he founds a metal-processing factory. It is managed efficiently, although the profits are largely distributed to the workers. Godin primarily produces patented cast-iron stoves.

»My basic principle is simple«, says Godin, »glorification du travail et emancipation du travailleur – glorification of work, and equal rights for the worker.«

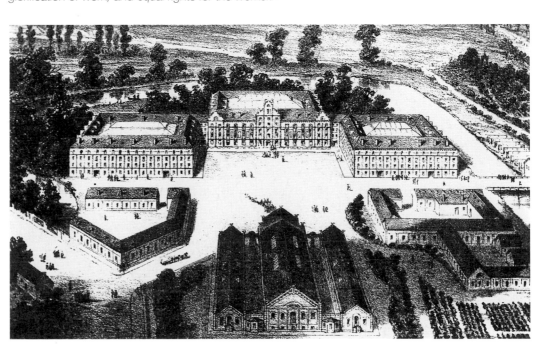

159. Jean-Baptiste André Godin, Familistère in Guise, 1859–85. Floor plan.
160. Jean-Baptiste André Godin, Familistère in Guise, 1859–85.

Godin leans on his own experience and on traditions:

»I borrowed many of Fourier's ideas and translated them into reality – including what he said about architecture.« We register all indications of a baroque palace as we approach the imposing plant (fig. 160). A large four-story building is located in a beautiful park, the concept is axial and symmetrical, the façades traditionally structured. But as we approach, very soon, we see the essential differences compared to the fantastic palaces of Fourier and of Considérant. The courtyards have glass roofs, and there are gallery streets on every floor here.

»These galleries«, says Godin, »are not just there for traffic but are public spaces, a kind of agora for communication between all inhabitants. And these come from all walks of life: workers, white collar employees, directors live side by side – and I myself moved into one of the apartments.« All the apartments can be accessed from the galleries and the pergolas. The roofed courtyards are truly imposing: Galleries and arcades, usually characterized by commerce, are here used for social purposes. These halls are places for communication, but especially for the many great festivals that play an important role in the community's life.

The astonishing thing about the building is its flexibility: Housing units can be combined and converted. Central heating and ventilation are surprising technological achievements.

»Fourier's Phalanx in no way resembles our buildings, for if one wants to found a harmonious community for 1,600 persons, one cannot use one of our traditional buildings, not even a large palace like Versailles or a big monastery like the Escorial. We built the three blocks in three stages – 1859, 1862, and 1877.«

Naturally they have every imaginable social and service facility: baths, swimming pools, a laundry, all of the proper size for the 465 apartments. In the *economat* people can shop at lower prices; in the store there is everything for people's daily needs, and a cozy informal restaurant is an added feature that contributes to conviviality. For single people there is a separate dormitory.

Optimum education is provided by a good system of infant nurseries, daycare centers, kindergartens and pre-kindergartens, and, of course, compulsory schools. In the Temple of Education these ambitions are represented symbolically, and the impressive theater serves not only entertainment, but also general education.

Godin explains why he built a complex that resembles a palace: »*Since it is impossible to make a palace from the hut or shack of every working-class family, we'll move the worker's home into a palace. Indeed, the ›Familistère‹ is nothing less than the social palace of the future.*«

In the »social palace« daylight floods every room. There are no dark rooms, no gloomy corners. The brightness of the room is the first prerequisite for cleanliness and hygiene.

Immediately behind the middle tract is the pavilion for the infants and toddlers, the nursery school and kindergarten.

Truly impressive is the huge children's hall, an airy hall with high ceilings and large skylights. The space is divided into six areas: four smaller ones for the babies, in lines of six cribs per row, and two larger sections for the children in two age groups. Approximately 30 of the smaller children have three or four attendants. In the middle there is a circular playpen. In the other section we see a group of older children dancing a round dance, while another group stands in a circle playing a game. There are not many toys, though.

In vain we look for collective institutions such as dining halls and community kitchens in Familistère, indications of a life of total togetherness. Rather, families have their own, beautifully furnished apartments and a considerable degree of privacy.

»When it comes to things that are used communally, we must take care not to restrict individual freedom. The tendency to be stingy is a danger we must struggle against.«

Godin tries to interpret the question of property in a different way: »*True equality does not mean that each individual is given an equal share, but that each is given a share that corresponds to his or her needs.*«

The next day Godin takes us to one of the big glass-roofed courtyards, where quite a few people have gathered. A stage has been erected, and actors are performing a scene from a historical play. The front rows are filled. Attractively dressed spectators are watching the play. But the flag-draped galleries are also crowded with visitors. Everyone is celebrating the first of May, Labor Day.

161. Jean-Baptiste André Godin, Familistère in Guise, kindergarten and day nursery, 1859–85.

162. Jean-Baptiste André Godin, Familistère in Guise, 1859–85. Section.
163. Jean-Baptiste André Godin, Familistère in Guise, 1859–85, Festival of Labor, 1867.

Now we have a chance to admire the surroundings of Familistère. Opposite the two projecting blocks are the farmyards and the utilitarian buildings, located right by the river. The slaughterhouse and meat store, sheds and stables, workshops and baking ovens are located here, and strangely, in the building on the right, this is where the restaurant, café, amusement center, and casino can be found.

Between the blocks and at some distance from the main buildings is the school, reflecting the clever educational system. The age structure has been rethought, a seven-part system has been developed, and the fact that the school has an auditorium and theater means it is used both for education and leisure activities.

And now a look over the bridge across the river: a laundry and swimming pool are located in a separate building.

We have time for only a short informative look at the extensive manufacturing plants. Up to 2,500 workers are employed here in a cooperative enterprise.

Godin himself is a wealthy man and is said to have something like five million francs in the bank. He explains his great idea to us: »Large properties are to be gradually eliminated by means of a progressive inheritance tax – and this is how we can get rid of social misery. We must promote worker participation and profit sharing.«

In 1880 we revisit the Guise plant and discover to our great surprise that Godin has transferred his factory to the workers and transformed it into a workers' cooperative. Thus he has single-mindedly implemented his idea of making the workers their own masters and making it possible for them to receive the proceeds of their work.

Again we are profoundly impressed by the reality of Familistère in Guise, though we find only a social island on which a few fortunate people can protect themselves from society, and it has been a long time since they worked in Godin's factory. At any rate, there were up to 1,800 inhabitants in Familistère, which was built in separate stages, roughly 100 apartments at a time. In the 1960s we call in Guise once more and are most surprised that long after Godin's death in 1888 there is still an iron factory here. Admittedly lifestyles have changed. And we visit the little town again in 2006, only to discover that the association was dissolved as late as 1968 and production stopped, while the buildings were used somehow or other.

The »social palace«, however, has been turned into a »utopia museum« at a considerable cost. In other words, in the long run none of the original idea has survived? Did it remain a utopia? Not at all – for again we note that utopias, models, implementations of this kind have been magnificent milestones on the road of social development.

Asch 1914; Choay 1965, 2001; Benevolo 1971; Hayden 1976; Dilas 1994.

Pierre-Joseph Proudhon (1809–1865). A people's bank, 1849, and a visit in the Swiss Jura mountains, 1872

»What is property?« asks Pierre-Joseph Proudhon. His answer is succinct: »Property is theft.« But he does see that there are certain distinctions. Not every piece of property must be damned, only dom, and in Proudhon's society all persons have an absolute right to that which they produce by their own work – but no one exercises that right over the means of production.

»For me, individuality is the criterion of social order, and politics is the science of freedom, of the personality. The root of property is in human nature and in the necessity of things. All human beings are proprietors, but property must be kept so small that it cannot become a means of subjugating others.«

Proudhon sums up his endeavors and demands in pregnant sentences:

Abolish the enslavement of human beings by machines.

Subject capital and the state to the control of work.

Guarantee the political equality of all citizens by the circulation of capital.

Design a public education system that raises the intellectual level of the entire nation and thus necessarily leads to the equality of all functions and capabilities in the service of the community.

The proceeds of production are distributed equally, with the burden on large industrialists, and in favor of a large number of small manufacturers. Goods, which are manufactured with the community's own means of production, are delivered to a kind of central exchange, the »people's bank«, in return for vouchers, and the people's bank also gives interest-free credit.

Society relies on »mutualism«, on mutual, free agreement with contracts where property is equally shared. And Proudhon's experience shows that the bourgeoisie and proletariat come closer to each other in the petite bourgeoisie, when there is reconciliation between the classes.

This social reform has made it possible that the state, this instrument of oppression, has lost its importance and been dissolved, while the economic system has basically been preserved.

Proudhon explains the three principles of a progressive urbanism: »First of all, there is the necessary struggle against the morbid pursuit of the past, in order to promote a global form of modern existence; then there is the need for rationalizing our behavior in the environment; and finally, we must recognize the role of industry in the city of the future.«

Proudhon understands that we care for and preserve museums, obelisks, and old architectural edifices. »But if we leave out of account the decorative values, over and above the building's use, then the masterpieces of architecture in Paris are without doubt the prisons of Mazas and the central market.«

For Proudhon religion has an important role: It is God who guides society by his eternal laws, and Proudhon wishes to proclaim his proposed reforms in the name of the Eternal, give them the solemnity that emanates from the power of an insight that overcomes everything.

»Human beings are subject to a predestined necessity – an absolute and irresistible order. But if this order is to gain acceptance, human beings need to discover it.«

Proudhon 1849, 1927; Diehl 1888; Choay 1965, 2001; Buber 1967; Servier 1971; *Nouvelles* 2001.

We find the connection to reality in a surprising place: in the Jura Mountains, in Switzerland. The village clock- and watchmakers combined their trade with farming and preserved their independence. Proudhon was tremendously impressed. It is here that he also met Peter Kropotkin. He was very interested in the latter's anarchist theses and, for a brief period, was pleading for the elimination of the state, a means of oppression. Proudhon had great expectations of the »people's bank«, a kind of exchange bank, but it lasted no more than six months.

As early as 1843 Proudhon writes about *Creating Order in Human Society*. He has friendly contacts with Karl Marx, but soon there are crucial differences of opinion.

Mikhail Alexandrovich Bakunin (1814–1876) and Pyotr Alekseyevich Prince Kropotkin (1842–1921). An anarchist (»collectivist«) society, c. 1860

Here are some of Bakunin's successes: Humanity has finally liberated itself and lives in perpetual peace without any constraint from outdated systems.

First we got rid of all religions, especially Christianity, because it promoted the »*impoverishment, enslavement, and annihilation of humanity to the advantage of the deity.*« ... »*We recognize only the absolute authority of science. Outside of science we declare everything to be false, arbitrary, despotic, and fatal.*«

»Science has become the property of all and is no longer the domain of predominant scholars. It has fused with the immediate and real life of all individuals.«

»Up till now the state, like religion, has been a necessary evil, but both have been abolished. The state, however, was not society, only its brutal and abstract historical form.«
The exploitation of some people by others has been finally abolished. »Exploiting people and ruling over them is one and the same thing, but we have also abolished governments, we've abolished states, and only by doing so have we recovered our freedom.

»The social organization we have created goes from the bottom up and is based on the ›association and federation of the workers‹.«

The free, godless internationale of labor immediately replaced power, though not by seizing property but by destroying the power of the state. Economic freedom followed immediately.

»All types of rule of people over people are now abolished. The means of production are communally owned and all products are the property of the entire society. Large private property had to be abolished. There is now solidarity as small groups of cooperative owners, and small owners work together.«

And there is a common-law brotherhood, just as there is common-law marriage.

»Anarchy is now a reality – though it is anything but chaos and terror – it is the emancipation of humankind.«

What has Prince Kropotkin achieved in his new society? A fundamental insight has gained acceptance: »All goods are there for all people. For all people have worked, each according to his or her ability, to produce the goods. Men and women have done their share of the work and that is why they have a right to a fair share of the goods – but this share is sufficient to guarantee their well-being. In other words, we have not distributed the goods in proportion to the contributed labor and volume of work, but to actual needs.«

Admittedly, Kropotkin again discarded his idea of coupons for labor instead of money, for he believes that such coupons could again exert a kind of pressure. The producers, who are both workers and owners, have organized as grass-roots communes, in a network of cooperation, and this system has made the state completely superfluous.

It is Kropotkin's achievement that agriculture has been taken into account in the social reforms. But landed property has been decentralized. In other words, land belongs to those who cultivate it, and farmers form cooperatives. State and feudal landed property has been abolished. »*History has given us the task of establishing free village communities.*«

The great synthesis of agriculture, industry, and the trades has now been achieved. However, industry no longer means the capitalist mega-factory, but takes the form of socially organized production with the full assistance of machines. There's no going back to manual labor, machines have been accepted – but they belong to the community. They are located in the village. Factories are built amid the fields, and the producers produce primarily for themselves. Men and women spend part of their working hours in the fields, under the open sky, where the air is fresh. No doubt a few concentrations of industrial plants are unavoidable, for instance, in the case of iron foundries or shipbuilding. But those are technical requirements, and do not serve the capitalists to dominate the market.

»*Everyone works in the fields and performs certain industrial tasks, and everyone combines scientific knowledge with knowing how to do a skilled trade – that is the endeavor of civilized nations.*«

In order to bring this about, education must be placed on a completely different basis. We are given interesting insights into Kropotkin's educational principles. The schools provide an ideal combination of intellectual and technical training. Everyone is encouraged to complete an apprenticeship in a specific trade.

»*Complete scientific knowledge is combined with complete knowledge of a handicraft.*«
Specialization is necessary, no doubt, but such training is not provided until a person has re-

ceived a general education in science and handicrafts. »Education intégrale« – a combination of intellectual and manual work is a reality.

»We were utopians – but we were right in believing that revolution would ensure that all human beings had housing, clothes, and food. The industrial crisis exploded in the very middle of the revolution, and there was ferment for more than twelve years, but progress could not be stopped.«

Bakunin 1974; Kropotkin 1912, 1921; Armytage 1961; Choay 1965, 2001; Buber 1967; Tod / Wheeler 1978.

The anarchy of Bakunin, Kropotkin, and their supporters was borne by a great wave of idealism, the conviction that human beings basically have ethical qualities and that people can live without any kind of rule.

Anarchy (anarchism) became the bugaboo of bourgeois society and there was continuing opposition to it. The recent resurgence of anarchism in the 1960s is linked to political terror, which is why it was bound to fail.

Wilhelm Weitling (1808–1871). The ideal Christian-Communist state (*Die Menschheit wie sie ist und wie sie sein soll*, 1838/39; *Garantie der Harmonie und der Freiheit*, 1849)

Is it even possible to implement all the social demands of Christianity? we ask. »Certainly. Christianity was already implemented, by the early Christians, and that's something we need to remember«, Wilhelm Weitling reminds and exhorts us. »The references are quite unambiguous, and Christ gave us a clear picture of a truly Christian society – read the Gospel carefully! We have understood and followed the commandments, and thus we now actually live in an ideal, happy society, leading a carefree, happy life characterized by justice, in the world of true communism.«

By no means did religion have to be destroyed; rather, it was used to emancipate humankind, for Christianity is the religion of freedom, of moderation, but also of enjoyment. »Christ is a prophet of freedom and love. Communally shared possessions and the abolishment of property are part of the Gospel. ›*Whoever of you does not renounce all that he has cannot be my disciple*‹ (Luke 14:33). And what does Jesus say to the rich man who fulfills all the commandments? ›*Sell all that you have and distribute to the poor*‹ (Luke 18:22). Jesus goes on: ›*It is easier for a camel to go through the eye of a needle than for a rich man to enter the kingdom of God.*‹

The letters, the Acts of the Apostles clearly state that the apostles, the early Christians, practiced the equality of all and the community of property: ›*We, though many, are one body in Christ, and individually members of one another*‹ (Romans 12:4–5). ›*Let no one seek what is his, but let each seek that which is the other's.*‹ And Acts 2:44 express the concept even more clearly: ›*And all who believed were together and had all things in common.*‹ The text continues, ›*They sold their possessions and goods and distributed them to all, as any had need.*‹«

We wonder whether the term »communism« referring to the Gospel statements is justified. And we ask, What is communism? Weitling gives us his definition: »*Communism is that state of a social organization in which all human powers, that is, all hands, heads, and hearts, every ability, every intelligence, and every emotion are set in motion to ensure for every individual – depending on the circumstances, which are equal for all people – as complete a satisfaction as possible of his needs, desires, and wishes or, in other words, as full an enjoyment of his personal freedom as possible.*«

Of course we cannot believe that the state through which Wilhelm Weitling accompanies us can be based solely on the Gospels. We ask Weitling to tell us something about its organization. He explains a carefully thought-out and intelligent concept of administration and organization. It goes without saying that it is based on the community of property, equal distribution of labor and of the goods produced by it.

The smallest social unit is the family, headed by the oldest family member. One thousand families form a family association and elect its administrative body. Ten such associations form the family district and elect the district administration. The latter elects a delegate for the congress of the great family federation, and the congress elects a senate, the highest legislative authority.

And thus it has become possible for the aristocracy to be abolished. There are no longer any rich or poor people, all are free to schedule their own working hours, people are able to travel at all times, and dance, theater, and other entertainments benefit all people. The equal distribution of labor and pleasure guarantees the most perfect social coexistence.

We've become very curious what the city looks like. First we visit one of the five blocks of houses, the so-called community building. Its floor plan is a pentagon, no doubt a rare form for a building. »In the middle is the association building«, Mr. Weitling shows us. »It houses the apartments and offices of the administrators, *the educational institution, the post office and transportation building, storerooms for supplies, apartments for visiting travelers and the industrial brigades, the people's hall with the speakers' tribune, the theater, the observatory, and the telegraph office. In the vicinity there is the community association's garden.*«

The sides of the community building's pentagon are occupied by the apartments of all remaining members of the family association. Every association represents a social and economic unit. The apartments, as we saw with our own eyes, are all spacious, appropriate to the family's needs, and attractively furnished. We are especially impressed that the apartments can all be heated to the same temperature.

Abundant provisions have been made for education and leisure time. We admire the ballroom and dining hall, the library, the exhibition halls, and meeting rooms.

Special attention is paid to the schools. Outstanding among these are the art and trade schools.

»The interior of all buildings must combine comfort, beauty, and economy«, adds Weitling. The streets inside the complex therefore have glass roofs to protect pedestrians from rain and wind, and there is a ventilation system for summer.

Just now, a wagon full of men drives past. Where are they going? »Field workers no longer walk to the fields but are taken there by horse and wagon«, Mr. Weitling informs us, »and they bring along portable tents that will protect them from rain and sun.«

Mr. Weitling praises the many practical advantages of community of property: It does away with all shortcomings, and the community kitchen functions much more economically. Farming and cattle breeding are pursued scientifically, and no one has to work more than six hours daily. People have time for travel to distant countries, and gradually everyone learns the universal world language.

»*Community of property*«, says Mr. Weitling in conclusion, »*is the salvation of the human race; it creates paradise on earth, as it were, by transforming duties into rights and nipping many crimes in the bud.*«

The realization of this paradise was only made possible by the Christian virtues, wise policies, courage, and brotherly love.

Weitling 1971.

Only a few biblical quotations lead us to believe that the early Christians had community of property, but they are sufficient for us to conclude that ideal communist communities did exist. Thus Wilhelm Weitling develops his almost effusive ideal.

A real attempt to create an ideal Christian state, but one that by no means claims to be a theocracy, is the experiment of the Jesuit communities in seventeenth-century Paraguay.

Moses Hess (1812–1875). The holy kingdom (*Die Heilige Geschichte der Menschheit von einem Jünger Spinozas*, 1837)

Something that history has long demanded has now actually happened: France and Germany, which have always belonged together, have formed a peaceful union. But humanity has created an even stronger union: Not only thought and existence, but thought and action have come together.

Moses Hess has founded a communism of a completely new type, though Marx and Engels ridicule it: »*The idea of communism is love, the law that governs our lives, applied to social life.*«

And Moses Hess has actually founded his state on this principle: It is the New Jerusalem. However, to our surprise, it is not found in the Near East but in the middle of Europe, in the center of the united countries France and Germany.

The holy kingdom of Moses Hess encompasses not only Judaism, but also a completely reinterpreted Christianity, indeed the whole world. It has indeed become an ideal kingdom, and we can see for ourselves that people live here in happiness and peace. We understand what makes this possible:

»*Politics is founded on holy, eternal principles and is maintained by devout and loyal people. Each person devotes his full strength to the fatherland. Villages are adorned with fine buildings and cities with lovely gardens. The entire country is a big garden. Men and women are bound by the tie of free love. In the holy kingdom, the restraint of marriage has disappeared, and marital union is no longer a chain of enslavement.*

The state has replaced the family in educating the young. Only when people no longer need to live under an external law because everyone carries the law within his heart – only then can each two parents form their own state again.«

It is not the long fought-for separation of religion and politics that is the ideal, but just the opposite: »*In this new, holy union religion and politics are one again. In the kingdom of God we lack neither the means nor the goodwill to create all the useful institutions we need: hospitals to heal all the fools and sinners, all the weak and sick, all those who need help and suffer deprivation. People have grown physically and mentally stronger.*«

Moses Hess is aware that this ideal life, that the prosperity attained by everyone was made possible only by means of machines. For the first time in human history it has become possible to overcome the material, to vanquish poverty.

In parting Moses Hess hands us his catechism. After all we have heard and seen we are not surprised to find that he has declared there is no contradiction between communism and Christianity.

Dirx 1982.

Moses Hess met Karl Marx and Friedrich Engels. In 1845 Hess and Engels published a newspaper together. But they soon parted company: Marx and Engels considered him to be a religious crackpot and went in a completely different direction.

In Wilhelm Weitling (cf. chap. 7.2) we find many parallels to the ideas of Moses Hess.

Karl Marx (1818–1863) and Friedrich Engels (1820–1895). The classless state, 1848, 1882, 1917

The process of disintegration among the ruling class, within the entire old society became violent and glaring. Part of the ruling class broke with this outmoded society, joining the revolutionary class, the proletariat. »*The proletarian movement is the independent movement of the overwhelming majority in the interest of the overwhelming majority.*«

The entire superstructure of strata that form the official society was exploded.

With pride and enthusiasm, Karl Marx explains that the theses of the *Communist Manifesto*, which he wrote in 1847/48 together with Friedrich Engels, have come true in every way: Thanks to the organizing of the proletarians of all countries the classless society has become a reality. »*Épatez la bourgeoisie*« – the bourgeoisie has been eradicated, the proletariat has won political power. Communism has done away with bourgeois property – private property.

Capital has been transformed into communal property that belongs to all members of the society. The means of production have been transferred into the hands of the proletariat. Accumulated labor is now a means of expanding, enriching, and promoting the workers' life process. The present rules over the past, not vice versa as hitherto. Through the nationalization of the means of production, those without possessions became subjects of the economy. People are now in a position to determine their own forms of public ownership consciously and rationally. Their relationships to each other no longer depend on heteronomy, but on their own wishes. The »market« has lost its omnipotence. Everyone works for everyone and is thus satisfied.

Each individual works according to his ability – yet no more than eight hours a day – and lives according to his needs – the second phase, communist society, has been attained. The proletarians of all countries have united. »*Gender and age differences no longer have social validity for the working class.*« The exploitation of children by their parents has been abolished, and women are no longer »*mere means of production*«.

»We have introduced the community of women – which has actually always existed.«

The expropriation of landed property has taken place, and the real-estate rent is used for public expenditures. The right to an inheritance has been done away with, the property of emigrants and rebels has been confiscated. The national bank, which holds the state capital, has the exclusive monopoly. The transportation system is in the hands of the state. Everyone is expected to work. Especially for agriculture, industrial brigades have been formed. The differences between city and country have disappeared. Children no longer work in factories, education is free of charge and public. »*The old bourgeois society has been replaced by an association in which the free development of each person is the requisite for the free development of all.*«

164. Frans Masereel, Revolt of the Workers, wood-cut, 1928.

And Karl Marx once more reminds us of the theoretical basis: »*It is not the consciousness of human beings that determines their existence, but conversely their social existence that determines their consciousness. Consciousness can never be anything but conscious existence, and the existence of human beings is their true life process.*«

Friedrich Engels takes another look back into the past as he explains the basis and development of society: »*The contradiction between societal production and capitalist appropriation comes to light as the contrast between the proletariat and bourgeoisie.*«

And Engels sees the end of state authority as a logical process. »*The proletariat seizes state authority and initially transforms the means of production into state property. In the process, however, it ceases to exist as the proletariat, it abolishes all class differences and class contrasts and thus also the state qua state.*«

And then, logically, development continued. »*The intervention of state power in societal circumstances became superfluous in one area after another and died a natural death. Instead of a government over persons there was now the administration of objects and the management of processes of production. The state has not been abolished, it is defunct.*«

Beyond this, however, Engels shows us the profoundly human aspect of this development: »The struggle for individual existence has stopped. Only in this way do human beings definitively leave behind the animal kingdom. This was humanity's leap from the realm of necessity into the realm of freedom.«

Marx 1848, 1872, 1890, 1894, 1921, 1932; Marx-Engels 1848; Engels 1882, 1945; Muckle 1917; Choay 1965, 2001; Buber 1967.

The assessment of the early socialists in the work of Marx and Engels is very ambiguous, but essentially quite critical. Friedrich Engels refers to Fourier, Saint-Simon, Owen, and Proudhon as the founders of socialism. He sees the clear development of socialism from a utopia into a science, and has given the utopians an important place in the development, but they did not represent the interests of the proletariat. Karl Marx on the other hand finds that being a utopian means not being capable of modern economic development.

Thus the utopians are at best a prelude – drawing attention to the problems without far-reaching effectiveness. The latter could be realized only through the theoretical and practical activity of Marx and Engels.

It goes without saying that Marxism was anything but a utopia, and yet the immense gamut between theories on the one hand and the huge spectrum of socialism, Marxism, and communism on the other hand justify discussion in the context of urban utopias and ideal states.

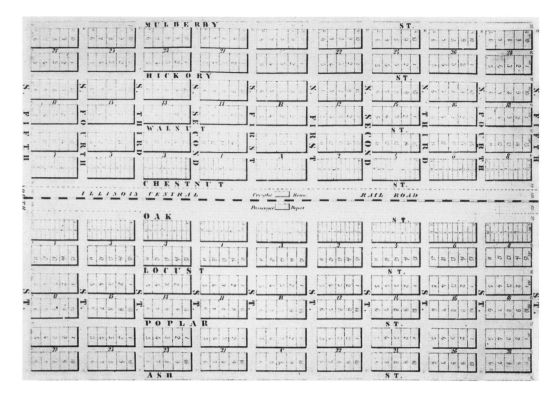

8. Dreamers, travelers, realists, c. 1850–1920

8.1. America, England

The Ilinois Central Associates. The Ideal Railroad Town, 1855

The director of the American railroad company is convinced: »The future belongs to the railroad and we will all obey it, because it serves our needs. And the towns of the future, too, will subordinate themselves to it.«

He's already developed the appropriate plans. They are rather simplistic: The Illinois Central Railroad whizzes straight from south to north and back again. All the blocks of houses are just as straight, each consisting of five large or ten small units in a grid that is repeated endlessly.

Longitudinal streets have names: Mulberry, Hickory, Walnut, and so on, while cross streets are simply numbered.

And the railroad stations are tiny: a passenger depot on one side, a freight house on the other side of the tracks.

Vercelloni 1994.

The rivers as the often only means of long-distance traffic have always been the occasion for founding towns. Now, during the pioneer era in America, railroads become an additional reason and a rigorous plan proposes the total marriage of the railroad and the town, a rational, modular structure.

Edward Akroyd (1810–1887). Akroydon, 1859

The textile manufacturer and mill owner Mr. Akroyd accompanies us to the village of Copley near Halifax in England. We feel as if we were back in the late Middle Ages: The long rows of houses, arranged in a square, ten in number, are parallel to each other and leave open only a narrow street between them. They are built in a romantic, Gothic style, not higher than two stories, with attic apartments and steep gables. The architects G. G. Scott and W. H. Crossland drew up the plans for this complex.

»It is not a village just for the upper classes, but for working people«, states the manufacturer. »The apartments have different sizes and are differently furnished«, continues Mr. Akroyd, »and that means different social strata will be brought into close contact. I am sure the lower classes can benefit by this.«

166. E. Akroyd, G. G. Scott, and W. H. Crossland,
Akroydon near Halifax, England, 1859–63. Sketch.
167. Henri-Jules Borie, Aérodome, 1865.

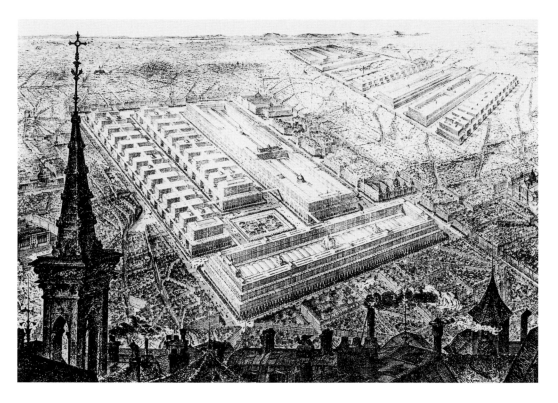

We are in a spacious square, a total contrast to the narrow lanes. Intersecting streets divide it into four green spaces, and there is a central fountain. »There is no castle, no church to mark the center, just a clear fountain for everyone's delight«, Akroyd explains the reason for the unusual village center.

We now visit the spinning mills where most of the townspeople work in beautiful halls under the best of conditions, as Mr. Akroyd assures us.

A model infrastructure has been planned. A school, church, and library provide education. There are gardens, green spaces, and fields immediately adjacent to the village.

Howard / Posener 1968; Bollerey 1977; Eaton 2001.

The village was actually built, though considerably smaller and with modifications. It is still in existence.

The reform towns express three ambitions of city planners: On the one hand, feudal architectural forms are adopted and reinterpreted, on the other hand the planners strive for a new architecture, and finally, as in Akroydon, there is a return to bourgeois medieval forms.

Henri-Jules Borie (c. 1865). The Aérodome, 1865

»With the Aérodome«, rapturously exclaims H. J. Borie, »we plan to improve life in the large residential centers. The air is bad here, traffic is noisy, and rents are very high.«

In Aérodome the houses along the boulevards are up to 40 m high and have numerous open spaces at right angles to the street. 12 m above street level the buildings are recessed 10 m, when, with a boulevard 34 m wide, the upper floors of the houses are 54 m apart.

»Let's imagine a second boulevard at that level, linked with the lower one. That way we get gigantic stepped buildings – we refer to them as inside and outside terraces, roofed with glass.« How do people deal with the great heights? There is a shaft connecting the floors. In it a steam-driven box moves vertically.

Choay 1969; Nouvelles 2001.

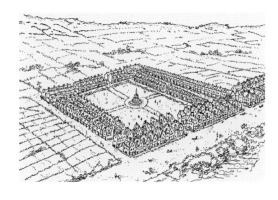

Henri-Jules Borie draws a blueprint for a city that is unusually densely populated for its time, in contrast with nineteenth-century tendencies to build more widely spaced towns. The public use of a second level is reminiscent of Asian and Native American architecture.

The steam-driven box anticipates the idea of the elevator, which is invented a little later in the United States and is driven by electricity.

Samuel Butler (1835–1902). The remarkable travels to the land of *Erewhon* (*Erewhon*, 1872), and a second visit to *Erewhon* (*Erewhon Revisited*, 1901)

We'll save ourselves the trouble of describing the long, adventurous journey to a strange kingdom. The land »on this side and beyond the mountain range« is called Aipotu. That's because in the language of these people our words are read backwards. In other words, we are in the land of »Utopia«, and the lovely woman who looks after us during Mr. Butler's friendly imprisonment, called Airam (or Yram), would of course be called Maria (or Mary) in our country.

»You must know«, Mr. Butler explains, »that in Aipotu being sick is one of the greatest crimes, and whoever commits this crime is imprisoned, of course. But on the other hand the population is very handsome. Everybody is good-looking, and my own healthy physical appearance, my blond hair, and blue eyes assure me the favor of the king and queen – for in this country these qualities are synonymous with a good character.«

We have indeed been struck by the beauty of the women. They are strong and majestic, of regal bearing yet graceful. And like almost all Erewhonians – including the men – they are dark-haired and dark-skinned. The many children we meet have a delicate, lovely beauty and seem unusually merry and lively.

While sick and infirm people are scorned and mistreated, evildoers, swindlers, even murderers are not socially discriminated against. Criminals are treated like sick people and can be assured of care. The victims of crimes, however –provided they're still alive, that is – can expect to pay fines for their misfortune.

There is an interesting institution, the straighteners. They can intervene in a quarrel, resolve conflicts, help, and give advice.

Sometimes it seems to us that the terms »beautiful« and »good« are simply interchangeable. And in the course of our extended visit in Aipotu we keep discovering that not only the words and values are reversed, stand on their heads, but that the entire population must be read »backwards«, as it were.

After an endless journey, we reach the capital of Aipotu. Great towers and fortifications give the town its special character. Tall, palacelike buildings predominate. A palace on a low hill is the house of the mayor. The huge garden is terraced, with broad stairs from one terrace to the other, ornamented with artistically perfect statues. Different kinds of shrubs, all new to us, have been planted in big stone vases. On both sides of each staircase there are rows of old cypresses and cedars, and then come vineyards and orchards.

We've now reached the extremely tastefully designed house of the mayor. In the middle of the courtyard is a pool with a fountain. The rooms we enter are spacious though somewhat bare, with high ceilings. The mayor receives us warmly though skeptically. While it seems we are prisoners, we are nevertheless able to study further strange aspects of the country in the months that follow.

Our first visit is to a »musical bank«, a magnificent building whose construction is peculiar but classic. We enter through an archway and see the majestic towers of the bank, an epic in stone and marble, across a green lawn. We are delighted and fascinated. Inside, there are painted glass windows. Strangest of all, men and boys are singing in one part of the building, accompanied by an organ; admittedly, it is a terrible noise to our ears.

We are then told of the strangeness of two currencies – without quite understanding them. Then we are able to be present at an unusual »festival« – everyone is very distressed, for they are troubled by the »ultimate inconvenience«: A child has been born. People swear at the child because of its birth and the godfather takes the blame for this misfortune upon himself. The child has come from a strange world of the unborn to be a burden in this one. The babies, represented by a lawyer, write a declaration of birth, beginning with the statement that the child was a member of the realm of the unborn, but entered the earthly realm through its own dastardly depravity and wickedly set about plaguing and torturing two unhappy people.

After all this we are no longer surprised when we are taken to the Colleges of Unreason, a fine and interesting edifice. Here, they waste the longest amount of time fostering and developing a hypothetical proto-language, instead of solving the many problems of society. But life would be unbearable if it were guided only by reason. »*It is not our job*«, explains one of the professors, »*to train the students to think independently. Our duty is to make sure they think like us.*«

We have long been struck by the fact that we have noticed no machines, fixed or movable, these achievements of the modern era, in this country.

»Five hundred years ago there was a civil war against the former settlers and owners of machines. We won! The machines have a kind of consciousness, just like people. That's why we had

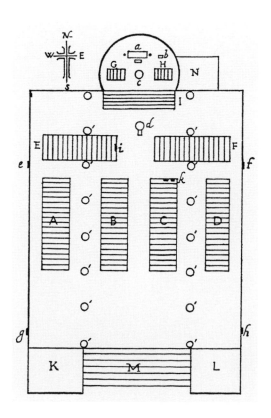

to destroy them all«, explains one of the professors. »A person can turn into a machine – and vice versa.« A look at the museum proves to us that they are familiar with the term machine. Here, beautifully arranged, are all imaginable, now historical, machines. The people themselves live approximately in a twelfth-century civilization.

What is more, not only human beings and animals and machines, but plants also have consciousness, of course. That presents no danger to us, however. We have spent enough time in Aitopu to get to know the land and the people.

Then we discover we are to be summoned to appear in a criminal court. Why? we wonder. It was because of the watch we own – in other words, a machine – or could it be that we are suspected of having measles? Whatever the case may be, it is time to take our leave. We manage to make a balloon and lift off before an amazed crowd of Erewhonians.

And so we return to our London home in a way that is no less adventurous than our journey to Aitopu.

We would definitely be very interested in finding out what became of the strange country of *Frewhon*, but a second journey seems too laborious, and we think Mr. Butler, who now calls himself George Higgs, can surely give us a credible report and the facts that interest us.

In fact, 20 years later, Mr. Higgs again undertakes the journey and tells his son John and us the most important news.

As expected, the long journey again involved encounters, adventures, new acquaintances, and curiosities. »Finally I arrived in the capital, now called Sunchildston«, Mr. Higgs reports. »And with astonishment I note all the things that have changed. First, there is the ›College of Spiritual Athletics‹, and in a store there are moral chest expanders against temptations; it is also possible to hire a certified nagger or have one's temper tested or be treated by a bore.

Another institution surprises me: Children who are too well-behaved and honest are sent to a deformatory, or at least whipped every time there is a slight mishap.«

The dislike, or even hatred, of machines, of everything that is modern stopped long ago. The great miracle for Mr. Higgs, however, is the report of his natural son George, whom he fathered with Airam (Yram) during his earlier visit, and George, whom he now visits, helps him in all perils and adventures.

While we do not doubt the truth of Mr. Higgs's report, we do question the effectiveness and purpose of many measures. However, we're used to the strange inversions from our first stay. »I think the temple will be of particular interest to you«, continues Mr. Higgs. »Naturally it is beautifully and carefully built. The richly ornamented main entrance is flanked by two tall towers. The towering south front has abundant and costly decorations.«

Mr. Higgs has brought a floor plan and now explains all the details. »A flight of stairs (M) leads to the building's entrance, which consists of a spacious nave, two side aisles, and an apse that is approximately three feet higher. In the apse is the altar table with two receptacles, one for the musical bank money, while the other is for offerings. Slightly in front of the table is the president's throne (c), placed in such a way that the president turns his back on the table, which indicates that the table is not a sacred object. In the apse there are a few pews (G and H) for the directors and their wives and daughters. In front of the steps of the apse there is a majestic pulpit with a lectern (d), and in front of this are more pews with backrests (E and F), again separated by gender. The nave and side aisles are filled with pews (A, B, C, D), and four side entrances (e, g, f, h) make it easy to empty the building quickly. Under each of the towers there is an additional room (K, L).«

Basically the interior is no doubt not very different from our churches, but Mr. Higgs describes a magnificent and unusual altarpiece: A fine carriage drawn by four horses seems to be ascending directly into heaven. It is the Sunchild soaring upward away from the earth.

Mr. Higgs gradually discovers the meaning of the painting and of the festival that is about to begin: »To my great surprise I learn that our balloon ascent 20 years ago gave rise to the belief that we are Sunchildren!« In the meantime the temple has filled with people. I am referred to as the ›Sunchild‹ of former days, and some think the temple should be dedicated to me. People vent their feelings in enthusiastic tirades or attacks.

In the meantime a wonderful solemn procession has formed in front of the temple. They wear magnificent robes, and there are priests and festive banners. In the temple, however, there is a tremendous commotion, but with George's help I manage to escape once more.«

Thus ends Mr. Higgs's second visit. Soon thereafter, in 1900, he dies. His sons John and George carry out their father's last will, and there is a loving meeting.

Butler 1872, 1910; Morton 1958; Schepelmann 1975; Trousson 1975; Heuermann 1984; Wuckel 1986; Seibt 2001.

The complete calling into question of a period and society is reflected in a kind of topsy-turvy world. It starts even with the names – Utopia becomes Aitopu – and ends with the assertion that plants have rights.

Some details are interesting as well: When we abstract the ironic exaggerations and abstruse scurrilities, we find astonishing prognoses: Today, too, the aesthetic is increasingly being given ethical dimensions. Diseases become »crimes« against society, made into obscene taboos. Many fields of study are turning into abstract, impractical oddities. Criticism and fear of machines (including computers and robots) plague us, religious practices are censured, and too often we hear that »the murder victim, not the murderer is to blame«. The »straighteners«, to choose another instance, would be referred to as »mediators« today, and children are not always regarded as a »blessing«.

Benjamin Ward Richardson (1842–1877) and I. B. Papworth. *Hygieia, the City of Health,* 1876

We know Mr. Richardson to be a competent physician, which is why it is not too surprising that health is the most important principle for his town. After all, he has every reason for making revolutionary demands: In England, industrialization with all its shadow sides has long since taken hold of the cities. Disease, early death, misery, immorality, and overpopulation have left their mark on the industrial towns.

Mr. Richardson's reaction is obvious: »In my town of 400 acres (100 hectares = 1 million m^2) 100,000 people live in 20,000 buildings. And it still makes the most sense to design such a town strictly as a chessboard.«

In addition to being loosely built-up, other hygienic measures in the broadest sense of the word include sports and educational facilities. In pleasing clusters, there are Turkish baths immediately adjacent to swimming pools, large halls for all kind of sports, as well as schools and libraries.

The method of construction of the buildings is clever: Instead of the traditional steep roofs they have accessible terraces. The chimneys are placed inside and are connected to wells. »The smoke from the chimneys«, believes Richardson, »is piped into these wells and thus detoxified.« In addition to the chimneys there are garbage shafts, and every apartment has cold and hot running water in the kitchen and bathroom. The bricks used to build the houses have perforations and are permeable to air, so that the houses themselves are also well ventilated.

The interior walls are painted in different colors chosen by residents, but any additional decoration is seen as superfluous.

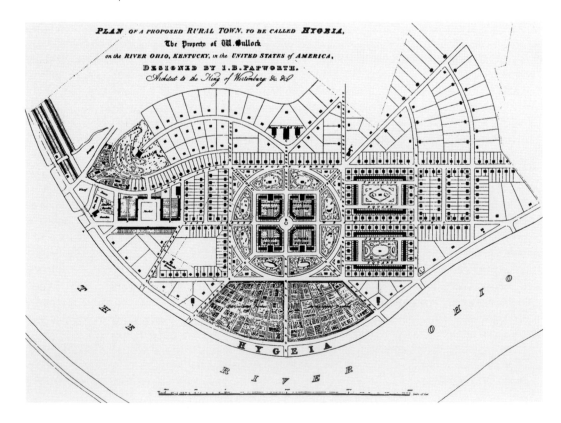

169. Benjamin Ward Richardson and I. B. Papworth, city of health, 1876.

The town has two wide main streets, planted with trees on both sides. There are railroad tracks for heavy goods traffic.

Richardson 1876; Choay 1965, 1969, 2001; *Utopia* 1978; Manguel 1981; Eaton 2001.

Fifty years later, we shall again encounter the concept that health goes hand in hand with architecture: Richard Neutra himself praised his famous Lovell House in Los Angeles (1927) as a »health house« and thus went down in the annals of the history of architecture. Today, dialogue about technology and architecture is dominated for long stretches by environmentally sound and healthy building design.

William Morris (1834–1896). *News from Nowhere*, 1884, c. *2000*

Maybe things got a bit too wild last night? At any rate, when we wake up the next morning we find ourselves on the bank of the Thames – a very changed Thames, to be sure. Blooming gardens and pretty houses are mirrored in the clear water. Woods, willows, and country houses radiate peace. We are somewhat confused – but a coachman offers his help. He's willing to drive us through the village of Hammersmith. And we are flabbergasted.

The houses are charming yet very solidly built, of red brick or half-timbering. The people are dressed in light colors, especially the women, and in the faces we clearly see that they enjoy life. Now we pass some impressive buildings: a gleaming, almost medieval hall, a central building topped by a cupola. It is the assembly hall and theater. Suddenly we catch sight of the silhouette of Westminster Abbey, followed by the Houses of Parliament. The coachman explains how they are being used today: as an auxiliary market and a fertilizer storehouse.

Having recovered from our amazement we enter a small shop to buy tobacco and a pipe. Children nimbly serve us – but we are even more surprised that we do not have to pay. Our guide solves the mystery: »Why should we pay anything? All the goods are in plentiful supply. Everybody owns everything, and envy and greed no longer rule.« Our guide adds: »Naturally there are also no thieves and no prisons, but also no divorce courts – after all, such courts only argue about property.«

What about marriage and partnership? »Why, marriage is also just private ownership, and especially ownership of the wife«, we learn. »It's become superfluous.« There is also no family. People are held together only by the bonds of affection.

And how is work organized? is our next question. »Work is not obligatory, everybody works when, how, and at whatever he or she likes.«

School and education are unfamiliar words for our hosts, as children learn without having to be part of an educational system and being locked up in schools.

And so we learn that there are no governments in the accepted sense. The entire nation is the parliament and in it everyone has equal rights. A police force has also long since become superfluous. And with the abolition of private property and of the government, people have developed a new attitude toward their neighbors. Art has regained the importance it deserves, and the citizens develop their appreciation of beauty.

Thus people live with joy in their work, in true brotherliness and love of peace.

Morris 1890; Bühler 1920; Choay 1965, 2001; Servier 1971; Trousson 1975; Berneri 1950, 1971; Heuermann 1984; Vercelloni 1994; Eaton 2001.

Once he returns to reality, William Morris describes the very real basis of his critique of modern society, which he formulated in 1894. Once again, he enthusiastically describes the ideal city:
»It would have a center with big public buildings, theaters, squares, and gardens. In a zone around the center would be the houses of the townspeople and smaller guildhalls, which in turn would be surrounded by parks and gardens; an outside zone that would also contain a district with public buildings whose gardens would not be clearly divided by boundaries so that this entire outside zone would form a green space with residential houses and other buildings scattered over it. Finally there would be the suburbs themselves, largely fields and orchards with small cottages, after which one would arrive in the open country with its isolated farms.«

The influence of Morris's paper was quite extraordinary. It contained many new ideas that affected not only the English reform movements, but also countries far beyond Europe, such as America and Australia.

170. William Morris, *News from Nowhere*. Frontispiece, 1892.

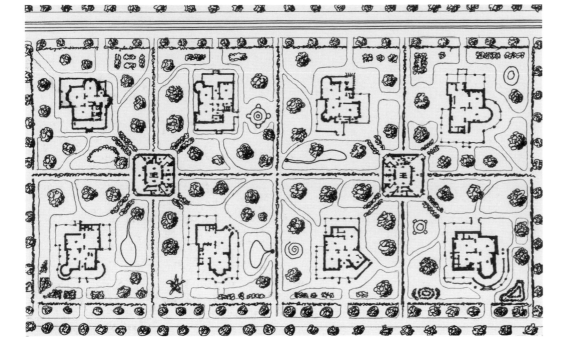

The Settlement Council. A unitary dwelling (Pacific colony) in Topolobampo, Mexico, 1885–95

»We believe that communal living can have very different forms«, the chairman of the settlement council tells us. »We didn't want to live in a big collective block. Rather, there was to be room for individuality to develop.«

It is true that each of the very attractive houses looks a little different, and each person has been able to structure the interior himself. »Each house has a different floor plan, and all the residents are very satisfied with their apartments«, the chairman says with conviction.

How is community expressed? »There is a common building for every four houses with a central kitchen. This saves a lot of work, particularly for women, and it is much more economical.« Beside the kitchen the communal building also contains a laundry, bathroom, and storage rooms.
What we like especially are the beautiful green spaces. There are some by every house, but people gather very frequently in central locations, and the children have access to the gardens at all times.

In the 19th century, with a wide range of visions from collectivism to individualism, the unitary dwelling represents an interesting interim solution that is again being discussed in the 20th century as well.

William Hesketh Lord Lever (1851–1925). Port Sunlight, 1888

We're all familiar with Sunlight soap, made by Lever Brothers – Mr. Lever produced 2,400 metric tons a week in the long factory buildings of Port Sunlight.

»A fundamental requirement for me is to create optimum living conditions for the workers. And appropriate housing is the first condition.«

But beyond this, Lord Lever believed that the most important thing was to fight poverty. Immediately adjacent to the factories, Lord Lever built a big settlement for the workers. Countless small romantic row houses form green courtyards. In the center there are a church and community rooms, and the railroad runs right by the township.

This housing settlement, too, was implemented with a few compromises, but the social expectations were not fulfilled. »Unilever« was created in 1929, and in 1952 further amalgamations created a huge group of companies headquartered in London and Rotterdam: More than 250 associated companies were formed.

172. Alice Constance Austin, sector of the city of Llano del Rio, California, USA, 1916. 1 community center, 2 parks, 3 residential buildings, 4 community facilities, educational buildings, 5 green streets, 6 streets for automobiles.

Paul Adam (1862–1920). The land of Malaise (*Lettres de Malaisie*, 1897)

Our journey is long – deep into the jungles of Borneo.
»According to my sources«, says Paul Adam, »students and supporters of Proudhon, Fourier, and Cabet founded this town circa 1850.«

Now it begins to make sense why in the tour that follows so many things are already familiar to us. It's almost a »déjà vu« experience.

In the town we are amazed at the luxury we find there. The comfortable houses are equipped with hot and cold running water and central heating. Electric light was probably retrofitted later, but the residents pride themselves on having invented a kind of gramophone long before Edison. The inhabitants' sense of beauty also seems to be well-developed: The walls are decorated with colored tiles, the floor is made of opaque glass, and the vaulted ceilings have discrete ornamental plasterwork. An oriel window looks out onto the streets. Paul Adam explains how the elaborate buildings came about: »There is a special department of national aesthetics that is in charge of the town's orientation in matters of taste. However, the artists do not express individual feelings, since the works are meant to represent the community's ideals. But this department also organizes a parade of beautiful young women every year for the delight of the citizens.«
It is the state that formulates what natural harmony is, and each person must obey the laws. The individual is subordinated to the state, yet there is total equality and community of property. Thus, money is superfluous.

Alcohol and tobacco are prohibited, of course. Something new, however, is the entertainment palace, where law-abiding citizens can devote themselves to group sex every week.

What happens to those who don't fit in? is our question.
»That's obvious. They're sterilized, and the criminals are drafted into the military.«
Adam 1898; Manguel 1981.

Surprising – and frightening at the same time are the totalitarian, dictatorial aspects that reappear constantly, often very vehemently. The sterilization of the »inferior«, for instance, clearly points toward fascism, as does the early nationalist education of the children – tragically all implemented half a century later.

Alice Constance Austin. The socialist town, in Llano Del Rio, California, 1914–38

Our guide to the Mojave Desert near Los Angeles is a highly imaginative and passionate woman, an architect and committed feminist. But this is no longer a desert: The colonizers have transformed it and it is »*as green as the plains of Ireland, unique and wonderful*«. An agricultural and industrial community with 10,000 inhabitants has developed here. Llano has become the metropolis of Antelope Valley, a »place of destiny« for all those who are looking for a home.

Ms. Austin is a competent guide. At first we cross a wide green belt that encircles the town. The strict circular geometry is continued in five concentric streets, crossed by no less than 32 radial streets, 64 of them on the periphery.

Your streets, we ask Austin, are rather narrow compared to Ebenezer Howard's – although in future they are expected to have a lot of traffic. »There's a reason for this. All business traffic including deliveries will be conducted underground, and so will railroad traffic, of course. And the whole infrastructure for the houses, and especially central heating, is located in the tunnels. Each family has a car, and cars are parked underground.«

We now approach the civic center, a carefully thought-out edifice. All the public buildings are lined up along a circular ring road. Each has a beautiful columned interior courtyard and is roughly the same size as the others, regardless of its particular function.

Our tour begins with the restaurant and market, then moves on to light manufacture and stores; then we view the church and temple, followed by the institutions of learning. The tour ends with garages and offices.

As we approach the center, we now stroll across well-tended green spaces with playgrounds. Small gardens also lie between the eight buildings we now encounter.

And now the passionate feminist gets a chance to speak: Directly adjacent to the large assembly hall that connects the buildings are the women's club and women's hall, right across from the men's club and the men's hall. Culture and city government are placed between these »poles«: the theater and library, bank and administration.

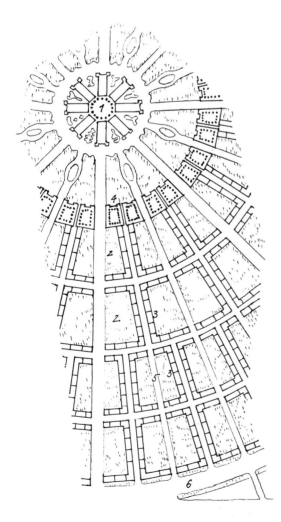

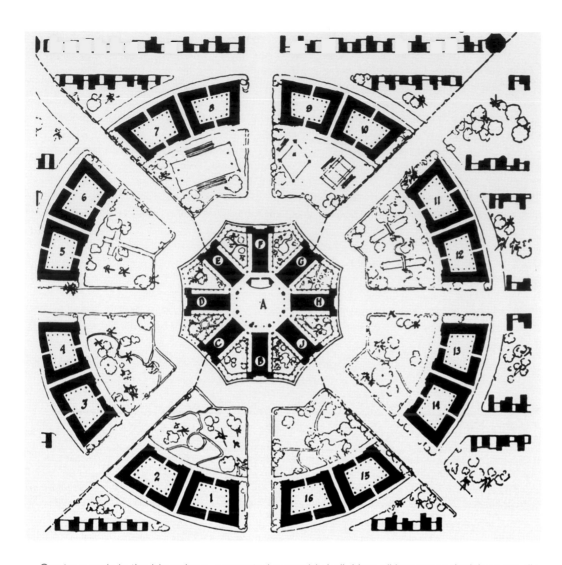

173. Alice Constance Austin, Civic center of Llano del Rio, California, USA, 1916, 1935. A assembly hall, B administration, C library and post office, D women's specialities, E women's club , F theater, G men's club, H men's specialities, I bank, 1 restaurant, 2 market, 3 groceries, 4 light manufacturing, 5 church, 6 temple, 7 college, 8 high school, 9 junior high school, 10 grade school, 11 elementary school, 12 school of philosophy, 13 hardware, accessories, 14 garage, 15 offices, 16 department store.

Our tour ends in the big column-supported assembly hall. Here all important decisions are discussed, and celebrations take place.

We now have the opportunity to look at one of the apartments, and are impressed by the varied and clever innovative planning. Austin is dissatisfied with the role of women in a sexist society. She rejects the traditional housewifely household. Laundry and cooking take place outside the house and are no longer the duties of women. »I despise our so-called civilization«, she states belligerently. »Every female personality is formed by paralyzing mental or intellectual oppression. Women are isolated in the home from early childhood and forced to adapt. Women must be emancipated from the endless and thankless daily grind of an unbeatable, stupid, and inefficient system that deprives them of a chance to work.« For the domestic life of a socialist woman she demands »*a peaceful and lovely environment in which she enjoys leisure and performs her duties as a wife and mother that are not dominated by cooking and doing the laundry*«.

It is quite surprising how often Austin stresses family education, for we find no public institutions for child care – children are supposed to remain in the bosom of the family.

The town has continuous street façades. We find the very different designs of the front of the houses surprising. Here, we have the illusion of being in an Italian village, while soon thereafter we seem to be in a Mexican pueblo. The public parks are very attractive, but there are also private open spaces near the houses, separate from the public green spaces. »The home gardens«, says Austin, »ensure privacy and prevent conflicts between neighbors and make the raising of children easier, for the private outdoor space can be seen at a glance from each room of the house.«

The homes have open sleeping balconies with awnings. People can enjoy the mild climate and the wonderful view of the mountains here. There is built-in furniture with folding beds that react to the touch of a finger. Floor heating systems provide cozy warmth. »Yes, I believe that residents should plan their private gardens according to their individual taste. New types of architecture have developed in basically new circumstances. But each resident can also design his or her housing according to his or her own imagination.«

174. Leonard A. Cooke, plan for Llano del Rio, 1915.
A civic center, B schools, C stores and hotels,
D clubhouse, E garages, F industrial and business
sites.

The land and the residential buildings are owned collectively. It was the only way to create all the technical facilities: central heat, laundries, a community kitchen. It is true that a certain similarity for all is assumed as regards the houses and accessibility of communal facilities. And every family owns a car.

Hayden 1976.

For the time it was very surprising that a woman architect developed a new urban concept and was so strongly committed to it. Austin's plan was certainly influenced by Ebenezer Howard, but it cannot be denied that it is ambitious and original.

Llano del Rio was actually founded in the US in 1914, full of hopes and expectations, full of hardships and setbacks. Instead of the beautiful, solid houses, they first built simple tents, wretched huts, or adobe clay houses. There were too many problems for Austin's ideal concept to be implemented – particularly when it came to financing by the communities, which were dirt poor. There was too little water for the big parks and sewer systems. The settlers could hardly imagine eliminating the kitchens. In 1917 the financial situation was so critical that it was impossible to think of implementing the »socialist town«.

An earthquake and floods destroyed the modest beginnings of the town. The residents moved to Stables, Louisiana, and founded New Llano. Job Harriman promoted the dream of a socialist utopia. A few productions were organized, and music and theater were fostered. Not until 1939 did the community fail due to financial problems.

Leonard A. Cooke. Llano del Rio, California, 1915

Once again we visit a – very different – Llano del Rio in the States.

We are familiar with the hexagon as the ground plan principle of a town, but Leonard Cooke encloses it inside a square formed out of the peripheral streets. Adjacent to this are the six square fields, each a grid of residential buildings. »I followed the geometry very strictly. It also helps me localize the public buildings. The squares of residential buildings have a school in the middle. Department stores and hotels are located in the spandrel triangles, and industrial and office buildings are on the corners of the big square.« The very center is occupied by the civic center, a castle-like building. Lovely green spaces break up the strict plan.

Geometric playing with the hexagon produces stars, which can be seen only from a bird's-eye perspective. The combination of the square and hexagon does not produce any convincing figures.

For Cooke there are initially no opportunities to implement his project. Cooke moves to Louisiana. In 1917 New Llano is founded. Four hundred people are housed in 75 buildings. A hotel, hospital, theater, printing works, as well as schools and workshops provide education and culture.

Conflicts soon erupt, but are not resolved. The settlement is doomed to fail.

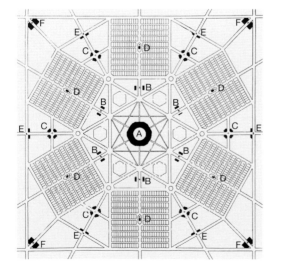

Edward George Earl Bulwer-Lytton (1803–1873). The coming race (*Vril: The Power of a Coming Race*, 1871)

Mr. Bulwer-Lytton assigns a professional engineer as our guide. The man has worked for many years deep underground, and now we descend into the bowels of the earth through a mine. A delightful world welcomes us, surprisingly bright, with clear streams, along whose banks there are vigorous trees and lovely flowers, meadows and woods.

Now we reach the town, built seemingly with great care, in a style resembling Greek but also Egyptian architecture. At the center there is a great hall. It is brightly lit and richly ornamented. The metal floor gleams wherever it is not covered by rugs. We go out again into a street formed by solid residential buildings on both sides, all with well-tended gardens.

We're curious to find out more about the society. In this troglodytic world the most intelligent person becomes the head of state. That means there are no wars, but one important aid is necessary: The engineer presses the »Vril wand« into our hands – this is a kind of magic wand. »Think intently about rising from the ground and flying.« And indeed, holding the Vril wand up in the air, we rise above the ground. »Vril is the wonderful force of nature that enables us to do so much, indeed almost everything, including defending ourselves against our opponents.« The people in this world have detachable wings with which they can fly out the windows and dance in the air.

And at once we get to see further instances of the miraculous power of Vril: The cool weather that prevailed when we arrived suddenly changes into mild temperatures. And the late twilight is suddenly illuminated by a brilliant Vril wand that plunges our surroundings into gleaming light. The Vril wand also gives people the energy they need, and it is obvious they live in an age of abundance.

In this society of *ana* and *gy*, men and women, crime is as unknown as poverty, and so there is no need for courts of law, prisons, or police.

During our tour we particularly notice the women, their build and stature. They seem to be more robust than the men. »That's actually true«, the engineer confirms, »and that's as it should be, for women choose their husbands, but make no use of their strength. The unions formed by the couples can be dissolved again at short notice at any time.« Women also have a very specific privilege: It is they who form the college of the wise; widowed and childless women especially are preferred candidates for this council.

Philosophy, history, natural sciences are favorite areas of study and research. Even more intensively, scholars devote themselves to the function and purpose of the Vril.

In the course of our tour we are astonished to see people of a very different type who seem to belong to another ethnic group, and we notice they have no Vril wands. We are told they are uneducated people, and the Vril people clearly distance themselves from them. Will this underground race, equipped with robots, not visit the surface of our planet some day?

One thing we find both amazing and disturbing is the work situation in a large factory. Highly developed machines do the heavy work, and the Vril wand is the actual driving mechanism. But we see only children doing the dirty work here, although the work is not difficult. »We've organized the children well. They're organized into bands under a chief, and every child performs the work appropriate for him or her.« The children are paid very good wages, which they save, and when they are grown up and ready to marry at age 20, they have a sizable capital and can spend the rest of their lives in leisure doing whatever they wish.

Private property is the right of each individual, but exploitation and poverty have been abolished.

The engineer now introduces us to an extremely prosperous, indeed rich and extravagant man – for goods are by no means equally distributed. Admittedly we are not quite convinced by his beliefs: »Very rich *ana* (men) like me are obliged to buy a large number of things that they do not need and to live in grand style. But we must bear our fate in this short transition through earthly life. Luckily my son loves great riches.«

Bulwer-Lytton 1871; Morton 1952; Schepelmann 1975; Wuckel 1986; Berneri 1950, 1971.

Bulwer-Lytton foresaw the future position of women with amazing acuity: Increasingly, in modern society, partnerships are actually short-lived, and also women play a decisive role in them. From our modern perspective, the unscrupulous use of child labor and the fact that it is possible to accumulate capital seem incompatible with an ideal state.

The Vril wand reminds us of the magic found in countless fantasy films, while the concentration of energy anticipates the principle of atomic fuel rods. Compulsory consumption as the alleged driving force behind the economy is expressed in an unusual way here, but is something we are absolutely familiar with in our day and age.

There is no doubt that, down to many details, Bulwer-Lytton was influenced by his great literary models – writers such as More, Bacon, and Godwin.

Edward Bellamy (1850–1898). Mr. West and Dr. Leete (*Looking Backward, 2000–1887*, 1888); (*Looking Further Forward*, 1890)

In 1887 Mr. Julian West fell into a deep sleep and reawakened in the year 2000. We accompany him through a new Boston and share his amazement at the radical changes.

We've found wonderful guides: Dr. Leete lives in this new Boston with his wife and charming daughter Edith, who also accompanies us. Thus we have no need to ask questions, for the astonished Mr. West from the nineteenth century, who has just arrived at the end of the twentieth century, asks the questions himself.

During our first walk we are immediately impressed by the beauty of Boston – how much the city has changed during these more than 100 years! For miles we see broad streets shaded by trees, with fine buildings. Statues stand in the large open squares and fountains splash. The public buildings are colossal in size, and have classic columns on all sides.

Mr. West begins his questions with a detail: »How is it that the houses have no chimneys and there is no smoke anywhere?« »It's been a long time since we had stoves. We have central heating, which is piped into the houses«, is Dr. Leete's answer.

The next question addresses essential problems: »In the streets there are no stores, no banks – what does this mean?« »You are speaking of very outdated institutions that we no longer know«, replies Dr. Leete. »Now it is time to speak about our economy.«

And so, with growing amazement, we hear about the most recent achievements. Industry and trade are run by a committee in which the entire nation is represented. The nation has organized itself into a single gigantic enterprise. The profits and savings benefit all citizens. After compulsory school attendance all citizens are expected to work from the age of 21 until 45, or 55 at the most.

But prior to this there is an entry phase: »*Before we choose our future profession, we are part of the class of ordinary workers for three years.*« »And what are you expected to do during this period?« we want to know. »*A little bit of everything, and none of it for a long time. We gather practical experience in every kind of work so that we are able to make a better career choice. This stage of work is great fun!*«

After these three trial years gaining experience comes the obligatory professional work. Work may be freely chosen, though only from a list of jobs needed by the community. Naturally the choice of a job is thus very conditionally voluntary.

»Does that mean one is forced to take the job?« Mr. West wants to know. »We wouldn't call it that«, Dr. Leete says reassuringly. »We all tend to take the work for granted. It is possible for people who are dissatisfied to change jobs, but those who do not want to work at all enjoy none of the advantages of society and are deported to another part of the country. But don't forget how bright and friendly are the factories we work in, and that the workers determine their own work! That's why we have hardly any malcontents.«

Before this compulsory period of work the citizens are in school, being trained, and their grades in school and during their apprenticeship determine their intelligence ranking in their later careers. After they have finished their obligatory work, that is, at age 45 or 55 at the latest, they enjoy a totally free life.

»But how is a fair balance of work achieved for everybody?« is Mr. West's next question. »*The balance is produced because the number of working hours in various trades is adjusted according to the difficulty of the work*«, we learn, »*Thus easy jobs that are performed in the most pleasant conditions have the longest working hours. For difficult jobs, however, for instance, mining, working hours are very short.*«

Still, the conditions for work and their inevitability seem very hard to us, and our guide frankly acknowledges this: »*If anybody wanted to avoid his obligatory work, it would be impossible for him to make his living. Yet such a wish is unthinkable. Anyone who wanted to make it come true would exclude himself from society, cut off contact with his peers, in short, commit suicide. But this practically never happens, for the mere knowledge of this makes everyone want to go to work, to serve the state.*«

We learn – and here, too, we can't help feeling uneasy – that the work systems are extremely rigidly structured, like an army. There are first-, second-, and third-rank workers. records are kept on every person's work performance, and one's promotion depends on this. Commendations, awards, prizes, and medals are meant to spur ambition and promote people's zeal in the service of the nation.

»Would you explain why there are no banks and stores?« we ask. »Instead of money every citizen has a credit card, and thus trade has become superfluous. Goods are distributed by the central depot – but are selected in district centers. Why don't we visit one?«

The exterior of the building gives no hint that this is a department store. We enter a huge hall whose tall ceiling is a glass dome. In the center, a fountain cools the air. Around the fountain there are chairs and sofas, where people are engaged in sparkling conversation.

We are amazed by the huge selection – but there are no salespeople in sight! »Take a look«, Edith points out, »there's a card attached to each item with all the information, and so all you have to do is order the merchandise – the order goes to the central, and from there the goods are sent through big pipes directly to the houses.«

»But how can a fair distribution of goods be achieved?« Mr. West pursues the topic. »Every citizen is free to spend his credit-card ration according to his wishes. It is true that all citizens have the same income, but it is up to each of them how they use it. Thus, for instance, the rents that the nation charges for the houses vary according to their size, elegance, and location, so that everyone can find an acceptable apartment.«

»*Are women given credit cards the same as the men?*« asks Mr. West.

»*Certainly.*«

»*Presumably the women's credit is for a smaller amount, since they often have to interrupt their work because of family responsibilities?*« wonders Mr. West.

»*Smaller?*« exclaims Dr. Leete. »*Oh no! Living expenses for all our workers are the same. That is a rule without exceptions, but if a difference were to be made because of the interruption you mention, the woman's credit would need to be bigger, not smaller.*«

»*The consequence of this seems to be that women are in no way dependent on their husbands for their livelihood.*«

»*Of course they aren't*«, responds Dr. Leete, »*just as children are not dependent on their parents, that is, except for their maintenance, for it goes without saying that they cannot free themselves from the duties of filial love.*«

All this, explains Dr. Leete, is the result of the nation's peaceful development: »Within one lifespan, our ancestors broke with barbaric social institutions and customs and adopted a social order that was more rational and more worthy of human beings. They abandoned their predatory habits, worked together peaceably and found a way of becoming rich and happy in brotherliness and through science.«

»But how can the organization of this community function if governments have been abolished?« Mr. West has more questions.

»*The nation's entire production and distribution*«, says Dr. Leete, »*is centrally administered, and nothing can ever go wrong because of how simple and wise the laws are, and because all the administrative work is in the hands of experts. There is a centralized, unified organization.*«

Our suspicion that the structures here are very authoritarian was subsequently confirmed. »Long ago, we did away with political parties and politicians, and thus eliminated demagoguery and corruption. The nation is the sole employer and the workers are used according to the existing needs of industry. Of course there are no state prisons.«

During our conversations we've been walking down a pleasant road, admiring the splendor of the city that indicates considerable prosperity. From a roof garden we see the new cityscape of Boston. Again we are impressed by the lack of chimneys and by the wonderfully clean air – thanks to the new heating system. And as we look around us, we see that the periphery of the city is quite sparsely developed and beautifully landscaped. At that moment, a shower falls over the city and we see something unusual: From the houses, watertight roofs are automatically stretched across the sidewalks.

»What's in that group of buildings on the outskirts?« we ask.

»Those are the sports facilities. A glass-walled swimming pool flooded with light, with a huge saltwater pool and fountains is in the center. Next to it are a few sports halls and gyms. Until the age of 21, everyone must participate in sports, for we want our young men and women to be handsome and strong. But the entire community also cares for the few who are weak or sick.«

Now we return to the home of Dr. Leete's family. After tea, the daughter, Edith, takes over the job of informing us and finally giving us a few delightful surprises.

At first, we have questions about the household,we don't see a kitchen, or household servants.

»That's all outdated«, Edith informs us. »The most delicious food is prepared in public kitchens. There are beautiful dinng halls, or you can have it brought to you. Public laundries, workshops, and other types of service make servants completely superfluous.«

Dishwashing, cleaning clothes, and doing the laundry are now things of the past. Clothes – even warm winter clothing – are made from specially manufactured paper, produced in the factory, and discarded once they can no longer be used.

»Of course we don't have so-called ›fashions‹. Even women wear the simple, practical men's wear.«

»*Please come with me to the music room now*«, Edith invites us. We follow her into a room without wallpaper, curtains, or portieres. The walls are paneled with wood and the floor is gleaming parquet. We expect to see entirely new kinds of instruments, but can see absolutely nothing in the room that could possibly be considered an instrument.

»*Please have a look a today's program*«, says Edith, handing us a card, »*and tell me what you'd prefer to hear. Just remember it's five o'clock now.*«

The card is dated »12 September 2000« and contains the biggest concert program I've ever seen in my life. The huge list is overwhelming. The listings for »five p.m.« contain only a small number of pieces. We choose an organ composition.

»*I'm glad you love the organ*«, says Edith, »*I know no other instrument that suits all my moods so well.*« She asks us to sit down on comfortable seats, crosses the room and presses one or two buttons. At once the room fills with the majestic sounds of an organ. We listen to the music with bated breath. We had not expected to hear such a magnificent work performed so well. »*Magnificent*«, exclaims Mr. West after the last mighty waves of sound have gradually faded away. »*The organ player must have been a Bach, but where is the organ?*«

»*Please be patient just a moment longer*«, says Edith. »*Before you ask more questions, I'd like you to hear this waltz. I think it's really sweet.*«

She is still speaking as the sounds of a violin fill the room, creating the magic of a summer's night. After the waltz is over, Edith turns to us.

»*The music you just heard is not at all mysterious. It isn't played by fairies and elves, but by good, honest, and extremely talented human hands. As with everything else, so with music, too, our principle was the highest achievement produced by the efficient collaboration of the most suitable talents. The city has a number of music rooms whose acoustics are adapted exactly to the various kinds of music. These rooms are connected by telephone with all the houses of the city whose inhabitants pay an insignificant fee. You may rest assured that there is no one in Boston who is not connected.*«

»*It seems to me*«, says Mr. West, »*that in my time we would have thought we had reached the pinnacle of human bliss if we had managed to invent a device like this. Namely that everybody could hear, in his own home, music that was not only perfectly performed and independent of a particular concert but also appropriate for each mood and that began and ended whenever the listener liked. It seems to me that if we had had such a fairy tale come true we would not have strived for further improvements.*«

After this magic experience, we return to reality and ask for more information about the social life and leisure of the city's inhabitants. »To spare ourselves useless expense, we have as few household goods as are compatible with our comfort, but organize our social life with unprecedented luxury. All industrial and professional associations have clubhouses as spacious as this one as well as resorts in the country, in the mountains, and on the coast for sports and relaxation in the holidays.«

We haven't heard much about the position of science and art yet – except for music. Edith is glad to fill us in: »On the average, people here live to the age of 90. After they reach the age of 45 or 55, they are no longer obliged to work – so that half their life is at their free disposal. Mostly they fill it with sports and entertainment, but also engaged in science and the arts. Every citizen can be a professional scientist, but the talent and hard work required are such that only those who are truly called to this profession are capable of pursuing it.«

On the next day, we are scheduled to go to Arlington, and see a new miracle: the electroscope. »What the telephone does for the ear, the electroscope does for the eye.«

Again we are seated on comfortable armchairs in a beautiful drawing room with white walls. It is getting dark, and already we are on a tour of the loveliest cities: Not only New York, Chicago, San Francisco pass before our eyes, but London, Paris, Cairo as well – we are connected to all the cosmopolitan cities. But naturally spoken messages are communicated as well, and we realize that church attendance has become superfluous now that there is the telephone and electroscope.

Beside his mother tongue every citizen also learns the global world language. Religious festivals and ceremonies are as superfluous as sects: Faith and philosophy are spiritual, and religious controversy has become a thing of the past.

The day concludes with a wonderful trip by airship over the countryside: The cities have become smaller, country life is easier now that there are electric plows, and because people have a vegan lifestyle cattle are superfluous.

We learn many more amazing facts, and are happy that Dr. Leete's hospitality makes it possible for us to think all this over in peace.

Bellamy 1888, 1897, 1967; Michaelis 1890; Blüher 1920; Trousson 1975; Manguel 1981; Berneri 1950, 1971; Berghahn 1983; Heuermann 1984; Wuckel 1986; Eaton 2001.

The title is irritating: Strictly speaking this is not a look back, but a look forward from 1887 to the year 2000 and we are in the strange situation of having actually lived in this era.

It is astonishing how many things that Bellamy anticipated 113 years ago have come true – though under very different circumstances. For in Bellamy's work we sense not only elements of socialism, but also of totalitarian communism, indeed of racism, things we have actually experienced in the last 113 years.

The system regulating work in Bellamy's book that is doubtless meant to be interpreted as compulsion has now become an unwelcome reality. The boundaries between the organization and regulation of work, between the cutting back of working hours on the one hand and compulsion on the other hand are certainly blurred, but Bellamy's descriptions inevitably remind us of the work systems in twentieth-century communist states. It seems Bellamy has anticipated, above all, the Soviet system of Stakhanovite work, a foretaste of totalitarian systems. And the vain hope that community ownership of the places of production can bring about prosperity for all, while organization can lead to the abolishment of government power, is proposed with surprising optimism.

The fact that Bellamy anticipates our radio is one of the amazing utopian ideas that have come true, and we find it in other utopian visions as well. A kind of movie theater is envisioned as well.

The mail-order system is also anticipated here.

The significance of electricity is anticipated, as is the system of »service houses«, such as those found in Scandinavia. Disposable dishes have become almost a matter of course for the fast food trade, and there have been repeated experiments with throwaway clothing. The reuse of textiles and commodities appears to be a precursor of modern recycling methods.

The sweet and strange love story between Mr. West and Edith toward the end of the book is surprising – we missed this part during our fictional tour. Bellamy adds a final revelation: Edith, Mr. West's wife, married a second time after he disappeared, and Edith Leete, it turns out, is the first Edith's great-granddaughter. But finally everything is discovered to be just a dream.

The book enjoyed tremendous popularity when it first appeared, and had an important political and social influence. In Boston, the fictional locale, a Bellamy Club was founded in 1888, followed by »nationalist clubs« in all parts of the country, where nationalism meant the nationalization, that is, state control of industry and agriculture.

On a small scale, Bellamy proposed municipalization (local control), that is, takeover of the means of production by municipalities.

We repeat the journey to the year 2000 once more, but our tour with Mr. West is not guided by Edward Bellamy and Dr. Leete, but by Richard Michaelis.

First of all we find, after Mr. West's 113-year sleep, that everything is indeed exactly the way Bellamy described it: There are no private, individual business enterprises. Everything is regulated by the state. From the age of 21 until the age of 45 everyone is part of the army of workers, money has been abolished, everyone receives his share in industrial work in the form of coupons, meals are prepared in large kitchens, clothes are washed in laundries, there is compulsory schooling up to the age of 21, there are no courts of law, lawyers, prisons, or tax collectors, and state government has been abolished.

Mr. West has been convinced by Dr. Leete of the advantages of all these and many other excellent institutions. He is enthusiastic, and we've shared his appreciation since our first visit. But now Mr. West is invited to give lectures on the terrible conditions in the nineteenth century, and gives detailed descriptions of what was wrong in that bygone society as opposed to the present one. He is very surprised, though, that there is hardly agreement, let alone enthusiasm, among his listeners – and cannot find an explanation for this.

At the end of the last lecture a certain Mr. Forest introduces himself to us and urges us to see the situation from a different perspective and not to give credence to Dr. Leete's propaganda. He begins to explain the facts and proves what things are like in reality. Mr. Forest maintains that society in 2000 has failed.

The egalitarian distribution of goods has prevented prosperity, working hours could not be reduced in the long run, the free choice of a profession is limited, and community of property led to authoritarian communism. Nepotism and corruption are the order of the day, corruption and tyranny have gotten to be a habit, while opponents of the system are ruthlessly persecuted.

Finally, religion has been abolished, marriage has been modified, and prostitution has spread. Mr. Forest was able to prove all his statements, and opened our eyes. We returned to 1887.

Michaelis 1890.

Rarely has the battle between utopia and anti-utopia been waged in so clear and polemical form. Richard Michaelis was the editor of the *Chicagoer Freie Presse*.

For him communism exists »as a form of government only among savages and cannibals«, and his critique of the totalitarian style of Bellamy's vision is completely justified.

Once more we set off on a journey. »Somewhat later« than in 2000 we travel to Boston, and this time it is Philipp Laicus who accompanies us. Naturally we intend to visit Mr. West. We're just in time for a great event: Mr. West has become increasingly fond of Edith Leete – and she of him. The marriage is imminent – and Mr. West has discovered that Edith is actually his great-granddaughter!

But first we go on another tour of Boston, and in the short time since our last visit a few things have changed: The machines have been improved and their number has increased, work hours have been cut to four hours a day, every citizen has music piped into his apartment, and much more. In other words, everything's coming up roses?

Mr. West is looking forward to the wedding – but his joy is dampened. There are no formalities, let alone a priest or church or religious ceremony. A preacher says a few words. The couple can get divorced any time, of course. »Isn't that living in sin?« wonders Mr. West. But Edith doesn't disapprove, not even when women sit in a public house, drink, play cards, smoke, and argue. Mr. West is now ordered to go to Cuba, which is an American colony, and with his lectures about the evils of the nineteenth century he is supposed to strengthen the new system. But Edith is not to accompany him, she is only 20 and school is absolutely compulsory till age 21. »That's not a problem«, says the president. »The marriage can be dissolved and a new one entered into in Cuba!« Mr. West objects – and Edith can now go with him after all if she promises to do volunteer service in the hospital.

After arriving in Havana Mr. West at once realizes how dissatisfied the population is with the new American system: impoverishment, slavery, and violence have spread, and Mr. West begins to have doubts, but continues to give his lectures. However, Edith's atheism is the cause of severe conflicts.

From Germany, visitors arrive in Cuba: Jesuits who are planning to study the school system. Edith has profound conversations with them. And one day the time has come. Edith professes: There is a God!

In the meantime social democracy in Germany has been overthrown. Perhaps Mr. West and Edith will go there?

Laicus 1891.

One more critical voice: Atheism, loss of rituals, a plea for the Jesuits, orthodox Catholicism are the motifs: Traces of the nineteenth-century Kulturkampf become apparent.

Herbert George Wells (1866–1944). *The Time Machine*, 1895, *802*, *701*; *Island of Dr. Moreau*, **1896; London in the 21st century, 1903;** *Modern Utopia*, **1905;** *Things to Come*, **1933;** *Men like Gods*, **1910**

In his rather small workshop in London the time traveler shows us his time machine: a strange, confusing device, a glistening framework made of iron. Individual parts are made of ivory, others consist of a transparent, crystalline substance, others again of brass and nickel, and the entire machine is equipped with small white levers, large wheels, countless rods, axles, tubes, and metal sheets.

The time traveler introduces his theories to us: »*Every real body has to have extension in four dimensions: It must have length, breadth, depth, and – duration. There is no difference between time and one of the three spatial dimensions, except that our consciousness moves along its line.*«

The time traveler has convinced us: skeptical and afraid at the same time we enter the time machine. One of the levers is activated and at once we are moving at lightning speed. Day and night alternate as rapidly as seconds.

After a dramatic and adventurous journey we land with a thunderous roar and amid hail and fog on a small lawn. The time clock shows the year 802,701.

The first thing we see is a colossal figure made of white stone, a sphinx whose wings are spread sideways. It is lying on a bronze pedestal covered with verdigris. Gradually buildings emerge from the fog, huge edifices with intricate parapets and tall columns embedded in shrubbery and trees.

A huge portal leads into one of the massive buildings. The archway is richly ornamented with sculptures that are already somewhat weathered.

The hail and fog have dispersed, and there is movement in the shrubs. Small, graceful men appear, barely five feet tall, dressed in purple robes with girdles. Men and women are dressed identically. We find the men very handsome and charming, but delicate and frail. They stand around us peacefully, and gaze at us in wonder, but we cannot understand their language.

We can now enter the fortress-like building to marvel at its interesting furnishings. First we find ourselves in a big hall whose windows are partially glazed with stained glass, while the floor is made of white metal slabs. In the hall there are large stone tables on which there is an array of many different kinds of fruit. We are invited to recline on some of the numerous cushions scattered on the floor and to help ourselves to the fruit. We eat like the many hundred other people in the hall. They are obviously all vegetarians.

Conversation is somewhat laborious, which is why we decided to go for a walk and climb one of the hills. The Thames has changed its course a little, and we see no villas, only large community buildings resembling palaces surrounded by big gardens. Between them are statues, obelisks, fountains – a veritable paradise.

The inhabitants are able to tell us little about themselves, but the evidence of our eyes is all the more impressive. We see no one working, there are seemingly no fights, no hatred, no envy – and no commerce, but optimal social provisions. Very soon, however, we learn the dreadful things that are concealed behind the scenes in this »paradise«.

Now we return from the hills to the marble sphinx – and freeze with icy terror: The time machine is gone! All our searching, calling, cursing, and questioning is in vain – we are seized by despair – and yet we are hopeful that we will find the device.

Then another terrifying adventure befalls us. During our walk we pass a ruin, climb on it, a dark passage arouses our curiosity – and suddenly, only a few yards away, an apelike creature with long white hair, its head down, runs past us. The creature abruptly disappears in a cistern-like shaft whose function had been unclear to us. After we have recovered from our initial shock, we come to the conclusion that the creature cannot be living underground all by itself.

After sleeping on the whole thing, we are determined to descend into this underground world. We venture into the shaft, in which rungs have been installed. With great effort we descend a good 200 yards, carrying only a few matches.

And indeed, here we meet with large numbers of these sinister creatures, called Morlocks: pallid, stooped, with large glittering eyes. Thunderous noise fills the narrow passages as we enter the deafening hall of machines, hot, oppressive, and dark. The Morlocks beset us from all sides, though we cannot guess what they want. We make our way to the exit and with our remaining strength climb up the shaft.

With a sigh of relief we can now understand what is going on here. This is a brutal two-class society: The Eloi are the people of the upper world, living in peace and prosperity, where all social problems have been solved. They are the aristocracy, and the Morlocks are the underground servants who make their clothing and all their necessities of life.

The Morlocks' subterranean world is purely mechanical industry, but the machines have required thought – and thanks to this thinking the Morlocks have revolted and are beginning to dominate the Eloi, who can enjoy their easy life only during the days. At night, they are threatened by the Morlocks.

It's high time to look for the time machine – and as if by a miracle we discover it in the pedestal of the sphinx!

It is easy for us to take our leave, and after a speedy return journey we land safely in London, in 1895.

We don't accompany the time traveler on a second journey in time, thirty million years into the future.

And luckily we decide not to take the third trip – the time traveler never returns from it.

Today, scientists are discussing something that seemed to be an unimaginable utopia a century ago: travel through time. New insights about the universe, about the nature of time and the fourth dimension according to Einstein (ideas that, though amateurishly, are touched upon in the story) make time travel possible, though for the moment only theoretically – a utopia that has come true. Stephen Hawking (1988, 1997) devotes interesting reflections to this topic, and J. Richard Gott (2002) gives his book the title *Time Travel*.

While many utopians dream of a classless society, H.G. Wells describes an extreme, two-class society. In view of the increasing escalation of the worldwide divide between rich and poor, this idea is by no means utopian.

And here's another disturbing modern-day reality: life underground. Though modern troglodytes do not spend all day below the ground, they do spend many hours there: not just miners or tunnel builders, but the hundreds of thousands of people who are subway conductors or work in underground shopping and entertainment centers.

The next journey takes us to the island of Dr. Moreau. He is well aware why he has retired to live here. We meet him in the middle of his remarkable experiments. »I have decoded human life. That is why I am able to alter the function of animals so that they become human, for I have surmounted the stages of the evolution of living beings.«

Shuddering, we turn away from the dreadful labs. A few years later we hear of Dr. Moreau's terrible end: He no longer had power over his creatures and was killed by a puma.

In recent years we have become familiar with the call »We have decoded life« – at least in its parts. Has the nature of life really been explained now that the genetic code has been interpreted? And how are we going to deal with this?

We return to London, which has totally changed. H.G. Wells accompanies us through 21st-century London, which has no less than 33 million inhabitants and is roofed with a huge glass dome. And the city is completely mechanized: There are elevators for vertical traffic, and automatic moving paths save people the trouble of long walks. It is possible to reach the city by plane. Theaters show moving pictures, cinematographic films, while in the homes there are devices that show distant events at close range.

There will be frequent projects to cover cities, to put a roof over them. Perhaps the most magnificent of all is Buckminster Fuller's idea of covering Manhattan with a giant »dome«.

The modern Utopia Mr. Wells now introduces to us is no flawless ideal state. »*There must also be tensions, conflicts, and waste, but they are far less significant.*« Wells describes a world state that has no national boundaries.

Both individualism and capitalism in their absolute form have been abolished, for, as Mr. Wells says, »*One system makes people into slaves of the cruel and the wealthy, while the other makes them into slaves of state officials, and the path of reason is possibly a wavy line down in the valley between the two.*«

The state takes care of the handicapped and the elderly, and salaries vary according to the value of the work performed. »Naturally a technician is paid more than a worker. Dividends are distributed to the members of the joint-stock company after a part has been laid aside for investments and taxes for the state. When an organization wants to devote itself to industry or farming, it can receive capital or land from the state.«

An individual's personal property is absolutely safeguarded, for, says Mr. Wells, »A person without saleable property is not free, and the extent of his property is an important criterion for his freedom.«

Money is by no means frowned on, it is something good and a component of personal freedom. Up to this point we were happy to go along with Mr. Wells's remarks.

But now he describes additional state provisions that we find increasingly disturbing as his account continues. For the state not only administers all sources of energy and makes them available for essential work, it also distributes work, controls, allocates, and administers all natural production, collects and distributes information. This thorough registration, exact cataloging, and compulsory reporting of all personal events may still be tolerable. But when Wells describes the institutions of marriage and education, we are no longer just amazed but horrified. For instance, those who add children to the community must prove they are personally productive and able to pay, in short, independent. A man must be 27, a woman 21 years of age, physically mature, healthy, morally irreproachable. If they do not meet these criteria and produce children nevertheless, the state assumes care of the children and the parents have to pay.

The parents of healthy children receive higher subsidies, while those whose children are mentally or physically defective are paid below the minimal standard: in other words, a brutal system of rearing children.

Mr. Wells explains the reason for this system: »*The process of nature where the strong cold-bloodedly kill the weak is replaced by the ways and means of modern humanity.*«

Society has to eradicate idiots, perverts, the unfit, and criminals, but it chooses not to kill or imprison them – they are exiled to an island, to monasteries and convents.

Once more we encounter the insanity of eugenic selection and a belief in the continuous selective breeding of the human race.

Wells's *Things to Come* shows us the new city, ruled exclusively by reason; that is why it is a simple, unadorned city, built in an international style. There's a lot about it that reminds us of *Metropolis*. The style is even more modern, and streamlined design predominates.

We remain in the city, but now we travel to the year 2054 – and now the city is hardly visible – there is open countryside, woods and meadows, as far as the eye can see. The explanation is that the city has moved underground.

And the journey continues to the country where *Men* [Are] *like Gods*. Now Mr. Barnstaple is our guide in this realm – where he ended up, as though by a miracle, while he was traveling on vacation. We find ourselves in a wonderful landscape – blooming meadows encircled by snowy mountains. This world is one of peace and harmony.

In vain, we ask him where the capital of this utopia is. People have returned to a rural existence, and this is probably the reason for their perfect community, their high intelligence and impeccable morals. In certain places people gather to study, motivate each other, or exchange views. These places consist of long rows of connected buildings, but are not towns. The utopians drive fast machines on highways, and planes zoom over the landscape.

Mr. Barnstaple has gradually gotten to know the country of Utopia and waxes enthusiastic about it. We learn a great deal about its public welfare system.

The societal, social, and moral ideas of the people in this country are far more mature than those in Mr. Barnstaple's own country, and thus they have become like gods.

»Authority is decentralized and there are no laws and no power that could impose them by force«, the Utopians declare. Private property has now disappeared, for it is an unbearable plague of humanity. »It is true that we own our tools and other aids, and everything necessary for everyday life, but there is no property to trade or speculate with.«

However, Mr. Barnstaple is astounded by the flawlessness of human beings in Utopia. People in this state have attained another, very different freedom – they are no longer deformed and oppressed. Their bodies and minds are incredibly beautiful, and disease and ugliness have been banished for good. They are refined and well-proportioned, and one has the impression that all of them are young, though many faces reveal mature strength. A handsome and intelligent boy by the name of Crystall has joined us in the meantime. He can tell us a great deal about the Utopians: »We've accepted the fact that human beings are essentially animals and that in their daily life they need to satisfy their desires and express their instincts to the full. The power of Utopian education does not begin until the animal has been satisfied and appeased.«

The »time of confusion« has long been overcome: It is the time before humanity attained its final perfection – and Mr. Barnstaple finds that it resembles the period in which »earthlings« now live and from which he comes himself.

Yet Mr. Barnstaple does not find it easy to affirm this life, so different in many respects: The fact that there is no marriage, that there is an attempt as it were to breed a healthy and beautiful human race, that the family has been abolished – or rather, extended to include all humanity – that is a mentality that worries Mr. Barnstaple in spite of all his enthusiasm.

»The driving force that led Utopia forth from the aberrations of human existence is curiosity, the play instinct, which in the lives of adults has grown into an insatiable thirst for knowledge and, to a large extent, creative urges.«

But now we return from a realm whose development is a good 3,000 years ahead of ours – but not far enough ahead of us that we, too, cannot reach it. Once more, full of yearning, Mr. Barnstaple sums up the world we have left: »*Serenity – beauty! All human achievements in perfect harmony ... The soul in accord with the universe ... All confusion resolved ... A world of intellects, crystal clear.*«

Wells 1886, 1895, 1899, 1900,1911, 1925, 1970, 2003; Manguel 1981; Klotz 1986; Eaton 2001.

The demand that instincts »be expressed to the full« seems to have been influenced by the new concepts of Sigmund Freud's and Wilhelm Reich's sexual theories.

Wells needs no island to escape everyday existence, consciousness, life's injustices: Rather, a kind of space-time alienation leads to another world. Two three-dimensional fictional worlds, Earth and Utopia, are interlocked more than three-dimensionally, interpenetrate each other. Actually, this utopia is located in London, but in what space-time dimension?

Between 1905 and 1916, Albert Einstein formulates his theories of relativity – might there be some connections?

Charlotte Perkins Gilman (1860–1935). *Herland*, 1920

Terrible things have happened, leading to the creation of Herland: Young girls have killed the men who tormented them, and then build a new society. The mother goddess Maaia becomes the land's patroness and grants a woman the ability to give birth to five daughters without a husband. This is the origin of Herland, which continues to get by without men.

Today three million women live in Herland. Their principle is absolute sisterhood. Love, patience, and affection characterize their life. The Over Mothers select the women who may give birth. Mostly only one child is allowed, but she receives an excellent education in the community.

The public buildings and residential buildings are quite magnificently furnished, for the women do not want their arts to be inferior to those of earlier times. They live in pretty little cottages surrounded by gardens.

Without exception, the women of Herland are attractive, though they do not resemble the traditional image of women. They wear their hair short and have simple, practical clothing, tasteful and dignified.

In the fields and meadows, we see no beef cattle. Why is that? »True«, says Miss Gilman, »we simply allowed those animals to die out – and we can do without hunting as well, for we are completely vegetarian.«

Now it is almost self-evident that in Herland there is no room for misery, poverty, and thus even dirt.

Gilman 1998.

The citizens of Herland are either androgynous or are able to reproduce by parthenogenesis – virginal birth – found in a number of myths and in Catholicism. Ms. Gilman does not tell us what their attractive beauty consists of. We also wonder whether killing the men was the only way to create a country of women.

8.2. France, Italy, Germany, Austria

Jules Verne (1828–1905). Professor Schultze in Franceville (*Les Cinq cents millions de la Bégum*, 1879); Propeller Island (*L'île à hélice*, 1895); (*Paris au XXe siècle*, 1863); the Barsac expedition to Blackland (*L'étonnante aventure de la mission Barsace*, 1880)

With Franceville Jules Verne and Professor Schultze, the planner, present us with the picture of an extremely pleasant, orderly city. »This order does not come about by itself«, explains Professor Schultze. »We have published exact and strict regulations regarding the form, construction, and building material of the single-family homes.«

And it is striking that the gardens with their nice beds are also neat and well-tended: There are regulations regarding them as well.

»For life in a city to be pleasant«, says Jules Verne, »a certain number of regulations are absolutely necessary.« And so Jules Verne shows us a city that was built according to strict building regulations, whose logic we cannot deny:

1. Every house is built at a distance from the neighboring lots. The space between houses is planted with trees, lawn, and flowers. The house belongs to a single family.

2. Every house is no more than two stories high. One house may not deprive another of air and light.

3. The façades of all houses are set 10 m back from the street.

4. The walls are constructed of patented tubular bricks.

5. The roofs are designed as terraces.

6. All houses have been built on a vault foundation.

7. The kitchens, offices, and adjoining rooms are arranged on the top floor with a direct connection to the terrace.

8. The interior design of homes is left up to each individual's imagination, but three causes of disease are prohibited: carpets, rugs, and wallpaper.

9. Every bedroom has a bathroom.

10. Every room has a fireplace.

The city plan is strictly geometric, but open to development. The streets intersect at right angles, are equally wide, and lined with trees. The houses are numbered. Every 500 m the streets widen by a third where there is a covered tram and bus stop on one side. Public gardens are planned for all intersections.

We notice that during evening strolls people sometimes leaf through a booklet. Professor Schultze informs us: »*The booklet lists the most important, scientifically based instructions for a well-ordered life in easily understood language. It s a fact that a perfectly balanced life is the basic prerequisite for good health, and that an alternation of work and relaxation is essential for the human organs.*«

The booklet draws up the basic rules for health:

»*– Avoid the use of toxic stimulants!*
Exercise daily!
Conscientiously do some intellectually stimulating work every day!
Drink only good, clean water!
Eat meat and unspoiled, simply prepared vegetables!
Get seven or eight hours of sleep a night on a regular basis!«

»And the citizens actually live by these rules?« we ask skeptically. »They have no other choice! The hygiene police sees to it – and everybody's watching everybody else.«

The visit on Propeller Island also teaches us that a modern life is not possible without sensible rules and regulations.

We're very curious to see how much Paris, which we last saw in 1863, has changed during the last century. Michel, a young man from a good family, has just settled in Paris, and is our reliable guide. »Yes, Paris is hardly recognizable and has become a very modern city: Look at the splendid buildings, up to nine stories high, some even up to twenty stories high, crowded together in the city. Some are hotels, capable of housing 20,000 travelers.« »Isn't it incredibly hard to climb that high?« »Not at all! Every building has an electric elevator, of course, and the cars glide to the top soundlessly. Electricity has conquered all of Paris, so to speak. Just look at the streets: Night turns into day. A mercury strip is electrified and gleams with incomparable radiance. The candelabra are connected, and Paris is suddenly aglitter with bright light.«

We've been admiring the wonders of traffic for some time: In the streets, horseless carriages speed by us. What makes them move?

Michel is glad to tell us: »Our gas cabs have a motor, in which air expands when gas is burned and thus moves the car. A steering wheel and a pedal help us keep tight control of the vehicle. Naturally there are also sturdy vehicles, meant for transporting heavy goods, but these are not allowed to disturb the peace after ten a.m.«

The houses are connected high above street level by pedestrian bridges, but suddenly a railway train rushes along one of the bridges.

»We have four railroad rings. The first encircles the old city of Paris; the second, 32 km long, connects the suburbs; the third, 56 km long, connects the outskirts of town, while the fourth, 100 km long, forms a net linking the bastions, but the old city walls were blown up a long time ago.«

All trains run on elevated tracks supported by elegant bronze columns. Underneath, pedestrians stroll and gas cabs drive on the streets.

At that moment, a train pulls in swiftly, almost noiselessly, but no steam rises from the locomotive. »The trains are driven by compressed air that is pushed through a large pipe, and the locomotive is coupled to the cylinder electromagnetically.«

On the banks of the Seine we are surprised that the water is dammed to a considerable height. »Yes, we built a dam, and the power station supplies us with water and electricity even when there is a drought.«

We return to the topic of electricity, and Michel describes a few most remarkable inventions: Letters no longer need to be copied by hand. There are special machines for that. Because of electric telegraphy, sender and recipient can get in touch directly, which reduces the number of letters sent.

175. Anonymous, after Jules Verne, *Paris in the 20th century*, 1863, 1996.

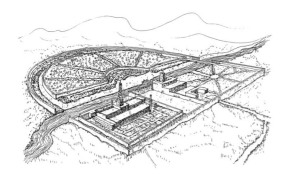

In the centers of all international stock exchanges there are columns with huge dials on which people can read the exchange rates of all stocks and shares.

In big halls there are electronic concerts with 200 electronic pianos played by a single pianist. And in Notre Dame not only the organ is played electronically: Electricity lights up the monstrance as well. The law also uses the electric current: The condemned are put to death by means of electricity. We wonder if this is a more humane way of killing.

The very next moment we are charmed by another invention: The pantelegraph transmits writings, documents, and drawings onto a white surface, and photographic telegraphy sends documents or plans a long distance away. These telegraphic networks cover the surface of the whole planet, including the oceans.

Michel must be very happy living in such a wonderful modern city, we imagine. »Not at all. Just the opposite – for morality, art, and science are in a very sad state. Illegitimate partnerships – and thus the children born from them — are increasing at a fast pace. There are no belles lettres, no paintings, no artists. The stock exchange, a magnificent building, has become the actual cathedral, for only money and profits are considered to be worthwhile.«

And how is Michel doing personally? »I spend all day next to an accounting machine. What saves me are good friends: In good conversations, with music and literature, we keep our intellectual existence alive.«

A very special adventure awaits us now. Monsieur Barsac is commissioned by the French government to find out whether the natives of Sudan are already sufficiently civilized to be given the right to vote. We have the opportunity to accompany him.

In the middle of the desert, however, we arrive in a completely unfamiliar town: Blackland – quite an astounding experience.

The town is structured strictly symmetrically – the axis begins with the palace of the ruler. A river divides it into a rectangular territory and a semicircular area for the population. The town is protected by a double fortress wall – but against what enemies?

We hear that the town, not including children, has 6,808 inhabitants, of whom 5,788 are Negroes (as they called them at that time) and 1,030 are whites: escaped prisoners, adventurers, the scum of society.

The semicircular part is divided into three sections. The aristocracy lives in the first, the Merry Fellows, organized according to military principles as a brutal police force. Around this first core, bandits, escaped convicts, criminals have formed a group.

The second section, the largest, is the town where the slaves live. Between the outside wall and an inner one 5,788 persons, all Negroes, vegetate. They all work in agriculture.

The third section consists of a semicircular strip, 600 m long and 50 m wide. This is where the whites who have not yet been admitted to the first section live. Here is the shopping district of the town, inhabited by 286 persons.

The rectangular section on the opposite bank consists of two parts: Fortress Garden with businesses that are vital for the town, and the palace territory with a block-like self-contained building, the barracks for willing slaves and Negroes. Opposite the palace there is the factory, about which we have more to say below.

Who, we wonder, is the ruler of this strange and sinister town? It is the immensely rich Harry Killer – as he calls himself – and he rules with terror and cruelty. We do not discover until later that terrible family circumstances were the reason he moved to the desert.

Tyranny is seemingly not detrimental to the town's practical qualities: We find a »*clean, well-kept town equipped with all possible comforts. Not one of the better homes is without a telephone, no house or hut lacks running water or electric light.*«

In addition there are other surprising technological innovations: We are particularly impressed by the flying machines, although they are the instruments of tyranny. The »aeroplanes« reach an average speed of 400 km per hour and have a range of 5,000 kilom.

We are familiar with the transmission of news by Morse telegraphy, but here it is wireless. Impressive but troubling are the *wasps*, small airplanes used in battle.

But how can all these marvels be developed in the desert? The dictator has a genius by his side: Marcel Camaret is an indefatigable inventor – it is even said he can make it rain.

We are able to see the factory, an autonomous, independent town, equipped with all imaginable inventions.

The workers, who belong to different nationalities, have come here voluntarily and receive princely salaries, however – they are never allowed to leave! They live in the factory, are confined to it, and have no contact with the outside world.

176. Jules Verne, the city of Blackland, Africa, 1880.

Thus, once more, our admiration for this town is dampened, and we realize it is ruled by force. What happens to the Barsac mission? His team is captured, then released again. A revolt is in the offing, Killer's family secret is aired and it is he himself in the end who triggers the town's destruction.

Verne 1863, 1879, 1887, 1895, 1996, 1977; Choay 1965, 2001; *Utopie* 1969

Franceville has strict building regulations – but they are no stricter than those in effect today and include urban development. Admittedly, a healthy lifestyle is just as important a prerequisite.

Jules Verne, the great visionary, forefather of science fiction, traveled all over the globe, visited the Moon, the oceans, and underground worlds, but had little interest in large cities. His 1883 essay about Paris was not rediscovered and published until 1994. How modest was his prediction that the population of Paris would one day number five million! Today close to fifteen million people live in the region.

Jules Verne was familiar with the beginnings of electricity, but his imagination accurately foresaw much later inventions: the fax machine, the Internet, television – as well as the electric chair. He anticipates the internal combustion engine – but does not envision compressed-air trains.

Above all, Verne's fear of the decline of culture, the power of stock exchanges and money is not unfounded.

The great inventor Camaret, politically clueless and close to insanity, dedicated to science alone, unquestioning in the face of force: an issue that concerns us in all dictatorships, a genial prognosis by Jules Verne above and beyond the numerous inventions.

With his *wasps* Jules Verne anticipated Ernst Jünger's *Glass Bees*.

Paolo Mantegazza (1831–1910). Anthropolis in the year 3000, 1897/*3000*

Speeding through the ether in an airship at a good 150 miles per hour, we've arrived safely in the Indian city of Anthropolis, the capital of the United States of the World.

What a splendid, modern city! In front of a large circular open space that forms its center are the most important buildings, carefully and representatively designed: the government palace, the Academy of Sciences, the Academy of Fine Arts, and the Temple of Hope. Seven streets radiate from this area, with the big hotels, storehouses and archives, libraries, and all the rest of the public buildings. The seven streets give the city its basic structure, but all the other streets are not straight or arranged at right angles, but winding, curved, adapted to each building, but all at least 20 m wide.

In spite of heavy traffic, the electric vehicles in the streets are noiseless, and on closer inspection we note that the streets are coated with a kind of india rubber. The streets widen into incredibly lovely squares planted with trees and flowers and decorated with statues and fountains.

After this first impression we are glad to have the help of an expert – the mayor of Anthropolis – to answer all our questions. At first we want to know why there are one-story and multiple-story residential buildings, all with small gardens. »There's a reason for this. The poor and unmarried live in the one-story houses, while the taller buildings belong to the wealthy and married people.« But all buildings have light, heat, energy, and water. The houses are all different, some designed in ancient styles, often in bizarre forms. »Yes, everyone can build and furnish his house according to his own taste. Look, there's a Gothic building next to a Pompeian house, and there's a Roman villa next to a small Baroque castle.«

It seems to us that the houses are not built of brick and stone, as in the nineteenth century. What about construction in this country? »It's very simple and quick: A liquid that gradually hardens is poured into the mold of the building. Depending on how wealthy the owner is, the liquid is a cheap substance or a material resembling marble and precious stones.«

Now the mayor takes us by electric tandem to the dynamic workshops. This is where all forces and energies are collected and redistributed as required: light, heat, water, energy. But the most amazing thing is a quadrant in the middle of the hall: On a big board In the darkened room, telegraphic dispatches suddenly appear in shining characters, announcing the energy requirements and other orders by the factories and houses.

As the mayor takes leave of us he recommends that we visit the department of agriculture. The very competent department head draws our attention to one of the global problems: »For three centuries now, we've had no war, and we use the free resources and energy among other things to improve the Earth's climate and fertility. But what is to happen to the endless forests, such as those in the Amazon region, or in the African interior? Should we destroy them and plant tropical fruit there? But that would have a huge influence on the climate of vast regions. On the other hand we need to worry – as Malthus pointed out – how we are to feed the growing population of the world.«

One of the first measures to prevent overpopulation is the regulation that – although each person is obliged to marry – a family may have no more than three children. This realization leads to our learning about one of the terrible drawbacks of this interesting city.

We visit »Hygieia«, a huge palace that is the health center. It is incredibly impressive how masterfully diseases are treated, suffering is alleviated, patients are counseled, and healthy people are examined. But a visit in the hygienics department gives us a dreadful shock. Here all mothers have to have their newborns examined. Most, but not all of them, are allowed to leave the department again with their children, provided with lots of advice. Just now the name of child No. 20 and its mother is being called. The child is placed on a table and illuminated by a pencil of rays, becoming as transparent as glass. Then the child's skull is transilluminated even more intensively. A monocle enlarges the brain cells. Now comes the physicians' assessment: »Sickly, nonviable child with lung disease – it is to be eliminated.« As the mother cries and sobs, the child is pushed into a black shaft, a spring clicks shut, a 2,000-degree airstream surges around the child – a little pile of ashes is all that remains. We are unable to conceal our horror, but the physicians are unmoved: »The elimination of children destined to suffer or to die prematurely – this alone is true compassion.«

But that's not all. The doctors tell us about another program that is supposed to inform us with certainty whether the child is prone to become a criminal or whether it is morally stable. »Born« criminals, too, are eliminated.

Our repulsion grows when we are shown the most recent invention: the psychoscope. »This allows us to read the thoughts of every person. It will finally put an end to lies and deceit!«

After all this we no longer feel like visiting the other city-states: the Land of Equality – including equality between men and women, where each day's schedule, clothing, and food are completely identical; the Tyrant City, full of soldiers, Turatia, the land of various types of socialists; Polygama and Polyandra, the multi-partner cities, Monachia, the city of nuns in the style of the Lesbian Sappho, Peruvia, the communist state, the Dynamo City of engineers and inventors, and maybe a few more.

Mantegazza 1817.

We are left in the dark as to which of the ideas that we find abstruse the author considers to be positive and which ones he rejects. Again, utopia and Dystopia overlap. Be that as it may, we are horrified by the brutal eugenics, the elimination of »nonviable life«, more than half a century before Hitler. And just as insane is the author's thesis of the »born criminal«.

Kurd Lasswitz (1848–1910). Images of the future (*Bilder aus der Zukunft*, 1878) and on two planets (*Auf zwei Planeten,* 1897)

The first journey with Kurt Lasswitz takes us into the distant future – the 24th century.

Even the vehicle by which we travel is a surprise: It is a flying car whose propellers can be adjusted horizontally so that we can take off vertically from the ground.

The city we are overflying is a loosely textured web of high-rises. We land on one of the rooftops not far from the luxuriant roof gardens that flourish everywhere. Between the high-rises there are extensive green spaces, but only a small part is used for recreation. Large areas, on the other hand, are used for agriculture, and thus an amazing synthesis between city and country has been achieved. The fertility is amazing, for the weather can be controlled by means of clever devices to produce optimal agricultural results.

We've long since come to realize that the world in the year 2371 is totally overpopulated. That is why it is necessary to use the earth's surface to the maximum. »*Every nook and cranny is devoted to growing grain and feeding beef cattle*«, explains Kurd Lasswitz. »*That is how we hope to avert a famine. That is why there are fields of grain wherever air and light permit.*«

This also explains something that struck us immediately: buildings standing on solid high columns. There are gardens even under the houses. Industry is located on the lower floors – these are very busy. Above them are private apartments. »*The crowning piece of all this*«, Mr. Lasswitz says with pleasure, »*are lovely gardens whose pure and healthy situation makes them everyone's favorite place to be.*«

The buildings are up to 25 stories, that is, close to 100 m high. The fastest means of transportation are air cabs, which we took to get here. Long ago they replaced the awkward balloon traffic. Once again we admire the adjustable propellers. However, the air cabs may not exceed the height of the buildings in flight.

In the meantime dusk has fallen. It is lovely to see the city bathed in light by spotlights. It is time for supper, and Mr. Lasswitz takes us to a nice restaurant. We don't see a menu. But we immediately find out how to order our food. »By the tables you will find various buttons with labels. That's where you can select your dish.« We push one of the buttons, and a few minutes later the food appears as if by magic from under the tabletop.

»The rise in population forces us to rationalize food production. That can only be done by means of food cooperatives. But people who are in a hurry can also take the universal energy extra-pill: Within a few seconds, they can enjoy several courses of a healthy meal.«

We return to the hotel, just in time for an astonishing performance. A beautiful lady is manipulating a complicated gadget – but we cannot see or hear anything.

»Come a little closer«, Mr. Lasswitz invites us, »and close your eyes.« Oh! Now we can feel it. Wonderful scents fill the room, called forth by Aromasia, a master performer on the Ododium, the scent organ, a keyboard of perfumes invented back in 2094 by an Italian.

As we cross the hotel lobby again, few notice a huge board with news items. But as soon as we have read them, the next item appears automatically on the board, and we are able to read about the day's events. »Just don't think that modern life is nothing but mechanical achievements«, warns Mr. Lasswitz. And so he launches into a long account of the moral and philosophical principles, the democratic social order, the polarity between »rational types« and »romantics«. Now Kurd Lasswitz shows us his special inventions: For one, there is the print telegraph that can transmit not only Morse code, but actual printed documents over long distances. Then there is a new type of artillery, powerful air hoses with a range of up to 250 km.

One experiment, though, is still being developed – a very special chemical substance that cancels the force of gravity.

»As we conclude our journey, I'd like you to join me on an excursion«, says Mr. Lasswitz. We get on board the flying machine again, it rises to great heights, and in less than three hours we have flown from old Europe to the Niagara Falls.

Our next journey requires a 1,500-year leap in time to the year 3877.

Of all the magnificent advances in all fields of technology and natural science, we are particularly interested in an incredible development: the direct manipulation of the brain. There are numerous »brain schools«. For two to three hours, students are subjected to galvanic currents in complicated devices. »*The theory of brain functions makes it possible to have a direct effect on the human brain. This effect has come to have an incalculable influence on the ideal structuring of people's lives.*«

The problem of how to feed the world's population has been ingeniously solved. People are not concerned that there are no forests, meadows, or fields. Thanks to the synthesis of protein, an unlimited supply of food can be produced – hunger has been conquered.

What about lunch? Mr. Lasswitz takes us to a »restaurant«. On the tables there are containers with wires wound around them. They are heated till they glow by galvanic currents. Around them are chemicals representing different flavors. We press the appropriate buttons and in a few minutes a delicious meal has been prepared. It is liquid, and we suck it through a straw, In the meantime strips of paper pass through a gadget, and we can read the latest news.

We do not have time to look at all the innovations. In conclusion Mr. Lasswitz tells us about the time travelers, about writing and reading psychokinetes, the brain organ, and similar wonders, and then it is time to take our leave.

Now comes the high point of the program: A very long journey takes us to the North Pole. We are amazed to find living creatures there. They come from Mars and have built a research station on the pole. We've established contact with the unusual guests, and they invite us to go to Mars. Our surprise has no bounds: The Martians live in an ideal type of state where enmity is unknown. And if a person doesn't like a place, he can move his mobile home somewhere else.

But the Martians, convinced of the perfection of their form of government, were also planning to conquer the Earth. The humans, however, were impressed by the Martian model and decided to establish a rational form of government based on that of the inhabitants of Mars. Now Martians and Earthlings live in peace.

Lasswitz 1948, 1971; Armytage 1968; Swoboda 1972; Ritter 1978.

177. N. Becker, A. Venir's *Look forward*, 1906. Title page.

Today, we call the »devices for lifting and lowering« elevators. Around 1868, when the book was written, Lasswitz, no doubt, was as yet unaware of the new American invention. The air cabs are probably forerunners of the helicopters, and changing wall newspapers anticipate television. A recurrent wish to establish everything that relates to the sense of smell – over and above food – as an artistic genre has been unsuccessful to this day.

Lasswitz anticipates the manipulation of the brain and artificial intelligences in his second book. He actually describes electrodes implanted in the brain that stimulate certain brain centers – an important field of research today.

A. Venir. A *Look forward* to Germany in the year 2006 (*Ein Blick nach vorn*, 1906)

It is the year 2006 and Mr. Venir has invited us to come to Berlin. »In recent years Europe has experienced a total social and political change«, begins Mr. Venir. »All class differences have been abolished, and the aristocracy and clergy have lost their power. The means of production have been nationalized, inheritance laws have been completely changed, workers have achieved profit-sharing in all the factories, university studies are free, and every worker's child can study at the university. So can women, of course, if they have good grades, and parents have no more say in the matter. Only those who are lazy or poor in school have to go hungry – and it serves them right! We are trying to improve the German race, which is why marriages between physical and mental degenerates are forbidden. And criminals are not incarcerated, but prevented from procreating.«

We refuse to get involved in a debate – we'd rather take a look at the city. Berlin has grown a lot in these past 100 years and we are especially impressed by the technology and traffic. Mr. Venir takes us to an elevator with which we descend 20 m deep into the ground to find ourselves in a spacious hall made bright as day by radium light.

»We are in the center for personal pneumatic mail«, explains our guide. »The cigar-shaped iron cars are hurled through the tubes by powerful electromagnets. At the interim points there are intercepting devices.«

There comes the speeding vehicle, we get in quickly, the driver presses a switch, and in six minutes we cover the 20-km distance to our destination.

»Look at those tall towers. They capture atmospheric electricity and the deep shafts below them bring the terrestrial currents up from the earth. These currents operate the pneumatic mail system.«

Mr. Venir has brought us out here to meet the officer Franz Rauchlos in a pretty restaurant. We listen with interest to his account of the past years.

»Germany has grown enormously, from 36 millions in 1855 to 150 millions today. We had to defend the vital interests of the nation. The mighty masses of Teutons must rule or perish. Well, I'll spare you the complicated political constellations, but it is not without importance that the Austrian emperor was shot by a Russian Pan-Slavist. There was a war with Russia in which we were victorious – and crushed Pan-Slavism for good.«

»An ingenious invention by Mr. Rauchlos was partly responsible for the victory«, Mr. Venir remembers. »Yes, that may be true. I developed a new cannon and was in charge of its production. The idea is to use the power of the motor of the self-propelled gun while it is standing still to dig a trench for cover – in other words, a kind of mole cannon. Within a mere two minutes the cannon has burrowed into the ground.«

The cannons can change their position at lightning speed in every kind of terrain. They move at a speed of up to 100 km an hour and shoot accurately at distances of up to 35 km.

We do not want to go on discussing military events, but prefer to hear about new traffic and information technologies. Mr. Venir and Mr. Rauchlos are only too happy to tell us.

»We all know the telephone. It is complemented by the teleprinter – on long paper strips, news appear in uncoded text. But the latest development is small illuminated metal sheets on which texts appear, so that there are completely new methods of transmitting news. Our means of transportation reach enormous speed on land, in the water, and in the air. You've seen our pneumatic mail system. Just as quickly, we flit over and under water. In the streets, there are electric mail coaches. But our most glorious achievement is the airships: slim tubes with gondolas hanging from them, the old ›Zeppelin‹ brought to perfection.«

Venir 1906; Ritter 1978.

177. N. Becker, A. Venir's *Look forward*, 1906. Title page.

The »novel« deserves attention in so far as it predicts, in 1906, events in the year 2006 – a time we have already reached! Therefore his prognoses can be checked, and it is amazing how incorrect they were – with a few exceptions. The German National and anti-Slavist tendencies are completely abstruse. In certain respects the totalitarian systems of the 20th century are heralded here, especially National Socialism with its preference for the Germanic race, its rigorous eugenics and sterilization. The political constellations are for the most part wishful thinking. At any rate, king and emperor remain on their thrones, but the period between 1870 and 2006 is largely peaceful, and it is not until the latter year that the big German-Russian war breaks out – a war in which all of Europe is somehow involved.

Stunning, however, is a prediction that almost came true: But it was not the emperor of Austria who was shot by a Pan-Slavist in 2006. Rather, the Austrian heir apparent was shot by a Slav in 1914, which triggered World War I.

Egon Friedell (1878–1938). The journey in the time machine (*Die Reise mit der Zeitmaschine*, 1905)

»I dared to write a letter to the great storyteller H. G. Wells«, Egon Friedell tells us. »I wanted to find out where his time traveler vanished to. But I received a furious letter from his secretary. Fine – I went time-traveling myself!«

First, however, Friedell explains at great length his theories about time and space and relativity – he's really read his Einstein! Finally, on May 4th, 1905, we can leave. We set off from London – the journey is meant to go into the past. The year 1840 is our first destination – bet there are problems with the complicated time machine and suddenly we land – in 1955! How much the world has changed during these 90 years!

»There was not a sign of growing plants: Far and wide, nothing but a homogenous, glassily shimmering surface. Not a sound around us in the air. For obviously there were also no animals, but on the other hand no gramophones, either.« And strangely, no city of London as far as the eye can see.

Then, we see a young man motionless in front of us, and ask him where London is. The man points toward the sky – and we catch sight of the sea of houses with covered markets, barracks, racetracks, theaters, cathedrals – floating above the earth! Gravitational energy has been mastered – the city has been able to leave the Earth below it!

Now the young man informs us about a number of achievements. People now work 22 hours – sleep is replaced by ultraviolet, at the automat atomizer there are oxygen snacks, and to get clean you go into the ultra-red field. We'd like to get to know the young man close up – but suddenly he's gone. He was only a projection.

We had had enough of this future and wanted to go back – but not so the machine – and suddenly we land in 2123. And again we have a strange encounter: two men with bronze-colored skin, obviously Egyptians, smart, well educated. An intelligent conversation ensues, and we learn that we have landed on an Earth of a different period! – For light does not travel in a straight line! Confused, inspired, engaged in discussion, astonished – and with more adventures under our belts, we land, rather relieved and glad, in the present – 1905.

Like Jules Verne, Egon Friedell tries to make the adventures plausible by means of a number of theories or at least explanations. Friedell was an actor, man of letters, and cultural historian, an important person in turn-of-the-century Vienna, of Jewish extraction. When the SS forced their way into his house on March 18th, 1938, he took his own life.

178. Fritz Lang, *Metropolis*, 1926. Drawing by Otto Hunte.

9. Art, expression, c. 1900–30

9.1. Germany. Switzerland. Austria

Artists in the ideal artists' colonies, 1850 to the present day

Aren't the nineteenth- and twentieth-century artists' colonies small towns in the broadest sense of the word? The artists wanted to translate into action the dream of the ideal society, born from the idea of sublime art, and human architecture, in unspoiled or paradisiacal nature, or in a city, or on its outskirts, was supposed to help this to happen. In fact, this vision was put into action many times all over Europe, but were the lofty goals ever reached?

Hundreds of artists' societies, associations, communities, and groups were formed, especially in the last century. Their idealism, their hope to improve the world, their public spirit very often have a utopian character – but they have become realities.

Thus we shall pay quick visits to at least a few of these societies that were formative for the cultural scene, but also for the idea of the 20th- and 21st-century artists' community, and we realize that some became »schools« or were connected to schools, and even their invariably short lifespan moves them close to utopia.

The school of Barbizon (c. 1850) meets at the edge of the forest of Fontainebleau, and Théodore Rousseau, Jean-François Millet, Charles François Daubigny, and Camille Corot prepare the way for impressionism. In Darmstadt Grand Duke Ernst Ludwig of Hesse assembles the artists, while Joseph Olbrich builds the ideal artists' settlement on Mathildenhöhe, a manifesto of Art Nouveau architecture.

In Worpswede painter Fritz Mackensen has discovered the beauty of the landscape (1889). Paula Modersohn-Becker enjoys living here, Rainer Maria Rilke is a frequent guest, the architect Bernhard Hoetger creates a romantic, expressive ambiance. The group cultivates and discusses an art that will improve humanity.

Hellerau near Dresden is significant not only as a garden town (1909). In Tessenow's Dalcroze Institute, students focus on movement, dance, healthy, graceful living.

For the Bauhaus in Dessau, the great synthesis of modern architecture and art, Walter Gropius creates the master houses not far from the magnificent school building.

Not all artists' associations of the period between the world wars established settlements. Some formed an inner city, as it were: the Blaue Reiter, De Stijl, Russian Constructivism and many others. Monte Verità, however, is worth a detailed visit (cf. chap. 9.1).

We could spend many weeks visiting additional interesting artists' colonies, such as Brannenburg, Murnau, or Grötzingen in Germany, Auvers sur Oise in France, Katwijk or Sint-Martens-Latem in the Netherlands, Kazimierz in Poland, or even Jirye in Korea.

The idea of artists' colonies/villages has not been abandoned by a long shot. Hundreds of small or larger communities, often only loosely associated groups, are active in our century as well.

Fritz Lang (1890–1976, film) and Thea von Harbou (1888–1954, script). *Metropolis*, 1926; Erich Kettelhut (1893–1960) and Otto Hunte (1881–1960)

Metropolis: We enter a mighty, glittering city, spacious, ambitious, inhabited by radiant young people, athletic and wealthy.

A massive Babylonian tower is the center of the city. Huge skyscrapers are clustered close together, connected by bold bridges with cars streaking across them. There are cars below as well, jam-packed in the canyons of the streets. Aeroplanes fly above, almost grazing the high-rises. Everything in the city is movement, dynamics, density.

John Frederson is the mighty industrial boss of Metropolis. But where are the machines? Together with the noble Maria, the leader of the workers, and Frederson's son, who is in love with Maria, we descend deep into the underground city. A powerful Moloch, a machine, both monster and edifice, has caught up the workers in its monotonous rhythm. The son is moved by the torture and imprisonment the workers are subjected to.

But the boss has a duplicate made of Maria. She is supposed to stir up the workers – but this also strikes at the heart of the city. The machine breaks, and masses of water threaten to flood the subterranean world. At the last moment Maria and young Frederson save the desperate workers.

Stamm 1903; Harbou 1925, 1984; Benson n.d.; Dethier 1994.

The magnificent images of this film – the city was constructed in the studio with the help of special effects – are supplemented by expressive preliminary sketches and drawings. There is hardly another film that has had as intensive and significant a relationship to architecture, to the city.

The expressive drawings of the Americans, but especially Sant'Elias's »città futurista« may have supplied the models here. But Fritz Lang completed and perfected these ideas and went far beyond the visions of his models. He has had many followers, the most obvious being the Japanese film *Robotic Angel* by Tezuka / Rintaro (2002), which directly references *Metropolis*. Cities of this type have long been realized today. High-rises have long surpassed the heights of Metropolis, and perhaps once America feels its cities have reached maximum density and height, the Asian cities will begin to overshadow Metropolis.

Fritz Lang calls the central building »Babylon« – it far eclipses the legendary tower.

Carl Zehnder (1859–1938). An Art Nouveau monument, 1909–18

Amid the turmoil of the First World War, Carl Zehnder shows us his monumental ideal city. We feel solemn and full of awe as we walk through the brightly lit, tall stone halls, which are domed and vaulted.

A number of architectural monuments are dedicated to the memory of great men. »Johannes Brahms is the greatest composer of the century that has just passed – I've dedicated a hall of honor and a monument to him, meant to express both the power and grace of music.«

Now we have come to a lake encircled by gentle hills. On the shore is a building both profane and sacral on a circular ground plan surrounded by minaret-like towers. The courtyard in which it is located is enclosed like a holy place by walls and arcades.

Nearby, and visible from afar on a massive foundation, there are four slim columns supporting a round platform on which a muscular young man stands, his hands outstretched toward the sky. The confusing and fascinating three-dimensionality of the transitions, intersections, and interpenetrations reminds us of Piranesi. But Zehnder wants to have nothing to do with Piranesi's *Carceri*:

»In the majestic, bright spaces I have always positioned ideal human beings: classically beautiful and lighthearted, but pervaded with spirit and faith, art and joy.«

In the meantime we have arrived in the actual city center. It goes without saying that in the wide street, which is like a forum, there are only pedestrians. Like them, we are delighted by the large pool. In it is a small temple with a four-horse chariot on top of it.

Now we are strolling up the steps to the upper platform. For some time, we have been looking at the truly immense rotunda whose dominant chord is a monumental portico. Sculptures, portals, columns, arcades accentuate the mighty perspectives that bring constant new surprises. »The city's vocabulary is not new«, admits Zehnder, »they're the age-old elements of the city, but I have completely reinterpreted them and created a modern city.«

It is indeed an imposing city, but one wonders where the many functions of our life, especially traffic, are located.

Zehnder 1918.

Carl Zehnder, probably only peripherally touched by the war in his refuge in Switzerland, creates architectures fit for monumental historical movies. His use of forms is reminiscent of the early Otto Wagner, while the atmosphere suggests turn-of-the-century symbolism and idealism.

Paul Scheerbart (1863–1915). The emperor of Utopia (*Der Kaiser von Utopia*, 1904)

What strange people these are! Our guide in Ulaleipu is the great author of *The Glass Chain*. Here, the emperor is Philandu, an original and humorous ruler over the large cliff city with spiral streets, tunnels, colonnades, and hanging gardens.

For the utopians, a glorious era has dawned. The country has a successful democracy and there is no militarism.

In Schilda, on the other hand, the lord mayor is in charge. It's quite an unusual town. The houses are triangular and there are no façades, for the pointed corners face the street. The same is true of the town hall and the railroad station.

But even more remarkable are the movable houses – indeed, half the town is built like this: Twenty big captive balloons hold a house aloft, including a restaurant. It's very amusing to dine up in the air or even to float away. Thus we see the buildings in ever new, surprising clusters, rising and descending. The airy town is lit by a thousand floodlights and is bright as day even at night. People travel by air car and fast electric trains that glide along like a cable railway on strong cables. Steamships and railroads complete the transportation system.

What impressed us the most, though, was a small device that recorded what we said and photographed us at the same time.

Then the rulers of the little towns have a ludicrous idea: They change jobs! The emperor of Ulaleipu becomes the mayor, while the mayor becomes emperor.

And then there is a gigantic artists' festival and it's hard to believe: Seventy million photographs are taken. But here comes an earnest admonition: »Such trivialities do not deepen art, but diffuse it.«

Scheerbart 1988.

Paul Scheerbart represents, on the one hand, the enthusiastic and dramatic side of expressionism, while on the other hand his work is characterized by irony, humor, and buffoonery, fine qualities that only rarely appear in architecture.

Bruno Taut (1880–1938). The Gläserne Kette. *Alpine Architektur*, 1917–23

»Get the masses involved in a great project!« In response to this inexorable appeal by Bruno Taut, with the help of all of Europe, people have begun building »Alpine architecture«: The highest Alpine chain from the Montblanc to the Po River plain has been transformed into a radiantly beautiful architectural landscape.

»In this great communal project everyone clearly sees the work of his hands: Everyone is at work building – in the true sense of the word. Everyone serves the idea of beauty –thoughts of the earth that bears the buildings. – Boredom disappears, and with it, squabbles, politics, and with them the heinous specter of war.«

Bruno Taut leads us through a dreamlike glass world. Enthusiastically, he announces: »*No material overcomes matter as much as glass. Glass is a completely new, pure material, in which matter is melted down and recast. It mirrors the sky and the sun, it is like bright water and has a wealth of possibilities – color, form, and inexhaustible character.*«

We walk past radiant community centers, transparent theaters, translucent festival buildings. The architects are the new global builders. Shining crystal structures and glass domes crown the peaks of the Alps, soar up to the light, transformed to light themselves, absorb the rays of light and transform them, creating a new house of the sky like the medieval cathedrals. We pay our first visit to a bizarre peak in the Alps. And Bruno Taut gives a rapturous description of the edifice:

»*Snow – glaciers – glass.*
Névés in eternal ice
and snow – superstructures
ornamented with
enclosures, surfaces
blocks of colored glass
flowers of the mountains.«

Paul Scheerbart, the poet laureate of the Gläserne Kette, chimes in enthusiastically: »*If we want to raise our culture to a higher level, we are forced, willy-nilly, to transform our architecture. And this will only be possible for us if we create spaces that are no longer closed-in. However, we can only do this if we use glass architecture. Then we would have a paradise on earth and would no longer need to look longingly for a paradise in heaven.*«

Up to this point we have been looking up to the mountains with a sense of wonder and enthusiasm. Now we are granted an enchanting vision of a broad valley nestled among the mountains like a huge flower. And, lyrically, Bruno Taut speaks of his architecture: »*Walls are placed up the slopes, made of colored glass in solid frames. The light that shines through them produces multiple changing effects both for the valley and for those who walk through it or travel over it by air.*«

Taut shows us the town's almond-shaped center: »*Down below, a lake with flower-like glass decorations in the water. The lake and the walls shine at night.*«

More marvels await us: Like needles or slim obelisks, tall columns rise into the sky from the mountaintops around the valley. »*Their tips are of polished crystal, and floodlights on the mountain peaks glitter brightly at night.*«

As we take our leave, Bruno Taut describes his architect's dream of the »Dead Palace«: »*I knew where I wanted to go. I therefore climbed undaunted up the roughly hewn rocky steps – and was soon at the top. And I was in front of the strong palace I'd wanted to have all my life. But I've never seen it as clearly as I did then. The palace sits on the mountaintop like a jagged, spiky helmet. I am very astonished. But – it is so silent here. I have never experienced such terrible iso-*

183. Wenzel August Hablik, the construction of the Air Colony, 1908.
184. Wenzel August Hablik, Airplane Towers. Silos. Artists' housing, 1921.

lation. The ruby columns catch my eye – and the wide halls are full of blazing heat. This, then, is the strong palace I have wanted to have all my life! It's all so dead! And a voice speaks to me:

›The art you dreamed of is always dead. The palaces have no life. Trees are alive – animals are alive — but palaces are not.‹

Therefore, I retort, I want what is dead!

›Yes!‹ I hear a voice calling – but I do not know whose it is.

I wanted quiet – peace! I call out wildly in terrible loathing.

›You will find peace soon enough,‹ I hear, ›don't be so greedy!‹

And I knew what I wanted – I wanted calm – without desire – a descent into the infinite!!! The dead palace shook – shook!«

Sites & Stations; Thomsen 1994; Stamm 2003.

Paul Scheerbart is the great protagonist of the Gläserne Kette – language and imagination, effusive enthusiasm are quite suitable for the work of the dreaming architect.

References in other Taut works allow us to give this drawing, too, erotic interpretations. We feel Bruno Taut's »An Architect's Dream« is an interpretation of Hablik's »Way of Genius« (cf. following chapter). It is remarkable that the idealistic enthusiasm for glass extends into World War II.

The new technologies, while they were the prerequisites for a new transparency, are stilted, spiritualized. The idea of »purity« addresses the ethical aspect, which is the foundation of the work of contemporary painters such as Mondrian.

Bruno Taut later took the path toward reality, into a very down-to-earth architecture that deals primarily with the construction of residential buildings, far from fanciful dreams.

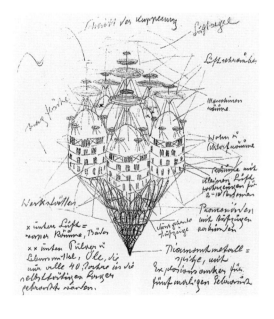

Wenzel August Hablik (1881–1934). The Airplane Towers, 1921, the Air Colony, 1908, and the Crystal Edifices, 1903–25

The silhouette of the town toward which we are flying is full of movement, colorful, many-faceted. The meaning of the towers soon becomes clear to us: Our flying machine, which can move both horizontally and vertically, docks at one of the towers, we get out by means of mechanical stairs, and the express elevator brings us into the city.

»I foresaw that air traffic would increase enormously«, Hablik is pleased by his prognostication, »and the towers allow the planes to land directly in the city.«

Hablik explains the color and movement, the dynamics and variety: «The city has everything the inhabitants need, but we've also located large silos here. However, the cityscape is given its unique character by the many artists who live here.«

But Hablik goes even further: He builds another, very different new city. He takes us to a huge meadow, where a remarkable structure rises into the sky: a lattice cone balances on a diamond-metal tip. Elevators take us to the top, to one of the domed houses that encircle a large central building. And already a slight tremor goes through the colony, the little town lifts off, and we are gently soaring toward the sea. Now Hablik gives us a tour of the small town. In the five cylinders in the lower part, many different kinds of workshops have been located. Above them are the residents' living rooms and dormitories, and just below them are the air-water rooms and baths, plus powder and oils, which are brought to the automated storage places every 40 years. Now the elevator has brought us to the promenade floor, and we enjoy a view of the landscape. We're especially interested in the mechanics that can move such a colony, and Hablik briefly explains: »The six domes contain the engine rooms; each engine moves a horizontally rotating propeller. The wings and the sails cause the town to soar gently through space.«

Now, far off, we see the sea and a wonderful castle, built by Hablik, appears. Like a mighty crystal it shines on the beach. Hablik's dream of the crystal edifice has been turned into reality here by the sea, but in the mountains and the desert as well: cathedrals of a new, pure religion. After a safe landing Hablik once more sums up his theses about architecture: »*We need new ideals. One of them is the* gesamtkunstwerk, *architecture! Not a ›box of bricks and emergency shelter‹ – but architecture as a living element that embodies cosmic laws. Our era demands that we solve entirely new problems and, truth to tell, these are not inconsiderable. For we are the ones who prepare the way for a new paradise on earth. Until recently the utopia of paradise belonged to heaven alone!*«

And filled with such sublime thoughts we walk the road of genius: over steep bluffs, over cliffs and crevasses, over bizarre rocks and pointed peaks, ravines and precipices, we struggle to reach the crystal cathedral-palace, light and freedom.

Thomson 1994; Eaton 2001; Stamm 2003.

»Upward«: Were one to sum up in one word the architectonic ideas of the expressionists, the Gläserne Kette, the enraptured dreamers, then it would have to be this one. As the soul ascends, so the creations of architecture rise into the heights, and like mountain climbers, architects too climb the rocks and glaciers. But that's not all: Wenzel Hablik and his colony soar into the air, articulating the architects' dream of weightlessness. Wenzel Hablik foresaw the rapid development of aeronautics, but like all prognosticators of flying he believes that it can take place in the context of a densely populated city.

Hermann Finsterlin (1887–1973). The color organ, 1920

On a vast plain, we approach a bizarre mountain formation, towering alien and isolated. But as we get closer, we see the radiant colors of the formation and realize it is a human settlement, an artificial mountain city. Finsterlin enthusiastically speaks of his concept of the city: »*Cities as form organs and color organs providing the most stimulating influences; cities as inspiration and guided dynamics, not fettered reflex, shall be the real expression of the architecture of the future.*«

But in addition to the mega-structure of the »city«, fantastic formations of houses give life to the vast landscape and form a giant sculpture garden. Finsterlin takes us from the »Casa Nova« to the »Red House«, the »Concert House«, past wonderful edifices where we need every bit of our imagination to imagine how they can be inhabited.

And the crazily, fantastically brilliant master explains his motives: »*I felt quite a very strange dislike for living in cubes, and for level surfaces, corners, and angles, and the boxes they call furniture. When I woke up or daydreamed I no longer wanted my eyes to rebound from vertical and horizontal walls, but caress complicated forms, as in the marvelous caves of my dreams or in giant organs, a rich, living, exciting environment.*«

Finsterlin 1920; *Stadt und Utopie* 1982; Thomson 1994.

185. Hermann Finsterlin, Communal Building, the city, 1920.
186. Wenzel August Hablik, Path of the Genius, 1918.

Hermann Finsterlin did not find the path to the real world of constructing buildings, and probably did not look for it either. He continued to be the single-minded representative of a three-dimensional, sculptural architecture, preferring rounded, soft, flowing forms to the bizarrely faceted, broken forms of the expressionists. Once more it becomes obvious than no clear boundary can be drawn between architecture and sculpture. Hermann Finsterlin starts out from modeled three-dimensional forms and considers them to be habitable, indeed, even defines them as a city.

Walter Determann (1889–1960). The early Bauhaus settlement, 1920

No, we are not going to visit the sharply defined, white, functional Bauhaus buildings of Walter Gropius – those won't be built for another six or eight years. Rather, we are visiting a highly imaginative settlement north of Weimar.

The plan that Walter Determann shows us at the outset seems more like an Aztec totem than the plan for a modern settlement: built strictly symmetrically, using bright colors and lavish patterns, and we have difficulty making out the buildings.

Once inside the settlement itself, we are astonished that the colorful pavements far exceed the green spaces. The center of the complex is a large building for theater and sports events, festivals, and exhibitions. »For this important building«, says the architect, »we chose the Bauhaus logo, a sparkling crystal resembling Bruno Taut's crystal structures. It not only reflects the rays of the sun during the day but emits light rays by night. It towers above the adjacent stadium, which

187. Walter Determann, Bauhaus settlement, 1920. 1 administration, festival, and exhibition halls, 2, 3 guesthouses and apartments for single people, 4 blocks of four family homes each, 5 dining and social hall, 6 indoor swimming pool, district heating, gym, physician, sick bay, 7 metal foundry, kiln for glass and pottery, 8, 9 manor, manor administration, 10 preparatory school for children, 11 openair swimming, 12 gate in the direction of Buchfart, 13 general workshops, 14 individual workshops, 15 playing fields, 16 theater and stadium, 17 Bauhaus logo, 18 lighthouses.

is simultaneously used as an open-air theater. Thus we have placed culture in the center of the complex.«

The more profane functions are located to one side of this center: the administration and the guesthouses. On both sides of the main axis are the detached family homes that are directly connected with the incredibly extensive workshop buildings, divided into individual workshops and general workshops. »The brickworks and the metal workshops are a little off to the side, across from the indoor swimming pool and the heating plant for the entire complex of buildings.«
Now we have crossed the settlement. When we reach the end, we look at the community buildings again.

Looking at the ground plan again, the eyes of the head, as it were, are formed by the schools. Between them are the sports and games areas.
Eaton 2001; Stamm 2003.

From the Renaissance we are familiar with the fact that town plans can become beautiful patterns. In the context of the Bauhaus it is unusual, though the early period of the Bauhaus did have some very expressive aspects. Determann's plan – the buildings can hardly be made out – becomes a painting, something between art deco and expressionism.

Uriel Birnbaum (1894–1956). The heavenly city, 1921

The architect built no less than 33 cities for his emperor, each one different, each more beautiful than the next, but the emperor was never satisfied.

»I'll show you three or four cities, the finest and most important«, Uriel Birnbaum promises us.

The writer now takes us to the top terrace of the Babylonian city, a compact, gray structure with stairs, terraces, and arcades. Up here, »The emperor and the architect« is revealed to us. We are looking up into the blue sky, which suddenly turns yellow. Huge rings become visible, and in their center a large gleaming globe appears. »Watch carefully, and wait and see what happens«, the architect tells us.

Sure enough, after a few minutes cubes rise one after another from the rings, massing in front of the rings, growing downward, with smaller volumes erupting from the larger ones. Windows open. And irregular forms grow from the lower bodies, spread and become rocks. Suddenly a huge fortress looms before us, almost inaccessible in these mountains, but shining in the most wonderful colors like a fairy-tale palace.

»But the emperor was not satisfied with the city, it was not his dream vision. And thus, one city after another is created, though never the ideal city of the emperor's visions.«

Now we race from one city to another. The »island city« rises from the sea, an enormous terraced tower; in the »red city« the houses are crowded together and form a hill surrounded by walls. The most stunning is the »glass city«. It, too, is formed from stacked-up volumes, but they are perfectly clear, transparent, sharply defined cubes, reflecting many colors, huge, precious crystals that fill us with rapture.

And yet, the emperor is dissatisfied, and the hapless architect is desperate. But in the end they are both forced to realize that there is only one ideal city: holy Jerusalem, the heavenly city.
Eaton 2001; Stamm 2003.

Uriel Birnbaum, too, was wholly dedicated to the enraptured poetry of the Gläserne Kette, and the mountains and crystals, domes and light are the main requisites of his architectural dreams.

Friedrich (Frederick) Kiesler (1890–1966). The City in Space, 1925

What a new way to experience the city! It is not a slab with houses placed on it, but a spatial adventure inscribed in a coordinate system. It is a completely new way of liberating ourselves from the force of gravity and, so to speak, experiencing the third dimension not only with our eyes but with every part of our bodies.

The old cities belong to the past. Kiesler pronounces a harsh verdict: »*Our houses are nothing but stone coffins rising up from the ground. One story high, two stories high – 300 stories high.*«

His condemnation of cities is even more severe:

188. Uriel Birnbaum, appearance of the »heavenly city«, 1921/22.
189. Friedrich Kiesler, Space City, Paris, 1925.

190. Fritz Malcher, *Heil-Land*, center of Muthmanns-dorf, Lower Austria, 1926.

»And our cities? Walls, walls, walls. We no longer want walls, barracks for the body and the spirit, a culture of barracks with or without ornamentation. What we want is
1. transformation of spherical space into cities
2. to be able to detach ourselves from the earth – the task of
the static axis
3. no walls, no foundations
4. a system of tensions in outer space
5. the creation of new living opportunities resulting in needs
that transform society.«

»Enough architecture has been made already. We don't want a new edition, no matter how cleverly designed. Instead of the former one-frontage models, instead of baroque lines – straight lines, and square windows instead of rectangular ones. The expert is bankrupt. What everyone is interested in is, How does one live inside these straight or crooked walls? What life – new life – do these four-frontage or X-frontage buildings give rise to?«

»Instead of ornaments, smooth walls, instead of art, architecture – I want none of that. I de-mand vital buildings, the city in space, functional architecture.«
Kiesler 1988; Nouvelles 2001.

The road to the three-dimensional city begins with Leonardo (cf. chap. 4.1). Otto Wagner and An-tonio St. Elia developed the third dimension from modern traffic. Friedrich Kiesler, whose layouts are related to those of the Netherlands group De Stijl, abstracts, aestheticizes, artifies space.

Fritz Malcher (1888–1933). *Heil–Land* (= Healing Land) in Lower Austria, 1926

Both the bashful and hard-working architect Fritz Malcher and Josef Napravnik, editor of the *Österreichische illustrierte Zeitschrift*, act as our guides. Napravnik saves us the trouble of de-scribing the eventful visit, as he enthusiastically speaks about the »New World« that has been cre-ated –why, we wonder – in an area near Wiener Neustadt, a very attractive landscape to be sure, but completely unknown.

Here is how the editor begins his account of the departure from Vienna:
»A long-drawn-out whistle, late passengers get on, the carriage doors close noiselessly, a sec-ond short signal – the train starts moving, the Künstlerhaus, Karlsplatz, and finally the patina of the Technical Institute and the mighty dome of the Karlskirche have vanished from view in less than half a minute although we are speeding along at a fair altitude in the overhead express train. The giant residential buildings of the 10th District, massive and ponderous, and settlements with gardens and single-family homes appear for a second, vanish, make room for a new view; we've hardly grazed Mödling when Baden welcomes us; we're flying at breathtaking speed across plains, past woods, toward our destination. A quarter of an hour after our departure we're there. The train stops elegantly, without a jerk or a jolt. The doors open.

We've arrived: Vienna's forest and garden city welcomes us. Sheltered from the wind, it stretches along the southeastern slopes of the Hohe Wand, fourteen km long, four km wide, with a population of half a million. There are no giant buildings. Nothing but the most modern single-family homes, gardens, and parks.«

Our editor goes on to describe the newest suburb of Vienna, near Wiener Neustadt: *»The swampy plain that lies in front of the Hohe Wand has become a lake: A dam in the Prosset Gorge has created this simple miracle. On the peninsula that projects into the lake is the arrival hall. Here we find all the buildings that serve public and cultural interests, arranged radially – imposing edi-fices.«*

The center of the semicircular island is the hall of music, a towering central building with a domed roof that reminds us of a sacral building – but in view of the fact that music is still consid-ered to be sacral, we see no contradiction here.

Interspersed with plenty of greenery, the very uniformly designed buildings are grouped around this center: The theater buildings, playhouse, and opera are complemented by the commercial buildings: The businesses, administration buildings, and hotels are not far from the docks. The democratic spirit of the First Republic is vividly represented in the community houses and the people's center, though without being dramatic, a quality that is reserved for the music building. From the station of the overhead express railroad that brought us here there is a connection to the main-line service, the city railroad, and to the lakeside train as well as the rack railroad. We

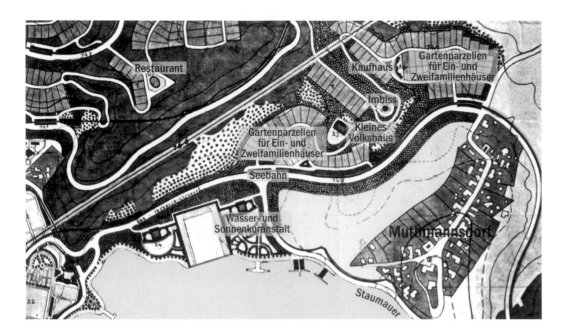

191. Fritz Malcher, *Heil-Land*, center of Muthmanns-dorf, Lower Austria, 1926.

take the opportunity to see the little town from above, and through the Leitergraben the train takes us to the Kleine Kanzel. The reservoir is only a short distance away and we recognize the dam wall that protects the village of Muthmannsdorf from the masses of water.

Above all, we get a good view of the settlement: It consists exclusively of one- and two-family homes standing in garden plots. For romantics and nature lovers there are »forest houses«. To be sure, it is not clear to us how half a million people are to be settled here at a future date without destroying the landscape.

At this point Fritz Malcher tells us about specific facilities available in this city of half a million. An airport is self-evident; enough room has been planned for freight railway stations, and ware-houses assure food supplies even in times of crisis.

»My city is rightly named ›healing land‹«, says the architect, »it is a region of health and healing for body and spirit. I took advantage of the wonderful air of the Hohe Wand and built a series of sanitariums and spas. Wounded war veterans are given preferential treatment. The area around the Hohe Wand has long been a favorite region for hikers and vacationers. Now mountain inns and tourist hotels are an added reason to visit this part of the country.«

The ample sports facilities are an added contribution to the healing and continued good health of the inhabitants. Water sports are available on the artificial lake. This is also the site of a large water and summer health resort. The large playing field is directly connected to the resorts, and from these, in turn, it is not far to the people's center and the department stores.

But, we are concerned, what happened to Gaaden and St. Peter am Moos with its beauti-ful frescoes? »We were forced to sacrifice them. The frescoes were removed and the rest of the valuable objects were salvaged, while the inhabitants all got a beautiful, new single-family home!«

Fritz Malcher really believed his plans would be implemented, and his painstaking planning goes far beyond a utopia. But neither the politicians of Lower Austria let alone those of Vienna would have been able to finance the project. Disillusioned, Malcher went to America. In New York he was at least able to have minor successes: A few of his ideas were incorporated in the planning of a City in the Age of the Motor for a population of 25,000. He did not live to see the completion of his monograph: In 1933 he died in New York.

Franz Sedlacek (1891–1945). The Town by the Sea, 1934

The painter gives us a tour of a charming little town. Here, he has gathered all the small idyllic dreams he's been able to salvage from history – as though world-shattering political events had not happened one year previously in Germany and this year in Austria!

We reach the town by boat. A breakwater and the quadrant of a promenade form a small har-bor, while a massive tower probably does not cast its light too far out to sea. Two of the cubical

192. Franz Sedlacek, The Town by the Sea, 1934.
193. Monte Verità, layout, c. 1927.

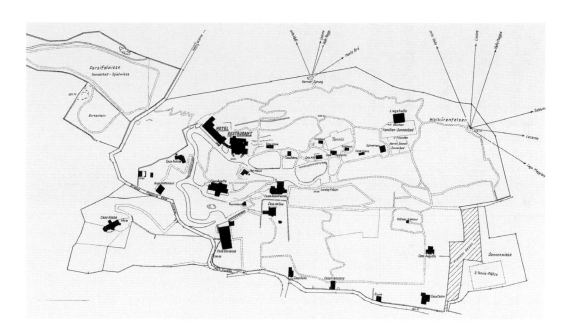

residential buildings form a portico, others ascend the landscaped slope. There are adjacent fields and vineyards. At the foot of a hill, there is a well-fortified castle, and at the top of the rocky hill, a ruined castle still dominates the small settlement.

Now we stroll across to the other part of the peninsula: The little square castle may have been modeled on the convent of Göttweig in Lower Austria. But now the painter reminds us of our own time: On the high, steep cliff, a radio tower with transmitter rises into an ominously stormy, romantic sky.

Hassfurther 2005.

Franz Sedlacek is part of the »new functionalism« movement of the 1920s and '30s that develops primarily in Germany and Austria and seeks an alternative, completely realistic style between expressionism, abstraction, and classic modernism. But Sedlacek most clearly signals his affinity with fantasy and shyly comes close to surrealism. He does not design the New City but creates a collage of a dream vision out of traditional elements. Fifty years later, Massimo Scolari, for instance, is his kindred spirit.

A hundred artists, thinkers, dreamers on Monte Verità, 1900–23, 1924–33

All of us have a dream, a goal we shall reach above all through our art: to create a new mankind, individuals full of harmony, embedded in nature and spirit. We need no power ruling over us, we shall live, a great community, in brotherhood and peace.

These are the lofty ideals the pioneers brought with them – and indeed: On Monte Verità something quite incredible, unique has come into being. Let us visit this place of marvels and innovations.

Ascona is our destination, and we approach Monte Verità, the mountain of truth, with high expectations. A barren, subdued landscape in the Swiss canton of Tessin lies before us as we climb the hill, past shacks, houses, villas, a hotel and restaurant. We are unable to recognize any sort of planning concept. Chance seems to have scattered the most differently designed buildings haphazardly – or should we say picturesquely? – across the hill.

The road from the center of Ascona takes us past a ruin, past simple or impressive houses bearing the names of the owners or poetic appellations: Casa Peace, Casa del Sole, Casa Semiramis, Château d'amour. The hotel is centrally located. At some distance from it are the staff building, hothouses, the gardener's house. There is an open air sun deck, and next to it a deck for family sun bathing and separate areas for men and women. These are not far from the Valkyries' Rock. The sunbathing meadow on the southwest, next to the birch grove, is called the Parsifal Meadow. We are struck by the fact that the houses have both traditional steep roofs and modern flat roofs.

Hotel Semiramis is five stories high. In spite of its flat roof it looks rather conventional, though it was built in 1910. Hotel Monte Verità is a quality building built in the international style, designed by

the renowned Berlin architect Emil Fahrenkamp. Casa Anatta, one of the most important houses, built in 1904, also has a flat roof.

The main building, however, it too built circa 1904, does not forgo traditional elements, such as symmetry and a loggia accessed by two curved staircases. Beside a restaurant it contains the library and writing, reading, and music rooms.

Let's get back to the utopia –we are then in the year 1889: This is when »Fraternitas« was founded. It is provided with its own building. The loose community somewhat resembles a monastery.

At the beginning of the 20th century we encounter lofty ideals by the dozens, as it were – what are the goals, the longings, the commonalities? The members' entire life, far from the metropolis, close to nature, is one of their unifying ideas, and »back to nature« is a recurrent theme.

The focus is alternative lifestyles, which are implemented single-mindedly. Healthy vegetarian food is one of the most important key points, air and sunlight therapy lead to open and high-minded nudity and graceful movement. Nature takes care of the healing processes.

All the principles that have to do with health, hygiene, and the body are given an idealized, even spiritualized overemphasis, however. One of the great dreams of humanity has come true here: life in complete harmony with nature and shaped by the power of the mind, experienced in community, in love and peace, a new model of the world.

Back to reality. We've already seen some of the completed buildings as we arrived. Which of the other spiritual ideals are expressed as architectural symbols? And what kind of people carry out the ideas?

First of all, »natural« living is a primary concern: Nearly everyone practices vegetarianism. People are building »air cabins«, primitive, open wooden houses. A kind of natural-healing sanitarium supplements the open-air activities. How successful is the synthesis with spiritual matters?

Spirituality often enough turns into spiritualism and occultism, and the »Black Chapel« is occasionally the site of strange phenomena and events. A mystical freemasonry, a magical Christianity, and various sects have affinities to this strange »town.« The healing power of physical movement leads to the beauty of movement, and this inevitably brings us to the dance, perhaps one of the most intense and important events on Monte Verità. In the realm of dance, we experience further, significant expressions of the ideals.

Emile Jaques-Dalcroze combines rhythmical gymnastics with dance and music. The decisive reform of dance came from Rudolf Laban de Varajs circa 1913 and was carried out into the world by the American Isadora Duncan and Mary Wigman.

Beside the nature idealists, the artists also showed their interest. They were inspired, or even healed, by air and light, but none of the great artists stayed for long, and a truly intentional artists' colony was never built, only scattered artists' houses.

Architectonic escapades in the form of temples with Art Nouveau emblems are, so to speak, the extreme wing of a conception of life that appears comical.

Whom do we encounter here on our tour through time? After 1869, several times, we run into the often fugitive anarchist Mikhail Bakunin, and then the revolutionary writer Erich Mühsam, in 1905. In 1911 we meet Pyotr Kropotkin, an anarchist like Bakunin, as he tries to repair his shattered health, together with August Bebel, the founder of the Social Democratic Workers' Party and Karl Kautsky, a pioneer of Marxism and socialism. With the radical socialist Gustav Landauer, the prominent, politically revolutionary forum is complete.

In 1907 we have a discussion with the proponent of Western and Eastern wisdom, Hermann Hesse, and circa 1920 we encounter the painters Marianne von Werefkin and Alexey von Javlensky. Almost reverentially we meet great minds such as the theoretician of archetypes, Carl Gustav Jung, and the writers James Joyce, Stefan George, and Rainer Maria Rilke.

The artists of the Bauhaus drop in only for short visits: Joseph Albers, Herbert Bayer, Marcel Breuer, Walter Gropius, Laszlo Moholy-Nagy, Oskar Schlemmer, and Paul Klee, as well as the dadaists Hugo Ball, Hans Arp and his wife Sophie Täuber, Hans Richter, and the Russian avant-garde architect El Lissitzky (1924).

194. Fidus, Temple of the Earth, 1901. Site plan.

195. Rudolf Steiner, 2nd Goetheanum, Dornach, Switzerland, 1924. Layout.

The painter Fidus demands – and this is true of most of the »Veritans« – »the unity of body and soul in the commitment to a transcendent principle«, and is convinced that Germans are especially qualified for this. The sentimental pathos of his »Prayers of Light« was also articulated in his paintings – slim youths, almost androgynous, their arms uplifted, hailing the sun, strange variations of symbolism and idealism that border on kitsch.

Borsano 1979.

Rarely had utopia and reality, fulfillment and failure, come so close to each other, indeed been almost indistinguishable: ideas, philosophies, concepts were for the most part utopias, but the people who were their proponents were a reality. A social reality – or were they out of touch with the realities of their time?

Once more, was this an attempt on their part to reconstitute a world within a world?

Between the turn of the century and World War I, Monte Verità was first and foremost a central proving ground for alternative lifestyles. »Dropouts«, health and nature freaks, reformers and crazies chose the Mountain of Truth as their refuge, as their sphere of work, as their destination for a longer or shorter period. Incipient communities failed or were only of short duration. Nevertheless, a kind of settlement, fairly unplanned, did spring up on the bleak terrain of Monte Verità.

Rudolf Steiner (1861–1925). The Anthroposophists in Dornach, Switzerland, 1925

»The world is in the process of gradual development«, Rudolf Steiner explains. »Our task is to reconstruct this development sensitively and with discernment, then we shall develop higher psychic abilities and with their help attain psychic insights.«

To us, it seems extremely difficult to translate such a complex spirituality into architecture. However, we are going to see a very concrete example.

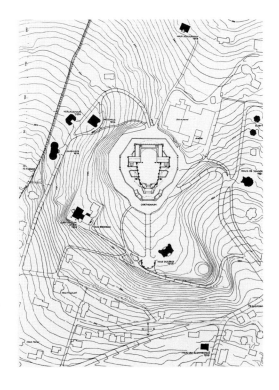

Hiking from Basel to Dornach, we soon climb a green hill. Like a fortress, the main building of the large group of structures, the Goetheanum, appears before us, powerfully dominating the region.

»Oh yes, this is the second Goetheanum. The first one, a wonderful wooden domed building, was destroyed on New Year's Eve 1922/23 in a devastating fire. We did not want to run such a risk for a second time. That's why we decided on a structure built out of concrete.« Rudolf Steiner himself drew up the blueprint, and the resulting building was incredibly expressive, powerfully modeled, and with hardly a single right angle.

»Human beings are spiritual beings, and neither the body nor the mind knows what a right angle is. In the human aura body and mind are present – and this is the explanation for many of the free building forms.«

It goes without saying that the stylistic idiom continues in the interior as well. In addition, there is a canon of strong colors that also reflects spiritual qualities.

But why do we call this a city? The Goetheanum is the center of a dramatic group of buildings: The sculptural Duldeck House is opposite; the so-called Glass House for the manufacture of glass windows dates back to the first Goetheanum; in the Furnace House the fireplace is transformed into a plant that resembles rising smoke. Loosely scattered, residential buildings surround the massive center, reminding us of Monte Verità, which we visited recently.

The Goetheanum »style« is not the original creation of Rudolf Steiner. Rather, it is related to the then prevailing expressionist movement, for instance, as represented by Erich Mendelsohn. Nevertheless the Goetheanum is one of the few buildings in which philosophy and architecture have been convincingly linked.

The style has had its dilettante imitators: Often only the windows and door lintels were made crooked, while the roof was buckled and jutted out: That alone made it the anthroposophy style. Rudolf Steiner is still relevant: Not so much his religious and philosophical theses as his biodynamic agriculture and particularly the Steiner (Waldorf) schools are still very much in vogue.

196. El Lissitzky, cloud hangers for Moscow, 1924/25. Photomontage.
197. El Lissitzky, plan of Moscow with the cloud hangers, 1925.
198. Mart Stam, cloud hangers, 1925.
199. El Lissitzky, Proun 1A, »Bridge 1«, 1919.

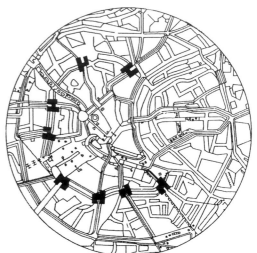

9.2. Russia

EL (Eliezer) Lissitzky (1890–1941) and Mart Stam (1899–1986). The cloud hangers (Wolkenbügel) of Moscow, 1924/25

With El Lissitzky we stroll along Nikitsky Boulevard and at the point where it widens into Nikitsky Square we stand in front of a truly architectonic event, the cloud hangers – at their feet, unhindered, flows the lively traffic of the new Moscow.

El Lissitzky has built skyscrapers of a completely different kind: On three massive pillars, two-thirds of which are glassed-in, with elevators and supply lines, rest the cantilevered, massive volumes. And El Lissitzky explains his basic concept: »One of our ideas for the future is to overcome the foundation, the feeling of being earthbound, gravity: The pyramid is an outdated architectural form, while a building that stands on the ground only at one point is the form of the future.«

And El Lissitzky continues his argument: »*Up to this point we have moved on wheels, subject to gravity, and now the propeller determines our locomotion – a soaring architecture has come into being. One day, gravity will be conquered, but until then the movement of the observer in space is the decisive aspect. The city consists of dying, old sections and growing, living, new ones. We want to deepen this contrast.*«

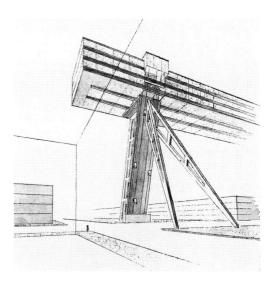

The cloud hangers give the city of Moscow a completely new, modern accent. They are a sign of technical progress and of the new society. The latest building materials have been used. »*The skeleton consists of new types of non-rusting steel that can withstand a great load. Also, we used chemically treated glass that passes light but screens out thermal radiation*«, adds El Lissitzky.

How was the artist El Lissitzky able to cope with construction-related problems? »I collaborated with my friend Emil Roth, an experienced designer, and he made many static sketches for me«, admits El Lissitzky.

Now we are driving down the ring street of Moscow and again we see the mighty towers, all eight of them. No doubt about it: Moscow has radically changed, has become a modern city, as it were. And here's another important detail that strikes us: Abstract color plays a fundamental role in present-day Soviet art, and so El Lissitzky has distinguished the eight cloud hangers by making each a different color.

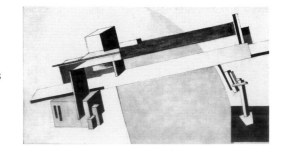

Now we meet the Netherlands architect Mart Stam. No doubt he advised El Lissitzky, perhaps even participated in drawing up the blueprint. We are surprised by his variant of the cloud hangers. The project is simplified, the constructive elements are clearly articulated.

»I find Lissitzky's idea of the contrasted, almost soaring offices wonderful. But I was the one who gave the construction its logic«, asserts Mart Stam.

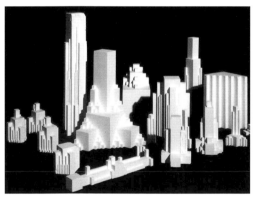

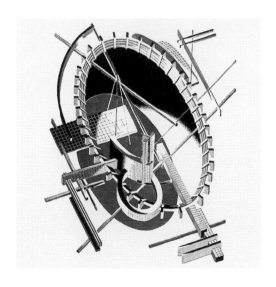

Back to El Lissitzky. He enriched Moscow in other ways as well: In every one of the districts we find a few »Proun works«, bridges, cubes, volumes, compositions, abstract yet useable by the community. The work was created around 1919. It represents a connection to the modern stylistic idiom of Western Europe.

The political aspect becomes apparent: El Lissitzky pays homage to the great Lenin, or rather, to his spirit of technical progress. In 1924 he builds the Lenin Platform, a lattice pile that dynamically juts out on a base; the speaker's rostrum for Lenin is at the upper end, and above it is a writing- and projection surface.

»My work definitely has a spiritual dimension«, says El Lissitzky. »It is a manifestation of the policy of industrialization and of the constructive spirit of the Soviet Union.«
El Lissitzky 1990.

El Lissitzky is one of the most important representatives of »constructivism«, the architecture of the Russian Revolution. Political, constructive, and formal aspects are part of its characteristic profile.

Of course, El Lissitzky knew the American skyscrapers from publications, and was also familiar with Western European architecture. But he clearly distances himself from the skyscraper: The horizontal line is even more dominant than the vertical line and houses the profit-making spaces, chiefly offices, no doubt.

In spite of the advice of the structural engineer Emil Roth, there is some question whether the blueprint could have been implemented according to existing drafts. It is therefore understandable that Mart Stam's construction appears to be more convincing.

Kasimir Malevich (1878–1935). The Suprematist city, 1927

We see no houses as we approach the city, and Malevich explains why: The city, too, has now become part of the nonobjective world. The Suprematist city consists not of little houses, but of abstract volumes, cubes, sculptures that create a cityscape of a completely different kind. Suprematism liberates us from the terror of objects and images.

We note, however, that the city reminds us of concentrations of American skyscrapers. »*The city*«, Malevich proclaims, »*has the form of an assemblage of the energies of the materials, with black and white predominating. I entrust the ultimate development of suprematism in the architecture of the future to the young architects.*«
Stadt und Utopie 1982; Dethier 1994; *Nouvelles* 2001.

Once more we recognize the close relationship between architecture and sculpture. Malevich supports this thesis, referring to his sculptures as »architectones«.

The assemblage in fig. 201 is a reconstruction consisting of seven old and eleven new sections (Paul Pedersen 1978).

Iakov Chernikov (1889–1951). The Soviet industrial cities, 1928, 1933

During our tour we initially believe we are approaching an enormous elliptical sports arena, but then we recognize the stairwells and individual floors, and know that this is a huge residential complex. Approximately in the focal point is the administrative center, rising vertically, combined into a magnificent composition by strong horizontal lines and an additional ellipse. Together with other beams, struts, panels, and lines, the result is a wonderful formal study somewhat reminiscent of Kandinsky.

Chernikov's words are hardly ideological: »This is simply the diagonal combination of lines, surfaces, and volumes. Thus we can expect a pictorial effect. I did not particularly strain my imagination, contrary to the visions the architects produce today, but simply created compositions.«
This statement becomes even clearer when we fly over the next city. At first we have the feeling as though the acute-angled star that forms the center were exploding, but at once we notice that these are streets leading off from the central square. The strong shadows and vivid colors intensify the impression of dynamic expansions.

As we come even closer and then stroll through the city, we realize we are dealing with a very strict, urbane, and architectonic concept: The city is divided into zones. Right angles are absolutely predominant. Factories, businesses, residential buildings, stores are designed as very clear cubes and arranged in additive series. Very unusual for a complete city is the vivid color scheme: Blue and red predominate.

Nouvelles 2001; *Visionen und Utopien* 2002.

We realize how incredibly and fascinatingly relevant Chernikov's work is today when we compare it with the »deconstructivists« (a label that is not very felicitous). These bars and panels, curves and planes, interpenetrations and intersections, rods and piles: That is precisely the stylistic idiom we find primarily in the work of Coop Himmelblau during the 1980s and '90s. We are reminded even more strongly of the early work of Zaha Hadid, whose coloristic ambitions clearly parallel Chernikov's.

On a different level, Chernikov also lives to see late realizations of his work and, together with Malevich, El Lissitzky, and Kandinsky, becomes the forefather of the deconstructivists.

Chernikov himself states that »an education in contemporary architecture may also consist in the realization of images from my own imagination.«

Chernikov does not offer us an ideology, or a concept of society, nor does he define any social issues or political opinions, which is surprising in the era of Soviet communism. With his »picture« he hopes to have a stimulating effect on the production of architecture.

Georgy Krutikov (1899–1958). The flying city, 1928

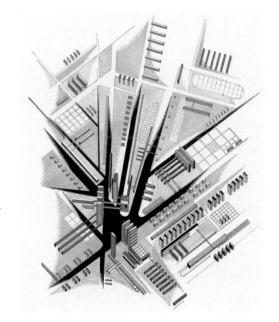

»*Without a doubt, as time passes, architecture tends to become more and more mobile*«, young Krutikov describes the starting point of his »*city of the future.*« The most intensive form of mobility is flying, and so the architect builds the flying cities.

»My new city has three elements: We are now approaching the large base ring that contains the industrial plants and integrates all horizontal communication systems.«

Placed on this ring as the second element are seven central masts that contain the vertical communication: elevators and stairwells, the power supply, and the waste disposal system.

The residential elements themselves, the third element, have been lifted off the ground and mounted on the masts. Steel cables stabilize the six-story towers. The lowest cone is reserved for community facilities, and over it jut the reinforced concrete slabs of the ceiling of each floor.

»There are lightly built cells that can be attached to the slabs. They are elements of mobile living, and at the same time they are vehicles, equipped with every comfort, that also take us to our places of work or to destinations outside the city limits.«

Three factors have made the building of the city possible: »For one, it was the progress of nuclear power; secondly, the rapid development of transportation technology; and thirdly, the vision of the further development of residential living«, explains the architect succinctly.

Nouvelles 2001.

Krutikov submitted his project, full of contradictions even between the text and the drawing, in 1928 as his architecture diploma project, at the peak period of Russian revolutionary architecture, and the renowned school »Vkhutein« under Nikolai Ladovsky showed a great deal of interest. There was no possibility of developing it further and so – such is the irony of fate – Krutikov became the curator of the state's department for the preservation of historical monuments.

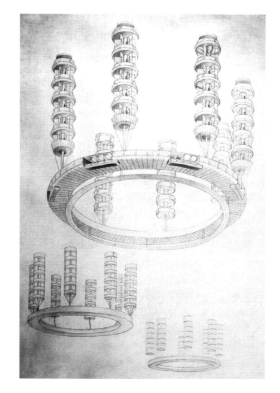

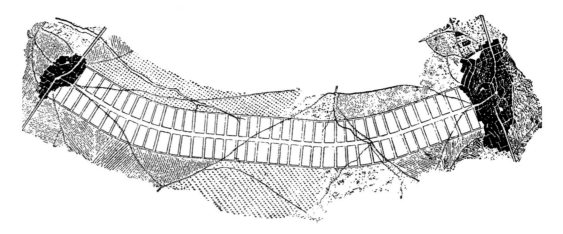

10. Innovators, visionaries, c. 1890–1940

10.1. Europe

Arturo Soria y Mata (1844–1920). The linear city (*Ciudad lineal*, 1882–1913)

The city's spine is a kind of street 500 m wide. It has railroad traffic and built-in lines for water, gas, and electricity. Landscaped boulevards and green spaces accompany the long street. The side streets are 60 m wide, while the actual residential streets are 20 m wide. Soria y Mata very eloquently publicizes his urban vision: »We started with a stretch almost 50 kilom long near Barcelona. But the Ciudad lineal is already being built all over the world. Because the city we are planning solves, in one swoop, all the problems that develop from life in large cities. It connects rural hygienic requirements and those in the large capitals. One thing is important – the railroads need to transport citizens free of charge or at bargain prices.«
  Soria y Mata 1968, 1910; Vercelloni 1994; Dethier 1994; Eaton 2001; *Nouvelles* 2001.

Through the centuries, we've seen central plans for cities: round or polygonal, with minor and infrequent deviations. A few plans for cities intended to be built by rivers, showed longitudinal tendencies. Fortifications have been an important motif: A surface as large as possible is to be enclosed by a small circumference.
  Soria y Mata has a forward-looking concept: The linear city can expand indefinitely and economically in two directions. Many disadvantages of this system have kept it from being implemented very frequently and on a large scale.
  There is a modest example 5 km long east of Madrid. Linear tendencies and especially the consequence of netlike links have become a standard model of urban growth and are again increasingly foremost in the minds of urban planners.
  Apart from rational urban planning, wide linear cities are developing all over the world between the large cities as a connecting link between urban areas. From Paris to Brussels, for instance, a single linear urban organism has now developed, and wide ribbon cities are beginning to integrate the globe.

Ebenezer Howard (1850–1928). The garden city of tomorrow (*To-Morrow: A Peaceful Path to Real Reform*, 1898; rep. *Garden Cities of To-Morrow*, 1903, 1920)

Ebenezer Howard invites us to a wonderful balloon flight: Only thus can we grasp the magnificent concept of his garden city.
  Mr. Howard explains the structural and social principles to us: »I managed to purchase 6,000 acres (2,400 hectares) of land and to build the city for 32,000 inhabitants there. Of these, 20,000 work in the agricultural green belt. The houses stand on 6- by 40-meter plots and were built by building societies representing the citizens' cooperative enterprises. Every citizen must also make a contribution to the public and social buildings. This great idea was only possible because the land was community-owned.«
  Half of the gainfully employed inhabitants work in the garden city, while the rest commute to the nearby central city, which, together with several garden cities, forms a larger organism to which we shall travel very soon.

All the products are manufactured in cooperatives, and thus the economy is based on the economic power of the workers themselves and has no need of capitalists.

Again, as it is so often, the circle is the basic figure for the city, though it is not intended to be strictly geometrical. And Howard supplements his explanations with a schematic plan: »*The actual town has a diameter of more than two km. Six magnificent boulevards, each of them 36 m wide, cut through the town as radii, dividing it into six districts that have a concentric layout. A railroad line surrounds the town, separating the big agricultural areas from the dairy farms and community gardens.*«

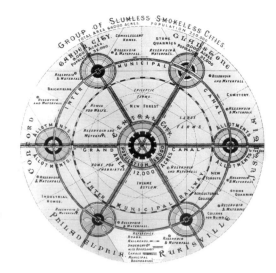

Our balloon has safely landed near a railway station. We drive a little further to the main station, in the process crossing a broad green belt that encircles the town and prevents urban sprawl. Agricultural areas are interspersed with woods and pastureland, community gardens and recreation areas. This green belt also contributes part of the food supply of the city.

The first ring zone we cross is reserved for the trades and industry: Furniture-, clothing-, shoe-, and other factories are strung together and connected by a railway branch line.

Mr. Howard draws our attention to the character of the peripheral zones: »In most cities many sections in this zone aren't exactly a source of pride: factories, warehouses, markets, coal depots, assembly shops, and the like. But here such plants are as well-ordered and clean as the premises of tradesmen.«

Now we come upon »Grand Avenue« – what an unbelievable dimension: It is 130 m wide and five km long, with landscaped boulevards on both sides. Grand Avenue and the side streets are wonderful residential areas: A type of single-family homes line the side streets, each with a small garden. The floor plans are curved and make the avenue appear even more imposing. Many were built by homeowners' cooperative building societies. Halfway down the avenue are churches, schools, and public buildings.

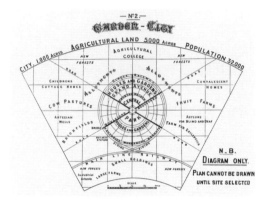

We now cross the innermost ring of the city and come to Fifth Avenue. Like all the streets in this city it is lined with trees, and it too has very fine, solidly built houses on both sides, each with its own generous-sized garden. But not one resembles the other. How is that possible, when they were planned uniformly?

»The city government asks only that the building line be observed and that houses be healthy. Every citizen can build them completely according to his personal taste and individual needs.«

Now we are strolling through the spacious, wonderful Central Park, admiring the beautifully designed playgrounds and recreation areas, all easily accessible by the inhabitants. The gem of this park is the »Crystal Palace«, a large glass hall that follows the circular form of the square and opens out to it. But the hall is by no means only an architectonic ornament, as Mr. Howard explains: »*In wet weather, this building is popular with local people, and the knowledge that this splendid roof is close by draws people to Central Park even in the most dubious weather.*«

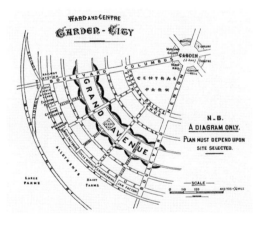

We now enter the spacious halls. Once more we are surprised, for we are standing in a busy upscale shopping street. We are impressed not only by the abundant selection of goods, but also by the beautiful indoor landscaping that alternates with the stores. We agree with Mr. Howard: »*This is where people come to make purchases that require deliberation and leisure.*«

Finally we come to the center of town, and Howard is aware that tradition requires a town to have a central point. But this is neither a church nor a palace, but a beautiful park with waterworks. The public buildings are grouped around this square: the town hall, a hospital, and the most impressive cultural buildings – concert hall, theater, library, museum – and each building in turn is surrounded by spacious gardens and directly connected to Central Park.

»My planning goes far beyond the garden city and comprises the entire surroundings. Cleverly scattered throughout are the new forests, orchards, pastures, and smaller landed properties.« And strangely enough, here and there, social and educational institutions appear: The industrial institute, the children's country hostels, convalescent homes, homes for the blind and the deaf, and even a special farm for epileptics are loosely sprinkled across the landscapes.

»We have now viewed a satellite town, but I think the central city and the project as a whole will interest you as well!«

Again we take the balloon and, favored by the wind, from a great height, we see the central city and finally the entire enterprise. »As I said, each garden city has 32,000 inhabitants, while Central City has 58,000 and the entire project has 250,000.«

The most striking element in Central City is not new to us, but still astonishes us: Two ring-shaped canals, which encircle the town, are connected by six radial canals that follow the radial streets. Waterfalls pour down from numerous reservoirs at the periphery to feed the canals. Although these convenient transport routes are available, people use the railway instead.

206. Ebenezer Howard, diagram of central city with garden city and satellites, 1898.
207. Ebenezer Howard, diagram of the garden city, 1898.
208. Ebenezer Howard, diagram of the garden city, detail, district and center, 1898.

209. Berry Parker and Raymond Unwin, garden city of Letchworth, 1903, 1910.
210. Anonymous, publicity for the garden city of Welwyn, 1917.
211. Louis de Soissons, after E. Howard, the garden city of Welwyn, 1917–19.

GARTENSTADT LETCHWORTH · BEBAVVNGS-PROJECT ·

① WOHNVIERTEL ③ LANDWIRTSCHAFT. ⑤ WIL-BURY FARM ⑦ PARK-ANLAGEN
② INDUSTRIEVIERTEL KLEINBETRIEBE ⑥ DORF NORTON ⑧ EISENBAHNSTATION

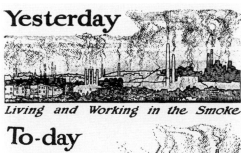

Yesterday

Living and Working in the Smoke

To-day

Living in the Suburbs – Working in the Smoke

To-morrow

Living & Working in the Sun at WELWYN GARDEN CITY

WELWYN GARDEN CITY

Howard's list seems to lack no additional social institutions: In the surroundings of Central City there are a college for the blind, a nursing home, a home for alcoholics, and a homeless shelter.

Rising higher in the balloon, we now understand the grandiose plan of the overall project: Around Central City, positioned by the canal that links the towns, we recognize the six satellite towns. One of them is the garden city we just saw. Each is based on a somewhat different concept; in two of them gardens clearly predominate over buildings. Now we can also understand that this group of cities, slum- and smoke-free, guarantees a sociable and healthy life.

In simple words, Ebenezer Howard describes the idealistic idea that underlies his garden city concept: »*The residents enjoy all the advantages of country living, healthy air, but especially cheap housing. A garden of their own gives them a sense of home, family life rooted in the land, and moral values. Nevertheless there is a lot of intellectual stimulation and every convenience offered by a bustling city based on the division of labor and connected with the large urban centers. Trees, shrubbery, and lawns give the town a semi-rural appearance. I am convinced that the ›marriage of town and country‹ has turned my ideal into reality: ›health – recreation – education‹.*«

Howard 1898, 1902, 1906; Choay 1965, 2001; Schumpp 1971; Tod / Wheeler 1978; Fishman 1982; Miller 1992; Vercelloni 1994; Dilas 1994; *Architekturtheorie* 2003.

And again we take a leap into the real world.

A few months after the publication of Howard's *Garden City*, in 1899, the »Garden City Association« is founded. In 1903, 40,000 acres (16,000 hectares) of land are purchased in Letchworth near Hitchin (Hertfordshire), and four years later, in 1907, the settlement is officially opened.

What is created here is indeed a garden city as envisioned by Howard, though it is completely different than the ideal plan: Berry Parker and Raymond Unwin plan and build this »city« not far from London in 1880–1903; it is still in existence. The first plan, up to 1903, still takes its bearings from axial, geometrical, and centered city blueprints with a main square in the center and streets that radiate from it. The second stage, east of the first, has irregular and loose groups of buildings. We are now able actually to walk through this settlement and perhaps admire beautiful home designs. But if we did not know, we would hardly be able to notice the difference between this and many – including many recent — suburban settlement experiments. The cooperative housing with a shared kitchen and dining room, and many of the social and communal institutions have long since vanished. The proposed circular geometry and the concept of the »city« have fallen by the wayside, and the loss of urbanity has been a problem to this day for hundreds of garden cities, including recent ones, that succeeded Howard up to the present, and last but not least in Germany and Austria.

In the case of Letchworth one fact was overlooked: More and more, agriculture is disconnected from the town and enters into a state of severe crisis, in spite of attempts to promote especially small businesses. The city expands, but the goals gradually become blurred, moral passion is diluted and is replaced by technological planning. Eventually Letchworth is neither a garden village nor a suburb nor a city.

In 1917/19 the garden city of Welwyn is founded and the publicity poster – »yesterday – today – tomorrow« – documents the planners' optimism.

The overall plan of Louis de Soissons tries to go on from where Howard's diagram left off, though he is hardly successful.

Soon it turns out that many people work in London – Welwyn becomes a bedroom community. And here is another implementation of Howard's ideal. Hampstead is a »garden suburb«. What is peculiar is that occasionally Howard's influence is only rudimentary. On the other hand, the theories of Camillo Sitte are quoted. The formal design is reminiscent of the romantic towns of Germany, such as Rothenburg ob der Tauber.

We've experienced hundreds of analogous ideas – and hundreds of implementations – up to the present day. Let's name just a few: As early as 1909 marks the founding of the garden city of Hellerau near Dresden by Richard Riemerschmid; around 1910 Ernst May modifies the garden city idea for Das Neue Frankfurt; Frank Lloyd Wright's Broadacre City (cf. chap. 10.2) was intended to be a gigantic green city; the »new towns« in England after World War II reinterpreted the idea, and so did Roland Rainer's garden city Puchenau near Linz, in Upper Austria.

We have experienced one, no, hundreds of implementations: The Crystal Palace, as described by Howard, is nothing other than our modern shopping mall – Howard probably knew this type from the »galleries« that were springing up at the time, streets where people could stroll and shop, which are enjoying increasing popularity again today.

Tony Garnier (1869–1948). The industrial city (*Une Cité Industrielle*, 1917)

The romantic dreams have vanished, the idyll is lost. In the »cité industrielle« the new era has definitely dawned. A huge harbor forms the city's boundary on one side. Here the wharfs have enormous roofs with rooflights. At the other boundary of the city are imposing industrial plants, an apotheosis of the new technology: tall smokestacks, a jumble of towers, silos, bridges, shafts, pipes, canals.

The railroad system is adjacent to the harbor and industrial plants. They are the city's first zone, and next to it is the second zone, the administrative area with connections to the railroad and the old town. But there is no tension, no competition with the old town, and the agricultural areas on the outskirts of town are also part of it.

The residential areas, the third zone, are separated from the industry by green zones. There is a hint of idyll here: The cubical forms of the international style are anticipated – Garnier is at least 20 years ahead of his time. We walk through quiet streets. There is no sign of separating fences, the little gardens are open and accessible to anyone, yet no one has a big garden of his own, though there is greenery everywhere between the buildings, people deep in conversation, playing children, peaceful citizens. The enmity between life and industry seems to have been suspended. Garnier's efforts to create »dignified housing for working people« have been successful: Hygienic and humane demands in the new industrial city have been met. The rigorous requirements for the apartments are most impressive: »*The bedrooms have a large south window, even the smallest room must be ventilated to the outdoors and have natural lighting. The walls and floors are made of smooth material, and all corners are rounded. The plots are half developed, and the other half is reserved for public gardens for pedestrians.*«

The residential buildings have a maximum of four stories. In vain we look for high-rises.

Tony Garnier informs us about the reforms of the new industrial city, which are invisible to us. »We studied the theories of Proudhon and Saint-Simon and reformulated them for our society, our city, we created orders and systems, but these are not rigid or brutal, but serve humankind. The land and goods, water, bread, meat, milk, and medications are distributed fairly. Naturally we pay attention to profitability, but only from the perspective of the happiness of the inhabitants. A concomitant of our social progress is that all citizens accept the rules. That is why we need no courts of law, no police, no prisons. After the disappearance of capitalism there are no thieves, swindlers, or murderers. We also need no churches. A positive socialism does not transcend human beings, we know only the religion of work.«

Life in the community was taken into consideration: The merely 35,000 inhabitants of the industrial town have opportunities for large-group discussions and to be educated together. The assembly rooms, together with the administrative buildings, form the first group of the town center, where a tower marks the town's heart, as it were. The social and cultural infrastructure is real-

214. Tony Garnier, *Une Cité Industrielle*, 16th study, 1899–1901. General plan.

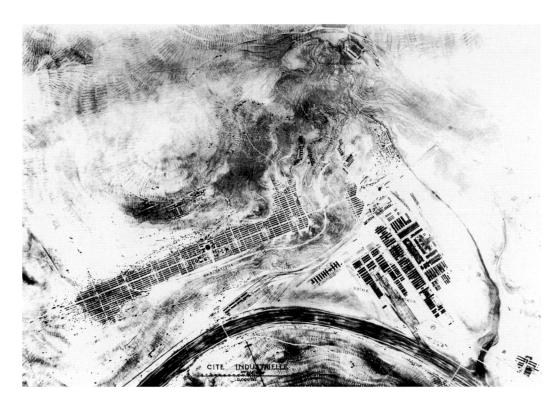

ly magnificent: There are meeting halls, all kinds of meeting places for clubs and political debates. In a gramophone hall it is possible to hear music at all times. The second group of the »heart of town« is formed by artistic and scientific collections, libraries and museums, none of which charge admission. The third group, finally, comprises the theaters, shows of all kinds, sports facilities, baths, hotels, and much more. All these carefully planned institutions provide the city's inhabitants with an incredible quality of life. And it goes without saying that the schools, too, have high standards. Boys and girls are educated together. The schools are directly connected with the residential districts and they, too, are surrounded by large green spaces. A streetcar operates at frequent intervals on the main streets. But the important thing is that all institutions belong to the public and are open to everyone free of charge.

Admittedly, what often attracts us to old cities – the ambiance of cafés, bistros, pubs – is missing, but we can find that in the old part of town, which is not too far away.

We are deeply impressed by this social and cultural progress, but we do wonder whether industry and production are getting a raw deal – and is all this affordable?

»We want to prove«, says Garnier, »that human alienation and the ugliness of the cities are not the inevitable consequences of industrialization, and the modern world is not incompatible with urban charm.«

The explanations Garnier gives us before we leave are very general: »Where the rivers join you'll find the factories, blast furnaces, assembly shops, and shipyards. They are connected to the town by an elevated railroad, and have their own station. Health facilities are protected from cold winds, as is the entire town, and are on the south side of town at an elevation. The hospitals are built in the pavilion system, embedded in green spaces. Our greatest pride is the ›Etablissement hélio-thérapique‹, a naturally based sanitarium, accessible to all citizens, of course. Accidents occur rarely, but if they do thorough provisions have been made: The town has a home for people with work-related injuries. All these elements – factories, hospitals, etc. – are positioned in such a way that they can be expanded at any time. Thanks to our efforts the society itself has complete control of the land, but also of food and medications. We have coupled functionalism and humanism, and have thus reached the ultimate, actual goal of the town: the happiness and prosperity of the citizens. Moral and social goals are definitely bearable, and our city is a living community. The progress of the social order was the precondition for the ›cité industrielle‹.«

Garnier 1917, 1969; Choay 1965, 2001; Schumpp 1971; Tod/Wheeler 1978; Vercelloni 1994; Dethier 1994; Faton 2001; *Nouvelles* 2001; *Architekturtheorie* 2003.

The projects Garnier actually implemented were of a quite different type: As the town planner of Lyon he had the opportunity to erect a series of groups of modern residential houses.

215. Otto Wagner, the metropolis, Vienna, 22nd Ward, 1911.

The idea of a functional separation of work, home life, recreation, traffic, and public institutions was Garnier's splendid vision. It is legitimately emulated in the *Charte d'Athène*, written under Le Corbusier's leadership in 1933/1943. Even if this manifesto was heavily criticized in the 1960s, it did represent – like Garnier's concept – a milestone in conceptional, urban thinking.

Garnier's urban fantasy is one of a number of exceptionally splendid prognoses: Images that came true in their entirety – and naturally over and above that – concepts that were implemented half a century later. The almost romantic maze of the technical plants is reminiscent of modern refineries.

Human socialism like that envisaged by Fourier gives way to a new society formed by industrial civilization, a realistic socialism.

In the decades that followed, we've often heard references to the »nobility« or the »religion« of work: These were slogans used by dictatorships.

Otto Wagner (1841–1918). The limitless metropolis, 1904, *2000*

In 2000 we find ourselves with Otto Wagner in a very different Vienna: The old imperial city has become a limitless metropolis with four million inhabitants. Its structure has been enlarged by increasing the number of »rings«. We are surprised that the city has now expanded far into the landscape of the Wienerwald, since we had regarded the green belt around Vienna as sacrosanct. But Otto Wagner doesn't see it that way:

»It seems more appropriate to give each individual district its adequate air centers in the form of parks, gardens, and playgrounds than to project an assumed belt of woods and meadows; after all, planning a belt that stretches around the city only amounts to creating a fixed containment that must certainly be avoided. The way we see it today, the expansion of a metropolis must be limitless.«

Then Otto Wagner explains the essential elements of a metropolis: Existing railroad lines were developed as elevated railways or tram lines in shallow tunnels; existing sewer systems were extended, and it was right that the city government gained control of the entire transit system.

Otto Wagner goes on: »Rapid transit was created, constant traffic between zones and constant commuter traffic on radial streets, so that any point can be reached with a single transfer. Elevators make it possible to transfer to elevated trains, streetcars, and subway trains. After all this was implemented, it is possible to say with certainty that by systematizing the regulation the city made sure there would always be free development.«

Otto Wagner's thoroughly rational thinking nevertheless does not permit functional onesidedness: *»However, one thing will absolutely have to become the main focus in urban regulation: Art*

216. Otto Wagner, the metropolis, Vienna, 22nd Ward, 1911.
217. Otto Wagner, the metropolis, a plan for Vienna, 1911.

and artists will need to be given a voice, the influence of the engineer, which destroys beauty, must be broken for good, and the power of the vampire ›Speculation‹, which nowadays makes the autonomy of cities almost illusory, must be seriously curtailed. Two things are a requirement for the administrations of large cities: First, a law of eminent domain, which is all the more attainable because every state will certainly fervently support the continuing prosperity of its metropolitan cities; after all, they are its largest and most reliable tax base. Secondly, procuring a city capital gains fund, which in turn automatically involves all the conditions of its backing, interest return, and security. As far as the law of eminent domain of the municipalities is concerned, this is divided into two parts: 1. the expansion of the city and 2. the amelioration of the existing section of the town. Funded as proposed, any metropolitan administration will be able to think of things that would contribute to the prosperity of its city and that our rapidly changing culture imperiously demands.«

An ample flow of funds has enabled municipal governments to erect ambitious buildings for the general public, the city's population.

As we continue our tour of the city we can see for ourselves that the new programs far exceed previous conventions. The large amount of public housing with all additional facilities is associated with public sanitariums, community centers, and, of course, all types of schools. Markets, trade fairs, and warehouses are proof of a prospering economy, while theaters, museums, and libraries contribute to educational opportunities. In the well-tended parks there are fountains, waterworks, observation towers, and monuments.

We would be interested in hearing how Otto Wagner solved the housing problem. Here, too, he proves to be both realistic and radical: *»The longed-for single-family homes in a still-longed-for garden city can never satisfy everybody. Whenever financial circumstances are difficult, when family size increases or is reduced, or when people change jobs, etc., the wishes of a population of millions change constantly. Wishes that result from these facts can be satisfied only by apartment houses and never by single-family houses. We must finally say it openly: Apartments in houses, on blocks that are divided into four to six plots and each of which has one front facing a garden, square, or park and is bordered by 23-meter-wide streets on three sides are definitely more appropriate for our lifestyles, especially if they are healthy, beautiful, comfortable, and inexpensive, than apartments built with the wrong premises. From our perspective it is simply tasteless to make tradition, sentiment, or a picturesque appearance the criterion for modern housing. The number of city dwellers who prefer to disappear in the crowd as a ›cipher‹ is significantly larger than the number of those who want to hear their faultfinding next-door neighbors in the single-family house wish them ›Good morning!‹ or ask them how they slept. Naturally the single-family home will not disappear from the cityscape; but it will owe its existence to the wishes of the wealthy elite. We must on no account leave the development of a city up to chance and to complete artistic impotence, as has been done up till now, when artistic endeavors are made out to be superfluous, or the growth of the city is at the mercy of the most terrible real estate profiteering.«*

We would do well to be somewhat skeptical here, for many observations show that many people prefer the single-family home, and city dwellers hardly wish to »disappear as a cipher.«

But Wagner is not totally radical in his conception of housing, for he has no objection to »the wealthy elite« having a »villa«. After all, he built two showy villas on large plots for himself. Otto Wagner succeeded in implementing his ambitious concepts for the districts, and we note with surprise that the Karlsplatz problem, too, has been solved.

Otto Wagner inveighs violently against romantic urban architecture and against *»those popular slogans – native arts and crafts, fitting in with the cityscape, keeping alive the soul of the city, etc., – mouthed by people who know and judge art only from textbooks, and who are clueless when it comes to urban planning.«*

Now we are strolling through the 22nd District, which was the first to be completed. Most houses are between four and five stories high, but there are also buildings of up to eight stories, and to our surprise we see pretty large skyscrapers at a few prominent points.

Why is it, though, that the countless blocks of buildings seem so standardized, so uniform? Surely this does not mean that the great master lacks imagination? Not at all, for he sees this quite differently: *»Our democratic system, where the general public calls for cheap and healthy apartments and is forced to live economically, brings with it uniform residential buildings.«*

What about the perfectly straight streets we've been walking along, aren't they very monotonous? There, too, Otto Wagner has a response: *»Deliberate, unmotivated bends in streets, irregular street and square solutions, and the like, allegedly in order to produce picturesque effects, are*

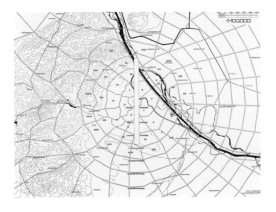

203

218. Otto Wagner, Artibus, design for a museum district, 1876.

artistically reprehensible, because busy people walk in straight lines whenever possible, and those who are in a hurry will surely be annoyed by even the smallest time-consuming detour.«

Now we stroll through the mighty main axis, one of the district's showpieces. A small square, formed by three public buildings, is our starting point, and now we are walking along a large pond, past poplars and tall hedges that provide cozy niches for sitting, toward our first destination, the main square of the district. A theater for 5,000 persons on one flank, a museum on the other are part of a complex of large public buildings.

We keep on walking, again along the pond and past public buildings, until we come to an obelisk on a tall pedestal. At once we are captivated by the monumental façade of the church with its modern portico. A low cupola and a tower behind it give the building its sacral dignity. Two U-shaped buildings frame the church square on the sides, and a large courtyard in the back makes it possible to view the back façade.

Five-story, U-shaped buildings flank the church and form one square each, flanked by the monumental central section. An additional spacious square adjoins the church in the rear, but that's not all: When we walk through the hall that fronts the square we again find ourselves on an ambitiously conceived square.

Beyond the city's architectural aspects, Otto Wagner is well informed about the city's qualities: *»The city's ›physiognomy‹ has the greatest influence on the cityscape. It has the difficult role of making the first impression as pleasant as possible. This impression, in turn, depends on the expression of the city's facial features – the pulsing life of the urban scene.«*

We are deeply impressed by this magnificent sample of the city, but Otto Wagner shows us a few more examples of his work, with which he has considerably embellished Vienna. His chief merit is probably the fact that he gave Karlsplatz, the eternal problem child of urban planners, its definitive character with the new City Museum and the carefully planned green space. Then there is the wonderful building of the Academy of Fine Arts, located auf der Schmelz in the 16th District, and the Museum of Modern Art.

The truly triumphal conclusion of our tour is the museum district Artibus, on which construction started as far back as 1878. It still bears all the traits of a monumental historicism.

After we cross the river by a six-arch bridge, we are welcomed by semicircular arcades, and adjoining them the long museum wings with all their annexes. The influence of Karlskirche on this church is undeniable. Now we go up the hill past murmuring cascades, and from a kind of pantheon at the highest point we have a glorious view of the fine grounds, feeling that we have been transported back to the 19th century.

Wagner 1889, 1895, 1896, 1899, 1902, 1909, 1912, 1914, 1915, 1963, 1964, 1979; Lux 1914; Peichl 1984; Graf 1985.

Should Otto Wagner be considered a »utopian«? The implementations of his projects are milestones of modern architecture and mark its beginning: the Kirche am Steinhof and the Post Office Savings Bank. As the planner of the Vienna city railroad, which still functions today as a subway system, he is one of the pioneers of a worldwide restructuring of the cities.

But Karlsplatz has remained an unsolved problem to this day, and even after World War II there has not been any really ambitious urban planning in Vienna.

Antonio Sant' Elia (1888–1916). The futurist city (*La città futurista*, *La città nuova*, 1914)

First, we meet the poet Filippo Tommaso Marinetti. His manifesto of futurism in 1909 is a great, dynamic outcry to a »new« era:

»We want to sing the praises of love of danger, of intimacy with energy and daring.

Courage, boldness, and revolt will be the essential elements of our poetry.

Up till now literature has praised philosophical immobility, ecstasy, and sleep. We want to praise aggressive movement, feverish sleeplessness, a running pace, the death-defying leap, the slap on the face, and the punch.

We declare that the glory of the world is now richer by a new beauty: the beauty of speed. A racing car whose body is decorated with big pipes resembling snakes with explosive breath, a car that starts with a roar and seems to run on artillery shot, is more beautiful than the Nike of Samothrace.

We want to sing the praises of the man who is at the helm, whose ideal axis passes through the earth, which itself races on its course.

The poet must glow, dazzle, and generously squander himself in order to increase the passionate fervor of the original elements.

Today beauty exists only in battle. A work without aggressive character cannot be a masterpiece. Poetry must be understood as a violent attack on the unknown forces to force them to submit to human beings.

We stand on the outermost foothills of the centuries! Why should we look back when we want to break open the mysterious gates of the impossible? Time and space died yesterday. We are already living in the absolute, for we have created eternal, omnipresent speed.

We want to glorify war – this hygiene of the world – militarism, patriotism, the destructive deed of the anarchists, the beautiful ideas for which people die, and contempt for woman.

We want to destroy museums, libraries, and academies of every kind and fight against moralism, feminism, and all cowardice based on practicality and self-interest.

We shall sing the praises of the great crowds excited by work, pleasure, or revolt; we shall sing the praises of the many-colored, many-voiced flood of revolution in the modern capital cities; we shall sing the praises of the nocturnal, vibrating embers of arsenals and shipyards illuminated by glaring electric moons; voracious railroad stations devouring smoking snakes; factories that hang from the clouds by threads of smoke winding upward; bridges that span rivers like giant athletes, that flash in the sun like knives; steamboats seeking adventures and scenting the horizon, broad-chested locomotives galloping along on the tracks like enormous steel horses bridled with pipes, and the gliding flight of airplanes, whose propeller flaps like a flag in the wind and seems to applaud like an enthusiastic crowd.«

Once again Marinetti speaks about speed (1913) and anticipates the hectic pace of our modern age:

»Getting used to the shortened views and optic syntheses that are produced by the speed of trains and cars ... loathing slowness ... love of speed ... Tell me everything in two words.«

And Marinetti wins over Antonio Sant'Elia for his futurism,. He influences, manipulates, inspires him. Sant'Elia, too, writes his manifesto as a revolutionary outcry, as a plea for a futuristic architecture in 1914:

I FIGHT AGAINST AND DESPISE:

the entire avant-garde pseudo-architecture that comes from Austria, Hungary, Germany, and America;

the whole classical, solemn, hieratic, stage-like, decorative, monumental, elegant, and accommodating architecture;

the embalming, the rebuilding, and the imitation of the monuments and palaces of antiquity;

the vertical and horizontal lines, the forms of the cube and the pyramid, which are static, ponderous, and oppressive and offend against our new sensibility;

the use of massive, voluminous, persistent, outmoded, and expensive building materials;

AND PROCLAIM:

that futuristic architecture is the architecture of calculation, of daring bravery, and of simplicity;

the architecture of reinforced concrete, iron, glass, plastic, textile fiber, and all those substitutes for wood, stone, and bricks that make for the greatest elasticity and lightness;

that futuristic architecture is therefore not a dry mixture of utility and functionality, but continues to be art, that is, synthesis, expression;

that oblique and elliptical lines are dynamic and because of their nature have emotive power that is a thousand times greater than that of vertical and horizontal lines, so that without them there can be no deeply dynamic architecture;

that decoration added on to architecture as an extra is an absurdity and that THE DECORATIVE VALUE OF FUTURISTIC ARCHITECTURE DEPENDS SOLELY ON AN ORIGINAL USE OF THE RAW, NAKED, OR GAUDILY COLORED BUILDING MATERIAL;

that we who are materially and spiritually artificial must find our inspiration in the elements of the completely new mechanical world we have created and whose most beautiful expression, most perfect synthesis, and most effective complement must be architecture, just as antiquity drew its artistic inspiration from the elements of nature;

that architecture is no longer the art that arranges building forms in accordance with predetermined criteria;

that architecture must be understood as the effort to bring the environment freely and very boldly into harmony with human beings, in other words, to represent the world of objects as a direct projection of the world of the mind;

that no habitual forms or lines can be produced by an architecture understood in this way, for the fundamental properties of futuristic architecture will be fragility and transience. THE HOUSES WILL BE MORE SHORT-LIVED THAN WE OURSELVES. EVERY GENERATION WILL HAVE TO BUILD ITSELF ITS OWN CITY: This constant renewal of the architectural environment will contribute to the victory of FUTURISM, which has already asserted itself in LIBERATED WORDS, SCULPTURAL DYNAMISM, MUSIC WITHOUT QUADRATURE, AND THE ART OF NOISES, and for which we fight incessantly against the doldrums of cowardice.

And here is how Sant' Elia continues to explain his – or Marinetti's? – ideas:

»... We need to rebuild the futuristic house from top to bottom ... an architecture ... whose sole justification is specific modern living conditions. We feel that we are no longer the people of the cathedrals, palaces, and assembly halls. Rather, we are the people of the big hotels, railroad stations, wide streets, enormous gates, covered markets, illuminated tunnels, superhighways straight as an arrow, and salutary urban redevelopment. We must plan and build the futuristic city like an enormous, noisy building site, flexible and dynamic in all its parts, and must approach the futuristic house like a gigantic machine. The elevators must wind themselves up the façades like iron and glass snakes. This house must rise on the brink of a noisy abyss: the street. The necessary connections between the floors will be provided by metal footbridges and very fast escalators. We are no longer receptive to the idea of monumental, massive, static forms. Rather, our sensibility is enriched by delight in light, practical, temporary forms and in speed. We no longer feel like the people of the cathedrals and palaces, but like those of the big hotels, railroad stations, gigantic streets, big harbors, indoor markets, brightly lit arcades, and healing operations.«

Now that we've heard Sant' Elia's passionate words, we are eager to tour the city – and we are not disappointed.

The train has been running underground for some time. A spacious railroad station greets us. We're going to take the express elevator to the top terrace of the high-rise now; from there, we'll have the best overall view. We travel in the dark for about ten stations through the lower and basement floors, but then whiz another fifteen floors in daylight up to the terrace.

The view of the city really is splendid. An axis that is several km long forms the basic structure. Four open shallow eight-lane vehicular tunnels and another, more elevated six-lane route take care of the heavy motor traffic.

Not only the railroad is located underground but the public municipal railroad, electric of course, is also on the lower levels and only appears on the surface here and there.

Now we look up at the sky, where for some time we have been observing the circling airplanes. And now we watch the landing maneuver: The airport is located in the axis of the streets and buildings, that is, directly in the city, and the connection to the trains is extremely short. Again we take the elevator fifteen floors down and get out right in the upper pedestrian zone. »Cars and pedestrians are strictly separate, and you can do your shopping here undisturbed«, Sant' Elia tells us.

Undisturbed is right: True, we can observe the dynamics of the traffic, but the newest vehicles on the streets are almost noiseless, and there are no exhaust fumes.

Bridges connect opposite blocks of houses, and there are escalators between the various levels. On the lower level there are shopping facilities and numerous cultural and educational institutions. We do miss green spaces and parks.

219. Antonia Sant' Elia, *città nuova*, 1913/14.
220. Antonio Sant' Elia, *città nuova* (*La città futurista*), 1914.
221. Antonio Sant' Elia, *città futurista*, 1914.

222. Mario Chiattone, the new city, 1914.
223. Mario Chiattone, modern metropolis, 1914.
224. Virgilio Marchi, *città fantastica*, 1919.

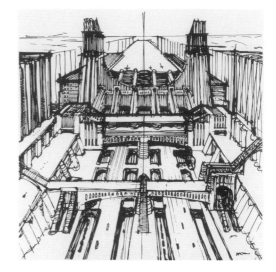

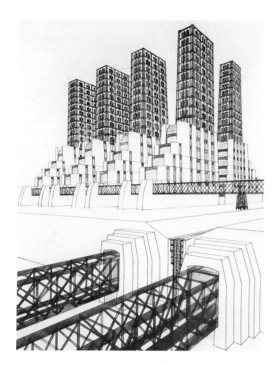

»The city is built so compactly«, Sant' Elia defends himself, »that one can be in the great outdoors within a few minutes.«

Vercelloni 1994; *Nouvelles* 2001; Eaton 2001.

Presumably Antonio Sant' Elia knew the work of Otto Wagner in Vienna. He probably never visited Vienna, but Wagner's many publications assured the popularity of his work. This would explain the amazing affinity between the »città futurista« and the work of Otto Wagner, especially the Viennese municipal railroad. A whole host of detail ideas and forms also shows a close resemblance to Wagner.

Conversely, Sant'Elia probably also influenced the Metropolis city in Fritz Lang's film (cf. chap. 9.1). It was a tragic irony of history that Sant'Elia, who had glorified struggle and force, was killed in the world war fighting against Austria.

Mario Chiattone (1891–1957). The modern metropolis (*Metropoli moderna*, 1914)

It's no surprise that Mario Chiattone is a friend of Antonio Sant'Elia, for Chiattone also created a wonderful *città futurista*.

Each of the five towering residential high-rises that we visit first is seventeen stories high. The six ground-floor stories housing offices, businesses, and public functionaries show a massive architecture, though the open narrow side has large glass surfaces. The eleven elegantly structured residential floors are set on top of this first floor as deliberate foreign bodies.

For Chiattone, too, the thoroughfares are essential structural elements, and they are elevated or below street level, go across filigree steel bridges or through tunnels.

»Let's remember«, says Chiattone, »that traffic areas are not leftover spaces, but that they are elements that determine the nature of the city, and have an enormous future ahead of them. They are also the indicators, indeed, the symbols for the city's future dynamics.«

The next section of the city is even a little more heavily built up, and its architectonic idiom is more consistent. Incredibly slim, dynamic, slender, almost Gothic in style, the skyscrapers rise from the web of traffic at their base. The formal idiom of the last building in the row is divided: The foundation beautifully articulates cylindrical cubes, while the slender superstructure is consistently transparent.

Stadt und Utopie 1982; Seibt 2001.

Antonio Sant' Elia and Chiattone had a joint exhibition in 1914 and are the founders and almost sole representatives of futurism in architecture (cf. chap. 10.1). Chiattone's formal, cubic articulation is even more consistent than that of Sant' Elia. Admittedly, it is hard to imagine what floor plans can be accommodated in the slim columns of his buildings.

Virgilio Marchi (1895–1960). The fantastic city (*Cittá fantastica*, 1919)

Virgilio Marchi takes us to the center of his fantastic city. It is the railroad station – no, it is much more – the core of the city from which the most important elements radiate: movement, dynamics, elementary communication.

»In this day and age, urban functions can no longer be seen in isolation. They overlap, connect, cross over, form networks and dense textures.«

Marchi's station by no means lacks monumentality, and perhaps his work still shows residues of a very pompous Italian art nouveau, yet it goes without saying that all the parts of the structure are planned in reinforced concrete.

Incredibly bold – and in this Marchi and Sant' Elia are kindred spirits – is the conquest of the third dimension. »We can no longer be content with the surface of the earth, there is too little room in the city. Take a good look at the building and you will be able to make out at least four levels in which people and machines move.«

True: We see movement on two track levels and three pedestrian levels, and in the interior of the building Marchi shows us how perfectly connected the floors are by elevators and escalators.

Dethier 1994; Eaton 2003.

No doubt about it: In Marchi's work as well, just as in Sant' Elia's, the vision of the vertical city has long since been fulfilled. In Marchi, too, we can expect a few additional, subterranean levels.

Ludwig Hilberseimer (1885–1967). The total grid, 1924

Our impression of this city is powerful, indeed violent. Motor traffic, 15 m below ground level, takes place on 50-meter-wide thoroughfares. The pedestrian walkways on the upper level connect massive high-rise blocks, each of them fifteen stories high and 180 m long. The street is seemingly infinite, without a visible end. People and cars become tiny accessories in the unending urban grid.

But Hilberseimer has good reasons for his system: »*The need to form a frequently enormous, heterogeneous mass of material according to a law of design that is equally valid for each of the elements demands that the architectonic form be reduced to its barest, most necessary, and general features. This means forms are restricted to geometrically cubical ones – the basic elements of all architecture. Forming large masses while suppressing their variety according to a general law is what Nietzsche understands by style as such.*«

Here is how Hilberseimer rejects every kind of artistic »design«: »*The problem today is no longer painting more or less good pictures or sculpting statues and creating aesthetic arrangements, but fashioning reality itself. Rational thought, functionality, the precision of economy, the qualities of an engineer in the world of today: these need to be the basis for general architecture. Constructivism is neither a new decorative art nor a new formalism.*«

Hilberseimer 1922, 1923; Dethier 1994.

Hilberseimer personifies the logical development of functionalism in the 1920s. One cannot help agreeing with many of his theoretical and literary views, especially if one keeps in mind the period during which he expressed them. His teaching in the US often provided the inspiration for them. But the blueprints seem to anticipate urban design in communist states, for instance, Stalin-Allee in Berlin.

Le Corbusier (1887–1965). Ville Contemporaine, 1922; Ville Plan Voisin, 1925; Ville Radieuse, 1930; Zlin, 1935; Rio de Janeiro, 1929; São Paulo, 1929; Montevideo, 1930; Algiers, 1933; Chandigarh, 1950–1964

The first city we are going to visit – the oldest – is the Ville Contemporaine, the »contemporary city« with a population of three million, built in 1922. Its implementation at the time absorbed a large part of a densely built-up suburb of Paris.

»With the Ville Contemporaine«, says Le Corbusier, »I formulated the fundamental principles of urbanism. I created rules by which the magnificent game of urban development can be played.«

First we arrive in the center of the huge grid: Le Corbusier invites us to visit one of the spacious terrace cafés – we sit in the shade of trees and have a wonderful view of the city center.

Around a large plateau eight glass-and-steel skyscrapers have been grouped, each of them 80 stories high. We are in the heart of the city, in its »brain«. This is where the municipal administration, large business headquarters, and offices are located.

The cruciform floor plans of the high-rises have zigzag wings. Light and air are among the maxims that govern life. Also, here in the center, traffic is bundled. Means of transportation that travel at different speeds and have different destinations are alternated.

Under the terrain there are three floors of railroad tracks. Railway traffic is separated according to the speed of each type of train: local traffic, commuter traffic, and long-distance travel.

Le Corbusier expounds his philosophy of the modern era: »*The mechanical engineering that has transformed our concept of time and makes speed its basic requirement demands that we found business cities: intensity, expansion, speed. The business district will be located at the place that is closest to all points of urban concentration: That place is the center!*«

In other words, Le Corbusier continues a perfectly traditional model – that of the centered city – but the center is primarily reserved for the administration. »*At the busiest points one finds the dominant buildings. These are the offices of the big companies preparing for business competition: order, organization, clarity, connection, Taylorism.*«

From our vantage point on the café terrace we can see the railroad station, a low and modest-looking building; beyond it is the racetrack, theater, and public halls, embedded in lush green spaces. But in the public squares we see only few people, for these centers do not belong to the community. They are primarily commercial centers. From them, following an odd though realistic hierarchy, radiate the other sections of town, far removed from democratic ideals:

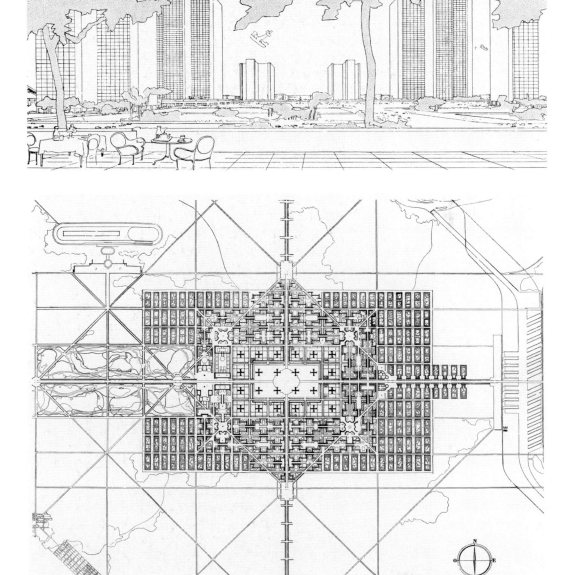

Plan de la ville de 3 millions d'habitants

226. Le Corbusier, Contemporary City, downtown terrace café, 1922.
227. Le Corbusier, Contemporary City, 1922. Overall plan.

The architect declares his support of this hierarchy: »The powerful, the leaders, have their headquarters in the center of the city. Then come the employees, down to the humblest of all.«

The city is completely car-oriented, which is why we can only finish our tour by vehicle. We are not too surprised that we cannot find any stores, workshops, or small industry here in the center, for occupation of the downtown area by office buildings and large companies is a clear tendency in the Ville Contemporaine.

Now let us take a closer look at the city's structure. Around the eight skyscrapers in the center, sixteen additional high-rises are grouped in strictly geometrical order: This is where the elite live, apartment buildings in a very broad sense of the word. Two-story housing units, prefabricated mass products, are inserted in reinforced-concrete frames »the way you put bottles of wine in a rack.«

Le Corbusier describes the residential high-rises very poetically: »*They float in a sea of trees. They are like passing steamers – magnificent mobile residential blocks of the modern era.*« He takes us into one of these housing units on the twelfth floor. Of course, it has a fine view of Paris and the distant surrounding landscape. The apartment is spacious and quiet and has all the conveniences of a huge luxury condominium. However, we do feel it is too poetic to refer to the pretty balconies as »hanging gardens«.

We go on to the roof terrace. Here, the view is even finer. Even more surprising, late in the afternoon, is the bustle of activity up on the terrace: People are playing tennis, swimming in a big pool, bowling and playing squash; the children have their sandbox, swings and slides. Two of the roof terraces are used rather differently: After dark, there is the kind of night life found in restaurants, casinos, bars, and night clubs – a kind of modern »salons«. Thus our impression is that a part of public life has moved from ground level to the rooftops of the skyscrapers.

Le Corbusier has added a second type of residential housing to the center: blocks of villas. Admittedly, these are apartment houses rather than villas, even if they are designed for upper-class clients. In a kind of zigzag pattern, as chains of houses, they create green courtyards, and the town houses, each consisting of two stories, are grouped in fours in an echelon formation, a total of eight floors. Altogether more than half a million people live in these zigzag houses.

Again we encounter a significantly high living standard. What is striking is that the bathrooms and toilets are small in favor of the »family center«, which combines living, eating, and cooking. As we continue the tour, another big surprise awaits us: The periphery of the »city of the present« is formed by garden cities – a concession to the »country cottage«? Or to Ebenezer Howard? Close to two million people live in the garden cities. The houses are prefabricated and have three stories. On the average the size of an apartment is 100 m^2.

Le Corbusier describes the duality of everyday life: »*I said that people create a two-stroke rhythm. They come from the periphery to work in the center of the city, and they return to the periphery to rest.*« Perhaps this helps us to understand the concept of the garden city in the Ville Contemporaine.

And another surprise, or rather a disappointment: There is, as it were, an additional, lower class – the inhabitants of the satellite towns, who have no share in the benefits of the contemporary city.

Thus we might say there are three classes of city inhabitants: The actual city-dwellers, who live and work downtown, the semi-city-dwellers, who work downtown and live in the garden city, and finally the suburbanites, who work in the peripheral factory zone and live in the garden city. We do express our misgivings about this strange stratification, but Le Corbusier regards it as a given.

Now to the next city: Le Corbusier takes us to the metro, which has long since been modernized. But where are we? Is it possible? In Paris! The Plan Voisin was implemented here – an old, uninhabitable part of town was razed. The principle of the street has been outdated for a long time, of course, and Le Corbusier's colossal work, begun in 1925, now stands on Avenue Saint Germain en Laye and the boulevard. It goes without saying that here too we again find a clear separation between the commercial city and the residential city.

Le Corbusier explains the name Plan Voisin as follows: »The Voisin brothers were the great French pioneers of aviation, and the city of today is totally dependent on modern traffic.« Again we are sitting with Le Corbusier in a pleasant café, this time in the middle of a lush, well-tended park. »*And above all, what is a human being?*« muses Le Corbusier. »*A human being is an unlimited potential of energy, placed between two contradictory and hostile forces of destiny: individuality and the collective.*«

Thus Le Corbusier once again underscores a dualism to which we are exposed in large metropolitan centers and which he himself was unable to resolve in his cities. However, he obviously

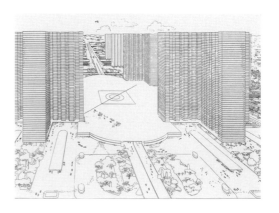

did solve another problem: »Let us prepare the cities for the imminent functions of the new speed. Simple speed (on foot or on horseback) has increased twentyfold (mechanical transportation). That is the great revolution. Cars create a new criterion of magnitude, of collective dimensions.«

We can easily walk to the center – but we do not find one that corresponds to the conventional idea; rather, the enormous central railroad station to some extent fulfills this function. It is covered by a gigantic platfom that serves air traffic. Just now, air taxis land and the passengers are brought directly to the trains or the garages or the local transit system – an ideal hub, and we also understand why a relatively small surface is sufficient for this purpose: The newest planes are able to take off and land vertically. The car expressway runs through under this platform. The hub is surrounded by four skyscrapers. The ground floors are vacant, and a good 60 floors stand on stilts, the *pilotis*, typical for Le Corbusier.

Le Corbusier formulates the doctrine of modern urbanism very pragmatically: »*Urbanization does not mean wasting money but rather making money.*«

We leave once again to roam through the new city as Le Corbusier falls into raptures: »*You are under trees amid large lawns, enormous green spaces. Clean air. Almost no noise. You can no longer see any houses. Through the branches you see enormous crystal solids, higher than any buildings in the world. Crystal, reflected in space, gleaming in the grey wintry sky, appearing to soar in the air rather than stand on the ground, a magical electric apparition at night. A subway runs under each of these bright prisms.*«

Down gently sloping ramps we have now come to the spacious terraces below the treetops. »*Cafés in the middle of the park's greenery, windows of luxury shops, a view of distant parts of the city. And the third ramp brings you to a third street, where the clubs and restaurants are located. No movement, calm, space, sky, light, serenity.*«

And on we go, to the Ville Radieuse, the radiant city, which was planned in 1930/31. Zoning has now radically changed. The city seems like a section of a linear city crossed by a central axis. Now the center is no longer reserved solely for commercial purposes, but includes extensive buildings for social purposes. Residential buildings are also given a place of honor in the Ville Radieuse.

When asked to prioritize the city's functions, Le Corbusier answers very succinctly: »a) housing, b) work, c) recreation (sports).«

In the Ville Radieuse Le Corbusier goes into specifics: »I strictly separated the individual functions: Heavy industry is located at the city's southern periphery; the warehouse zone is a connection to the factories, and a green belt separates them from the residential areas. Travel and tourism – railway, hotel, airport – form a zone of their own, which is directly adjacent to the commercial part of the city.«

Le Corbusier's many contacts, plans, and completed projects for Moscow probably also changed his social approach. Here we find not only an emphasis on the social milieu, but also new aspects of living: Communal and collective aspects are given new importance. Le Corbusier seems to have lost his enthusiasm for capitalism, but even an intensive community life needs order and hierarchy. Le Corbusier proposes a syndicalism headed by intellectual workers. »*The city is a humane city because it is classless.*«

The series of high-rises that the architect built here are well suited for communal services, and the buildings become »commune houses«, as it were.

»*But here lies the cornerstone of the modern organization of housing: For kilometers, directly above the pillars of the apartment houses, an entire floor is reserved. That is the floor set aside for community services.*«

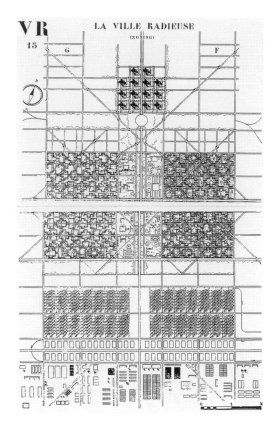

Now we have the opportunity to observe the daily schedule of a family. The lavish breakfast was ordered the day before and is delivered directly to the apartment in thermos containers. After the morning meal the family – a couple with two children –leaves the apartment together. The children are dropped off on the ground floor in the kindergarten and in elementary school. Now the apartment is cleaned and cared for by the service staff. Dirty clothes are picked up by the laundry, the table is set. The husband eats lunch in the cafeteria, the wife in a café-restaurant, while the children eat at school. After work the husband goes to a political club, the wife picks up the children and enjoys the late afternoon in the rooftop swimming pool. There the husband meets them. Supper has already been delivered to their kitchen by pneumatic post.

Trucks bring consumer goods from the country or from the factory directly to the station of a »hotel organization« that supplies the needs of 3,000–4,000 inhabitants at a time. It maintains storerooms, a cold-storage depot, and above all it runs a canteen kitchen.

In his views on women, Le Corbusier shows himself as the very opposite of progressive. True, it seems very friendly of him to demand absolute equality and only five hours of work for women – but it must be housework, and »*a woman is supposed to go to her stove, her children.*« Yet even so, gainful employment for women has come to be taken for granted.

And again the poetic optimist Le Corbusier tries to fill us with enthusiasm for his ideas: »*A new day begins: productive, relaxing, joyful, healthy – the day in the life of people of the machine age in the ›radiant city‹. One city replaces another. Human lives alternate: activity and the end of activity, once every day. I think neither of the rich or the poor – but of human beings.*«

Not the garden city, but the landscaped metropolis was one of Le Corbusier's basic concerns, and for his »Ville Radieuse« he once more demands: »The radiant city is a green city. I was the first to proclaim that the modern city must be a gigantic park, a green city.«

Because of the way the skyscrapers are grouped, only fifteen percent of the terrain is built up, while the rest is natural landscape, garden, park, playing fields.

Now Le Corbusier takes us to two cities that could not be more different and also completely contradict the Ville Radieuse and the Plan Voisin.

We're going to fly to Czechoslovakia, into the Zlin valley. But why this small provincial Bohemian town of all places? It derives its fame from the largest shoe factory in Europe: In 1894 Tomás Batá founded an enterprise that became world famous as a result of its employment benefits, worker participation, but especially its streamlined production.

Le Corbusier is lavish in his praise of the Batás: »*The Batá factory is not just a plant that manufactures industrial products, but the creation of a harmonious society.*«

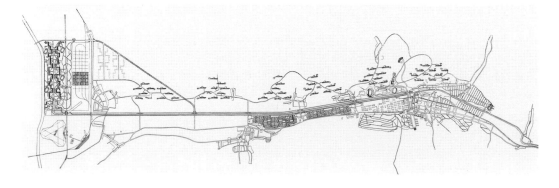

230. Le Corbusier, The valley of Zlin. Urban development plan, Czechoslovakia, 1935.
231. Le Corbusier, La Ville Radieuse, 1930/31.

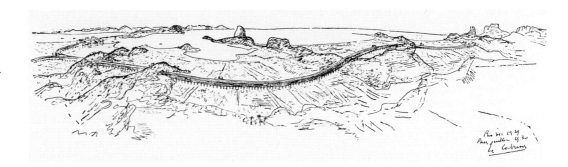

As we fly over the town, which was expanded in 1935, we are surprised that Le Corbusier, for whom the center of a town was important, planned a kind of linear town. Le Corbusier gives his reasons for this urban form: »*I wanted to systematize the network for freight transport by rail, water, and road.*«

The eastern flank of the town is formed by the characteristic chains of houses. In the central part blocks of high-rises are loosely placed in the landscape, while in the western part we find a series of the most varied configurations in terms of urban development.

How far does the influence of the great company head extend in the private lives of people? One detail makes us sit up and take notice: »The cultivation of vegetable gardens by workers is strictly forbidden; open spaces between houses should simply be planted with grass.«
The last stages of our journey are really not suitable for a tour.

In 1929 construction was started on the city wall of Rio de Janeiro, and here the new synthesis became a reality: House, city, and street have been fused into one; for over 30 km a millipede winds its way through the landscape, standing on *pilotis,* bringing to a close the old city of Rio like the Great Wall of China; cars speed on the roof, with gigantic viaducts for majestic freeways stretched between the mountains and the sea. But Le Corbusier is able to see the lyrical aspects of this city as well:

»*The sight of the distance: The fine, wide series of buildings – and, running horizontally above them, the freeway, which extends from mountain to mountain and stretches its hand from one bay to another! The airplane has become jealous: So much freedom always seemed to be reserved for it alone!*«

As we continue our flight around the globe, Le Corbusier once more explains the reason for the colossal dimensions: »Our cities need new standards«, he demands. »It is not the addition of little houses but the great, sweeping gesture that has been characteristic of new and of old cities.«

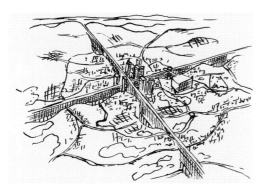

Not unlike Rio is the imposing picture of Algiers: It, too, is a giant snake winding parallel to the sea, on the plateau, down the expressway, and below it, vertically reachable by short roads, a narrow linear city. By this road we reach the new center, which also follows the dynamics of the curved structure.

Very different is the hyper-structure of São Paulo: Now we have street structures as straight as an arrow, a gigantic cross that overlies the city and at whose intersection the city grows vertically into the air.

In comparison to São Paulo, Montevideo in Uruguay looks almost modest: It seems as though a giant apartment house had penetrated the mountain, a massive edifice that incorporates primarily the large commercial center shoots out of the mountain, toward the ocean. During our flights over the cities Le Corbusier is taciturn. He says: »*I prefer drawing to talking. Drawing is faster and leaves less room for lies.*« And already he has captured the basic ideas for his cities on his sketch pad.

Let us take a 20-year leap forward and stroll through Chandigarh, the new capital of Punjab . Le Corbusier has created a magnificent *gesamtkunstwerk*. His masterful architecture predominates; the interesting new city has been built in accordance with the bold urban development design. The people, the climate, the functions, social aspects have all been confidently integrated; the country's history is given clear expression, and the idiom of reinforced concrete has been rearticulated.

Le Corbusier 1964; Hilpert 1978; *Stadt und Utopie* 1982; Vercelloni 1994; *Nouvelles* 2001; *Visionen und Utopien* 2002.

But Chandigarh was actually built, wasn't it? Why is it a utopia? The qualities that were praised above have been achieved only very imperfectly. Chandigarh actually does have fascinating architecture, but not a *gesamtkunstwerk*. Le Corbusier implemented only the capitol, while the other buildings were designed by Indian architects. Also, a circle of slum shacks, clay structures, and emergency housing has sprung up. The social situation is problematic, the climate was not adequately dealt with, the buildings are partly in ruins, dimensions and distances have not been taken into account.

None of the cities based on prewar blueprints were built by Le Corbusier – and nevertheless he exerted an enormous influence on modern urban development. Le Corbusier's cities are truly radical, his razing of a segment of Paris far exceeds Baron Haussmann's consistent plans for Paris.
On the other hand his rapturous description of the »crystals« is reminiscent of the poetry of the *Gläserne Kette* (cf. chap. 9.1).

The *Charte d'Athènes* with its demand that functions be separated – clearly alluded to above – has been harshly criticized, but has also been historically misunderstood.

Rudiments of the great urban visions have been isolated in the »unités d'habitation«, turned into solitaire buildings: Marseilles, Berlin, Nantes-Rezé, Firminy. But important ideas were never implemented: the internal shopping streets, the society of the roof landscapes, the lush parks.

Zlin with its extensive factories is a reality. But Le Corbusier's urban development was implemented in a barely rudimentary fashion, although it would have taken a perfectly concrete direction. In contrast, the plans for Rio de Janeiro were fairly certainly doomed to remain a utopia. And yet there is one unusual implementation on the smallest scale, though not by Le Corbusier: A test road for cars has been built on the roof of the Fiat auto plant in Turin.

236. Le Corbusier, Chandigarh, India, administration center, capitol, and mud hut, 1952.
237. Louis Sullivan, regulation regarding the height of skyscrapers, 1891.

10.2. America

Hugh Ferris (1889–1938). An expressive New York, 1929

At first glance we can barely tell the New York of Hugh Ferris from the 21st-century one: skyscrapers as far as the eye can see, and the observation of zoning laws.

Soon, however, we do notice that it is a different city: Here, German expressionism, Fritz Lang's *Metropolis*, and Antonio Stant' Elia have left their mark.

The skyscrapers are cut like huge crystals, magic light falls into the canyons of houses. The façades are pleated, tilted, creased like the buildings in an expressionist film. The skyscrapers tower as high as monuments, and traffic moves on different levels. And on the connecting bridges are the apartment houses.

»My city«, says Ferris, »resembles a plain peppered with mountains. The massive centers, which cover several blocks, rest on broad, six-story bases. I've transformed the roofs into blooming gardens, unless they are shaded by skyscrapers up to 300 m high.«

During our tour we come to the Civic Circle, a vast park landscape for the recreation of all city dwellers and users. At the periphery of this park are shopping centers and centers for art and science. At the same time we can participate in the city's busy life while enjoying the beautiful gardens.

Kimpel 1984; Eaton 2001.

If we look at present-day New York with its increasing areas of concentration, with Central Park and the cultural and commercial activities at its margins, and especially with Daniel Libeskind's new, very expressive blueprint for the new WTC – it is a new utopia! – then Ferris anticipated only a few trends.

Seven Architects: Louis Sullivan, M. Green, H.H. Vreeland and others. The third dimension, 1900–1925

It is quite true that we only fly over all these cities instead of walking through them on foot: All of them, one way or another, have conquered the third dimension, and we follow it in the sky. For not only the buildings have gigantically shot into the air, but people themselves experience the city as if affected by the altitude: as pedestrians or in a vehicle – best of all in a plane, and ours is able to speed through the ages.

We start as early as the 19th century, and Louis Sullivan's skyscraper city seems somewhat chilly and simple: Not surprising, for as early as 1891 he clearly demonstrated how to deal with the increasing height of skyscrapers.

238. Hugh Ferris, *Metropolis of tomorrow*, 1929.
239. M. Green, H. H. Vreeland, and J. B. Mc Donald, *New York in the year 1999*. Drawing, 1900.
240. N. Pettit, *King's Dream of New York*, 1908.
241. Francisco Mujica, *Hundred-story city*, 1928.
242. David Butler and Stephen Goosson, Film: *Just Imagine*, 1930.
243, 244. Richard W. Rummel, *Future New York*, 1913. Metropolitan traffic solutions.
245. Anonymous, *Amazing City*. Periodical, 1939.

238 239 240
     241 242
243 244 245

From 1900 we fly to New York in 1999: At the south tip of Manhattan, the skyscrapers have shot up in large numbers, but, as M. Green, H. H. Vreeland, and J. B. McDonald explain, they have not renounced art and decoration yet. They are interconnected by overpasses, open and covered ones, and the traffic here is as busy as on the ground-level streets of the city.

We remain in New York. Around 1908, Mr. Pettit began to create King's Dream for the future: The buildings are now simpler, tighter, straighter. Gigantic airships glide over the city.

Richard W. Rummel has a lot to show us, first of all, again, in New York: Bridges crisscross between the buildings, and the streets lie deep below in the narrow canyon.

Now we do descend a little farther down, into one of the streets that is no longer quite as narrow, and the city has now been provided with no less than five public right-of-ways: Two are underground for the railway and utilities, the next is for the streetcars and cars, and the two levels above are reserved for pedestrians, who can look down on the street and participate in the busy traffic optically. Some bridges stretch diagonally across the street eight floors up.

Circa 1928, Francisco Mujica built his city in the »New American Style«, and the skyscrapers definitely have more than a hundred stories. On the level that is reserved for traffic twelve lanes are available for cars, and here, too, there are bridges over the broad streets. The endless street leads directly to the airport.

David Butler and Stephen Goosson take us to the just-imagine city of film (1930). The Gothic repeatedly inspired expressionism, and America. It is therefore no big surprise that the metropolis of Buttler / Goosson seems like an assemblage of Gothic towers.

Our flight ends in an interesting way: Deep below us is the base street of the Amazing City, developed in 1939. In spite of the narrow streets, there is plane and helicopter traffic.

The conquest of the third dimension, the vertical, is the most important criterion of the new city. It was Leonardo da Vinci who discovered it. Antonio Sant' Elia perfected it, and the architects and visionaries of the 1920s are obsessed by it. Yet how rarely it has been actually realized in the above-ground urban realm during the past century!

Daniel H. Burnham (1848–1912). The new Chicago, 1909

We fly low over the new Chicago: There is nowhere for the eyes to stop, all the buildings have 20 stories. Only the city hall towers over this endless steppe – or should we call this a splendid order? Very few diagonal roadways battle the dogma of the right angle. However, the fact that Burnham and his team succeeded in getting their plan accepted in spite of overall private capitalist interests demands our respect. We are even more impressed that in important ways the team encouraged a new awareness of community in an America whose society tends to be individualistic.

Kimpel 1984.

There is no doubt that a right-angled grid is an urban prototype that goes back thousands of years and will continue to remain popular, no matter how much we rebel against it at times. The question is only what is the cutoff point beyond which crowding, monotonousness, repetition become unbearable, and the qualities of the city – including aesthetic qualities –begin to deteriorate. We must, however, keep in mind that we perceive the city not as a plan, as a model, or from a bird's-eye view, but from a mobile perspective, for the most part 1.5 m above the ground, though the speeds at which people move vary a great deal.

Richard Neutra (1892–1970). Rush city and rush city reformed, 1923–1927, 1935

How different is the character of the city compared to the magnificent luxury villas the architect will build in the 1930s!

We can drive along the wide streets at considerable speed. The traffic – on which the city is based – is well planned. The blocks are aligned in a totally linear way, a remarkable parallel to Ludwig Hilberseimer's city, which was developed at the same time. And the different traffic levels in the work of both planners may have been inspired by Sant' Elia. At any rate this is a kind of linear city of a type previously conceived by Soria y Mata.

Although the rigidity of the blocks and the endless agglomeration of the buildings are disturbing, Neutra has not denied his humane and idealistic ambitions completely: Family homes are in-

246. Daniel H. Burnham, the new Chicago. Drawing by Jules Guerin, 1909.
247. Richard Neutra, rush city reformed, 1923–1927, 1935.

cluded in the concept, as are schools, of course. Mobile markets ensure local availability of supplies.
Eaton 2001.

The broad, linear street and the simple, cubical blocks of buildings are from now on the determining factor in the new city, which is characterized by transportation and economy. The connecting bridges, like those envisioned by *Metropolis* and the American utopians, have a hard time trying to link the divers elements of the city.

Frank Lloyd Wright (1867/69–1959). Broadacre City (*Living City*, 1934)

»*Individuality is the fundamental integrity of the human soul*«, Frank Lloyd Wright formulates his dogma, »*and democracy is the true gospel of this individuality.*«

And for Wright this individuality depends on one's own plot of land. »Men, women, and children are born to set foot on their own land. There's a piece of real estate waiting for every unborn child after its birth. Each of them should get an acre (4,000 m²) of land. Only in this way is democracy truly made real. Broadacre City is the city of the new freedom. This does not mean a return to the ›subsistence economy‹. Neither is it a return to rustic life.« Rather, according to Frank Lloyd Wright, Broadacre City reflects the true form of the machine age, but it has »gone to the countryside«, grown into the landscape.

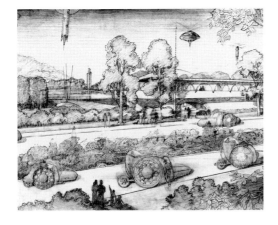

Through Broadacre City we ride in Frank Lloyd Wright's elegant Chrysler, for, contrary to the master's statements, public transit is available infrequently, and in front of the representative houses we also see two or three cars – in other words, this is a town where cars totally predominate. But we do see other vehicles that seem rather strange to us. They are equipped with two wheels as high as a man, while a third, small wheel is used for steering. At first glance it looks like a snail.Countless disc-shaped helicopters – the latest models –provide individual air transportation. »Cars give us new freedom«, says Frank Lloyd Wright, »and help us to master time because they are now fast and flexible.« »Broadacre« – oh yes, but we actually see no sign of a »city« during our romantic drive, nor of a recognizable, dominant center. What we think of as »urban« seems to have been completely retracted, and only a few high-rise office buildings predominate above the buildings that have few stories and are integrated in an absolutely rectangular grid.

»*The true center (the only centralization allowable) in the Usonian democracy is the individual in this true Usonian home.*«

And Wright continues: »*Every citizen can make his house a harmonious whole, as appropriate to him as to his purse – to his ground as to his God.*«

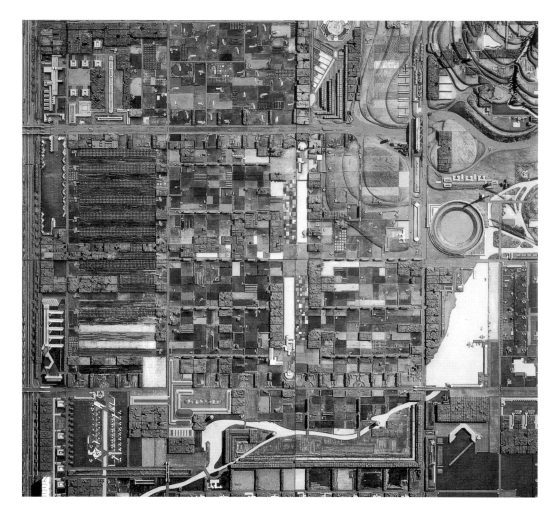

250. Frank Lloyd Wright, Broadacre City (*Living City*),1934, 1958. Model site plan.

In fact, the size of the plots seems to be about 5,000 m², but these are not merely ornamental gardens: many kinds of citrus fruit are planted, enough to satisfy the needs of each family. And on many plots we see a grazing cow or other animals.

The autonomous core family is the base, but it is not condemned to isolation, for Wright has seen to it that there are many kinds of social institutions. To be sure, the great idea of joint owner-ship, of the cooperative, the commune is not consistent with Wright's individualism.

»Simply having a place to live is not enough«, explains the patriarchal Grand Old Man. »We've also made sure that there are jobs. There are innovative farms, small yet profitable industries, and especially trades. The miracles of modern transportation technology – cars, planes, and heli-copters –cause space and time to shrink and make it possible for everyone to work in private in-dustry. Thus the unhealthy and undemocratic concentration of the cities has become superfluous. In Broadacre City, within a radius of ten to fifteen minutes by car, the inhabitants have everything they need and are at complete liberty to choose: schools, factories, shopping, cultural activities, entertainment.«

Wright is proud of the big changes he is bringing about, which are far from completed: »I have transformed the wretched suburbs of the United States into green, blossoming paradises where everyone can develop in a completely individual way! Today's large cities are monstrous aberra-tions, destructive for efficient production and human values.«

Mr. Wright says that everyone can develop to the full – but surely he means only wealthy fami-lies? »Not at all: Even with all this individuality we have developed rational technologies. The houses are completely within the means of middle-class, indeed of working-class people.«
And after a short drive we stop in front of a far more modest home – which, to everyone's sur-prise, is not fenced in.

»This is one of the many poorer families that live here. They were given a plot of land and a new start. They have built a minimal, simple house that they can expand later on. A vegetable garden gives them an extra income. They've bought a cheap used car, and the husband works in the factory. The family has found its self-respect, and in less than a year no one will be able to call them poor.«

251. Frank Lloyd Wright, Broadacre City (*Living City*), 1934, 1958. Location on the river.

The factories are private or have cooperative owners. They are small enterprises, always in the vicinity of the workers' homes, but can be reached only by car.

Of course not all the houses are the same size, and are categorized in a surprising way: »The size of the houses varies from ›one-car‹ to ›five-car‹ houses. But this is not a hierarchy, for they are all quality buildings and there are no poor people.«

Frank Lloyd Wright now takes us through the landscape in a wide arc and we arrive at quiet lakes – on whose shores there are office buildings. We drive through lovely woods, and the white cubes that gleam among the trees are the factories. Churches, hospitals, and schools seem to grow out of the rolling fields of grain.

We ask where the needs of consumers are met. »Shops have been reduced to the required minimum and are located at rural intersections.« We now reach the »great roadside market«, and from the start Mr. Wright emphasizes that it cannot be compared to ordinary supermarkets. Rather, this is a permanent »country fair« under a giant roof. Indeed, we find the most diverse enterprises of a decentralized economy here. Each producer has his own booth, and here we see the small farmer selling his fresh produce, the craftsman and his wares, and manufacturers with their machine products. Right next door there are restaurants, cafés, and cabarets.

For Mr. Wright the roadside market is »*the most attractive, educational, and entertaining, single, modern unit that to be found among all the features of Broadacre City.*« There is no competition. Rather, buying and selling is a kind of entertainment, a game with a number of different friends, a ritual of social solidarity. A joint economy becomes an event, a daily festival.

»However, the roadside market is only one meeting place for the community«, explains Mr. Wright. »There are many communication points, but they are not centralized and the real social center, as always, is the family in its home.«

Mr. Wright shows us one of these meeting places, and we see extensive grounds including golf courses, racecourses, zoos, aquariums, planetariums, galleries, theaters, and restaurants – in other words, yet another kind of centralization.

What about education and schools? Our drive continues, but we do not arrive at a central school, for Wright, violently critical of traditional schools, has implemented quite a different idea. »Every elementary school has upwards of 25 but no more than 40 students, without a fixed curriculum. The school's focus is on individual activities. The fatal separation of manual and intellectual work has been abolished. Simple everyday tasks such as cooking, gardening, and drawing have replaced mechanical learning.« And it is a given that the ground-level school buildings are spacious, transparent, interchangeable, and flexible.

»*Eye and hand, body and what we call Mind thus becoming more and more sensitive to Nature ... Spirituality and physicality, the Broadcare boys and girls would become the Coefficienty of a naturally, Creative humanity.*«

The traditional universities are closed. Rather, no one builds them in the first place, or else they are turned into community centers where, in small institutes, higher education is offered in research projects as a »vision of society«.

Another form of education takes place in design centers. Here, young artists and designers can experiment with the most advanced industrial technologies working in cooperation with factories.

Wright has great expectations of the role of architects and artists. »Artists and architects have been assigned an almost prophetic role. They recognize developing trends and have very important contributions to make to a new society. And the person who sees to it that the land is fairly distributed, so that every citizen owns a piece of land, would have to be an architect.«

Choay 1965, 2001; *Stadt und Utopie* 1982; Fishman 1982; Vercelloni 1994; Eaton 2001.

Wright's Taliesin East and West may be regarded as an implementation of his educational ideals. In 1932 he invited 23 young men to work with him. They were students, apprentices, but then primarily his collaborators, draftsmen in Wright's projects, and the »family« is at the same time the office and studio under Wright's patriarchal direction.

In spacious residential areas like Oak Park near Chicago, with Wright's representative houses, we see a variant – though hardly a democratic one – of Wright's Broadacre City.

Moreover, in the dispersed, spread out single-family homes in every small town, we see modifications – or perversions – of Wright's ideas. Basically, in the United States, the dream of Broadacre City is present in every settlement of single-family homes.

Ebenezer Howard started the railway era with his concepts, and Frank Lloyd Wright anticipates a city totally dependent on cars.

11. Policy, violence, c. 1870–1945

11.1. Germany, Austria

Ferdinand Amersin. The land of freedom, 1874

On a visit to the capital of the country, which is in Africa, we are surprised how symmetrical and centered the town plan is. »The actual town«, explains Ferdinand Amersin, »is divided into twelve different districts, each of which is a sizeable town in itself.« A network of intersecting, broad streets going in the four cardinal directions runs through the town.

We walk down one of these twelve radiating streets. They are wide and are formed by attractive façades behind which there are not only apartments but also public assembly rooms, administrative offices, and similar facilities. The façades are interrupted by well-kept parks with lovely vegetation, canals, and drinking fountains. In the middle of town there is no castle or church, but, strangely enough, all the local kindergartens and teaching gardens. Thus the impression we get is that this town promises a healthy, comfortable, and pleasant life.

To be sure, the political organization is rather surprising. There are ordinary citizens, super-citizens, and old citizens, whose votes in elections have differing values. But all citizens are obliged to come to plenary meetings, and must pass a citizens' examination. When anyone receives an inheritance, part of it goes to the community.

It is not the parents, but the community that educates the children. Hopelessly crippled children are killed painlessly.

Amersin 1874.

Once again the benefits received from the state are juxtaposed with the dictatorship of education and the cruelty of genocide. The fact that attendance at meetings is compulsory reminds us of 20th-century dictatorships.

Theodor Hertzka (1848–1924). Transported to the future (*Entrückt in die Zukunft,* 1895), Freeland as an image of a social future (*Freiland. Ein sociales Zukunftsbild*, 1890)

It's a long journey we must take with Theodor Hertzka: We're off to the equatorial interior of Africa, or, to be more precise, to the mountains of Kenya, east of Lake Victoria. That is where we find Freiland, the new state.

During the journey there is time to listen with amazement to Hertzka's remarks. After the country had existed for a year, there were already 95,000 inhabitants, while today there are more than 200,000. Hertzka explains the economic system: »The community has provided the capital for production. But the principle of total personal freedom or of justice was not violated. People have renounced profits, but without introducing communist control instead. Now there is no obstacle on the road to a free society. Land, capital, and means of production belong to the state, and every inhabitant has an equal right to the jointly shared land and the means of production.« »*We here in Freiland*«, proudly declares Theodor Hertzka, »*have managed to assure that our working classes enjoy the entire proceeds from their work no matter how high the proceeds – what is more natural than using as many machines as our technicians can invent?*«

Now we have arrived in the ideal state of »Freiland«, and right now we love the capital, called Eden Valley. The first thing that strikes us are the well-kept parks and many green areas. Scattered here and there among these are the villas, which are naturally surrounded by gardens.

We now have the opportunity to take a closer look at the pretty private houses. Though they are all built in the typical, half Moorish, half Greek »Eden Valley style«, they are different in size and differently furnished.

But even the production centers are skillfully built. We are totally amazed when we visit an iron rolling mill. We enter a massive building whose architectonic forms are perfection itself. Inside there are magnificent halls, flooded with light and air, in which many hundreds of men are occupied – doing what? At first we are not sure. »*This is where the sheet metal from which the walls of the geodrome are built is rolled and riveted.*«

Here? Well, where is this sheet metal? »*In the underground rooms: Here, workers merely operate the machinery. The racket, the heat, the fine metal dust created in the process are too much for human ears and lungs. What would be the use of controlling the forces of nature if we were incapable of transferring the aggravating, unhealthy part of all labor to the machines?«*

Along with these cool, rational, and humane reflections, there is also evidence of imagination and romanticism, as we discover on a walk through Eden Valley. Again and again we are charmed by the enchanting gardens.

Hertzka shows us *»a fairy garden covering an area of about a hundred square kilometres, filled by tens of thousands of delightful, elegant little houses and hundreds of fantastically splendid palaces; also, there is the intoxicating scent of every imaginable kind of flower and the singing of countless nightingales – which were imported from Europe and Asia.«*

Broad streets and squares, and large, airy terraces make for a pleasant stay outdoors. Everywhere residential buildings and parks are harmonically combined, and they are so spacious they remind us of lifestyles that in the 19th century were only available to the rich and were therefore increasingly moved out to the periphery of the cities. Here in Eden Valley such estates are lined up along a highway, which means that the undesirable division into town and country architecture does not exist here.

Hertzka 1890, 1891; Berneri 1950, 1971.

The ideal towns are mostly very far from Europe: We had to travel to dozens of islands, many distant, often unknown countries. Theodor Hertzka takes us to Africa.

By now it goes without saying that production is organized in the form of cooperatives, with the workers sharing profits, and that everyone is prosperous and contented.

Eugen Richter (1838–1908). A social democratic future, 1890, 1892

Eugen Richter gives us a tour of the new Berlin. Social democracy has definitely been victorious and we observe this »most perfect« of states. But very soon we notice that this committed, liberal politician is unstinting in his harsh criticism of »socialist« achievements – his comments are formulated in such a way that it takes close attention to hear the critically ironic undertone. True, not all his criticism seems justified; often certain actions and facts become absurd and comical – and at the same time alarming and oppressive – only because he exaggerates them.

What does this social democratic present look like? In Berlin we meet an old, friendly typesetter who is happy to tell us about it in his more than modest apartment:

»The rotten social order of capitalism and of the system of exploiters collapsed! There was joy on all sides among the entire population! ...

»We walked outside, under the linden trees. The cheering would not end! There was not one discordant note to disturb the festivities. The police force has been disbanded. The people themselves maintain law and order in an exemplary manner.«

Yes, and the city of Berlin has changed, of course, has become even bigger and more beautiful! Sure, instead of the statues of the Humboldt Brothers we've erected the figures of Karl Marx and Ferdinand Lassalle! And Frederick the Great has been replaced by Karl Liebknecht! We've turned the Erfurt party program into a reality!

All means of production, real estate, machines, and means of transportation have now become the property of the state or, as we call it now, society. All people have the same rights and duties. For example, they have to work from the age of 21 to 65. The state cares for children, young people, and the old.

Doctors and lawyers, too, are maintained by the state. They work for the public free of charge. The military has been disbanded, the collection of taxes proves to be superfluous; instead, the state keeps the surplus of the profits of socialist production. *»A new and glorious future is before us. People have no problem choosing a profession. Posters directly ask them to do so. It's up to each person what profession he chooses, but only if quotas allow this. Naturally the place of work is determined by the state.«*

But our typesetter does not want to hide the drawbacks: *»Oh well, every once in a while there may be a mishap. My daughter-in-law Agnes had quite a bit saved in her bankbook for her dowry. But suddenly the bankbooks were declared to be null and void! Agnes is totally crushed! Well – I guess our new chancellor will find a solution!«*

And his son hasn't exactly had an ideal career: *»Franz got a job as a typesetter – but not in Berlin. There's only one newspaper left, Vorwärts, which is sent to every household free of charge. Franz had to move to Leipzig – you see, his critical remarks on Castle Square didn't exactly help* him, either. But of course the marriage to Agnes, who has to stay in Berlin, is off for the time being – Franz is pretty mad at the politicians, but you can't really blame him.«

And our friend hasn't heard any good news about the neighbors, either: »See, in our neighborhood a couple was even divorced, but marriage is now a purely private relationship. Of course, you can enter into it and get divorced at any time. Naturally when there's a planned organization of production and consumption married people can live together only as their jobs permit, not the other way around.«

And our neighbor now speaks of his own problems: »Yes, I admit that my own choice of a profession wasn't too smooth. I did find a job as a bookbinder, but only as an apprentice, not as a master. It's just that a big company doesn't need that many master bookbinders! More people registered in Berlin as hunters than there are rabbits within a radius of ten miles. They had to cast lots. There have always been horse and dog lotteries, but here for the first time they drew lots for people.«

What about jobs for women? we ask. »That's not a problem, they work in state workshops.« The kids? They're in state daycare centers and schools. The laundry? They wash it in central laundries! The food? The main meals are eaten, exactly regulated, in state kitchens. In all 1,000 Berlin kitchens the same food is served, to 1,000 persons at a time. The state kitchens are an admirable achievement! »*It's a great feeling that in all the state kitchens of Berlin, on the same day, the same food is being cooked everywhere!*« Naturally the portions are the same for everyone. There are no second helpings! If you want extra food you simply don't understand the social democratic principle of equality!

»My wife, though, wasn't really okay with that. She says the food is like army rations. See, women always find fault with food they haven't cooked themselves.«

Now we have an opportunity to visit such a kitchen. For a money certificate we get the food coupon and numbers. Once the right seat is vacant, we pick up our food. Police make sure the food is distributed quickly and in an orderly manner, and watch the clock to make sure that the limited time allowed for eating the meal is observed.

But we are struck by the fact that the policemen in the kitchen today draw attention to themselves in a rather unpleasant way. There doesn't really seem to be a big crowd in the state kitchen today, does there? »I'll be glad to explain: Today, the self-employed workers are striking because they're not receiving the ›full remuneration for their work‹, so their noon and evening meal has simply been cut.«

Naturally society needs its entire workforce, and so it goes without saying that emigration is forbidden by law. The law is strictly observed, so they shoot at fugitives.

There's something strange about the work in the workshops, though – for those are places for killing time, easy does it, so the guy next to you can catch up. People think you're stupid if you work hard and show eagerness! But this spirit of egotism is just a legacy of the old society! Soon the tree of social democracy will flourish joyfully, cast its cool shade over all mankind, and make people happy.

Then, suddenly, moving day had arrived, and a furniture wagon stood in front of the door, come to get our furniture. We had thought the furniture was private property! Well, said the mover, Where would we get the furniture for all the new institutions, for children's education, caring for the elderly, nursing the sick, etc.? You get to keep the table, beds, and chairs anyway. »I suppose so – after all, Bebel did teach that household effects should be limited to bare necessities. And that was what we now had – I mean, our new apartment. It's a lot smaller and darker than the old one, and faces the back. We don't need a kitchen, because the state kitchens are to open tomorrow. But it was all above board. Why complain?«

»*This mawkish sentimentality is not in keeping with the spirit of the new era. Now that all men have become brothers and millions embrace each other, we need to lift our eyes, above the narrow petit bourgeois circumstances of a long-gone, outmoded time. Unfortunately, when we moved, we again had to leave behind more household goods. The new apartment was too small. But we mustn't let it worry us. In the new society, instead of a limited, miserable private existence we need to organize a magnificent public life. We've finally got to realize that.*«

We've been listening to the old man with astonishment, and we promise to come back a week later, for he has a lot more to tell us.

When we return for another visit, he seems both excited and happy. »Well«, he says, »they did it!« Did what? »Just imagine – Franz and Agnes managed to escape, and they've arrived in America safe and sound!«

Richter 1892; Berneri 1950, 1971.

Eugen Richter has been actively involved in politics: he was the leader of the liberal party in the German Reichstag in Berlin. The book, at any rate, was successful: Hundreds of thousands of copies were sold in Germany, and the English translation was also a gigantic success.

From the very first page of the book it becomes clear that Eugen Richter is not portraying a desirable future but rather that his work is a satire describing the Berlin of his day and ironically extrapolates the theories and emerging practices of socialism.

We must admit, however, that many of the regulations were reinforced not only in the early socialist states and in the dictatorships, but also in the democracies. In view of rising unemployment a person's free choice of a workplace has become relative in our time as well. Naturally working mothers are dependent on public childcare, and in many factory cafeterias, very strict order prevails. Eugen Richter's ironic vision in 1892 has thus come true in more ways than seem desirable to us.

Arnold von Passer, (Franz-Levy Hoffmann). A journey of discovery to Europe (*Menetekel*, 1893/*2398*)

The date is 1898, when we succeeded in founding the Freiland state here in Africa. Its beneficial work during the centuries that followed had worldwide effects. In Africa itself beautiful cities were founded. The capital, Thomasville, was named after the great utopian Thomas More. Deserts were reclaimed, meadows and forests were created, gardens and parks blossomed everywhere, and the economy prospered. Both the blacks and whites are a highly cultural nation and live together in peace. The date is now 2398.

We'd like to know what things look like in the Old World. An expedition consisting of citizens of German extraction tries to find out, and we join them. After a swift sea journey our ship lands in Hamburg. To our great shock, we see a ruined city, a city of the dead, oppressive and eerie. Only at night are there signs of life. What has happened? We go deeper into the country. The sights that meet our eyes everywhere are very similar: Germany is a wasteland inhabited by poor, wretched, starving people. Our expedition moves further south – the scene is the same wherever we go – but one day we meet a family that has preserved a precious chronicle. It gives an account of the last century, and now everything becomes clear to us!

At the end of the 19th century Germany was the mightiest empire in the world. And the workers had long ago expressed their views. Social democracy had begun a beneficial triumphal march. Of course all the problems had not been solved by a long shot. Suddenly, a short paper was published. In it, a member of parliament, Mr. Eugen Richter, describes the »social democratic pictures of the future« – but in what grim colors! His thesis is that the social democratic state replacing the capitalist one must inevitably bring about its downfall. The triumphal march of all social democrats seemed unstoppable – yet suddenly, there came a great about-turn, triggered by Richter's pamphlet. The socialist delegates were arrested, the movement crushed, all its achievements revoked. By 1901 the process was complete: Social democracy no longer existed. The situation of the workers became indescribably bad. Around 1930 a worker was a consumptive individual, while by 1970 he was a wretched creature who inspired pity and horror. No wonder that art and culture, too, experienced a decline. Yet ten percent of the population – big industrialists and big landowners – lived in unheard-of luxury.

Want and misery escalated, poverty and hunger held sway over the whole country, and capitalism could not get the situation under control.

Reading this report, our expedition was shattered. But they believed that there was new hope. »*The social ideas have not vanished. They are still alive in Africa, where they have borne glorious fruit. There, such things as wealth and poverty, or class differences, do not exist. In our country everyone enjoys what his work has created, and no one can take away the fruit of his hard work by force or trickery. From Africa, new light will stream over this dark continent and give it back to culture once more!*«

And this actually took place: »*Each year, on the soil of the devastated German empire and the other European states, more and more settlements that get their inhabitants from Africa have begun to flourish. In the new state that is being created here there are neither rich nor poor, neither Germans nor Frenchmen, only happy and contented human beings.*«

And then it is 2398: we are in Africa, in the great national hall of Thomasville near Lake Victoria/Nyanza, and in a magnificent festival people are celebrating the 500th anniversary of the founding of the state of Freiland.

Passer 1893.

Arnold von Passer references the gloomy picture of social democracy drawn by Eugen Richter (cf. chap. 11.1) and tries, in a somewhat clumsy literary form, to counter it passionately and drastically. He also cites Theodor Hertzka's *Freiland* (1890) and Edward Bellamy's vision of the future (cf. chap. 8.1).

Passer undoubtedly was not aware of the thesis (which has recently been disputed again) that the origins of Homo sapiens are to be found in Africa. That is why the idea that Germans from Africa want to colonize a devastated Europe with an ideal form of communism is all the more peculiar.

Theodor Herzl (1860–1904). The Zionist ideal state of Oldnewland (*Der Judenstaat*, 1896)

It's another long journey – the Zionist Oldnewland is located in present-day Israel, and we begin our excursion in Jaffa, modern Tel Aviv. But Theodor Herzl has provided us with unusual and interesting guides: Friedrich Löwenberg, a desperate Jew, once a regular in a café in turn-of-the-century anti-Semitic Vienna who has since fled from that city, and the ungainly German Mr. Kingscourt – a.k.a. Königshof, who for twenty years has been roaming through the world with Dr. Löwenberg and then spent a long time living on a South Sea island.

And now, in 1923, they head for Palestine in their yacht, land in Haifa, and experience one miracle after another.

For it is a miracle that immediately upon arrival in Haifa Dr. Löwenberg runs into David Littwak, the little Jewish boy from the Viennese café whose life he once saved. Welcomed with open arms, the guest has thus found a friend and expert guide through the new Palestine, a well-to-do citizen of Oldnewland, who will be by his side during the coming days – and probably much longer.

We are happy to follow the triumvirate Löwenberg-Kingscourt-Littwak, who will soon be joined by family and, at times, many friends. From the beginning, we are impressed by the large size, the life, the beauty, and the prosperity of the city of Haifa. Before us is a big square, formed by lovely arcade buildings, with a lush palm garden in its center and rows of palm trees along the sidewalks. The people who crowd the square are very diverse: Europeans and Chinese, Persians, Arabs, many in their colorful and picturesque ethnic garb. Cars glide by without a sound and suddenly, overhead, we hear a soft hum: The electric cable railway runs above the square.

Now we pass by a few more stately buildings: the maritime court, the department of trade, the employment office, the administration of the education system, and the city planning department, particularly charming with its loggia and frescoes. »This is where the engineer Steineck, our city architect, resides. He drew up the city plan and was able to draw on abundant resources«, explains David Littwak.

We are surprised by a detail in a few houses built in the Moorish style: densely woven wooden lattices. »Yes, this is where a few Mohammedans live, including my dear friend Reshid Bey«, explains Mr. Littwak, »and he is a member of our new society. I'd be glad to tell you more about it.« So a Mohammedan is the member of a Jewish society?

From the house we hear wonderful singing – it is Reshid Bey's wife – who, however, is confined to her home – yet lives with her children in a happy family.

»We've seen your public buildings. That must mean you have a lot of public servants?« we ask.

»We do, but there are also many honorary offices, and paid positions are given only to competent applicants.«

In the streets we find hardly any small stores, let alone the kind of bazaars we are accustomed to in the Orient.

»We didn't directly forbid retail trade, but it is inefficient and we have established large department stores and mail-order businesses.«

In the meantime we have arrived at the spacious home of Littwak, whose hospitality we shall be able to enjoy during the next days.

By now we have recovered from the journey and our first walk, and thus we welcome an invitation to an evening conversation at Mr. Littwak's house. Naturally our first question is about the political system of the »new society.« »We live in a mutualistic society«, says Mr. Littwak, »and that means that the cooperatives determine the economy and the finances. That's an optimal form between individualism and collectivism. *The individual is not deprived of the stimulation and the joys of private property, and nevertheless he can ward off the superior strength of capitalism by working together with the members of the cooperative.*«

Is there unemployment here? »In our country everyone has the right to work«, Mr. Littwak informs us, »but of course everyone is also obliged to work, and there are no beggars. And it goes without saying that the poor and the sick are provided for.«

The emigration of so many Jews has had a positive effect on Europe as well – at least that is what is claimed. The Zionist movement was equally salutary for those who emigrated and those who stayed behind. In the countries which had »too many Jews« »a remarkable social relief had occurred« and above all – anti-Semitism was now definitely a thing of the past.

As we say goodnight to our host, a pleasant experience awaits us: We are given an earpiece and hear the latest news, the stock market prices – and an advertisement for jewels.

The next day, Reshid Bey also joins our conversation circle, and he, no doubt, is the right man to answer our question: »Haven't the former inhabitants of Palestine been ruined by the immigration of the Jews? Have they not been forced to move away?«

»What a question«, responds Reshid. »For all of us it was a blessing. Primarily for the landowners, of course, who were able to sell their plots of land at high prices to the Jews. The poor Arabs have become much happier. They can have decent food, their children are healthier and learn something. None of their faith and their old customs have been destroyed.«

Our skepticism has not been completely eliminated yet. Surely the Mohammedans must regard the Jews as intruders? »The Jews have enriched us, why should we be angry at them? They live with us like brothers, why should we not love them?«

We now also meet the architect Steineck personally – we've already passed by his charming office building. He is happy to tell us about his work: »We draw up the plans for the workers' houses and for the station buildings. For a start, simple designs that could be produced quickly had to be sufficient, though this didn't leave much room for beauty.«

Not until later was Steineck able to show his qualities »in the functional, graceful, and sometimes majestic conception of larger townships and cities.«

For the present, 500 barracks of a new system were ordered from France: They could be put up in less than an hour and pulled down even more quickly.

»First I went to Sweden and Finland to buy timber for construction and to Germany and Austria to order steel. Then I found some young graduates at the Swiss, German, and Austrian institutes of technology.«

A few weeks later the construction office in Jaffa was running, with a staff of a hundred civil engineers and draftsmen, and the new tasks were clearly spelled out.

»Gradualy we were able to think of more ambitious building projects«, Steineck tells us. »You've seen a few of the representative public buildings already, I believe. But we've also designed some rather elegant houses for the citizens and given them the estimates.«

Honest prosperity developed to an amazing degree, and thus beside luxury hotels there were soon marble villas with lush gardens, elegant palaces, and spacious country homes – »architecture flourished«, Steineck states enthusiastically.

The architect points out one more interesting detail: »Under our streets we have hollow spaces to contain every possible already existing and future wiring and pipes for gas, water, and sewers, electric wires and the telephone.«

On the next day we get a lovely guided tour to Tiberias. The beautiful, well-kept landscape is a delight to see. But we do have one urgent question: What is life like for people in the country? Surely the farmers haven't died out – or craftsmen either. »The craftspeople are half farmers too. Both farmers and craftspeople are joined together in cooperatives. The goods they produce are delivered by the cooperatives to the big department stores, mail-order businesses, and exporters.«

Thanks to its medicinal springs, Tiberias had become a world-class health resort. Here, too, we recognize by the buildings that the religions exist peacefully side by side: Stately mosques, churches with the Latin and Greek cross, and synagogues show their stone splendor.

A second excursion takes us from Jaffa to Jerusalem, and our expectation of a lively, fascinating city is not disappointed.

The Old City has remained largely intact, and we see the Church of the Holy Sepulchre, the Mosque of Omar, the turn-of-the century cupolas, towers, and roofs, but the streets are paved, well kept, and clean. There are no private houses here, as everything serves welfare. There are pilgrim guesthouses for all denominations, Christians, Mohammedans, and Jews.

But now we come to a large, splendid, modern building – the so-called Peace Palace, a building for the many needs of the inhabitants and at the same time a peace memorial. This is where international conferences and peace negotiations take place.

But even mightier, more splendid is a building that gleams white and golden: the Temple. »It has been rebuilt because the times have been fulfilled.«

Its roof is supported by marble columns; as in the days of old, it is built of blocks of limestone. In the forecourt is the bronze altar and the »iron sea«, the huge water receptacle.

Of course, our intense interest in the city has not effaced our sympathy for our hosts: The death of Mr. Littwak's mother has affected us deeply, while the sincere affection of the German grouch Mr. Kingscourt for Fritz, Mr. Littwak's little son, has delighted and amused us greatly – and finally Dr. Löwenberg's romantic interest in Miriam, Mr. Littwak's pretty daughter could no longer be ignored. Plenty of reasons for the two globetrotters to settle in Oldnewland.

Herzl 1896, 1985.

»If you wish, it will not be a fairy tale«, Theodor Herzl, who is regarded as the founder of the Zionist movement, addresses his readers even on the title page of his book.

It was no fairy tale: In 1897 the first Zionist World Congress takes place in Basel. It was possible to win over England and Germany for the ideas of a new state. In 1948, 53 years after Herzl wrote the book and 25 years after Dr. Löwenberg's fictional journey, the state – not of Palestine, but of Israel – is proclaimed. It was no fairy tale – for all the technical achievements, the flourishing of the cities, the prosperity have become a reality.

It was a fairy tale – for this new state is very far removed from the boundless harmony, the peaceful coexistence, the indescribable happiness described by Theodor Herzl. And yet he has only described what can be reached directly with a capitalist-democratic background.

Herzl has predicted so many details: the phonograph, the supermarkets, the solar collectors. However, Herzl could not foresee the horrifying course of history. Twenty years after 1891 the dreadful First World War is unleashed, and even the fictional year described in the book, 1923, is followed by dictatorships, another world war, genocide – the greatest crimes in human history.

It was a fairy tale – for the dream of the end of anti-Semitism brought about by the creation of a Jewish state is further from realization than ever.

Josef von Neupauer. Austria in the year 2020 (*Österreich im Jahre 2020*, 1893)

Our guides on this journey are Mr. Julian West and Mr. Forest from Chicago – by the way, you'll recall Mr. Bellamy, who told the story of his 2440 journey to Boston.

On 13 July 2020 after a successful trip we cross the Austrian border near Salzburg. After touring the beautiful town, which has a permanent population of 1,500, we go on to Tulln and after a short stay there reach Vienna. Our Viennese friends, Mr. Zwirner and Dr. Kolb, have found us a lovely place to stay, and the very next morning, expertly guided by our friends, we begin to familiarize ourselves with the imperial capital. What we learn fills us with astonishment.

We had been aware that Austria is a communist state, although the imperial family continues in power. It is a system we regard with some skepticism.

»Austria is no longer ruled by one class«, explains Mr. Zwirner. »A long time ago, it was turned into a people's state, where all the citizens are equal.« Then how can individual qualities unfold – in art, in various skills, for instance? *»Birthrights have been abolished so that each person can be honored and rewarded according to his merit. So that natural inequality is to be able to develop fully, all artificial inequality – caused by subjugation – has been abolished.«*

We could not understand, however, why there is still an influential nobility in Austria, and even a Habsburg emperor.

»The nation itself voted by a large majority not to abolish the nobility. With all the authority they have, the aristocracy and the imperial family are now characterized by kindness, sound common sense, and culture, and the old privileges have been abolished. They are citizens like everyone else.«

Women have been given a very different position. They have founded a women's assembly where they discuss their problems. They do not deny their position as women and mothers, but they vehemently and successfully bring forward their demands and wishes and are fully eligible to vote in every respect.

Schooling and health care have reached a high level. The physician of each community is responsible for the prevention and cure of all diseases. Once a year he must examine all the citizens and report on their health. We wonder if the checkups, indeed, the surveillance – for instance of teeth – do not go too far.

Work is compulsory from the age of nineteen to the age of sixty-five – with many exceptions. So there are privileges after all? Daily work schedules have already been reduced to eight hours. The population is distributed according to where work is needed. People are assigned to jobs. Only what the nation needs is produced. Everyone must share the work to the best of their ability, and receives provisions from the total production. The state is the universal owner.

The new Vienna consists of districts that are all the same size. Clusters of four large residential buildings surround a palace that is used for administrative offices, reading rooms, and dining halls. Between these buildings are gardens and swimming pools. Only two or three wings of the exterior buildings extend as far as the landscaped streets, where no trucks or carriages are allowed. Only streetcars run in the streets.

Like street cleaning and garbage collection, heavy traffic does not begin until late at night, and this work, like a number of other services, is done by pensioners, who have younger men working under them.

A drive along Ringstraße is instructive: The stock exchange – which is now superfluous – has been transformed into a school building, while the police station is a student hostel. At the university, theology and law have been eliminated, for the visible Church has been dissolved in favor of the invisible one. Most churches were torn down or given a different purpose. The traditional administration of justice is no longer necessary. The people's tribunes live at city hall, and in parliament the nation votes by communities. Mostly, however, this is where European congresses meet.

The city is completely changed. Of course, the old majestic 19th-century buildings are still in place and Ringstraße is still as magnificent as ever. The streetcars still go around in curves, but are not driven by steam, let alone horses, but are pneumatically driven, i.e., by compressed air: the air vessel is pumped up again at the stops from pneumatic tubes. The switches can be worked from the driver's seat.

By the important public buildings there are large areas roofed with glass, many of them connected by underground corridors. But everywhere in public smoking is strictly forbidden.
In addition to the pneumatic streetcar we learn about a number of other interesting innovations. For instance, the telephone system has been fully perfected, and a dense network makes fast long-distance connections possible. The annual acquisitions of the libraries amount to twenty million books, and libraries have a total of 400 million volumes. The libraries are connected by a system of tubes so that books can be sent pneumatically.

While Austria at the beginning of the 21st century has won our approval in many ways, one strange regulation has definitely dampened our respect.

Again we encounter the strange endeavor to alter and improve human characteristics by means of genetic practices – something anticipated long ago in Plato's works. It was decided, in order to avoid cretins, cripples, and people who are unfit to work, that only a certain number of the healthiest girls and boys should be allowed to marry. The selection of a partner begins in early childhood: Selected future spouses are allowed to let their hair grow long, while the others get short haircuts. Transgressions – such as unauthorized pregnancies – are severely punished. With many new impressions, but with very mixed feelings, we leave Austria.

Neupauer 1893.

Many motifs known since Plato's time are picked up again, especially the age-old yearning for ideal communism. What is strange about this story is that communism is linked with an ideal Habsburg monarchy. Now that 1984 is a few years behind us and the year 2020 is almost here, it seems even stranger that Neupauer had not the slightest clue about the most important and catastrophic events that were to take place in the period between 1893 and 2020.

Hugo Bettauer (book) (1872–1925) and Karl Breslauer (film) (1888–1950?). The city without Jews (*Die Stadt ohne Juden*, 1922)

We've arrived in the state of Utopia, in whose capital   but we immediately recognize it – it's Vienna! We're planning to stay for three weeks, and we have good contacts with the politicians, and get direct information.

But we are also able to gather interesting snippets from the press: *»An insane fever of greed has come over the speculators. Inflation and rising prices weigh heavily on the state and on the population. The big black marketeers have wild parties, while the majority of the population lives in poverty.«*

Now we have the opportunity to speak with the federal chancellor in person. He belongs to the Christian Social party.

»We want an ideal city without poverty and misery. And the Pan-Germans in the parliament have convinced me: Only a city without Jews, who are to blame for all the misery, can be an ideal city. For, you see, in spite of decades of oppression they've managed to occupy the first place in the world because they're so smart! Tomorrow we are voting on their expulsion – it's the only thing that can save us!«

On the next day we are deeply shocked to learn that the anti-Semites in parliament, the Pan-Germans and many Christian Socialists, have won a clear victory: The Jewish Law has passed! Now, with extreme cruelty, the Jews are forced to leave the city by December 25th. As they stream to the railway stations and the borders, they are filled with despair and hopelessness. Where are they going? To London, to Paris, to Prague, and to Zion.

»The city is free of Jews!« the Pan-Germans cheer only a few weeks later. »The aliens have left the country!«

And yet – the recovery of the state is a long time in coming! Even in the first days after the expulsion Austria begins to feel its effects. There is no support from American anti-Semites, while the Jews in the big world banks boycott the country. The currency does not recover, and cultural life is at a standstill.

We speak with the business people and they confirm: »Yes, business is bad. Since the Jews went away, elegant life has stopped. Other countries no longer buy our goods, the Austrian *krone* keeps falling, and we have to introduce new taxes.« The coffeehouses are almost empty, the Viennese girls mourn their generous Jewish friends. In the fashion stores they're trying to switch to loden coats and dirndls, and cultural life is laid low.

Only a few weeks after the expulsion posters suddenly appear in the city: The »Union of True Christians« calls for the abolition of the law of expulsion. Many citizens agree and put pressure on the politicians.

We learn a remarkable secret: Leo, a deported Jew, has returned as a French painter. The posters are part of his campaign. Gradually a mood swing makes itself felt. The press and population demand a new parliamentary vote – and succeed.

Is there still a chance, perhaps? Hardly – though apparently the anti-Semites have a majority of one!

Leo, our »French painter«, keeps agitating and takes liberties, »Jewish liberties«, as he calls them: He gets Deputy Bernart, a solid anti-Semite, blind drunk. Bernart misses the sitting and the law is annulled. And Leo marries his middle-class Christian wife.

In 1920/23, when Hugo Bettauer wrote the book, and in 1923, when H. K. Breslauer made the movie, Hitler's seizure of power was in the distant future, though not anti-Semitism, which goes back for centuries and millennia. Bettauer's catchy, often ironic portrayal must be understood against the background of a city where large numbers of Jews had participated in cultural life since the turn of the century. But the city, or rather, cities without Jews become a horrifying reality: Gradually, after 1938, Jews were actually completely removed from Austrian cities and towns.

Bettauer's anti-Semites were almost »human«: The Jews were allowed to emigrate and did not end up in the gas chambers.

Breslauer's silent movie seems somewhat simple-minded and yet embarrassing today: Ten years before Hitler and almost 20 years before Auschwitz, the film shows almost prophetic scenes of horror: »Aryanization«, deportation trains, columns of suffering people. Of course the »happy ending« gives rise to concern: The parliament is manipulated by a Jewish trick.

An interesting detail: Hans Moser, soon to become the great Viennese film comedian, even during the Nazi period, plays the role of Deputy Bernart, appearing in a short, expressionistic scene. The film and the book have a touching happy ending. The reality, however, was the greatest murder tragedy in history.

There was no happy ending for Hugo Bettauer, either: In 1925, he was shot by a National Socialist – one of the first victims of the Nazis in Austria.

11.2. England, Israel

Ignatius Donnelly (1831–1901). *Caesar's Column*, 1892, *1990*

What a wonderful city lies at our feet! New York has ten million inhabitants – the biggest city ever to exist!

As we approach by airship, we look at the millions of lights. They are not produced by electric dynamos, but by the magnetism of the planets themselves, but this power returns to the earth again without losses – human beings have only borrowed it. Because of the glowing lights, day and night are now almost impossible to distinguish.

Once we arrive in the city, we are astonished at the traffic. Horses and carriages have long since been excluded; under the commercial streets are the routes of the trains, which are pulled by motorized smokeless and noiseless electric cars, separated into passenger and freight trains. At every street corner electric elevators go down to the tracks. In addition, high above and alongside the houses there are tracks on steel columns, where diagonal elevated railways race above the city.

There are two kinds of airships: The anchored ones with their fish-shaped metal balloons run on wheels, suspended from big cables strung in the air. Where they cross the sea, the cables are held by balloons anchored on man-made islands. The free-floating airships, cigar-shaped balloons, have no connection with the earth; the balloons have sails and electric motors. Parachutes with boats hanging from them provide safety. With these airships, the distance between London and New York can be covered in an incredibly short time – just 36 hours.

In New York we stay in a luxury hotel. The elevator is the size of a living room, a musician is playing the piano, we go up to the roof terrace, but immediately find ourselves in a tropical jungle: Flowers scent the air in the greenhouse, birds are twittering, there is the sound of music, and radiantly lovely girls stroll up and down. After admiring the amazing panorama, we return to the dining room. It is a good 100 m long and there is complete silence.

We sit down, and a mirror appears before us on which dishes from all over the world are listed, all numbered. Our table is equipped with hundreds of buttons – we press the button for the dish we want and very soon the table opens up and the desired dish emerges, though there is no alcohol.

We go back to the hotel lobby and are confronted with another surprise. Again we are standing in front of a mirrorlike surface and suddenly the most incredible, current pictures from all over the world appear, accompanied by the news. In the meantime, English has become the world language.

We've noticed for some time how pleasant the air is in the hotel: Air is piped in and out through tubes arranged in pairs. All the houses also have hot water. The heat is collected deep underground and piped all over the city, where it is also used to heat the buildings.

While we admire all these arrangements, we wonder about the purpose of certain little pavilions in the parks.

»When people are tired of living, they swallow a pill prescribed by a doctor, go to one of the pavilions, take a bath, lie down in bed, await death and wake up in the great beyond. The bodies are removed hygienically and do not pollute the rivers.«

On the other hand, we are impressed by a pneumatic mail system that gets all kinds of information to their destination incredibly fast.

In a strange incident on the streets of New York we meet an unusual man – let's call him Max. He dampens our enthusiasm for New York and shows us the horrifying, unimaginably wretched reverse side of the city. He takes us to the outskirts, to particular sections of town. Boundless poverty, unimaginable squalor, deprivation, and despair, combined with crimes of all kinds, disease, and early death. Miserable wages, heavy labor, and cruel exploitation are the inevitable fate of the poor.

There is no prospect of improvement, for the actual power is in the hands of a corrupt, all-powerful secret society led by a dictatorial prince.

Max shows us newspaper article from the year 1889 that urgently warns against coming catastrophes – all in vain!

But our friendly guide, Gabriel Weltstein, knew what the solutions for the problems were: Interest and usury should be abolished, the personal ownership of money should be restricted in favor of social and humanitarian institutions, the ownership of real estate should be limited in favor of the community. Trade and industry should be transferred to cooperatives, the international currency should be standardized by using paper money. Gold and silver should be devalued, and food should be produced chemically. With amazement and skepticism we listen to our friend Weltstein's interesting remarks long into the night.

But now we return to an appalling reality and learn of a powerful secret society directed against dictatorship and exploitation, against aristocracy and power. Yet the society in turn has become a totalitarian power with millions of members. A violent man, Caesar Lomellini, a giant in stature, enormously talented, heads the society. Already opposing forces are organizing. These are the powers of plutocracy and aristocracy, who own the »Demons«, the latest devastating airships. We are filled by great horror and manage to escape in time.

We were right to be scared: Gabriel Weltstein later tells us about the terrible events, the horrifying future of America and Europe:

Gabriel Weltstein's passionate appeal for peace was in vain. The insurgent troops of the workers and proletarians, of the rabble and of destruction are advancing toward the city – the citizens and the aristocracy are surrounded. In vain they hope for the Demons to save them: As a result of betrayal they have fallen into the hands of the insurgents: Bombs and poison gas rain down on their encircled enemies, and there is unimaginable carnage. It is a dreadful revenge for centuries of even more disastrous oppression.

But Caesar, the insane leader, has a monstrous idea of how to dispose of the corpses: They are piled up into a huge tower and then cement is poured over them. This is »Caesar's Column«. An inscription announces: »Erected by Caesar Lomellini, commanding general of the society of destruction. In memory of the death and burial of modern civilization.«

The revolutions spread. For Gabriel Weltstein America becomes unbearable – he flees to Europe – and finds the same situation there. His last refuge is Africa! And there at last the ideal society can be created.

Five years later, we revisit our friends Gabriel and Max, and their families, in the little town of Lincoln and share their happiness in the boundless idyll. It is based on true social reforms: common property, education, solidarity, faith in God, peace.

»The broad streets of the town are planted with trees, not merely shade trees, but fruit trees whose abundant harvest is available to all who feel like having a piece of fruit. No matter how humble, each cottage is surrounded by a garden where friendly flowers and vegetables are grown for the household. We don't have any proud palaces that cast cold shadows on the hard work of those who are inferior, no splendid carriages to arouse the envy and jealousy of passersby. A spirit of brotherly love prevails here. People are in the habit of singing and being cheerful at work, for the dark shadow of poverty has no power over them. Women, too, like to sing as they prepare supper, for after supper they're off to the theater. What radiant, rosy faces, both young and old. The people here are happy, and like to joke and tease in a spirit of fun; everybody has a friendly word, a witty remark for their neighbor. And so people walk through life, their hands folded in gratitude, toward a peaceable death, and the face of God blesses them as he looks down from his throne of stars.«

Donnelly 2003.

Donnelly obviously sympathizes with the brutal conspirators and revolutionaries and their abstruse hatred – he sees them as liberators – a duplicity that is not infrequent in human history. Once again, the fact that the evil and humpbacked co-conspirator is Jewish probably signals a proto-fascist anti-Semitism.

After the horror, for the end of the 20th century, Donnelly offers us an idyll worthy of Queen Victoria's reign or late 19th century family magazines. We've already had Donnelly's future year, 1990 – but were the yearning visions all that far off the mark?

And the real events of this turn of the century? Was what Donnelly described – airships in battle, gas warfare, mass destruction, cruelty, the fury of war, revolution, the destruction of civilizations – really so utopian? And then there was the growth of the cities (the population of New York has grown not to 10, but to 25 million!), subways, night turned to day by neon lights (Tokyo, New York, Shanghai), traffic on several levels, and much, much more.

On the other hand: We were not destined to enjoy the social idyll, the paradise of love.

Aldous Huxley (1894–1963). *Brave New World*, 1932, and thirty years later *Brave New World Revisited*, 1959

What a pleasure to experience a logically planned affluent society with Aldous Huxley! Everyone has a share in the luxury, and anxiety, misery, and disease have finally been overcome!

The handsome and proud people we meet are the result of planned breeding. Even as test tube babies they come into the world as members of a class, from Alpha to Epsilon: from the intellectual leadership elite to the slave labor, yet all of them are happy.

»And that, exactly, is the secret of happiness and virtue – to enjoy doing what one has to do. All conditioning has one thing as its goal: to influence people in such a way that they love their inevitable social destiny.«

After arriving in Central London, we immediately go to a squat gray building only 34 stories high. In large letters, the sign on the door informs us: »Central London Hatchery and Conditioning Centre«. We also learn the motto of the World State: »Community, identity, stability.«

The director himself receives us – the only way to gain access to the huge baby factory. »The first place we will come to is the fertilization room, and then you will see the incubators. And over here is the week's supply of ova. The egg is treated according to Bokanovsky's Process, which yields between eight and 96 buds, meaning embryos, and the same number of human beings, completely identical.«

The division, the categorization of human beings, was presented with absolute conviction: »Alpha children work much harder than we do, because they're so frightfully clever. Betas have to work less, and the Gammas are stupid. Delta children can only manage a few assignments, and the Epsilons are totally stupid.«

But no matter what befalls people, they have soma, a true magic potion that corrects even the smallest breakdowns in happiness. And yet: Things go wrong in the breeding process and the result is outsiders who suddenly appear and utter the taboo word »mother«.

And a »Savage« asks the remarkable question: What have you sacrificed for your happiness? And the Controller has to admit: Well – art and science, and religion, of course. In the old days there used to be a so-called God.

But that's not all you have sacrificed, says the Savage, there is something even more precious: *»I don't need comfort. I want God, I want poetry, I want real dangers and freedom and virtue. I want sin! I demand the right to be unhappy. Not to mention the right to old age, ugliness, and disease.«*

It is understandable that the Savage is doomed to fail: Banished to a lighthouse, he ends his life tragically.

Thirty years later, in 1959, we return to the »Brave New World« once again and with horror we have to realize that many of its terrors have become a reality: in the communist states, under National Socialism, in dictatorships all over the world: Hyper-organization has produced the standardization of human beings. Individuality is dissolved, the collective has priority, people are obliged to obey the political system, propaganda exerts enormous power, the media are instruments of dictatorships, brainwashing is common practice, yet the regime tries to make people believe they are happy. »Hypnopaedia«, a kind of sleep »instruction«, or rather, sleep manipulation, has gone beyond the experimental stage. In other words, this is really a »Brave New World.«

Huxley 1932; 1953, 1959, 1960, 1981; Swoboda 1972.

Should we revisit the »Brave New World« in 2006? Then everything is not really so bad, is it? The big dictators have long been overthrown! Except that there are still plenty of totalitarian systems – in the »West« other dangers are more menacing than ever: surveillance of the citizens, total control, the stress of advertising, proliferating organization, the »transparent human«, total registrations, computer terror of various kinds, biochemical manipulation.

It is true that there is no »soma«, but there is an enormous range of drugs that help people attain a similar state of »bliss«.

The title of Huxley's novel is taken from Shakespeare's Tempest: »How many goodly creatures are there here! How beauteous mankind is! O brave new world that has such people in't!«

Huxley, of course, uses the words ironically – the »brave (fine) new world« is a powerful dictatorship, and much in his book is reminiscent of Zamyatin's »Single State«. To us those who want to break out seem like heroes, martyrs, winners – or fools.

But the cruelest and perhaps the most dangerous reality of all is genetic manipulation – the cloning of human beings, designer babies, the new Superman.

252. Richard Kaufmann et al., Kibbutz Nahalal, Israel, 1928, 1936.

With young Israelis in the Kibbutzim of Israel, 1909 to the present day

Why, if we have been traveling through the utopian cities, do we visit a clearly rural settlement, a kibbutz? If we extend the term *city*, as we have done frequently up to this point, and interpret it as the differentiated and structured coexistence of human beings that comprises economics and politics, culture and education, the unique phenomenon of the kibbutz cannot be omitted.

This was one part of the dream of a new Jewish state: A kibbutz was to be not only a political and organizational structure, but also a new form of living together and of managing the community's affairs. *Kibbutz* means community, a »gathering« of a completely new type. It is intended to be a community based on the principle of mutual aid and social justice.

The basic principles were summarized in seven points:

1. Women and men have the same rights.
2. There is communal production, consumption, and education.
3. Members »work for themselves«. There is a closed labor market.
4. The workforce is at the disposal of the community.
5. Each member works according to his / her capability, each receives as much as
he / she needs.
6. The self-administered collective operates in accordance with democratic principles.
In this social system people share the work and the property.
Once more we step outside the realm of utopia into one of the most powerful realities of human life in our time.
Infield 1956; Moholy-Nagy 1968.

Our first journey takes us back to the year 1909. We are in the Jordan Valley, where we see the first settlement of this kind, characterized by commitment, thrift, and poverty. Forty years before the founding of the state of Israel, Zionists who come primarily from Eastern Europe have gathered here.

The basic principle followed by all the other kibbutzim has already been clearly articulated here and is explained by our young guides: »Two things are important for us. They are inseparably linked: a collective economy and living together in community. Only in a true community will we be able to cultivate this land. We have created an effective grass-roots democracy.«

Proceeds from the surplus, once the kibbutz's own needs are met, are spent centrally, in accordance with the needs of the collective and the members. »Each gives according to his / her abilities and receives according to his / her needs.«

253. Karel Čapek, *R.U.R.*, scenery at the National Theater, Prague, 1921.

Development during the decades that followed was slow, difficult, and full of privation. After the founding of the state of Israel in 1948 more than 270 kibbutzim were founded all over Israel. Close to 130,000 people have chosen this way of life, though that is no more than three percent of the population.

The kibbutzim have long since expanded their functions, and are no longer devoted only to agriculture, but also run industrial plants, factories, and hotels – once again, we can classify them as urban communities.

But what if we remove this superb model from its agrarian context and place it in an urban one? Is that a utopia too? Not at all, for it has been implemented. We now go to Ef'al.

The year is 1947 – the state of Israel has not been officially proclaimed yet – and we travel to Tel Aviv, the former Jaffa, which we know from a tour with Theodor Herzl (cf. chap. 11.1). The kibbutz Ef'al is located in a suburb of the seaport, and about 80 male and female workers have tried to transfer the rural settlement model to the city.

»We could count on the help of national organizations«, the head of the plant tells us, »and thus we initially managed to build the residential houses, with more than 70 apartments. Naturally we could not copy the rural layout, and the economic system is somewhat different.«

The members cannot all work in the same factory. They are employed in different professions in the city. About half the members commute to Tel Aviv every day. One feature they have kept, however, is a community fund of which all members get their share, each according to his / her needs. »In the community we have gained psychic and economic security«, the members assure us convincingly.

And how have members who have a higher income dealt with losing part of it? »Admittedly we've had a number of problems, and we've modified a few things«, confesses one of the members. How many other people want to adopt this urban model?

»Once more we have to confess that so far we're the only ones who've adopted this particular form!« And how have you modified the idea?

The model has remained flexible. We've been open not only to industrialization, but also to tourism. And gradually a stronger individualism has developed. The collective spirit certainly did suffer as a result, but we have more freedoms, are more family-oriented, though this may mean more work for the women.«

11.3. Czechoslovakia, Russia

Karel Čapek (1890–1938). *R. U. R. (Rossumovi Universálni Roboti)*, WUR (*Werstands Universal Robots*), 1920, 1922

The purpose of our visit at *Rossum's (Werstand's) Universal Robots* is to see the head of the powerful enterprise. But we wait for him in vain: The great master has long since retired from the worldwide company. A member of his experienced research, development, and marketing staff is glad to provide us with information: »*Back in 1920 old Werstand (Rossum) traveled to a distant island in order to study marine fauna. By means of chemical synthesis he tried to reconstruct exactly the living matter that is protoplasm. Suddenly, he discovered a substance that behaved very much like living protoplasm, although its chemical composition was different. This was in 1932.*«

His robots are not mechanical machines but are made of organic, colloidal jelly. The technician explains the advantages: »*In your opinion, which worker is the best from a practical standpoint? The cheapest, of course! The one who has the fewest needs. We've invented a worker with minimal needs. We've simplified him, thrown out everything that does not directly serve work. In doing so we've thrown out people and invented robots. They're mechanically more perfect than we are, they have amazing common sense – intelligence, but they have no souls. The invention of an engineer is technically more flawless than a natural product.*«

Helena Glory, the daughter of the president of Europe, has found us in the meantime. She wants to get to the bottom of the secret of how robots are produced, and so we hear new information about the robots. Helena is shocked. She thinks of the robots as human beings: »Why don't you make them happy? They should be treated as human beings!«

The answer is that they're only robots, they will always be machines, they have no soul, no emotions, feel no pain.

»But look how far we have come. The robots produce so much of everything that things no longer have any value. There is no poverty. There is also no longer any work. Everything is done by animate machines. The robots dress and feed us, build houses, write numbers for us, and sweep the stairs. People do only what they love to do, they will live in order to achieve perfection.«

But a new shock confronts Helena: »Is it true that no more children are fathered or born?« »Yes, that's true. We can live without that aggravation.«

For a long time, we've had a premonition that something terrible is in the offing. Now we are shocked by the following news report: »In Le Havre the first organization of robots has been founded, and a call has gone out to robots all over the world.«

And the appeal is successful: As we look out the window, we are seized by horror: Slowly and in silence, a vast troop of robots is approaching the factory! And here's another shock: Suddenly they are all armed! As they storm the factory and kill the engineers, we hear them cheering: »*The power of human beings is at an end. A new world has begun. The age of robots! The rule of robots! The humans gave us too little life! Robots, to work!*«

What about people? Have they been wiped out? And Helena has burned the secret of the robot factories! Will human beings become extinct?

Then we meet the male robot Primus and the female robot Helena, and one of them is to die. But how strange – each wants to sacrifice himself for the other. They are filled with love for each other – are they still robots? Or are they the Adam and Eve of a new race?

Čapek 1920, 1922; Manguel, 1981; Wuckel 1986.

Fears of magical-mythical creatures, spirits and gods are among the basic components of utopias, they become dystopias. With the articulation of the age of technology, fears of the machines and their anthropomorphization take shape as robots who have become independent. Karel Čapek presumably derived this term from the Slavic languages, using it for the first time in his plays. The topic is more relevant than ever today: The fear of being dependent on computers and gradually being controlled by them has long since crossed the boundary between science fiction and reality.

254. Karel Čapek, *WUR, Werstand's Universal Robots*. Title page of the German edition, 1922.

Yevgeny Ivanovich Zamyatin (1884–1937). The single state (*My*, 1920)

The man D 503 – he is the great constructor of the spaceship »Integral«, which is to carry the system of the State into outer space – has invited us to visit the »Single State«. It is ruled by the Benefactor – assisted by the Guardians – and is surrounded by a huge Green Wall. Of course no one here knows that outside the Green Wall there is a second world, an almost untouched wilderness where a small number of people develop quite naturally.

In the »Single State« all is well regulated and ordered, and D 503 describes the life for us: »*Every morning we, millions of us, get up as one man at the same hour and the same minute. At the same hour we, a host of millions, begin our work, and end it at the same hour. And, fused into one million-handed body, we lift the spoons to our mouths at the same second determined by the Table of Hours, go for a walk at the same time, gather for the Taylor exercises in the auditoriums, go to bed.*«

There are still two personal hours left, though an order will be found for those, so that »*then the Table of Hours will cover all 86,400 seconds of the day*«.

All people wear a clearly visible gold badge with their number. On the back of it there is a watch, which is already a component of the human mechanism.

The houses have completely transparent glass walls, and the Guardians of the State, instruments of the government, can see what is taking place in each apartment. We express our horror about the destruction of intimacy, but D 503 reassures us: »In the hour of sexuality one is allowed to draw the curtains, though only on regular sexuality days.«

But how do people know when these sexuality days are? we'd like to know. »That, too, is sensibly regulated. The Bureau for Sexuality analyzes the hormones of every citizen and draws up a table of these days. Then one receives a booklet of pink coupons. Each coupon entitles one to an hour of sexuality – for each ›number‹ (meaning, person), for one belongs to all and all belong to one. However, women may have children only if they meet certain standards. If they ignore this law, they are put to death.« But isn't this lack of freedom, aren't these constraints terrible? »No. Human beings have an innate instinct for lack of freedom. Happiness exists only when there is no freedom, or freedom exists only without happiness – there is no other alternative!«

But ultimate happiness has not been attained yet, even after the end of the Two Hundred Years' War. »We're just a few steps away from the ideal. That won't arrive until – nothing happens anymore.«

We take a closer look at the city. The Green Wall, made of opaque glass, is its boundary. We are impressed by the big auditorium, formed from 66 concentric tiers.

The glass operation office resembles a huge bell, but it is not organs or limbs that are operated on, but, far more progressively, the soul, the imagination, the demonic, are expertly eliminated. The glass city we walk through is flooded with light. Long cubical residential blocks of houses form the straight streets, and we keep encountering gray-blue uniformed marching columns. We look in vain for restaurants: Healthy naphtha food keeps the »numbers« strong.

Now D 503 introduces us to his girlfriend I 330, a pleasant meeting. He is glad he has already received the pink coupon for sexual intercourse. But his joy is marred because I 330 is suffering from a dangerous disease – »soul« – and has to see a doctor.

Now we have the opportunity to watch a festival. It is the »Day of Unanimity« and of the election. Who is going to vote for the Benefactor again? All hands shoot up. And who is against him? Nobody! Or rather: One hand is raised: It is I 330's! Only with great difficulty D 503 manages to save her from the people's anger and the police! But the appearance of contentment is deceptive.

There is an insurrection, and D 503 is persuaded to join the revolutionaries. The hijacking of the spaceship »Integral« by the insurgents fails – an excursion over the Green Wall was of short duration, and I 330's inflammatory speech goes unheeded. But the alleged followers of the Benefactor call through the streets: »The disease is called imagination! It is the last obstacle on the road to happiness! The obstacle has been removed!«

»Long live the Great Operation! Long live the Single State! Long live the Benefactor« And so D 503's imagination is surgically removed. The insurgents are brought back into the »Benefactor's machine« under the »gas bell«.

Can there ever be happiness in freedom?
Zamyatin 1920, 1952; Eaton 2001.

Yevgeny Zamyatin was active with the Bolsheviks – though he had imagined the Soviet state to be different from Stalin's dictatorship. For, he is convinced, people long for love, motherhood, and poetry.

Zamyatin's prophetic gift is astonishing. Years before Stalin and Hitler (and also before Huxley and Orwell) he portrays the pandemonium of the totalitarian state: constant surveillance in the glass house, secret police, brainwashing, sexual dictatorship and eugenics, unanimous elections, the spaceship, electronic music, the Iron Curtain, and arbitrary torture and death. No wonder, therefore, that the book was prohibited in the Soviet Union.

Andrei Platonov (1899–1951). On the road to *Chevengur*, 1928/29

Our guides are Andrei Platonov and Stepan Kopyokin. Together we arrive in Chevengur and, to our surprise, find a town that has, so to speak, totally dedicated itself to socialism or, more correctly, to communism. Platonov describes life there: In this society there is no affluence, we almost have the impression of a certain degree of poverty, but all the inhabitants live in brotherliness, and work is done completely voluntarily, for the people, bonded in friendship and comradeship, devote their attention to the soul. Women are not seen as an object of beauty and desire. Rather, they live with men in friendship but without love. They can choose their husbands themselves.

»Well, that sounds very nice«, says Kopyokin, »but is that true communism if human suffering continues to exist?« – »What do you mean by that?« Platonov asks him. – »Look, there's old Titysh. He's so lonely he has to live with a cockroach. And then there's the grieving mother whose child is dying in her arms – wherever you look there is still human suffering.«

»Yes, but how can human suffering be abolished?« retorts Platonov, »You can't expect that of communism, can you?«

»*Communism*«, announces Kopyokin, »*is the glue that binds the bodies of the proletarians, but when all is said and done things are exactly the same as under imperialism.*«

We share our guide's skepticism, but he wants to stay in Chevengur a little longer.
We leave the town, but we sense more and more »*the hopelessness of the Chevengur experiment, and we are not convinced that an ideal society has been established here*«.

Months later we hear that Kopyokin constructed a few more useful machines and implements, but the experiment ended as a result of the attack of an unknown military division. Kopyokin dies in the battle.

Ten years after the October Revolution and five years before Stalin's seizure of power, a poet dreams that communism might eliminate human suffering – an expectation of salvation that far exceeds previous millenarian thinking.

Stanislav Gustavovich Strumilin (1877–?). The community palaces, 1930

»*Two elementary principles are the precondition for a society and consequently for a city*«, postulates Stanislav Strumilin, »*the collectivization of workers' lives and the total emancipation of women*.«

The city is laid out in the form of a square with an area of three km², so that it is possible to reach the center from every direction within ten minutes. Therefore there is no need for a subway, electro-buses, or elevators. Everything is very simple and easily accessible.

The inner city comprises the manufacturing plants, the communal apartments, the central offices for electric power, radio, and telephone services, the culinary center, the bread factories, the library, an institute for 3,000 students, fifteen boarding schools for 6,000 students, a hospital, a large department store, a theater, a club, and a stadium. These cover an area of no more than 300 hectares, half of which is green space.

The various circumstances under which they are utilized require different solutions, but the communes take the form of »large buildings« and are organized like sanatoriums or hotels. That means that not only meals but also all necessary services for the families are centrally organized.

The city is divided into »micro-districts«, and each district provides services and has its own preschool and school. Roofed pedestrian-only roads and squares guarantee absolute safety. The »community palaces« are quite large: No less than 10,000 persons live in each unit. Units are no more than three stories high. All service facilities are located in the semi-basement: office, health care center, post office, hairdresser, laundry. On the second floor, one wing houses the children's apartments, while another houses older inhabitants. The third floor has two- and three-room apartments for families, the fourth floor has single rooms for young workers, students, or other unmarried persons.

Within twenty years, it will be possible for each individual to acquire living space of from 16 to 18 m². Human beings are social creatures, but in the apartments provisions have been made for workers to retire to a quiet room to rest and relax.

The common cafeterias are good for daily human contact, but everyone can also prepare his or her own food on a private hotplate.

In the community palace there are opportunities for many kinds of contacts and interests – for instance, scientific, literary, musical, choreographic, and sports activities.

»We have found a sufficient number of people who were glad to move into the community palaces of their own free will«, concludes Strumilin. »And it is important that everyone enjoy living here in friendship with everyone else.«
Choay 1965, 2001.

Drafts, sketches, ideas, theses dealing with communal living existed long before Stalin's seizure of power. The ideas of Plato and his many successors often inspired such visions. The implementations were very modest, and under Stalin people returned to the petit bourgeois family.

K. Ivanov and the construction committee of the Economic Council. The Soviet Communes, 1925–29

The great pioneer in Russia's new culture and the Soviet Union respectively, El Lissitzky, explains the infrastructure to us: »*The birth of the machine is the beginning of the technological revolution that destroys manual crafts and becomes crucial for modern large-scale industry. Our revolution begins in October 1917, marking a new stage in the history of human society. The basic elements of our architecture are part of this social revolution, not of the technological revolution. In our country, the new architecture does not continue an interrupted tradition, it stands at a new begin-*

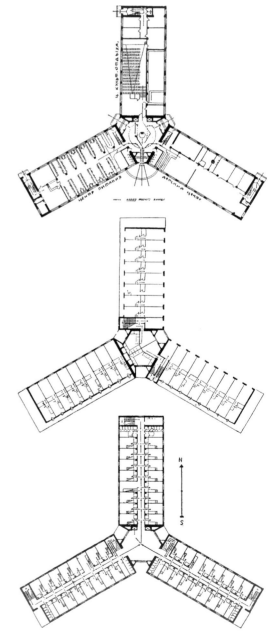

255. K. Ivanov, T. Tochin, and P. Smolin, (Institute of Civil Engineering), residential building-commune, 1925–29.

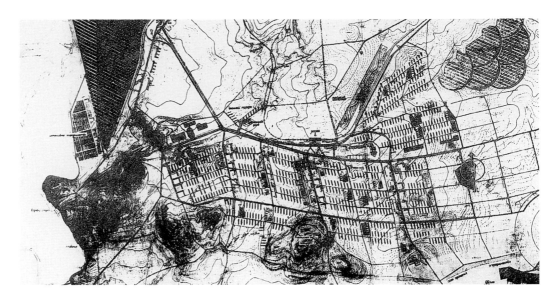

ning and its task is not merely to construct buildings. It needs to grasp the new forms of life so as to participate actively in the birth of a new world by creating buildings commensurate with this world. Soviet architecture has moved forward toward reconstruction.«

Past Leonidov's Lenin Library, Tatlin's Monument to the Third International, Vesnin's Pravda Building, and El Lissitzky's speakers' platform for Lenin we come to the big communal settlements, imposing residential apartment blocks scattered loosely in green spaces.

Comrade Ivanov describes the successes with enthusiasm: *»We have abolished all contrasts between various types of residences, from the dark basements of big-city workers to apartments that cover an entire floor, or private villas.«*

Now we have a chance to visit one of the communes, and understand why the housing units are so very small: »Cooking has been moved from the individual kitchen to the communal cooking laboratory; the main meal of the day has moved to public dining halls, children are educated in nurseries, kindergartens, and schools. A house here is no longer a sum of private apartments, it has become a house commune.« The traditional bourgeois family has been dissolved into its functional components, which are placed in the hands of the collective. People spend their free time at the club, in lecture halls, at the cinema.

Now we have time to visit the types of buildings erected by the Economic Council and notice their extreme thriftiness: Many communes have communal baths, but all have beautiful community rooms. »We have reached an initial goal: We've doubled available housing, and each inhabitant of Moscow has at least 6 m² of living area.«

El Lissitzky 1936; Vercelloni 1994; Eaton 2001.

Thus the communist utopians perfect the two-and-a-half millennia old ideas of Plato. Yet the implementations are modest: None of the architectural projects were actually built. One student hostel and a few blocks of residential housing are the undistinguished sum total of the implementations.

Mart Stam (1889–1980). Magnitogorsk, 1928

»My dream has come true«, states Mart Stam with great satisfaction. »I've escaped from the capitalist or hypocritically social democratic Western Europe to the new, ideal society of rising socialism in the Soviet Union. My ambitious plan for Magnitogorsk has been accepted, and building has already begun. Between the traffic arteries, residential areas have been created, in great uniformity as is appropriate for a classless society. At some distance from the housing, the gigantic rise of Soviet industry is unfolding. An enormous educational thrust and the collective spirit of the society have created the new Soviet citizen!«

Vercelloni 1994.

And what was the reality? Mart Stam is deeply disappointed by the task he was set: Forced collectivization, the dictatorship, a lack of resources, unsurmounted poverty make it obvious that he had misjudged the situation. In 1934 he leaves the Soviet Union, never to return.

Nikolay Milyutin (1899–1942). The Soviet linear city, 1930

Fifty years have already passed since Soria y Mata developed his idea of a linear city. Milyutin takes up the theme and reinterprets it. »A linear conception of the city makes organic growth possible – that was the premise for a Soviet city«, declares Milyutin.

Crisscrossing this linear city we look in vain for something like a city center, but we can clearly distinguish the individual zones Milyutin has been explaining to us: »The railway is our present and future – that is the most important axis, along which all the industrial plants and the needed administration are located. A wide strip of green space with sports and recreation areas creates a link to the residential areas with community facilities. It goes without saying that the restructuring of Soviet principles has brought with it the restructuring of culture and everyday life!«
Vercelloni 1994.

As a matter of fact there had been concrete attempts to build a linear industrial city – for Magnitogorsk in 1928 and for Volgograd in 1930 (cf. chap. 11.3). However, the projects were developed by Mart Stam.

257. Nikolay Milyutin, Soviet linear city, 1930.
258. J. Bronstejn, P. Kuzonyanc, V. Pereyaslov, M. Cerkasov, G. Lyudvig, Palace of Technology, 1933.
259. A. Samoylov, B. Efimov, G. Barkhin, and G. Obrazcov, Palace of Technology, 1933.

Soviet Architects. The Palace of Technology, 1933

The buildings through which the architects conduct us are not palaces in the traditional sense of the word. Rather, in an excess of technological enthusiasm, entire cities were built.

J. Bronstejn takes us directly to a large round arch portal with a mighty supraporte. Now we enter a forecourt with a fountain that inevitably reminds us of the »paradises« of early Christian churches. We walk through another arcade portico and now stand in a courtyard of majestic dimensions.

»Classical symmetry is still valid«, Bronstejn tells us. »It is in no way inconsistent with functionality and usability. We are now approaching the monumental Building for Technology and Society. It may remind you of a shattered column.«

On the way there we notice an inaccuracy in the symmetry of the construction. »Symmetry is not a dogma. Here, I merely introduced a transverse axis that links the river bank with the main axis.« The enormous square is reminiscent of an ancient arena or its transformation in Rome, the Piazza Navona.

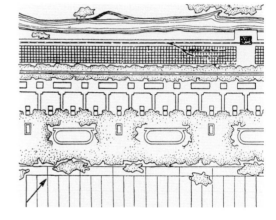

The associations in A. Samoylov and B. Efimov's project are different. They conjure up the drafts of Antonio Sant' Elia, though there is a strange stylistic contradiction: While the bridge for the streetcar represents an elegant technical steel and concrete construction, the structure that spans it is incredibly massive and heavy and expresses a severe, dictatorial pathos.

This dilemma also characterizes the town designed by the team of Georgiy Volfenzon. An endless row of houses is spanned by huge nonfunctional arches whose giant columns are topped by strange little decorative turrets. In contrast to these, the two-story buildings that flank the street have a largely practical structure that approaches the Western International Style.
Mosca 1991.

Architects such as G. Barkhin come from a revolutionary Russian constructivism. The year 1933 also brings Stalin's seizure of power, which means the end of progressive architecture. We can imagine against what obstacles the progressive architects had to struggle.

Vladimir Alexevich Zhukov (1886–1967) and Vladimir Georgevich Gelfreich (1885–1967). The Stalinist City, 1933

Are you sure we haven't gone back two or three thousand years in history? Is this Egypt, Mesopotamia, or Rome? No, we are in the city of the great dictator. The monumental buildings of the universities, party headquarters, and government buildings have become the model, the standard for the entire metropolis.

»We reject formalistic experiments, playing around, and abstractions«, challenges Zhukov. »Our city is an expression of the working class – realistic in form and socialist in content.«
But your classicism and pseudo-Rococo is also playful, isn't it? is our question. »We've simply conquered bourgeois art and made it serve our permanent revolution!«

So it is no surprise that the most colossal building is the Palace of the Soviets in Moscow: A gigantic cube, supported by arcades, spreading in extensive terraces, and visibly dominated from afar by the triumphal column of Lenin.

It did not take long for Stalin's dictatorship to liquidate the bold ideas and projects of progressive constructivism. As early as 1933, the year of Stalin's seizure of power, Stalinist architecture had already been clearly articulated.

Ivan Fomin. The Academy of Sciences, Moscow, 1934

This imposing project, an apotheosis of science, was created as a result of a competition. We approach the large, almost deserted square, first passing the entrance buildings that flank it. The temple-like building stands on a three-arch rustic base.

»Time after time, antiquity has been our teacher«, emphasizes Ivan Fomin. »In the flanking buildings, I was very definitely influenced by the architecture of antiquity, but I also kept in mind the tradition of Russian classicism«, Fomin justifies himself.

Now we stand on the square whose vastness is both fascinating and oppressive. Our eyes come to a rest on two high steles. A temple façade with double columns and a widely drawn tympanum forms the border of the square.

Mosca 1991.

Ivan Fomin's 1934 project avoids the gigantic monumentality of a Stalinist architecture that has already become popular. Rather, it is inspired by Russian classicism, and one cannot help also being reminded of French revolutionary architecture around 1800.

The brothers Aleksandr (1883–1959) and Viktor Vesnin. Red Square, Moscow, 1935

What, someone has dared to compete with the magnificence of the Kremlin, the beauty of the Cathedral of St. Basil? Yes indeed – the Vesnin brothers create a building that puts to shame all other architecture – the building of the Narkomtyazprom, the People's Committee for Heavy Industry, was erected as a 36-story building following the 1935 competition.

At first we see a group of four massive towers placed on a six-story base that has arcades running around it. The individual towers are connected by bridges on two floors. Between the towers, on the lower floor of the base, there are gigantic groups of figures representing the struggle and victory of the Soviet Union. The building with its elegant glass façade is completely part of the trend of the International Style.

»Every task always has more than one solution«, say the Vesnins, »and that is why we also designed a variant. Here, the building is compressed into a compact but articulated body whose exterior is more powerful and monumental.«

And besides, we notice, the political aspect has been taken into account to a greater degree, for the terraced foundation forms a huge grandstand for demonstrations on the Red Square.

260. Georgiy Volfenzon, Arseniy Maksimov, Yuriy Savitskiy, Palace of Technology, 1933.
261. Ivan Fomin, Academy of Sciences, 1934. Competition.
262. A. and V. Vesnin, building of the People's Committee for Heavy Industry on the Red Square, Moscow, 1935. Competition.

The most surprising thing about the project are two classicistic temples on the flanks of the complex and turned away from it, representing only slightly modified combinations of the Brandenburg Gate and the Neue Wache in Berlin.
Mosca 1991.

The Vesnin brothers are among the main representatives of constructivism, of the architecture of the Russian Revolution. They created interesting designs, such as that of the Pravda Building in Moscow. Now that Stalinist architecture began to exert its despotism – voluntarily or not – they did an about-turn, responding to the dictator's predilection for things big. The »pastry-cook style« is not yet mandatory, but the triumph of might when it comes to historical buildings is ruthless.

11.4. Italy, Germany

Giuseppe de Finetti (1892–1952). The Arena District of Milan, 1933

»Even today, the city is meant to be a monument. But churches and palaces are no longer needed – let's make residential buildings and businesses into monuments!« And Finetti builds high-rises on wide foundations, 25 floors high or more, with columns and porticoes, and terraced toward the top. Mussolini has just gained power in Italy – is this what the architecture of the new regime will look like?

We cannot help comparing de Finetti's work with Vesnin's buildings on Red Square, but under Mussolini architecture takes a considerably more moderate course. Initially it is close to the International Style.

Adalberto Libera (1903–1963). Castelfusano, Rome, 1933/34, and Aprilia, 1936

We have not noticed the lovely shaded green spaces that adjoin the large complex of buildings, for we have been strolling down a more than a kilometer-long façade along the river bank A connoisseur of Italian architecture, Oliver Cinqualbo, has been our guide, and now takes stock of our tour: »*It is the end of a long and hot day. The sky is turning orange. Like many others, we have come to the river to breathe a little cool air. You can hear the cars driving down the expressway by the sea and, behind them, the rustling of the pine forests. The sandy beach has been formed by the retaining walls of the highway that were treated like a long façade. At regular intervals openings allow pedestrians to walk up to the top level. And here there are six dominant towers, which appear to be very far apart, although the placement has a certain rhythm. The towers are elevated above the ground by pillars. The façades, still bathed in sunlight, reflect a light that prevents us from distinguishing every detail. The six blocks are reflected in the sea, massive and smooth, with enough space between them to be autonomous, yet similar enough to be a whole. We have now come halfway. A floating bridge invites us to cross it. But primarily it marks the symmetry axis, which is indispensable for the entire complex.*«

In the distance we now see a man's silhouette: It is the architect inspecting his work. He is Adalberto Libera, for we are in the riverbank development of Castelfusano near Rome, planned in 1933/34.

We are glad to meet with Libera and hear some of his comments: »I believe the principle of repetition in architecture is age-old and is not supposed to indicate monotony but rhythm. That was my rationale for creating six towers that are elevated above the ground. They produce good balance between the masses and the long horizontal line of the riverbank development.« We are interested whether his work has any political connection with Italian fascism. »The project was sponsored by the Mussolini regime, and there is no doubt that the architecture, which I call ›razionalismo‹, is related to modern political movements, while at the same time it picks up historical motifs.«

Our second visit is to a town designed in Libera's studio – Aprilia in the Alban Hills south of Rome. »Yes, this city, too, or rather its general settlement, was supported by the regime.« Here we find a completely different concept. Two large quadrangles at a street axis form the strictly orthogonal basic figure.

We visit the larger of the quadrangles, the actual center. It represents the public sector. »The three forces of society are present here: the religious aspect in the form of a church, the civil

263. A. and V. Vesnin and S. Lyascenko, building of the People's Committee for Heavy Industry on Red Square, Moscow, 1935. Competition.
264. Giuseppe de Finetti, arena district in Milan, 1933.
265. Adalberto Libera, urban planning for Aprilia, 1936.

of the town hall, and the political in the form of the House of Fascism. The church and the fascism building have been given a tower each, while the town hall is articulated as a massive block of a brick building.«

The public buildings are surrounded on three sides by apartment houses. On the ground floor columns stand in a kind of arcade, faced with gray stone. They support the dazzling white cube of the top floor. The second quadrangle, much like the first, consists of apartment houses.
Dethier 1994; *Nouvelles* 2001.

The fascist architecture of Mussolini is of a completely different nature than those of Stalin and Hitler. Classical borrowings have been reduced, geometrized. For the most part, columns have not been used. Clear geometry predominates. A reinterpreted International Style is developed further in »razionalismo« and continues well into the 1990s, indeed to the present day. For E 42, the Esposizione Universale 1942, important buildings and squares built in a characteristic authoritarian and traditional style were created that are at times reminiscent of the paintings of de Chirico.

Hanns Dustmann (1902–1979). The New Vienna, 1938–41

Since 1940, Baldur von Schirach has been the Gauleiter of Vienna, and so it is understandable that his brother-in-law Hanns Dustmann was commissioned to redesign Vienna, a task he carried out down to the smallest detail in accordance with the »Führer's« wishes, though not always with the latter's total approval.

We begin our visit in the Old Town, which escaped big changes, but did undergo certain minor ones: Heldenplatz, or Heroes' Square, was completely redesigned and now includes the Gauforum, the Party's cultural district headquarters. The two equestrian statues – Prince Eugen and Archduke Karl – are definitely accepted as heroes. They've been moved into a transverse axis in front of the Neue Burg. A »Viennese Valhalla« was erected in the new focal point of the square close to the Volksgarten: The Temple of Theseus, raised on a high granite pedestal, now forms the architectural boundary of the Heldenplatz, which is completely paved in order to provide a stable area for large demonstrations.

The Gauhaus [district center] of the NSDAP [National Socialist German Workers' Party] was built on Ballhausplatz. The hotel for the heads of the Party is on Karlsplatz. And from this vantage point we also get an idea of the impressive south axis, a wide avenue on which we are now driving: It ends at the new central railroad station, which combines the southern and eastern railway traffic while also integrating the western and northern rail system. The visual boundary of the axis is formed by a huge building whose ground plan is octagonal.

In order to get a sense of the huge expansion in the north we have to take a helicopter, and from above we now see that the Old Town provides a kind of hinge between the city's northern and southern expansions. The north-east expansion, which begins by the Danube Canal, is laid like a wide ribbon of grid across the 2nd and 20th district; beside the Reichsbrücke a new bridge goes over the Danube, to a majestic conclusion: The Party Forum in Floridsdorf eclipses all the imperial buildings in Vienna by its huge size.

Back to Leopoldstadt: Both ends of Ringstraße are extended in a straight line, provide boundaries for the new city and lead into the bridges across the Danube. Between them is a grid city that reminds us of the blueprints of Otto Wagner and is also interspersed with monumental buildings.

»The Führer supported my plans, although he fears competition with Berlin and shows a preference for Linz«, the architect, Hanns Dustmann, tells us. »But he immediately realized the advantages of destroying Leopoldstadt: The most important Jewish quarter of Vienna was thus liquidated. He said, and I quote: ›I've gotten the Jews out of Vienna already, and I'd like to get the Czechs out as well.‹«
Wagner, W. 2000.

We'll save ourselves further visits to the expansion of Vienna: Neither the grandiose ideas of German-born planners, nor the rigorous axial systems of Franz Schuster, Erwin Ilz, and Robert Oerley, nor Walter Strzygowski's blueprints, which were intended to be perfectly concrete, seem worth a visit, since they hardly go beyond Dustmann's blueprint.

Hitler did take a fancy to the splendid axial plans, but, aside from the fact that there were no funds available before the beginning of the war, Berlin naturally had priority. There, Albert Speer began work on planning »Germania«.

To be sure, the basic idea of expanding Vienna toward the south and north is in principle not utopian: These developmental trends – though not in monumental axes, but in agglomerations of high-rises – began in the 1960s, and have not been concluded to this day.

Albert Speer (1905–1981). The New Berlin – Welthauptstadt Germania (world capital Germania), 1937–43/*60*

As we approach the former Berlin by plane – the capital of Europe is now called Germania – we can already sense the majestic dimensions of the city's new district. And so, at least roughly, we are able to get an overall view of this new city: 38 km long, it stretches over Berlin and is up to seven km wide.

Upon our arrival we are met by a national hero, architect Albert Speer, who has, as it were, re-created the city following Adolf Hitler's precise instructions. Enthusiastic and amiable, the great master welcomes us: »This is a fine opportunity to get to know the new ›Germania‹: You can take part in celebrating the fifth anniversary of Germany's victory over her enemies. During the procession through the magnificent east-west axis we can see the most important buildings.«

We agree to meet the next day – April 20th, for the day of the victory, the capitulation of the Western and Eastern powers and of America in 1945, has been cleverly linked with Hitler's birthday. We plan to meet at 9 a.m. at the south railway station, before the start of the festivities. Albert Speer has time for further comments: »As far back as 1937 the Führer commissioned me to begin planning. Work proceeded quickly, and we started construction in 1941, in the middle of the war. But then we had to interrupt work for two years, though immediately after the final victory, in 1945, it continued with full strength. We have a huge very economical work force available to us – the prisoners of war – and enormous material resources – the reparations paid to us. Thus we achieved a miracle: Within a mere five years we have turned Berlin into the new capital of Europe, Germania.«

We have a little time left, and we look at the architecture flanking the enormous station square – and the railway station itself. The main floor is defined by a row of columns in the classical style, while above them is a recessed penthouse floor. But why, we ask in surprise, are there such tall glass walls behind the columns? »Our National Socialist style, which is based on the eternal values of Aryan classicism, is totally capable of integrating new technology, for instance in the form of glass walls«, replies Albert Speer.

As we walk through the square building, we glance at its monumental south side. There is a semicircular square in front of it.

»It's time to welcome the Führer!« the architect reminds us. So we have time for only a short look at the other buildings around the station square. But already the square has filled with thousands of people – only in the middle a circular area is left open – and already we hear the whirring of the helicopter. It lands, and immediately the SS form a lane of honor as Adolf Hitler alights – and already there is much cheering, calls of Sieg Heil resound. Accompanied by Goering, Goebbels, and two generals, Hitler gets into his open limousine. We've already seen the enormous triumphal arch that completes the station square. Its architecture seems somewhat crude, reminding us of the Roman, world-dominating Janus arches of ancient times, though at a height of 117 m and width of 170 m it far surpasses all ancient monuments of the same type. Is it dedicated to a triumphant Hitler?

»Not at all«, says Albert Speer. »We consecrated it to the undefeated German army in the world war, and the Führer personally produced the first draft back in 1925.«

Hitler's car crawls along toward the triumphal arch, past the trophies, consisting of captured tanks and cannons. The populace forms a column, and as he passes the triumphal arch, there is more loud cheering from the crowd.

Albert Speer has the privilege of following the victory parade in a car at an appropriate distance, and we listen with interest to his remarks. On the left is the large octagonal plaza with ho-

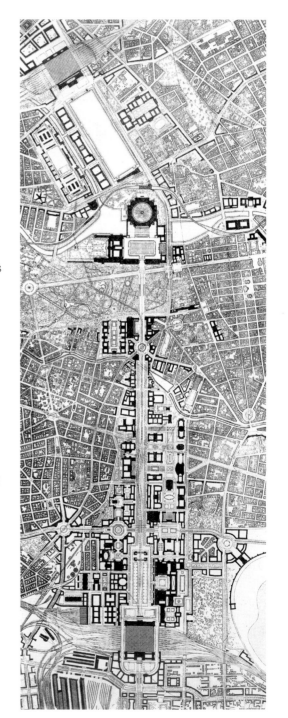

tels, theaters and concert halls, and the building of the KdF (Strength through Joy) organization. On the right are the sports and recreation area and the public swimming pools. The »Führer« is a great opera lover, you know. He attends Richard Wagner premieres at every opportunity. That's why it was only natural that he had a new opera house built – there it is, on the left.

We've been driving very slowly and thus we were able to observe more and more crowds of people emerging from the side streets in ordered groups and adding their numbers to the triumphal procession.

»Here we have two particularly interesting buildings«, Speer points out. »We are aware of the great international importance of industries and have therefore located them here along the new Germania axis: on the left, the AEG – General Electric Power. And again we are surprised by the name of the architect: It is Peter Behrens, who already demonstrated his affinity for totalitarian architecture in 1912 with his German embassy in St. Petersburg. Then, on the right, we have the administration building for Agfa Photo Products.«

The next point of interest is the round plaza. »I did not design it all«, Speer tells us almost modestly. »Wilhelm Kreis built the Soldiers' Hall on the left here – the big, almost Romanesque tun inside is worth seeing. He also designed the army headquarters with its powerful tower. Meanwhile, the Hermann Goering Reichsmarschall Building next to the Soldiers' Hall comes from my drafting tables. On the round plaza there are buildings serving a number of different functions: Beside administrative buildings there are also a few cinemas.«

The following section of street is a very different surprise: We drive through an old park that has just started turning green. »Nature, too, is important for us. And so it was obvious that we should include the Tiergarten park.«

Already we are approaching the »Führer's« palace and the Reich chancellery – but the feature that has long captivated us is a huge cupola that dominates the axis more and more as we come closer. »We've built the largest dome of all time: The diameter is 300 m and it is 290 m high – which means it could easily have room for St. Peter's Basilica inside it.«

We are now driving through the portico of the Reich Chancellery. »Here, at the end of the left wing, is the entrance for the Führer's guests. They are led through the staterooms, accompanied by SS guards of honor, and the guest walks almost 500 m until he reaches the Führer's study. From here one has a view of a magnificent garden with waterworks, a greenhouse, and the private theater.«

On the right of the forecourt we see a very familiar building: It is the Reichstag, which was incorporated in the planning as a historical keepsake.

On the enormous square in front of the domed building, more crowds have arrived in the meantime. They are allowed to enter the »dome«. Hitler drives up to the portico of columns and enters the building.

»The Führer retires for a short time. Meanwhile the festive populace has been gathering in the hall. We have created room for 250,000 persons. Still not enough – however, the rest of our national comrades can follow the Führer's speech with the help of loudspeakers and movie screens here in the square.«

The architect takes us into the building through the side entrance. Indeed, the cupola – though strongly reminiscent of the Roman Pantheon – is incomparably effective. We are privileged, and so two of the only 200 seats for prominent guests are reserved for us.

There is no need to describe Adolf Hitler's speech – it is an apotheosis of victory for the Führer, the nation and Fatherland, and there are constant interruptions as the crowd cheers and shouts »Sieg Heil«. The final cheering turns directly into the three anthems: The German national anthem and the Horst Wessel song are followed by the new hymn of victory.

Now the masses of people stream out of the domed hall onto Town Hall Square. The two massive towers of the town hall dominate the huge complex. Two pylons form a connection to the north railway station. Across from the town hall is the Military Academy. »The town hall was designed by German Bestelmayer. You'll be amazed to hear who was the architect of the Navy Headquarters: none other than Paul Bonatz.«

We really are surprised by the way the architect of expressionism, who designed the Stuttgart railway station, has switched to the would-be classical, totalitarian architecture of the Hitler buildings.

»The town hall is reflected in a vast pool of water – but for present great events we've transformed the pool into a festival ground.«

At this point we get an overview of the colorful festival crowd. The participants are now forming big groups and figures. Naturally the formations of the army, navy, and air force take up the dominant positions, followed by the SA and SS, Hitler Jugend and Bund Deutscher Mädel, and other organizations.

However, the great diversity and color come from the many folklore groups from all parts of Germany. »The fostering of folk traditions«, says Albert Speer, »is a vital concern of the Führer, and a new culture of folk tradition has developed.« Now, however, we see ethnic costumes, flags, and banners that seem somehow unfamiliar. But our host explains: »Those are representatives of the conquered but now friendly nations that have sent their delegations to Germania.«

Dance and music groups form in many places, and their merry hustle and bustle is again interrupted by cheering: On the balcony of the town hall tower, Hitler appears once again, giving his attention to what is happening below.

A series of German folk songs and Adolf Hitler's departure finally conclude the demonstration, the participants wander off in all directions, and special trains and buses fill with people.
We can't help admiring Albert Speer, though our admiration is tinged with criticism. »Well, what you have seen is only a small part of the new Germania. You will be in the city for two or three more days, so be sure to see the east-west axis with what is left of the historical Berlin. You must definitely visit the new university and the large housing developments. A staff member from my GBI, the General Building Inspections office, will be happy to accompany you.«

Larsson 1978, 1983; *Stadt u. Utopie* 1982; Vercelloni 1994; Dethier 1994; *Impossible Worlds* 2000.

I have no comment: The 1933–1945 »implementations« make this unnecessary.

12. Naïve worlds, c. 1880–

12.1. A private cosmos

Folk artists. The nativity towns, 15th century – present

The wonderful nativity town we wander through reminds us of many others: certainly not of Bethlehem, the birth place of Jesus, perhaps sometimes of Jerusalem, but most of all of a romantic little town in the Alps, nestled in the landscape, with hills and cliffs, woods and meadows – an ideal place imagined and built by an ordinary man. And naturally before we get to the stable with the Holy Family we first meet the shepherds, and soon after that we also encounter the Three Wise Men, a free and charming interpretation of the Gospel.

The town is an idyllic utopia, with local characteristics, an enchanting piece of folk art. It is found in Christian homes and in churches. Of course, devout Christians do not consider the central event that is represented to be a utopia, but one of the great realities that express God's saving grace.

Ferdinand Cheval (1836–1924). The Palais Idéal, Hauterives, France, 1879–1922

How many people dream of creating their own world! Ferdinand, *le facteur*, the mailman, takes us to his private »Palais Idéal« and tells us that he worked on it all his life. All on his own, he has turned his dream, his utopia into a reality.

How unimaginably difficult it is to build a city, a world! And yet there are still people, individual persons, lunatics, geniuses, visionaries, who build their »world« themselves:

»I am a mailman in the town of Hauterives. That's why I spend all day on my rounds and find a thousand things. Why shouldn't one build a palace from them? Well, and I've read quite a few books – so I built architectural models of primitive cultures and they're just incredible.«
We run into a young art historian, Monsieur Weiss. His descriptions make up for the mailman's silence:
A towering termites' nest that seems to have been glued together from secretions. Stones, shells, roots, mosses. Poured over it is a gray dough, kneaded, churned up – everywhere one senses the hands that joined these scraps together. Initially one grasps this whole, this confused construction, and senses the secret order that guides the movements of the hand. One's eyes feel their way over the interlaced forms, discover faces, human shapes, limbs, animals, but only as faint suggestions at first. The stuff that dreams are made of. The first encounter. Here something is coming into being. A world of ideas.
The reality of a self is being created here. My self is my imagination. I dream. From impulses and thoughts I build forms. All of it intertwined, tangled, cluttered with impressions from the diurnal world.
Everywhere the forms turn and dip, rise, spread, turn into ornaments, plants, fruit, have eyes, stretch their limbs, move forward, pull me deeper into corridors, shafts, alcoves. There are memories of stalactite caves, grottoes in gardens, Etruscan gravestones, aquariums, and all of it is transformed into something unique, incomparable. I am inside a dream.
Jouvé 1981; *Eccentric Style* 2002.

These »architectures« do not fit the definition of the city, which is inseparably linked with society, isn't it? Maybe. And yet Monsieur Cheval has built more than, something different than, a city: He has dreamed a world, his world, indeed his cosmos – and he has turned it into a reality.

St. EOM (Eddie Owens Martin, 1915–1986), 1935, 1957

So often, in the old days, God gave instructions what should be built and how. Why shouldn't this be possible today as well?
»Well, something like that happened to me. A spirit told me: »*Call yourself St. Eom from now on, and be a Pasaquoyan, the first in the world. And build Pasaquan!*«

But it was not until 1957 that St. EOM actually began work on his world – and the spirit guided his hand. The wonderful Pasaquan, the world that became a »monument for all primitive peoples«, was created in Buena Vista, Georgia.

For St. EOM it really does become a closed imaginary world, and behind its walls »*I feel cut off from the outside world, here I can live in my own world, and wherever I look, I see something beautiful.*«

High walls surround the area, covered by rhythmical and yet constantly changing ornaments in green, yellow, black. At the entrance, giant sculptured heads stand guard. We enter the courtyard. The walls, the turrets, everything is occupied by colorful monuments, abstract constructions, cosmic symbols.
    Visionen und Utopien 2002/03.

A magic directive is the motivation for creating a world of enchantment: We think of the divine commands that led to the creation of the Tabernacle, the temples, and churches.

Simone Rodilla (Rodia) (1875–1965). Watts, Los Angeles, 1960

It should be possible to somehow use everything that is being produced – in such a way that there is no waste and that even the scraps of waste can be incorporated, together with found objects – perhaps even creating a work of art! And Simone Rodilla managed to do this!

»It's incredible how much waste there is in my profession«, Rodilla, a tile setter, tells us. »I collected everything, plus stones and seashells, and built towers and a garden.« That is how the Watts Towers came into being, a wonderfully colorful magic garden.
    But how can a person live in something like this? »I built a simple small house next to it, for my wife and me. And the colorful courtyard next door was just for my imagination.«
    Eccentric Style 2002; *Visionen und Utopien* 2002.

Once the work could be considered to be complete, Rodilla disappeared without a trace, not to reappear until a short time before his death in an American small town. But the Watts Towers were a central meeting place during the critical years of the Watts riots, and so the solitary work of art was given that social significance that we have missed in the »naïve« artists. It was declared a historic landmark years ago.

Howard Finster (b. 1916). Paradise Garden and the Folk Art Church

An architecture that costs practically nothing – isn't that a utopia too?

We visit Reverend Howard Finster in Summerville, in the state of Georgia, and he shows us his small, very personal »city«, an anti-city as it were, consisting of things non-perfect, nonessential, unpretentious, accidental, and playful.
    »Those are just a couple of old wooden shacks«, he says modestly. »But there's so much lying around in the world – so a person makes himself comfortable.« The shacks themselves are hardly visible, covered as they are all over with the trash, the litter of the car society: hubcaps and license plates predominate, junk, found objects, worthless stuff: That's how simple it is to implement the dreams of the new city. And one component of it is the World's Folk Art Church.
    Eccentric Style 2002; *Visionen und Utopien* 2002.

The »objet trouvé«, a principle in modern art, is a guiding principle here as well, where there is no museum or art market. Worthless objects, found by chance, create deeply moving »worlds«.

273. St. EOM (Eddie Owens Martin), Pasaquan, monument for all primitive peoples, 1935, 1957.
274. Simone Rodilla (Rodia), Watts Towers, Los Angeles, USA, 1960–1980.
275. Howard Finster, Paradise Garden, USA.

Farmer Josef Hinterhölzl. The mechanical cosmos (1960–1980) St. Martin, Upper Austria

There's not too much happening on a farm. Imagination – now, that must be a lot more exciting!

Yes, that's how Josef has been spending his spare time. He's created a lovable little world, set in motion by a brook that flows by the house: rattling, whirring, turning, and clattering – life is motion! Farmer Hinterhölzl had no models, and these are not actually architectural structures. He seems to have created a movable, dynamic, mechanical town as a model of the future – wheels, axles, pulleys, transmissions, levers, all moved by water. If the brook is diverted, it all stops. There are also moving figures – but it is not they that move the wheels, but the wheels and levers that move them.

Thousands of allotment gardeners, 1850 to the present day

Imitation of the world, homemade nostalgia, a yearning for faraway places given concrete structure, domesticated architecture, alternative building, personal articulation: those are the intentions of the architects – and very often they are utopias.

The »man in the street« builds mini-worlds in the front yard; or charming little wooden cottages, rock gardens, magical worlds in the community garden. Don't turn up your nose at the garden gnomes: They are magic, fairy-tale figures, miraculous creatures.

Chris Burden (b. 1946). Pizza City, 1991–96

Near the ocean the city gets very narrow – as narrow as a slice of pizza. The idyllic little town we are visiting seems very familiar. »It's not just a European town«, says Chris Burden. »You'll find it includes Eastern, North African, American, and futuristic elements. It's a multicultural town of the spirit, a response to life in Los Angeles.«

Toward the center the town becomes more and more compact. Factory chimneys and church towers, half-timbered houses and office buildings, steep gables and flat roofs coexist side by side. Thus not only regional but chronological styles as well are placed peacefully side by side.
Burden 1996.

Pizza City is an eight-meter-long, wedge-shaped miniature town. It is built at a scale of 1:220. Chris Burden has collected Christmas decorations, toy train sets, paper models. Its outline resembles a slice of pizza. The crusts at the edge are the mountains, and there the town becomes less compact. We are fascinated by the seemingly carefree and accidental juxtaposition of all sorts of functions and building styles. Burden's reproduction of the »world« resembles the dream architecture in the front yards of cottages. There, it is naïveté, while in Pizza City there may be an element of calculation.

12.2. The worlds of children

Fairy–tale cities

These are the truly imaginary cities: cities that arise in the minds of children when they are abducted into the world of fairy tales, myths, legends, and stories. These cities are quite close to the other unreal cities – the dream cities we adults are also allowed to visit.

But aren't a lot of fantastic things happening in the cities? The house takes the place of the city and vice versa. Thus we may regard fortresses and castles and forts as a kind of city. They share structural differentiation and social structure with the city. And, just like a city, they are mysterious, frightening or protective, menacing or hospitable, hostile or accessible.

Fairy tales, miracles, and fantasy are not dead: Films have been responsible for their unexpected revival. »Fantasy« is a very broad category. And the Harry Potter boom at the beginning of the 21st century proves how interesting magic and enchantment still are.

Walt Disney (1901–1966) and his myriad successors. Mickey Mouse and his friends and buddies, 1926, amusement parks in the big cities, and world fairs

Initially, we do not encounter Mickey Mouse in the big cities, but in the idyll of the rural village.

But Walt Disney did not remain in the idyllic rustic world – he, too, built his own city. »My figures gradually capture the city – not only the city of our day, but also the city of the future«, says Walt Disney, and hey presto! we find ourselves in one of these cities, dazzled by an abundance of forms that could hardly have been devised by an architect. There are the bold vaults of cupolas, the sweep of ledges, sloping pillars, curved roofs – a turbulent, organic architectural landscape.

The Land of Tomorrow was built by Herbert Ryman. There is not a single right angle here and gondolas hang from monorails and flit overhead. The ground level belongs to the pedestrian, who wanders from one attraction to the next, past well-tended parks.

Walt Disney proposes we go up in a balloon to get a panoramic view: We have a favorable wind now! And as we soar gently over Disneyland it does make us think of a city, even though everything is artificial: the castle in the middle, houses, palaces, churches, intermingled with houses in all kinds of styles, nestled in a lovely river landscape.

And yet it feels strange to be in a »town« where people don't know each other, everyone lives only for a few hours – a place that becomes a ghost town at night. Still, Disneyland is a kind of city. We find it in Anaheim near Los Angeles, in Florida near Cape Canaveral, in Paris, and in Hong Kong. We'd love to visit those »towns« of entertainment and pleasure that are much older than Disneyland – the amusement parks of the big cities: formerly (1929) Coney Island in New York, Tivoli (1843) in Copenhagen, the Prater in Vienna, Luna Park in Moscow, and many more.

281. Chris Burden, Pizza City, 1991–96.
282. Herbert Ryman, entry to Land of Tomorrow, Disneyland, Los Angeles, USA, 1954.
283. Herbert Ryman, Land of Tomorrow, Disneyland, Los Angeles, USA, 1954.

284. Frank R. Paul, City of the Future, 1942.
285. Herbert Ryman, Disneyland, Los Angeles, USA, 1954. Bird's-eye view.

There are high-class fairgrounds that become representative of times and nations: world fairs, prestige-laden cities that, since the first great London fair in 1951, have become demonstrations of architecture.

But we've experienced quite different Disneylands as well: Dream worlds are also present in a hundred holiday villages, in the preservation of the façades of old buildings as the buildings themselves are demolished, in Potemkin villages, in the hypertrophied protection of historical monuments, in the continuing eclecticism of architecture – an interface between reality and utopia! But that's not just something for kids and for summer holidays any more.

Frank R. Paul. The science-fiction city, 1942

Frank R. Paul and his amazing cities lend reality to so many human dreams, primarily those of architects

»Naturally it is possible to build the dream cities: dynamic, majestic, overpowering, colorful«, says Frank R. Paul enthusiastically. »We've overcome the idyll – speed and geometry have triumphed.«

In fact, it's a repertory of solid geometry – and of Pop Art: globes, cylinders, cones, parabolas – but there isn't a »house« in sight.

The cone buildings, crowned by globes, have cantilevered landing strips for flying objects. Street vehicles are located lower down and away from the spacious plazas, which have beautiful fountains and gardens and are lined with arcades.

But how can the air space be so crowded with flying objects without there being collisions? »That's not a problem – all the vehicles are completely computer-controlled. That's why accidents are out of the question.«

The pencil – and now the computer – of the comic book artist create fantasy cities far more rapidly than do films. These are continuations, extrapolations, hypertrophied forms of cities that have existed for a long time, but are now largely being divested of their functionality and thus take off into the realm of fantasy. They are cities that are modeled on the formal aspects of expressionism, organic architecture, deconstructivism. The artists try to give the city a new dynamism: curves, bizarre forms, angles, diagonals, penetrations. But it is a vocabulary we are all familiar with.

13. A new era, after 1945

13.1. Japan. China

Kiyonori Kikutake (b. 1928). The floating city Unabara, 1958, the Underwater Cluster, 1958, and the Marine City, 1958–63

»The future of humanity is on the ocean«, Kikutake is convinced. He shows us three different types of marine cities. Admittedly we are able to view them only briefly and at a distance as we flit by on our express yacht.

»First we'll go to Marine City 58, the first ocean city, which I developed back in 1958. It consists of spherical and cylindrical pontoons, linked into a huge circle. The cylinders are partially submerged under the surface of the water and contain factories and large warehouses as well as apartments for aquatic people.

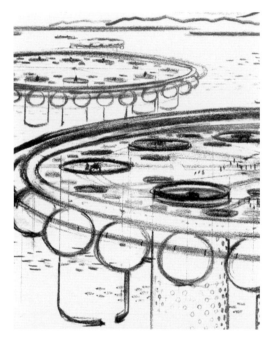

In 1963 I built the ›tower community‹, ten 55-story towers in the middle of a large city, yet we immediately leave for Marine City 63, for there very similar towers stand on circular and elliptical, artificial islands. The towers may remind you of corncobs. The entire island is formed of clusters of tower blocks, and we've combined of few of these into a real city. We began the biggest of the projects as far back as 1960. We've called it ›Unabara‹.«

The architect now heads for a big island in Sagami Bay near Tokyo.

»Here I hardly used the geometry of the circle at all«, explains Kikutake. »Wait till you see when we take the helicopter in the harbor.«

This really is quite a different picture. Two fairly concentric, but completely irregular rings surround a kind of center. The 500-meter-high tower houses the energy center, and an artificial sun illuminates the city. The inner ring island is occupied by apartment buildings and their auxiliary facilities, while the outer ring contains all production centers.

»This ring will be extended further«, Kikutake tells us, »and will soon be the center of the production belt on the east coast of Japan – an industrial city with half a million inhabitants.«

The island has taken on two additional functions in the energy sector: While the use of solar energy has long been taken for granted, the latest methods are tried out and developed here. In recent years you don't hear much about the tidal power plants anymore. More generally ocean wave energy is used in Unabara. Also, seafood is farmed, a true alternative to traditional fishing. We ask about housing on the island.

»A kind of ›sail‹ constructions are the basic structure: curved frames made of steel hollow sections strung with steel tubes resembling the strings of a harp. The circular residential units are attached to these vertical tubes.«

»We've developed flexible units called ›mova‹ because they denote movement. We can make them fast to the web of the suspension girders, which are connected by a vertical slab that provides the infrastructure.«

The almost endless curved 20-story façade looks like a corncob on its side. The knobby, gradually tapering façades move toward a center comprising all social and service facilities and visible from far away due to its tall curved towers. From the helicopter we can clearly see that the

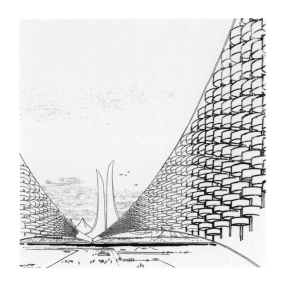

»movas« combine to form six-point stars. Between and partly under the blocks of housing there is ample space for public life and gardens, parks, and playing fields.

Our journey over the ocean continues. The distance between Osaka and Kitakyushu is over 400 km, and this entire length is spanned by a vast, floating linear city. This impressive large-scale project can be seen from a magnet suspension railway. It takes us 40 minutes to cover this distance.

»This city«, says Kikutake, »is a complement to the numerous coastal towns already inhabited by more than seven million people. It is built on rectangular floating platforms, half-submerged pontoons.«

The well-balanced infrastructure next to low-rise residential housing is taken for granted: Cultural institutions, universities, hospitals, airports, schools, and a large supply of consumer goods are cleverly interspersed with clusters of housing units. Kikutake pleads for his bold projects: *»The marine city is a proposal for the world of tomorrow. Fresh air, a healthy, mild climate, a magnificent natural landscape, a horizon that gives one a global feeling, the blessings of the sun from dawn to dusk have left their mark on a new human race.«*

Dahinden 1971; *Nouvelles* 2001; *Traum* 2003; *World Architecture,* no. 32.

Kikutake was very close to the implementation of a large project: For the 1975 marine exhibition in Okinawa he built »Aquapolis«, a large, floating exhibition. Only a modest section of it was implemented, however. The 1989 Monaco floating concept can also be regarded only as a model.

Kiyonori Kikutake was one of the most important members of the Metabolists; together with Kenzo Tange, Kisho Kurokawa, Fumihiko Maki, and others he attempted links with the Japanese philosophy of transformation, change, and movement. Purely technological in nature are drilling rigs and research stations, long known for being floating structures.

In the tourist industry as well certain projects have a chance of being implemented – for instance, »flowtels« floating hotels with docks, cinemas, and restaurants for the oil state of Dubai.

Hydropolis, too, is being planned for Dubai; the 220 suites are located 15 m below sea level. Additional plans are currently being drawn up and the road to an underwater city that is completely underwater is technologically speaking a definite possibility.

Floating architectural structures have long been a promising trend. Is it only lack of space that compels people to settle the ocean? Perhaps we feel the urge to return to the primeval element we originally came from: in the development of each individual and in the course of millions of years.

289. Kiyonori Kikutake, Marine city of Unabara, residential and communal buildings, 1960.
290. Kiyonori Kikutake, 400-kilometer linear city, Osaka-Kitakyushu, Japan, 1990.

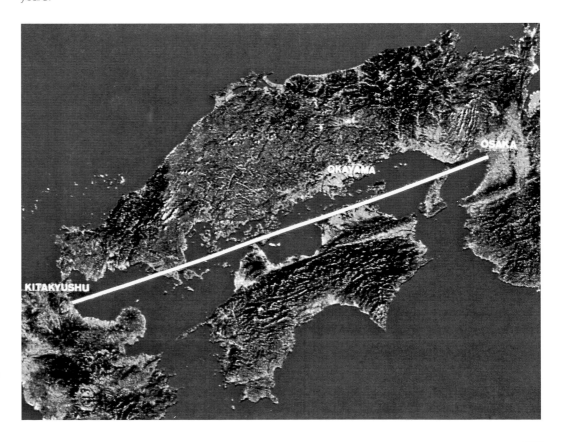

Kenzo Tange (1913–2005). Tokyo Bay, 1960, and New Tokyo, 1961

The overall concept of Tokyo Bay City can only be grasped from an airplane. Kenzo Tange explains: »I connected both shores, Tokyo and Yokohama, by a large double link, a kind of spinal column and conveyor belt, but also the stage for urban life. While cars, subway trains, and railway trains speed through the lowel levels, we can stroll at our leisure on the upper levels. The link between the two cities is subdivided into eight areas. The station is on the mainland and is directly connected with the subway systems. Then comes the first area – office buildings – and a new station and seaport are the second and third area. At the same height as the dry land but also as the underwater level of the link, and connected with each other but projecting into the ocean are the two new airports. The government district, area four, is again followed by office buildings – zone five. Shopping centers and hotels form the sixth area, and then there are more office buildings. The leisure center, again docked to the other shore, is the eighth zone.«

After landing we can see for ourselves that dense urban areas form these axes. These are structural vertical systems that we later find repeatedly: Strong support and supply towers, erected in a square grid, provide vertical communication. The office bridges, far above the terrain, span the space between them. The expressways are located on the periphery of the link, on the shore. The areas between them serve stationary traffic and contain spacious landscaped recreational spaces.

Housing developments branch out of this densely built-up urban area: skyscrapers with broad bases that seem to stand right in the ocean. These »branches« radiating from the wide link have some growth potential, though it is limited. We are able to view only a very small section: The pro-

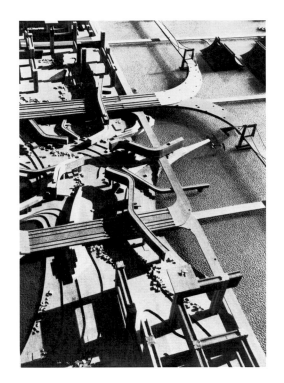

jecting lower floors of the high-rises have terraces; green zones and pedestrian areas are not disturbed by the traffic on the lower levels.

The lower pedestrian level houses stores, social facilities, restaurants, and community buildings as well as parking lots and monorail stations, so that the dark zones are well used. The projecting parts of the buildings, however, are, as it were, broken open in different places. Here even interior areas are open to the sky: This is where kindergartens, schools, and parks are located. The apartments all enjoy a lovely view of the ocean. They are privately owned, while the lower-lying levels are common property.

How can the idea of the Metabolists – of whom Kenzo Tange is one – have an effect? Where is the change and transformation they advocate?

»We did not fix the housing areas. They are interchangeable units that can be adapted to the needs of the residents. Residents can also design their ambience completely individually: In that case they receive only the concrete platform with utilities supply points, and everything else is left up to their own creativity.« Our tour ends at the junction point to the mainland – a dense, fascinating, three-dimensional space heralding a new urbanity.

Next, Tange takes us to the new mainland city of New Tokyo. Like the ocean city it projects into the sea like a mighty bridge. It would be impossible for us to have a clear view of it if we had not taken an aerial tour of the city. The city numbers ten million inhabitants, but its growth was restricted by planners and politicians. Thus it is not possible for it to expand indefinitely.

Kenzo Tange regards the transportation of people and goods as the chief problem of cities. »*The rapid pace and the scale of contemporary life demands a new spatial order in our cities. The structure of the city has come to terms with the transportation system and architecture. The street and the buildings are organically linked.*«

Cook 1970; Dahinden 1971; Schumpp 1971; *Stadt und Utopie* 1982; *12 Villes Prospectives*.

The idea of a linear city is transferred from the land to the ocean. Growth is limited by the shorelines, but the city can be expanded on land. The structure resembles live rails from which electric current can be tapped.

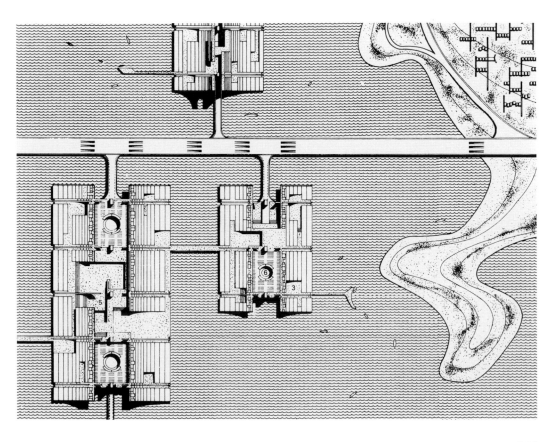

293–294. Kenzo Tange, A. Isozaki, K. Kamiya, H. Kon, N. Kurokawa, and S. Watanabe, expansion of Tokyo, 1960. Detail: residential blocks.

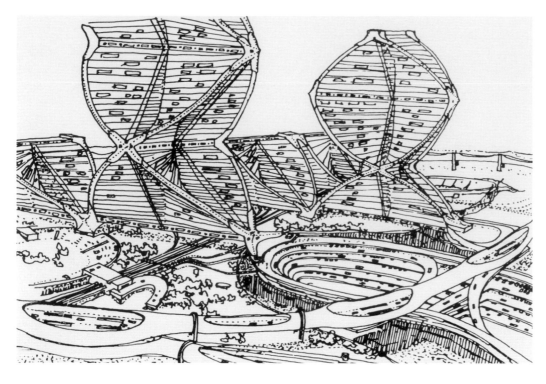

Kisho Kurokawa (1934–2007). Towering Wandclusters, 1959, and the Floating City, 1961

It's a little difficult to grasp the complicated configuration of the Wandclusters, but Kurokawa helps us: »The form comes from the biological microcosm: The helix of the DNA was the inspiration for the spiral twist.«

»We began construction in 1959. Initially we called the structures ›wandclusters‹, then ›ville en hélice‹, helix city. Every spiral connects with another by means of platforms and public pedestrian spaces. This is meant to be a city of joy.«

Optimistically Kurokawa speaks of the qualities of his city: »There is no car traffic in the cities. People stroll from terrace to terrace among lush vegetation. Housing units are attached to the terraces. Public space is habitable and can be modified.«

Kurokawa now takes us to the new city of of Kasumigaura on the north side of Tokyo. The »ville flottante«, the floating city, consists of massive rounded forms linked by bridges and tunnels. An extensive network of man-made islands thrusts into a lake 100 km north of Tokyo. The trira-diate split-level houses are built on these islands. Their top levels are linked, and these are the connecting roads between the individual high-rises.

The mega-structure, the overall plan, consists of thirty-floor buildings. At the top or on the tenth floor the buildings are connected by a large continuous network, a communication infrastructure. Driving a car on the rooftops of the gigantic structures, one discovers the panorama of the landscape. The buildings' territorial scale takes the place of the districts of a traditional city. »I draw the new forms from nature. Water lilies, spiders, radiolarians are potential inspiration for my forms.«

Cook 1970; Schumpp 1971; Dahinden 1971; *Stadt und Utopie* 1982; Thomsen 1994; *Nouvelles* 2001; Eaton 2001; *12 Villes Prospectives*.

In 1961, when Kurokawa created his drawings, the system of the DNA double helix was barely known. We may assume that the name he gave his city is a much later interpretation. The drawing and the model barely correspond, and reconstruction is somewhat difficult. Kisho Kurokawa succeeded in implementing only a few of his early projects. One of them is the Nakagin Capsule Tower, which is formally more like the »plug-in« and »clip-on« ideas of the Archigram: The tower was built in 1972 and has an affinity with the Metabolist movement, one of whose chief representatives Kurokawa is. Attached to the support and supply towers are 144 capsules. These are not conventional apartments but cells for employees who live on the outskirts, for instance, or temporary quarters for single people.

In the pavilions of the world expo, Kurokawa was able to implement and at least hint at the Metabolist ideas of change.

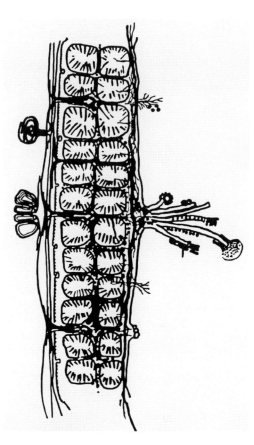

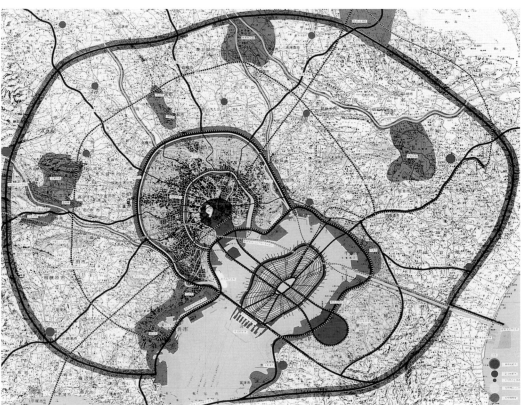

Arata Isozaki (b. 1931). The Bridge City, 1960 and the Aerial space City, 1960

As we come from the old city we can see the tall towers of the bridges from afar. »Those are the support and supply towers. Between them stretch the residential buildings«, explains Isozaki. Like steel bridges they connect the individual towers and have a similar static function. The ground level remains free for all types of communication, for the community buildings, and for large parks. But the remnants of the old city can also remain undisturbed under the bridges for as long as they are needed until they are finally absorbed by the new city.

All traffic, including stationary traffic, is banished below the ground. Above ground is an interesting combination of big platforms forming public plazas, green spaces, and community buildings. »The towers are about 80 m apart and have a diameter of 12 m. We chose to link them together freely, and so the city grew logically a stage at a time«, explains Isozaki.

»By contrast, in the next city, which is being built now, we are going to use the same system while choosing a strictly geometrical ground plan.«

»Actually it's a classic principle«, says Isozaki. »What I have in mind are ancient columns with their architrave.« To prove this, Isozaki has placed his space city in an archeological field in Italy without having an impact on the temple ruins.

The aerial space city, the Metabolist city we visit next, is quite different. It is an immensely imposing structure. The support and supply towers are massive and tall. The higher they are, the longer the girders corbeling outwards. And from these projecting girders, the cells hang like huge kernels of corn. But Arata Isozaki points to another dimension: »Metabolism is a concept in Japanese philosophy: We're interested in the constant change, the permanent transformation in life and in architecture. However, there is also something lasting, constant, eternal: This is represented by the massive columns, supporting, supplying power, while the capsules are interchangeable, movable, changeable.«

Because of the overhangs that get larger toward the top, the »clusters in the air« – another way Isozaki refers to them – might actually evoke associations with Japanese temples.

Schumpp 1971; Dahinden 1971; *Stadt und Utopie* 1982; Klotz 1986; Thomsen 1994; *Nouvelles* 2001; *Visionen und Utopien* 2003.

Arata Isozaki articulates two fundamental principles that we encounter repeatedly in the 1960s: the support and supply towers between which the residential buildings are suspended, and mobility thanks to interchangeable cells, promoted by the British Archigram group as a »clip-on« system. Tradition ranks high in Japanese culture. Linking the »clusters« with Japanese Metabolism is probably not completely convincing. Even this prominent and busy architect has failed to implement any visionary projects.

300. Arata Isozaki & Associates, City in the Air, Shinjuku, 1960.
301. Arata Isozaki & Associates, Bridge City in Archeological Field, incubation process, 1960.

302. Arata Isozaki & Associates, business district Marunouchi, Tokyo, 1963.
303. Arata Isozaki & Associates, business district Marunouchi, Tokyo, 1962. Section.
304. Arata Isozaki & Associates, City in the Air, one of the units, 1962.
305. Arata Isozaki & Associates, City in the Air, Metabolism, 1962.

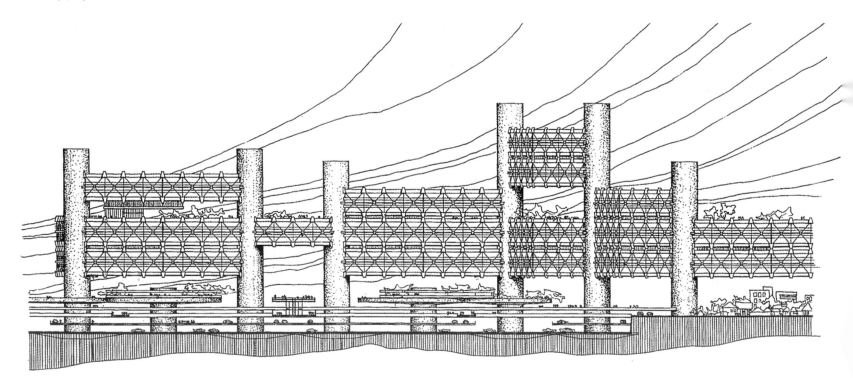

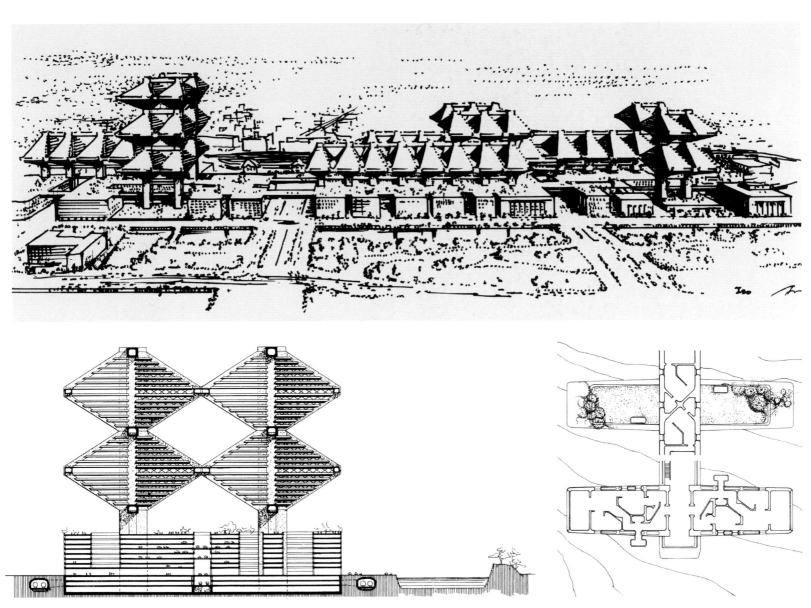

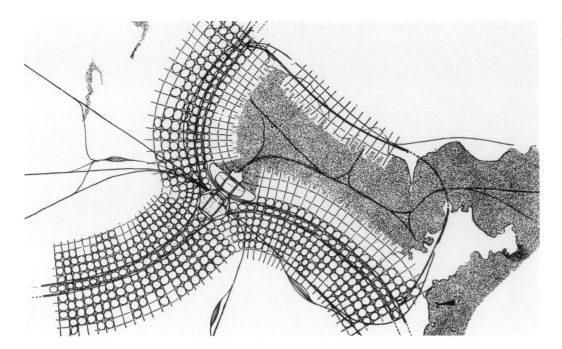

306. Y. Akui, T. Nozawa, K. Amamoto, T. Akaiwa, linear city for Tokyo, 1964.

Y. Akui and T. Nozawa. The linear city near Tokyo, 1964

As we approach the new city by air, we have an informative view: Starting out from a center, three wide curved ribbons reach into the landscape with an almost dance-like flourish. Two of the ribbons end directly by the ocean. But what are the endless rings that seem to be connected into what looks like a textile weave?

»Urban structure is defined by the transit system«, states Akui. »This one is a loose-knit network of streets with rings between them, allowing an optimum flow of traffic.«

The core of the city comprises the airport where we are now landing. Like the harbor and the railway station, the city center is shaped by traffic.

During the flight we recognized the mega-structures that rise over 50 stories high at the intersection points of the network. They are, as it were, four triangles with 45-degree angles docked at a central core for traffic and utilities supply.

Now we take a leisurely drive through the huge development. The rings contain not only large green spaces but also every kind of sports, entertainment, and leisure facilities.

The pyramid-like buildings rest on a bridge-like foundation floor that is at the same time a pedestrian promenade and houses all the service facilities. Here there is also a garage for our car. An express elevator takes us to the top terrace.

»The city can easily grow in three directions. One of the neo-›mastabas‹, as I'd like to call the residential pyramids, has about 25,000 residents.« Access to individual apartment cells is through a kind of pergolas. We wonder why there are no public squares. Akui tries to reassure us: »Right, we have no romantic medieval squares as gathering places. They are outmoded. Now let's go to the ›spine‹ of the city, the ribbon-like center.«

And in fact the character of the buildings changes here: The office and commercial buildings stand closer together, interspersed with business and shopping zones, and at various points there is something like a public life. These office zones merge almost seamlessly with industrial zones, and it goes without saying that these are invariably environmentally friendly production centers.

Dahinden 1971.

If we can trust the overall ground plan, there are close to 500 housing units, each with 25,000 residents. That would mean a city with more than twelve million inhabitants, an unimaginable density in the indicated area.

Individual traffic moves along streets supported by concrete haunches and dominates the structure. Both the residential buildings and the green spaces seem to be encircled by these streets. Here, too, we wonder why a large number of apartments have a purely northern exposure.

The idea of a linear city, which we first encountered with Soria y Mata in 1884, has been turning up repeatedly in recent years.

307–309. Kuniaki Suda, Hiroshi Toyomura, Yoshiyuka Haruta, mobile cell towers, 1967.

Kuniaki Suda, Hiroshi Toyomura, and Yoshiyuki Haruta. Mobile cell towers, 1967

As our helicopter landed on one of the high-rises, none higher than 35 stories, the scene we saw held no surprise for us. From our current position we have a clear view of the new city. The base – the commercial district – is formed by a carpet-like, relatively low network of domed buildings and cubes with green spaces and small open areas between them.

The architects provide more details about the tower blocks: »Each tower has a core of four massive, interior shafts containing the elevators, the entire supply of utilities, and the waste disposal. These shafts are the only static elements.« We go downstairs from the top platform to the residential floor just below to take a look at one of the maisonette-type apartments. Through the entryway we enter a spacious living room with a large adjacent terrace. A spiral staircase takes us one floor down to the bedrooms. We are surprised to find enough space for a family of five.

»We are now in the largest type of apartment«, the architects explain. »The special feature here is that the bedroom section can be enlarged or reduced in size at any time. It consists of individual cells that are simply attached in various different arrangements below the living room platform.« A permanent crane on the roof we noticed when we landed can bring this about in a very short time.

The bath cell is among the different-sized sleeping cells. But we look in vain for a kitchen.

»Cooking at home is a thing of the past«, say the architects. »First-rate food is prepared centrally and transported to the dining rooms on each floor.«

We walk down a corridor directly into one of the dining rooms, resembling an elegant but simple restaurant. On every other floor the space between the elevator towers is used as a kind of lobby, serving the communication of the house residents.

»For small everyday errands they do not have to go down to the business and shopping area«, say the architects, taking us to a bridge that connects the individual towers. Sure enough, we find all the necessary small businesses here, along with post offices, doctors' offices, and kindergartens.

Dahinden 1971.

The study was an entry in the competition »Urban Residences for a High-Density Society«, sponsored by the journal *The Japan Architect* in 1967. We may therefore assume that the authors meant their contribution to be actually implemented rather than be a utopian vision.

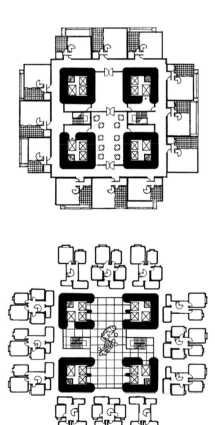

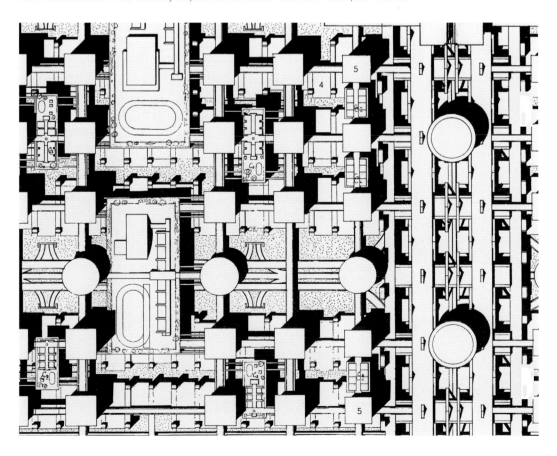

Kuniaki Suda, Hiroshi Toyomura, and Yoshiyuki Haruta. Mobile cell towers, 1967

The team of Tadaaki Anzai. The city of round towers, 1967

310, 311. Team of Tadaaki Anzai, round tower city, 1967.

Driving toward the city with the early morning sun in our eyes, we first see an immense mass with a barely differentiated silhouette. Only when we get close up we recognize the huge round towers. Standing on something like a three- to four-story pedestal whose base covers the entire area of the city, these are up to 90 stories high and reach a height of close to 300 m.

We ride up to the level of the top terrace, where the architects graphically explain the construction concept. »The construction is simple: The horizontal circular rings are attached to eight reinforced concrete tubes. Completely flexible residential capsules are docked on these, while the vertical tubes hold the elevators, stairs, and all utility supply and waste disposal lines. Opposite each reinforced concrete tube plus once between them, vertical concrete bulkheads provide stabilization. These are the reason for the distance between every fourth cell unit: The distance after each cell unit makes it easier to replace it.«

We now ride up to one of the residential floors. The horizontal rings form the access lanes, and from here we can visit one of the residential units. We come directly into the big living-dining room formed by three capsules. A kitchen and a combination WC and bathroom are immediately adjacent. A spiral staircase goes up to the top floor: Here, too, the architects have chosen a maisonette type. The four capsules with the bathroom as the fifth are sufficient to house a family of five. Small round windows and French doors provide lighting.

»Of course this is our largest unit. But we could just as easily order single rooms similar to hotel rooms«, the architects reassure us regarding the dimension.

The express elevator takes us eighteen floors down. Here the tower has a distinct horizontal recess where communal areas and landscaped terraces are located. At last we land on the upper level of the foundation building, a busy urban scene. Every aspect of the infrastructure is represented here: a big selection of stores but also schools and leisure activities, interspersed with greenery. And naturally all traffic is restricted to the lower floors.

Dahinden 1971.

This project, too, was a submission to the 1967 competition »Urban Residences for a High-Density Society« sponsored by *The Japan Architect*. Again it is clear how topical the flexible capsule system was at the time.

Although sociologists postulated that density of buildings does not have to mean social and communicative density, »urban density« became an incontrovertible dogma of prospective urban development in the 1960s and 70s.

No overall ground plans are available for the above project, but it is hard to imagine that with the density of the towers optimum lighting is possible for apartments and other utilizable spaces that require natural light.

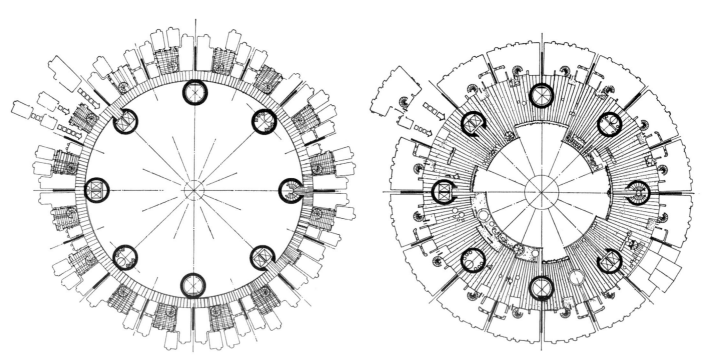

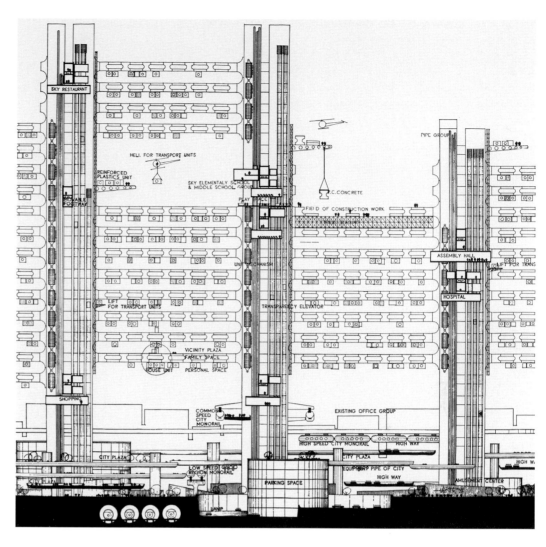

The team of Akira Shibuya. Dense Metabolism, 1966

By now we are quite familiar with the system: Again we have tall towers between which, like bridges, housing and other usable spaces are strung. Shibuya creates three closely integrated residential levels: From the access level one enters the spacious living-dining room with an adjacent large terrace, the massive residential section formed by the box girders, which are far apart. The kitchen element is a movable cell, and so are the bedrooms and studies that are attached as room cells on the underside of the box girder and can be arranged at will.

Directly under them there is another level: public space – promenade and walking path. We find it hard to imagine that private rooms, particularly bedrooms, project directly into this space without there being physical and psychological tensions. Akira Shibuya has a different view of things: »We've always been familiar with the horizontal vicinity of private and public space. Why shouldn't there be a vertical vicinity as well?

»Another thing: In recent decades a completely new relationship between privacy and community has formed. Admittedly it is still developing.«

Still skeptical, we turn to the other facilities.

Traffic is very carefully planned: There are three different types of monorail, corresponding to three speeds: high-, average-, and low-speed monorails running on different levels. Admittedly it is surprising that the highways, on various levels, go through the middle of town, since completely noiseless and emission-free cars are still in the development stage. Many facilities, such as restaurants, shopping malls, schools, meeting halls, hospitals, family and neighborhood spaces seem to have been distributed quite arbitrarily in the densely populated structures. The architects explain why this is so: »It is true that we do not need to work out ingenious locations. In our system we can rearrange things at any time.«

We are able to observe an interesting scene: Just now, a permanent crane brings a prefabricated concrete part and sets it precisely in place. One of the box girders is now in its final position. At the same time a helicopter brings a room cell from the warehouse. It is now simply clipped onto the supporting structure.

Dahinden 1971.

This is another submission to the above-mentioned competition. The parallels in all the submissions are striking. The issue of energy technology, particularly in America and Japan, hardly played an important role before the 1973 energy crisis, which explains many economic and ecological problems.

The team of Kunihiko Hayakawa. A New Society, 1966

Though the city is built according to a consistent standard rectangular pattern, we would not be able to find our way without expert guidance: The density of the buildings can scarcely be surpassed and completely absorbs open spaces and even green spaces. It reminds us of the fantastically bewildering, expressive, baroque spatial fantasies of a Piranesi.

As we approach by helicopter, we can detect something like systematic order in the cylindrical centers. We learn one of their functions: The wide corbeled platforms are landing strips. We land on one of them. Under these platforms communal areas extend far down to the lower residential floors. The apartments above them are coupled to the cylinders.

»We are convinced«, say the architects, »that we need not only a new architecture but also a new society, and we have implemented it here! We all know the traditional extended family has long been outmoded. Families have long since forfeited their function as educators. We've implemented an entirely new structure.«

And so the architects first show us the »dormitories« – the areas to which children move at an early age to be raised by the community.

But other age groups and social situations have their specific remedies in the view of the planners: teenagers, single people, young marrieds with or without babies (the latter are not yet raised by the collective), single parents, seniors, the disabled: they all have their specific lifestyles and have therefore been assigned the appropriate living quarters. In addition, the appropriate communal areas –especially those located in the cylinders – are available to them.

»Naturally we've created an exquisite administration«, the architects proudly claim. »Every change in the social profile is registered and we take the necessary action.«

The size and equipment of the communal areas are truly impressive. We also have a chance to see one of the sleeping cells and are startled to see that they are barely larger than a sleeping car compartment.

Dahinden 1971.

This project was also submitted to the competition »Urban Residences for a High-Density Society«. Societal considerations flagrantly contradict modern ambitions and the latest developments: Integration, communal lifestyles, and intergenerational living have commendably become the leading trends in today's society.

The minimal cell – like a box for sleeping or the compartment of a sleeping car – has actually been implemented several times in Japan. The dissolution of family ties and the fact that people are assigned sleeping cells are not new phenomena: This socialist collective idea was frequently discussed in the initial phase of Soviet architecture, though it was rarely implemented.

Hidezo Kobayashi. The Submarine City, 1980

Like Kikutake's Unabara, Kobayashi's city is also below sea level.

Coming from the lovely, untouched landscape past sailboats and motorboats, we enter the underwater world through huge transportation tubes. A dense network of traffic tubes connects the individual junctions. Here urban activities take place. We note that the city is totally dominated by the traffic network. »That is quite true«, explains the architect. »The city is nothing but communication, and we've worked out many different communication types.«

Stadt und Utopie 1982.

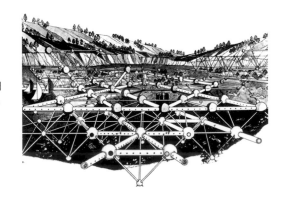

Kobayashi's city reminds one of lattice structures, and it is hard to imagine how this type of homogenous network is supposed to function. It is also unclear where residents are actually meant to live and work.

Shin Takamatsu. The Ocean City, 1990

Naturally we begin by overflying the city. Here in the ocean it is no doubt logical to use a circular form.

However, Takamatsu is not satisfied with this geometry. »I think the interplay of geometric forms as formerly advocated by Le Corbusier really forms the basis of architecture: In the embracing circle I have placed the big, round air-conditioned domes. The major part of the housing development is under them and thus protected.«

From a small marine airport we take speedboats into the harbor. The interplay of forms is certainly wonderful, as if masculine and feminine symbols were in continuous dialogue. Domes alternate with pointed cones and tall cylinders. This is where offices and businesses, cultural institutions and consumer services are predominantly located. The ocean as a quiet harbor or, beyond the circular zone, as a turbulent sea is ever-present.

De Vallée 1995.

Large geometric forms, especially the circle, but also archetypes such as cones and cylinders play an important role in Japanese architecture. The understandable plan to deal with overpopulation by moving out onto the ocean was not put into effect.

Meinhard von Gerkan (b. 1936). The Luchao Harbor City (Lingang New City), China, 2003–20

The little sports plane we ride with von Gerkan is ideal for a visual tour over the new city, which projects far into the ocean 60 km from Shanghai.

We realize at once that again a perfect circle is the underlyng principle, and follow a number of concentric circles to which eight huge lobes have been joined like the petals of a flower. But only three of the lobes are intact and complete, while the other five seem to have been completely or partially swallowed by the ocean. We cannot make out a center – or rather, where we would expect a center there is a huge expanse of water in which there are small islands with flat buildings. »Those are cultural and administrative buildings«, says von Gerkan. »The actual center is unoccupied – or rather, it is reserved for the most ancient element of all, water, the ocean. It is the future ›Lake Luchao‹.«

Between the lobes, characterized by very uniform and almost exclusively rectangular buildings, large wedges of greenery are left open for parks, gardens, and recreation areas. Charming little rivers and lakes enliven the landscape.

Is there even the remotest chance that such a huge project will be implemented? »*China is like a utopia, eager to enter unexplored territory*«, says von Gerkan.

314, 315. Shin Takamatsu, Marine City, 1990.
316. Meinhard von Gerkan, Luchao Harbor City, 2003–20.

In only two years, the two- to three-meter-deep ocean was filled in with earth and sand, and an eight-meter-high dike was erected on the ocean side as protection from typhoons. Admittedly residents cannot see the open sea.

Our plane has now landed in one of the private airports and we begin our tour. After a first green zone we reach one of the residential districts, consisting almost entirely of apartment blocks with open courtyards. »We are in one of the elegantly structured residential districts. They have nothing massive about them, though close to 300,000 people live here. In 2005 the population was 80,000, and by 2020, the district will have 800,000 inhabitants.« The apartment houses are extremely simple, almost all built of the dark fired bricks typical for Shanghai. They create an impressive contrast with the great glass surfaces.

On we go through a broad ring of green spaces to a closed ring of somewhat taller but very uniform buildings: Here, apartment buildings are interspersed with a variety of office buildings, businesses, cultural and entertainment venues. No building is more than eight stories high.

We now enter the innermost circle directly by the lake surrounded by a wide sandy beach. We feel in the mood for a vacation. »*It's like the Copa Cabana*«, says von Gerkan. »*You can sit on the beach in the middle of the city and swim, surf, or sail and just have fun.*«

One single element is so high it dominates the scene: In the middle of the lake, the steel »cloud needle« towers 300 m high – and it actually does spray water from it tip, thus producing a cloud.

Our tour ends in an elegant lake restaurant. We ask von Gerkan whether problematic new towns like Brasilia and Chandigarh haven't caused him concern.

»Luchao Harbor City is quite different. We've made sure that the city has plenty of life, dynamism, development, and communication.«

The building of Luchao Harbor City has actually started. Probably this kind of project is now possible only in Asia, where the most incredible utopias are turned into a reality.

317. Incheon-I city, South Korea, 2005.

318. Qufu Aquacity, South Korea, 2005.

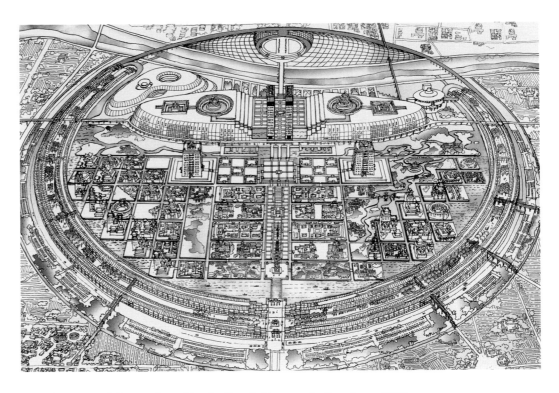

The planners of the marine cities in South Korea, starting from 2005

We cannot possibly get a clear idea of the two new Korean cities unless we go by private plane. First, we fly over Incheon city. Even from a distance the plan of this huge man-made island becomes clear: It is an ellipse – and of course symbolically represents the egg. A highway crosses the island. It is a connection with the mainland city, the airport, and neighboring towns. The business center is in the western part surrounded by green spaces. A gigantic sea wall protects the island. The apartment houses are added on in the form of a huge horseshoe. Four 20-story residential high-rises are firmly moored. This superstructure houses the industries. The garages are near the apartments, as are the markets and the community and cultural hall. The roofs are equipped with sun collectors. In the small ellipse axis, the dominant feature is a 50-story office tower. The inner harbor is on the large axis. The harbor basin is independent of the ocean thanks to locks. The luxuriant green spaces are possibly only temporary. In future they may be developed further, but enough of them are to be kept available for leisure and tourism, which is being promoted especially vigorously.

We are no less surprised by Qufu Aquacity. It seems as though it was modeled on Venice, for the gigantic circular wall completely encloses an expanse of water in which the sections of the city seem to float like square islands. The city has two focal points: the university district and tourist facilities. The latter include the big cultural center with the monumental temple axis. The very modest housing developments form the concluding rings. Parking lots are nearby, followed by green spaces and the traditional buildings. A monorail connects all points, and the center is a pedestrian zone.

Metamorph 9 2004.

Surely this is no utopia? After all, the cities are already under construction. We do not currently know whether and to what extent the plans can be implemented: Once again it looks like the boundary has been crossed between a utopia and an ideal city.

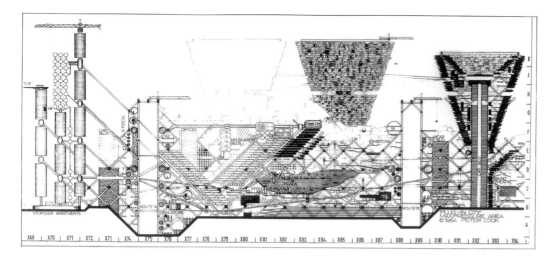

13.2. England

Archigram: Peter Cook (b. 1936). Plug-in-City, 1964–1966; Ron Herron (b. 1930). Instant City, 1965, and Walking Cities, 1964

Once again, tall towers mark the new district of London. »Architecture must remain flexible, mobile. We've invented the ›plug-in‹ and the ›clip-on‹ system: The flexible elements are simply plugged in and provided with all utilities from the supply tower as they would be by a socket.«

The Plug-in City is an extremely dense, even confusing structure, rightly called a »city«. Only the fact that Peter Cook is our guide prevents us from getting hopelessly lost. We can make out a basic structure – a loose-meshed grid of diagonal tubes that provides support for the many cell elements. Up to 20 stories of residential cubicles are inserted here. At the top of the supporting framework the express monorail glides soundlessly, and in the area next to it the expressway has been suspended.

But these are not the only means of transportation: A raised express monorail speeds past along the riverbank, a local line links all parts of the city, and a railroad brings in mainly heavy cargo. Smaller differences in levels are bridged by escalators.

»Why does the crane at the top still run along the crane runway. Isn't the city finished?« »Right«, says Cook with conviction, »because it will never be finished, like any living city. It is in the process of continuous transformation, and in order to bring changes about rapidly, we need the permanent crane. It does have another function, though: It lifts goods from delivery vehicles and drops them into the diagonal tubes. From there they are distributed directly to warehouses.«

These diagonal tubes also have a direct condition with the freight station. But only half of the tubes are used to transport goods. The other half contain diagonal elevators serving different levels, and all the utility supply lines and waste disposal lines also run through the diagonal tubes.

The elevator now takes us to the main pedestrian level in the lower third of this complex. Here we see a colorful assortment of businesses: Stores, boutiques, cafés, and restaurants alternate with the necessary day-to-day service facilities.

The residents cannot complain about a lack of cultural and community institutions: The local monorail takes us past theaters, cinemas, exhibition halls, schools, libraries, and assembly halls. Naturally there are also excellent restaurants.

Giant plug-in towers dominate the rest of the city. The more than 60 levels corbel outwards toward the top, so that the top twelve stories, like a crater, form an inner courtyard. It goes without saying that here, too, the permanent crane makes a rapid exchange of residential cubicles possible.

The massive load-bearing cores of the towers are designed differently. While all the towers have the function of receiving the mobile cells, the office and hotel towers also house the entire mechanical equipment in addition to the elevators, ending in the computer headquarters. In the residential towers, on the other hand, the massive core is designed to be a parking facility.

Now we witness a strange scene: In one of the big loops of the base structure a large foil expands, begins to grow, swell, and take shape. »Today there will be a big concert, and the inflatable hall protects us from the weather. We can adjust its size depending on the number of concertgoers«, Peter Cook explains.

»There is also another type of pneumatic structure: In the upper regions of the base framework, similar to the pneumatics of cars, there are built-in balloons that can protect various parts from inclement weather.

Now we continue our investigation on foot. To our surprise, the structure of free spaces and shopping zones is almost romantically detail-oriented and carefully differentiated. In vain we look for larger green spaces. »We can manage without them«, says Peter Cook, »for our city is so compressed that we can be in the country within a very short time, in a real, not simulated, natural setting.«

Now we have an opportunity to see some of the cubicles close up and from the inside. The technological equipment for modifying rooms is far in advance of current technology: All parts of a room used to modify spaces are electronically controlled. It is possible to make several daily changes.

Suddenly, to our surprise, a huge shape appears on the Thames, then another and another. Peter Cook explains: »That's not a ship but an office building mounted on a gigantic hovercraft. It goes wherever it is needed at the moment.«

The cylinder-shaped structures have a varying number of floors. These in turn are variably connected with a core. On the lowest level are the forum and assembly rooms; the motors for the hovercraft mechanism are installed in the foundation floor.

Peter Cook speaks of the lifespan of the architecture: »There have never been buildings that lasted forever, not even in ancient times. The lifespans of our building elements have been exactly calculated: The foundation framework will be used for 40 years, the railroad will be replaced by a more efficient system in fifteen years, the shops can be changed in a short time and will probably not be used for more than three years. The hovercraft building will be operational for ten years but can be fundamentally changed after five years. The core of the high-rises will last for 20 to 25 years, but we will replace the plug-in elements every three or five years.«

The next day we get an even clearer impression of how flexible, modifiable, and mobile the design of the city is.

At Ron Herron's invitation, we leave London in the morning, and arrive in a small country town 400 miles to the north.

»There's a big youth festival here today!«

»Where is it supposed to take place?«

»Wait, let's go and have a drink!«

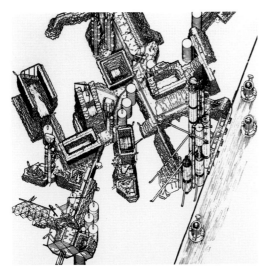

And as we sit in the pub, we hear the thundering of trucks. On the big campus, large packages and boxes are being unloaded, machines are unpacked and coupled to plastic packages, compressors start up, and enormous halls are inflated before our eyes. Cranes come driving up and raise the roofs of tents being set up, large screens are unrolled and raised, and speakers' platforms are opened up. In the trucks we see huge items of technical equipment. An infernal but precise process has been set in motion.

But there are other technological surprises: Ron Herron displays the entire arsenal of resources that have allowed him to turn the little town into a metropolitan event in a few short hours.

Balloons are lowered from helicopters and immediately filled with gas. These hold up a huge awning over part of the terrain. Also, fresh from the central kitchens, food and beverages are delivered by air in special containers to keep them hot or cold.

Here comes another surprise: An enormous »cigar« appears on the horizon. An airship similar to the old »Zeppelin« approaches and hovers over an area that has been left vacant. Now huge screens descend from the body of the airship. They, too, are used as projection surfaces.

»It is important for me«, explains Ron Herron, »that these events do not take place in the open country but in the middle of town, integrated with the town such as it is.«

We go for a hike through the lovely surroundings and return toward evening. Sure enough, the Instant City is finished, the first guests begin to arrive, and the event can start!

»The Instant City has other functions as well«, says Ron Herron. During the day there are classes, educational events, and information. A few evenings are also devoted to high-brow offerings: concerts, movies, and plays.«

Herron concludes: »*The sun of the provinces might become the exciting scene, with the old metropolis becoming a cultural as well as physical embarassment.*«

We are even more amazed by the next day's events. Ron Herron takes us down to the harbor. From a distance, we can see massive egg-shaped structures strewn with dots that turn out close up to be hundreds of windows.

»Next week our Walking City will get under way – a complete city. It will head for America and drop anchor in New York. Then the huge telescopic tubes will be extended and form a dense communication and supply network. The Walking City is an autonomous structure. It can be a real ›city‹ wherever it is located, and perhaps it will travel on to South America a year from now.«

Ron Herron now invites us to visit a unit. Like the big ocean liners of the past, the units of the Walking City – about the size of a city district – have a distinctive infrastructure. The planners have paid special attention to education and leisure: All types of schools with libraries and research facilities are represented. There are first-rate cinemas, theaters, and exhibitions. A luxurious shopping mall has everything a shopper might want.

In the meantime, the sky over the harbor has cleared and we accompany Ron Herron to the imposing technical command headquarters from which this marvel is electronically controlled. »Make us a spring day!« requests Ron Herron. At once the huge glass dome over the center folds like a fan and we look into the clear sky. And now we understand that the luxuriant trees, flowers, and other plants in the gardens of the center have good chances of prospering.

To some extent, we can imagine the differentiated technology located underwater. But there is one thing we would like to know: the mechanism that moves these colossal structures.

»We've developed an entirely new system – the details are still absolutely secret. I'll just say that it's more or less a combination of the hovercraft and rocket principle. That means the city can move on water and land. We can plow through oceans or visit deserts.«

Cook 1970; Dahinden 1971; Tod/Wheeler 1978; *Stadt und Utopie* 1982; Klotz 1986; Thomsen 1994; *Architectures experimentales* 2003.

The Archigram group had an enormous influence on the young generation of architects, including the Austrian scene (cf. chap. 13.8). They clearly inspired Japan, where we recognize modest attempts to work with the module system.

The idea of the Instant City, though not necessarily inspired by Archigram, has actually been implemented: For gigantic demonstrations, for mass concerts small towns are created, at least in technical terms. For example, Marc Fisher has made a name for himself with these events. In his use of light, color, sound, and space he by far surpasses anything offered by today's cities.

The Walking City extrapolates the autonomous »city« of the ocean liner – which filled Le Corbusier with such enthusiasm – on a giant scale.

The fact is that Ron Herron never published anything about the inner structure of his Walking City. The question of the mechanism that made it move also remains open. Projects that use the system of the ocean giant as their starting point are therefore probably somewhat closer to reality than Ron Herron's virtuoso designs for a traveling city.

322. Archigram / Ron Herron, Walking City, 1964.
323. Peter Cook, the Outriders of Layer City, 1981.
324. Peter Cook, the city as a responsive environment, 1972.

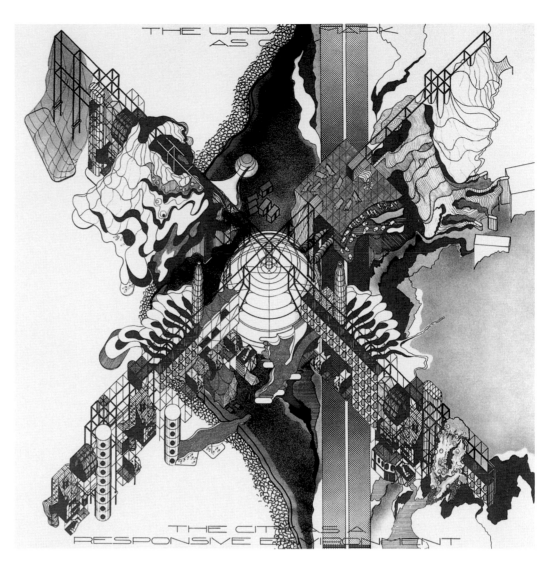

Peter Cook (b. 1936) and Christine Hawley (b. 1949). The city as a responsive environment, 1972, and Outriders of Layer City, 1981

The basic structure of the city is clearly recognizable from the plane: It is a large cross, composed of a vast number of modular cubes and spanning a big domed building in the center. But this rigid spatial grid now seems to dissolve in a mixture of landscape and sculpture. And as we wander through the »city as a responsive environment«, we have trouble orienting ourselves. Like sleepwalkers, or rather, like people in a dream with all its unreality we walk, soar, fly through these urban spaces. Is this a built environment? Is it already a landscape? Is it nature? Has it crossed the boundary into art? Peter Cook guides us through a magic world. Is this a battle of principles: square rationality against proliferating three-dimensionality – or have the planners achieved a synthesis, integration, identity?

»We've come to a reconciliation«, says Peter Cook, »the old dialectics have led us ad absurdum, the tensions still exist, but they have become exciting, adventurous.«

Nearby, we come to the Outriders of Layer City. It is a bold structure with towers, arches, and domes, fantastic – and yet many parts are cut out of small square grid surfaces, as though made of squared paper.

»We need reconciliation not only with nature but also with history. And unlike the postmodern architects, we can remember columns and arches, turrets and domes.«

Inventionen 1981; *Stadt und Utopie* 1982; Klotz 1986; Thomsen 1994.

Peter Cook has been developing his ideas for four decades in lovely continuity: Technology and imagination have always been interfused. Peter Cook succeeded in implementing his first, late – too late? – project together with Colin Fournier: the Kunsthaus Graz in Austria, which garnered him praise as well as criticism.

Hal Moggridge. The British Sea City, 1968

In the east of Britain is the county of Norfolk. Here, we take a shuttle boat that brings us to the harbor of Sea City in 20 minutes. We're in the middle of town. The uninviting fortress-like more than 60-meter-high wall we saw upon arrival shelters a respectable-sized little town inside its huge omega loop.

»There are 30,000 people living here«, Hal Moggridge tells us. »We have created a pleasant, peaceful ambiance: The high wall protects the town from rough seas and lies in the sea like a giant shell. In front of it there are also plastic pontoons, nine-tenths full of water, acting as a breakwater.« If necessary the opening of the wall, like a harbor portal, is protected from high waves by a veil of compressed air.

The planners have chosen two different constructional systems. Since the sea is no more than 9 m deep, the big town wall stands on fixed reinforced concrete pillars. However, in the center, which is protected from waves, the buildings were erected on triangular pontoon elements that can be combined at will.

The lovely terrace apartments with their lush greenery are reminiscent of lakeshore developments. They are all oriented toward the interior – the islands – and thus toward the communal and office buildings and the green spaces and recreation areas. The cinema, theater, storehouses, and especially the large power plant, fueled by natural gas, are located in the dark zones of the town wall.

Dahinden 1971.

It is noteworthy (though this is not a significant indicator that the plan can be carried out) that the project's initiator is the famous glassworks Pilkington Brothers Ltd., which has its own research and development department. At least this is a guarantee that the concept of the project is sound.

»Sea City was designed in 1968 for the Pilkington Glass Age Development Committee by architect Hal Moggridge and engineers John Martin and Ken Anthony.«

Zaha Hadid (b. 1950). Executing God, 2000

The city to which Zaha Hadid takes us is breathtaking. It eclipses and improves upon New York's Times Square and the Ginza in Tokyo, and transfers them into a wild landscape of curves, ramps, and loops. Zaha Hadid regards this city with optimistic and passionate eyes: »*Anarchic and chaotic, it is a pirate utopia – but it is our future, and it's marvelous.*«

Zaha Hadid has created a complete city, the most extreme example of her formal dynamism: curves, bundles, folds, overlapping layers, junctions: The entire repertory of fantastic visions of space has been implemented here.

»*It is a city of extremes*«, says Zaha Hadid. »*the most important obsessions are spirituality, shopping, and television. It is a city of paradoxes, magicians, skyscrapers, magic and technology alike, a city of witchcraft and science. It is the bubbling fusion of Los Angeles, Mexico City, Bombay, and Tokyo. In the city, teams of clairvoyants, psychologists, astrologers, chaos theoreticians are at work.*

All traditional ideas about urban structures have collapsed. The total city is kept in motion solely by the forces of the market.«

Impossible Worlds 2000.

If we recognize films as a type of implementation, then Zaha Hadid has come very close to one. The film's producers Marc J. Hawker and Isabel Whitaker invited her to design the city of the Executing God for a feature film. The Japanese designer Hideyuki adapted the formalism of Zaha Hadid for the film.

325. Hal Moggridge, Sea City, 1968.
326. Zaha Hadid, Executing God, 2000.

13.3. France, Netherlands, Belgium, Spain

Constant (C. A. Nieuwenhuys) (b. 1920). New Babylon. The hyper architecture of desire, 1959–74

We get our first overview of the New Babylon as we take an aerial tour of Amsterdam with universal designer Constant (his civil name is Nieuwenhuys). The outlying districts and suburbs are overlaid for long stretches with a very irregular, low structure.

We land on one of the large flat roofs and now have a close-up view of a rather bizarre, almost chaotic structure. But it is filled with hustle and bustle, incredible activity. Why is that?

»I don't want to build finished cities«, Constant explains. »We only make available the large structure and then, almost playfully, the space is occupied and given form. It is an ›object of mass creativity‹, that is, it is the Babylon of collective teamwork before the confusion of tongues.« Constant derives his strategies from our present situation:

»I activate the enormous creative potential that is present in the masses. I recognize the facts, such as the rapid growth of the world's population and of traffic, the total urbanization of the planet.

We need to throw overboard all conventional, traditional orders and concepts such as axes, symmetries, classical aesthetics. The character of buildings and complexes is somewhere between a flexible cluster of tents and a permanent building site.

For some time now we've been moving toward a nomadic existence. I created the ›Dynamic Labyrinth‹ for movable urban situations. New Babylon is a global city. It is the entire planet Earth. Life is an unending journey through a world that is changing rapidly and constantly appears in a different form to us.«

Every change can only take place in a chronological dimension, and this is an important factor in New Babylon. But the »time« of New Babylon is that of slow human passing. »What we have here is a microstructure in constant change where the factor of time, the fourth dimension, plays a considerable role.«

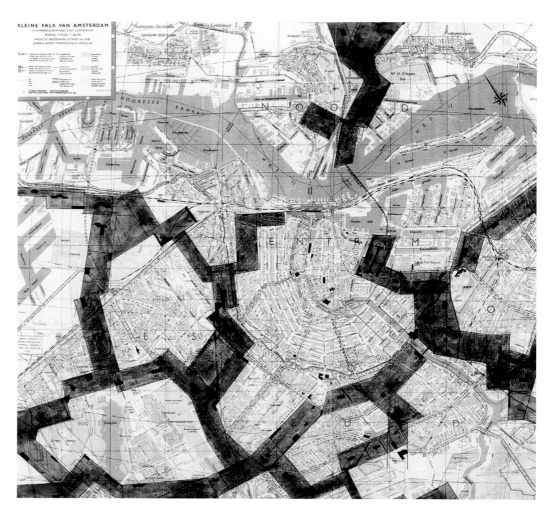

327. CONSTANT (C. A. Nieuwenhuys), New Babylon, urban development of Amsterdam, 1968.

All human activities have a chronological structure. In New Babylon they are playful, not functionalistic, and time can also acquire a new profile in space. »Collective space is a place of inquiry, adventure, and play, where the sense of time is interpreted differently.«

However seriously they present themselves to us, Constant wants to dedicate his cities to »homo ludens«, a playful human being according to Jan Huizinga: »*For it is probably clear that functional cities created during that long period of history when human life was dedicated to being useful in no way correspond to the very different needs of the creative race of homo ludens. The environment of homo ludens must above all be flexible and changeable, guarantee complete freedom of movement, permit every change of place and mood, every kind of behavior.*«

The part of town through which we are walking is raised above the ground. Below, traffic flows independent of the buildings. The apartments are located in the raised three- or four-story platform, and it is easy to switch the apartments. Planes land on the terraces and there are also playing fields here.

The system consists of individual sectors as its basic elements. The constructional macrostructure, which has few supporting pillars, provides enormous freedom for the microstructure of the interior spaces. There are surfaces at different levels one above the other connected with each other and with the terrain, as well as with the fixed cores used for service and for the supply of utilities that represent the junctions of the large network structure. The sectors primarily have extensive areas for social and communicative activities – above all for playful actions – and also form a network. The lower level is reserved for traffic, but also for a large number of nature reserves with small patches of woods, gardens, parks, and ponds.

The public spaces represent an interplay of volumes, stairs, platforms, and corridors. They can be modified at any time. Color, light, sound, and climate can be constantly altered as well.

Constant now leads us through adventurous, stimulating spaces and describes the experiences that lie ahead: »*We will find a large number of irregular spaces, elevators, forgotten corners, indeterminate areas, cul-de-sacs. There are unexpected surprises everywhere. You come here because of the adventure. You can discover yourself in the soundproof room or in the screaming room with its loud colors and rebounding sound. You can go to the echo room, the picture room, the meditation cell, the relaxation room, or go to the area for erotic games. During a longer stay this is how you can cleanse your heart and mind.*«

Constant's ambitions go far beyond structure: »New *Babylon is not an urban planning project but a way of thinking, of imagining, a way of looking at things and at life.*«

The district we are touring now is quite large, but we see that construction is still going on. »New Babylon is never finished, and the network can span entire regions.«

A little to one side from the fascinating web of New Babylon Constant takes us to a group of transparent shapes whose form reminds one of UFOs.

These are the Spatiovores, consisting of a lower bowl and a domed bowl, each supported by three pillars and raised above the ground. A dynamic, spatial interplay develops between the two bowls as the levels and spaces penetrate each other, cross, and overlap.

Constant likes to reminisce about the time when he was a militant artist. Together with Asger Jorn, Corneille, and Karel Appel he founded the artists' group »Cobra«.

Constant is committed to advocating his theses on urban planning and architecture. Before we leave, he hands us his manifesto, »Urbanism of unity«:

»– *The ›urbanism of unity‹ defines itself in complex and permanent activity, which conscientiously re-creates the human environment. Housing problems related to traffic, recreation, and work can be solved only in terms of social, psychological, and artistic aspects, as well as a synthesis on the level of lifestyle.*

– The ›urbanism of unity‹, independently of all aesthetic considerations, is the result of a new kind of collective creativity. The development of this creative spirit is the precondition for an urbanism of unity.

– The creation and development of a favorable environment is the immediate task of creative people today.

– We must use all means, create all conditions that serve an action of unity. The coordination of artistic and scientific means must lead to complete unity.

– To construct a specific situation is to create a temporary micro-environment and a play of events for a singular moment in a person's life. This is inseparable from building a general environment, which is relatively long-lasting, in the ›urbanism of unity‹.

328. Constant (C. A. Nieuwenhuys), New Babylon, 1968, Structural model.
329. Constant (C. A. Nieuwenhuys), Spatiovore (space eater), New Babylon, 1959.

*– A built environment is a means of approaching the ›urbanism of unity‹, the indispensable
basis for developing the building of situations – playful or serious – in a free society.«*
Dahinden 1971; Tafuri 1976,1999; *Stadt und Utopie* 1982; Klotz 1986; *Sites & Stations* 1995;
Constant 1997; Wigley 1998; *Nouvelles* 2001; Documenta 11, 2002.

In countless sketches and drawings, in graphic mock-ups Constant presents his »New Babylon«.
The mock-up as a quasi – i»real« three-dimensional representation is the first clear step toward reality.
Constant went no further – and he shares this fate with urban planners whose work on space cities
more or less parallels his own: Yona Friedman, Eckhard Schulze-Fielitz, Günther Domenig/Eilfried
Huth.

But Constant took an additional step into reality. He returned to the point from which he set out:
Art is a reality of different kind.

André Biro (b. 1926) and Jean-Jacques Fernier. X-City, 1962–64

The peaceful landscape through which we are driving seems endless: It turns into a well-kept
park that is touched only by the supporting pillars of the houses: The city seems to float.

Here is what the architects tell us about the idea behind the city: »*Ninety-nine percent of the
terrain is open countryside, with only the recreational buildings occupying the surface at ground
level. Neverthelesst there are 1,000 inhabitants per hectare. The city has a continuous, growing
structure that can potentially develop in a linear or volumetric way. It's the only way we can deal
with future problems.*«

Unlike in a linear city, no direction for growth has been predetermined. A »shoot« can grow out
of any of the junction points, as on the trunk of a tree, and then extend in an undetermined dimension.

»The constructional principle is simple«, say the architects: »X-shaped reinforced concrete
plate girders form the basic structure. The basic element is fitted between every two such supporting pillars: This is a series of stepped terrace apartment units whose »night part« faces the
open countryside, while the »day part« faces the pedestrian area, the zone of encounter with others.

We express our concerns regarding privacy. For the »day part« we would demand a certain
degree of intimacy – will this not be impaired by the pedestrian zone? »Society has changed«, the
architects believe. »We've learned to live together harmoniously in community, which is just as important as individuality.«

If the land is given back to vegetation, then where does the traffic go? We've hardly heard any
traffic noises. »Cars have been noiseless for years, and they move in a tunnel that horizontally
connects the intersection points of the X support pillars. The monorail, also noiseless, runs on
tracks on the underside of the tunnel.«

This seems like an ingenious solution, but is not without disadvantages: Cars need long,
space-consuming ramps to reach tunnel level.

Now we take the elevator twelve floors up straight to a community terrace. From here there
are walkways across the rooftops through the entire city. Now we can see the many »hanging
gardens«, spacious terraces, balconies, and loggias of the apartment buildings. The buildings are
arranged in ground plan formations that are bent and broken in various ways, so that it is hard to
find a right angle. From here we also see that the buildings are organically embedded in green
spaces, gardens, and parks. We imagine that each apartment has a lovely, free view.

Only communal facilities such as schools, department stores, administrative buildings, movie
theaters, and assembly halls occupy a small part of the ground-level surface.

»We've chosen a different stylistic idiom for these buildings«, the architects explain the reason
for the architecture. »Curved, organic, often playful forms indicate special functions and are substantially different from apartment buildings.«
12 Villes Prospectives 1965; Dahinden 1971.

We keep coming back to the problem of city growth. The system of a linear city was elaborated early
on (cf. chap. 10.1), initially seemed to make sense, but did not really catch on. Biró and Fernier have
also proposed a type of linear city, from the point of view of potential growth. However, the pattern is
not precisely linear. It is a structure in which branching lines close into rings, an interesting version of
the linear city.

Edouard Albert (1910–1968) and Jacques Cousteau (1910–1997). A man-made island in the Bay of Monaco, 1963–67

We set out from Monaco with M. Albert und M. Cousteau and a moving walkway in a tube 15 km below the sea transports us the five km to the »Île flottante«.

We've already had a good view of the layout from the helicopter we took earlier: It is a pentagon put together from numerous smaller pentagons. This rare geometry reminds us of its few forerunners, for instance the Villa Caprarola near Rome or the Pentagon in Washington.

The selection of this closed form indicates a distancing from the rest of the world, but is also the spatial implementation of a new, unaccustomed, mathematical form. Is this even a city? For what we see during our tour are chiefly recreation facilities and research labs, with only a small number of interspersed apartments for the staff and hotels for visitors. Whatever the case may be, the constructions and forms are interesting, and so we are happy to take the tour since the underwater explorer Cousteau is an expert who definitely knows about the water. Together, he and the architect Albert explain the construction: »More than half of the pentagonal island, which has an exterior diameter of 220 m and an interior diameter of 115 m, lies underwater – the float, which consists of a framework of tubes dynamically anchored by five huge concrete cubes and slack cables. Wind speeds of up to 185 km/h are not a problem. The constructional core is a kind of steel crown 25 m wide, and a 100-meter-high tower rises above the island.«

During our visit the sea is quite calm, and yet we feel the gentle swaying of the island. What will be the effect of rough seas? »The waves can be up to 10 m high. At that point the safety system automatically becomes operative: The 40 swimming pools, which contain 13,000 m^3 of water, are emptied and the island rises 10 m out of the water and is protected from the waves.« From the harbor and the beaches we stroll through the heavily built-up island. Comparing this to other leisure cities we are struck by the lovely transparency of most of the buildings: The clubs, restaurants, exhibition halls, and sports facilities look like giant crystals, and the sea is always present. And there is a particularly wide panorama from the glass tower that rises above the complex at one of its corner points. It is a lighthouse, scientific observatory, and residential tower, but also has room for public plazas with tall trees, shrubbery, and lawns.

The research labs, strangely placed next door to movie theaters and nightclubs, are all located in the lowest floor under the surface of the water, where all the functions that need no daylight are housed. Once again we move at sea level and enjoy watching life on the beach from a lovely seaside restaurant.

»The fact that the island is so self-contained«, says Mr. Albert, »provides us with a kind of calm lake that is at the same time connected with the sea in many ways.«

Dahinden 1971; *Nouvelles* 2001.

Settling an island is a recurrent idea among those who wish to create an ideal society. Usually a shipwreck, an escape, a chance discovery are the reason for such a settlement. In recent times, people have been creating man-made islands, mostly brilliant technological feats, yet the ancient idea of the island no doubt still persists.

The architects of Architecture Principe, 1963–1968, Claude Parent (b. 1923) and Paul Virilio (b. 1932). The Fonction Oblique

Our first visit is to the »Vagues«, the waves, and Claude Parent is our guide. The buildings loom on the horizon at a distance of 20 kilom. As we come closer it feels as though a whim of nature has tossed the cliffs of a towering mountain into the landscape – a gesture so violent it is observed only in geological events.

The soaring dynamism of plates, disks, layers, and cubes we are familiar with in skyscrapers has been transferred to an explosive gradient. We would not be surprised if the sloping plates were the runways of spacecraft.

As our car races down the road, Parent passionately pleads: »*Let us leave our cities! That is the only true political action! Let those useless and private agglomerations fall into dust! The new cities with their truly closed-off spaces, protected, autonomous, are the nuclei of new human groups, efficient centers for the 21st century.*«

Claude Parent now takes us to the »Grandes Oreilles«, the big ears or seashells that have alighted in the level landscape like gigantic primeval birds. The apartments are housed in

332. Edouard Albert and Jacques Cousteau, island in the Bay of Monaco, 1963–67.

333. Claude Parent (Architecture Principe), The Big Ears I, The Shells, 1966.
334. Claude Parent (Architecture Principe), Turbo-City, 1965.
335. Claude Parent (Architecture Principe), The Wave – La Vague, 1965.

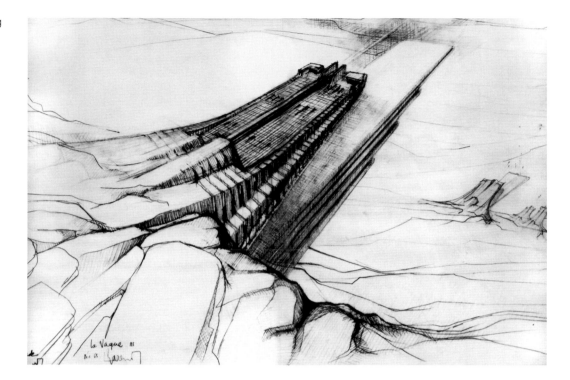

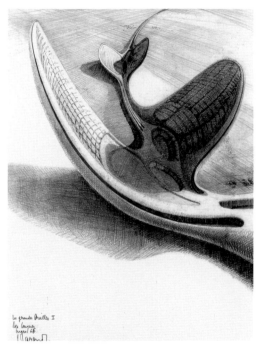

the dynamically and sinuously curved wings. Up to 26 stories high, they rise above the ground. The base, again modeled in curved forms, contains all the community institutions. Now we are on our way to the next city, through a wonderful landscape where meadows and fields follow dramatic cliffs and forests almost untouched by human hands.

But Mr. Parent has already pointed out the striking silhouettes of the buildings on the horizon: Like enormous fans or open hands the Turbo-City rises up to 40 floors into the sky as we face its convex exterior. We've been driving below ground level for some time, and now arrive in the central garage. The express elevators at first rise vertically, then change to a diagonal direction. After arriving at the top we are on the large communal terrace. We not only have a fine view of the landscape but can also see the concave interior sides, which are more than terraces: the hanging gardens are broadly staggered. Every resident enjoys views in two cardinal directions: a distant one of the landscape, and a view of the center of the complex, in which the lowest floors house all the cultural, educational, and commercial facilities of the community.

We ask about the dimensions and the number of residents of the gigantic complex. Here is the architects' answer: »We have close to 2,000 residential units – housing for about 5,000 people. A conventional suburban housing development would take an area of 130,000 m², while our project occupies not even 3,000 m² of land, and even in the projection 30,000 m² are sufficient.«

As a counterweight to the diagonally salient volumes, broad concrete bases serve as foundations. Between them are garages with direct connections to the elevators and energy supply centers. »I call the buildings ›turbines‹«, explains Mr. Parent, »because they do not constitute balance but produce a dynamics that corresponds to our industrialization. But they are also related to the social turbulence in our society.«

The buildings are arranged approximately in a circle and form the boundary of an interior space that is available for all community activities and communication. On some of the levels there are community assembly rooms. They have no special function, but are a response to the demands of social life.

»Nature« does not enter into the »turbines« themselves, but a wild, untamed environment is immediately adjacent to the buildings, and the possibility exists of having green spaces within the city.

Inner views are dynamically designed to be downward, upward, toward the center, and on a slant, but never horizontal, except for the communal spaces.

»Architecture is not biological in nature«, Parent holds forth, »it is pure creation, but it can also not be equated with the object, it is an anti-object. Architecture brings people together, it is the essence of human group formation. Architecture is not integrated in the building site or locale, it exists for itself, but together with the landscape it creates a connection with nature in quality and dimension.«

Mr. Parent believes that architecture has a very important mission: »*It must leave existing cities and promote new urban groupings, it must dominate the landscape and become an antithesis of natural relief, forming an artificial landscape relief.*«

Paul Virilio works in the Architecture Principe for a few years together with Claude Parent. For the most part it is Virilio who formulates the definitions of the »fonction oblique«, the oblique, tilted, dynamic function: »*We're experiencing the end of the vertical and horizontal line in architecture, and we are inventing a new vocabulary. The third spatial potential of architecture, the new spatial order, is the slant. We no longer build Euclidian but rather topological architecture. There are no simple geometric forms. Edges and corners, but not orthogonal ones, are what matters.*«

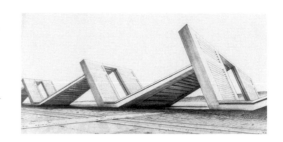

When we approach the »Cité Oblique«, the »oblique city« of Virilio, it seems as though the city's structure is made up of massive slabs that shore each other up. Close up, we realize that these are enormous houses about 25 stories high built on a terraced slope. The completely flat parts house the community facilities; the gentle sloping parts contain the places of work, while the apartments are located in the steep slabs. The terrain itself is left free for huge traffic arteries and for green recreation spaces.

Paul Virilio now takes us to the Nautacité (1966). »*The period when our spatial environment was only physical in nature is long past. Today we also need a psychological environment, where human activities can unfold in a new, psychological domain as well.*«

That is what Paul Virilio regards as the main function of his Nautacité – a gigantic city seemingly »floating« on an endless plain, oriented toward the vast spaces of the atmosphere. The surrounding area is reserved for continental highways and solar energy collectors. Even from a great distance we were able to see the massive complex, an unimaginably large sculpture whose effect is powerful but also chilling. Only when we have taken the elevator into the interior can we get an overview of its spatial qualities and their unaccustomed scale.

M. Virilio explains the city's basic system: »*Level 0 serves the exploitation of the soil – primarily agriculture. The warehouses and silos, parking garages and water reservoirs are located on level 1. On level 2 are the central energy supply, manufacturing plants, and air conditioning systems. The upper regions are design to hold mobile solar energy collectors, and also there are places for strolling, playing fields, intercultural centers, universities, and the administration.*«

All telecommunication systems are installed in the two slanted towers. The two slanted blocks are primarily for apartments. The main levels are continuously connected by slopes and counter-slopes.

Architecture Principe 1966, 1968; *L'Avenir des villes* 1964; Virilio 1966, 1996; Dahinden 1971; Parent 1981; *Sites & Stations* 1995; *Architectures experimentales* 2003.

The term »oblique« means not only tilted, slanting, crooked, but also ambiguous, hidden, infinite. There are different methods of creating terraces large enough to be called »hanging gardens«, as in the days of Semiramis. Only rarely is a natural slope available – in such cases there are convincing implementations. The architects of »Architecture Principe« venture to carry out a few bold, static experiments. But they're interested not only in the terraces, but also in the city's significant dynamics in the middle of the landscape.

»Architecture Principe« succeeds in carrying out a project that cannot easily be brought into line with the architects' principles: The Church of St. Bernadette in Nevers, a bunker-like concrete »New Brutalist« structure. Claude Parent surprises us in the 1980s with amazingly subtle, imaginative, and poetic architectural drawings (the Oreilles, too, reappear here) and a few residential buildings. Paul Virilio becomes a theoretician, and his philosophical essays, such as the one on the topic of »speed« have provoked much interest.

Martin Pinchis (1907–2005). The Space City (Ville de l'espace, 1964)

The dream city of the future has become a reality, and Martin Pinchis, sculptor and architect – it's almost impossible to tell the disciplines apart anymore – speaks of his convictions.

»*The remarkable qualities of modern sculpture call for new and radical solutions in architecture that have quite a different connection with the past.*«

Indeed, the city we are approaching is not even remotely comparable with any of the historical cities. It is true that like many Italian cities it is also situated on a gentle hillside in an almost unspoiled countryside, but the silhouette seems to be upside down as it were: From a massive foundation three, four, five multi-story terraced buildings project boldly into the blue sky.

336. Paul Virilio, Cité Oblique, 1965.
337. Paul Virilio, Nautacité, 1965.

338. Martin Pinchis, future city, space city, 1964.
339. Jean Claude Bernard, Ville Totale, 1965.
340. Yves Salier, Adrien Courtois, and Pierre Lajus, Ville Tripode, 1966.

The last of these terraces raises huge frames, open windows into the sky; each of the frames is four or five stories high.

»La ville future, la ville de l'espace!« is the simplest formula for Pinchis. But sculptural monumentality must not go so far that the city becomes ossified. Pinchis sees new potentials here. »The uniqueness of our era is only short-lived, while our energy bubbles over as we envision more and more possibilities for building, destruction, and renewal.«

It goes without saying that the credo of the 1960s, urban density, is one of the precondiitions for compact space cities and that is why it makes sense that it is expressed in cultural terms. And Pinchis adds: »*A city is not a landscape strewn with buildings. We must develop a new city without destroying essential qualities and characteristics of the basic concept of a town. Our era allows the construction of new concentrations based on radically new principles, which revive those of the past as well.*«

We are now in the center of the dynamic sculpture. Notwithstanding the expressive monument, we have a sense of enormous movement. The unexpected aspects of the space are the main reason for this. But the secondary architecture especially expresses movement – for instance, the three-dimensional, totally flexible apartment modules, suspended from gigantic masts and stretched from one building to another. They seem to vibrate and gleam.

With all its dynamism, however, the city does not seem fragmented. It is dense and compact, and every use of space was avoided.

Martin Pinchis promises to show us more cities that have sprung from his imagination, and again we board the plane. But we refrain from landing. The cities are certainly beautifully structured and impressive, but do not offer any essential quality that would make them superior to the skyscraper cities found all over the world.

Architectures experimentales 2003.

»Gestural« architecture is nothing new. It is perfectly legitimate to remember such architects as Erich Mendelsohn – admittedly, his dynamic designs have been adequately implemented architecturally.

Jean-Claude Bernard. The Total City (La Ville Totale, 1965)

»I've turned the Parent / Mirabeau system upside down, so to speak«, explains Mr. Bernard. »I've created a wide foundation with three basement floors for traffic and energy supply systems. On the other hand, my towers, merely 25 floors high, become narrower toward the top.« In Bernard's city, too, every apartment has a wonderful view of an unspoiled landscape, and the many offerings in the densely built-up center create a fine urban experience. But residents also find the security and peace they seek here.

Mr. Bernard hopes that his city is a »poetic creation« that is both logical and mysterious. The »internal labyrinth«, as the architect calls it, is meant to remind us of old urban neighborhoods. Many of the workplaces are housed in the city's broad foundation, thus there is a new balance of urban functions – and again without impinging on the surrounding countryside.

L'Avenir des villes 1964.

Jean-Claude Bernard's Ville totale is no doubt one of the utopias that could easily be implemented because they use modern technology and have a realistic economy. When we think of American and Asian cities with their vast infrastructures, we realize that this project has long become part of our reality.

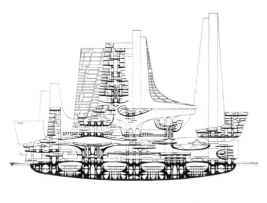

Yves Salier, Adrien Courtois (1921–1980), and Pierre Lajus (b. 1930). The Tripod City (La Ville Tripode, 1966)

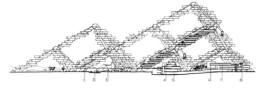

The city rises a good 35 stories – over 100 m – above ground, over a lovely, flat landscape . But it is not a massive pyramid. Rather, we see the sky and clouds through huge frames formed by the residential cubicles. These cubicles are attached to the base structure, which consists of massive box girders that provide communication – containing slanting elevators, stairs, and escalators – and that also provide the entire energy supply and waste disposal system.

»Modern architecture has long been familiar with the third dimension, meaning primarily the vertical line«, says M. Salier. »With our Cité Tripode we've conquered this dimension for urban development as well.«

The slanting elevators give direct access to the apartments, but from them we also reach the pedestrian walkway that runs though the whole city and takes us to communal areas as well as to offices and schools.

The architects continue: »Like a tripod, the city is set on the earth's surface only at certain points. Hexagonal and diamond-shaped open areas are formed, but only a third is occupied by traffic. The rest of them are green spaces and recreation areas with communal buildings.«
Dahinden 1971.

The tiresome issue of dark zones in houses on terraced slopes and hills is here resolved in an interesting way: The »hill« is simply hollowed out and turned into a framework. The plug-in system is modified further here, and the share of the weight-bearing structure in the total structural expenditure seems to be particularly high.

Jean-Paul Jungmann (b. 1935). Dyodon, 1967

This is a city of fantastical creations, sumptuous, swelling forms. We touch the exterior »walls«, pneumatic, double-walled, air-filled structures, membrane cushions that we also find in the interior.

Jungmann's settlement lies on the shore of a big lake. Its soft, rounded forms compete with the hills of the landscape. »*I call my housing ›Dyodon Habitation‹, after the fish that inflates itself when it is in danger. The complex promises to become a refuge of middle-class comfort, something between a ship and a house of pleasure.*«

Inside the building we really do find – in addition to the usual living rooms – every imaginable comfort: a solarium, a small observatory, a climatized room, a winter pool and and a winter garden, an aviary, a library, and an acoustic shell.

In another type we visit, a few functions are outside the Dyodon: The central Dyodon is complemented by smaller, pneumatic satellites attached by hoses to the main building. Autonomous exterior rooms are joined to the main structure – a winter pool, the refreshment hall, the gambling salon, nurseries, the guest room, and the art gallery.

»*The inflated houses are extremely flexible. A volume of one cubic meter weighs no more than seven kilograms*«, explains Jungmann. »*The houses can be erected in almost every kind of terrain, in every climate, and they can also be suspended or float on the water.*«

For his structures Jungmann uses the air-cushion system, i.e., a double-walled, or rather double-membrane construction. The membranes are under constant overpressure, which is adjusted according to the function of the parts.
Dahinden 1971; *Stadt und Utopie* 1982; *Inflatable Moment* 1999.

The second pneumatic system, single-walled membranes under constantly adjusted overpressure, has found numerous uses, such as air-inflated stadiums for sports and exhibitions, expeditions, and temporary buildings. The use of such stadiums has so far been drastically limited because the structures are not fireproof or thermally insulated. This is also true of the double-membrane cushion structures described above.

Nicolas Schoeffer (1912–1962). The Cybernetic City (Ville cybernétique, 1969)

»*My ›Cybernetic City‹ has three forms*«, explains Nicolas Schoeffer, as we drive through charming municipal areas. »Living, and particularly sleeping, is a horizontal activity, so to speak, *and so I've chosen low buildings, no more than four stories high.*«

We do not find the following arguments quite as convincing as Schoeffer explains: »*Most work is done standing up, which is why the working part of town consists of transparent tower buildings.*« In various locations there are strange buildings with organic forms – the third type of structures. »*I've given the buildings for recreation and entertainment free, sculptural forms. They are meant to be clearly differentiated from the rationality of work and day-to-day existence. Museums and an art school, theaters and movie houses, libraries and conference centers will be characteristic features of the cultural city centers.*«

One form in particular attracts our attention: a globe that gently ends in a little hat. »*I am sure you have the right association: It represents a well-rounded woman's breast, for the building is the center for sexual leisure activities. The musty smell of porn shops and bordellos is definitely a thing of the past! In the concept of my building, curves predominate. Visitors are plunged into an audiovisual bath where the air is pleasant and scented. Sound, colored light, and fragrances pulse in an agreeable, slow rhythm. On the ground floor there are dance halls and a hotel as well as a restaurant.*«

And were you thinking of Ledoux' ›maison du plaisir‹, whose layout is in the form of a phallus? »Maybe, because Ledoux, at the beginning of the Enlightenment, also saw sexuality from very new perspectives.«

As we approached the city we had our first glimpse of a scaffold-like tower between whose struts nestle metallically gleaming cubes. Schoeffer has invented a new word for these types of buildings: »*Spatiodynamism is the use of space by employing visible rhythmical and structured scaffolding and transparent or translucent surfaces or bodies fitted into the spatiodynamic whole.*«

What is the meaning of the strange flashes and glitter? »*The tower buildings*«, says Schoeffer, »*are at the same time constructivistic light sculptures. Cybernetically controlled, they emit different types of light signals into the urban space.*«

Les visionnaires de l'architecture 1965; Schoeffer 1969, 1970; *12 Villes Prospectives* 1965; Schumpp 1971; *Stadt und Utopie* 1982.

Schoeffer did not build the new city, but the cybernetic tower and a few light installations were actually implemented. The cultural centers, like Schoeffer's sketches, have long become common property – though without the »center for sexual leisure activities«.

Yona Friedman (b. 1923). The Space-lattice Cities (Villes Spatiales, 1958–66)

Our schedule for visiting Yona Friedman is rather hectic. We get through some of the visits by rapid helicopter – for instance, the first stop, Paris. It's a good thing we come by air, for we can see that the suburbs of Paris have long since vanished and a vast carpet of low lattice structures has been superimposed on the former layout of the city. Naturally there are appropriate landing strips for our flying machine. From the transit center the metro takes us directly to the station Seine-Espace. And when we get out on level 4, the former street level, we see above us the gigantic lattice structure, already densely occupied by volumes, extending high above the Old City of Paris.

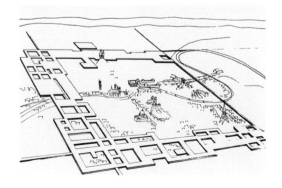

Here is how Friedman describes his concept: »What is crucial for the spatial city is something I call ›spatial infrastructure‹: a multi-story space-frame-lattice that is supported by pillars at widely spaced intervals. This infrastructure forms the fixed part of the city. The mobile part consists of walls, foundation slabs, and partitions that make it possible to tailor space to individual needs.« »*The building is essentially mobile. The type of use desired by the consumer or by a group must be possible and feasible.*«

Friedman lists the most important guidelines:
»*The design of the ›ville mobile‹ follows three criteria:*
   1. *Buildings must touch the ground on a minimum surface.*
   2. *It must be easy to dismantle and move buildings to another site.*
   3. *Buildings must be modifiable according to the wishes of the individual resident.*«

279

345. Yona Friedman, Space City, expansion / building over the city in the south of Manhattan, New York, 1964.
346. Yona Friedman, Bridge City over the Canal, 1963.
347. Yona Friedman, Ville Spatiale, bridge city with harbor, Gibraltar, 1963.
348. Yona Friedman, Space City, expansion / building over the city in the south of Manhattan, New York, 1964.

»I want to duplicate the original surface of the city with the help of the raised floor plans. Every building used is not necessarily an obstacle to modifiability, but a point of departure or arrival for each resident.«

Now we arrive at a huge construction site – and at the same time a demolition site. »A ›quartier spatial‹ is being erected above the former demolition district as we speak. One part is already completed. There, workmen are already beginning to demolish the old neighborhood. In its place, commercial and cultural centers will be erected.«

We are amazed at the incredible formal variety. There is no unified planning in the new Ville Spatiale. *»Only the basic structure with a totally flexible infrastructure is planned in a unified way. But the secondary structure can be modified completely individually according to the tenant's wishes. The givens are a grid measuring 3 m vertically and 6 m horizontally.«*

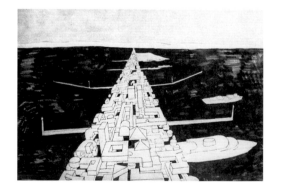

What we experience as we wander through the Ville Spatiale is an amazing sense of space, a new three-dimensionality. The upper level of the spatial grid, which has optimum sun and light, is devoted to apartments; the middle layer is occupied by public institutions and businesses, while the lowest level consists of green spaces, the circulation of the inhabitants. In Paris, there are still old buildings slated for demolition under the grid.

»The conventional city is dead, it's a nineteenth-century concept«, asserts Yona Friedman. »We have simply built over Paris. The old city may die below – here, a new freedom has been born, and in the spatial grid everyone can choose his own ambiance.«

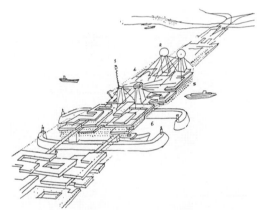

Now it's back to the airport. We're off to Calais. Here we see the event of the millennium: France and England are linked, but not by a dark tunnel, but by a bridge city, up to 1 km wide. It is raised 25 m above the sea and the total height of the eight plugged-in levels is an additional 25 m. All cultural institutions and communal buildings are on the lower levels. Above them are the offices and businesses, and on the top floors are the apartments. From the topmost terrace we enjoy the view of a vast seascape. We don't have the time to visit Dover, an hour's trip, or London, a trip of 70 minutes.

We're not surprised that Friedman has linked Europe and Africa by quite a similar Gibraltar bridge. Our next destination is the new airport, Calais-Global. The booking of tickets, check-in, and boarding are completely digitalized and take 20 minutes.

The flight to New York by supersonic jet takes three hours. Even during landing we can see what Yona Friedmann wants to show us: a very different type of slum clearance. Now, the Space City spreads over the north of Manhattan, seven stories high, raised a good 15 m above ground. Level 0 is still reserved for the usual heavy car traffic. Pedestrian assisted traffic, with various mechanical aids, and pedestrian traffic itself are located on levels +1 and +2. The different types of express traffic, both private and public, are invisible, located on levels –1 to –3.

Friedman's system has stood the test of time, which is why the docks in South Manhattan were extended by adding a large space city, or rather replaced and built over. »Naturally I am particularly interested in unusual situations, for that is where the usefulness of the space city is demonstrated especially clearly«, explains Friedman. »That is why we first visited Paris, Calais, and New York. But now let's look at the space city prototype, so to speak, freely developed, for instance in the desert of Nevada – and here you can see the concept of the new city particularly clearly.«

The planned infrastructure does not limit the city. Rather, it allows builders to implement every imaginable type of city. But the type of city can be altered again at any time. »*This freedom of transformation can be carried out in accordance with the residents' criteria, reflecting their living conditions at the time*«, Friedman reiterates. »*Billions of combinations are possible, including elemental, three-dimensional forms.*«

Friedman asks a controversial question: «*What could we build instead of the existing city, which is difficult to modify?*«

He believes, however, that the question should be rephrased: »*What could we add to it?*«
For Friedman architecture has a very important societal component. He pleads for broad participation: »The future user himself learns an interpersonal language. This language shows him what consequences he can expect from his project. He will therefore be in a position to plan for himself, without recourse to an expert.«

L'Avenir des villes 1964; *12 Villes Prospectives* 1965; *Les visionnaires de l'architecture* 1965; Dahinden 1971; Tafuri 1976, 1999; *Stadt und Utopie* 1982; Klotz 1986; *Nouvelles* 2001; Eaton 2001; *Visionen und Utopien* 2002; *Architectures experimentales* 2003.

Yona Friedman's space city is probably one of the most publicized and least implemented ideas of the euphoric late 1950s. Long before the movements of the 1960s there were widespread reports about the availability of urban space for citizens, marking new, urban freedom. The fact that urban planners built over historical cities shows an almost aggressive confrontation with history. The close proximity of neighbors is based on the idea of a new urban solidarity. Perhaps we can regard Moshe Safdie's Habitat or the communes of the 1960s as implementations of these ideas.

In Austria Günther Domenig and Eilfried Huth very concretely worked out the technological problem of the space lattice city (cf. chap. 13.8), but it was not economically feasible.

Yona Friedman also carried out a few projects together with Eckhard Schulze-Fielitz (cf. chap. 13.4). The two pioneers' ways of thinking were very similar. It is quite surprising that no later than 1974 Yona Friedman's work took an entirely different direction. In his book *Utopies réalisables – Feasible utopias – rejection of familiar models of the future* he views utopia exclusively from an ecological and humanitarian perspective and develops his idealistic ideas for a better world.

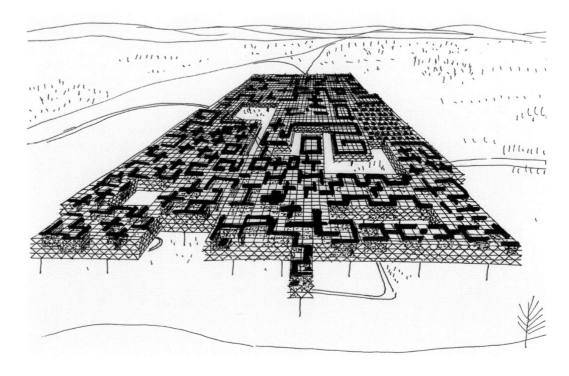

Guy Rottier (b. 1922). A future Nice (Nice futur, 1966–69)

»We had two basic ideas« explains Mr. Rottier. *»One was to use the bed of the Le Var River as a site for the housing and recreational buildings and, nearby, places of work. The other was to close the airport and replace it with a resort.«*

The riverbed is a public place and was used for a city over 20 kilom long. The endless housing development »Le Serpent«, the Snake, actually does stretch the whole length of the winding riverbed.

As we flew over it on our information-gathering trip we were able to see the incredible size of this linear city. It starts in the densely built-up residential districts »Ariel« and »Venise«, directly near the city of Nice. The expressways also follow the course of the river.

From the small airport where we land we drive to one of the typical parts of town in a small segment of the »Snake«. And in several places we see people obviously still working on their houses. Though the project seems enormous, it offers many opportunities for individual development.

»The construction is very simple, consisting of unworked concrete and wooden girders, but there are no spatial partitions and no façades. Water and air are piped in, and gas and electric power are supplied, through vertical columns. Every resident is free to design his apartment according to his needs; the individual levels are a garden, as it were, in which he can erect his house. He needs no floor or roof, only the vertical protective elements. He is free of all constraints as far as building regulations and aesthetics are concerned.«

This freedom is also the reason many people are still busy working on their space. The »Snake« is not the only architectural type used. We have long been interested in a dominant feature of this city, the »Helix«, a gigantic spiral – a seemingly dynamically moving 240-meter-high residential high-rise.

Nouvelles 2001.

The »linear city« of Soria y Mata is reinterpreted here, and the space lattice city of Friedman, who was the co-author of the project, again tries to plead for the freedom to tailor urban spaces to the needs of residents.

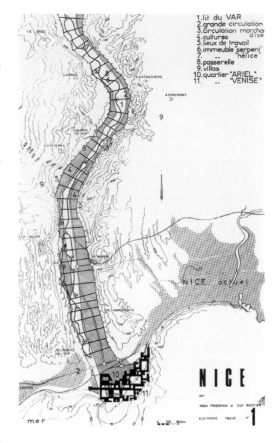

Chanéac (Jean Louis Rey) (1931–1993). The Crater Cities (Villes Cratères, 1963–68)

Different-sized rectangles form the grid of the city, but once we enter one of the courtyards we are confronted with a completely different geometry: Rounded, curving forms, including circles and ellipses, are predominant in the houses built on terraced slopes, scarcely more than seven stories high, but swooping up to a height of 20 stories at the corners.

»The Ville Cratère is an artificial landscape made of six elements«, Chanéac tries to systematize. »There are ›traffic canyons‹ corresponding to the former streets. The ›artificial hills‹ are built on the sides of these canyons and keep out the noise of traffic. On these hills are the buildings with offices on the street side and apartments on the courtyard side. An ›artificial plateau‹ has been located on the upper ledge of the artificial hills, intended for quiet traffic – pedestrian sidewalks and moving walkways. But mainly this level comprises communal and consumer facilities. Together these elements create a vast urban landscape.«

Chanéac is especially proud to show us that his years of experimentation with plastic modules have borne fruit here. The »cellules parasites« are mobile capsules, permanently in place or temporary, which allow volumes to be expanded to a surprising degree.

The apartments on the lower floors have very big terraces, so that up to four such plastic modules can be erected for supplementary needs such as play modules for children or hobby modules.

Chanéac goes below ground level only minimally, with long-distance traffic. Local traffic, open and visible, takes place at level 0, which is at the same time the pedestrian level between the dynamically rising rectangular blocks. Levels 2 through 8 are occupied by offices and businesses on the street side; there are also service facilities and storehouses, so that the dark zones can be well utilized. On the garden side, terraces are staggered from the second to the top floor, and face the lovely interior park.

»I think we should activate people psychologically as well. I see potential in creating an ›artificial landscape‹, a modification, continuation, and intensification of the natural landscape.«

Dahinden 1971; *Architectures experimentales* 2003.

350. Guy Rottier (with Yona Friedman), a future Nice, 1966–69.

351. Chanéac, Crater City, 1968. Cross section.
352. Chanéac, Crater City, 1963–68. Floor plan model.
353. Chanéac, Crater City, 1968. Detail of cross section.

»Landscape« is still one of the deepest longings architects have. We need to expand this term to include elements that have nothing to do with »nature«. Chanéac, for instance, creates an architectural and sculptural landscape that with its planted terraces is a close approximation of nature.

Thus Chanéac invents a variation of houses built on a terraced slope – a design that is so often advocated but far too rarely implemented.

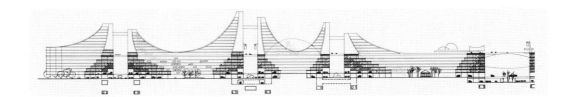

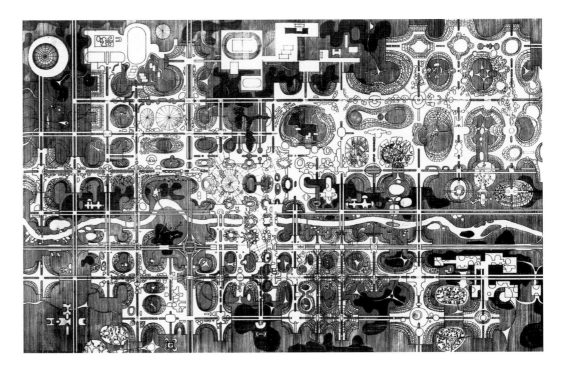

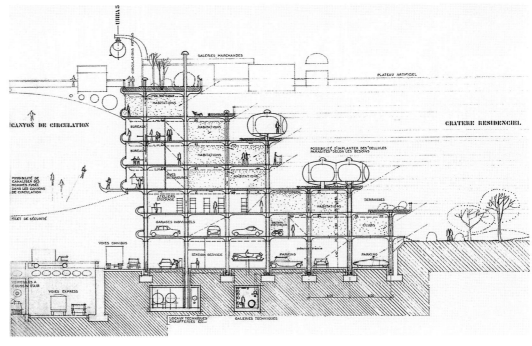

Paul Maymont. Paris under the Seine (Paris sous la Seine, 1962), the Suspended City of Paris (Ville suspendue, 1963), the Floating City near Marseille (Ville flottante, 1964), the Circular City Thalassa (1964), the Floating Cities of Tokyo (Villes flottantes Tokyo, 1963) and Kyoto, and the Lunar City (Ville lunaire, 1964)

The sprawl of Paris far into the surrounding countryside is one of the central problems of urban planners. A number of interesting solutions have already been found.

Paul Maymont has gone deep down and into the sky. His new housing development is located underground, under the Seine, to be exact. He places more than twelve stories under the riverbed. All traffic levels are above the bundled energy supply lines. Above them are all kinds of communal, commercial, and educational institutions. This removes traffic from the city itself and gives it back to strolling Parisians.

Now we accompany Paul Maymont to the outskirts of Paris. Here the architect introduces us to a truly daring project: The new city of Paris, putting a stop to further urban sprawl.

The huge cones whose silhouette glides gently from the top to the base are visible from a distance. Paul Maymont's postulation seems to be a commonplace: »*The problem of the city is a problem of density: We must build upward.*«

Maymont speaks about specific technological possibilities: »*Steel cables are the solution for the future. They allow us to suspend very heavy weights. The cables have been suspended from a central mast. Housing units have been hung In this basic structure, along with business streets, hanging gardens, and man-made hills.*«

In part, areas that are being redeveloped are overbuilt with cones, and the residents have simply moved into the upper regions.

Maymont is also optimistic regarding the »atmosphere« and believes that picturesque charm might unfold here as it did in historic cities. »*On the outskirts of Paris we've been experimenting and gaining experience – which we applied on a large scale in the Floating Cities and the Ring City.*«

We meet Paul Maymont the next day at the underwater railway station in Marseille. In ten minutes we are in the center of the Ville flottante – and again admire the archaic archetypes of the massive buildings. »Water is the future habitat of humanity«, explains Paul Maymont. »When Earth becomes too small or polluted, our big chance is on the water!«

The Ville flottante, the Floating City, was easy to recognize from very far away: There is a high central tower from whose top a silhouette curves down to the broad base, similar to what we saw on the outskirts of Paris. How do you get the city to float? »The city has eight stories below ground level – and these lie under the surface of the water, acting like a huge pontoon«, Maymont responds. »An air cushion for shock absorption is between the water and the bottom of the caisson, and this makes possible a suspended city whose modules are hung between the pre-stressed cables. The cables in turn are suspended from the central mast.« The central mast contains all energy supply and waste disposal lines. An express elevator brings us to the observation platform above the 50th floor – i.e., more than 350 m above sea level.

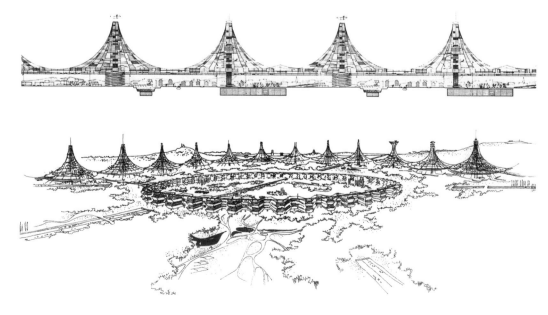

354. Paul Maymont, the Suspended City of Paris, 1963.
355. Paul Maymont, Thalassa, a city with half a million inhabitants, 1964.
356. Paul Maymont, Paris under the Seine, 1962.

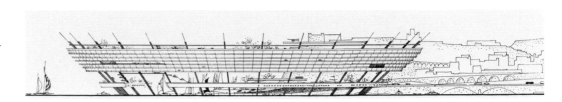

Looking across the water, we see three more giant cones still under construction. How large is this city intended to be?

»*We're planning to erect up to 20 cones 300 to 500 m in diameter. At that point the city will have between 15,000 and 20,000 inhabitants.*«

»You don't know our biggest project yet. Let's fly over the building site so that you can get a sense of a new city with half a million inhabitants – the city of Thalassa .The concept is truly impressive, but also convincing: A gigantic ring city surrounded by greenery no more than six stories high, with a surrounding semicircle of twelve suspended cities of the curved cone type we inspected at close quarters earlier.

It goes without saying that there are a corresponding number of jobs available for the half-million inhabitants, primarily in the tower buildings. Around the city is a 120-hectare forest, but in the center of town there is also a huge park, discreetly interspersed with playing fields and recreation areas, with educational and cultural facilities.

A long journey now takes us to a large Floating City in Japan. A very pleasant trip by speedboat takes us to the first of six city rings of Tokyo. From the landing, simultaneously the private marina, we are brought directly up to the roof by slanting elevators – and here is the helicopter landing strip as well. We have a good view of the mighty round of one of funnels, approximately 180 m in diameter but only eight floors high. The floors look as though they are skewered on slanting support pillars. All municipal community facilities are housed on a mezzanine floor. Paul Maymont explains a special feature of the city: It is assembled from modules and, like the cone city near Marseille, supported by multi-story submarine caissons, underwater floats anchored on the ocean floor whose top decks almost go up to water level.

»The entire structural system«, says Maymont, »has one characteristic that is eminently important for Japan: It is absolutely earthquake-proof.« Naturally the individual floors of the caissons are used, for garages, storage space, energy supply centers and for recreational activities that do not require sunlight. »*The rental space is located in the four suspended rings, and their tilt allows sunlight to fall continuously on the large plaza surrounded by buildings. All apartments have terraces facing inward and a splendid outward view of the landscape. The city is growing steadily and soon a traffic network will link points on the Bay of Tokyo. After the first six funnels, each housing 20,000 residents, more will be built until the city has a total of half a million inhabitants.*«

Paul Maymont has developed further the idea of the floating city, but again only an overflight gives us a halfway clear impression of the concept's scale.

Approaching by plane from far away we are initially misled, for we have the impression that we are heading for a reconstructed, Central American, pre-Columbian city. But the mighty archetypes house everything a modern city needs: apartments, places of work, leisure and educational facilities.

Admittedly we are not able to visit the most daring and exciting project: It is the Lunar City, the first attempt to settle the planet. »The ring-like building has room for 1,000 residents. The skeleton consists of steel tubes – and again of prestressed steel cables. Steel and plastic plates form the shell. The interior is air-conditioned and creates a small oasis.«

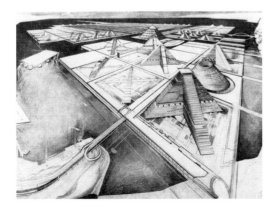

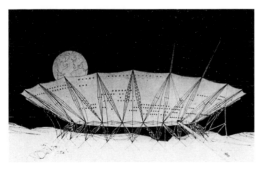

L'Avenir des villes 1964; Cook 1970; Dahinden 1971; *Stadt und Utopie* 1982; *Les visionnaires de l'architecture* 1965; *12 Villes Prospectives* 1965.

It seems that a rich imagination inspires Paul Maymont to plumb the broad spectrum of 1960s utopias.

Maymont goes below ground: The substructures of the modern cities actually form separate cities. Maymont builds upward: The inexorable urge to go higher, particularly in Asian towns, is a reality. Maymont goes out on the water: Floating Cities are realities when it comes to the technological sphere and have long been designed for residential and tourist apartment complexes. Finally, Maymont goes to the Moon: There has been silence regarding the settlement of the Moon, but official planning goes on largely unnoticed.

G. A. Jellicoe (1900–1980). Motopia, 1961

»Why does traffic, in order to be ›harmless‹, always has to be located underground?« wonders G.
A. Jellicoe. »I developed a better and cheaper system: Traffic moves above the houses, but not
along costly lanes, but directly on the rooftops.«

Together with the architect we get into the new car with a difference: The »silent car« has absolutely no emissions and its tires are practically noiseless, though only when used together with
the new whisper road surfacing.

And sure enough, after driving up the ramps to the skyways we can hardly hear, even with the
top down, the steady traffic that streams across the rooftops. And we enjoy the wonderful view,
not only of the strict geometry of the buildings of Motopia, but also of the big parks, with educational and leisure facilities amid the greenery.

Stadt und Utopie 1982.

Modern traffic technologies and urban planning are directly connected. The transition from steam to
electric locomotives meant a turning point in regional planning. Something similar might happen in the
case of cars. The visual presence of cars in cities need not be rejected wholesale.

Rem Koolhaas (b. 1944) and Zoe Zenghelis. The City of the Captive Terrestrial Globe (Ville du Globe captif, 1972, and Exodus, 1972)

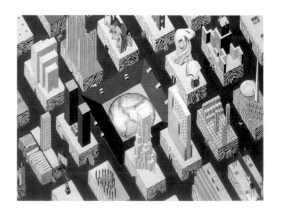

We stroll through a grid of streets consisting of uniform, closed, blocklike cubes of polished granite that can be entered only through small gates. What could be concealed inside? But when we
look up, we are surprised to see so many familiar buildings – representing all of recent architecture, they stand on the blocks, pedestals as it were.

Rem Koolhaas and Zoe Zenghelis boldly dip into the treasure chest of the 20th century and
present chiefly buildings that have not been built.

These include the scenery for an expressionist filmmaker, and Le Corbusier's skyscraper from
the Ville Radieuse. A high-rise looks into the interior of a church by Angelo Mangiarotti. Hermann
Finsterlin's fantastic formations perch delicately on a rooftop, and not far from them the pointed

362. Rem Koolhaas and Elia Zenghelis with Madelon Vriesendorp, and Zoe Zenghelis, Exodus or the Voluntary Prisoners of Architecture, 1972.

tower of the Trylon and Perisphere from the 1939 New York World Expo rises into the sky. The cubic landscapes of Kasimir Malevich's Architectones that tower over El Lissitzky's speaker's platform are impressive.

In the center of this architectural symposium is the captive terrestrial globe, below the level of the large plaza, separated from the architecture scene of the 20th century, confined in a kind of tetrahedron. How are we to interpret it? Here is how Rem Koolhaas sees it: »*The weight of the past can be made bearable only by being incorporated in tangible, palpable modernity. The mass exodus from the field of utilitarian architecture opens up a bright prospect.*«

After this instructive tour of architectural history we are confronted with very different dimensions: In a city jet that starts vertically we overfly London and have ourselves been part of an *Exodus*: Between three gigantic, parallel slab-like buildings with huge terraced landscapes lies a part of London, also captive; the huge building walls create clusters.

»*Our city*«, *says* Rem Koolhaas, »*gives prominence to specific aspects of the modern city, functionalism and capitalism, and at the same time criticizes them. Exodus is a symbolic narrative telling of the creation of an ideal metropolis that exerts a powerful attraction on the inhabitants of a real city – a run-down London. However, two big insurmountable walls prevent them from entering – they are the voluntary captives of the architecture.*«

Koolhaas 1978; *Inventionen* 1981; *Visionen und Utopien* 2002; *Architectures experimentales* 2003.

We remember Charles R. Cockerell's *The Professor's Dream*: He, too, imagined that a city could be a collage of the most prominent buildings in history.

Admittedly in Rem Koolhaas this montage has something ironic about it: We are not only chronologically placed in a historical grid, traditions, and memories, but we've domesticated the globe itself. The city of *Exodus* reminds us of the »continuous monument« of the Italian group Superstudio: The extreme positions of innovation are exhausted far beyond the limits of the conceivable – though in the totalitarian states there are enough examples of this radicalism. Many were not carried out, or not in their entirety.

François Schuiten (b. 1956). New Brussels, 1980

Is this another Metropolis? »Well, yes, there are certainly tensions«, admits François Schui-ten, »but this contrast between the old and the new is one of the attractive qualities of our city.«

We are standing in a small, historic square with narrow houses, each of them triaxial, but we go up a narrow flight of stairs to the attic and the view from the window is really overwhelming. The city seems telescoped, compressed. We can hardly make out the streets. But the architects have given free rein to their imagination in designing the slender skyscrapers. Spirals, cubes, cylinders, discs create a formally interesting vocabulary. The highways over bridges on high stilts crisscross through the city as automatically piloted flying objects flit soundlessly above and below the bridges.

Dethier 1994.

Strange – we are cast back into the 1920s and '30s: crowded skyscrapers, connecting bridges, overpasses, zeppelins: a very new kind of nostalgia.

Three planning teams and Marie-Hélène Jourda (b. 1955). The North City of Paris, 2004, 2014, 2034, 2064

What is supposed to be so special, or utopian, about this city, this suburb? Doesn't it resemble the many new developments, urban expansions, suburban structures?

It is not so much the formal manifestation but rather the process of planning that is so amazing and special. The city has become metamorphic and permanent, a city that changes constantly and at the same time endures.

»We started implementing our planning in 2004, and here before us are aerial photos of the city in 2014 and in 2034. Well, in 2064 we can clearly see what incredible metamorphoses the city has undergone. We must say that it's a living city. There's hardly another like it. The secret is this: The city has accepted both the past and future.«

»*We understand and respect the past*«, explains a team member, »*but we also love discovering the future, and have realized that permanence and metamorphosis are not opposites.*«

Our 2034 visit to the city – Saint Denis – is rather short and very strange. It is true we enjoy the »green lung« of Paris that has spread here, but it is partly a jungle, and there are shacks and floating huts in the moor. The inhabitants call themselves »shepherds« and use backpacks and dollies. Thanks to the 25-hour week – most people work only three days – the region is a popular destination for Parisians.

Strolling through the city 30 years later, in 2064, we sense its dynamism and liveliness, but also a little of its temporary and transitory nature. Paris North has totally changed. The region has become quiet and peaceful. The »green lung« has kept it that way. Saint Denis has become a rural place, though its inhabitants are now wealthy members of the middle class. Every imaginable leisure activity is available here, and there is an elegant hotel for the guests. A unique barter economy of the region's own products has developed. Active clubs and and organizations promote communication, and the place is a favorite vacation destination for people in the worlds of art and finance.

Here is a big surprise: The European Union has decided to settle 200 families from crisis zones in Central China here – as honorary citizens, not as immigrants. How will the tension between preserving their national identity and integration be resolved? Will the newcomers create a village within a village? A new challenge faces the city.

Jourda 2004; *Metamorph 9* 2004.

The Parisian architects, especially Marie-Hélène Jourda, are committed to »métamorphose durable«, lasting change, and have taken the initiative to do some unusual teamwork. Ms. Jourda again spells out familiar ground rules: maximum density, but not necessarily high-rises; a mix of activities and inhabitants; taking into account environmental concerns; use of renewable energy; three-dimensionality as a concept of the city. But all these problems must be approached universally and globally.

»During the planning we simply created a game. Three teams, each consisting of five members, took part – architects and other experts. Certain programs and ground rules were given. We respected that and we inspected the area very meticulously. But here's something strange: We didn't

363. François Schuiten, New Brussels, 1980.

364–366. Three planning teams, the north city of Paris. Models 2014, 2034, 2064.

spend more than two days working on the model. We barely knew each other, and yet we worked together in an exemplary fashion.«

The focus was work on the model, but conversations, discussions, and reflections were equally important. At all times the »players« were aware that one cannot plan a »finished« city, nor were they able to answer all the questions.

The playful element in architecture and even more in urban planning has always been controversial, since cities strictly follow political and social maxims, which do not indulge in playfulness. But every once in a while there are »sandpile planning sessions« that cannot be described as utopian at all. Admittedly it is debatable whether an urban district can be planned »from scratch« in two days even if the fifteen planners are experts; in the utopian realm, however, it is a wonderful process.

Vicente Guallart and Spanish and international («Star«) Architects. Sociópolis, the city of the future, 2002, 2010

We're off to the outskirts of Valencia in Spain. Vicente Guallart has developed the master plan and an elite group of international architects left their calling cards here and built a town of 2,500 housing units.

Guallart argues, and we agree: »In the 21st century we must build completely differently, not only technologically and artistically, but from a social point of view – that aspect must regain its importance once more.«

What are the architects' ideas concerning the society of this young century? What innovations and what goals do they have in mind?

Sociópolis is truly an ideal city. The ancient dream of people living next to and with each other has finally been fulfilled – no barriers, no prejudices, no social differences prevent the residents from living together peacefully. Not only is this the ideal city, but this is a model of the »world« that will gain general acceptance.

Naturally, »normal« families and couples predominate, but the needs of single people and single parents are addressed as equally important. There are special provisions for large families, immigrants from many cultures are welcome, there are no barriers for the disabled, and senior citizens can enjoy their old age in individual ways. What is more, the old and the young help and respect each other.

Communal living accommodations for various age groups or for meaningful socially mixed groups are available for those who wish to live in small intentional communities. It almost goes without saying that there is first-class care, counseling and assistance in all situations, cultural and athletic offerings, playgrounds, and shopping opportunities.

As we approach the city we observe that the formal aspect at any rate is still important: not only is there a range of dfferent geometric volumes, but also there is room for expressive and even biomorphic structures. »Naturally all forms are possible, but that isn't what it's all about. Our guideline is rather: ›My house is my neighborhood, my neighborhood is my house‹ – in other words, we are practicing very new and yet old forms of communication.«

Even as we stroll about in the public spaces we notice how many old people we meet in the company of young ones: walking, playing, chatting, relaxed and leisurely, as though everyone really had time for everyone else. »Well yes, we're a slow city. Our experence is that it's possible to combine one's professional and everyday life without being in a rush.«

Even as we enter the landscaped, park-like terrain, we are struck by the fact that we do not encounter a single car, only an occasional ambulance. The broad paths belong to the pedestrians, cyclists, scooter riders. We see completely new types of fast and maneuverable wheelchairs. Those who can't walk or use wheels take one of the electric trolleys, which are free of charge. »Here we have created an 150-unit old age home. One hundred students or singles live in the round tower. But the rich variety of social and cultural facilities keeps ghettos from forming and encourages contact between the residents.«

Thus the ancient concept of neighborhood, long believed to be dead, has been resurrected here. Neighborhoods here are relatively small, easily manageable units. »We have successfully followed the precept of our century: We must create a new synthesis between nature, technology, and social institutions.«

The architects keep coming back to another concern: »We create a bit of city life in the country, and a bit of country life in the city.« It goes without saying that the latest high-tech methods are used in the city, and of course all citizens benefit from these.

367. Vicente Guallart and 12 architects, Sociópolis near Valencia, Spain, 2003–10. Model.
368. Vicente Guallart and 12 architects, Sociópolis, Valencia, Spain, 2003–10. Simulation of final expansion.

Again we switch to the real world: The city is actually being built. In 18th- and 19th-century architectural fantasies, such as those of John Soane, Charles Cockerell, or E. S. Field (cf. chap. 6.2), the idea emerged that the designs of the best and most famous architects of all time should be brought together in an ideal city. Something like that is happening here.

The architects who have deposited their buildings here do not represent all periods but (almost) all countries. It is difficult to imagine how this conglomeration of completely heterogeneous structures could ever become a »city«.

The total area is divided into thirteen mostly narrow, long lots. The reason for their shape is the original agrarian structure of the region. Here the architects have neatly placed their little houses side by side, without the least regard for each other, let alone structure – or overall planning. As we stroll through the area – and that can be regarded as reality – we are struck by the formal aspects of a few buildings: for one, there is Greg Lynn – with his lush biomorphic norms.

»This is an architecture of plants instead of caryatids«, Greg Lynn explains his stylistic idiom. The decorative and almost baroque vocabulary is continued in the interior as well.

At the periphery of an atrium, there are four towers containing apartments partially combined with workshops. The façades are partly made of semitransparent textiles (workshop, atrium), and partly of metal grids and ceramic material.

The Netherlands group MVRDV presents its green spaces on the upper levels – raised vegetable gardens that increase the size of agricultural land. Toyo Ito houses his apartments and community institutions in large overlapping cylinders. Master planner Vicente Guallart builds a flexible, multifunctional tower. And Willy Müller erects a tall building with a supermarket and recycling level.

And what's futuristic about it? The fact that the infrastructure, which is old hat by now, has been slightly improved? There's nothing futuristic about building 150- or 100-unit accommodations for old people, the disabled, or singles, when it is well known by now that single-function conglomerations are passé.

And the sixty-four-thousand-dollar question is whether the tired idea of neighborhoods can actually be revived. The planners give special emphasis to a center for autistic people – why this group in particular, we wonder?

A purely pedestrian city of this size hardly seems realistic. Painfully long distances hardly contribute to social life, and electric trolleys would create enormous traffic jams.

Speaking of social life – the most important question is still: Which sections of the population could afford to live in this city? Many questions are still open – the future will provide the answers!

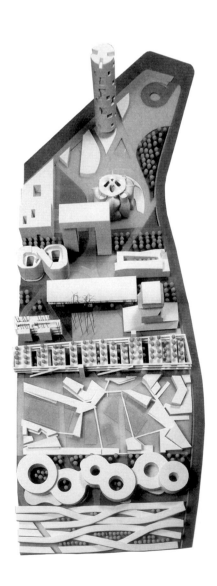

13.4. Germany, Switzerland

Merete Mattern. The urban landscape of Berlin, 1955–59, Ratingen, 1967, Bratislava, 1968, and Fort Lincoln, Washington, D.C., 1969

In her own words, Merete Mattern's idealistic motivation is more than a commonplace: » *I couldn't understand why people live in less than beautiful spaces, imprisoned in dark houses, square rooms with roofs over their heads, closed tight towards the top.* «

The part of Berlin we're heading for now seems to be a gigantic game of pick-up sticks, a confused pile of firewood. Merete Mattern is interested in more than an interesting, expressive stylistic idiom: »*Human beings and human society are ›partly autonomous‹ members of a biological, micro- and macrocosmically controlled environmental system; every cultural system implies an intervention in a natural system, and the task of architects and city planners is to continue reintegrating culture and nature on a higher level.* «

If we believe that nature is a free and expressive interplay of forms, Mattern's urban expansion really does have a biomorphic character: We are unable to discover a single right angle in the urban pile of sticks from which a tower rises in the center, as it were on the mountaintop. This stylistic idiom is condensed in chain-type houses that form beautiful, dynamic open spaces.

Next, we visit Ratingen near Düsseldorf, where we see a similar urban structure. The park landscape directly merges into the lush vegetation of the terraced apartments, which house close to 25,000 persons.

Mattern's stylistic idiom is revealed particularly impressively when we overfly Bratislava, which has close to 160,000 inhabitants. »I tried to create something like new climates inside and outside this part of town«, says Mattern. »The tall ridges, protection against the wind, the specific plantings on buildings and on the ground, the way wind and sun were taken into consideration all contribute to a synthesis of nature and architecture.«

Mattern went a step further in the town of Fort Lincoln in Washington, D.C. The buildings here are an organic continuation of the hill landscape, accented by individual towers. The latter are not there merely for visual reasons – they also store solar energy, which is tapped when necessary. This way, and also by means of man-made rain from these towers, the urban climate can be modified.

»In the center of town, instead of a church or palace, there is a music and information center serving local inhabitants to express themselves in conventional and new media«, says Mattern. A complementary project is still being developed. It is meant to promote the total mobility of the modern urban population. The compact communities are universally mobile, so that they can settle at short notice on water or land.

Dahinden 1971; Werner 1981; *Stadt und Utopie* 1982.

Mattern's work, which goes back to the 1950s, continues the expressionist tradition, but surprisingly seems to anticipate the deconstructivist movement of the 1980s.

The fact that Merete Mattern submits her projects to competitions could be an indication that she does not consider their implementation to be impossible.

369. Merete Mattern, urban landscape, Berlin, 1955 to 1959.
370. Merete Mattern and Team, project for Ratingen near Düsseldorf, Germany, 1967.

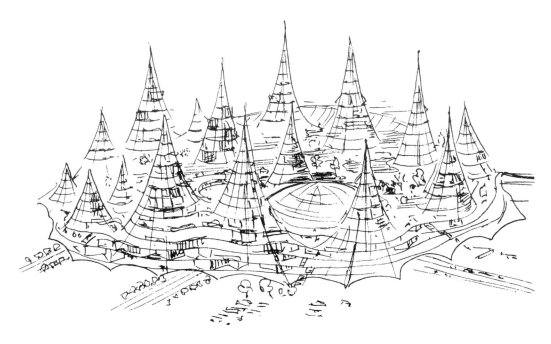

Frei Otto (b. 1925). The Arctic City with a climate shell, 1959, 1971, and the city of suspended roofs, 1960

The long journey was worth it: From the airport of Arctic City, the arctiexpress brings us directly into the city without our missing the pleasant temperature of the plane. We are in an amazing world: The houses with their gardens stand in rows and groups amid lush vegetation, a moor with abundant trees and shrubbery.

When we look up, we see the answer to the mystery: A fine net stretches above a vast area. The meshes of the polyester net are filled in with double-shelled insulating pieces of plastic. An impressive, noiseless air-conditioning system creates the almost Mediterranean climate. The clean cold air drawn in from outside does not need to be purified. It is heated and raised to the necessary pressure by atomic energy in large subterranean generators, flows below ground level as it heats it, to the blow-off vents – the stale, cooled air is blown out again.

»Of course we can also produce something like seasons«, says Frei Otto. »It is easy to regulate the air temperature. However, the difference in temperature between outside and inside should not be too great. In the polar nights we can imitate sunlight under the dome, and vice versa: In summer movable sails provide protection against a superabundance of sunlight.«

At a width of 2,000 m, the dome covers a surface of three km^2. It is 240 m high, making it possible to build a few high-rises as well. At this time, Arctic City has 20,000 inhabitants, and 10,000 more may be added. As needed, more domes, connected underground, will be added. The small town is hardly different from a European one. We are pleased to note that there is no automobile traffic.

»Vehicles, and especially delivery trucks, have to pass through an air lock. They then park underground. On the surface there are only conveyor belts and electric cars for internal traffic. This is how we keep the air clean.«

But why do people have to settle in the Arctic of all places? Isn't there enough room on the Earth? »There are certain reasons for it«, Frei Otto informs us. »What tempts people primarily is the search for mineral resources – oil, uranium, and diamonds. And of course another reason is a

373. Walter Jonas, the funnel city of Intrapolis, 1960.

series of important research projects in a number of different fields. Finally, strategic and prestige issues motivate a number of nations to have a presence here.«

Our journey now takes us to a city of a very different character. Tall, central tent formations are grouped around a dome.

Frei Otto assures us: »The city actually does have something to do with tents, for the buildings are cable net structures. The logical result is the curve of the silhouette, with lower floors that project for some distance.«

The housing units are suspended and offer every comfort. The strong central support pillar provides the infrastructure. The central, fully air-conditioned dome contains a rich spectrum of community facilities, interspersed with large green spaces and recreational areas.

Schippke 1970; Cook 1970; Dahinden 1971.

Otto's roofed-over Arctic City is a parallel, but also an alternative to Buckminster Fuller's geodesic dome over Manhattan. In Frei Otto's design the shell is held by excess pressure – in other words, it is a pneumatic construction. One wonders how high the excess pressure in the interior has to be to keep the climatic shell in place. Examples implemented to date have never exceeded the dimensions of sports and exhibition halls. In the field of cable net construction, Frei Otto has successfully implemented an important project: The large sports halls in Munich show that the roofing becomes complicated and difficult, while foundations and / or bracing take up an enormous amount of room. The concept for heating the Arctic city does seem to be oversimplified. Moreover, confidence in heating by atomic energy has declined considerably. However, the project has gained a certain degree of concreteness because the German company Farbwerke Hoechst has expressed its interest.

Walter Jonas (1910–1979). The funnel city of Intrapolis, 1960/65

The ground level is now reserved for cars and green spaces. With Walter Jonas we speed to the root point of the funnel city. The car is automatically removed and an express elevator, first vertical, then slanting, brings us up to the penultimate floor: Walter Jonas welcomes us in his apartment, which has a large, luxuriantly landscaped terrace. He explains his intentions: »*The name Intrapolis refers to the fact that there is increasingly less space to counteract the imbalance created by too much extroversion and to give space to the introversion we all psychologically need, Here, we mean to restore balance.*«

The »districts« of the funnel city are grouped around a central square, a patio in the interior of the building. The square is landscaped with many trees and shrubs, and this level also houses the schools and kindergartens. The rest of the floors consist of apartments, each of which has an open space. The topmost ring, the large roof terrace, is landscaped and intended for the use of the community. We stroll along a promenade past cafés, restaurants, and kiosks. And from this circular path there are bridges to the next unit – these are the city's most important means of communication. An apartment needs to be a place of self-contemplation and individualization. People who wish to rent or buy an apartment simply buy the necessary square-meter volume and build their home according to their wishes and needs.

»Above all, it is necessary to keep the surface of the Earth unspoiled in spite of the rise in population. The funnel city touches the Earth's surface only on a small surface.«

The city is a structural-engineering challenge: The base – the foundation – is a flat-bottomed four-story structure, a counter-cone, in which the reinforced concrete cantilever girders are anchored as a type of wall disks. The slabs of the individual floors are inserted between them.

The above-ground core, a continuation of the underground part, comprises ten stories. This is where the administration, cinemas, supermarkets, and the hospital, on the top floor, are housed.

»My ›Cité intra‹, the funnel city, is universal. As we speak, this type of cty is being built on the surface of the ocean in North Africa. We might build it just as well in a swamp or moor. And it goes without saying that it is possible to add on to the Cité intra: In Honolulu we are currently building 38 of these funnels, giving us a city of over 100,000 inhabitants.«

»You have now seen the round-tunnel city. Now I'd like to show you the second type. It's preferable to view it from the air.«

The uppermost promenade terraces include a landing strip for helicopters, and Jonas has already requisitioned a special machine that can attain the speed of a small jet. We now fly over Bremerhaven. The southern outskirts are quite unusual: There is no endless urban sprawl but rather a compact, geometrical large-scale grid of six funnel cities.

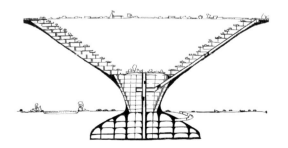

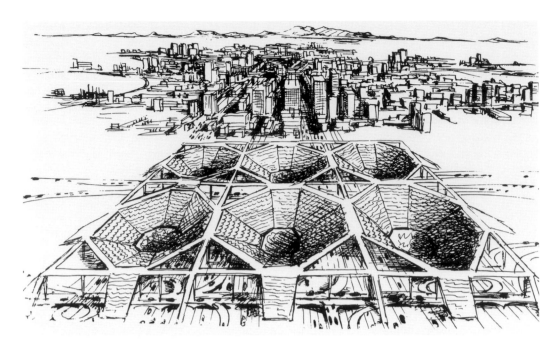

374. Walter Jonas, the funnel city of Intrapolis, 1960.
375. Werner Ruhnau, air-conditioned city, three-dimensional load-bearing structure with dwellings suspended over existing older buildings. Ruhr district, Germany, 1964. Model.
376. Rudolf Doernach, the biotectal city, 1964.

»Basically the principle is the same«, explains Walter Jonas, »only here instead of a circular form I chose a hexagon. That is how I can shore up the funnels one against the other even better.«

The top platforms, where many facilities offer leisure, educational, and social opportunities, have been logically interlinked. Slanting ramps and elevators connect them with the ground level.

Les visionnaires de l'architecture 1965; Dahinden 1971; *Stadt und Utopie* 1982; Thomsen 1994; *12 Villes Prospectives* 1965; Schippke 1970.

Walter Jonas was very close to implementation: In 1970 implementability was tested and the German Renters' Association began planning ten Intrapolis units. Was the builders' lack of financial resources only a pretext because people got scared of their own boldness?

The exterior sides of the funnel are occupied by corridors that encircle it and provide access. The peripheral funnels also have no view of the surroundings. This is not a problem if, like Walter Jonas, we look at life as being more introverted with respect to space and the community. The »outside« is occupied by a stream of traffic as it is.

One questionable aspect continues to be the fact that the quality of the housing probably varies greatly depending on which direction the apartment faces.

Werner Ruhnau (b. 1922). An air–conditioned city in the Ruhr, 1964

Werner Ruhnau has based his work on one of Yona Friedman's space cities in the Ruhr and raised them to a very different level by a sensational move: He has corrected the weather. »We installed rows of connected balloons and then built spray rocket stations. The landing runways for planes run at right angles to the main direction from which low-pressure areas in our zones mostly approach. Gathering fronts are fought with rockets or occasionally from planes by seeding with silver iodide.«

The city is heated by infra-red radiation.

12 Villes Prospectives 1965.

Weather modification has been a recurrent idea in recent decades. The notions of Werner Ruhnau, who has spent a great deal of time working on compressed-air ambiance, probably have only theoretical value. The important conclusion to draw here is that humanity is still practically powerless in the face of vast natural catastrophes but also of everyday weather. Together with the French painter and all-round artist Yves Klein, Ruhnau developed additional projects involving »aero architecture«.

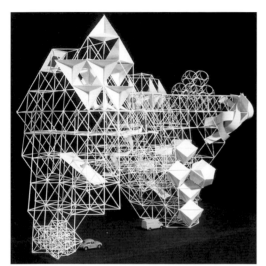

Rudolf Doernach. The Biotectal City, 1964

Free, organic, biological forms greet us as we visit the city. Doernach speaks very optimistically about the effect of his architecture: »It is no longer a stiff, constructed, fixed environment, but like a biological organism continuously changes. This growing, shrinking, and adapting will loosen up societal rigidity.«

Our first journey takes us to faraway northern regions of eternal ice. By a process of gas condensation Doernach has produced artificial icebergs and melted many varied and strange spaces in them that could be used commercially.

Near Marseille, on the open sea, Doernach has built his Hydropolis I, employing reusable pneumatic constructions as a kind of framework. A proliferation of microorganisms is established on these pneums, comparable to corals perhaps. These form a sufficiently massive frame for the city and give it a fascinating, sculptural appearance.

Hydropolis II was created in a similar way, but here plastic foam was used as a framework. After the structure was reinforced, this was melted away.

»The city must meet the conditions of the complex, dynamic process called ›life‹«, says Doernach. »That is why it must be a functional likeness of a human being.«
Dahinden 1971; *Stadt und Utopie* 1982.

Many of the utopian city projects are completely capable of being implemented by using all possible technological means, if we disregard the economic and social problems involved. On the other hand, as far as the organic and biological sphere is concerned, there seem to be hardly any indications that controlled growth is not possible on such a large scale.

In his fantasies Doernach goes a step further: »Perhaps it would be important for peace studies to address the development of self-reproducing, fruit-bearing houses for developing countries.«

Eckhard Schulze–Fielitz (b. 1929). Space City, the Cité spatiale, 1960–65

Schulze-Fielitz worked with Yona Friedman; they jointly developed a few projects, and so the architects' arguments are very similar. Both planners begin with a neutrally usable lattice structure consisting of modular elements. The structure can be very flexibly filled according to need.

Schulze-Fielitz takes us to the outskirts of Berlin, where he has succeeded in implementing an imposing, large-scale project. For the longest time, we drive through a lush green landscape before approaching the compact structure. How is it possible that there is no chaos in the midst of this individual freedom?

We realize the planner's intentions during our walk: the tension-filled contrast between the total efficiency of the prefabricated lattice structure and the total individuality of the often droll and kitschy »implants« of the users. »The constructed space, that is, the basic structure, and the non-constructed space, improvisation or individual adaptation, are coordinated by the modular system. But in a free society perfect planning is neither possible nor desirable. That means unpredictable development, tailored to the needs of the residents.«

»The space city is an agglomeration of various spatial structures that follows development. The characteristic style of the structure organizes the inevitable proliferation. There is freedom in the infinite possibilities of the combination.«

The compact city not only promotes contact and communication, but also offers economic advantages: Heating becomes more efficient, and automatic air-conditioning becomes possible.

Once more, Schulze-Fielitz praises the advantages of his city: Multi-story inhabited load-bearing structures bridge large spans by their great static height. In the centers where there is dense traffic, the town is detached from the ground, and vehicular traffic moves on the ground itself. It is possible to solve traffic problems because it becomes possible to have higher density in population centers by building over traffic surfaces and water courses, by keeping entire levels free for traffic or parking, and by rigorously separating various types of traffic.«
Dahinden 1971; *Architectures experimentales* 2003; *12 Villes Prospectives* 1965.

Flexibility, modifiability, and variability have increasingly preoccupied architects since the beginning of the 1960s. One of the standard systems consists of filling in fixed supporting structures with flexible elements of many different types. There has been only minimal implementation, in Japan and at exhibitions.

377. Eckhard Schulze-Fielitz, Space City, 1960 to 1965.
378. Eckhard Schulze-Fielitz, diagram of the Space City, 1959.

Wolfgang Döring (b. 1934). The city of PVC cells, 1965

Plastics are finally gaining ascendancy, after many setbacks in the 1960s. Finally structural engineering and fire hazard problems have been successfully dealt with.

»We've developed the new technologies and continued to develop structural engineering«, declares Wolfgang Döring proudly. »And thus it was possible to stack and interlock serially produced residential modules up to twelve stories high: We've created new districts at a third of previous construction costs and in one-fifth the time.«

We express our surprise at the equilibristic trick of stacked and projecting modules. »Naturally we can't avoid using solid structural engineering; each main block and all building parts connected with the ground have an inner structure: an interior steel construction forms the basic framework, only the projecting parts are held in place by a system of steel cables that at the same time stabilize the entire system.«

»It's like compelling automobile designers to go through an apprenticeship as cartwrights before beginning their studies in order to learn how to build horse-drawn carriages.«

Domus 4/1967; Wedewer, Kempas 1970; Dahinden 1971; *Stadt und Utopie* 1982.

Like so many others, this concept was developed before the big 1973 energy crisis. Later there would have been objections to the large cooling surfaces.

The ascendancy of plastics was surely one of the great utopias. Wolfgang Döring is by no means one of your utopian dreamers. He's an experienced architect who has worked very specifically on prefabrication and new technologies. He can look back on a series of achievements. He did not succeed in implementing the stacked houses, let alone a whole city of them.

Jules Egli and Josef Lackner (1931–2000). The Anticity, 1964–66

We're in perfect agreement with the analyses Egli and Lackner share with us at the outset: »*Nothing is static – isolation is deadly... Human beings and the natural world around them together form a harmonious whole. Let's stop building developments all over the landscape. From now on environmental planning must leap in a vertical direction. In ›cities with a future‹ there must again be a ›home‹ for the human heart and spirit.*«

The result of these reflections, however, is very surprising, for even at a great distance we see a massive block with a silhouette that stands out. The impression from close up is as though a high-rise had simply come crashing down in the middle of the landscape. The fact that the countryside is directly adjacent to it is an additional argument for the Anticity: »*This design regains the wide landscape for every resident. The people and their city are part of a whole, part of the landscape in which they are rooted.*«

Now we are facing a huge wall almost half a kilometer long. Up to ten stories of individual, cell-like residential units are stacked on top of each other. Egli and Lackner show us one of the housing units: In principle, they are maisonettes; we like the three-dimensionally curvy figuration of the details: The stairs, kitchen and bath, entryway, and storage rooms are modeled in colorful plastic and add sculptural accents.

But our admiration is somewhat dampened: »Unfortunately this is a prototype we were not able to produce. It's too soon – we don't have the technology to do it.«

So, as we view another housing unit, we have to be content with the type of conventional maisonette apartment we've seen in many other buildings. The architects speak of the tremendous economic advantages, and we learn more about the construction and infrastructure. Excellent provisions have been made for leisure, shopping, community activities, and games – with an ever-present view of the lovely natural surroundings.

Anti-Stadt 1966.

The architects' theses may have been quite innovative 40 years ago, or at least not common property – but for us, today, they seem to be commonplace, and did not have very much to teach us.

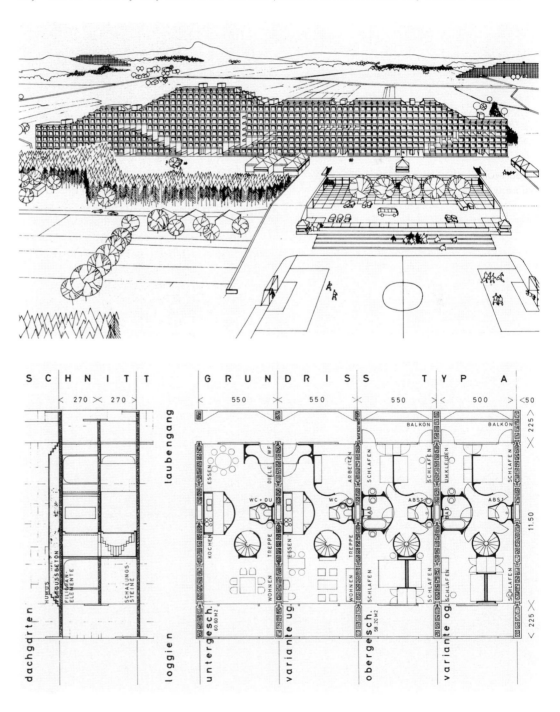

380. Jules Egli, Josef Lackner, Anticity, 1964–66.
381. Jules Egli, Josef Lackner, Anticity, 1964–66.
Floor plan and section.

382. Fritz Haller, Total City – integral urban, final expansion of the quadrinomial unit of the third magnitude, 1968.

Fritz Haller (b. 1924). The Total City – integral urban, 1968

Before we take off to get an aerial view of the gigantic grid city, which has six million inhabitants, Fritz Haller tries to expound his mathematical system to us. It is hard for us to judge whether the huge number of figures and geometrical diagrams is actually a sign of optimal, rational urban planning.

»The deciding factor is prevailing ›orders‹«, explains Fritz Haller. »These begin with units of zero order – family space – and go on to units of the first, second, third, fourth, and fifth order. The units accumulate systematically. In the end, the new six-million city came into being.«

We now fly over this monstrously large structure, Construction Phase Z, with its endless grids. These are embedded in green recreational spaces with lakes and rivers and open country. Admiittedly, the landscape and topography seem a little strange, almost denatured, and Fritz Haller confirms our observation, explaining: »We leveled hills and undulating terrain and corrected the courses of rivers.«

Of course, we have no sympathy for these consequences of a truly »total« city. The dominant features of the city are the countless high-rises comprising 24 residential floors and 1,250 residential units each, hardly distinguishable from conventional buildings.

But after our landing, which, of course, is not possible directly in the city, we are able to experience the ingeniously devised traffic system. Fritz Haller shares the following information with us: »People walk short distances. For somewhat longer distances, there are moving walkways at various speeds. However, the absolutely innovative medium is the automated freeway. It consists of electronically steered four-person electric vehicles. These automated vehicles run on a multi-story system of traffic lanes. At their departure and arrival points the automated vehicles are stored in a kind of paternoster elevator. From these the vehicles swing into shared traffic lanes, forming a loose procession of 20 units.«

It is really fascinating – we are reminded of a ballet – how the little cars now separate, rejoin each other, form new clusters, and are in constant, swift motion.

Haller 1968.

In the Total City we experienced something that had always worried us: the transformation of a system, of a diagram, of a mathematical calculation into a seemingly »perfect« city.

We are reminded of an early example that was never built: Ludwig Hilberseimer's gigantic big-city visions. The attack on natural topography during the last three millennia is possibly a factor of urbanization. Today we find it hard to understand, since we now have a different relationship to the natural landscape.

NASA team. Lunar station, 1970
Frei Otto (b. 1925). Pneumatic lunar station, 1972

The great challenge followed soon after Neil Armstrong's 1969 lunar landing: We were called on to study possibilities for human housing on the Moon. And together with other experts and institutes we submitted our proposals, which were tested at the next lunar landing.

A NASA team developed metal containers, and initially four units were joined together, a completely autonomous group with all that a town requires. But Frei Otto's starting point was to work with pneumatic shells, and so, thanks to their minimal transportation weight, he established a type of towns on the Moon.

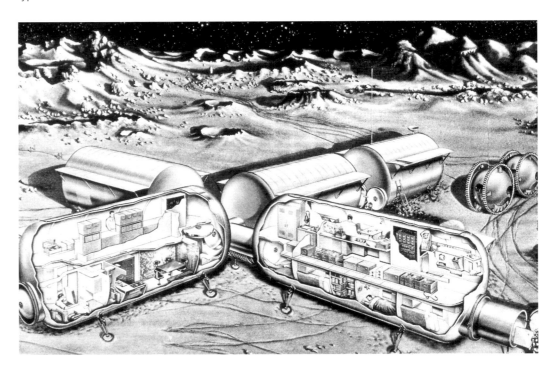

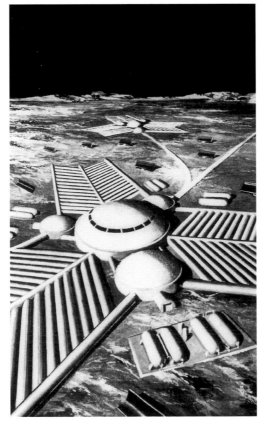

383. NASA team, lunar station, 1970.
384, 385. Frei Otto, pneumatic lunar station, 1972.

Doubtless these were utopias, although their technical feasibility was definitely within the bounds of possibility. Drawings from the 1970s seem somewhat naïve to us today and seem like something akin to science fiction. Space technology and science, and space research have experienced an enormous upsurge since then, but no one now speaks of human settlements on the Moon.

Justus Dahinden (b. 1925). Radio City, 1970, Kiryat-Ono, Tel Aviv, 1971, and New York 1972

No, Radio City has nothing to do with radio, though it does have to do with the radii of the circles and paraboloids of which the city was composed. »*This climbable macrostructure of the urban functional unit*«, says Justus Dahinden, »*is seen as a natural prototype. The interior of the hill assumes the function of an urban public space and houses facilities that meet general needs in a stimulating audiovisual milieu.*«

The outside of the gigantic paraboloid is faced throughout with housing units. A slanting elevator brings us to the top terrace, which has a helicopter landing strip. From here, we overlook the architectural landscape that spreads before us like a geometrized mountain range. The lush vegetation planted on the terraces reinforces the impression that we are looking at a natural landscape. But we find it difficult to imagine an interesting dynamics explained by Dahinden: »*The city can grow or shrink, for units can be continually added or taken away. It is therefore not possible that the core of the city is blocked by its own substance, as happens with cities today.*«

From the terrace we take the elevator five stories down and find ourselves on a kind of ridgeway that horizontally connects individual residential districts. From one of the comfortable apartments we enjoy one more view of the beautiful landscape, then leave for the center of public venues. Our first impression is an amazing flood of light. It almost feels like being in the open air. »*The building's dome*«, says Dahinden, »*is closed with a kind of air cushion under the upper thrust collar. At the same time the air cushion can be used as a film projection surface.*«

The next town, Kiryat Ono, is located in the conurbation of Tel Aviv. Our helicopter lands smoothly on the upper level. We observed while approaching that the architect has retained the principle of Radio City but simplified it substantially: The base of a single huge cone forms this leisure city. All residential functions are fulfilled by many kinds of variable containers consisting of flexible plastic modules. We take the panorama elevator to the lowest level, and even the elevator ride is an experience in itself, since we see glimpses of the large number of activities that are taking place here this late afternoon. Down below we are dazzled, confused, and fascinated by the wealth of sensual impressions. There is something bewildering about the way these overlap acoustically and visually.

»*The public space of communities*«, says Dahinden, »*is a ›manipulable volume‹. We have total mobility here. Only the indoor swimming pool and the ice rink are permanent facilities, but here, too, retractable platforms make different uses possible.*«

386. Justus Dahinden, Radio City, 1970.

387. Justus Dahinden, Kiryat-Ono leisure city, Tel Aviv, Israel, 1971.
388. Justus Dahinden, Piper-Pile Project for waterfront, New York, USA, 1972.

In contrast to the circular form of the complex at large, the secondary structure follows a triangular or hexagonal pattern. A lattice structure is placed on the massive base with underground garages and air-conditioning. Again, a transparent dome is the upper boundary. Greenery is reserved only for the terraces of the housing units and seems to be banished from the recreation area.

We now witness an interesting scene: Large exhibition walls soundlessly slide to one side and are stacked in a bundle; immediately, elements of a platform slide from another bundle and are grouped around an unfolded revolving stage: An experimental theater is giving evening performances.

Again we go up, this time to the »control center«, and the stage manager demonstrates further mobility tricks: movable platforms for scenery, retractable projection walls, all kinds of light and sound effects, screen-like partitions for active community activities.

Dahinden does not share our concern about a glut of offerings, overstimulation, hedonism – stress. He concludes by saying: »*Leisure must be seen as a time of liberation; it can be attained wherever society is in control of systems instead of being controlled by them. True leisure is a time of learning as well and is inseparable from work. It is a daily occurrence. Leisure activity implies participation, a change of roles, and playful, creative productivity without a profit motive, in all realms of life other than people's daily jobs.*«

Our next journey also takes us overseas, to New York. We assume that even here Dahinden was averse to high-rises. Our visit on the waterfront of the Hudson River confirms this: The »Piper Pile«, the result of a competition, once again pays homage to the idea of the hill city.

»I avoided the conventional high-rise form«, declares Justus Dahinden. »We created a hill-shaped leisure city above piers that are no longer used. Outside, terraced housing modules have been inserted in the load-bearing reinforced concrete superstructure. The conical ring is raised above the water.«

At the foot of the residential hill, a busy marine life unfolds. There are interesting views of the city from the terraces. Between the residential modules certain areas are left open for lush vegetation: The poplars and cypresses are a few meter high already. »*There is transit under the two piers that have been bridged. The piers are available at all times for the recreation of Manhattanites*«, explains Dahinden.

What is planned for the huge dark zone of the core? We can see for ourselves – and in spite of all differences, the leisure and educational area reminds us strongly of Kiryat-Ono.

Dahinden 1972, 2005.

In fact Justus Dahinden did successfully implement a recreation center on a small scale: the »Schwabylon« in Schwabing, the artists' quarter of Munich. It stayed in business no more than eight years, and finally failed.

What has endured – though not in every case — is a similar type of complex: the large movie complexes with restaurants, shopping, and games that have sprung up by the thousands all over the world and have reached dimensions close to those found in Dahinden's visions.

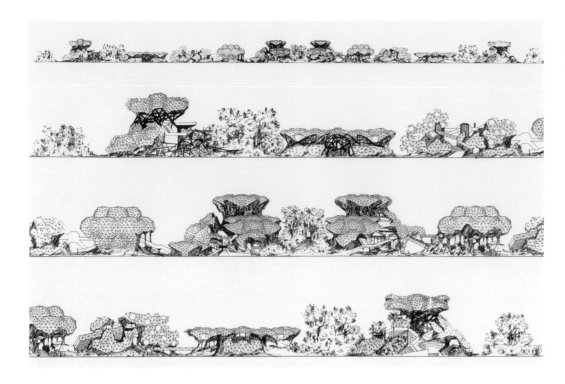

389. Günter Günschel, settlement of Teerhof in the Weser island, Bremen, Germany, 1978.
390. Leon Krier, Atlantis, 1987. Picture by Carl Laubin.

Günter Günschel (b. 1928). The settlement of Teerhof on the Weser island, Bremen, 1978

From afar we seem to see the silhouette of a dense forest against the morning sky. As we approach, we see that the forms are much more varied, more three-dimensional, and luxuriant: This is sculptural architecture of a very special kind.

»People often say that structural consistency and three-dimensional architecture are opposites. I believe that with this small suburb I've proved it's just the other way round.«

Now we are close enough to see that the richly differentiated silhouettes consist of very distinct lattice structures, whose basic form is dome-shaped formations that overlap and penetrate each other. The center in particular with its communal venues is of interest to us. We have a wonderful experience of space: After going up wide, commodious stairs, we enter an expressive interplay of light and shadows. Transparent glass domes alternate with the twilight of niches, caves, and ramps, a virtuoso synthesis of construction and sculpture.

Inventionen 1981.

For long periods, the tension between structural, functional and sculptural, emotional tendencies defines the architectural scene after 1950. Günter Günschel attempts an interesting synthesis, something that is still a rare phenomenon.

Leon Krier (b. 1946). Atlantis, 1987

»Yes«, says Leon Krier, »I conjured up the past – Greece, Rome, the Renaissance. But why shouldn't we give new life to the greatest architectural monuments of all times and reinterpret them? In the old cities everybody feels much happier, so why don't we build ›old cities‹? There is only one true architecture – classical architecture. In Roman archiecture especially we find everything we require and can use today.«

The timing of our visit is just right. At this very moment preparations are being made for a big opening ceremony. They're unrolling the red carpet, palm trees grace the arcades and landings, well-dressed men are having discussions, and on the steps under the dramatic arch there is a table for the ceremony. Expectant people are standing on the balconies.

Before the ritual begins, we have time to look at the architecture. The stairs are flanked by wooden arcades on the right, and by a hall of round arches on the left. On the portal building in front of us there is a temple with a wooden roof framework. Behind it is a mighty ten-column temple on a massive foundation. If we follow the perspectives toward the back, we find another tem-

ple with a wooden roof, an obelisk, a columned hall, and finally a steep pyramid: The sun is reflected in its golden tip, and over it all is a bright blue sky.

Thomsen 1994; Vercelloni 1994.

The brief period of the so-called »postmodern era« in the 1980s gave rise to a new eclecticism. The classical vocabulary was sometimes alienated, treated ironically, and reinterpreted, but conservative trends were clearly apparent. The fine work of Leon Krier, and to some extent of his brother Rob Krier, must be seen in this context.

Hans Dieter Schaal (b. 1943). The public municipal stage, 1980

We can't help thinking of the urban visionaries of the Italian Renaissance, especially Sebastiano Serlio with his theater cities, when we walk through the streets of Hans Dieter Schaal.

The streets are a conglomeration of modern styles, peppered here and there with historical »Italianità«, and a trace of de Chirico. But it is remarkable that in the end all this colorful formal diversity combines into a completely reinterpreted harmony of cntrasting styles, like old parts of town where the centuries stand peaceably side by side.

Hans Dieter Schaal tells us what ideas were behind his urban visions: »Turning imagination inside out, making dreams accessible, sharing them with others: street space as a public stage. Creating places whose form, content, and meaning are as complex as human beings themselves.«

And we are happy to admit that this walk between past, present, and future gave us extraordinary pleasure.

Inventionen 1981.

Urban planners, curators of monuments, and architects have been putting a lot of effort into preserving and producing the harmony of the city. But that harmony has been an illusion for a long time now. Hans Dieter Schaal takes us to a lovely variation of a »collage city«.

391. Hans Dieter Schaal, Stadtbühne (municipal stage), 1980.

Francesco Marino di Teana (b. 1920). The city sculpture, 1965

In Marino di Teana we meet an excellent sculptor. His sculptures are abstract volumes, steles, tension-filled arrangements. »It has long been common knowledge«, argues di Teana, »that the compact center of the city, and especially of the American city, is actually a sculpture.«

This phenomenon has now become worldwide: The Asian megacities, too, have city centers, concentrations in volume and mass, so that we can now perceive them as plastic art. »Architecture becomes sculpture – and yet it is possible to think of this the other way round: Using the formal principles of sculpture as a starting point, we arrive at architecture.«

»We can make a building out of any good sculpture, can declare plastic arrangements to be a city«, says Marino, and his new city is actually a huge ensemble of significant volumes. Provided with all services, every group of buildings has 15,000 to 20,000 residents. A distinguishing feature, however, is that the city is now surrounded by a natural landscape and there is no urban sprawl.

L'Avenir des villes 1964; Wedewer, Kempas 1970; *Stadt und Utopie* 1982.

There are no cities that are »one hundred percent modeled« sculpturally. Their artistic character is the result of our projections and our interpretations. Sculptural city centers are primarily the result of economic, political, and societal forces.

William Katavolos. The Chemical Marine City, 1960

And again we encounter fantastic, lush forms like huge sea flowers. But, as Katavolos explains, the backgrounds are now different: »*Chemistry opens up new possibilities in architecture ... Forms burst into existence like explosions. My architecture is immediate, constantly capable of change in terms of desired stability, predetermined directions, and predictable periods of time.*«

Katavolos envisions a great goal: the synthesis of human beings and their environment, the dissolution of the boundary between subject and object. Both have one thing in common: biochemistry. »I have liberated architecture – and the human race – from the force of gravity and from immobility, and have taken life back to its origin: the ocean.«

Colossal, ring-shaped cities spread on the ocean. They resemble enormous corals or crystals: both elements that manifest growth under completely different conditions. »And my buildings grew in a similar way«, Katavolos tells us. »They are chemical processes in a macroprocess.« He describes the formation of these cities for us: »*The new city grows on the ocean from large circles of an oily substance. In the process, patterns are created. A plastic mass is poured into them. Subsequently, a network of stripes and discs develops; this expands into bulges and shells, finally forming cavities for various purposes.*«

We visit one of the residential capsules and are not surprised that the interior consists entirely of chemicals, that is, of synthetic elements. We do miss one thing: the kitchen. »Cooking is a thing of the past, and has long since been replaced by chemical reactions with a large number of different basic substances.«

We are also struck by the fact that there are no windows. »*Chemicals in hollow walls that heat, cool, and purify the air*«, says Katavolos, »*replace the windows.*«

The interiors, without added artwork, are formally amazingly diverse. The structure of the ceilings is reminiscent of that of crystals; the floors develop like corals; the ornamental pattern of the

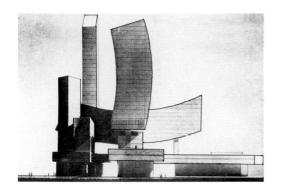

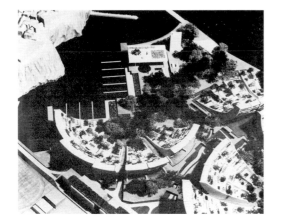

surfaces traces the lines of tensile stresses. »*These structures*«, says Katavolos, »*stretch over us weightlessly. The floors are fixed in place and contain everything people need to live. A large number of appliances are contained in this fixed modular grid.*«

The architectural structure is in the process of continuous development: The growth is produced by self-producing and self-reproducing structures.

Schumpp 1971; Dahinden 1971; *Stadt und Utopie* 1982.

Here, too, as in the work of Rudolf Doernach, the point of departure is the use of biological growth. Admittedly Katavolos can see a few concrete starting points: »substances that expand tremendously, then catalyze and harden when appropriately treated with certain activating agents«.

In the meantime, chemistry has made tremendous progress, but the 1960s enthusiasm for plastics and chemicals, like the craze for atomic energy, quickly waned in the 1980s at the latest. For hygienic, psychological, and environmental reasons, the type of houses envisaged by Katavolos can hardly be imagined, let alone produced, today.

Manfredi Nicoletti (b. 1930). The Monte Carlo satellites, 1966

It is quite understandable that the small principality of Monaco looked toward the ocean when planning its expansion. Of course, Monaco is a very special kind of »city«: Above all, it is a place visited by holidaymakers, who spend a short or longer period here. The island is flanked by two harbors – one French, the other Monegasque. No more than 20 stories high, the little town has a clearly defined silhouette without towering over the old part of town.

»I wasn't planning to create a sentimental idyll, but still make the sky, the sea, and the park landscape accessible to all inhabitants«, the architect explains his intentions. After parking in the underground garage, standing on one of the roof terraces, we can see this for ourselves. The curved terrace segments stand next to each other or back-to-back. They rise gradually from the park landscape that is continued in the luxuriant landscaping of the terraces. Each residential terrace has a view of the nearby park or the open sea. The rear of the segments is reserved mostly for office space.

»The construction is quite conventional«, says Nicoletti. »The trestle-like reinforced concrete frames stand in a giant tub that at the same time contains the three lower stories with the garages and technical equipment that are directly anchored on the bottom of the sea. Between these frames are inserted the ceilings of these stories. The spaces, which have few supporting pillars, provide an opportunity for free floor plan arrangements.«

Back to the lower floors now: Supermarkets, hotel lobbies, boutiques, community rooms, restaurants, movie theaters are accessed from an inner street. For public life in open spaces and for more sophisticated special services there is a large-scale series of squares that are penetrated by green spaces. This is where people hang out, meet, and get to know each other.

»We haven't isolated ourselves from the city. That is why there is a long, quiet zone for trade and industry as a connecting link«, says Manfredini as we drive back to town through this innovative, pleasant industrial zone.

Dahinden 1971.

The project seems carefully thought through and structurally defined inasmuch as it may be regarded as something that can be implemented. Compared to the idyllic, artificial »holiday towns«, it may be economically feasible as well.

Adolfo Natalini (b. 1941) of Superstudio (1966). The Continous Monument (Il Monumento Continuo, 1968) and the twelve ideal cities, 1971

An unimaginably vast edifice looms like three gigantic slabs over New York. Here is how Natalini describes the »Monumento Continuo«: »New York for instance: A superbuilding stretches across the Hudson and the tip of the peninsula and connects Brooklyn with New Jersey. Another building, at a right angle to the first, provides additional space. All the rest is Central Park. That is enough to include the entire rebuilt space of Manhattan. A group of old skyscrapers is preserved as a reminder of a time when cities were built without a unified plan ... And from the bay we see New York through the ›Continuous Monument‹ in a vast plain of ice, clouds, or sky.«

393. Marino di Teana, city sculpture, 1965.
394. Manfredi Nicoletti, Monte Carlo satellite, 1966.

395. Adolfo Natalini and Superstudio, Continuous Monument, 1968.
396. Adolfo Natalini and Superstudio, Cone City, the 12 ideal cities, 1972.

The best way to view this monument is from one of the latest city jets. This new cookie-cutter city seems to have come off a conveyor belt. But Natalini is not satisfied with Manhattan, with New York. He has great plans, which he enthusiastically describes: »*The structure will extend over the entire world. Its static perfection moves the world by the love it conveys, by composure, calm, and sweet tyranny.*«

We didn't have the time to visit the twelve ideal cities, but the Cone City does interest us, since we have often seen the circular urban ground plans. We've never seen the consistent geometrical layouts found in Natalini's work, though: expansive, encircled by a farm belt, the city lies in the countryside. The flat cone with its terraced houses reminds us of a Chinese hat. The other cities, Natalini assures us, are no less magnificent and extensive.

Cook 1970; *Stadt und Utopie* 1982; *Inventionen* 1981; Dethier 1994; Eaton 2001; *Nouvelles* 2001; *Visionen und Utopien* 2003.

After World War II, the radicalness of this urban utopia is by no means rare. In the 1960s and 70s especially, long before urban »globalization«, architects are considering the potential destruction of the old cities and at the same time envisioning the creation of structures that span the Earth (cf. chaps. 13.3 and 13.8).

Archizoom Associati (1966–74). The No-Stop City, 1969–1972

As we fly over the large terrain of No-Stop City, a very strange scene unfolds below: Each of the individual, additively repeated parts of the city has completely different elements: a small, rustic, traditional group of houses, and next to it cube-shaped buildings, all embedded in greenery. Looming over these relics are enormous, completely self-contained, square boxes with land-scaped roofs: the actual city.

»We've created the definitive integration of the city in the methods and spaces of industrialization. The giant industrial containers are artificially lit and air-conditioned, but nevertheless permit endless variations and an extreme creative freedom.« That is how Andrea Branzi sees the underlying principle of his No-Stop City, which is intended to go beyond previous standards of the traditional city.

»In our city the process of composition, the expressionism, the aura are radically limited, reduced almost to zero. This is in keeping with a society that is bereft of traditional values.« No-Stop City is an »amoral« city, without qualities, where individuals can create their living environment in a creative, free, and personal way.

»*No-Stop City came about as a result of scientific analysis*«, asserts Andrea Branzi. »*We regarded the urban artefact as the result of a purely quantitative process, independent of the quality of the architecture. We transferred the typology of the factory and supermarket to residential buildings. Architecture does not represent society. Rather, it contains it and leaves it certain freedoms. Nature, outside the urban model, becomes completely autonomous again.*«

Andrea Branzi now formulates his view – and that of the group – covering a wide range of themes: »*Making architecture does not exclusively mean making houses or, in general, constructing useful things. Rather, it means expressing oneself, communicating, debating, and freely creating one's own cultural space. All individuals have the right to create their own environment.*«

Klotz 1986; *Architectures experimentales* 2003.

The group Archizoom Associati has successfully implemented many projects – in the realm of design and the world of objects. Because the boundaries of the disciplines are fluid, designers are involved with architecture and vice versa.

Aldo Rossi (b. 1931). The city of de Chirico, 1978

It's a hot day. We're wandering through the city with Aldo Rossi. The sun blazes down on the treeless squares. The sharply outlined geometric forms cast hard shadows on the pavement of the squares that are now deserted in the burning midday heat. We feel we've been transplanted into one of the *Metafisica* paintings of de Chirico or Carrà.

A large, cubical block with square windows bars our way: No doubt it contains the public institutions and meeting places for the people, who are not visible at this time. Behind them are five one-story rows of houses – schools, offices, small stores. A steep cone forms the boundary. Its chimney has been transformed into a phallic tower. Behind it is another endless row of shady arcades with a massive adjacent octagonal tower, like an extended telescope.

The only two-story residential buildings are raised high above the ground and stand on slim concrete discs and round traffic towers. This clearly defined typological order is then broken up: Gabled houses, the kind we are familiar with from traditional architecture, seem to respond to the hieratic rigidity with their free architectural volumes.

Visionen und Utopien 2002.

Aldo Rossi has many successful implementations to his credit. We almost have the impression of the reverse process: Rossi creates the collages of his visions from the built houses.

Constantinos Doxiadis (1913–1975). Ecumenopolis, 1970

»How did an urbanized world with nineteen billion inhabitants come about?« asks Doxiadis. His prophecies have been fulfilled. »*All the cities of the world have finally merged and formed a system of corridors that encircles the globe like a single, connected city.*«

We've lived to see total urbanization – and yet it is not destructive, for the Earth is divided into three regions:

»*1. A ›universal city zone‹ that takes up less than five percent of the Earth: That is ›Ecumenopolis‹. 2. An ›agricultural zone‹, inhabited by two billion people who produce the food with the full benefits of technology. And 3. a ›nature zone‹ consisting of forests and uninhabited reserves that preserves the integrity of the environment and especially guarantees the gigantic quantities of water we need.*«

Schippke 1970.

Doxiadis recognized our ecological problems very early, even before the great energy crisis. He, too, proposes a global network of linear cities.

13.6. America, Africa, Asia

Burrhus Frederic Skinner (b. 1904). *Walden Two*, 1948

»The dissatisfaction that induced me to write *Walden Two* was personal«, states B. F. Skinner. No doubt, however, it was also the situation after World War II that motivated a search for new lifestyle models.

Skinner does not deny that he got the title and idea from Henry David Thoreau's famous *Walden*. We don't need to travel very far to get to *Walden Two* – we reach the commune by train and bus. »Walden Two«, explains Mr. Skinner, »is communally owned, of course. For the agricultural buildings and dormitories, the architects made simple sketches for us.«

When we visit one of the apartments, we see that it is well designed and comfortably furnished. The kitchen is modest, for meals are prepared and eaten together. »Naturally all the people here are industrious. They all choose their work themselves, but depending on how disagreeable the task is, they are awarded a different number of points. Thanks to hard work and organization, no one works more than four hours a day.« The commune is administered by a rotating and self-renewing board, the »planners«.

When we go past a cultural center, we are surprised to see how busy things are even in the afternoon. We listen to part of a concert, then watch the rehearsal of a play, and finally go to a reading. »The short working hours leave a lot of time for culture and entertainment«, our guide tells us. »Play and sports give us physical and psychological health.« We see no sour faces, no tired citizens, no sad figures, and are willing to believe that prosperity, harmony, and good cheer prevail in this town.

Skinner 1948.

It is unusual for a finished literary utopia to be translated to reality point for point, as it were. In 1967 a group of eight people gather in Virginia full of hope and idealism to found the agricultural commune Twin Oaks, based on the imaginary model of *Walden Two*. What Skinner probably does not mention are the full-scale problems of the initial period and personal conflicts experienced by the commune, first headed by Kathleen Kinkade. There are also material, financial, and technical problems: In contrast to the novel *Walden Two*, envy, jealousy, worry, and rage have not vanished – they are daily experiences. Work, power, sexuality cannot be dealt with as peacefully as the model describes. For all those years, the commune's members have to struggle with very human problems. Nevertheless, the commune grows to 40 persons. They build two large dormitories, a basement for storing food, and a freezer. They mostly grow their own food.

From *Walden Two* – which remained an ideal – they take the idea of common property, joint meals, the point system at work, and a number of other things.

Were they successful in turning the utopia into a reality? At any rate, there are concrete places, buildings, people who live an alternative life. Of course, they are far removed from *Walden Two*. Though the Israeli kibbutzim were not influenced by Skinner, it is possible to find in them a sufficient number of analogies to *Walden Two*.

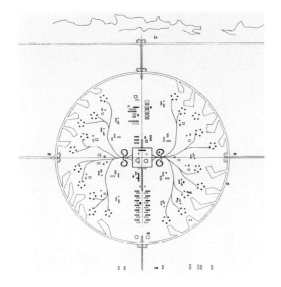

Lucio Costa (1902–1931) and Oscar Niemeyer. Brasilia, 1955; and Oscar Niemeyer (b. 1907). The Ideal City

The design created by Lucio Costa is magnificent and bold. As we fly over the city, we might think it is the magnified shadow of our plane reproduced on the wide plain. Costa confirms our impression: »Yes, I was thinking of flying – a huge bird spreading its wings or an enormous plane landing.«

At present, 200,000 people live in the new capital of Brasília, while the entire region has a population of two million. Now we ride to the top of the observation tower. From above, 220 m up, we have a lovely overview. »My friend and student Oscar Niemeyer designed wonderful buildings for the city, a universe of modern architecture.«

In the east, the towers of the parliament building dominate the large federal district, the Square of the Three Powers. The imposing cathedral connects earth and sky. Not far from it, outside the »eagle«, is the university and diplomat district. The heart and limbs are formed by the cultural and entertainment district, flanked by banks, offices, the commercial zone, and the hotels. In the west are the barracks, the central railroad station, and small industrial plants. The two great »wings« of the residential districts in the south and north are framed by plantings of flowers, the botanical garden and the zoo, and the riding club. The airport, cemetery, yacht club, and trade fair grounds are located far outside the city.

Pedestrian and automobile traffic are strictly separated, the town is divided into zones, the buildings take the climate into account, and the entire city is filled with dynamic, urbane life.

»It is a seamless city, built for the benefit of its people«, says Lucio Costa, not without pride in his well thought-out planning.

But why do we include Brasilia among the utopias? After all, it was actually built! That is true. But not much is left of the bold plans, especially of the dreams of a new urbanity. Oscar Niemeyer did actually build his excellent representative buildings. But Niemeyer is deeply distressed about the city as such: »*The people have transformed the shape of the city into great chaos. In the side streets, the architecture is terrible. The banks have pushed through a terrible state of affairs.*«

The 1964 military coup completed the disaster. Niemeyer, a dedicated communist, fled to Israel and designed his Ideal City.

399. Oscar Niemeyer, City of Tomorrow, 1979.
400. Lucio Costa (Oscar Niemeyer), plan for Brasilia, 1956. 1 Square of the Three Powers, 2 government buildings, 3 cathedral, 4 cultural sector, 5 entertainment district, 6 bank and office district, 7 commercial district, 8 hotels, 9 radio and TV transmitter, 10 sports, 11 municipal square, 12 barracks, 13 railroad station, 14 warehouses and small industries, 15 university city, 16 embassies and legations, 17 residential sector, 18 duplex houses, 19 duplex super blocks, 20 botanical gardens, 21 zoological garden, 22 bus terminal, 23 yacht club, 24 palace of the president, 25 hotel, 26 fair grounds, 27 racecourse, 28 cemetery, 29 airport, 30 golf club, 31 south sector of individual houses, 32 graphic and design industries, 33 north sector of individual houses, 34 suburb »Parkway Mansion«.

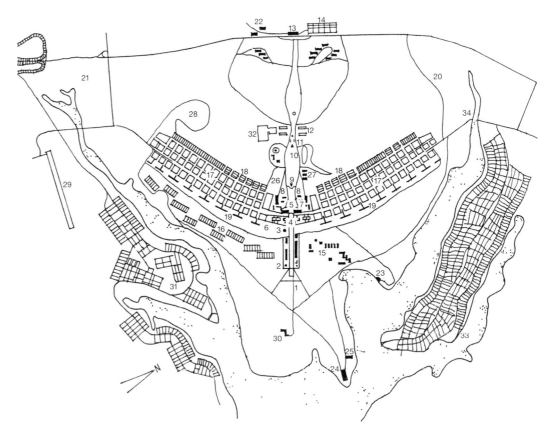

»Here, too, we should fly over the city to recognize the system«, says Niemeyer. We take a small private plane to the Negev desert. Niemeyer took over the large system of coordinates from Costa and allocated it to the bulk of the traffic. The north-south axis is the backbone for all the public buildings, office buildings, culture, and leisure. From the north-west axis the streets branch off like the branches of a tree, leading to residential districts, identical tower blocks embedded in greenery. The office high-rises and tower blocks provide accents in the city. The axes intersect in the center and expand to form a large square. The inhabitants have cars, but thanks to a perfect public transit system these are used only for long-distance driving.

Niemeyer felt that the actual plan for the Negev, like the preceding description and a few other urban development drafts, could definitely be implemented, although they were shaped by the visionary optimism of the 1960s. However, none of his projects after Brasilia materialized.

Young people in Haight Ashbury, 1962; and the Hippie settlements of America, 1960–80

»Wandering aimlessly up Haight St., over to the free store at Carl and Cole, then back to Masonic for a cream pie and a coke, or to the Panhandel for a Digger stew ... An admixture of homemade, spiritual group theory and actors' life theater which turns the participants into celebrants.« What an enchanting life we encounter – and how convincingly the Protestant ethic is lived here – the religious virtue of the individual, a modest life, and finding happiness in work and in community.

»We are certain that we will create a new world, for our generation, for ourselves, for our community«, says our guide enthusiastically. We have great expectations of »flower power«, and the peaceful flower children.

»This world will be radically different from the past middle-class mentality of this century. We will live in a new consciousness and in love, helped by art and drugs.«

Haight Ashbury is the ideal place where this new scene was able to unfold.

The end of the utopia: Haight Ashbury actually became a reality. We can really visit the »city« now – it actually deserves this name.

What an unusual scene greets us! A charming conglomeration of scarves, colorful cloths, ribbons, ponchos, fantastic musical instruments, bells, beads, shells, Indian requisites meets our eyes. Much of this is produced here, made by hand in the communes that have been established here since 1960, whose members were referred to as »hippies«, the ones in the know. The young people walk barefoot, part their hair on the side, and wear handmade clothing with their blue jeans. »Initially most commune members were artists«, explains our guide, »but our group was very popular, and soon there were close to 15,000 of us.«

How did people deal with the drug problem that had such enormous fascination for this generation? »At first, alcohol and marijuana were sufficient, but then we used LSD and mescaline as well. That didn't always work so well, and in 1966 we opened a ›Psychedelic Shop‹.«

Although many preferred a life of idleness to the hectic pace of modern life, others also produced handmade crafts: jewelry, clothing, leatherwork, posters.

We stroll through the area, a love-in park where communication is very open. On this fine summer day, most sleep outdoors.

Three years after our first visit we return – but how great is our disappointment! Hard drugs have left their mark on the social structure and health. There is increasing violence at the hands of outside groups. At night people prefer to stay at home. There are more and more dangerous diseases, and hopelessness spreads gradually. The houses are now dirty, dilapidated, and rat-infested. Loafers and beggars, addicts and criminals hang around in the streets.

Deeply disappointed and depressed, we leave the failed experiment that began so hopefully. Still, we are by no means totally discouraged and want to see other hippie »cities«. We're particularly interested in the Drop Cities. These communities formed on the hills of South Colorado and were in existence from the late 1960s to the early 70s. They are typical of the so-called »international communities«. The founders were University of Kansas and Colorado art students and writers. They had no intention of founding a large community, but mainly wanted to live cheaply, have time, make art. Their amazing »architecture« goes back to none other than Richard Buckminster Fuller. We again find the »geodetic domes« here, referred to as »domes«, homemade from car roofs, simply assembled from wood, cardboard, sheet metal – they even got the Dymaxion Prize for their work!

401. Anonymous, Hippie Domes, after »Dymaxion«, Richard Buckminster Fuller, USA, c. 1965.
402. Anonymous, Boat City, Sausalito, Los Angeles, USA, c. 1965.
403. Woodstock Music Festival, 1969.

404. Paolo Soleri, Hexahedron, city for 170,000 inhabitants, 1970.
405. Paolo Soleri, Mesa City, 1971.

We find some »architecture« at the Morningstar Ranch as well, with its peaceful, nature-loving people, who have largely withdrawn from society.

The Himalayan Academy has settled in a former brewery, and the yogis, led by a guru, devote themselves to a Hindu-Christian spirituality. As one of the yogis succinctly says:

»The ultimate goal of all members of the community is to achieve perfect self-realization or union with the Supreme Power (God) of the universe, through the practises of yoga, meditation, and physical exercise.«

In the colony of Waldo Point in Sausalito near Los Angeles we find a very different, colorful, and cheerful type of boat people. Here we meet artists and dreamers, screwballs and hippies.
I am sure we could continue our journey endlessly, and would be surprised to see that many more dozens of »utopias«, better characterized as dreams of a different life, actually materialized.

But let us conclude our tour in Twin Oaks, *»... a society that creates people who are committed to non aggression; a society of people concerned for one another; a society where one man's gain is not another man's loss, a society which is constantly trying to improve in it's ability to create happy, productive, creative people.«*

However – we are not at our destination yet, for we must not leave out a truly incredible utopia: the fact that music unites almost half a million people peacefully in one place. That, too, became a reality.

In August 1969 a hopeful crowd full of the enthusiasm of love, eros, and music – half a million! – assembles in Woodstock, 150 km from New York. The ideological spectrum runs the gamut – yet under the imaginary banner of »love, peace, and brotherhood«, for 72 hours, the audience celebrates the greatest musical event of all times together with 32 bands. Drugs, chaos, and rain were hardly able to dampen the flower children's enthusiasm.

The most important, now legendary, stars were Janis Joplin and Joan Baez, Jimi Hendrix and Ravi Shankar, Santana and Ten Years After – and dozens of other bands.

Paolo Soleri (1919–2003). The Hexahedron, 1970, Mesa City, 1971, the Asteromo, 1960/70, and Arcosanti, 1969

Of the 30 cities, the »arcologies«, planned by Paolo Soleri, we are able to visit only the most important ones.

We begin with the Hexahedron. This compact city, shaped like a double pyramid, the tips pointing up and down, rises up to 1,200 m above the ground and looks as if it had been composed of a thousand crystals. In the lower part are public institutions and work places, while the upper part consists of apartments that all look out upon the wide, unspoiled countryside.

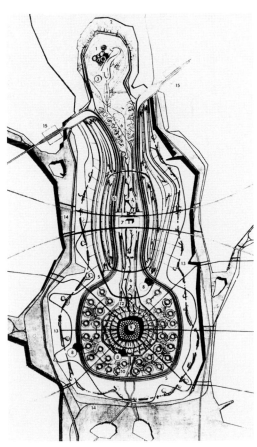

Between the two pyramids there is a high gap, where public life takes place: An express elevator brings us to this level in the middle of the complex. We stroll down the promenades, through the well-kept parks with their cafés, restaurants, and playgrounds. In the center of this area are the cultural center and community buildings.

Soleri explains an underlying principle of his: »I've attained a maximum population density. There are close to 3,000 inhabitants per hectare. In other words, the 57 hectares of developed land have more than 170,000 inhabitants.« All the »arcologies« together will in the end provide housing for eight million people.

Our ride up to the top platform brings an added surprise: It almost seems as though we were looking at a green mountain. The big terraces are so lushly landscaped that to some extent they already seem integrated into the natural landscape.

Our next stop is Mesa City, the city of the theologians: From above it resembles a biological shape. As we approach, we see a densely inhabited, lively, three-dimensional city with a population of two million. The dimensions are immense: the city is 35 km long and 10 km wide. One of the main purposes of Mesa City is the study and utilization of cosmic energy and natural forces.

»The great philosopher, theologian. and ethnologist Teilhard de Chardin has always deeply impressed me«, Soleri tells us. »One thesis was important for my work: the idea of a civilization that includes the individual. I wanted to implement that in my buildings as well, beginning with Arcosanti.«

Our journey resumes: In an enormous campus lies Asteromo, the space city: It is ready to take off into outer space and can house as many as 70,000 people. Its longitudinal axis is 2,600 m, while the largest diameter is 1,400 m.

»Asteromo is more than a city: Actually it is an all-inclusive living space, for it includes not only gardens but also farms, as well as work places, research labs, and water reservoirs.«

We would love to see some of the other cities as well – for instance, Veladiga, the city of the dam, Babel II B with its calyx of petals, Arcoforte, Arcvillage, Arcollective, Archibuz, Novanoah, and many others. However, we have to be content with Soleris's concluding statement. He speaks of the underlying principle of his bold reflections: *A societal pattern is influenced, perhaps even dictated, by the material pattern in which it is situated. The natural landscape is not the appropriate space for the complex life of a society. People must design the cityscape in their own image: a physically compact, dense, three-dimensional package, not a thin layer of organic matter.*«

Cook 1970; Dahinden 1971; Schippke 1970; *Stadt und Utopie* 1982; Soleri 1988; Eaton 2001.

We conclude our tour in Arcosanti, in the Arizona desert – a comparatively small settlement with 1,500 inhabitants. But now, after the huge dimensions of the megacities, we have reentered the real world: Here, Soleri has implemented his campus »city«, an open living space in an exciting landscape. In 1969, after working with Frank Lloyd Wright, Soleri buys land in Arizona and begins developing and building it: Arcosanti is a ceramic city, as it were: Fired clay of all shapes surrounds us –bowls, bells, ornaments, figures. In three large concrete bowls students, visitors, and architects meet to talk shop. We recognize the semidomes from the gigantic Arcosanti blueprint. Here, the priorities are quite different: It is a city of movement, art, research. The big semidomes, reminiscent of the Roman Pantheon, house workshops, studios, meetings, theater, and staged events.

»The theater is just as important as the studios«, says Soleri. »This is how we respond to the universal demand for art and show the significance of creative, artistic work.«

Arcosanti has grown very, very slowly, and the homes of the artists on the edge of the campus have nothing at all in common with Soleri's wonderful blueprints.

We greatly admire Soleri's persistence in pursuing an unattainable goal until the day he died. Hundreds of students and young artists helped with building, and the campus seems to be a lifesize and yet tiny model for the imposing monument that is Arcosanti.

Soleri could show us yet another implemented project: an early work dating back to 1953, the ceramic factory in Vietri sul Mare, Italy.

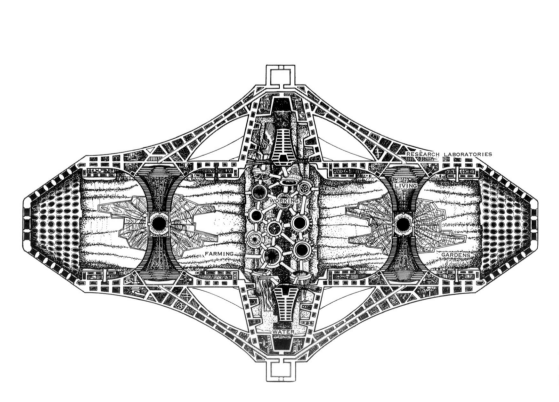

406. Paolo Soleri, Asteromo, space city, 1960/70.
407. Leopold Gerstel, Ziggurat study for a terraced building, Israel, 1963.

408. Jan Lubicz-Nicz and team, project for Tel Aviv, 1963. 3rd construction phase.
409. Jan Lubicz-Nicz and team, project for Tel Aviv, 1963.

Leopold Gerstel. The Ziggurat, 1963

From a distance we actually have the impression that we are approaching a ziggurat in ancient Babylon, though not quite as steep. The ziggurat may also have been modeled on Central American pre-Columbian temples and the stepped pyramids of the Egyptians. »The early cultures dedicated their monuments to the gods and rulers. Today we erect our compact buildings for the people, for society«, says Leopold Gerstel.

Of course, the built mountain, a step toward God, ascension to heaven, are no longer the most important themes. Rather, one of the methods of contemporary architecture is to build terraces in an appropriate and meaningful way. Close up we see that because the architectural volumes are divided into small sections, the terraces, balconies, and bay windows give the massive structure a scale and form a beautiful contrast to its monumentality.

Every apartment has lovely open spaces and a view of a distant panorama. The building is crowned by community facilities with a large terrace. What is concealed in the core? This question has been the downfall of many terrace blueprints. »Come and I'll show you how useful dark zones can be«, says Leopold Gerstel. Every cubic meter actually has been put to use: not only for garages and power plants but for many functions that do not need natural light: shopping malls, supermarkets, a cinema and theaters, but also clubs and restaurants.

The contrast between the tremendous freedom and openness that we enjoy from the terraces of the apartments and the almost cavern-like enclosed space in the interior creates a delightful tension.

Cook 1970.

The magical, mythical significance of the ziggurat, the ancient Oriental temple mount, has been given a new modern interpretation: Since the turn of the 19th century, the terraced house has been one of the most popular forms of housing, but constantly encounters economic and functional limitations, thus often coming close to a utopia.

Jan Lubicz-Nicz. The »Spoon City« of Tel Aviv, 1963

When the first construction phase of the new city was started, the political situation in Israel was very different. A new traffic plan and city expansions were proposed.

»Actually we built two completely different cities«, explains Jan Lubicz-Nicz, »an inner city and a maritime city. Large traffic axes with extensive parking lots connect these cities. They are thus integrated in the traffic network of Tel Aviv.«

The inner city announces its presence from a distance: The compact buildings that form its dramatic silhouette seem like huge spoons. Before our car disappears in the vast underground garage, we have grasped the basic principle of the spoons: On one side they soar steeply, ending

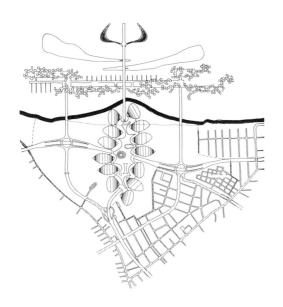

in a slender high-rise; on the other side, however, a cascade of terraces drops to a point where the building is just a few stories high.

Lubicz-Nicz confirms our observation: »Toward the city center office high-rises tower up to 55 stories high, while the outside terrace apartments have a view over the landscape – the city, the sea.«

From the underground garage the elevator takes us directly to the middle of town, whose form is reminiscent of a huge village green. Urban life is promoted by cultural and commercial facilities: theaters and cinemas, museums and exhibitions, schools and libraries, and a synagogue. Naturally there are cafés and restaurants and all kinds of shopping opportunities, all in all enough venues to provide vibrant urban life.

»We began the first phase of building with six towers, followed by six more. The thirteenth tower is now ready for occupancy, and thus the growth of the inner city is now complete«, Lubicz-Nicz informs us. »Now close to 20,000 people live here.«

We leave our car in the garage and stroll toward the sea down a promenade. We don't notice any striking landmarks; rather we enter an almost idyllic town whose houses have a maximum of five stories and stand on a long man-made island. Every house has direct contect with the water. Two more islands are in front of the densely built-up development, which consists of small buildings. These islands have no buildings and serve recreation and water sports. There is another architectural landmark, however. We reach it by a moving sidewalk. Two gently curving complexes of buildings lie in the middle of the sea – hotels for more than 2,000 guests, offering a varied leisure and entertainment program. Automobile traffic is banished underground. Moving sidewalks and electro-buggies assist pedestrian traffic. All deliveries take place underground.

»We tried to develop a broad spectrum of urban life«, says Lubicz-Nicz. »In this day and age, there should be no more dogmas regarding urban housing. Rather, there should be many more alternatives allowing people to freely choose between forms of housing.«

Dahinden 1971.

The project stands on the border between reality and utopia, since it was specifically planned for Tel Aviv. The architects have addressed another very real problem: the large number of different types of housing and urban heterogeneity.

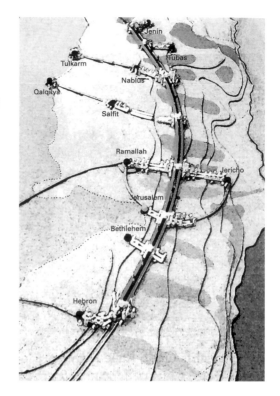

Doug Suisman. The new Palestinian state, 2005

Designing a New Palestine – what crazy audacity! Yet somebody did take this risk and make it a reality – the dream was fulfilled after the great peace. Doug Suisman was commissioned to do the planning – but naturally that wasn't the end of the matter. It was political will on all sides, peace, and tolerance that made it possible.

What was the background for Mr. Suisman's planning? The first commission came from the RAND Corporation, the powerful US research company with its 800 scientists. The project was instigated out of a conviction that the time was ripe. And as a matter of fact all the politicians, Israelis and Palestinians alike, became interested. The prerequisite – a stable peace – had been created long ago. And the financial problem was also solved: A total of 33 billion US$ were invested. The architect's idea is as bold as it is simple: »High-speed trains link the big and small towns, markets, and villages. Directly connected to the localities are farms and nature reserves.« In a large arc, the ribbon of traffic, with the cities it links, swings through the vast landscape.

Mr. Suisman brings us to the Hebron railway station where we board the rocket-like train, equipped with all imaginable luxuries. But the speed is not fast enough to keep us from seeing the fertile fields and beautiful rural villages.

We pass Bethlehem and Jerusalem, and stop in the double city of Ramallah-Jericho. The city has developed magnificently. Modern buildings have sprung up. They do not copy the West but have found their own stylistic idiom.

»Until now, Palestine existed as a dream or a nightmare«, Mr. Suisman reminds us. »But the Israelis themselves realized that this state must be created, and the Americans actively supported them and promoted our plans.« The ardently longed-for »day after peace« has actually arrived now, and the planners were ready.

Wanting to see the rest of the railroad line, we board another train. We do have a question: How does one reach out-of-the-way villages and towns? »Naturally there are also local lines with lower-speed trains. Right now, we are near the local line to Salfit and Qalqilya.«

410. Doug Suisman, blueprint for the Palestinian state, 2005.

Past an impressive Nablus, we go to our final destination, Jenin. We've traveled 110 km. »Of course, it is primarily Palestine that has gained from this«, admits Mr. Suisman. »The life of the population has improved in every way: There is more work and more schools. Food and water supplies are now guaranteed. The healthcare system, housing, and traffic have been developed: We've founded a successful state – and that's important for the whole world.«
New York Times 7.4.2005.

Once more we realize that without a political will urban and regional planning really does remain a utopia and that today, in 2006, »life after peace« is as distant as ever. The fantastical nature of the plan is not altered by the fact that Doug Suisman presented his ideas at the White House, to the EU, the World Bank, and to interested Palestinians and Israelis.

Richard Buckminster Fuller (1895–1983) and Shoji Sadao. The cylinder towers of slum redevelopment in Harlem, New York, 1965; Tetra City, 1966; Triton City, 1968; and Old Man River's City, 1971

Now North Manhattan also has its own unmistakable silhouette in Harlem. From our plane the towers of slum redevelopment are visible from afar. There are fifteen residential tower blocks, each 110 stories high. A total of half a million inhabitants are supposed to have their homes here. »Bucky« explains the principle of design, definitely not new but amazing in these dimensions: »In the middle is a mast with all traffic and power supply systems. Just now, it carries a projecting coping at the top, from which the 110 ceilings are hung on steel cables, and on these stand the prefabricated housing units. The apartments do not begin until the tenth floor. This is where the express highways lead. Raised above the ground, these connect the individual towers.«

We are able to view one of the apartments and admire the glorious panorama of the Hudson from a small terrace. Admittedly, as we stand on one of the topmost terraces, the strong wind almost blows us down. The infrastructure for each tower goes without saying: supermarket, community rooms, cultural centers, schools. It is also understandable that Americans like to have their cars close by: That is why they drive straight up to their apartments by way of spiral ramps in the core.

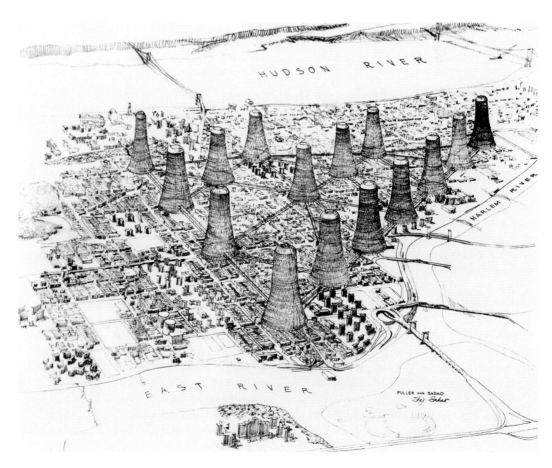

411. Richard Buckminster Fuller and Shoji Sadao, slum redevelopment in Harlem, New York, USA, 1965.

»In three years, with the most modern technology, we planned and implemented the entire project«, Fuller tells us. »It took us the first year to prepare the prefabricated parts.«

What happened and is happening to the former housing here? we ask. »Part of it has already been demolished, creating parks, green spaces, playing fields. And by the water, new harbors were created, with large playing fields and recreation areas between them.«

Dahinden 1971; *Sites & Stations* 1995.

As is so often the case with the brilliant designer Buckminster Fuller, the daring technological feat and interest in structural questions are in the foreground, while the physical and psychological conditions take the back seat.

The idea of filling the voluminous core of the skyscrapers not only with the load-bearing and power-supply structure but also with a gigantic spiral ramp for the cars seems surprising and naturally necessitates expensive air-conditioning systems; emission-free cars might reduce the problem in future.

With »Bucky« we fly to Tetra City, an urban pyramid that overshadows the Egyptian pyramids. As we approach, we quickly realize our mistake: It is not a pyramid, but a tetrahedron – in other words, the ideal form whose every side and angle are equal. It is no less than 3,000 m high, towers in the clouds, and even has its own climate. Close to 300,000 families live here – that is, more than half a million people. With our small plane we are able not only to fly over the gigantic building, but circle several times near its top. We can distinctly see that the tetrahedron represents the basic structure even on a small scale: A dense weave of steel rods forms the delicate network of the outer shell, and we can also see that the mountain is divided into four sections. »These sections also structure the interior. They are equipped with huge ribbons of light that illuminate the inside«, explains Fuller.

We have landed, and the express train takes us to the railroad station lower down, from which we can directly reach the center. But this is not one of your customary commercial plazas, not a crowded business district – rather it is a spacious park landscape comprising the entire infrastructure. We are astounded how lush the vegetation is in the core of the giants. But the artificial light has the crucial qualities of daylight and thus ensures that there is an organic ambiance.

»We created a truly gigantic structure, but residential life here remains individual«, says Fuller. »All residents get 180 m² of living space and 90 m² of garden each – and they are free to do what they like with it. The simplest solution, of course, is for them to insert movable modules, like trailers, totally mobile.« A building of such dimensions also poses a problem in terms of construction

413. Richard Buckminster Fuller and Shoji Sadao,
Old Man River's City, 1971.
414. Richard Buckminster Fuller and Shoji Sadao,
Triton City, 1968.

time. But the structure allows building to proceed in individual layers. It is a process of growth that is not exactly defined chronologically

Later that evening we revisit the city hill. Our impression of the illuminated mountain that also reveals parts of its inner structure is no less imposing in the dark, and Bucky's associations are interesting: »It's a constructed mountain that glows like a refinery at night.«

Dahinden 1971; *Sites & Stations* 1995.

Buckminster Fuller does not explicitly address the question of how the huge spaces inside the towers are to be utilized. What kind of urban life can develop here? What physical conditions are given for the rapid 3,000-meter change in height? How is it possible to grow vegetation here? Was the project simply a daring intellectual and technological feat, designed to show what structural exploits are possible nowadays?

Buckminster Fuller is able to give convincing reasons for Triton City: »You must keep in mind that probably 80 percent of the American population of cities over a million live close to bodies of water – so it is natural to expand cities into the ocean!«

Buckminster Fuller's Triton City conjures up ancient seascapes. This time we approach the city from the ocean side. The triangle is the basic figure for the floating islands, whose buildings are diverse, assembled from efficient modules and expandable at any time. They are linked to existing cities.

A basic unit has between 3,500 and 6,500 inhabitants. Three to six units are joined into a city, giving a total of between 15,000 and 30,000 inhabitants. And three to six cities have a population of 90,000 to 125,000 each.

»Mind you, in Triton City I've reduced individual traffic and separated it from pedestrian traffic. The public facilities, schools, cultural buildings, markets can all be reached on foot, and all doors open on to a 50-meter-wide, hanging pedestrian street. I've calculated the costs: I can manage with 8,000 dollars per person.«

We leave the city at dusk by one of the newest local planes and see the three huge, incredibly impressive triangles below us. They are lit from inside with white and colored light that changes from time to time. The buildings glow like magic crystals linked by beads.

Dahinden 1971; *Sites & Stations* 1995.

Buckminster Fuller frequently transfers the constructional microstructure to the macrostructure. Thus triangular elements become figures of the ground plan.

Our next stop is the eastern part of St. Louis. Old Man River's City is an enormous circular cluster, but we might as well call it a city. The compact settlement is 1,500 m high, and the base diameter is also 1,500 m. It has 125,000 inhabitants. The 50 levels of terraces decrease in size toward the top. Radial bridges connect all pedestrian levels. Communal facilities and technical essentials are located in the interior of the terrace stories.

»Every apartment has an outside terrace«, Fuller enthusiastically tells us. »You have a glorious view of the landscape. It's like being on the hills of Hongkong or Berkeley. The terraces are sepa-

415. Cesar Pelli and A. J. Lumsden, Urban Nucleus, Sunset Mountain Park, USA.

rated by trees and shrubbery. Naturally all services are provided, and there are also job opportunities in offices and workshops, businesses and restaurants.«

A tall, transparent dome spans the entire city, based on Fuller's system, of course. »This kind of city«, says Fuller, »is similar to an ocean liner: It needs to include every facility for life and survival.«

Sites & Stations 1995.

The circular aquatic city is already familiar to us from our earlier travels. Buckminster's utopias, however, have a concrete basis – the reasoning of a brilliant engineer.

Cesar Pelli (b. 1926) and A. J. Lumsden. The terrace city Urban Nucleus in Sunset Mountain Park, California, 1965

The Santa Monica Mountains in California: a harsh yet exciting landscape, without buildings of any kind. Then a hill appears on the horizon, seemingly ribbed like a huge venetian blind. The top of the hill is crowned by a flat, calm silhouette.

As we suspected, the ribs are large terraces that wind their way uphill like reptiles. »Our task was to develop an area of almost fifteen km^2«, says Cesar Pelli. »We realized that we could not use the building regulations of Los Angeles, which stipulate low density. We succeeded in building a condensed hill town with terraced apartments.«

But how was it possible to circumvent the general preference for single-family free-standing homes? »From the spacious terraces, each apartment has a unique view; each ensures privacy and can be designed to suit individual needs. Moreover, we offer a lively, urbane milieu«, promises Cesar Pelli.

We have parked in one of the garages at the base, and an express elevator brings us to the city center in a matter of minutes. The main square is surrounded by stores, cafés, and restaurants. On the top floors are offices, banks, the post office, and hotels. A school and a library, a church, a theater, and a cinema provide education and culture.

Even though distances in the center are minimal, a moving pathway is an extra convenience for pedestrians. It goes without saying that the center is also accessible by private and public transportation; parking garages, service stations, bus stations, and power companies are logically housed in the dark zones, as is a central computer system.

The cascades of the terraced apartments are interrupted several times by large plazas: Landscaped recreation areas create the space for urban community life.

»The inhabitants like to go to the center for shopping«, says the architect, »but we've developed another system mainly for small everyday purchases: There is an arrangement resembling the old pneumatic dispatch system for the most important goods, electronically controlled, from the supermarkets to the individual groups of floors. But that's not all: We've also installed a central kitchen, and after preparation the food is also sent out pneumatically.«

From the helicopter landing strip we finally go off on a tour and now see that the city actually does hug the topography like an armadillo. Wide tongues or mighty cascades go tumbling down the hill, interrupted again and again by landscape that has been left in its natural state.

Dahinden 1971.

Terraced buildings have been controversial for many years. While there are numerous implementations and their number is rising, the final word is still out. Pelli/Lumsden start with an ideal situation that is found very rarely: a topography with the ideal gradient. Still, vertical or slanting transportation presents a number of problems.

Engelbert Zobl, Helmut C. Schulitz, and Dale Dashiell. The caravan city in the Mojave Desert, USA, 1967

A fine tissue with large, dark, but sometimes transparent cubes and with a dramatic silhouette is outlined against the clear sky as we approach the city riding through the Mojave Desert.

»We believe we've reached a maximum of flexibility and mobility for an urban agglomeration«, state the architects. »Our modules are as easy to move and adapt as a house trailer and can be bought and equipped just as individually. A perfected computer system indicates which positions in the spatial lattice are still available – something like an electronic furniture catalogue.«

In the meantime, we have reached the connectors for the transportation system. These are linked and allow traffic to switch between the main transportation level, the secondary level, and the levels with the conveyor belts. These horizontal transportation levels are directly connected with the vertical ones – elevators at different speeds. The latter are very helpful during our tour, for

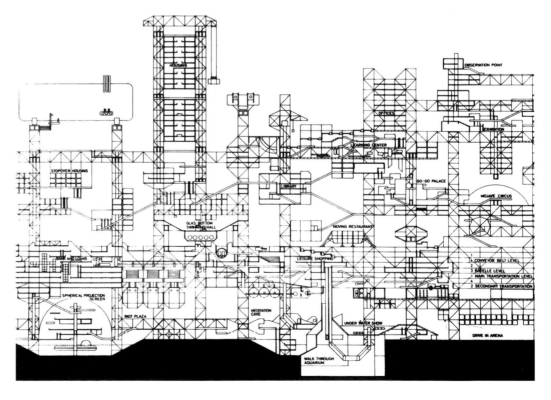

416. Engelbert Zobl, Helmut C. Schulitz, and Dale Dashiell, Mojave Desert, USA, 1967.

all the institutions are not on the same level, but distributed, seemingly accidentally, throughout the supporting framework of the structures.

We first visit one of the tower blocks: At this moment, one of the caravan modules is being lifted by a permanent crane and placed in the selected position. Admittedly only the top stories enjoy a completely unobstructed view of the landscape.

While a crisscross tour now takes us through the structure with its attractions, the architects explain their intentions: »*What we're interested in is a self-regulating structure, as it were, an undefined agglomeration of urban components that not only satisfies the needs of modern consumers but can also be adapted to the requirements of an unforeseeable future.*«

The instrument of this adaptation is the optimum disposability of the facilities, including even the restaurants, which are also mobile. The differentiated learning center, formerly referred to as a school, can conform to all educational and societal needs, and so can the libraries, offices, exhibition halls, and the large-scale recreational and shopping center. The meditation cave, Exuberance Square, or the go-go palace could also be moved to different positions. Even the location of the cinema and theater can change.

The only facilities whose location is fixed are those requiring extensive technological equipment: the accessible aquarium with its underwater show, the circus, the projection dome, the indoor glass swimming pool, and the observatory on one of the upper platforms.

Dahinden 1971.

Very early, we can see a trend toward a society focused on personal experience. Recreational facilities are prioritized over residential space, at least in the graphic representation.

Michael Frayn. *A Very Private Life*, 1968

People are afraid of total collectivization and loss of individuality – but now the reverse is happening. They want to live a totally and unrestrictedly individual existence – and in order to achieve this they have retreated completely into their own private space. Everyone has built a wall around himself and his family and thus keeps society and its demands at a distance. The walls have become more and more impenetrable. All over the world every family that can afford to has created its own, completely individually controlled environment.

But that's not all. After people have built their »castle« by raising external walls, they also erect internal walls, so that family members can isolate themselves from each other.

People now meet only technologically by means of holovision – that makes direct encounters superfluous, for they see their partners three-dimensionally, of course in color, on the monitor. That isn't enough: Erotic encounters also take place by means of these channels, which are also very »hygienic«.

But the electronic devices have not eliminated insecurity, dissatisfaction, and depression. That is why people have learned to construct certain chemical screens within their own bodies. They can withdraw behind these into an inner protected area, where everything is under control.

»One girl, pretty Uncumber, wanted to know what is actually happening ›outside‹. She escapes. And what does she find outside? Environmental pollution, depravity, suffering, and misery. So she returns back to the private security of her walls.«

Most historical, social visions that have to do with an ideal city were characterized by public-spiritedness, solidarity and communication. What we have here is its antithesis. The American elite actually do live behind high walls that surround their homes, which are accessed through underground garages. And it is a fact that the electronics boom does not protect us from increasing isolation.

Moshe Safdie (b. 1938). Habitat Puerto Rico (1968–71); Keur Farah Pahlavi in Senegal, 1975–78; and Simpang New Town near Singapore, 1994

Habitat Puerto Rico looks almost like a new Babylon. But the architect used the topography of a hill as the basis of his hill city. »I didn't cover the entire hill with buildings. There's still a lot of greenery left«, comments the architect, then explains the constructional system: »I created concrete modules whose cross sections resemble compressed hexagons and can also be combined in wonderful ways in the vertical plane. At 22 metric tons per module I have provisionally reached

a minimum weight. The modules can be transported on special low-bed trucks on the highway or on barges by water – this way the city can gradually grow, but of course also shrink again.«

We have driven halfway up the hill by big winding roads, get out of the car, and look at the town's charming layout. It reminds us of Mediterranean hill towns, and no doubt was modeled on them. The town's courtyards and squares are a beautiful combination of public and private space. Especially appealing – and certainly also inspired by the Mediterranean region – are the roof-scapes, which are accessible to residents. »Their particular charm«, says Moshe Safdie, »lies in the fact that in the vertical plane the modules are staggered every half story so that short con-necting stairs equalize the individual levels.«

We have gradually climbed to the top of the hill city and can imagine the fine view the apart-ments have of the distant panorama. And in a café on the plaza we enjoy a view of the sea and get a good overview of the town. Businesses, restaurants, and communal facilities surround the square. The plaza gives access to the fourteen-story high-rises. There is also an open-air am-phitheater with a view of the sea and the landscape.

Cars are banished to the interior of the hill, but access streets go to each individual housing unit – a total of 800 prefabricated elements with private terraces.

We have our doubts whether a single architect can build such a huge city single-handedly.

»I believe I've created a huge variety«, counters Safdie. »You'll find a whole range of houses and apartment types. Naturally housing directly near the water is preferred, but all the homes look out at green spaces.«

We're very impressed by Habitat Puerto Rico, but put off for another time visits to the Habitats in Israel and New York, based on very similar concepts. For we want to visit two more gigantic cities, beginning with Keur Farah Pahlavi in Senegal. From a private plane we see that a linear city has been implemented here.

»It is natural«, explains Safdie. »The sand dunes stretch along the Niayes waters, a green oa-sis, for more than 2 km, and the network of houses has developed along the regulated waters and is influenced by traditional building forms.«

What is the motive for creating such a city here? »It's actually an industrial port, near the phos-phate mines and oil refineries. Soon the population will have increased to a total of 200,000. Many of the people work in the factories.« For the most part, the city is a pedestrian zone. The harsh landscape has been made an integral part of it.

Simpang New Town (1994) in Singapore has a completely different character. Like a boom-erang it lies by the ocean, housing 125,000 people. The commanding large structure, shaped like a horseshoe, is a link between the ocean and the lushly landscaped city.

This center is dedicated to recreation and community life. It is continued in two extensive wings as a sports harbor and a houseboat settlement.

Dahinden 1971; Safdie 1996.

Project Puerto Rico is not quite as utopian as it seems: at any rate, 30 units were actually complet-ed – after which the building contractor pulled out.

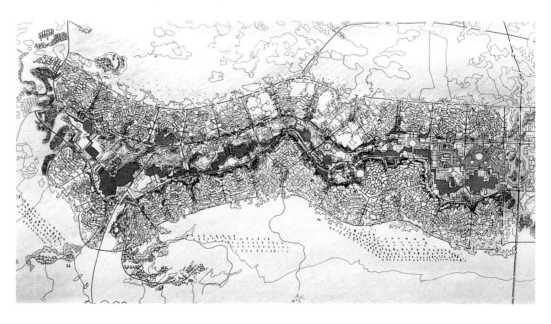

417. Moshe Safdie, Habitat Puerto Rico, 1968–71.
418. Moshe Safdie, Keur Farah Pahlavi, linear city, Senegal, Africa, 1975–78.

419. Moshe Safdie, Simpang New Town, Singapore, 1994.

Moshe Safdie implemented a notable project before designing Habitat Puerto Rico: in 1967 he created Habitat '67 for the Montreal World Fair. Safdie does not use space lattices, but stacks the self-supporting modules on top of each other to a height of ten stories. Admittedly, the concrete modules are very heavy. The result is a series of appealing configurations. The roofs formed the terraces for the floor above. Of course, the interesting density of the development meant that to some extent neighbors had an unimpeded view of each other's space. The first construction phase consisted of 158 housing units made up of 354 concrete modules. For the second construction phase, totaling 1,000 housing units, the system was modified, but the project never materialized. On the other hand, smaller developments in Israel were actually implemented.

The urban planning projects in Senegal and in Singapore are borderline utopias, for they were developed quite rationally as plans that could definitely be implemented. Moshe Safdie is anything but a »utopian« and has produced a very impressive series of works. In the more recent, large housing developments, however, he no longer uses the »Habitat« concept. The architecture of the representative, public buildings in the US, Canada, and Israel is realistic and high-quality.

Stanley Tigerman (b. 1930). The Instant City, 1968, and the floating Urban Matrix, 1969

The term »Instant City« doesn't seem entirely plausible to us. It tends to make us think of something flexible and provisional.

Tigerman is in every way »Bucky's« equal when it comes to massive geometrical architecture. »My buildings are not pyramids«, he explains, »but gigantic triangular slabs that shore each other up. These triangular frameworks contain the functional volume, apartments with the inserted infrastructure. Between the slabs, on a sunken level, are express and access roads.«

The construction was simple: The triangles have 200-m-long sides and are 16.5 m deep; the primary structure consists of 65 cm thick, fireproof steel tubes. This structure stands on individual concrete pyramids that transfer the load to concrete slabs. Diagonal steel cables take up the tangential thrust.

We take the slanting elevator and at several stops Tigerman explains the vertical structure: »The garages are located four stories below ground level. The first three upper floors are reserved for city government and offices, schools and light industry.«

We get out and walk past the pretty stores that invite passersby to go on a shopping spree. We then ride past five office floors. The last section houses the apartments, all of which have a wide, sweeping view of the landscape. From the restaurant at the top there is another lovely panoramic view. »You can see the wide green spaces and recreation areas at the foot of the pyramid, both a natural landscape and park. They're within easy reach, which makes individual terraces quite superfluous.«

The pyramid form is also the basic element of the floating city »Urban Matrix«. The pyramids are inverted and connected with each other in a huge egg-carton system. This rests on a massive pontoon several floors high. Its upper level is a spacious public plaza. »I chose reinforced aluminum for the structure in order to keep the floating island as light as possible. Octagonal tubes with a diameter of 5.50 m form the exterior framework. The entire transportation of persons and goods takes place within these eight tubes.«

As a matter of fact, one of the slanting elevators brings us to the top floor, and a moving pathway takes us to the next slanting elevator. Now we notice that in various places two pyramids are placed on top of each other and in some spots a third layer has been stacked on top, each layer having 24 stories. The system comprises more than 160 pyramids.

The fully automated transportation system makes cars superfluous. These can be parked in a large car park on the shore. An express road connects it to the traffic junctions.

»The city is completely flexible. At present its character is very commercial: Most of the pyramids contain offices, and the pontoon, mostly underwater, houses factories and industrial plants.«

420. Stanley Tigerman, Instant City, 1968.
421. Stanley Tigerman, Urban Matrix, 1969.

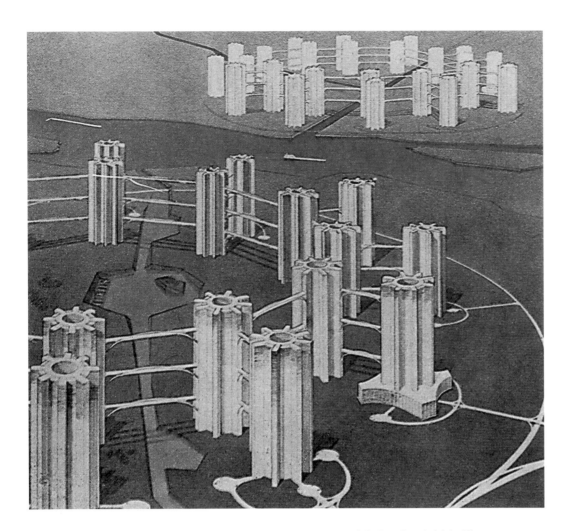

Tigerman shows us one of the most beautiful apartments: It is four levels high. The rooms are of different heights and the space is brilliantly designed. Again, we have a view of both the sea and the plaza, for the apartments are located on the periphery of the artificial island.

Stadt und Utopie 1982; Dahinden 1971.

The question remains open whether the residential sections of Instant City (which has nothing in common with the one designed by Archigram) are actually adequately shielded from traffic noise. If the housing units were oriented toward the east or west, then all of them, unlike other similar projects, would have adequate natural sunlight. There is also the question of open spaces near individual apartments and around schools and kindergartens. The construction drawing shows that the building could definitely be implemented using conventional structural design methods.

Vernal M. Tyler and Carl Asiala. The City of Reason, 1970

From the mother city the U-Rapid brings us into the U-Water Ring 1 of the city in seven minutes. »We're going to change to the O-Water Ring 3, so you'll have the best view of our new city«, our guides advise us. The transfer functions perfectly: UW1 to VR4, then Vertical Rapid Elevator 4 and from there to the OW3, and we're seated comfortably in noiselessly moving containers in a glass panorama tube.

It's almost too fast for us to be able to take in the complex in its entirety: Arranged in a circle there are twelve towers 160 m in diameter and 120 stories high, that is, roughly 400 m. The complex has a population of 250,000. One underground and three aboveground express railways connect the towers. Parking is located in the underground floors, but cars are used only for external traffic.

We notice that the towers look very rigid and schematic. »Not at all« say our guides. »That may be a superficial impression, but you can purchase very different types of apartments, and moreover you can plan the apartment just the way you want it. And naturally there is a first-class infra-

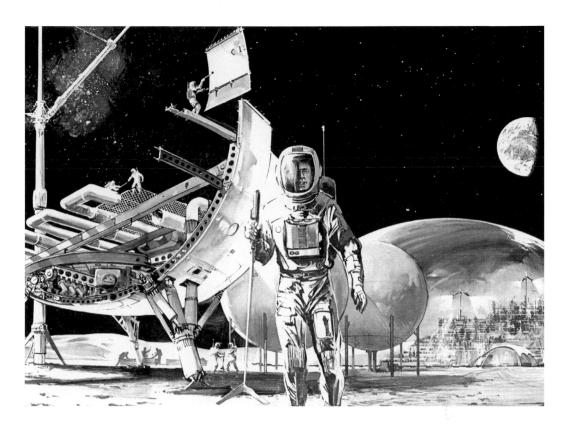

structure. We've especially emphasized venues for education, culture, and communication.«
It also goes without saying that the technology is state-of-the-art.

What about open spaces? »We're in an aquatic ring city here – the water is the recreation area. But the neighboring city is terrestrial: It's in an almost unspoiled landscape.«

In conclusion, Vernal M. Tyler enthusiastically exclaims: *»From every floor of our housing developments you have an unobstructed, grandiose view.«*

Schippke 1970.

Sometimes it is necessary to get close to science fiction, and occasionally maybe even cross the boundary to it when interesting urbanistic concepts are presented. There is a suggestion of considerable euphoria here – which was still prevalent when the book was published, in 1970. There are constant references to the legendary year 2000. Well, this is 2007 – which part of the prophecy has come true, and what has turned out completely differently?

Paul Lowman. The Lunar City, 1970

One hundred years after Aldrin another space capsule lands on the Moon – to visit the almost completed Lunar City. Paul Lowman of the American Goddard Space Flight Center played a substantial role in its development, and he is our expert guide.

»The first ›settlers‹ on the Moon were the scientists, of course, and primarily the astronomers. Initially they had to put up with living under the surface of the Moon, in relatively small, connected capsules. The next phase consisted in simply roofing over the craters of the Moon. Geodesic domes modeled on those of Buckminster Fuller were the ideal structures!«

Ahead is a third stage in settling the Moon, the boldest of all: An immense transparent dome arches over the terraced city. And to our surprise the individual levels, like hanging gardens, are overgrown with luxuriant vegetation. Our guide explains: »Minute traces of lunar dust cause the plants to proliferate. Also, we are able to obtain water from deep within the Moon.«

Schippke 1970

After the euphoria of the lunar landing imaginations have gradually calmed down. However, in the US, research on the settlement of space has been continuing almost unnoticed. Depictions of the colonizing of the Moon are becoming more concrete.

Philip Hammond, Ulrich Schippke, and the US Department of Agriculture. The Atomic Agrarian City, 1970

Naturally walking or driving through the city is out of the question. We can observe its gigantic dimensions only from the air. The first thing we see from a height of 1,000 m is one of no less than 3,000 man-made islands equipped with nuclear power stations that supply nineteen billion people with energy. But why have the power stations been built out in the ocean? »It's the only place where, without major problems, we can obtain the huge amounts of cooling water«, says Professor Hammond. »Moreover, we do not take up precious land.« And somewhat euphorically he adds, »*This is not simply an additional source of energy, it's a new dimension for the human race.*«

The availability of energy makes it possible to have huge agrarian machines, large factory farms that stretch for miles parallel to roads and track systems. Machines for sowing, harvesting, and processing, run on endless rails like craneways and are fully automated. But this agrarian system is still weather-dependent. That is why there are enormous glass dome structures, which are completely independent of the climate and topsoil: They create their own optimum growing conditions.

Schippke 1970.

The drawing has the usual naïve character of science-fiction portrayals. Now that our imagination is roaming in the future, there is also the question of alternatives to atomic energy.

Yet the future already seems to have begun: The US is already in the process of planning the first offshore atomic island in New Jersey. And experiments with synthetic foods have been going on for decades as factory farms are being developed by the US Department of Agriculture. Of course, the increasing »green« movement with its emphasis on »natural« foods has been strongly opposed to this trend.

James Wines (b. 1932) of the group SITE (Sculpture in the environment). The highrise of homes, 1981, and the greening of Manhattan, 1979

From far away the ten-story building seems like an ordinary high-rise. Close up we can hardly believe our eyes, however, and James Wines is delighted by our amazement. He explains the reasoning behind the structure: »Well, we know that the individual single-family home is every citizen's dream – and we help them achieve this dream. We simply built a huge shelf with topsoil in lieu of floors, open on two sides. Then people came, each with their little house, finished, already built, in the style they preferred!«

Quite true: What a wondrous, comical mix of all imaginable styles – plus, homeowners have a small piece of land they can call their own. Naturally they do not have to give up technical comforts. Connection to the central infrastructure is not a problem.

But what about all-round natural sunlight? »See for yourself«, says Mr. Wines, »all the little houses have optimum sunlight, for the north side is occupied by technical equipment, and service and communal facilities, which do not need natural light.«

425. Philip Hammond and Ulrich Schippke, nuclear power plants on man-made islands, and factory farms.

426. James Wines and SITE group, highrise of homes, USA, 1981.
427. James Wines and SITE group, The greening of Manhattan, USA, 1989.

Before we get to the core of the building, we walk through a lush garden landscape, more wilderness than park, and an ideal place for children to play. The elevator brings us to the roof terrace, and again we are surprised by the prolific greenery and flowers.

We stop briefly on the sixth floor to visit one of the homeowners. He's decided on an alpine cottage surrounded by a little garden to match. At the moment, he is enjoying the sunset. But that doesn't mean he lives in isolation. Mr. Wines emphasizes how important the role of communication is. »This is a vertical community that can house diametrically opposed human needs, so that homeowners can use the cultural advantages of an urban center without having to give up the individual privacy of a house and garden in the suburbs.«

If the high-rises with their little gardens were a big surprise, we are completely flabbergasted at the next place we visit.

We approach Manhattan from the water side, and while the familiar silhouette is not new, it always fills us with admiration and enthusiasm. But as we gradually approach, we do a double take: The sharp outlines of the skyscrapers are blurred, flicker in a strange, green, almost impressionistic light – do our eyes deceive us?

Gradually we realize that the houses and skyscrapers are overgrown with plants – flowers, shrubs, trees: New York is now a green city.

How is that possible? we ask. »We've developed a new serum after years of research. Now plants no longer need soil, since a thin layer of this preparation is sufficient to produce a hypertrophy of vegetation.«

Thomsen 1994; Vercelloni 1994; *Visionen und Utopien* 2002; *Architectures experimentelles* 2003.

Is this really a city? We keep encountering situations where a »house« becomes a »city«. It is hard, and perhaps not that important, to draw a distinction. For a short time, there was a plan to implement such a project: Battery Park in New York was considered as a possible site.

The full expression of individuality in an urban setting has repeatedly been the subject of debate. »Stacked city lots« are also discussed, as a kind of borderline case of participatory building.

We have known about the greening of buildings for a long time – though only with vegetation rooted in soil. Thousands of suburban homes on the periphery of large cities have actually turned into green cubes enveloped by vegetation.

In a few temples in Angkor Wat, Cambodia, and again in Teotihuacán in Guatemala, the plants have triumphed dramatically: The temple buildings have been occupied, shrouded, broken up by the force of the vegetation.

Lebbeus Woods (b. 1940). Centricity, 1986, the Cyclical Cities, 1987, and Aeon, 1981–84

What an incredible city! Guided by Lebbeus Woods, we feel confused and alienated – and yet we have a sense of déjà vu. Is it the spatially irritating, absurd structures of Piranesi's *Carceri* we are reminded of? Is it the technocratic silhouettes of the oil refineries with their towers, struts, pipes, frames, and ladders? Is it the huge industrial containers of gas and liquids? Is it the parallels to the »deconstructivism« of the early Coop Himmelblau buildings? Or to expressionistic 1920s film architecture? Or are we on the set of the latest science-fiction movie? Whatever the case – we have dozens of associations: Admittedly it isn't easy to imagine this as an inhabited city.

The first city we visit is Centricity, which has already been in existence for 20 years. Irritated and fascinated at the same time, we move in the spaces that are given strong physicality by light and shadow. We do not ask Lebbeus Woods whether Centricity is functional, for we would no doubt get only aphoristic answers, such as the following: »Centricity*: That is the unified area. Centricity is the adjective and the noun, the changer and the changed. A Centricity of universal science exists within the present space-time continuum.*«

Nor do terms like »geomechanical tower« or »protomechanical tower« or »biomechanical tower« help us decode Woods's remarks. So we abandon ourselves to amazement at the sight of his proliferating, brilliant stylistic idiom. We feel that Woods's reflections, not always easy to understand, exist independently of his architecture: »*New patterns of urban forms and city life develop from concepts of time and space, which we consider to be a space-time continuum. Energetic form is the basis of a universal science, universcience, which includes all individuals and whose principal instrument is the study of architecture. Its interactive sphere is the* CENTRiCITY*. The goal of the study is knowledge, and the goal of knowledge is the completed work.*«

Now we pass some towers, perhaps those with the central photon accumulator, called QUAD and D-QUAD: They are biomechanical and biodynamic towers with quadropolar and deformed quadropolar forms that correspond to the centrisymmetrical forms (circles) and eccentrisymmetrical forms (ellipses). They are also part of Centricity and form the »unified urban field«.

Before continuing our journey we take a plane and from above see to our surprise that ten circular rings are the structural elements overlying this confusingly expressive city.

Consequently we are no longer surprised by the excessive variety of forms in the next city, Cyclical City. Lebbeus Woods explains a few details. Again we struggle to understand his trains of thought, ranging between science, fantasy, and poetry: »*Forget the traditional so-called ›laws‹ of statics, aesthetics, and proportion. Feel your connection with the new experience of space and time. The number four is an ancient magical element: The four elements make up the world. Our existence moves through the four ages of life. And the same irrational substance is inherent in the circle. An architecture of dynamism, of geo-, bio-, mechano-dynamism, moves as a unit in the direction of an order or disorder. It is a combination of the dual metric measurements, of the geometry, biometry, mechanometry of the time-space complex.*«

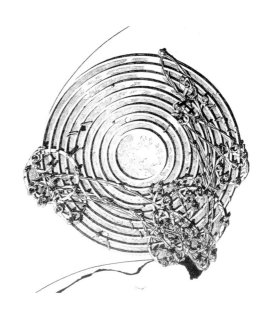

And Woods tries to elucidate the elemental significance of light: »*Visible light is a wave phenomenon, constant to matter and energy: Mattergy can be universally experienced in an urban
environment. Visible light is formed by architecture, which reveals an essential order, being a form
of visible light of metric transformations. The architectonic mathematics – archimatics – of visible
light is the basis of the general principles of a universal science. Architecture and the urban forms
of a universal science reveal the time-space transformations of metric light.*«

And now Woods takes us to see his AEON: A globular balloon has lifted the city of cross and
square into the clouds.

Lebbeus Woods takes leave of us as he quotes almost classical and charismatic guidelines:
»*We need create nothing but vision*« and: »*There is beauty of form only where there is beauty of
idea.*«

Woods constantly seduces us to follow him on poetic escapades: »*Perpetually soaring upward, precipitous, hard; growing out of the stone and rock or growing into it; or made of metal,
glass, crystal; sculptural, dome-shaped, balloon-shaped cupolas; globes like those of diving
boats; pyramids; airships like flying arks, sailing, gliding, soaring; extraterrestrial architectural bodies that are not concerned with accustomed geometries; others that phallically penetrate the
earth, form underground laboratories, pierce the surface like the shoots of plants, fly off as rckets
and explosive devices, spreading their payloads of ideas far and wide.*«

Woods 1987, 1992; Thomsen 1994.

Virtuoso drawing and fascinating graphics have a solid role in modern architecture. Once a drawing
goes through the transition to an autonomous work of art this all too frequently means it is no longer
buildable. The drawings of Lebbeus Woods evoke associations with science fiction films, and there
are also clear similarities to the work of the Swiss film architect H.R. Giger, though this is not necessarily a direct influence.

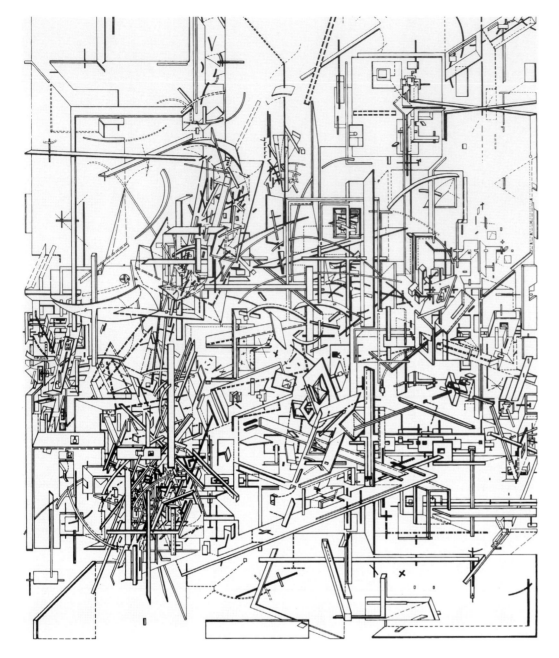

Daniel Libeskind (b. 1946). Little Universe, 1980

What an incredible, magical city – though at first it looks like chaos. Yet soon we gain completely new insights. Then we recognize an order, a basic structure committed to right angles, and rods, bars, slabs, poles.

Above and below them there is a plunging cosmos of arches, junctions, teetering, flying architectural elements, so that we, with our biological bodies, are hardly able to find our way here amd are afraid of being an involuntary part of this systematized explosion that again becomes an implosion, however, a condensed and crisscrossing complex.

Is there a suggestion of Piranesi here? »*Certainly*«, admits Libeskind, »*he proclaims that rather than being focused on pleasure or usefulness, architecture is deeply related to the voice of the spirit.*«

Modern architecture is no longer horrified by extremes and excess. Libeskind, too, thinks in relative terms: »Micromegas – that is, tiny giants – like giant dwarfs, inhabit my ›little universe‹, a universe that like the coming reciprocal primeval bang, has shrunk into a house full of miracles.«

Klotz 1986.

We cannot help thinking of another comparison, the stylistic idiom and probably also the process character of expressive deconstructivists. Libeskind draws his fantasies in 1980; but Philipp Johnson does not bundle the phenomena of deconstructivism in an exhibition until 1988, and so it is only logical to invite Libeskind to participate. However, Libeskind is not content with the drawing alone: The Jewish Museum in Berlin is his breakthrough into reality and marks the beginning of his career as an international »star architect«. We shall meet him again in chapter 13.6.

Phil Hawes (b. 1934). The Llegada Piedras (EcoVille), Oracle, Arizona, 1990

On the long, impressive drive through the Arizona desert Phil Hawes finds the time to expound his views on ecology. They are principles, almost commonplaces, with which we have been familiar for years. Still, there are a few points that arouse our interest.

»We've completed the ›Biosphere 2‹ project in Arizona, and now we are planning a truly ecological community, which we call ›EcoVille‹. What we are interested in is garbage: It can also be seen as a resource, only it is located in the wrong place, at the wrong time, and in the wrong concentration. We are now in the last phase of the industrial revolution and have to complete it by total cleansing. We can no longer return to primal nature, but we must live in symbiosis with it.«

Phil Hawes now tells us about his model experiments in small neighborhoods, where participants explored the enormous importance of the locations where food is produced and of the transportation of food.

»*And so EcoVille was planned as a group of urban clusters with greenhouses and agricultural areas. The latter overlap for up to 500 m with the urban centers, which makes it easier to control the recycling of food and makes it possible for farmers to participate in urban life, reduces transportation costs, gives townspeople access to the rural landscape and helps them to understand the processes of food production.*«

We can already make out the silhouette of the little town on the horizon, but our amazement increases with every kilometer as we recognize the details: Is this another Disneyland or one of Hundertwasser's quirks? Little gabled cottages, crooked arcades, turrets and domes, romantic squares and narrow lanes form a strange conglomeration that seems garnished with green spaces. The globe that forms the center of the town, however, is imposing: It serves the community, entertainment, and fun.

Underground access roads bring us directly to the center: Like the rest of the town, it is a pedestrian zone. A subway takes care of all short-distance travel. Only the elderly and disabled use small electric vehicles.

432. Phil Hawes, Llegada Piedras, Arizona, USA, 1990. Project for Oracle.

»We've overcome the fatal urban separation of functions: Residential areas, offices, businesses, and factories coexist perfectly, for all sources of environmental pollution have been completely eliminated.«

As we continue our walk, we are surprised when Phil Hawes takes us into a supermarket – what's so special about that? Hawes explains a principle that embraces both the realm of ecology and ethics:

»People should buy what they need. We would like ›consumers‹ to become ›customers‹, purchasers, buyers, patrons.«

And that also explains why the supermarket is not flooded with a glut of merchandise.
The planners have also implemented another very important aspect: When we take a few of the products from the shelves, we discover that printed on the packaging – which is limited to a minimum – are very precise, legible, and easily understood facts about its contents, weight, origin, and manufacture, guaranteeing that it was organically and ecologically produced.

We conclude our visit in the large globe, take transportation to its observation level, and see the green fingers of surrounding wilderness areas reaching into the little town that lies before us like a fairy tale.
Architectural Design 63/1993.

The eco-house and the energy-saving house have gone through considerable development in the last decades, even if a full broad-based breakthrough has not occurred to date. The eco-town is the subject of constant discussion, promotion, and design. The idea of transforming existing cities is probably utopian, but so is the founding of new eco-towns. Typically such urban concepts are mostly romantic, idyllic, and nostalgic in character – verging on kitsch. A dedicated urban planner, Phil Hawes has succeeded in implementing a few model situations.

Lazarus Long (b. 1912). New Utopia, 1995, 2000

Even on the luxury liner that brings us to the Caribbean island southwest of the Cayman Islands, the ruling prince of New Utopia describes his realm in glorious color:

»New Utopia today is a world center of international business, and is the headquarters of big firms, huge insurance companies, important corporations. The power and imagination of entrepreneurship, the profitable businesses, the freedom to make money characterize the city-state. And it was all made possible because we collect no taxes – except a 15-percent import tax.

Well, I don't think much of democracies with their lack of freedom and oppression. I have created a constitutional monarchy, the first in 200 years. This form of government protects citizens from abuse and guarantees stability. But we get along with a minimum number of politicians, and the government functions like a well-run business. The only citizen elections take place when they believe that their freedoms are restricted.«

Asked about the level of social welfare, Prince Lazarus explains: *»We do not need a welfare system. Everyone can take care of himself and knows his own interests and needs perfectly.«*

We are now approaching the island and are already able to recognize the massive substructure: A huge concrete plaform, standing on pillars and anchored in rock, supports the buildings. In the meantime we have landed in the harbor. We can see the magnificent silhouettes of the houses, and feel we've been transported to a new dream world, a collage of 19th and 20th century architecture.

We step directly from the ship into the luxury yacht of Prince Lazarus I, then slowly tour the town – by water. As a matter of fact, a new Venice has been created here, but one far more splendid than its old, sinking, dilapidated model.

The buildings have been arranged in incredible concentration, in condensed, interlinked, overlapping, interpenetrating combinations. But the plazas left free between them are enlivened by restaurants, cafés, hotel gardens full of happy young people.

Stone bridges and dramatic round arches bearing symbolic figures span the canals. Monumental domed buildings reminiscent of Otto Wagner, high-rises overgrown with flowers, office buildings in various styles make up the island's motley panorama.

»Attached to the luxury hotels are the casinos, but also cultural facilities. There are plenty of first-rate theaters, spacious exhibition halls, and festival halls for films and music.«

Prince Lazarus takes it for granted that all institutions have been conceived with an eye to tourism. *»We needed an initial 200 million dollars to get the island started. We began by building*

433. Lazarus Long, New Utopia, 1995, 2000. Center by the river.

the airport as well as the hotel and harbor. The areas have been divided precisely and rationally: We need 1.2 million square feet for the offices and commerce, 1.3 million square feet for the apartments and homes of every kind, and 1 million square feet for the hydroponic farms. In addition there are the areas required for the airport, harbor, cultural buildings, research institutes, and shopping centers.«

Our high-speed yacht, which has slowed to a comfortable crawl for us, takes us through the most important canals of the city. Traffic on the water is busy, and the buildings and activities are all directly linked with the blue, crystal-clear water.

Prince Lazarus is not content with architecture alone, for New Utopia is an incredibly lively city.

Even upon arrival we were struck by how many young people live in this city. »Yes, that's true«, the prince, who is himself well advanced in years, is pleased. »We are a youthful, even immortal city. A big clinic is studying the problems of prolonging life – and the research has been quite successful. But of course job opportunities and leisure activities are tailored to the needs of the young.«

The events and leisure activities listed by the prince make this quite evident: *»Every four years we have a gala event, a big birthday celebration. There are big prizes – not cars, but ships. Our Mardi Gras festival rivals that of New Orleans. Winter marks the beginning of the big arts and culture festival. Fine golf courses and tennis courts are available to everyone. In a big arena there are all kinds of competitions.«*

Now our ship lands near one of the inviting café-restaurants, and we realize that in the well-kept squares palm trees and tall plants provide shade.

On our return trip the prince once more praises the climate: »The water is very calm here, mostly as smooth as a mirror. Hurricanes come roughly once every seven years, but all buildings are securely constructed, and there are no floods, since the city stands on a platform.«

And before we take our leave of him and set off for the airport, the prince proudly speaks of his empire: *»We've built a new land in a wonderful climate, a perfect paradise. New Utopia.«*
Impossible Worlds 2000.

»Prince« Lazarus Long is a character in one of Robert A. Heinlein's novels. The entrepreneur Woodrow Wilson Smith has adopted this pseudonym.

Did Lazarus Long actually imagine he was so close to realizing his utopia? We can compare this project with Leon Krier's Arcadia (chap. 13.4). Krier probably also intended his project to be implemented, though, in spite of the postmodern era, he meant the architecture to be considerably higher in quality.

There have actually been implementations: The big holiday villages, for instance the Club Méditerranée, are very similar in character and represent a hedonistic and autonomous world beyond all global problems.

The idea of a peaceful paradise was actually realized in an amazing project, truly a built utopia: the American experiment »Celebration«, a »city« of peace, wealth, prosperity, and perpetual harmony. The counter-model of the city of eternal youth, as it were, is the American »town« Laguna Woods, a kind of old age home grown to urban dimensions that guarantees boundless contentment in old age (cf. chap. 13.7).

Ross Cortese. The Leisure World of Laguna Woods, California, USA, 1964–present

»Yes, this really is about creating the ideal town for old people! In the mild landscape of California we've succeeded in creating the best possible conditions for all those who want to enjoy their old age in peace and quiet!«

Mr. Ross Cortese welcomes us with these euphoric words – and at the same time we are back in the real world: This ideal town did become a reality – but how ideal is it?

In Mr. Cortese's private jet we circle above the town. We don't find the hundreds of little houses nestled amid the greenery particularly surprising. After all, this is par for the course in America. »This is really a small town«, Mr. Cortese informs us. »More than 18,000 people, 11,000 women and 7,000 men live in the 500 cottages. The total area is 2,100 acres or 3.3 square miles.«

But why do you believe that it's an ideal town? »That's simple: because here you find everything you need for your daily life, leisure, fun, and health!«

After landing and a short bus trip we actually get to see the town for ourselves. Coming from the east we pass a luxurious mall, the health center, and the hospital. After parking in a ramp we get into speedy golf carts and continue our tour past the Lutheran and the Catholic church and the golf course, directly into the community center.

»You'll find just about every activity here – enjoyable and constructive pastimes the whole year round«, Mr. Cortese praises this institution.

Not far away are the shopping center, the garden center, the stables. For spiritual recreation there are a Methodist and a Baptist church, also a Jewish temple and the house of »Christian Science«, while the Presbyterian church is west of the community center.

Two big golf courses provide the most popular and healthiest sport played by the elderly. The visible symbol of safety and surveillance are the twelve security gates. No one may enter without checking in.

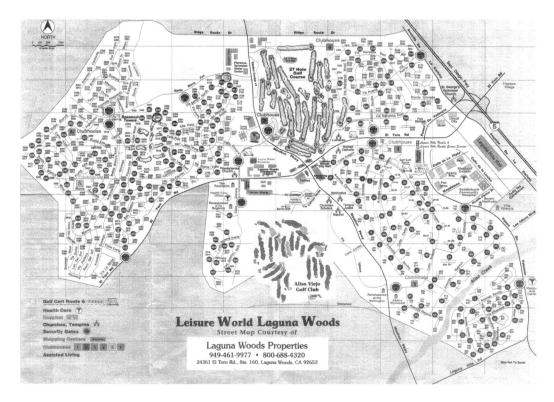

434. Ross Cortese and teams, Leisure World, Laguna Woods, California, USA.

435. Bodys Isek Kingelez, the new city of Kimbembele Ihunga, Kimbeville, Africa, 1994.

Now we drive along the periphery for a short stretch. At some distance from the rest of the buildings, somewhat isolated and very quiet, are a special type of cottages with few people outside them. The answer to our inquiry is a little disturbing: »Leisure World is a totally active and dynamic place. But of course not everybody can keep up as they get older. We've settled those who are in need of care here on the periphery.«

We're interested in concrete statistics, and Mr. Cortese is glad to oblige. Residents need to be over 55 years old. At the moment the average age is 78. Leisure World opened in 1964 and was completely settled by 1999. The inhabitants pay between 300 and 600 dollars a month depending on their income.

Of course we can understand Ross Cortese's enthusiasm, but we were not quite convinced and many questions remained unanswered.

Monocultures, whatever their type, have been increasingly criticized in recent decades. We cannot help feeling that the old people have been shunted off into a giant, seemingly perfect ghetto. Here we meet with a counter-model to the kind of community progressive forces all over the world strive for: integration, synthesis, multifunctionality.

Laguna Woods is not an isolated case, of course. Ross Cortese founded six more such settlements: two additional ones in California, and one each in Maryland, Virginia, Arizona, and New Jersey. In addition, there are many more models in the US, all of them tackling the problem of the elderly.

The St. Joe Company. Celebration, 1990

We have finally succeeded in building the city of pure, untroubled happiness!

Well no, of course it's not a utopia. After all, we've been wandering through this little Florida town, and it's inhabited, here and now, by flesh-and-blood human beings! What a fine life they have! In elegant, classicistic houses (800,000 to 1 million US$ each), with well-kept gardens, in secure communities, with friendly neighbors, and a perfect infrastructure – yes, indeed, this is where the truly happy American families live! It's not far from the airport and Disney World, and Market Street with upscale shopping is close by, as are the most fashionable sports facilities and elite cultural events; and in Artisan Park people can do arts and crafts.

Then why is this a utopia nevertheless? This aseptic prosperity, this carefree sense of security, this seductive backdrop are reserved for a new, artificial aristocracy, a shrinking minority of American society, a tiny fraction of the world's population.

Bodys Isek Kingelez (b. 1948). The city of Kimbembele Ihunga (Kimbeville), 1994

This journey takes us to Africa, to a little-known city – but let's forget all our preconceptions about African cities – here the African Kingelez has realized his dreams. He praises the advantages of his city.

»We haven't had any racist or social prejudices for a long time. Therefore there is no crime, and police and jails have long since become superfluous. The city has finally become rich – and still there is a political and economic balance.«

Boring gray houses, monotonous skyscrapers, streets as straight as an arrow are also a thing of the past: All the buildings have strong colors, exciting ornaments, pleasing patterns, and interesting forms. Public buildings have eccentric configurations, rigid street grids have been dissolved in dynamic, organic spatial landscapes, filled with life and joy. Much of this seems to have been built by playful children.
Documenta 11 2002.

And again – as in all the »utopian« centuries – a familiar nostalgic idea reappears here: no social prejudices, no crime, no police, no prisons. In Kingelez's city we are reminded of the colorful building blocks of children, but also of the bright world of Pop Art, the designs of Archigram, the theses of trivial and banal architecture in the 1960s. However, the demands of architects that cities should become more cheerful, more colorful, more improvised and flexible have rarely met with much success.

Belgian team Kinshasa. The imaginary city, 2000

How can we even speak of a city here? Where are the apartment houses, government agencies, office buildings, supermarkets? And our Belgian friends – a researcher, a filmmaker, and an architect – restate our question and add to it: »Can a city exist without architecture consisting of built houses? How modern is our modernity? How universal can urban planning be? Can urbanity be incorporeal?« Using as their example Kinshasa, the capital of Congo, the former Belgian Congo with its two million inhabitants, our friends show us an »imaginary city«. They introduce us to a different concept of a city. »A Western city is for the most part defined by traffic, engineering, and technology, by sanitary systems and consumption. All that is necessary for the urban identity.«

Yes, certainly, but what might be the alternatives? How could these factors be pushed into the background? »In this city, or in large sections of it, urban space unfolds and designs itself, as it were, there's a very specific infrastructure in which even errors, conflicts, and even breakdowns have their place.« We stroll through the city, which consists primarily of sprawling districts that we might refer to as slums. But obviously the city exists outside conventional urban architecture, and the explanations of our friends are not very easy to understand: »Kinshasa goes far beyond narcissistic architecture. The most important infrastructural unit is the human body. It is the only ›structure‹, as it were, constantly in process of being built and perfected. It is at the same time a marketplace, street, garage, and church: That's the imaginative city.«

But how does this phenomenon become concretely visible? »People are very concerned about physical aesthetics. Sports, bodybuilding, clothes are very important.« So people are completely self-absorbed? »Not at all. The six million inhabitants of the entire region have strong social relationships. They've created an impressive community.«

But no doubt people have few spiritual, non-material relationships? »That's not true, either. The visible world is reflected as if in a mirror and creates an invisible world. People live in dualistic fields of tension, between reality and its double, between the visible and the invisible, between day and night.« But all this hardly has a metaphysical basis, such as a religion, does it? »Wrong again. The people are devout Christians with many pre-Christian relics, all kinds of magic and mysticism. They're convinced that the dead are not dead. Thus the cult of the dead has great significance. People are preoccupied with the Apocalypse and apocalyptic visions.The ›église de réveil‹, the church of awakening, is a very strong spiritual force and has its own TV channel and a strong public presence.«

We continue our tour of the city, which seems to be almost endless, and waver between shock at the poverty of the inhabitants and fascination at the vibrancy of this »imaginary city«.
Metamorph 9 2004.

The analyses of the Belgian research group are fascinating, but a crucial question remains unanswered: What is supposed to happen, what can happen here? Should development – or lack of it – be allowed to take its course? Should one intervene? But how?

Harvey Ferrero. The big agricultural structure, 1990

We race across the plains of the Midwest – and there it is: The gigantic buildings with their multi-layered slabs, cubes, and volumes seem to be caught up in something stormy, urgent, thundering. And at the edge of this mighty, dramatic spectacle a menacing monster stands in the middle of the fields: wildly echoing and shooting the rays from its crown into the sky.

Harvey Ferrero is searching for an authentic American architecture, but he gives us only a few verbal hints: »*We're still building as we did a hundred years ago. I almost have a nervous breakdown when I see what technologies and materiel were used for a terrible purpose in the Gulf War – or in the America's Cup regatta. We should work with them in architecture – new lightweight materials that move, change, and react to a constantly changing and modified environment. All these new structures are beautiful and in tune with the American ideal, which is tied to individualism and a love for wide open spaces.*«
Architectural Design 63/1993.

Harvey Ferrero tells us nothing more detailed about the type of agriculture involved. It seems almost anachronistic that such a progressive town, which uses the most modern materials, is created for a traditional economic system.

436. Marketplace, Kinshasa, Congo, 2000.
437. Harvey Ferrero, large Midwestern agricultural town, 1992.

Dagmar Richter (b. 1955). A Century City for Los Angeles, 1991

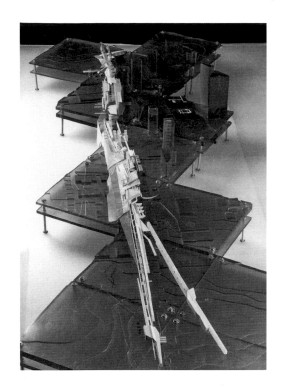

Again we need to take our first look at the new Century City from the air: A confusing bundle of surfaces, cubes, struts, slabs shoots across a highway over the city and landscape, clearly a »deconstructivist« design.

»*The city is, as it were, a blood sedimentation of various interacting ›traces‹. The city looks like an airy puff pastry of ›traces‹ that alternate each time they are recorded.*«

»*The city*«, continues Richter, »*is a medial text that changes through its producers and users.*«

There is no functional program. That is why this new city has returned public space to the inhabitants of Los Angeles. The top level is covered over with a translucent wall. Suspended from this linear structure is a series of vertical surfaces that create a sound barrier against the noise of the freeways. Also suspended is a genealogical library. The interior level, on the other hand, presents an artificial landscape with light and shadow plays.

Richter 2001; *Architectures experimentales* 2003.

Can real »city plans« still be drawn up today? How long ahead can we plan? Progressive urban planners try to express themselves in structural images, computer simulations and three-dimensional models, verbal programs, and politico-economic policies, leaving open as much as possible (cf. chap. 13.10).

Norm Nixon. The Freedom Ship, 2002

Norm Nixon, the head manager of the Freedom Ship, gives us a choice whether we come by ship or plane. Since we're talking about an island in the ocean, we prefer to go by ship.

From our ocean liner we catch sight of the gigantic structure that moves slowly in the ocean. As we gradually get closer we are able to distinguish close to 25 floors; we have a hard time estimating the length, which is certainly not less than 1,500 m. »There are 40,000 people living here«, Norm Nixon says to our surprise. »They have many reasons for wanting to be part of this ocean community. Foremost among these is wanting to see the world without ever leaving home. Above all, a business community has grown here. What is sensational is that there are no taxes, fees, or charges.«

We've approached the Freedom Ship and now the motor yachts dock and bring us into the harbor. From there we go to the elegant reception room with an upscale restaurant, and we are surprised by the lovely view of well tended parks, pools, and palm trees. There are at least 80 hectares of green spaces and productive land on the ship. There is plenty of room for outdoor sports and games.

It goes without saying that the entire »city« infrastructure is carefully planned: schools, universities, libraries for education; cinemas, theaters, museums for culture; hospitals and sanitariums for health care; and, naturally, a luxurious shopping mall to meet the diverse needs of consumers.

Norm Nixon shows us a few of the apartments, which are opulent. The splendid, ever-changing view of the ocean seen from each apartment is, of course, one of their outstanding features. »*Not everyone here on board is a rich tax-evader*«, Norm Nixon reassures us. »*Remember that the crew, service personnel, and their families total more than a thousand, who all live on the ship.*«

Our initial misgivings that we will never manage to walk all over the ship on foot soon vanish: We board an electric train that brings us to the overhanging bowsprit – free of charge, of course. We ask Norm Nixon what happens to the enormous quantities of garbage – that must cause terrible pollution of the ocean, right? »*Our ship is an example of environmental responsibility. Our complete recycling system prevents even small amounts of pollution to enter the ocean.*« Norm Nixon offers plenty of idealistic interpretations that far exceed the advantages of a tax-free society.

»*By building the Freedom Ship we didn't just build a big ocean liner, we created a society that offers its members a new, wonderful, unprecedented lifestyle. The ship is not a separate state, however, but sails under the flag of an existing state. And the citizens of the ship are subject to the laws of this state. The captain, however, has special authority.*«

The ship's construction is not revolutionary by any means. »*We didn't intend to demonstrate the kind of high-tech imagined by the designers. We built a simple barge, from a traditional steel structure. We don't expect high speed, but security and solidity.*«

438. Dagmar Richter, Century City for Los Angeles, 1991.

One wish, or dream, which is becoming more and more pronounced in view of what is happening in large cities, seems to have come true in the Freedom Ship: »The ship is not targeted by criminals and terror of any kind. We have an FBI agent on board in charge of a 2,000-man security force. The ship is the safest place you could ever live on.«

The old notion of developing the ideal society on an island has been given a new interpretation in this modern project. The ship as a largely autonomous structure, equipped with all that is essential for life and constituting something like a community, or at least social relationships: That is something the ship has in common with a city, which is why ocean liners have always been a kind of floating cities.

A fascinating hypertrophy of this idea is the Freedom Ship as a totally mobile society. We've already encountered a floating city, inflated to a gigantic size: the Walking City of the Archigram Group (cf. chap. 13.2).

In the Freedom Ship there would clearly be three castes: the immensely rich, permanent inhabitants, the staff for the entire infrastructure, and visitors and tourists.

439. Norm Nixon, Freedom Ship, 2002.

Visit. New York 11. 9. 2001

It is September 9th, 2001, a fine, sunny day, and on this, the second day of our New York visit, Christiane and I, planning to do the obligatory tour of Manhattan. The majestic panorama keeps sending us into raptures – the white towers of the World Trade Center rule the skyline.

On the following day, September 10th, we visit downtown Manhattan, have a pleasant snack in the garden near the World Financial Center. It's a lovely, warm late-summer day. And then we walk over to the World Trade Center: The express elevator rushes us up to the top floor, we stand on the terrace with its fine panorama of the dreamy sculptured landscape of Manhattan, photos for our archive, then back to the carefree, colorful, restless city.

The agenda for September 11th is to go uptown; another sunny day. We take the bus to Columbia University.

A woman gets on the bus and tells the busdriver that a plane has crashed into the World Trade Center. Must be an amateur pilot who's lost his way. But at the university there's a strange excitement – nervousness, people running back and forth, talk, hectic movement.

Then we are sitting in front of the TV in the university's community room, unable to comprehend what we are watching on the screen. It is so hard to imagine, so shattering, so horrifying that one wishes it were just a horror movie – but this unimaginable catastrophe has become reality: For already we see, as we leave the building, the gigantic cloud of smoke over downtown Manhattan. The cloud bears witness to the unmistakable atrocity: Two planes controlled by terrorists have rammed the towers of the World Trade Center. Within minutes, the towers have collapsed, burying 3,000 people under them.

And here, once more, a tragic utopia has become a reality that goes far beyond anything anyone can imagine, invent, or fear: destruction, death, annihilation. The new Babylon has collapsed, not because of the wrath of God, but as a result of hatred and despair, fanaticism and injustice. And this day, which we experienced directly here and now, this day – September 11th, 2001 – has changed the world.

The world architects. The new utopia of Babylon, 2002–10

Barely a year after the second of horror, the elite of world architects is called upon to rebuild the New Babylon. Naturally it makes no sense economically to leave the site vacant as a memorial – it is one of the most expensive pieces of real estate in the world. In other words: The new »World Trade Center« is no utopia, is it? It must rise again, mustn't it, in one form or another? Such was the prevailing opinion soon after the 2001 catastrophe, and soon the architects were hard at work. Seven made the last cut.

It is now 2007 – but none of the projects has been implemented – what a gigantic utopia the bold designs proved to be! In other words, a good reason to pay them all a short visit!

The United Architects: Foreign Office Architects« created a heavenly city. Their skyscrapers resemble their predecessors the most closely – a group of buildings that touch at a few points and are linked by a large public plaza 240 m above the ground.

SOM give the skyscrapers that they assemble into an irregular group sharp bends, breaks, slanting angles, cladding the cores with obliquely structured glass sheaths.

Peterson / Littenberg do without specific architectural styles, adopting the forms of Battery Park City and thus the traditions of the 1930s.

The group THINK-Design also takes up the theme of the twin towers. But there is to be a new focus: The World Trade Center is also supposed to become a World Cultural Center. At 640 m it is the highest building in the world.

In the project by Richard Meier the remembrance of the catastrophe is intended to be in the foreground. The five towers form a powerful, monumental gesture for the skyline of Manhattan that competes with Cesar Pelli's World Financial Center.

Norman Foster takes up the theme of the two towers. The clarity and sureness of his design has garnered him a great deal of support. The towers carefully touch only at two points. The public space at the base is very effective.

Surely not all the designs have remained utopias? Daniel Libeskind's project is going to be implemented, isn't it? For a while, it seemed that it would – though substantial changes are being planned.

440. World Trade Center, terrorist attack, New York, USA, 11. 9. 2001.

But gradually, under pressure by the investors, chances of implementaion have dwindled. In other words, we are visiting Utopia!

The press, the public, and many politicians were thrilled by Daniel Libeskind's project. One of the lovely faceted towers rises to a height of 400 m; it is directly connected with a needle tower, brilliant as a crystal, 600 m high, which is, as it were, the vertical memorial. The horizontal memorial, on the other hand, is sunk deep between the towers. The rocks that used to form the foundations of the Twin Towers have been exposed. The traffic streams past the memorial site – past and present, tragedy and hope are linked.

Back to reality now – yet none of the seven projects that made the last cut win the race! Disappointed and embittered, Daniel Libeskind, so close to the goal, realizes that though a fellow competitor is awarded the contract – the huge architectural factory SOM (Skidmore-Owings-Merrill) – the father of the somewhat simple project is C. Whitehead, the former US secretary of defense. Its height is determined by simple symbolism: 1776 is the year of the American Declaration of Independence, and that will be its height in feet. Just this once, we include a non-utopia.

Based on a later competition in 2005, the winner, Michael Arad, was given the task of designing the open space, though only after substantial changes.

441. United Architects, project for new World Trade Center, New York, USA, 2002.
442. Richard Meier & Partners, Eisenman, Siegel, and Holl, project for new World Trade Center, New York, USA, 2002.
443. Foster + Partners, project for new World Trade Center, New York, USA, 2002.
444. Daniel Libeskind, project for new World Trade Center, New York, USA, 2002.
445. David Childs of Skidmore, Owings and Merrill, Freedom Tower, World Trade Center, New York, USA, 2007, 2010.

441 442
443 444 445

13.7. Russia

The NER group. Moscow, 1967

On the outskirts of Moscow three towers, unequal in height, dominate a rather diffuse landscape. They highlight a residential and industrial district.

Adjacent to the towers is a fanshaped structure comprising 20 floors of apartments. Spatially rectangular structures alternate with sculptural figurations. It is obvious that open public spaces, while not clearly articulated, do exist.

»Our diversity and abstraction are a protest against Stalinist architecture«, explains one of the group's members as he leads us through the large squares, which, though large, do not overwhelm the residents.

Architectural Design 10/1968; Cook 1970.

Stalinist architecture was jettisoned long ago – at least by a few young, progressive groups. That is why we are not surprised by the passionate adoption of the stylistic idiom of the West.

However, there are only faint echoes of the great era of Russian constructivism.

A. Shipkov and E. Shipkova and others. The Siberian residential pyramids, 1967

We're traveling in a special jeep through the endless winter landscape of Siberia. Why, we wonder, do people have to settle in this snowy wilderness? Isn't it true that the Soviet Union has unlimited land reserves in moderate climate zones? »Naturally, this is not an architect's whim, but a practical necessity. Many years ago we started mining the mineral resources of Siberia, but people live in wretched huts. So we've built a new city.«

Already, huge pyramids have appeared on the horizon. At first, there are two of them, 25 stories high. How did the Shipkovs solve the problem of apartments with a northern exposure? »There are no apartments with a northern exposure – the pyramid has apartments on three sides; but the fourth side is fully glazed, and light streams into the large common space, which is completely air-conditioned.«

We park in the underground garage and now arrive directly on the plaza that has an almost Mediterranean feel: trees and shrubs, meadows and flowers, playing fields and recreational areas. The social life that unfolds here also reminds us of the South.

All social institutions – education, administration, and commerce – are housed on the lower floors. We visit an apartment and are surprised by the big terraces – in this climate. »Don't ge the wrong idea about the climate. In summer the days can be pretty hot, but the inhabitants use the terraces even when temperatures drop below zero«, says Shipkov. The pyramid has close to 600 housing units, for a total of almost 2,000 persons. An express train provides shuttle service, and there are connecting passages from both railway stations directly to the pyramids' entrance lobby.

L'Architecture d'Aujourd'hui 3/1968; Moholy-Nagy 1968.

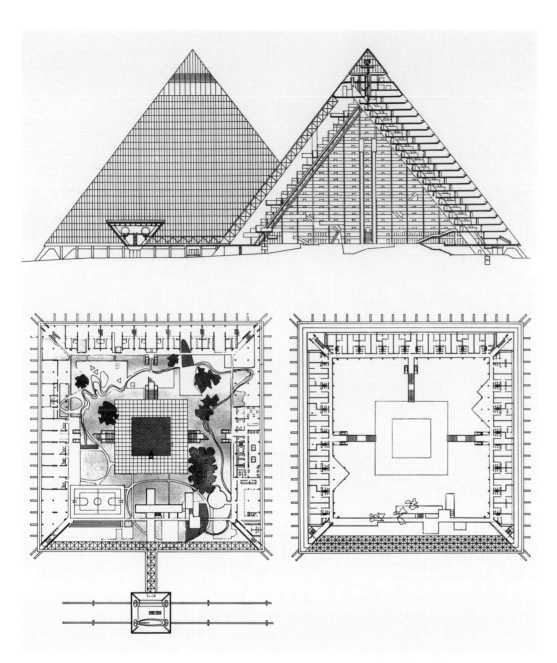

The pyramid as a house-city, as a rigid form of concentration, is something we encounter over and over. The magical, mystical interpretations of the pyramid form do not apply in Siberia: Here, the pyramid is the optimum form available in view of the climate and available technology.

V. Kalinin, Y. Ivanov, P. Kovalyov, V. Magvidov, and V. Tarassevich. The New Moscow, 1966

We meet the leading architect in a hotel on the periphery of the city. The elevator brings us to the hotel's roof terrace. What we can see from here, however, does not give us a clear idea of the vast restructuring of the city: We see the huge residential blocks, endless slabs that seem to be raised above the ground and point directly toward the towers of the Kremlin outlined in the distance.

We are therefore glad to see the landing of the helicopter. We do not grasp the overall concept until we fly over the city. »There are a total of twelve residential blocks, like enormous rays, imaginary pointers at the Kremlin as the center, without ever reaching it. They are intercepted by a large ring, the newly built second ring of the city.« The city inside the first ring with the Kremlin as its center remains largely intact, but is accentuated by a group of three slender high-rises that now tower far above the silhouette of the Kremlin.

The first and second ring – which include beltways for private transportation – are diagonally linked by relatively low groups of buildings.

After gaining an overview we land on one of the roofs of the second ring. The architect invites us on a walking tour, which covers only a tiny part of the gigantic development, however. Here we find a rich infrastructure for all aspects of urban living: education, culture, business, leisure, and, of course, restaurants seem to be ideally placed, especially because the apartment blocks are directly connected with the service ring. They are built on stilts, so that the city below them also has a chance of surviving for an extended time before new structures replace it or the green spaces spread.

»The apartment blocks form a significant and efficient link between the center and the periphery«, says the architect, »and thus we have overcome the eternal dichotomy between the urban center and its sprawling outskirts and we have also brought residential areas closer to workplaces again.«

We'd like to hear more about the traffic situation. »Our famous Moscow metro has been expanded, of course«, explains the architect, »but we've added one more mode of transportation.« We get to see it immediately: Along the undersides of the residential blocks, monorails whizz past soundlessly, providing a smooth connection between the individual rings – the new first and second service ring and the outside rings. We board one of the monorail cars. Fully automated, they leave at very short intervals and go to the end of the long, narrow blocks of housing. Here, a model apartment convinces us of the excellent standards of the new housing.

We are now on the top – the 20th – floor. Since the first level is raised a good 50 m above the building site, we are more than 100 m above ground and have another broad view of the magnificent urban concept. The monorail is vertically linked with the subway, and within a few minutes we are back at our hotel. »With this concept«, claims the architect, »we've discovered an ideal method for growth and development in individual stages. We don't need to brutally raze entire urban districts. The new overstructures will gradually absorb the old parts of town.«

Dahinden 1971.

The project definitely has a precursor: El Lissitzky's Cloud hanger design (with Mart Stam) from the period of Russian constructivism also uses the basic concentric structures of Moscow as its starting point.

The project was created long before the end of socialism, but left Stalinist architecture far behind. Of course, the ambitiousness of such urban planning does not come up to the potential of Russia today.

449. V. Kalinin, Y. Ivanov, P. Kovalyov, V. Magvidov, and V. Tarassevich, the New Moscow, 1966.

13.8. Austria

Carl Reinhart (1890–1968). The Lifelong City, 1962

As we overfly the city, we realize it is linear in character, though with a beginning and an end.

»The size of the city is strictly limited«, explains Carl Reinhart. »No more than 25,000 people will be living here once it is finally settled, and there will be no urban sprawl.«

For Reinhart the shape of the city is by no means a formal concern. »The linear form of the city is by far the most efficient. A circle line makes it possible to gain quick access to all parts of town. The main axis stretches from southeast to northwest, resulting in the optimal situation of living spaces.« Private transportation has been reduced to a minimum, and railborn vehicles transport people and goods. A single streetcar in both directions is quite enough. Freight traffic moves underground.

We begin our tour with the railroad station, post office, hotel, and the city administration. The latter is the only high-rise, and has a representative function. Office buildings, banks, and credit unions are grouped in strict hierarchy. Trade fair exhibition halls are also located here. All buildings have underground garages. We enjoy the view of the spacious complex from the two-story lobby, looking down at the forum, agora, and open-air stage. The theaters, museums, and exhibition buildings are here as well.

The belt railway is also conveniently located. We board one of the comfortable cars and get a fine overview of the residential section during the ride. »We did not build any residential high-rises; instead, we chose the optimal form of house: two-story single-family row houses grouped around an atrium.«

There are only three types of housing:
a) kitchen, living room, bedroom for childless couples or couples with one child;
b) as above, plus a children's room, for a maximum of four persons;
c) as above, with larger rooms and a second children's room, for up to six persons.
Dormitories for unmarried people are available for single people.

Each group of residential complexes is provided with all services, such as schools, kindergartens, playgrounds, a post office, and stores. »*Among the special features of the new cities are seminars providing continuing education after people leave the statutory schools. They take the place of secondary schools.*«

A wide recreation area surrounds the city in the form of a green belt. Even in the transition zone to the city forest there are clubs and restaurants.

We proceed to the end of town, but we don't feel there is any truth in Carl Reinhart's thesis that this is where we will find those buildings and institutions that are better left far from everyday life. We feel it is indefensible that old age homes are shunted off to this part of town and that the church, too, was built here – or is there an assumption that with increasing age people go to church more frequently? It is as if, by locating hospitals, a crematorium, and the cemetery here as well, the planners were »taking care« of the decease of the residents who are dumped here.

Reinhart 1964.

Carl Reinhart has presented features that seem very precise and quantified. Admittedly they hardly reduce the utopian character of the project. Nevertheless Reinhart anticipates a series of very commendable innovations – for instance, the reduction of personal transportation.

Reinhart's clusters of buildings with a central semi-public courtyard are a continuation of the tradition of Viennese government housing between the world wars.

450. Carl Reinhart, the Lifelong City, 1962. 1 Open-air theater for 2,870 persons, 2 railway station, post office, hotel, administration, and rooms for festive occasions and public events, 3 three blocks of buildings, eighteen floors each, three assembly halls, 4 lobby, 5 trade fair exhibition halls, 6 theaters, museums, exhibitions, 7 clubs, restaurants, 8 gym, 9 boys' school, 10 girls' school, 11 green belt, 12 post office, police station, ambulance, reading room, 13 kindergarten, 14 public restrooms, 15 recreation area for office buildings, 16 apartment blocks, 17 apartment buildings with inner courtyards, 18 central heating system and laundries, 19 Skylight of the underground garage, 20 clay tennis courts, 21 wading pool, 22 office blocks, 23 deliveries, 24 refuse, 25 church, 26 old age homes, 27 cemetery, 28 crematorium, chapel.

451. Hans Hollein, city for the south-west of the USA, 1960.
452. Hans Hollein, Compact City, 1964.
453. Hans Hollein, Aircraft-carrier City in the landscape, 1964.

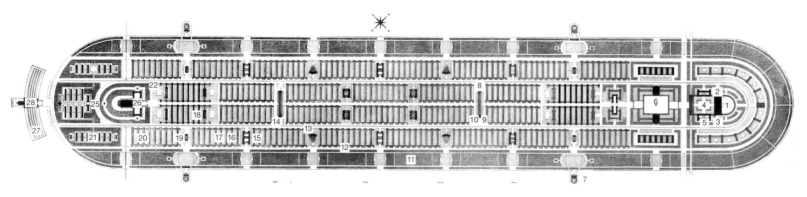

Hans Hollein (b. 1934). The Compact Cities, 1963/1964

We approach Vienna from the Kahlenberg heights. From here, we have our first overall view of the city on the Danube. But its contours have changed radically: Historic landmarks like the pointed tower of St. Stephen's Church have been joined by modern landmarks. The compact structures of the new section of town sit on strong, pedestal-like supports; sculptural and molded, they dominate the city – multifunctional complexes of buildings. And yet there is something solemn, even sacred about them.

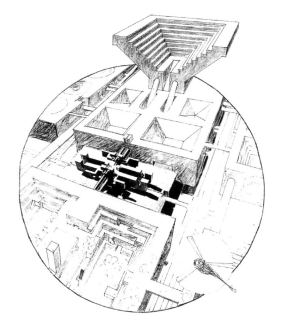

That is Hollein's intention: »*Architecture is a spiritual order, given reality by building ... All building is ritualistic.*«

Now we ride through the gentle hills of Burgenland, which exude great calm – but very soon we become attentive once more, as a dark silhouette rises against the sky: a Compact City – yet the form seems familiar. »It's an Aircraft-Carrier City«, explains Hollein. »We can easily transform the dimensions in very similar forms – it could just as well be a tea set.«

The third city we visit is the most sophisticated and most interesting. Hollein outlines his principles: »*Building is a fundamental human need; it is manifested in the erection of sacred buildings, in marking the focus points of human activities – which is the beginning of the city.*«

From this focus, this hinge of the city, tubes shoot toward the adjacent buildings: strands of communication that link the diversity of architectural manifestations into an open unit. Toward the north it is a block with courtyard terraces and finally, again connected with tubes, a projecting horseshoe of terraces for apartments and offices. Toward the south there is an adjacent block with terraced courtyards.

As our helicopter lands we have another overview of the city center, which, though compact, has great sculptural variety. Hollein shares his striking theses with us: »*Architecture dominates space – dominates it by shooting upward, by hollowing out the ground, soaring over the land as it corbels outward, spreads in all directions. Dominates it by its mass and its emptiness. Dominates space by means of space. Today, humanity dominates the infinity of outer space.*«

This urban concentration is not only a new, visual experience that can be compared with that of the historical cities. Rather, today density has quite a different function, which Hollein describes as follows:

»*The development of the human race is embodied in the city. People who are at the height of civilization and culture strive for an even more concentrated and more compact city, an even more natural, undeveloped countryside. Today we can finally leave our miserable huts and settle cities that soar, strong and powerful, above the landscape or dig deep into the earth at certain points.*«

Hans Hollein 1995; Hollein-Pichler 1963; *L'Architecture d'Aujourd'hui,* May, June 1966; Cook 1970; Feuerstein 1988.

Hans Hollein's career began with his 1960s urban visions, and he has become one of the most important architects of the 20th/21st century. Hollein has built no cities – but have none of his urban visions actually been implemented? With virtuosic skill Hollein has proved that every house is also a city: His museums especially are condensations, concentrations, derivatives of the urban – models and at the same time implementations of what a city can mean.

Walter Pichler (b. 1936). The underground city, 1963

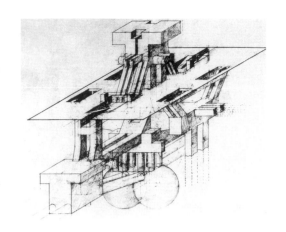

The urban building before us is splendid and monumental, but it is only the part of this compact city inhabited by the elite. The part of the city for the ordinary people, almost as large as the other one, is located underground. Here is how Walter Pichler explains his concept – which can only too easily be misunderstood: »*Architecture is an embodiment of the power and longings of a small number of people. It's a brutal thing... It will be a constraint for people, they will feel stifled by it or they will live – live as I understand the term.*«

How are these theses supposed to be compatible with our new society, with democratic systems? Don't they sound like the pronouncements of dictators? And Walter Pichler feels that his view of architecture is a fact whose reality we need to deal with constantly. These are not prophecies, but facts that continually confront us in urban life. »*Architecture is born of the strongest ideas. It is a weapon.*«

If we examine the history of architecture from this point of view, we find it difficult not to agree with Pichler. »*It is a brutal thing that hasn't used art for a long time. Architecture ruthlessly uses the strongest means available to it. Machines have taken it over, and the people are merely tolerated in their realm.*«

We might regard these vague statements as a pessimistic analysis of today's reality.

Yet we descend into Pichler's troglodyte cities. Wonderful spaces surround us – bright, spacious, free. A pleasant, artificial climate, music, scents envelop us. Does the underground city of the »ordinary people« have »quality of life« as well?

Hollein-Pichler 1963; *L'Architecture d'Aujourd'hui* 1966, 2003; Cook 1970; Feuerstein 1988; *Architectures experimentales* 2003.

Walter Pichler created a »city« of a completely different kind: He built his world in St. Martin in Burgenland: Houses in the countryside, a mix of traditional and modern elements, almost sacred buildings, house his sculptures – a city of art.

Our reality offers enough examples of the troglodyte aspects of Pichler's dark visions, of course: For a long time, every cosmopolitan city on this planet has comprised an underground city. These underground cities are not reserved for traffic alone: consumption, manufacture, leisure, even education have long since moved down deep below the cities.

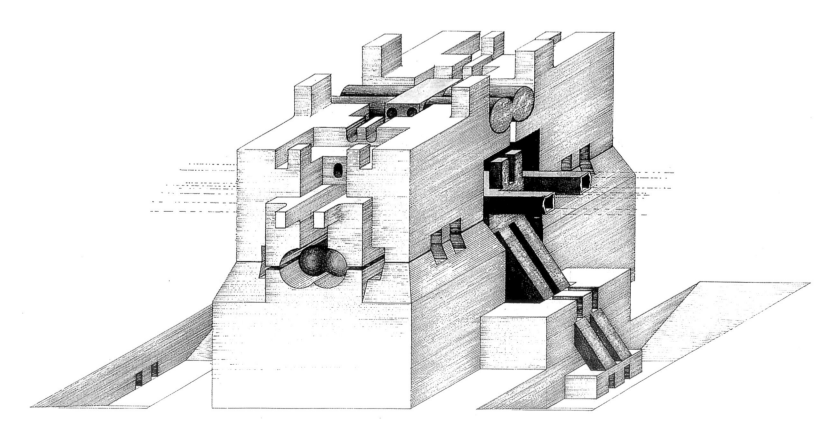

454. Walter Pichler, entrance of a subterranean city, 1963.
455. Walter Pichler, core of a city, 1963.

456. Laurids Ortner, The 47th City, 1964.

Laurids Ortner (b. 1941). The 47th City, 1964

Laurids delivers his passionate polemics against the old cities: »*You live in a city, dirty, loud, unhealthy, alone. You are sick without knowing it, sick for lack of enough sunlight, air, greenery. It is possible to calculate how much dust you consume daily, what percentage of your skin cannot breathe, how your physical condition changes because you do not exercise enough. No one can calculate the changes in your head, the atrophy of your psyche. But I hate all cities, Paris, Vienna, New York – all of them – except for the 47th and the 43rd and the 44th and 45th. Those are cities for you and me. Beehive cities that change constantly. Here you can live better, think, kiss, and love better.*«

Accompanied by Laurids, we reach the 47th City in an unaccustomed way: we buckle on a rocket belt and go directly by air. »*It's wonderful here, but where is Laurids?*« we hear as we arrive – but here comes Laurids whizzing in with his rocket belt. »*Hey, hey, let's go to the 43rd!*« the others call. »*Ursula is there with her new rocket belt.*« And already we are rushing over to the 43rd, and Ursula really does have not only a new rocket belt, but a new capsule as well. It's orange red, and she's had it installed high up.

»*You buy your house the way you buy a car*«, Laurids promotes his product. »*It can be picked up and installed within ten minutes – lots of sun, lots of air. In two minutes you're at the office, in three minutes you're in the country: just buckle up, go to the window, and jump. There is no more fascinating feeling. I'm happy in the 47th.*«
Urban Fiction 1966; *Haus-Rucker* 1992; Feuerstein 1988.

In the 1960s and '70s the Haus-Ruckers managed to implement many projects: globes, capsules, oases, in the context of events, happenings, performances. After a phase when they created landmarks, such as abstract sculptures, there has been a gradual change: to solid architecture, so to speak. Is it still possible to track down traces of the »heroic« era?

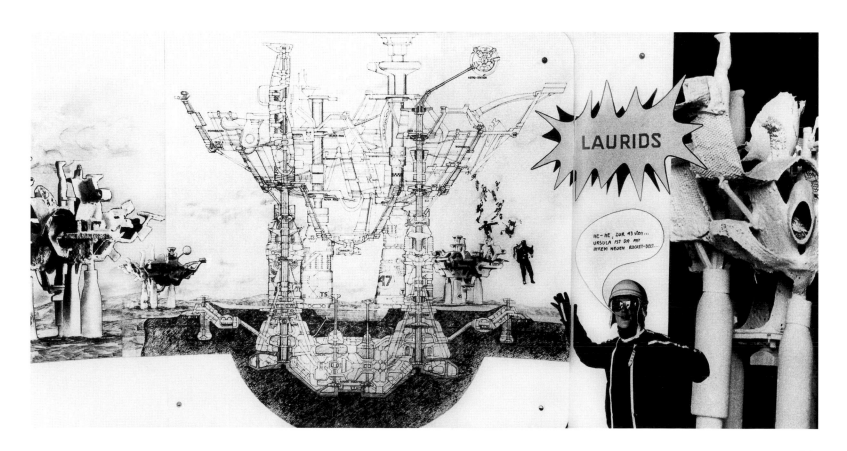

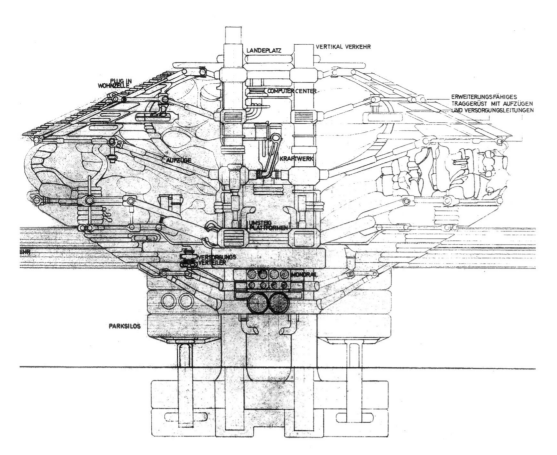

457. Wolf Dieter Prix, Urban system 2, 1966.
458. Wolf Dieter Prix, Urban system 1, 1966.

Wolf Dieter Prix (b. 1942). The city in space, 1966

For a long time now, the city has stopped being an additive collection of houses. It is now a complicated system of horizontal and vertical planes that primarily form the strands of communication. »*The city*«, explains Wolf Dieter Prix, as we move at great speed by monorail in an underground tube, »*is a pulsating volume in which a unit – a neighborhood with central facilities – is repeated in variable ways. Urban structure is spatial. The city has a spiritual and physical center that determines the significance of the city: culture, politics, commerce, industry.*«

We have now reached the transit center. Many different modes of transportation converge here. From the parking ramps, too, we can directly and automatically access the urban transit system, particularly vertical traffic. Express elevators take us to the top platform next to the helicopter landing strip. Here we have a magnificent overall view of the city. The city center we are standing in lies below us like a tortoise, its outside faced with residential blocks.

»What is the actual heart of the city today?« asks Prix and answers: »We moved the central power station for the entire city into the unlit middle and positioned the computer center above it.«

We can see individual tower blocks far in the distance. We can clearly distinguish the vertical load-bearing and supply structure. Prix points out: »Not all compartments are occupied yet, but there are enough of them to justify clipping the units for kindergartens, schools, and stores in place.«

We do like the fact that there is no traffic noise: Horizontal modes of transportation run inside tubes, mostly underground, and the vertical ones are completely noiseless.

Urban Fiction 1966; Feuerstein 1988.

We couldn't help being reminded of Archigram with its plug-in and clip-on system. There is no question that Prix's inspiration came from London. The project was developed at the Technische Universität Wien. Soon thereafter, together with Swiczinsky and Holzer, Prix created »Coop Himmelblau«, which is still in existence.

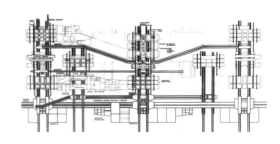

Haus-Rucker-Co (1967–88). Pneumacosm, 1967

What a surprise! During our tour around Manhattan with Laurids (Ortner) and Zamp (Kelp), an un-real landscape of translucent globes suddenly appears – four or five superimposed rows of them. What is this? The Haus-Rucker-Co have actually convinced a developer to implement their revolutionary idea: pneumatic units clipped on to a supporting frame. Pneumacosm now exists as a dynamic urban expansion.

»The places we live in have become fixed in conventions, settled into a sedentary mode that places us in shackles – it is up to us to liberate ourselves from them«, hopes Laurids. And Zamp adds: The module is a new opportunity: it implies both urbanity and individuality. Our pneumatic residential module functions like a lightbulb – and resembles it: you simply screw or plug it into the socket.«

»The balloons«, explains Zamp, »have a 12-m diameter, and the internal pressure is between 1/1000 and 1/5000 atmospheres above atmospheric pressure.«

We now have an opportunity to visit one of the units: Through a cylindrical entryway, made of polyester, where there are various outlets, we reach another rigid area that contains wet rooms. From here we enter the living space itself, differently designed in each module, though all the modules have the pneumatic shell in common – it connects directly but in different ways with the neighbors, the city, the sky, the sea.

Cook 1970; Dahinden 1971; Feuerstein 1988; *Architectures experimentales* 2003.

A frequent process in experimental architecture: The prototypes are actually manufactured, the Haus-Rucker team builds the »Yellow Heart«, and the prototypes are then imagined or drawn on a larger scale up to and including the construction of a city.

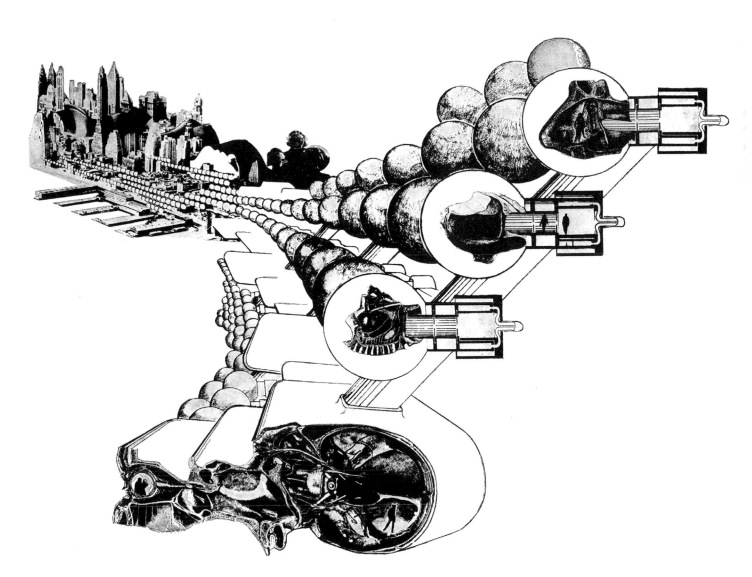

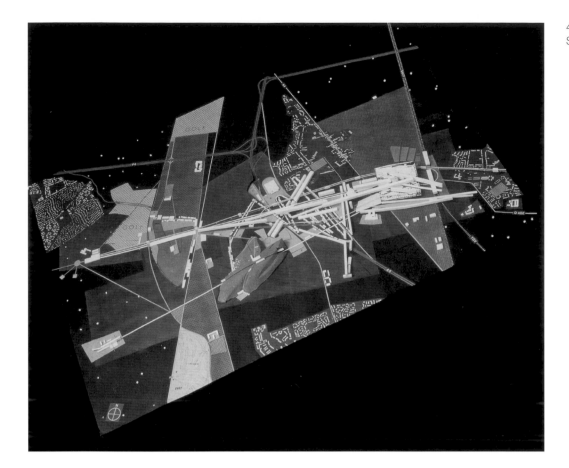

Coop Himmelb(l)au. Mélun-Sénart (Paris), 1987 and the Wolken Himmelb(l)au, 1968

Coming from the center of Paris, we reach Mélun-Sénart by metro. The station is directly in the center – no – there is no center in the usual sense of the word. Rather, we are immediately in a city that has conquered the third dimension both on a visual and experiential level. Structural struts, intersections and overlaps, overlying planes and planes that penetrate each other, passageways and barriers form a fantastical texture, but colors and lights also help us to orient ourselves. Between them, again and again, we find »clouds«, pneumatic constructions, overhanging roofs, floating glass shapes, improvised globes and tents. *»For us, a city is a city only if it gives you a sense of variety and discrepancy«*, Wolf Dieter Prix begins his statement. *»High and low, compact and empty, loud and soft, heat and cold, tenderness and hardness, confusion and clarity, captured in potential structures.«*

At first by car, then by the elevated metro, we follow the »lines of force« of the city that is committed to a new concept of dynamics. And gradually we do discover a few focus points: The heart of the urban development is at the point from which the boulevards radiate; the networks of cottages are located inside two additional lines of force.

The complex of ridges of lofts, new and forceful, unexpectedly slashes through the urban structure of the existing network of provincial houses. The dynamic elements that expand urban life are unforeseeable.

Finally everything transitions into three-dimensional zoning. This open verticality with its many levels combined in diverse ways rises to a height of 20 m and is largely determined by public and social space.

Cook 1970; Coop Himmelb(l)au 1988/1990; *Nouvelles* 2001.

Coop Himmelb(l)au (Wolf Dieter Prix, Helmut Swiczinsky) are among the most important representatives of the »deconstructivists«, a recent trend in architecture, roughly between 1980 and 1990. For their entry in a competition, the Mélun-Sénart Project, the group received the first prize. In other words, there was a concrete reason for the project, but it was never implemented.

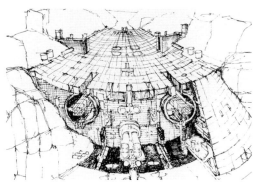

Raimund Abraham (b. 1933). The Megabridge, 1965, the Metropolitan Core, 1963/64, the Glacier City, 1994

We meet Raimund Abraham near the railroad station, the point of departure for the Megabridge on the coast of France. He takes us a little further east, from where we can see the imposing perspective of the tubes that span the English Channel. The massive tubes are not underwater, they rise above the water, forming the Megabridge. They are enveloped by tens of thousands of housing units for people who live on the ocean, with an open view of sky and water, directly linked to all necessary services.

The tubes in the interior, in the center, handle the entire communication, local and long distance traffic, by car and rail, and of course the technical infrastructure, an efficient collector, runs parallel to the tubes.

Here is how Abraham explains his fundamental ideas: »*The scale of architecture can no longer be based on the physical dimensions of the human body, but must be based on the new media of perception, on all the senses, on dreams. Architecture must become multidimensional and transplantational.*«

Back to the railway station now – which looks more like an airport – and into the luxury train. The train races through the huge tubes – from the continent to the island.

We catch sight of the imposing Metropolitan Core, the new compact city, an anti-satellite city. But first we get off the train on level three – the level of the station. The express elevator brings us to the top floor of the central tower, and we are standing in the big info-dome of the Metropolitan Core. And from here we have a lovely panoramic view of this »heart of the city«: A wonderful landscape of communication towers, and between them the globes of the top floors, reserved for the varied social functions.

Raimund Abraham tells us about his concept of the city: »The cities start underground like a huge, multi-cylinder machine, they break through the ground, through the horizon, like a swelling molecular structure. Parts of the structure remain underground, however.«

Just a look – as we fly over it – at Glacier City. It is located between the steep walls of a broad valley. An enormous sail, a membrane, which spans the city, serves as a protective shield and as a collector of solar energy.

Abraham 1967, 1996.

In Raimund Abraham's work, the phase of dream-reality, virtuosic drawings, followed the 1960s period of bold urban projects. An apartment building in Berlin and a cluster of residential buildings in Vienna were his first important implemented projects. The crowning achievement of his work to date is the Austrian Cultural Institute in New York. The spectrum between fantastical drawing and built architecture is full of great tension.

461. Raimund Abraham, Megabridge, 1965.
462. Raimund Abraham, Glacier City, 1994.
463. Raimund Abraham, Metropolitan Core, 1963/64.

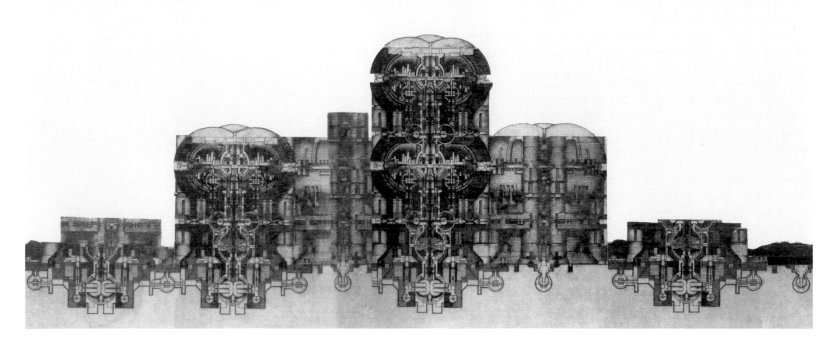

464. Friedrich St. Florian, Interchange 2, 1966.
465. Friedrich St. Florian, Vertical City 2, 1964–66.

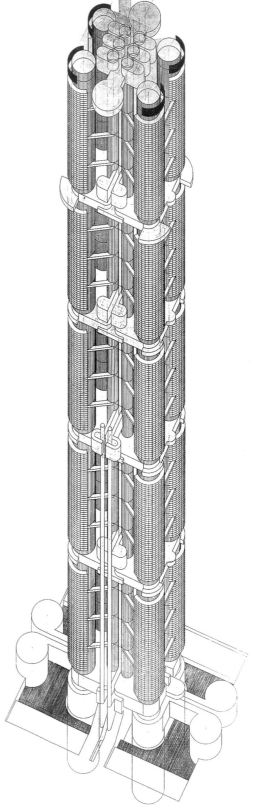

Friedrich St. Florian (b. 1932). The Vertical City, Boston, Massachusetts, USA, 1966

We did not take the tunnel route, but came by helicopter, landing on the transfer platform directly by the express elevators. This is not a skyscraper, but rather a vertical, autonomous, compact, diverse city with an optimal infrastructure. The wish to overlap all urban and human functions and to have them close to each other has finally been fulfilled.

»You have just been introduced to one of the key elements of the Vertical City«, Friedrich St. Florian points out to us. »Interchange 2 links the regional air connections and the vertical transportation systems of the city.«

Five vertical elements with four cylinders apiece are stacked on top of each other. A break has been planned between the elements. Here people can come outside on the terraces and access public institutions. The four cylinders that have residential and office functions in a conflict-free mix can easily be reached by vertical traffic, which is bundled in the center (together with all supply and waste disposal systems). For the tower city itself, cars no longer have any meaning. We do realize cars exist: From the stop on platform 4 the elevator brings us directly to level U3, where we observe the lower end of town, Interchange 1: All horizontal means of transportation, such as the interrail, monorail, rocket trains, magnetic railways, cars, etc. have their stations here – cars can be parked here, and we can transfer directly from the elevator to the interrail by going up a short escalator.

Urban Fiction 1966; Abraham/St. Florian 1967; Cook 1970; Feuerstein 1996.

Once private urban cars no longer have total autonomy, the principle of changing from one mode of transportation to another gains in importance. Many architects have devoted their attention to this principle. Friedrich St. Florian shows us a logical transfer system. There are countless very similar implementations today.

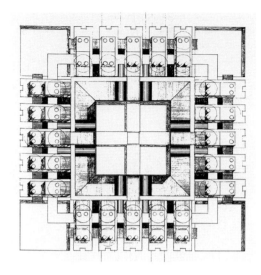

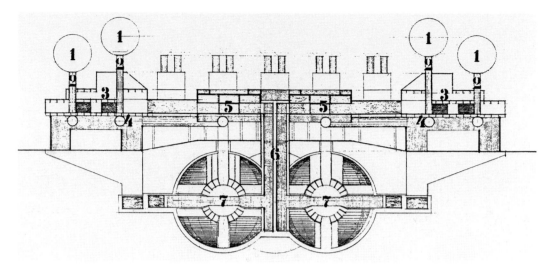

466. Klaus Gartler and Helmut Rieder, Campo Mondo, 1965. Plan.
467. Klaus Gartler and Helmut Rieder, Campo Mondo, 1965. Schematic section. 1 flying cabin, 2 docking on Campo Mondo, 3 labs and workshops, 4 collection channel: energy, water, waste disposal, 5 technical center, 6 elevators, 7 storage space. for water, energy, and food.
468. Bernhard Hafner, Tower City, 1966. Transfer station.

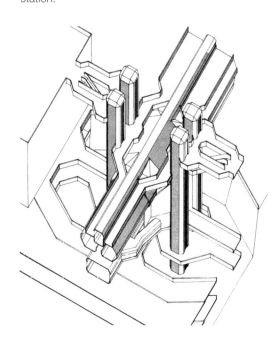

Klaus Gartler (b. 1940) and Helmut Rieder (b. 1940). Campo Mondo, 1965

In Berlin we boarded one of the strange, globular capsules and flew in the direction of Graz by means of rocket propulsion and electronic, unmanned control systems. We knew what to expect: The whole city is underwater, only the castle hill still juts out. But towering on the hill is a massive building: Campo Mondo, the docking station for the capsules.

»These ground stations are distributed across the whole planet«, explains Klaus Gartler, as we approach the enormous square, and Helmut Rieder adds: »They've been equipped with all the technical and social infrastructures: schools, businesses, assembly rooms. When we dock our capsule, we find a complete, viable city. Two issues were important for us: the potential inclusion of labs and workshops, and energy, water, and food supplies. This makes us largely crisis-proof.«

Near the Campo now, we can see that dozens of capsules have landed here and we are directed fully electronically to the next position.

Since jobs in specialized professions are located far apart, they involve moving one's family to a new home. This problem is solved by using housing modules that are capable of flight. Our project is dedicated to the new, mobile society.

Urban Fiction 1966.

Naturally utopias may be not only »non-places«, but can also move beyond all reality. The idea of placing cities underwater, of flooding them, appears again and again from the 1960s through the 1980s, with various rationales: as aggression against the historical city, as a radical new beginning, or out of the conviction that cities are past saving. But how was Graz supposed to be flooded? How were the capsules suppsosed to be powered? And why would a capsule land in the middle of the ocean?

Bernhard Hafner (b. 1940). The Tower City, 1966

»Today we must make our cities more compact both maximally and optimally«, says Bernhard Hafner. »One of the great opportunities in new urban development is the rediscovery and reinterpretation of the vertical line.«

Bernhard Hafner's vertical cities are low-density and flexible. Their most important elements are the transfer stations, where people change from one transportation system to another and thus also change to a different speed of travel. The framework, the basic system, the power and traffic routes are given. But that leaves a lot of room for the creation of individual details and individual lives.

Urban Fiction 1966.

The change of modes of transportation becomes a synonym for the mobility and diversity of the city. »Change« – in many respects, is a key concept of the 1960s.

469. Günther Domenig and Eilfried Huth, residential development of Ragnitz, Graz, Austria, 1965. Model with modules.
470. Günther Domenig and Eilfried Huth, residential development of Ragnitz, Graz, Austria, 1965. Hygio-bile.

Günther Domenig (b. 1934) and Eilfried Huth (b. 1930). Ragnitz-Graz, 1965

From Graz, the capital of Steiermark, it takes us half an hour to reach the suburb Ragnitz. Günther Domenig, with Eilfried Huth by his side, steers us through what remains of the poorly constructed village buildings. Very soon the scenario changes: It is true that the new building we are now approaching from the south is no more than eight stories high, but the dense system of struts leaves no doubt that the structure is very special. »We're still in the process of finishing the south section, so that you can easily study the system.«

The elevator takes us up to the top platform, and we have a fine overview: the imposing still-empty spaces of the framework, reinforced concrete lattice girders with vertical, cruciform stabi-lization supports. The two dimensions of communication, vertical and horizontal, are clearly distin-guishable. Three vertical tracks contain the passenger elevator, the freight elevator, and all the plumbing. The dominating horizontal features, on the other hand, are the upper and lower street, which provide access to the stairwells. And there we notice that a large number of modules have already been plugged into the space lattice. As Domenig and Huth point out, »There comes Hygiobile II/35/Z, the complete bathroom; it's lowered by a crane and will be inserted in space No. 234/35/0 of the lattice frame.«

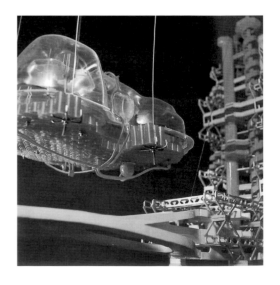

On the top level of terraces we stroll over to the already completed north section. Domenig and Huth describe the basic general and structural ideas: »*Our environment, but particularly the dense city centers are subject to cybernetic closed-loop laws. In the control system, for example, the sum of all individuals, the elements of the organism, which are in communication, are charac-terized by their element functions and their system fuctions. The most important among the ele-ment functions of the inhabitants are the individual private sphere, individual work for the commu-nity, publicly installed usability by individuals, and the public sphere.*«

The architects have thought through in detail the crucial problem, that of availability, and have arrived at a vey difficult solution: »We introduced an alternative goal. To achieve that goal, the area being developed and the air space that goes with it needs to belong to each community (city, etc.) as a kind of meta-property, or else there needs to be a guarantee that it will not be affected by land speculation. Individuals may choose from what is available and use their building volume as a kind of sub-property, without reference to the land.

»The element functions of the housing system are the communication structure, the supporting structure, primary and secondary, the housing volumes, the interior furnishings, and the service zones.«

»The goal of our study was primarily as follows: We coordinated industrially prefabricated elements of a communication center into one whole, and thus also fulfilled the function of orientation and identification. From the function by way of construction we reach the form and reflection.«

The supporting structure was industrially prefabricated as a primary structure in concrete, and the secondary supporting structure is also made of concrete. However, steel structures would also have been possible.

The concept of the housing volumes is very innovative. As a result of new environmental regulations, it is possible to purchase and finish the construction of a building under a kind of lease within the framework of the public meta-property. There are several possibilities: It is possible to freely develop individual activities inside the buildings, or to choose from a selection of industrially produced finished and semi-finished parts for the climatic shells.

Another possibility is for the community to construct preplanned housing units as a kind of publicly funded housing, with a number of variants that are then available for rent and occupation. »Here is another goal of our study: By creating a climatic shell prototype, which shows the greatest adaptation, variability, and mobility, the industry had an incentive to bring a large supply of climatic shells on the market in order to satisfy the many different individual wishes for comfort and form, and in order to be able to facilitate a speedy and economical implementation of housing programs within a framework of great individual freedom.«

For the architects it was important to include the residents' personal manual contributions. Such work was done outside regular working hours. This authorized personal work led to new creative activity and a stronger sense of identification. Because industrially prefabricated parts were chosen, however, there were only very modest possibilities for individual contributions. In the finished section of the building we are able to view the housing units. They are not predetermined – the use of the apartment is dictated by mobile appliances and modules that are bought as consumer goods and discarded again, somewhat like cars. Basically we saw three categories of modules: modules for sleeping, living, and playing; furniture for storing all utensils; and finally the hygiobile, the bathroom-toilet module, which is mobile and has a gray-water filter and electric garbage burner.

We're impressed by the »concentroom«. The architects explain the multiple possible uses of this module: »*It is a minimal mobile room – a consumer item, manufactured and sold like cars or refrigerators. The air-conditioned room, intended for one person, makes possible optimal, concentrated activity and a space for watching and listening to audiovisual news and information while at the same time being acoustically and optically isolated. This concentroom is expanded for two or three persons for joint activities, or opens into the surrounding space to become a technical item of furniture. The modules take records, tapes, a magnetic tape library, television and radio, films, microfilms, and slides. Such modules can also be used in schools, institutes, and libraries for teaching and learning.*«

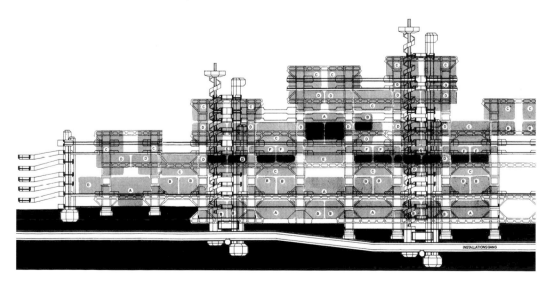

471. Günther Domenig and Eilfried Huth, residential development of Ragnitz, Graz, Austria, 1965. Comprehensive section.

»An individual discipline – architecture – gives rise to interdisciplinary activity in all areas, as a reflection of our consciousness. That is why the development of technology or the development of art or the development of a socially conscious humanism are in a reflective relationship to each other. This is why architectural creation is not ›reserved for a few individuals ...‹ but is a communal activity. This presupposes that, first, ›modern architecture‹ enters our consciousness as a symptom of a new communal development and is not regarded as a fait accompli according to outdated criteria; and second, that the public will be educated – a process that needs to be accelerated – allowing everyone to make informed choices.«

The new city is not a technological showpiece, but is based on complex sophisticated, societal reflections, which Domenig and Huth try to explain: Can the wish for single-family houses be realized even in dense housing developments? Domenig and Huth, at least according to their statements, used the floor plan of single-family homes even though they did not design the homes as detached houses.

In compactly built-up areas, a considerable number of parts of buildings necessarily receive less sunlight or none at all. These have been sensibly devoted to commercial and public use: stores, offices, organizations, workrooms, libraries, gyms, clubs, and even a church have been integrated in the overall plan in close vicinity of homes. *»What's important to us«*, emphasize the architects, *»is the intermingling of the private sphere with the public sphere. Only such a combination makes urban life possible. Artificial alleyways on the top floors that go past children's playgrounds and old age homes and include landscaped roofs go through the housing development. These are connected to the ground floor.«*

At the periphery of the residential buildings, the architects point out an important factor that provides flexibility: Here, it is possible to convert and add on modules and room dividers when families increase or decrease in size, or their needs change.

Domenig & Huth 1967; Wedewer & Kempas 1970; Dahinden 1971; Klotz 1986; Feuerstein 1988; Domenig 1991; Thomsen 1994; *Utopie* 1969; *Architectures experimentales* 2003.

Domenig and Huth actually did intend their project to be realized. Since it had been worked out in precise detail, there were definite prospects, and a builder was interested. However, after concretely going over the calculations – no doubt unique for projects of this type – it became apparent that for a publicly funded housing development the cost-effectiveness ratio of weight-bearing / supply structure and utilizable floor space is not acceptable.

In the 1987 Neufeldweg housing development in Graz we can, perhaps, still make out the rudiments of the space lattice structure. The idea of a »stacked single-family house« occurs repeatedly, a kind of consolation prize for the unattainable little villa. What is not mentioned, however, is the fact that certain important criteria of a »house in the country« cannot be met.

Günther Feuerstein (b. 1925). Salzburg-Superpolis, 1965

»I love Salzburg«, says Günther Feuerstein. »I love the city and the Land of Salzburg, particularly the countryside around the city – both need to be preserved – which is why I developed Superpolis.«

The new compact city has a high capacity for residential units, administration, and jobs in a very intensive mix of functions. That way the historic city is preserved, and above all, all urban sprawl is contained. From the airport the express railway takes us directly into the center of

473. Günther Feuerstein, Salzburg-Superpolis, 1965.
Bridgehead.

Salzburg-Superpolis. The tunnel opens wide; we get on an automatically controlled electro-car
and program our horizontal and vertical routes and our destination. Later we take the express elevator. Even as we ride up to the top terrace, we get a good overview of the open, transparent,
flexible, yet monumental new town.

Up on the terrace we are captivated by the enchanting view of the old town, but also of the adjacent countryside with its parks and gardens – truly still unspoiled nature without disfiguring construction. »We are now on the highest terrace of the administration center«, explains the architect,
»but it is at the same time a large shopping center. The bridge over the Salzach and the part of town
on the opposite bank are primarily reserved for housing, as well as for educational institutions.«

How do people deal with the city's imminent growth? Initially Superpolis will become more and
more compact. Then, however, the outdated part of the old town will be renewed with dense development, and growth is possible in the other direction as well, always on condition that there be
high urban density.«

We go down ten floors in the elevator and cross the bridge on foot. Signs and signals, information and visuals guide us, and the city's adventurous three-dimensional space offers one new
aspect after another. The bridge city forms a link between both parts of the town. Once again we
enjoy two equally wonderful views: the silhouette and structure of the old town and, on the other
side, a completely unspoiled natural landscape. »Let's take a short tour of the countryside«, invites the architect. Again we board the express railway. After a ten-minute ride, the train stops in
the lovely landscape.

From Café Visio we have an informative view of the new silhouette: The dominant center is not
merely a diverse, three-dimensional architecture. Screens and monitors are showing current
events in images and print, only some of which contain commercials. From a small center on the
other bank, weather reports are being sent, coded but understandable.

Even from a distance we can see that particularly the bridge section, individual levels, terraces,
escalators, and elevators are bustling with activity.

»Superpolis is a flexible city«, says the architect in conclusion. »Most of the buildings are mobile modules. They can be replaced, but above all it is possible to add on to them. The city has
not reached its full density yet.«

Feuerstein 1966, 2003.

Werner Höfer (b. 1941) and Walter Prankl (b. 1935). The fourth skin, 1968

474. Werner Höfer, Walter Prankl, the fourth skin, 1968. Model of a city.

Two more typical children of the sixties? Not quite. It's true that they do not lack imagination, but instead of rousing slogans, provocative sketches, and interesting experiments their projected city is based on realistic reflections about history and the present.

»You might say there are six different ›skins‹ enveloping our individual or collective bodies«, declare the architects: »The first skin is the one we're born with, the second is our clothing, and our smallest mobile space is the third: the cell, the womb, or the car. The fourth skin is the city with its surrounding countryside, the fifth skin is the Earth, and finally the sixth is the cosmos.«

When we approach the city, our eyes gradually perceive the silhouette: pyramid-shaped terraced houses up to sixteen stories high; ten of these are devoted to residential units, while the top stories, shaped like towerlike structures, are reserved for community services and restaurants. These pyramids are accompanied by five-story residential buildings that form spacious, beautifully designed, semi-enclosed courtyards with luxuriant vegetation. All open-air areas in the city are completely closed to traffic. Traffic, including the subway and light-rail transit, is restricted to the extensive underground floors, a complex subterranean city.

The ground floor is reserved for commercial services, intermingled with cultural venues and restaurants.

»We believe a city's open areas need to be much more strongly articulated«, claim the architects. »So we have created various distinctive landmarks that improve orientation, especially meeting places of many different magnitudes: very small, small, medium-sized, and large.« The smallest are the kiosks and espresso bars, the small are stores, restaurants, small movie houses, and childcare centers, the medium-sized are neighborhood shopping centers with department stores, hotels, libraries, and schools, and finally there is a big one: the downtown city center.«

The urban hierarchy proceeds smoothly from the main center by way of the pyramids to the low housing developments, which are sharply delineated and allow no urban sprawl. There is also a kind of transition to the countryside: delightful small gardens.

Höfer/Prankl 1968.

The spectrum of Austrian architectural visions is extremely broad when it comes to elaboration: It ranges from ingenious sketches of ideas to precisely thought-out floor plans and rational reflections. The project described above is obviously one of the latter.

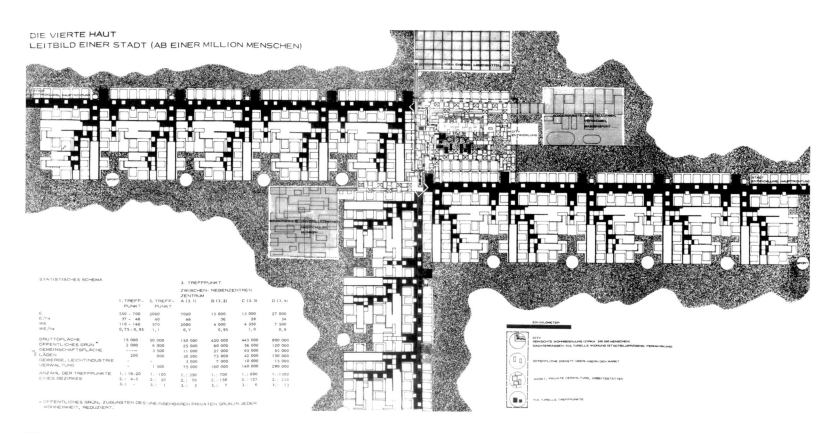

DIE VIERTE HAUT
LEITBILD EINER STADT (AB EINER MILLION MENSCHEN)

STATISTISCHES SCHEMA

	1. TREFF-PUNKT	2. TREFF-PUNKT	3. TREFFPUNKT ZWISCHEN-NEBENZENTREN ZENTRUM A (3.1)	B (3.2)	C (3.3)	D (3.4)
E	550 – 700	2000	7000	15 000	13 000	27 000
E/ha	37 – 48	40	48	36	29	34
WE	110 – 140	570	2000	4 000	4 350	7 500
WE/ha	0,75 – 0,95	1,1	0,7	0,95	1,0	0,9
BRUTTOFLÄCHE	15 000	50 000	150 000	420 000	445 000	800 000
ÖFFENTLICHES GRÜN	2 000	6 000	25 000	60 000	56 000	120 000
GEMEINSCHAFTSFLÄCHE	-----	3 500	11 000	27 000	65 000	55 000
LÄDEN	200	800	30 000	75 000	42 000	150 000
GEWERBE, LEICHTINDUSTRIE	-	-	3 000	7 000	10 000	15 000
VERWALTUNG	-	1 500	75 000	160 000	140 000	290 000
ANZAHL DER TREFFPUNKTE EINES BEZIRKES	1.: 16–20 2.: 4–5 3.: -	1.: 100 2.: 30 3.: 1	1.: 350 2.: 70 3.: 3	1.: 700 2.: 150 3.: 7	1.: 600 2.: 125 3.: 6	1.: 1300 2.: 250 3.: 13

* ÖFFENTLICHES GRÜN, ZUGUNSTEN DES UNEINSEHBAREN PRIVATEN GRÜN, IN JEDER WOHNEINHEIT, REDUZIERT.

EIN KILOMETER

CITY
GEMISCHTE WOHNBEBAUUNG (ZIRKA 100 000 MENSCHEN)
DACHTERRASSEN: KULTURELLE WIDMUNG (STADTBILDPRÄGEND: FERNWIRKUNG)

ÖFFENTLICHE DIENSTE ÜBERLAGERN DEN MARKT

MARKT, PRIVATE VERWALTUNG, ARBEITSSTÄTTEN

KULTURELLE TREFFPUNKTE

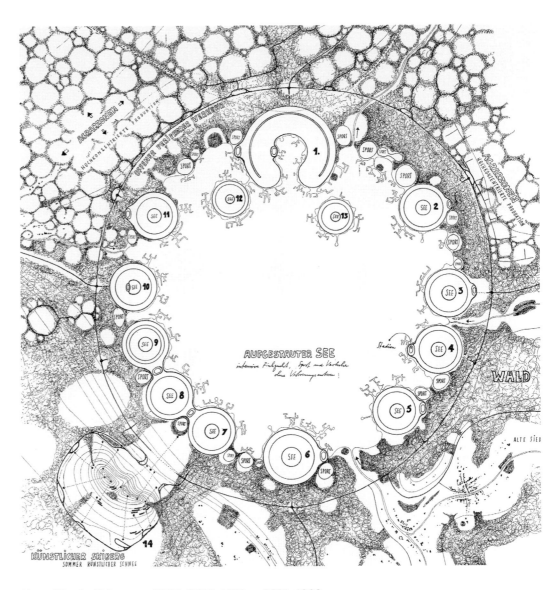

Hans Bischoffshausen (1927–1987). Million 2001, 1968

»My background is art, but my concept of art is universal. That entitles me to take a critical look at the city.«

And Bischoffshausen really has invested a multitude of ideas and concrete observations in his concept of a city. He sees the individual districts of the city as huge discs between 130 and 500 m high. All of them are grouped in a ring around an artificial lake 12 km in diameter. In the center of each circular disc is a smaller lake, like an eye. Coming from the countryside, we run right into the imposing housing development. »Forest, meadows, and zones of very intensive agricultural production directly adjoin the densely built-up crater forms«, adds Bischoffshausen. The residential craters represent the connection between elements of nature, as it were, a link between woods and water. The big lake creates a potential for an additional means of transportation: Silently, boat buses glide over the water, intended only for passenger transit. A huge traffic ring connects the units underground by means of every imaginable mode of transportation.

And it goes without saying that provisions have been made for air transportation: soundless planes, overcoming the force of gravity, fully automatic, provide express and individual transportation.

Though he is an enthusiastic advocate of technological innovations, Bischoffshausen also makes allusions to the calendar and the cosmos: »Twelve centers, named for the months of the year, establish an expanded infra-urban, vertical, and horizontal connection. The towns on the periphery are named for the planets.«

Pedestrian auxiliary traffic is equipped with all technical innovations: moving pathways, escalators, slanting elevators, elevators; the speeds of all these modes of transportation can be adjusted.

What is the city's population? we ask. The answer is precise: »Every crater, depending on its size, has between 50,000 and 60,000 inhabitants. 350,000 persons live in the ›capital‹, a peripheral center, paradoxical as that sounds. Thus the city has a total of a million inhabitants.«

A visit to the »capital« is most impressive: In addition to the housing and in beautiful synthesis with it, cultural and educational life is first-rate. These facilities are not centralized, for the district craters also have the necessary infrastructure.

The numerous jobs are distributed according to an exact system among all the crater units. The apartments themselves by far exceed conventional standards. A high degree of flexibility goes without saying. Homes are fully air-conditioned, and air-conditioning is automatically controlled and equipped with anti-parasite and anti-fungal installations. Naturally all homes are on the electronic network. Every housing unit has a landscaped terrace with automatic irrigation.

Now we go up to the top terrace, which can be accessed by all citizens and their guests. We enjoy not only the delicious buffet, but also the magnificent panoramic view of the city and the almost unspoiled countryside beyond.

trigon 1969; Feuerstein 1988.

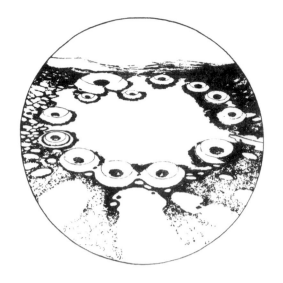

Compactness, concentration is one criterion of 1960s urban visions, while the other is a love of archetypes, especially the circle, though its symbolic content is not articulated.

Helmut Ortner (b. 1937), Karl Plötzl (b. 1937). The city of the Residential Mobiles, 1968

»We're going to visit the biggest RV city to date«, announce Ortner and Plötzl. »It will soon have reached its maximum size of 160,000 inhabitants.«

Our helicopter lands in the town's airport. Within a few minutes the express train takes us to the center, formed by an impressive building used for cultural events and as an administrative center.

We're even more interested in the immediately adjacent clusters of RVs that give the town its name and are its characteristic feature. The town's silhouette is pleasantly structured: The highest buildings are 23 stories high, but we find twelve-story ones as well, and the blocks are connected by bridge buildings. »The essential thing about our cities is the system of RVs. They meet the demands of modern living:

»*1. changeability,*
2. capability of being enlarged or reduced in size,
3. exchangeability,
4. mobility,
5. independence – individually tailored design.«

In an exemplary manner, Ortner and Plötzl have removed the process of building from its medieval context and surrendered it to industrialization. The architects consider Konrad Wachsmann and Jean Prouvé to be the real pioneers of the 20th century.

If there is one building form suitable for industrial mass production, it is the room module. »We did not pursue lovely utopias with multistoried modules made of synthetic materials.« From the start, Ortner and Plötzl were realists. »Structural physics and fire prevention rule this out from the start. Our modules consist of 7.5-cm-thick steel panels foamed in place. Inside there is a 5-cm-thick laminated panel with layers of fire protection panels on the inside.«

»Thanks to logically consistent industrialization«, Ortner and Plötzl say delightedly, »we've been able to decrease construction costs by 25 percent as compared to conventional buildings.« Decreased construction costs were largely due to an 85 percent prefabrication of modules, while the load-bearing and supply structure was built locally, using pairs of reinforced concrete pipes with suspended access lanes of precast concrete units.

»The pairs of concrete pipes carry the main head beams for the wire rope constructions over cantilever girders«, Ortner and Plötzl explain in more detail. »The residential modules are mounted on the bearer cables by means of coupling mechanisms.«

The steel cables for suspending the modules also represent an important innovation as compared to similar modular systems, such as those used by Archigram.

In conclusion, Ortner and Plötzl take us through a few apartments. It is really impressive how many different designs are possible in spite of the use of modular units, something that is made possible primarily by link-up systems with the hinges. Last but not least, we are happy that the architects decided to create a colorful and varied architecture.

Ortner/Plötzl 1968; Feuerstein 1988.

476. Hans Bischoffshausen, Million 2001, 1969.

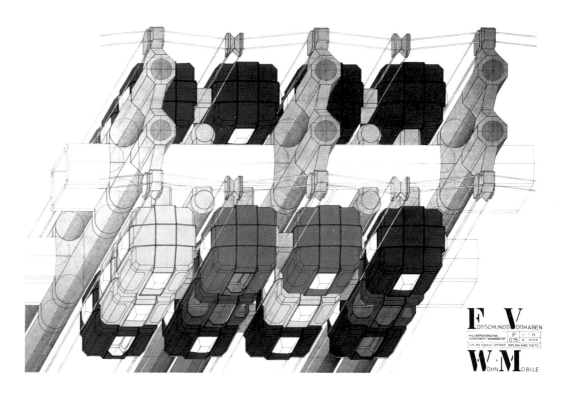

Though the project was developed in 1975, shortly after the 1973 energy crisis, many questions,
such as that relating to the many cooling surfaces, were left unanswered. There can be no doubt that
the project was inspired by the clip-on and plug-in systems of the Archigram group, but the highly
imaginative and artistic approach of the London group was replaced by serious attempts to be more
specific, with the goal of implementing the plans. At any rate it is amazing that at the time this type of
project was publicly promoted by the Residential Building Research division of the Austrian Ministry of
Building.

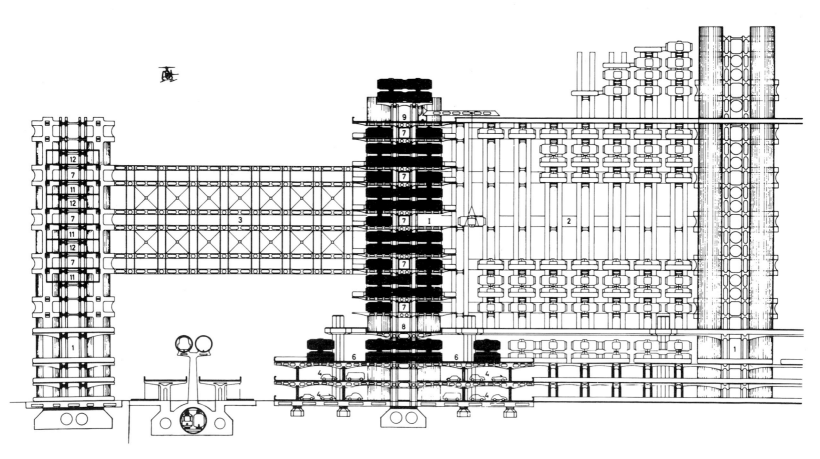

Herbert Prader (1928–1980) and Franz Fehringer (b. 1928). The Hexagonal Residential Modules, 1969

»We are convinced that the linear city is still largely relevant, and our modular city proves it«, say the architects.

»We started out with hexagonal residential modules and found they provided an optimal modular construction system«, Herbert Prader tells us as we drive into the underground garage of the »urban framework«. The elevator brings us to the city's top level, to the terrace café. Here we have the best view of the complex, for we are standing exactly between the two modular high-rises, which are at this point about 250 m long. This modular high-rise, up to 60 m high, has a beautiful, complex silhouette. A play of horizontal and vertical lines is placed in front of the apartment modules: Behind the vertical stair- and elevator towers lie holizontal pergolas. In turn, these are connected by means of slanting bridges directly with the center, the city's framework.

»If need be, the city can go on growing«, says Franz Fehringer. »*We now have available a surface of 800 by 1,000* m*, and by the time construction is finished there will be a total of 2,500 apartments with 8,000 inhabitants.*«

We especially like the well-kept green spaces between the city's framework and the residential high-rise: These flourish partly on natural soil, partly on terraces above the garages.

The architects take us into one of the residential modules and explain the construction: »*Our starting point was airplane construction. We created the load-bearing structure from two steel sheets, each of them 2.5 mm thick. The total thickness is 15 cm, with insulating layers of synthetic foam. Due to favorable structural engineering, we are able directly to stack up to 25 units, with staggered half floors. That means we can do without the expensive supporting structures used in other projects.*«

A residential module has a total interior height of 5.40 m, so that two levels, of which the second is mostly a loft, can be installed. We can see for ourselves that there are definitely opportunities for individual layouts. »The principle is not new«, confesses Franz Fehringer, »but I believe we have discovered a fine design: One side of the module turns toward the community, the city, while the other side turns toward nature, the landscape. According to our plan the link between these will be parks and playing fields, schools and recreation areas.«

trigon 1969; Dahinden 1971; Prader / Fehringer 1972.

During the 1960s, a time of change, Austrian government agencies experienced a thaw in certain areas. The secretary of the Department of Buildings commissioned a few very »utopian« projects, including the Hexagonal Residential Modules. The starting point, very specifically, was to selectively cull prefabricated architecture and to plead for more compact cities.

480. Carl Pruscha, Linear Global City, 1962–64.
481. Carl Pruscha, Linear Global City, 1962–64.
Traffic junction.

Prader and Fehringer showed once again that many »utopias« had been very carefully thought out. They proved it in a substantial research project carried out from 1966 through 1972.

The idea of stacking the modules reappears constantly as an alternative to load-bearing frameworks, but here, too, it seems doubtful whether it is possible to stack up to 25 modules in this type of light structure, especially if both sides are open or made of glass. The architects assumed there would be 3.5 persons per module – but the size of the households is closer to less than two persons.

Carl Pruscha (b. 1936). The Linear Global City, 1962–64

We've covered hundreds of km by air, and what we see on the grund along the whole distance is a very similar system: Two parallel tracks of varying width stretch across the country for thousands of kilom.

»You might say they are life strands, lines of force for the cities. They provide communication and energy, and cities everywhere can be connected to them as though to two-core power cables«, explains the architect.

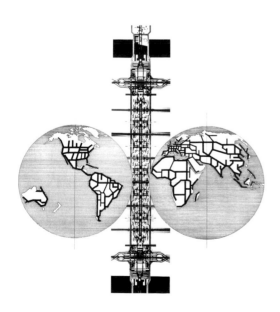

Even from a great height, we now realize that »links« have formed between the strands, cities of great density and enormous significance. No, these are no linear cities of the type we have already visited. Rather, they are »crossbeam cities« that have sprung up between the lines of force. But the city is not limited to the area between the strands. Its emanations are far-reaching – culture, sports, education, and amusement have their venues even outside the double tracks, and industry in particular has moved to these locations.

The intersections of the tracks have a special importance: the junctions assure that traffic functions smoothly; moreover, they are striking buildings. The cities themselves are mostly characterized by very dense high-rise landscapes. We wonder if there are any open spaces and parks.

»You don't need parks: On the one hand, every apartment has a private open space, and on the other hand you can be out in the countryside by super-metro within a few minutes – thanks to the compactness of the cities there is no urban sprawl.«

The famous concept of »networking« has been given a completely new meaning here: A traffic network does not link just individual points and places. Rather, the global city becomes a gigantic network that envelops the entire globe.

»Cities are dynamic fields of interrelated forces«, says Carl Pruscha in conclusion. »Global lines of force have become carriers of secondary developments among polarization centers that attract each other – interfaces of pathways of different speeds in evolution and movement.«
Urban Fiction 1966.

The total urbanization of the earth is by no means a utopia: The world's population is still growing, and as it grows cities swell to become monstrous conglomerations – admittedly not to the extent we have seen in Pruscha's global city.

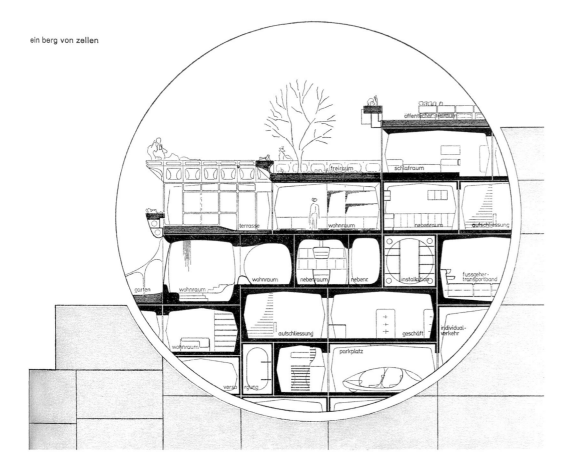

Hans Peter Schlosser (b. 1946). The Mountain City, 1969

Our express universal vehicle carries us from north to south across a wide plain. Suddenly, a green hill appears before us, with a mighy tower at its top. »What we see is not a hill with a look-out tower«, explains Hans Peter Schlosser. »This is a hill city with a dominant high-rise.« But it is only when we approach within two km that we see the »hill« is roofs and terraces overgrown with luxuriant greenery. This landscaped hill rises gradually to a height of 80 stories – a good 250 m – and the tower, another 80 stories high, rises into the sky over the lush cascades of green.

»The city is a mountain«, postulates H. P. Schlosser, »a mountain and a network of different re-lationships, a tangle of needs whose surface is formed by human housing. The city is a green mountain whose hills are inhabited by human beings, whose belly provides for these people, a vineyard, landscape created by human beings.«

484. Herbert Missoni and Franz Cziharz, urban spinal system, 1969.

Coming from the highway, we immediately drive into the underground garage and from there a fully automated transportation system brings us to the programmed destination, the top terrace. We really have the feeling that we are in a lovely landscape, and nothing troubles the almost arcadian atmosphere. Yet the mountain not only conceals the apartments in its outer shell, but also we find all service facilities in the compact structure; in particular there is a large number of jobs. Thus the hill city has also become a model for autonomous, integrated living.
trigon 1969.

The »re-creation« of the world in architecture always leads to a mountain: the pyramid, the ziggurat, the terraced house. Hans Peter Schlosser, faithful to the trend of the 1960s, compresses the city into a high mountain range – the idea is totally relevant again.

Herbert Missoni (b. 1938) and Franz Cziharz (1939–1998). The Spina, an urban spinal system, 1969

Our actual destination is the city of Dortmund, for that is where the Spina was first implemented. Our informational flight in a small private plane makes the principle clear: a city, or rather urban belts over the city.

»Parts of the periphery of Dortmund were dilapidated, substandard, no longer acceptable according to the latest standards. That is why our idea was implemented. From two starting points, two urban strands have gradually inched their way forward, finally meeting at one point.« That is the basic principle of Missoni and Cziharz. Narrow, long tracts branch off these strands, like fishbones.

We transfer to the subway, which causes the curves in the city's spine. We get out at one of the stops, roughly in the middle – there is no actual center. On the elevator, we pass various traffic levels until we reach the pedestrian level, and are now on a busy shopping street lined by high buildings.

»We are now in the area with the highest urban density, the ultimate concentration of work, commerce, education, and culture. But the height of the buildings decreases like a descending slope and ends harmoniously in low housing developments that turn directly into park landscapes.« So say Missoni and Cziharz.

And actually the character of the city does change as we stroll along the diagonal street: The high-rises make way for four- to six-story buildings that finally end in a series of small row houses.

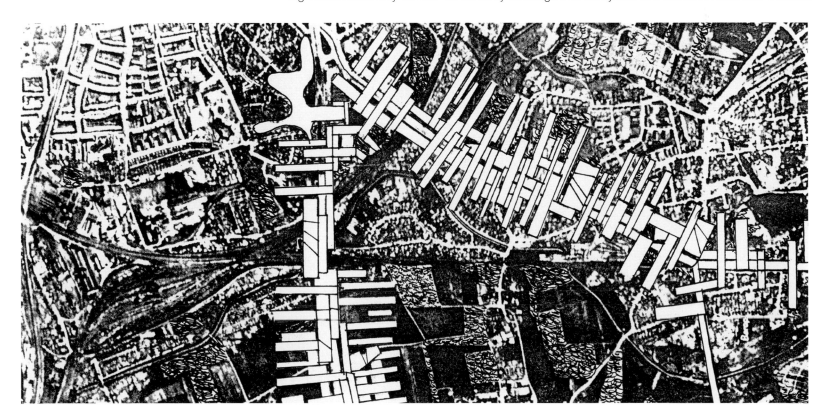

The Spina system allows enough room between the blocks for open spaces. Here is how the architects express their main concern: They strive for »*freedom of choice of individuals settling in the field of tension between calm and movement, between nature and technically structured activity space, between anonymity in the area of greatest activity and privacy on the periphery.*«
trigon 1969; Feuerstein 1988.

Urban concentration was one premise, and limitless growth the other. The result is the reemergence of the idea of the linear city. In the project of Missoni and Cziharz it is the spine of traffic that is capable of growing, but functional elements also radiate at right angles to it.

Franco Fonatti (b. 1942). The Sensomobile City, 1966–69

Fonatti explains his motivation for the artistic aspect of his architecture: »*Art should be pitted against the positive sciences as a form of gaining insight that is on an equal footing with them.*«

As we study Fonatti's Sensomobile City, there is no doubt: It is a linear city, but not one that has endless, additive ribbons, but rather tension-filled spaces. The communal and public buildings and their sleek cubes predominate, while the residential areas form a gently modeled band. The strands of traffic are absorbed, embedded in the strung-out volumes. An »insistent« architecture, in other words, an architecture that stubbornly insists on form, creates interesting forms that remotely remind us of Hermann Finsterlin, of expressionism.
Fonatti 1974.

As with so many architects of the generation after World War II, drawings represent an important medium, bearing out the frequent assertion that modern Austrian architectural drawing has a special quality (Hollein, Pichler, Abraham). Many architects are content with this medium. For most, including Fonatti, it is an introduction to, and a part of, built architecture.

Helmuth Gsöllpointner (b. 1933). The mobile Steel City, 2003

We approach the dramatic silhouette of the Steel City from the water side and watch the most wonderful mirror effects: The entire city is mirrored in the water and the individual buildings mirror each other in the many-faceted, fissured, split, furrowed façades. Under the partly clouded sky, mirror glass and high-grade steel parts now present a fascinating spectacle of constantly changing light.

Very soon, however, as we approach we notice that it can't be only the play of light that is responsible for our constantly changing impressions. Rather, the silhouette as such seems to be changing.

»Yes, that's true, too«, Gsöllpointner confirms, »the city's volumes are totally mobile. I've invented a complex system for telescoping volumes, somewhat resembling Japanese puzzle boxes, but even more complex. The volumes can be modified in various time rhythms – days, weeks, months.« As he speaks, a towerlike element is pushed up into the sky while a slanting cube is retracted and a horizontal body corbels outwards.

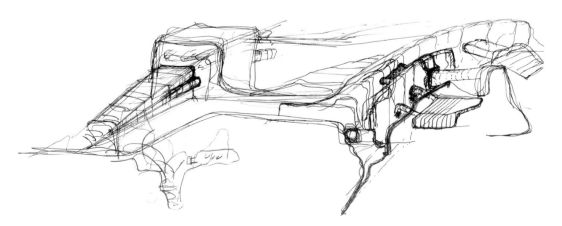

485. Franco Fonatti, Sensomobile architecture, 1969. City fragment.

When we arrive in the city, we are surprised by the relatively loose development. The city is divided into eight districts, and between the buildings that form the silhouette there are many green spaces with low residential buildings. As we stroll through the city, we again experience the strange changes of the ambiance.

Gsöllpointner 2003.

We've already come across the mobile city several times: In Lissitzky's Monument to the Third Internationale three cylinders move rhythmically; Ron Herron's Walking City is mobile in its entirety; and a few blueprints by Coop Himmelblau include the concept of mobile, extendable building parts. Helmuth Gsöllpointner comes from sculpture – like so many artists of the city – and has actually implemented these ideas of telescoped dynamics a hundred times, from very small hand objects to sculptures as high as houses. For the steel city, 40 real objects were assembled spatially in a collage.

Gerhard Rühm (b. 1930). A new Vienna, 1968

With Gerhard Rühm we drive out to the Upper Belvedere. From here, we have the best overview of the new city, which consists of huge high-rises. But there is no doubt where we are: We can clearly read the name of the city, formed by the buildings – WIEN. Now Gerhard Rühm explains his »project to build a new city of WIEN [Vienna]«.

»The plan is to construct four buildings. The first is in the shape of the letter W, the second of the letter I, the third of the letter E, and the last in the form of the letter N.

The buildings have the same height as Vienna's Stephansdom [St. Stephan's Cathedral], and the cubic columns and passages have the same diameter as the tower – roughly at mid-height. the buildings are completely closed toward the outside and are only connected underground, so that the sight of the inhabitants does not spoil the picture.

The first building houses the administration and its numerous officials.

The second building is used for contemplation. from the loudspeakers, all the possible combinations of the letters W, I, E, and N are heard in muffled arbitrary but uninterrupted sequence, for instance, *wien*, *ein*, *wein*, *nie*, *wen*, *wenn* – as well as longer words like *weinen* and *nennen*. when meaningless combinations produce words in a foreign language, such as the English word *new*, they are pronounced accordingly, for the city is supposed to be cosmopolitan.

In the third building, the sexual life of the inhabitants takes place. the lowest horizontal passage is intended for heterosexual partners, the second, above it, for gays and lesbians, while the top one is for masturbators who are provided with bugging devices that transmit acoustic events from the lower passages as requested. but the building can also be arranged differently and more diversely. For example, there might be torture chambers for masochists, etc., etc. since new generations are not wanted, labor and delivery rooms, nurseries, and similar facilities are superfluous.

In the first column of the fourth building, the old and sick inhabitants await their death. from above, to pass the time, come the sounds of light music. when people collapse, an apparatus vacuums them up, whereupon they slide down the slanting passage – it extends sufficiently

486. Helmuth Gsöllpointner, variable Steel City, 2003.

deeply into the ground; the best location for this last building would be near a river that would immediately wash away the bodies. Black habits could hang from the ceiling of the second column from which crosses would be dropped after them.« (1968)
 Stadt und Utopie 1982.

Universal genius Gerhard Rühm, who loves to experiment and has a great sense of humor, is one of the important artists of our time: He has a virtuoso command of language, music, graphic arts, and their subtle interfaces. In 1958 he cofounded the legendary literary movement the »Wiener Gruppe«.
 His excursion into architecture is provocative and unique. We are familiar with baroque monastery ground plans in the form of letters (IHS). Rühm erects the letters and makes a city out of them. It is easier to understand the project in the context of the atmosphere in Vienna during the late 1960s: experimental architecture, Viennese actionism, literary happenings, etc.

Otto Mühl (b. 1925). Friedrichshof, Burgenland, Austria, 1972–87

A few hundred »Mühl communes« are already in existence, and like many other important models of alternative societies, this one has not remained limited to Austria and Europe, but has long since spread to America; a first in an Asian country, three communes are being formed in India. Otto Mühl, an elder, master, guru, boss, and patriarch rolled into one, describes the theoretical and social background of his vision.
 »Naturally there's no getting past our forefather Sigmund Freud, but in practice we can outgrow him by far and tap into other sources of inspiration. The first and foremost of these is Wilhelm Reich and his sexual theories.« But doesn't Wilhelm Reich attempt a rapprochement to the theses of Karl Marx, while the Mühl communes for the most part distance themselves from them? »Wilhelm Reich's most vital idea, the abolition of sexual oppression, is our starting point as well, particularly his revolutionary position on sexual freedom as a way of totally detaching from bourgeois conventions.« Reich even questions the tabooing of incest and of sex with minors. Admittedly, he clearly deviates from psychoanalysis.
 Otto Mühl and the members of his communes actually did set off a landslide of sexual »liberation« in their communes.
 »Our first and most important task was to dissolve the nuclear family, the nuclear-family society, and the breaking up of couple relationships with their constraints, conventions, and mechanisms of oppression. Free sexuality, starting with the commune, is now taken for granted, and universal community of property is a logical consequence of the processes of emancipation.«

However, isn't this a return to the ancient models, starting with Plato, which all failed, if they were even ever implemented?

»We developed the models further and articulated them in a new way based on a critique of modern society – that is the secret of our worldwide and lasting success.«

Again Otto Mühl refers back to Wilhelm Reich, particularly his concept of the »*armor-plating of the human character structure promoted in patriarchal, authoritarian civilizations*«.

We can certainly not deny that Otto Mühl has become a prominent representative of these same patriarchal structures, yet thanks to his experimental methods, with often ecstatic self-presentation in the action analysis, the members of his communes succeed in breaking up the »armor-plating« of individuals.

Gradually a rich vocabulary of experimental practices has developed. Dance and body language, a large degree of nudity and loss of inhibitions, and the free use of profanities are part of the repertory of so-called action analyses. Their early stages are massage, rolfing, caresses, kisses, but also blows and slaps – all developing freely and spontaneously, where regression and infantilism are perfectly acceptable.

At times, art plays a decisive role. It is often also part of the processes of liberation, and Mühl himself is frequently a universal artist beyond bourgeois concepts of art, but he now criticizes art in the harshest of terms. »*The artist is without exception a person who shows his damaged sexuality by anal-sadistic acts. In a communal society where every person can develop genital and social identity there can be no artists and no art. art and artists are produced by being raised in a nuclear-family society; that society forces members of nuclear families to search for the meaning of life outside social reality.*«

The all-encompassing 20th century reform of society was far-reaching, and Otto Mühl will no doubt be recorded in history as a peaceful revolutionary and an apostle of liberation. But now we are confronted with a reality of incredible dimensions, a gigantic success and a catastrophic defeat.

Otto Mühl comes from the movement of »Viennese actionism«.His material actions in particular were a strong focus for the group that included Günter Brus, Hermann Nitsch, and Rudolf Schwarzkogler. Mühl's last actions took place around 1971. After 1970, the first Mühl commune

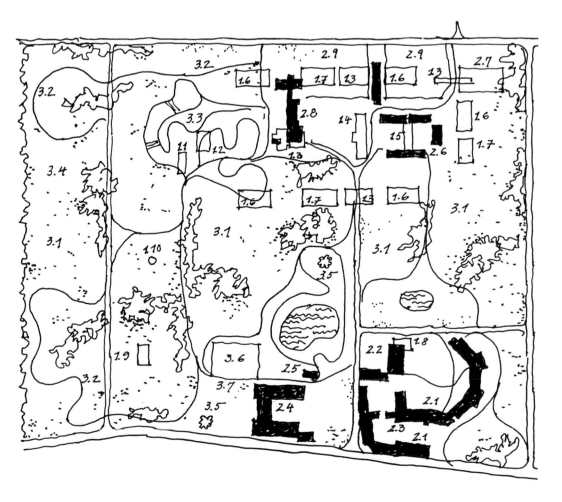

488. Friedrichshof, a former Mühl commune, Burgenland, Austria, 2005. 1. The old Friedrichshof, 1895, 1.1 manor house, 1.2 manager, 1.3 services, 1.4 draft animals, 1.5 shed, 1.6 Farmhands, 1.7 stables, 1.8 school, 1.9 Slovak house, 1.10 well, 2. the new Friedrichshof, 2000, buildings, 2.1 apartments, 2.2 seminar room, 2.3 seminar hotel, inn, 2.4 museum, 2.5 sauna, 2.6 stables, 2.7 riding hall, 2.8 various buildings, 2.9 building sites, 3. the new Friedrichshof, 2000, open spaces, 3.1 garden, leisure, farming, 3.2 jogging path, 3.3 sledding hill, 3.4 tenant, 3.5 gardens fireplace, 3.6 playing field , 3.7 playground.

develops on Praterstraße in Vienna. It meets with lively interest in the subculture and quickly grows in size – the apartment on Praterstraße becomes too small.

And now comes the real success story: Friedrichshof, an old farm in Burgenland, 20 km from Vienna, is purchased in 1973. With a living space of over 3,000 m^2, rather run-down, it is restored by the commune members. Thanks to amazingly hard work and good management it becomes a flourishing enterprise.

The community grows, its practices are developed – action analysis, self-presentation, sexual liberation in action analyses, in the life of the commune are key concepts. The commune's forefathers Freud and Reich are far outstripped and overshadowed by concrete events. Action analysis has continued to develop: from bodywork to self-presentation, and on to ecstasy.

An old storehouse is the scene of happenings: Individual or couple actions are celebrated in the presence of the entire commune. The couple relationships that still exist are dissolved for good, promiscuity becomes a matter of course.

The commune gets an incredible amount of publicity, especially in Germany. Visitors, but also »patients« arrive at Friedrichshof, and many »branches« are established. By 1982 there are 35 groups with close to 600 members in fourteen cities – Paris, Stockholm, Strassburg, Düsseldorf, Heidelberg, Copenhagen, Zürich, Genf, Amsterdam, Lyon, London, Hamburg, Berlin, and Vienna. Children are engendered and born, with the fathers uncertain for the time being. Education is completely repression-free.

As we tour Friedrichshof, Otto Mühl gives us a truly impressive and convincing picture of the commune and its intensive life. Again, he sums up the four basic principles: community property, free sexuality, actionist psychoanalysis, and direct democracy.

Fleck 2003.

Fourteen years later, in 1987, we revisit Friedrichshof, and now the picture has changed fundamentally. First of all, we are surprised that Otto has just married Claudia. They're looking after Lili, their disabled child. They have founded a small branch commune, a refuge, on one of the Canary Islands, La Gomera.

Countercurrents have become noticeable in the late 1970s: Private property has to be reintroduced; the appearance of AIDS forbids sexuality outside the groups, couple relationships resume once more. Graphic art comes back into fashion, more and more people leave the commune, fathers are revealed by means of DNA tests.

Above all, we now take a more critical look at the position of Otto Mühl: His authoritarian, patriarchal attitude can no longer be denied. It is possible that for many commune members the father image represents psychological help. But Mühl expanded his sexual practices and it is hard to believe that only therapeutic and ideological aspects are involved when he practices a type of »ius primae noctis« and copulates with each incoming woman member. Yet he does not do so only with women, but also with twelve- to sixteen-year-old girls – and this proves to be his nemesis: They do not keep silent and insist that they did not do it of their own free will. The result: Otto Mühl is sentenced to seven years in prison and returns to Gomera at the age of 67, broken in health and spirit. Most people have distanced themselves from Otto Mühl long ago.

After crises, conflicts, and lawsuits, the commune of Friedrichshof fell apart, was quickly dissolved in 1991/92, and was sold. The commune members, as best they could, found bourgeois jobs. A monumental failure – in other words, the commune was a utopia after all.

But now, in 2006, Friedrichshof is defined completely differently: It has become a »place with wide horizons«, a loose community that has left all extremes behind.

Anton Schweighofer (b. 1930). Stadt des Kindes (the City of the Child), 1968–74

Purkersdorf is a rustic small town just outside Vienna, but even before we reach its center, we turn off the highway, to be greeted by architecture of great simplicity and amazing quality.

The administration is located in the largest building. The head of the City of the Child is our tour guide. »This is a good time, now in the late afternoon, and you will see that this is really a small town«, our guide says delightedly.

»I thought of what a street is basically«, Anton Schweighofer explains. »In principle all public institutions are on the left side of the streets, while family homes are on the right.«

Around this time the street is full of hustle and bustle. A young family is coming down the street on their way to the swimming pool. Afterwards there is going to be a football game at the

489. Anton Schweighofer, Stadt des Kindes (the City of the Child), Purkersdorf near Vienna, 1968–74.

playing field. The gym is crowded, too, and the local athletic club has reserved it for two hours. At the cultural center, folk theater professionals are rehearsing a scene from a play by Nestroy, to be performed tonight, with adults, children, and teenagers from the City of the Child. Behind the scenes, people are painting a simple backdrop. And of course, when the weather is nice, there is an open-air performance on the theater square.

The dining room is also designed simply and without ostentation. Our guide invites us to have a delicious snack. In the adjacent club room, a lively discussion is in process about the activity program for the coming weeks. It will be another couple of hours before the disco opens.

The architect explains the underlying principle of individual homes. »Transparency and open spaces were important for me. I believe such things deeply affect the lives of young people and especially promote a sense of community. Still, every resident must have private space available to him or her.«

We really enjoy going up and down the stairs and through the halls, and have an interesting exchange of ideas about the »caves«, and intimacy.

»We've now arrived at the second important phase, and are completing the process of integration«, the architect confides. »A school and a kindergarten are being built locally, and the little Lederer mansion is being converted to a residential and training center for mothers and educators.«

Feuerstein 1988; Schweighofer 1989; Österreicher 2003.

The development, unquestionably an architectural masterpiece, hardly functioned as described above. Nor was it expanded, and thus actually remained a utopia. As so often in the present-day architectural scene, the implementation of the physical construction of the vision is successful, but the social and societal hopes and ideals have not been fulfilled.

The City of the Child represents a counter-model or alternative model to the various types of children's villages. Not a rustic idyll with pretty little cottages, but a compact complex with many types of offerings was intended to help problem children housed here to change their lives.

The seductive and novel idea behind the vision was integration: The population of the »outside world« was invited to use the public facilities, indeed the entire complex, thus promoting communication and contact. Things hardly worked out as expected, and personnel and pedagogical problems finally resulted in the »city« being closed. The architect and many fellow protesters were opposed to the demolition of the complex, and the building was preserved, its function barely changed. A new tract of gardens and residential housing are the town's economic basis.

13.9 Writers, filmmakers, artists

George Orwell (1903–1950). *1984*, 1949

George Orwell takes us to Oceania, we are in 1984, in the future, and Oceania is the former London. We are deeply depressed at the sight of the houses, streets, and squares: We walk past huge numbers of dilapidated buildings. The walls are sometimes propped up with wooden posts, the windows boarded up with cardboard, the roofs patched with corrugated iron. We are all the more surprised by four massive buildings, pyramid-like towers made of white concrete, close to 300 m high.

»Those are the four ministries«, Orwell explains. »Minitrue, the Ministry of Truth, Minipax, the Ministry of Peace, Miniluv for the Ministry of Love, and Miniplenty for the Ministry of Plenty.«

Now we meet Mr. Winston Smith, a citizen of this city. He can tell us about life in 1984. At first we want to know the meaning of the huge posters we have been seeing everywhere: the face of a man about 45 years old with a bushy black mustache and powerful, appealing facial features – a face whose eyes follow you everywhere.

»Look at the text on the poster over there: It explains everything.« The giant letters read, »Big Brother is watching you.«

How is this supervision implemented? we ask. »The television sets work both ways: That is, we not only see, but are also seen at all times. And also there are thousands of microphones in the apartments, in the city. Of course it's impossible to turn them off.«

Winston invites us to a special event. We enter a large hall where seats are arranged around a huge TV screen. »You are now going to see the daily Two Minutes Hate. That's Emmanuel Goldstein, the Enemy of the People. A renegade, once the dictator, then sentenced to death for counterrevolutionary machinations, he escaped« – catcalls, screams of rage, curses, yells fill the hall as we enter.

What are the goals of the ruling party, in very general terms? »The basic motto of the system is extremely simple: ›War is peace – freedom is slavery – ignorance is strength.‹«

In concrete terms Mr. Winston expresses how this applies to political reality: »*The Party has two goals: the conquest of the entire planet and the definitive elimination of any possibility of independent thinking.*«

In your opinion, how can these goals be reached in practice? Understandably Mr. Winston keeps a very low profile, for »*whatever the Party considers to be the truth is the truth. Reality can be recognized only through the eyes of the Party*«.

And Mr. O'Brien, initially the confidant and later the torturer of Mr. Winston, is completely convinced: »*We know that no one seizes power with the intention of relinquishing it again. Power is not a means to an end, it is an end in itself. People do not establish a dictatorship in order to guarantee a revolution; they have a revolution in order to guarantee the dictatorship. The goal of torture is torture. The goal of power is power.*«

But how do you deal with all the contradictions in thinking? we now ask. »That's pretty clear: There is ›doublethink‹, which means we totally accept that two contradictory statements are true.«

We have many more questions, but George Orwell intimates that they cannot be addressed here and now without harming Mr. Winston.

Well, we encounter Mr. Orwell again a year later. He gives a brief rundown of the subsequent fate of this secretly rebellious citizen: »Mr. Winston committed two egregious errors: For one, he began to keep a diary, full of guarded, but also open criticism of the system. And he met the lovely Julia, who was outwardly loyal to the Party, had illicit meetings with her, and fell in love with her. He paid for this: Imprisoned under horrifying conditions, he underwent inhuman torture ordered and carried out by O'Brien.«

But the goal was reached. And in the end, after the great victory over Africa, Mr. Winston had to admit: »*But it was all right, everything was all right, the struggle was finished. He had won the victory over himself. He loved Big Brother.*«

Orwell 1949.

Not the place, but the time of our journey is a fiction. The magical year was awaited with literary interest – but history had thankfully developed in a completely different direction: Five years later, in 1989, communism in Europe collapsed. Yet we are still filled with fear: fear of the power of the multinationals, fear of the power of fascism, fear of Stalinism or whatever has replaced it. And a new dread now attacks us, fomented by many politicians – the fear of terrorism. This fear is used to legitimize the redefinition of the fears described by Orwell. »Big Brother is watching you!« has been given a new meaning. Since 11. 9. 2001 other, no less horrifying fears have sprung up worldwide: the menace of various kinds of terrorism. Under the pretext of fighting it, new systems of surveillance, which attack the freedom of the individual, have developed in the »free« world.

Ray (Douglas) Bradbury (b. 1920), *Fahrenheit 451*, 1953; François Truffaut (1932–1984), film, 1966

We are probably in a city in the American Midwest between St. Louis and Chicago visiting Mr. Montag in his lovely home. Admittedly it is not very cozy: The walls of the room are huge screens, but they are not just for watching television – the inhabitants of the house are also watched: observed, kept under surveillance. And the city itself does not feel particularly comfortable. In the streets young people race around wildly in their turbo-diesel cars, destroying and killing. Informers keep the citizens under surveillance. And a mechanical hound in the streets can extrude his deadly steel needle.

Montag is a fireman, which is nothing unusual. But what he does as part of his job is rather strange. His task is not to put out fires, but to set fires – to burn books. For books are strictly illegal. When they are discovered, singly or by the hundred, the jet of kerosene hits them without mercy, and often their owner as well. It doesn't hurt the houses, for they are all fireproof.

»The consequences are clear, you see«, says Mr. Montag. »*Less school, less pressure to study, no more philosophy, no history, no languages. Why learn something if it's enough to press a button or flick a switch?*« On the other hand, there are more sports for everyone, more mass rallies, more movies. »*A book in the house next door is like a loaded gun. You've got to destroy it. Got to tear down the spirit.*«

Clarisse is a pretty, somewhat strange young girl. Montag likes her a lot. She has many stories to tell about her uncle: »*In the old days, houses used to have a front porch. That's where people sometimes sat at night, chatting or rocking in their rocking chairs. The porches have disappeared. The gardens too, by the way. People talked too much and had time to think.*«

One day, Clarisse vanishes – Montag is in despair. But that's not all: He gets hold of a book, but does not hand it over to be burned and is thus doomed and has to run away. Where? Already, he's been discovered: The mechanical hound and the thugs are after him. Montag runs to the river, dives into the water and swims away. He climbs the bank and follows the railroad track. In the dark, he sees a fire in the fields, a blessed fire at which men are keeping warm, refugees like him: scientists, poets, professors. Montag is accepted into their circle. But what's the use? The books are lost, aren't they? Not at all: Every one of his buddies is a book, carries a book in his head, memorized, and Montag, too, has something to contribute: Ecclesiastes, the Book of Revelation. The world of the spirit will survive.

Fahrenheit 451 1953.

Recent history shows that book burnings are not a utopia: On huge pyres, the Nazis burned primarily the works of Jewish authors. Ray Bradbury writes an apotheosis of culture in the most adverse of circumstances. Truffaut's film was shot in 1966 with Oscar Werner and Julie Christie.

Ernst Jünger (1895–1998). *Heliopolis*, 1949, *The Glass Bees*, (*Gläserne Bienen*, 1957)

We are given the great opportunity to meet not only Ernst Jünger but also Mr. de Geer. In the utopian society of Heliopolis he is the nonconformist. »Yes, I've traveled through all the utopias«, he tells us. »I've gotten to know them all. But now I'm looking for a new utopia.« Does he have any idea where it can be found? we ask. »I believe that at the moment I am in the middle of a conflict that has arisen between the proconsul, an aristocrat, and the governor, a popular hero.«

Do they represent the two large social classes that still face each other with all social tensions? »It's not that simple«, replies de Geer. »The proconsul and governor both want to represent not only the army but also the people. Both support technology and the interests of humanity.«
Is there now a new dichotomy that needs to be restored to harmony? And who will resolve it,

who will be the ruler in the long run? »The ruler of the state is a God-the-Father figure. He works for peace and has invited the rulers of the entire world to a large peace conference.«

Is there a chance of world peace or is it all an illusion? we ask skeptically. The solutions of the conflict are up to the »Parsees« – they are devoted to the spiritual realm, while the »Mauretanians« , the technicians, represent power. These two groups seem to have insurmountable differences. Thus people place all hopes on the »best men« of the state, the intellectuals, who seek contact with the kingdoms of this world – so there is hope!

We continue our tour – accompanied by Richard, who is looking for a job. He wants to accept the offer of the great magical mechanic Zapparoni. We are invited to visit his mchanical magic realm.

We rest in a wonderful garden and are amazed to discover that the bees in the garden are made of glass, slightly larger than biological bees, and fly thanks to a complicated mechanism. »Isn't it absurd to have mechanical bees?« wonders Richard. »Is it possible to combine the old mechanical perfection with the new technological one? One of them must no doubt be sacrificed.« But Richard finds the way out: He is a member of the »old« human race with all the technical knowledge of the »new« humanity.

Jünger 1949, 1960, 1991.

Should the »Parsees« be seen as the Jews, while the »Mauretanians« are Nazis? Then they are definitely irreconcilable. In this day and age, however, we can no longer regard spirituality and technology as antagonistic forces.

Stanislaw Lem (1921–2006). Strange worlds in the cosmos

It is wonderful that Stanislaw Lem wants to be our guide during our rambles, no – journeys, no, not that either – during our trip into the unreal future worlds here and in the universe. However, he warns us: »The kind of cities you probably imagine, such as Paris or Florence, don't exist anymore; at least, they are no longer of interest to us.«

It's true that the places we visit all over the universe are no less interesting. First, we visit *Solaris*, 1972, and then we are surrounded by *Perfect Emptiness*, 1973. We read the *Star Diaries,* 1973, and listen to the *Robot Tales*, 1973, visit the *High Castle*, 1974, and are glad at the news of *Peace on Earth*, 1986.

Admittedly, Stanislaw Lem was right: Only vaguely, something like a city, a settlement, or architectural structures loom here and there – and yet it is clear why we end our trip deeply impressed.

Lem 1988.

Stanislaw Lem was one of the most famous science-fiction authors of the 20th century. His work combines an amazing knowledge of technology and the natural sciences with high literary quality. Have any of his visions come true up to this point? Only few of them have been fulfilled – but let's wait another hundred years!

Ursula K. Le Guin (b. 1929). The planet of *The Dispossessed*, 1974

We have to commute back and forth between two planets, two countries, two cities: In Anarres there is no property, no marriage, no government, but also no justice and no prisons. And Ursula K. Le Guin reports enthusiastically: »Men and women are finally equal. This is the key to harmony and peace. There is no ruling elite and no property.«

But what a pitiful sight Anarres is! A poorly built wall surrounds the wretched harbor with its rocket launching pad, warehouses, garages, hostels, all dirty and depressing.

Now let's visit the other planet / city-state, Urras. There is some prosperity here; everything has to be bought here, unlike in Anarres. The tops of the city's towers are shrouded in mist, trains race along on elevated tracks, the streets are lined with walls of glass and stone, and thanks to electric light the city is bright as day. The city's inhabitants are 16,000 students – males only – whose society is hierarchically structured. The citizens are well-to-do and live elegantly and in luxury.

Anarres was home to the brilliant physicist Shevek, but the country, completely focused on community, has isolated itself too much from the outside world. If Shevek wants to translate his knowledge into action, he must travel to the planet Urras. Here the communications technologist is welcomed with open arms – but he cannot bring along any money from his home planet Anarres. Shevek's lectures and research, as well as his person, are met with enormous interest in Urras. He is able to translate his mathematical theories into practice. Yet at the end of the day Shevek does not feel at home in Urras – he cannot decide in favor of either of the two societies.

Le Guin 1974.

This journey probably also crosses the borderline to »science fiction«, but the idea of the »dispossessed« is a very clear reminder of the societal models we encountered in earlier journeys and thus provides interesting continuity. When all is said and done, however, none of the ideal states can bring a lasting paradise.

Margaret Atwood (b. 1933). *The Handmaid's Tale*, 1985, *1995*

We are in the once wonderful university town of Cambridge, Massachusetts. We are aware, of course, that the conservative Christian movements in the US repeatedly exhibit fundamentalistic and totalitarian traits. Yet the development of recent years is terrifying beyond measure.

The societal changes of recent decades, defined as signs of moral and ecological decline, provoke resistance and displeasure: There are those who claim that declining population numbers because of atomic contamination, abortion and pills, AIDS epidemics, homosexuality and feminism, alcoholism, drug addiction, prostitution and pornography, consumption and entertainment, the influence of the Jews and people of color will inevitably lead to the downfall of the nation. A coup by conservative extremists allows a horrendous regime to be established. The city is called Gilead. We are confronted with a cruel totalitarian theocracy.

The main evil causing the decline was equal rights for women. This flaw is the first to be remedied: women are dispossessed, their bank accounts transferred to their husbands; they are deprived of the right to work and ordered to remain at home. Women in unmarried partnerships or divorced women are called up to do work service for the state – or assigned to bear children to the husbands of infertile women. If they are also barren or give birth to handicapped children, they are sent to death camps together with old and sickly women.

»Offred« can accompany us only with her voice, recorded on a tape that was found by chance. She was condemned to be a »handmaid«; worse yet, she is forced to be a walking womb. She belongs to Fred, the »Commander« – hence her name, »Offred« – and since his wife is barren, is supposed to provide his offspring – according to an old biblical tradition: Hagar, the maidservant, also bore children for Abraham when Rachel was infertile. But eroticism or sexual gratification, romantic feelings or other emotions during the sex act are undesirable, attraction and orgasm are unnecessary, only a frivolity, and she laments: »It's only the insides of our bodies that are important.«

The institution in which she is confined is strictly guarded and surrounded by a high wall on which the executed opponents of the regime are hanged.

Life consists of sermons and Bible study, begetting and birth ceremonies. There are no books, no music or films, and no theater.

Cigarettes and alcohol are unhealthy, cosmetics, fashionable clothes, personal property and social life are superfluous and hence prohibited.

Thus life has hardly anything to offer: household meetings, shared meals, bleak shopping trips, church attendance. What options does Offred have left? What resistance is possible? Only memories and daydreams? Of her mother, husband, daughter? But now something strange happens: A kind of love for her oppressor and bedfellow flares up. Yet Offred does not become pregnant – for Fred is sterile. So Fred's wife pairs her off with Nick, the Commander's bodyguard and driver – and a quiet love grows between the two: Nick helps her to escape. But what does the future hold for her?

Not until the 1980s do women gradually begin to write utopian fiction. The point of departure is usually dystopias, visions of horror, scenarios of dread. Interpretations, questions, and solutions are offered from a feminist perspective. Margaret Atwood sets two cornerstones: the Old Testament insistence on offspring and the cruelty of modern dictators – between which women are crushed.

Italo Calvino (1923–1985) and Marco Polo. The *Invisible Cities* (*Le città invisibili*, 1972)

Marco Polo, the man who talked to the Mongol ruler Kublai Khan, sketches 25 cities of many different kinds. Italo Calvino takes us on a tour of these cities. Unusual as the life of the inhabitants may be, we are only interested in the fantastic architectural styles. Italo Calvino / Marco Polo themselves describe these cities, so that all we, the chroniclers, need to do is listen. But of course we picked only those cities that particularly fire our imagination.

»In Smeraldina, the aquatic city, a network of canals and a network of streets overlap and intersect. In order to get from one place to another, you always have a choice between the land route and the one by boat. Since the shortest line between two points in Smeraldina is not a straight line, but a zigzag that branches out in intertwined variants, each person has not two, but many routes open to him or her. The number of routes is even larger for people who sometimes cross by boat and at other times walk instead.

Thus the inhabitants of Smeraldina are spared the monotony of walking down the same streets every day. But that isn't all: The network of passages is not laid out only on one level, but follows the ups and downs of small flights of stairs, balustrade pssages, humpbacked bridges, hanging streets. Because of a combination of segments of a number of different overpasses and elevated highways each inhabitant has the pleasure of a different route every day to get to the same destinations. In Smeraldina lives that are the most bound by habit and the most uneventful pass without repetition...«

»If you walk three days toward sunrise, you are in Diomira, a city with 60 silver domes, bronze statues of all the gods, streets paved with pewter, a crystal theater and a golden rooster that crows from the tower every morning...«

»The city of Leonia makes itself new every day: Every morning the citizens wake up between clean sheets, wash with bars of soap that come straight out of the wrapping, dress in brand-new dressing gowns, get completely intact cans from the most perfected refrigerators, hear the latest fairy tales from the newest radio models. On the sidewalks, wrapped in clean plastic bags, what remains of yesterday's Leonia waits for the garbage trucks. Not only empty toothpaste tubes, burnt-out lightbulbs, newspapers, containers, and packaging, but also boilers, encyclopedias, pianos, sets of china; Leonia's prosperity is measured, more than by the things that are produced, sold, bought day by day, by what is thrown out every day in order to make room for new stuff. So one wonders whether Leonia's true passion is indeed, as they say, the enjoyment of new and different things rather than getting rid of, removing, cleansing oneself of a constantly returning impurity. The fact is that sanitation workers are welcomed like angels and their function – the job of eliminating what is left of yesterday's existence – is greeted with silent respect like a ritual that demands reverence, or maybe it's just that once stuff is thrown out nobody wants to give it another thought.«

»You could talk about the city of Dorotea in two ways: You could say that four aluminum towers rise from its walls, which flank seven gates. Their drawbridge is placed over a ditch whose water feeds four green canals that flow through the town and divide it into nine districts of 300 houses and 700 chimneys each. You could comment that the marriageable girls of each district marry young men from other districts and their families exchange the goods that are the exclusive property of each: bergamots, caviar, astrolabes, amethysts. Based on these data you can make calculations until you know everything about the city – its past, present, and future.«

»In the center of Fedora, a metropolis built of gray stone, stands a metal palace with a glass globe in every room. In every globe, as you look into it, you can see a blue city, the model for another Fedora. These are forms the city could have assumed if for one reason or another it had not become the city we see today. In every era, there has been someone who, looking at the Fedora of his time, imagined how an ideal city could have been created here, yet even while he was building his miniature model, Fedora was no longer the same as before, and what had been a possible future yesterday was now just a toy in a glass globe...«

»The traveler who does not yet know the city of Zoe awaiting him along his route wonders what the royal palace will be like, and the mill, the theater, the bazaar. In every city of the empire every building is different and differently built; but as soon as the stranger arrives in the unknown city, looks at this forest of pagodas and garrets and haylofts, and follows the maze of canals, gardens, and rubbish heaps, he can immediately tell which are the princes' palaces, the temples of the high priests, the tavern, the prison, the slum. This – according to many – confirms the hypothesis that all of us carry in our minds a city that consists only of differences, a city without figures and without form, and the individual cities fill it up. This is not true of Zoe. At any point in this city you could sleep, manufacture tools, cook, accumulate gold coins, disrobe, reign, sell, consult oracles. Any one of its gabled roofs could just as well cover the leprosarium as the baths of the odalisques.«

»I do not know whether Armilla is like that because it has not been completed or because it's been destroyed, or whether magic or a whim is the hidden reason. The fact is that it has neither walls nor ceilings nor floors: It has nothing that would make it look like a city, with the exception of plumbing that rises vertically where there should be houses: a jungle of pipes that end in faucets, showers, siphons, drains. A few sinks or bathtubs or other fixtures gleam white against the sky like ripe fruit still clinging to the branches. One could say the plumbers had finished their work and left before the bricklayers arrived; or that their installations, because they are indestructible, had survived a catastrophe, earthquake, or the work of termites…«

»The ancients built Valdrada on the shores of a lake, with houses, all veranda, one above the other, and elevated highways whose balustrades face the water. When a traveler arrives, he therefore sees two cities: one upright above the lake and one reflected upside down. No thing is or happens in the one Valdrada that is not repeated in the other, for the city was planned in such a way that every one of its points is reflected in its mirror, and the Valdrada down in the water not only holds all the recesses and projections of the façades that rise above the lake but also the interiors of the rooms with ceilings and floors, the perspective of the corridors, the mirrors on the wardrobes…«

»The city of Sofronia is a combination of two half-cities. In one are the big roller-coaster, the flying carousel, the Ferris wheel, the Ride of Death with the motor bikers headfirst, the circus dome with the trapeze suspension tackle in the middle. The other half-city is built of stone and marble and cement, with the bank, factories, big houses, slaughterhouse, school, and all the rest. One of the half-cities is fixed, the other is temporary, and when its stay is over, it is dismantled and removed, only to be rebuilt on open terrain in another half-city…«

»Once you've arrived in Fillide, you'll enjoy looking at the great variety of bridges that cross the canals, each different from the others: humpbacked, covered, on pillars, on boats, hanging and with perforated railings; at the great variety of windows facing the street: double-arched, Moorish, lancet-shaped, ogives, with lunettes or rosettes above them; at the great variety of surfacing: pebbles, flagstones, gravel, white and blue tiles. At each point in the city there are surprises for the eye: a caper bush coming up from the fortress wall, the statues of three queens on a ledge, an onion dome with three little onions on top. ›How fortunate are those who have Fillide before them every day and never cease to see all the things it contains!‹ you exclaim, full of melancholy at the thought of having to leave the city after you have barely glanced at it…«

»After wading through the river and crossing the mountain pass, the man suddenly stands before the city of Moriana with its alabaster gates, transparent in the sunshine, its coral pillars that support ledges faced with serpentine, its villas made of pure glass, like aquariums, where the shadows of the dancers swim about with silvery scales under medusa-shaped chandeliers. If this is not his first journey, the traveler already knows that cities like these have another side: A short walk, and you see Moriana's hidden face, a field full of rusty metal, burlap, nail-studded beams, sooty pipes, piles of cans, fire walls with faded graffiti, skeletons of chairs without their cane seats, ropes fit only for hanging oneself from a rottem beam…«

»When you come to Tecla, you see little of the town behind wooden fences, burlap covers, framework, metal scaffolding, construction boards attached to ropes or placed on sawhorses, ladders, tangles of wire. When asked, ›Why is the construction of Tecla taking such a long time?‹ they answer, as they continue to heave buckets, plumb walls, sweep long paint brushes up and down: ›So that the destruction won't start.‹ And when asked whether they are afraid that the city will disintegrate and fall apart as soon as the scaffolding is removed, they add quickly and softly: ›Not only the city …‹«

Calvino 1972.

Italo Calvino's beautiful language makes a miracle happen: The cities materialize before our eyes, we see them even though they are invisible, and we have surely seen some time and some place, even if only in our dreams.

Roy Lichtenstein (1923–1997), François Schuiten, Benot Peeters. The Comic-book City, 1965, 1984
Massimo Iosa Ghini (b. 1959). The *città fluida*, 1989
Eric and Marc Moreno. Arboris, 2004
Thousands of comic-book characters

490. François Schuiten and Benot Peeters, city near Samaris, 1984.

491. Roy Lichtenstein, *This must be the Place*, 1965.
492. Massimo Iosa Ghini, città fluida, 1989.
493. Eric und Marc Moreno, the Regulator, 2004.

»*This must be the Place*«, Roy Lichtenstein exclaims. Which place does he mean? »*Just the Place*« – that's all we are told, but we see that it must be a special place: the New City!
The forms of this city are compact, strict, simple, contoured: Segments of circles, cylinders, curved surfaces, towers – seemingly a conglomeration. We are reminded of the banality of the comics the inspirations come from. And yet this city gives us a colorful, living picture. It is a compendium of surfaces and bodies with barely recognizable exterior spaces. The city seems to be deserted, and we do not know where the voices come from.

Quite different is the city in which François Schuiten is our guide. There is a mix of periods, of styles, Art Nouveau with lovely French-Belgian details – but the buildings are dissolved in steel and glass, covered with glass roofs.

Massimo Ghini takes us into the vivid, dynamic world of a seemingly exploding, colorful architecture that by far surpasses expressionism around 1910/20 and leaves even the deconstructivists of the 1970s far behind.

Eric und Marc Moreno tell moving, spine-chilling stories that take place in eerie, oppressive cities, shaped entirely by an already antiquated but still fascinating 19th/20th century technology.

A lot of new ideas come from painting and sculpture. They are always protests against the empty functionalism of many contemporaries. Pop Art hardly left any mark on architecture, though it did influence architectural drawing. Roy Lichtenstein is one of its main representatives.

He's a very nice, friendly man, reliable and pleasant, working in his office day in and day out. But he invites us to come on a nocturnal walk with him: And now we see him flitting between the high-rises, in the streets, across highways. Within seconds he is where he is needed: His power is in demand, and so are his speed and inventiveness, but above all his helpfulness and his kind heart.

What superb fantasies film designers come up with. Colorful, dynamic, living cities: These, too, are dreams, but they are utopias that can be implemented. And isn't the film itself reality?

Philip K. Dick (1928–1982). *Do Androids Dream of Electric Sheep*, 1968, and Ridley Scott (b. 1937). The city of the *Blade Runners* (film: 1982/*2019*)

Incredible things have happened. Long feared, they have now become a reality: A group of androids has fled to Earth from the space colonies – they must be pursued, captured, destroyed – and that is the special mission of Rick Deckard/Dick Tracy.

But the cities where the chases take place are so unbelievable – they are the new megalopolises: huge, run-down. Eerie, dark, menacing cities, clouds and mist, rising vapors, agitated, flickering lights; we sense danger, hate, murder: cities of anxiety and torment.

The neon lights make the canyons of streets darker rather than lighter, danger lurks everywhere – is it still possible to live in such a city, is this not the antiroom to hell? And yet we cannot deny its fascination, and we are not sure: Perhaps these are really the cities of the future? The urban landscape seems to be boundless, there is no end to the city. What is so fantastic about it is a new, ever-present three-dimensionality. Not much happens on the »ground«, while a lot is going on in the underworlds of the street and in the airy heights of the residential towers built out of discarded high-tech and the refuse of our civilization – told by freaks, punks, business people. We notice materials that are strangely virtual. The walls seem to be made of prestressed materials. Steel, glass, and garbage do not seem to contradict each other. The architecture of the big companies is strange: The Tyrell Corporation's buildings resemble pyramid-shaped microchips. In the long run, the space of the city is not transparent, but that is no longer necessary, for people communicate mainly by means of videophones.

Rick Deckard, seemingly brutal and unscrupulous in his chase, becomes unsure of himself: How can he tell androids from human beings? Where is the dividing line between men and machines? And lovely Rachel – is she an android too, and doomed to die? And is Rick really sure he isn't an android himself?

In Ridley Scott's magnificent 1982 film, Harrison Ford played the leading role, and his team created a virtually »real« city of terror. The film combines science fiction and the new wave of nostalgia, a surprising combination that we will encounter one more time.

Osamu Tezuka and Rintarô. The New *Metropolis ziggurat*, 2002

We enter the New Metropolis – and a lot is already familiar to us from Fritz Lang's *Metropolis*. But how much more powerful this city is, how much more mighty its towers, how much more hectic the traffic, life, and technology. Again the human race has diverged into two branches. But now robots are the disenfranchised members of society, living in separate worlds from the humans. The ruler of the worlds commissions the construction of a childlike blond angel, Tima. The perfect robot girl, she is to take over world government and to destroy the world and herself. She does not know what kind of a creature she is, but she loves young Kenichi, who saves her from destruction – and the blond robot is filled with human emotions.

495. Jeph Loeb and Jim Lee, Batman in action, 2002.
496. Osamu Tezuka, Rintarô, *Robotic Angel*, 2002.

The reminiscences of Fritz Lang's *Metropolis* are quite deliberate – he has hardly any rivals when it comes to the magnificent scale of his architecture. The film is one of a number of Japanese manga computer trick movies. *Robotic Angel* was directed by Rintarô (see Hayashi), and Osamu Tezuka was the author of the 1946 manga *Metropolis*.

497. J. R. R. Tolkien and P. Jackson, *The Two Towers* (*The Lord of the Rings*), 2003.

John Ronald Reuel Tolkien. *The Two Towers: being second part of the Lord of the Rings*, 1954, and Peter Jackson's film *The Two Towers*, 2003, of Middle Earth

In vast worlds, fantastic landscapes, toward endless horizons we follow brave Frodo in his adventures with the mysterious ring. Once, however, we also experience a city: the two towers that stand mighty and isolated in the landscape. Between these towers, evil holds Middle Earth in thrall, and battles and adventures continue to the happy end.

The kind of arduous work of designing and crafting film scenarios we are familiar with from *Metropolis* has long become outdated. It is true that the buildings for the film were erected at locations in New Zealand, but they were reduced in scale, and it is the computer that completes the architectural illusion.

George Lucas (b. 1944) and Jonathan Hales with Edvin Natividad. The cloned warriors of *Star Wars* and Coruscant, 2002

Coruscant, with its dark »entrails«, is a mighty city. All our senses are attacked, all the walls have monitor screens installed in them, we are exposed to constant electronic bombardment. The rich and mighty live in the exclusive heights, but the »lower« classes are housed between the foundation walls.

In Coruscant there are no private planes, only monorails, which go diagonally up and down the buildings as well. And in the city's canyons we also find warehouses, industrial buildings, and nightclubs. This is a place of shadows and dangers. We are now in the center of Coruscant, and we immediately remember where we have already walked through such spaces: It is not the technology, but the light and space that seem almost a copy of Giovanni Piranesi's fantastic spatial compositions. We are standing approximately in the middle of the city center looking down into dark Dantean depths, ravines, precipices.

Among these many levels, ramps, rails, roadways we lack any point of reference to the earth. We are overcome with a presentiment of the spacelessness of the space capsule. And when we look up, we gaze at floods and cascades of light, radiant and mysterious. And through this very compact, urban world flit soundless monorail trains, digitally controlled, available at a moment's notice, with automatic steering. There are also »gliders«, high-speed two-person vehicles that move through the air.
Star Wars 2002.

Film technology and planning gained a great deal: Concept Art and storyboards are joined by animatics, three-dimensional animated sequences, moving storyboards; digitally produced images are superimposed on them, and a rough version of the film, previsualization, is created. The method comes close to virtual reality, or rather, it *is* a kind of virtual reality. The stylistic influences of architectural history are remarkable: We've already mentioned Piranesi; the halls and palaces remind us of early metro stations and bank buildings in the latter part of the 19th century; and finally, Oriental architecture is frequently present.

498. George Lucas, Edwin Natividad, the city of Coruscant, 2003. Interior of the landing platform.
499. George Lucas, Edwin Natividad, the city of Coruscant, 2003. Street scene.

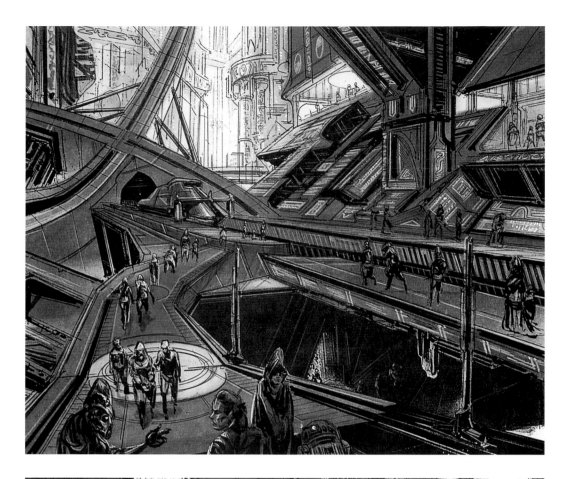

13.10. Virtual reality. Computer city

Many inventors. The virtual city: one, 1837, 1872 – present

It's an age-old dream: finding a way of communicating across long distances, even infinite spaces when no people are present there. The idea became a reality long ago.

Basically, the »virtual city« will soon be 150 years old: The telegraph, followed soon thereafter by the telephone, creates the first useful method of telecommunication: Particularly between cities a net with an invisible, sophisticated structure develops, a kind of – virtual – overall city. Television and video-phones are the next steps: An optical feature is added to the networks. With the exception of early visual and acoustic signals, for the first time people who are not in the same place can now communicate visually as well, with their bodies, their faces.

Electronics experts. The virtual city: two, 1960 to the present day

We were not satisfied: We wanted the exchange of messages, news, ideas to happen over greater distances, become more compact, more intensive.

Something like a quantum leap, a revolution in communication has taken place: A new generation of electronic communication, first »analog«, then »digital«, has encompassed the world. But does this mean »cities« have now been created? With the Internet, and the capabilities of e-mail, a completely new structure has been created; we do not see a real city, but the »global village« prophesied by Marshall McLuhan as early as the 1960s has become a reality. The imaginary, virtual, digital cities of our time seem to be confusing, complicated, inaccessible, indeed chaotic.

In principle, however, they are a reality, and confront us daily, even hourly.

Progressive architects. The computer-generated city – the virtual city: three, 1970 to the present day

We now visit the cities generated by computer following a notion of the designer. Our impressions are so new and run counter to our formal ideas of a city, so that we have trouble finding our bearings. Yet we are thrilled by this new urban world. We are hardly able to describe it. It cannot be compared to anything we have encountered heretofore.

The new City was created on the computer monitors of architects and is truly virtual – how can we find our way within it?

At times it seems quite conventional and »normal« – indeed, like many cities, it simply consists of houses. But there's something else as well: We're in a different world! Here, there are no right angles. Lines, curves, bodies flow and stream, we are in an unprecedented world of forms, col-

500. Greg Lynn, *Stranded Sears Tower*, 1993.

501. Haus-Rucker-Co, Mind Expander II, precurser of the cyberspace helmet, 1968.

ors, and sounds. This new world has found its own language: blobs and bubbles, folds and splashes, blots and scribbles, pliant and supple – beyond the traditional terminology of architecture. Don't we have a sense of déjà-vu? Where have we seen this before? Friedrich Kiesler, Hermann Finsterlin, Coop Himmelblau?

Mayrhofer 1991.

The pioneers of computer planning have hardly done any urban planning, but have only designed buildings. It is doubtful to what extent computers can be of assistance in creating »ideal cities«.

The new experts: virtual reality, the virtual city: four (1978/*2020*)
William (Ford) Gibson (b. 1948). *Cyberspace and Cyberpunk*, 1977
Jaron Lanier. *Tele-Immersion*, 2000

Every city is a virtual reality, artificially created, and the first step toward this reality was taken 6,000 years ago. And then came the next steps toward artificial realities: religion, dance, theater, followed by cinema and television. But always, a »real reality« existed at the same time.

Will this »real reality« be abolished now that we have reached the 21st century? Will it become superfluous? Will the physical world in its entirety be transformed, digitalized, liquidated? We've already visited the first stages: telephone, television, internet. The process continues. We have visited a first phase of the 21st-century digital city. But we have to reinterpret the term »walking tour«, since it takes place on the monitor screen, in the »cave«, on the panorama monitors, in the helmet.

This city has no geographical location – it is a perfect integrated network of non-places: that is, u-topos, utopia that has become a digital »reality«.

We no longer walk through utopia in reality, but only illusionistically. The house and apartment – in so far as they can still be referred to as such – are naturally integrated in the LON, the »local operating network«, the total linking up of the »human environment«. The »infranet« enables us to carry out »facility management«.

All input technologies of virtual realities amount to the fact that movements – of the eyes, hands, faces, and bodies – are transmitted. The user has to perform certain movements. That is necessary in order for his semiotic body to become active at all. Thanks to the computer, the physical movements are transmitted to the data body at such speed that the time this takes or uses remains below the discrimination facility of the human senses. The real body, the »fleshly body« and the »data body« can overlap.

Now we risk an excursion into virtual reality and enter cyberspace. We sit in comfort in our cyberseat. We've put on our helmets, so light and airy we can't feel them. The HMD, or head mounted display, a kind of video headset, is the main component. It communicates sensory information for our head: optical, acoustic, and olfactory impressions. We have put on sensory overalls that envelop the whole body like a space suit and transmit all haptic and thermal experiences. We've slipped our hands into the data gloves, but have not activated them yet. We don't need a remote control: The sensors react acoustically to our speech, though admittedly not to our thoughts alone.

We can now begin our walking tours. We command, »A view of the Belvedere« – and immediately find ourselves in front of the splendid Viennese baroque castle with a view of the city, which is now surrounded by a dense garland of high-rises. We enter »sunrise«: A red sun is rising above the city. We turn our heads: There is a wonderful panorama, and as we look up into the sky there are scattered little white clouds. »Supercity« is our next command, and in an instant we are in a city with the most glorious modern architecture, surpassing anything built today – but is this city really only virtual or has it already been built?

But enough of the houses! »A walk by the lake«, we whisper – and in a flash we are strolling on a lovely path by the lakeshore, while mountains and forests rise on the other side. »A swim in the lake« – and we dive into the water whose coolness laps against our space suit as we watch fish and pebbles on the lake bottom.

Too boring for you? We input the command »adventure«: Robin Hood, Karl May, Bonny and Clyde, Superman, Star Wars, the Titanic: It's all available and we're right in the midst of it – and barely survive. »Lunch« – delicious smells fill our nostrils, the meal is in front of us, invisible rays touch our tongues and palates, we taste the exquisite dishes, while a pill satisfies our hunger. Now we feel like eating some real food, however, including ready-to-serve meals. No problem –

502. Stelarc, Amplified Body, Laser Eyes, and Third Hand, c. 1985.

the refrigerator-computer has long since signaled what groceries are needed, and the pneumatic dispatch system delivers them within a short time.

Do we need a doctor? The remote diagnosis is perfect, the data are all displayed, the treatment is convincing.

If we want to play a game, we can choose from thousands of them, including those involving partners, from table tennis to bridge.

»Siesta« – and here is darkness followed by light in the lovely dreams we wished for.

»Partnership« is the next command, and already a beautiful young girl stands before us: tender words, erotic touch that we feel pleasurably on our bodies.

We do wonder, though, whether the »teledildonic« technique has been developed sufficiently for us to be able to say: We've tried 'em both – and the comparison stood the test.

The next day is a working day, when we have to go to the office – no, that's a thing of the past. Telework is something everyone takes for granted, but instead of speaking we use complicated keyboards. There's a conference this afternoon: All the participants are there punctually, and in addition to the striking minds who are present, all the necessary papers appear as well.

It is obvious that our children don't walk to school: They're sitting at their own receivers. Telelearning and teleteaching are a matter of course. Everyone is connected to the education highway.

In the afternoon, we go on a shopping spree – certainly, but we don't have to leave the house: There's Paris and the Rue Saint-Honoré, London and New Bond Street, New York and Madison Avenue, Vienna and the Kohlmarkt – we can choose – and the goods are so close you could almost touch them. Three days later they arrive at our house.

And then there's another change of scene. »Leisure World« appears: an endless selection of entertainment and fun: »outdoor fun«, a total leisure city of nature and art through which we stroll. Is there still even a need to create a real ambience? Isn't the digitalized world enough?

Do we want to see the latest art trends? In living color we experience the most recent – virtual – gallery openings.

Feel like going to church this Sunday? There are 35 denominations to care for our souls via headset.

It goes without saying that we can chat with our friends anytime we like. At night, we go to the theater. What's playing? We'll decide that ourselves: The set, scenery, actors, themes, music, plots are selected by us and given a new production from a selection set. Does all this still seem incomplete and half-baked? William Gibson is a big help – or rather – he introduces us to his world of »cyberpunk« – a truly adventurous world, the world of the »neuromancers«!

We meet 21-year-old Case in Chiba, a horrendously beautiful, wild city between Tokyo and Osaka, and have the craziest adventures. The experience of a global nerve system as described by Gibson gives us the perspective of cyberspace, a disembodied world, a simulated substitute for physical reality in exchange for simulation. Gibson tries to express the essence of cyberspace concisely, but his metaphors tend to be on the poetic side.

»Cyberspace. A consensual hallucination experienced daily by billions of legitimate operators, in every nation… A graphic representation of data abstracted from the banks of every computer in the human system. Unthinkable complexity. Lines of light ranged in the nonspace of the mind, clusters and constellations of data. Like city lights, receding …«

In Gibson's novel people create cyberspace by plugging into interconnected computers by way of a neuronal interface. The complete immersion in cybernetic space described here seems to anticipate the immersion of virtual reality implemented as of the late 1980s as computer technology of space simulation. To a certain extent, cyberspace becomes a marketplace: It is a public »space« to which everyone has access at all times, in which everyone can act, and everyone can exchange views and information. Admittedly – at this time only those who have money and / or programming skills can freely move in this »metaverse«, the new parallel world.

Gibson has some advice for us: He wants us to turn to the man who predicted virtual reality. Jaron Lanier can be of assistance, he coined the term »virtual reality«. We get additional information from him and his team. Gibson is glad to be our guide.

Jaron receives us in his eccentric loft in New York. But before we begin our conversation, he has a surprise for us. »You wanted to speak with our friend Timothy at the university in Los Angeles, didn't you?«

Oh yes, of course, but what's so special about that? The videophone is old hat by now! Afer a short talk, Jaron takes us into a room, one of whose walls is taken up by a screen. We sit down in comfortable chairs – and within minutes the wall opens and Timothy is before us – we're about to stand up and shake hands with him, but he is virtual – in real time and actual size! »Yes, it's another step toward virtual reality«, declares Jaron not without pride. »I call this ›tele-immersion‹. But we're still far from our goal.«

And Jaron explains: »Virtual means that something exists only as an electronic image, but otherwise has no concrete reality. It seems to be there, but is not there. Virtual reality is not the computer. We are speaking about a technology where with the help of a computerized pickup a common reality is synthesized. »It reshapes our relationship to the physical world on a new level, no more and no less. The subjective world remains intact. This has nothing to do directly with what is happening in the brain. It has to do only with what is perceived by the sensory organs.«

Mitchell 1996; Lem 1969, 1985; Gibson 1987, 1989, 1997; Waffender 1991; Lanier 1991; Benedict 1991; Novak 1991; Rheingold 1992, 1994; Schaufler 1993; Duschlbauer 1994; Lindo 1994; Rabl 1995; Kotzab 1995; Featherstone 1995; Rötzer 1995, 1998; Andrews, K. T. 1996; Barloewen 1998; Mörtenböck 1998; Maar 1998; Schaffer 2000; Mulder 2000; Maresch 2001, 2002; Aigner, W. 2002.

Colloquially the term »cyberspace« is today used mostly as a synonym for the Internet or specifically for www – the World Wide Web. In the fields of technology and social sciences, however, the tendency is to distinguish the Internet and World Wide Web as infrastructure from cyberspace. Here, cyberspace appears as a virtualized impression of space that has no topographic locality. The social, factual, spatial, and temporal perception of those who enter cyberspace is virtualized. The film *eXistenZ* plays with the possibility of cyberspace and opens ever new visual spaces to the viewer. In the *Matrix* films (Larry and Andy Wachowski), the excessively dynamic action is fused with cyberspace.

Cyberspace describes a global space of data networks, wires, transfer junctions, programs, data packages – a space that can be perceived with the help of specific techniques by human consciousness and that can be traveled in a certain sense.

We have already become acquainted with the Internet as a model of the fictional and idealized conception of one cyberspace and thus we can understand cyberspace as the future of network communication.

Cyberspace, the field of communication and interaction, is understood as a geometric space with a Cartesian system of coordinates, and accordingly it is programmed and can therefore be perceived by users only thus and no other way. »Cybernetic space« is modified by metaphors, myths, and models into a technological, social reality. Does cyberspace denote a dichotomy to our »reality«? Are we not part of these systems, affected by them and actors in them? Are we constructing cyberspace as a digital, chaotically developing multiverse of infinite, digital constructions of reality and potential reality? (Aigner 2002)

Does »virtual reality« lead in the long run to the vanishing of bodies? Or even to a »realm of pure intellect«? In any case, we are dealing with a new polarity: On the one hand there exists the physical body, the »body of flesh«, on the other hand there is the »data body«, the semiotic body of signs and symbols. The two are connected by an electronic umbilical cord – to the dividing line where the two bodies are identical.

And what might be the next stage? »Away from the biological body, from the Earth and into cyber-space, to new bodies and brains, and in the end to expansion into the universe« (Wachowski 1999).

William Gibson wrote his »cyberpunk« stories as long ago as 1977, full of strange and abstruse de-tails. Today, 30 years later, we still haven't really managed to create the »cyber city« about which we began to fantasize back then, but William Gibson was convinced it would by far surpass the real city.

The expected developments leading to a perfect virtual reality in the form that had been described did not materialize: experiments with various boxes, with screens, with three-dimensional sensory re-lays are actually technically a long way from the perfect, digital virtual reality.

Back to the future once more. For now we are no longer separated, distanced from the systems. Rather, we are physically integrated in these networks, our nervous system is connected to the electronic organs, the network has entered our bodies, which have been transformed into a bio-neurotechnical logical interface. Implants, brain chips, new plug-in techniques – the nanotechnol-ogy in entrails and soft tissues completely erases the boundary between humans and machines. To put it more precisely: Man has become a machine, a cyborg.

The cyborg, a total fusion of the cybernetic and the organism, has never gone beyond a few perfor-mances, but has conquered a wide territory in literature and film. The costly performances of the artist Stelarc are along the same lines as a cyborg, but their tremendous cost clearly shows their utopian nature.

Sim City (1995, 2003) – Computer games of little and big kids, 2007. The virtual city: five

Before we take a tour of this city, we ourselves must first create it. Before us is the big open countryside where the city is to be located, a boring, flat surface. So we first create a topography: Rolling hills and lovely valleys come into being around the future site of the city. A pretty lake will provide clean air and relaxation and opportunities for sports. We also make sure there are woods, meadows, and fields on the future outskirts.

What should we build first? Our budget is not very sizeable yet, so we start by building hous-ing, a few compact blocks. The schools are built at the same time. But naturally jobs must follow immediately: Industry, trades, and commerce get their buildings, and it goes without saying that traffic routes are built parallel to these. But already a crisis approaches: An earthquake we would never have expected badly damages the new buildings. The damage is soon repaired, and now magnificent cultural buildings are created on the lakefront. But we wonder whether we have not undertaken too much. For the power and water supply is not yet completely in place. And we re-alize something else: The crime rate is rising – we have neglected our security system! And there is a violent controversy about the use of nuclear energy, but also about the nuclear threat. Will it soon be necessary to build massive geodetic domes for our safety?

And now another safety issue preoccupies us: In one part of the city a huge fire has broken out. The damage is enormous! How could that happen in a city that was so carefully planned? Now we remember and in a flashback we realize we followed public opinion, which rejected the additional budgets for increased protection against fire – and actually also for increased funds for crime prevention. And we finally give some serious thought to the question whether following public opinion might not be a road to disaster.

Meanwhile our city has grown to such a size that we are sure we can solve every problem – and thus actually face the future with great optimism!

Sargeant 1996.

This is the other kind of virtual city: In computer games we really do get the impression that we can re-create the cities, and even the whole world, and like the film they have one foot firmly planted in the real world. Finally we have the city well »in hand« – in the true sense of the word. We can influ-ence, control, stage-manage what happens in the city, the streets, and the houses: by simply press-ing a button.

503. Manfred Wolff-Plottegg, the Binary House, 1989.
504. *Sim City*, 2000, functional, 1995.

Admittedly, we cannot (yet) influence and control the image, the nature of our communication partner.

The game *Sim City* referred to here is, of course, a »good game«, in which everything can be controlled positively. There are also all kinds of horror and catastrophe cities.

The new experts. New realism – the virtual city: six

»We are now no longer concerned only with generating new forms. The virtual reality of the 1970s, too, is passé«, say our companions. These are Marcus Novak, Hani Rashid, Kas Osterhuis, Peter Weibel, Kolatan, MacDonald and many others.

»On the contrary, we are trying to develop a ›real virtuality‹«, says Manfred Wolff-Plottegg. »We need to generate new functional aspects, create networks and new inventions. The infatuation with forms that was characteristic of the 2000's decade is outmoded. We are reminded of the processlike nature of architecture again. That's something we debated back in the 70s!«

We think in these process categories, after all – and we are surprised: The city generates itself in many points, often with the help of the computer. The computer also often helps us to understand the city better and make certain processes visible. And we take a critical look at new situations: How do we cope with various speeds: the intoxication of high velocity versus the praise of slow motion, non-simultaneity versus perseverance, the overlapping of present and past versus timelessness.

»Our task today should be to go from the ›functional‹ to the ›informational‹ city – a direction in which we have been moving for a long time. It will be less important to make ›images‹, which is the great temptation when we use a computer; rather, it's about a computer-processed-city, developments, processes, growth models, simulations. It's also about durability, sustainability, also variability, a ›liquid city‹, a ›transarchitecture‹.«

Wolff-Plottegg now tries to explain his Binary House: »*The lines, the plans of the Binary House may be regarded simultaneously as a floor plan, elevation, section, axonometry, perspective. The Binary House itself – though in existence – has no dimension. Its lack of dimension is in direct relation to the namelessness of the lines. The Binary House is abstract architecture. This architecture is timeless.*«

Stephen William Hawking (b. 1942). Time travel, 2020 – the virtual city: seven

The brilliant researcher, thinker, and physicist claimed as far back as 1990 that time travel is very likely. Now he has created the real possibilities and we have the opportunity to take part in two time trips – admittedly both are only short stays in the past and future.

The first journey – at our special request – takes us to Cluny. We are able to experience the wonderful, long-destroyed cathedral in its original three-dimensionality and splendor – a spatial impression of overpowering beauty.

But the journey into the future, though short, is deeply moving: We find ourselves in 2020 in San Francisco, the headquarters of the ecumenical world religions. There is a threefold celebration: the foundation of the Palestinian state, the complete emancipation and equality of women in Islam, and the ordination of the first twelve women Catholic priests by the new African pope.

Once again we encounter surprising boundaries. Technology and magic are no longer conflicting opposites. The two spheres increasingly prove to be closely intertwined. We are familiar with a similar phenomenon: While commerce has been spiritualized, (pseudo)spirituality has been commercialized. There actually is something approaching a journey into the past: The abbey of Cluny was reconstructed as a computer animation at great expense.

13.11. Spirituality

People of the spirit: the (imaginary) places of the spirit

Even after the Enlightenment, people are still asking questions regarding the world of the spirit, a new spirituality, the New Age. These questions have become very important in the religious communities of America, and the new rationalism and pragmatism of the period after World War II have not provided conclusive answers. It is difficult, indeed almost impossible, for us to separate imagination from fantasy, enthusiasm from fanaticism, piousness from false piety, spirituality from spiritism, parapsychology from the belief in the supernatural, inspiration from insanity.

The spirit has no place, let alone a city. But since we have seen that every city is at the same time a community – we can also assume that every community is a city in the broadest sense of the term: imaginary, virtual, spiritual. This legitimates us to pay a visit, albeit a short one, to the »spiritual« cities as well. Previously, we've already encountered the great world religions in all sorts of forms. Now we ramble through a few of the hundreds of religious groups – communities that are active today.

If we wanted to travel to all the new, spiritual cities and realms, many months would not be enough. Let us therefore fly over the many revivalist movements, sects, youth religions, and special communities, and let us look at the incarnations of the spirit.

First there are those communities that remain more or less within the orthodox framework of Christian denominations or of the Bible: Taizé is discussed in the next chapter; the Cursillo movement developed in Spain; in England, there was the MRA, or Moral Re-Armament, and in Italy there was the Focolare movement. Should we also visit Opus Dei, considered to be a right-wing, fundamentalist Roman Catholic movement? The New Apostolic Church sees itself as the newly instituted salvation work of Christ, the Pentecostal movement places the outpouring of the Holy Spirit in the center of devotion. The Seventh-Day Adventist Church goes back to the American William Miller and his calculations of the last days; Jehovah's Witnesses hope for the peaceable kingdom of God on Earth. The Grail movement knows reincarnation and karma, and the world consists of divine radiation; the members of »Opus Angelorum«, the work of the angels, founded by »Mother« Maria Bitterlich in 1947, are in actual dialogue with the divine beings; the AMORC sees itself as descended from the 17th-century Rosicrucians. The Church of Scientology, founded by L. Ron Hubbard in 1954, claims it can attain absolute freedom through clearing the consciousness.

The number of sects and special communities in the US is huge: The »Children of God« (1969) prepare for the end of the world, and the Moon sect fights against communism and wants to create the »kingdom of God on Earth«. The Amish renounce the achievements of civilization and live according to strict social rules that partly date back to the 16th century.

Countless movements originated in Asia, but have gained a foothold in the West. The Hare-Krishna movement has its center in India and is related to Hinduism. The Bhagwan movement combines Eastern and Western thought, and the members of Transcendental Meditation (TM) hope for an age of enlightenment. The Divine Light Mission worships the Guru Maharaj as the Lord of the Universe. For the Bahai Religion God is absolutely unattainable; the oneness of humankind is to be realized in an all-encompassing community.

We must not generalize, but many groups depend on central, charismatic founders or leaders, frequently with Messianic claims to leadership and totalitarian, or at least authoritarian, structures. Many groups have a strict requirement that members live together and have community of property. We have thus come full circle from the many social utopias we discussed in previous chapters. Religious enthusiasm easily turns into fanaticism, and the latter can even lead to crime – from an outsider's perspective.

Some of the groups are geographically localized, but for most, their actual locality – and in a certain sense a u-topos – is heaven, paradise, nirvana.

Peter and Eileen Caddy. Findhorn, 1962, 1975, 1985

The times of utopia – if you can call it that – the times of searching, thinking, looking for Peter Caddy's irrational, metaphysical world are long gone. We step directly into reality.

And the road to the village of Findhorn, on the northeastern coast of Scotland, is also very real, accompanied by rain and storms that are said to prevail here for a large part of the year. But when we enter the gate of the »camp« of Findhorn, our bleak mood changes. Not because of the strange ambience, but because of the many people we meet, still strangers to us. They have one thing in common: We sense an unusual radiance, great peace, and order.

We have the same reaction to Peter Caddy, who welcomes us warmly and calmly. Not a guru, not a sectarian or a nature freak – but a charismatic human being. His (second) wife Eileen – they found each other by divine providence – is no doubt a peaceful, capable housewife. But very soon we realize that she is the spiritual head of the family and indeed of the whole community.

The legendary fertility and beauty of the gardens is world-renowned, legendary, and embued with mystery, which is why we are primarily interested in them. The weather has improved, and Peter is happy to take us on a walk through the extensive gardens, which were first started in 1963. It's true that there are no 40-pound cabbages and the delphiniums are not 3 m tall. We also do not see 65 different kinds of vegetables rumored by the press to be growing here, but the lushness of the vegetables and lettuces, the beauty of flowers and shrubs, the height of the trees are impressive nonetheless.

How is all this possible given the barren, poor soil in this part of Scotland? The answer is surprising enough: »Of course we use good natural fertilizer. But the secret lies elsewhere. We live in loving community with God. He is the center of life. But there are also magical beings helping us: The divine and powerful Pan; the king of the elves, who rules the world of nature spirits; and especially the Devas, the master builders of the plant world.«

And Eileen, who has now joined us, credibly confirms: »God speaks to me. But I am also in constant conversation with our spiritual helpers. We cooperate with them.« The persuasiveness of her words appeases our skepticism: Is it possible that such astonishing devotion to the spirits of nature still exists in the 20th century?

We remember the message Eileen received in one of her meditations: »*I am spirit, I am everywhere, in everything and in everyone. There is no place where I am not present. Once you have fully realized and accepted this insight, you will know that the kingdom of heaven is within you. Your external search will come to an end. Everything you long for lies within you. Life will become clear and simple. If you stop and fall silent, you will discover everything you seek within you.*«

We now return to the center, planned along very simple lines: Forty trailers stand in the huge parking lot, fourteen simple bungalows were built, and at this time 130 members and 40 guests are living here. For community activities there is a sanctuary, a dining hall, and a community center.

Did you have to overcome a lot of obstacles when you created the gardens and the community? »Certainly, but God helps us in all our troubles and is by our side in all ›manifestations‹. We demonstrate God's plan, it's all divine guidance.«

The community is committed to four basic rules: no narcotics, no smoking in community spaces, no negative thinking, unconditional love.

The next day we have the opportunity to visit the education conference meeting in Findhorn. The conference is not just about theoretical discussions, but includes personal statements bearing witness to spiritual experiences. An Irish girl weeps with gratitude as she remembers her experiences, a young man tells about Christ's energy.

Deeply impressed but still skeptical, grateful and yet filled with doubt, we say goodbye to our hosts. One question – perhaps a blasphemous one –still comes to mind: If God causes the barren soil of Findhorn to produce bountiful harvests – why does he not do the same for devout people in the hunger zones of Africa and Asia? Can the theologians answer this question, we wonder. However, ten years later we revisit the colony. It has grown, and there have been many changes. Findhorn has kept its »light-bringing« function and has become a magnet for thousands of seekers – and skeptics. The fundamental tasks remain, they have expanded: environment, education, community, spirituality. The community totals more than 200 members. Additional large properties and a hotel for the guests have been purchased, many seminars have been offered, the organization is tighter, more exact and thorough. Close to 14,000 visitors come to Findhorn every year. New, self-governing groups formed as far back as the 1980s. The Findhorn Foundation basically supports the organization of the Findhorn community.

Hawken 1975.

Among the countless efforts to bring about a »New Age« of spirituality Findhorn has a special position. On the one hand the belief in a world of spirits seems completely anachronistic, while on the other hand organic gardening and environmental awareness are very relevant today. Admittedly one cannot deny that the movement has the characteristics of a sect.

Frère Roger (Schutz-Marsauche) (1915–2005). Taizé, France, since 1949

Utopia seems to be so simple, so self-evident: developing a new model for all religions, all denominations to live together! And above all, young people of all nations are to help bring it about! Was this utopia realized in Taizé? We wanted to see for ourselves.

We had so been looking forward to experiencing in person the famous charisma of the venerable Frère Roger and had planned our trip to Taizé for the summer of 2005, filled with joyous anticipation.

But soon we were plunged into a tragic reality as we heard the terrible news: During worship, a woman had hurled herself at the celebrant and kept stabbing him. Shortly thereafter he died.
We are thus denied the tour with Frère Roger. A pleasant younger German Brother, Frère Alois, born in 1954, is now in charge. He tells us about the charismatic lifework of Frère Roger and about Taizé. Taizé is more than a small village in southern Burgundy near Cluny. It is a miracle achieved by a prophet, an Evangelical Reformed Christian.

»Yes, success is possible. We've proved it here in Taizé: We've developed, particularly with young people, a new model for people of different faiths to live together.«

Three great ideals are first and foremost, recalling the monastic vows: poverty, celibacy, simplicity. But wasn't Frère Roger counting too much on young people's capacity for enthusiasm, and ignoring the reality of life in the world? »The power of faith emanates primarily from the young – faith is the great opportunity to change the world«, Frère Alois interprets Frère Roger's ideas.

Frère Roger began his work in 1949 with seven brothers. Today more than a hundred belong to the community – Protestants and Catholics. But visitors to Taizé who have experienced it and received new inspiration here number in the tens of thousands. Taizé is actually a city, a utopia that has become reality. It is not the already realized kingdom of God, it is not a theocracy with secular claims to power:

For however much the community has found its expression, in Taizé itself as well as in many brotherly meetings, peace and understanding and worldwide religious unity are still its deepest longing, its greatest utopia. Frère Roger's Taizé was implemented in a specific place, but hundreds of Christian revival movements have remained u-topoi, not geographical locations – or else invisible, spiritual places: a spiritual type of virtual reality.

Sri Aurobindo and the »Mother«. Auroville, 1970

Again a mighty circle seems to give the city its shape. However, when we take a closer look from a bird's-eye view, we can make out spirals, rotations, segments: The basic structure is a cosmic spiral form. The city is to be given back to the divine spirit of the cosmos. That is the idea of the great father, the mystic and philosopher Sri Aurobindo.

The great master wonders: »*When will the world be transformed into the model of heaven?*«

And he answers: »*When all of humankind turns into boys and girls, in community with God, revealed as Krishna and Kali, the merriest boy and the strongest girl of the group playing together in the garden of Paradise.*«

And here, not far from Pondicherry in India, a reflection of Heaven might be felt in the community. It was the »Mother« who had great visions of this new city and soon knew what it was to be called: »*Auroville might be the first realization of human unity based on the teachings of Sri Aurobindo, where people of all nations would be at home.*«

When we meet with Sri Aurobindo, he is silent and wrapped in thought. »The Mother« is all the more talkative. She introduces us to the powerful, spiritual city and explains the place in more detail: »I created a very modern city that quickly grew to a population of 2,000. It keeps growing and will soon have reached its limit of 50,000 inhabitants.«

The people we meet are calm and composed, cheerful and trusting. They need no government, no administration, no money. The Mother's authority is sufficient. Basically, the people are self-sufficient, or there are autonomous small groups. There are no taxes, and each person contributes to the welfare of the others.

»*Auroville is intended for those who long for the supramental and strive to achieve it*«, says the Mother. Amazed, we wonder how such a large city can be organized, built, administered?

The Mother answers: »*Do not ask me about the organizational and administrative details. I can only tell you that everything was ready down to the last detail and is only waiting to come down.*«

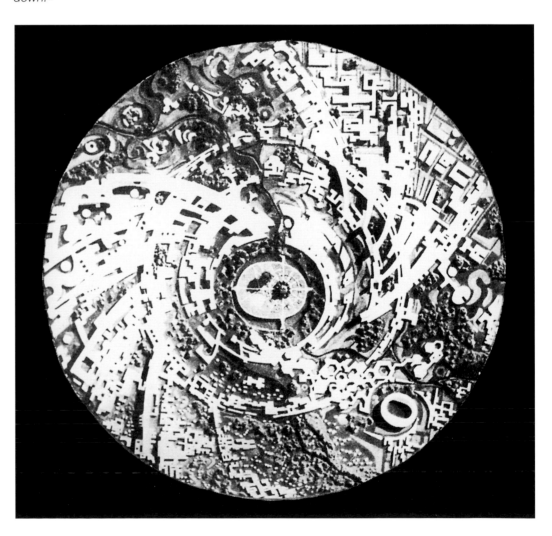

505. Roger Anger, Auroville, India, 1965 version.

After we had a large-scale, bird's-eye view of the city, the Mother sketches its four-part layout: The pavilions of the nations, with the Indian one leading the way, the buildings for culture, the residential district, and the site for small industry form a harmonious whole.

We walk through the residential areas with totally different houses and huts. There is no automobile traffic, but there are many skillfully laid-out plantations. »We are now approaching the center, the Matrimandir, the town's spiritual central point«, the Mother prepares us.

First, we go into a lush garden surrounded by a circular wall. Here, the Matrimandir rests in a clear pond. From above, it had looked like a globe, but now we see that the form is more oval. The structure is built of brilliantly white marble that reflects the sunlight. We descend the steps, go through a tunnel and up a winding staircase in the middle, only to find ourselves in the wonderful domed room. A perfect crystal globe, barely a meter in diameter, lies in the center. Through a small opening at the vertex, a small sheaf of the sun's rays fall on the globe and are reflected, diffused and refracted, onto the dome. There is no other light in the room.

The symbol of the Mother, a hexagonal star with a flaming center, is engraved in the floor. The building is also a kind of mandala, a spiritual center of integral culture.

But what is the Matrimandir? The Mother explains that it is »a symbol for the response of the Divine to the longing of humankind for perfection. The union with the Divine as it is manifested in a progressive human unity is above all religions«.

And the Mother again describes the ideal: »It is our great goal to reach human unity, a unity of the entire person. One of the ways to do this is spiritual and material research.«
Auroville 1976; *Stadt und Utopie* 1982; *Visionen und Utopien* 2002/03; Thomsen 1994.

Auroville was actually implemented – but what a vast difference between the »holy« city of the spirit and reality! It was after Sri Aurobindo's death in 1950 that the Mother »saw« – rather than invented – the city. The Matrimandir was built as a center: In 1972–73, a huge pit was excavated, 19 m deep, with a 50-meter diameter. Four massive reinforced concrete pillars, not the symbolical twelve slender columns, support the roof. The last sections of the four pillars of the Matrimandir were finished on November 17th, 1973 – and on the same day, the Mother died.

In January 1975 the concreting of the lower section was completed. The rest of the construction dragged on, and the official opening of the project took place. The Matrimandir represents the sacred center, so to speak, and it also marks the zone of peace. The idea of the Matrimandir first appeared very early, but it was originally a simple cylinder with a cone-shaped roof borne by twelve columns. The circular layout was retained, but now one enters between the pillars and goes into the room down ramps.

The Mother, a native of France, commissioned the architect Roger Anger to draw up the plans. The first model, a strictly right-angled, rational complex, was rejected, as was the second one – designed in 1966 – and a similar one dated 1967, centrifugal in character. A very free, diffuse »city« developed. The actual year Auroville was founded is considered to be 1968 – February 28th, to be precise. The first pioneering period is characterized by a down-to-earth, simple style with folkloristic traits. Natural materials, predominantly clay, were preferred. Then three- to four-person huts were built. The »forecomers« used bricks and planted a tree nursery.

A few settlement projects were soon implemented between 1967 and 1973: »Promesse« was created in 1967, additional residential units followed in 1970. In the »Aspirations« settlement a school was built as well in 1970, and an idealistic educational system was established. In 1971, a health center and a community center were created. The latter supplies schools as well.

Small crafts businesses and apprentice training workshops were organized: a metal workshop, printing office, wood worker's shop, and, in 1972, a needlework center. In 1971 the »Bharat-Nivas«, the pavilion of Indian culture, was built, in 1973 plans for the large residential complex Auromodel were revised, and finally the education center Aurodevenir and the community house »New Com-munity« were built.

In the 1970s and '80s there was quite a lot of experimentation, modern architecture was adopted, and reinforced concrete was used as a matter of course. More than a hundred settlements, groups, communities came into being. For Germany, Sebastian Wagner designed a pavilion. The original design of the city has probably largely remained a utopia.

Auroville was slated to have 50,000 inhabitants. At the opening ceremony in 1968, close to 5,000 people from 124 nations were present. But only about 1,700 people from 44 nations live in the town on a permanent basis. Of these, 1,300 are Indian. But huge numbers of visitors come to Auroville every year. They probably need to be differentiated: There are true seekers, interested people, spiritually involved individuals, but also emerging signs of banal tourism – the curious, hitchhikers, pseudo-esoterics. And reports and opinions vary: positive voices about the community, complaints about lack of human contact and alienation.

507. Diamond World Mandala, Tibet, 9th century.

There are attempts to continue implementing the originally planned zones: the industrial zone, the international zone, the culture zone, the residential area, and the green belt. The planners are trying to involve the local population, though they are obviously only partially successful.

Even after all kinds of setbacks, friends and residents still honor the ideal concept. »We want to be a universal city where men and women from all countries are able to live in peace and progressive harmony, transcending all faiths and denominations, politics, and nationalisms. It is the intention of Auroville to make human unity a reality.« Is this experiment a success or a failure? An awe-inspiring, but unique and nonreproducible project? A model for similar foundations all over the world? The spiritual, social solution of the problems of cities, communities, and society?

Buddha and Shiva. The Mandala and the Sacred Mountain

The dreams of the heavenly city are as relevant as ever: They are celestially perfect, comfortable, pleasant, healthy, peaceful, safe – certainly, this is what a city should be like –many cities come close to the ideal – but they are not places of the spirit.

508. Mandala of the Simhanada Lokeshvara, Tibet.

arupadhatu

rupadhatu

kamadhatu

Let us therefore conclude our travels by visiting another celestial city. We began our pilgrimages with Jerusalem, and now we travel through a diagram and climb up into a heavenly edifice – and also remain in the virtual cities with which we began our journeys.

The mandala is the wonderful image of the temple, the city, heaven, the world of the gods, indeed the cosmos. It is a step on the path to spirituality, the temple of Buddha or Shiva. We enter the city by one of the four gates in the wall that are open in the cardinal directions. We walk past gods and demons, past the enlightened and monsters. We come into the city. It is both square and round, built out of the strength of the soul, filled with the peace of heaven.

We go up into the Borobudur stupa in Java, a holy city, guarded and cared for by hundreds of Buddhas. It tells us many stories. And it is a mountain we climb, coming closer to heaven with the help of the holy ones. We ascend the steps of the great square and are now in the spiritual care of the circle. We are close to heaven – we are already in heaven – as we would be in a medieval cathedral. Or, to put it differently: Our thirst for essence has been quenched.

Utopia and reality, architecture and spirituality are identical.

Bibliography

Abensour, Miguel, *Les formes de l'utopie socialiste-communiste*, Paris, 1981.

Abercrombie, Patrick, *Greater London Plan 1944*, London, 1945.

Abraham, Raimund, and Friedrich St. Florian, *L'Architettura sperimentale*, Rome, 1967.

Abraham, Raimund, *Works 1960–1973*, Vienna, 1973.

Abraham, Raimund, *Ungebaut / Unbuilt*, exhibition catalogue, Bozen and Innsbruck, 1986.

Abraham, Raimund, *(UN)BUILT*, Vienna and New York, 1996.

Adam, Paul, *Lettres de malaisie*, Paris, 1898.

Adam, Paul, *La Cité prochaine*, Paris, 1904.

Affeldt-Schmidt, Birgit, *Fortschrittsutopien*, Stuttgart, 1991.

Agulhon, Maurice, *Une ville ouvrière au temps du socialisme utopique, Toulon de 1815 à 1851*, Paris, 1970.

Ahrbeck, Rosemarie, *Morus, Campanella, Bacon. Frühe Utopisten*, Cologne, 1977.

Aigner, Carl, *Vergangene Zukunft – Design zwischen Utopie und Wissenschaft*, Krems, 2001.

Aigner, Wolfgang, *Reality-Switching (RS)*, Krems, 2002.

Akroyd, Edward, *On Improved Dwellings for the Working Classes with a Plan for Building*, London, 1862.

Alberti, Leon Battista, *De re aedificatoria, libri decem*, Florence, 1485.

Alberti, Leon Baptiste, *L'Architecture et art de bien bastir ...*, Paris, 1553.

Alberti, Leon Battista, *Ten Books on Architecture, reprint*, London, 1955.

Alberti, Leon Battista, *Hypnerotomachia Poliphili*, London, Cambridge, MA, 1997.

Allain, Mattié (ed.), *France and North America, Utopias and Utopians*, Lafayette, LA, 1978.

Alpers, Hans Joachim, Werner Fuchs, Roland M. Hahn, and Wolfgang Jeschke, *Lexikon der Science Fiction Literatur*, Munich, 1980.

Amersin, Ferdinand, »Das Land der Freiheit«, in: same author, *Weisheit und Tugend des reinen Menschentums*, Graz, 1874.

Amersin, Ferdinand, *Im Freistaat oder Gesetz und Sitte der Freiheit*, Triest, 1880.

Ames, Russell, *Citizen Thomas More and his Utopia*, Princeton, 1949.

Ammannati, Bartolomeo, *La città, appunti per un trattato*, Rome, 1582, 1970.

Anderson, Edith, »Feministische Utopien«, *Sinn und Form* (Berlin), 1/1982.

Andreae, Johann Valentin, *Reipublicae Christianopolitanae descriptio*, Strassburg, 1619.

Andreae, Johann Valentin, *Reise nach der Insel Caphar Salama und Beschreibung der darauf gelegenen Republik Christiansburg*, Esslingen, 1741.

Andreae, Johann Valentin, *Christianopolis*, Oxford, 1916.

Andreotti, Libero Xavier Costa, *Situacionistas – arte, politica, urbanismo. Situationists, art, politics, urbanism*, Barcelona, 1996.

Andrews, Edward Deming, *The Community Industries of the Shakers*, Albany, Philadelphia, 1932, 1972.

Andrews, Edward Deming and Faith Andrews, *Work and Worship. The Economic Order of the Shakers*, New York, 1974.

Andrews, Keith Thomas, *Browsing, Building and Beholding Cyberspace*, Graz, 1996.

Annecke, Ute, *Utopie, Richtiges im Falschen?*, Cologne, 1995.

Les Années Pop 1956–1968, exhibition catalogue, Centre Pompidou, Paris, 2001.

Die Anti-Stadt, Bauen ohne Bauland, Wetzikon, Rüti, 1966.

Antonis, Adrian, *Wilhelmostadum*, the Netherlands, 1647.

Apollonio, Umbro, *Il futurismo*, Milan, 1972.

Archigram, »Symposium zur Ausstellung«, Vienna, 1997.

Architectural Design (London), 10/1968.

Architectural Design, (London), 63/1993.

L'Architecture d' Aujourd' hui (Boulogne), 1965, May, June, 1966.

Architectures experimentales, exhibition catalogue, Collection du Frac Centre, 1950–2000, Orléans, 2003.

Architectures Formes Fonctions, Paris, 1968.

Architectures Non Standard, exhibition catalogue, Centre Pompidou, 2003/04, Paris, 2003. .

Architekturtheorie im 20. Jahrhundert, Wien, 2003.

Arendt, Hannah, *Elemente totaler Herrschaft*, Frankfurt am Main, 1958.

Armytage, Walter H. G., *Utopian Experiments in England, 1560–1960*, London, 1961.

Armytage, Walter H. G., *Yesterday's Tomorrows: A Historical Survey of Future Societies*, London, 1968.

Arndt, Karl John Richard, *George Rapp' s Harmony Society 1785–1847*, n. p., 1972.

Arquitectura Radical, exhibition catalogue, MuVIM, Valencia, 2003.

Art & Design – Art & the City, London, 1996.

Asch, Käte, *Die Lehre Charles Fouriers*, Jena, 1914.

Ascher, François, *Métapolis ou l' avenir des villes*, Paris, 1995.

Asimov, Isaac, *Cosmos Utopia: the Edge of Tomorrow*, Bergisch-Gladbach, 1988.

Atelier P+F, Prader.Fehringer.Ott, *Hexagonale Wohnzellen*, Munich, Innsbruck, 1984.

Atlantis, Modell für die Kunst des Lebens, Frankfurt am Main, 1987.

Atwood, Margaret, *The Handmaid' s Tale*, Boston, 1985.

Augspurger, Hans-Jürgen, *Die Anfänge der Utopie in Frankreich und ihre Grundlagen in der Antike*, Bamberg, 1975.

Augustinus, Aurelius, *City of God* (426), London and New York, 1963.

Auroville Today, Tamil Nadu, India, 1989.

Austin, Alice Constance, *The Next Step*, Los Angeles, 1935.

Bachstrom, Johann Friedrich (Fridericus), *Das Bey zwey hundert Jahren lang unbekannte nunmehro aber entdeckte vortreffliche Land der Inquiraner*, Frankfurt am Main and Leipzig, 1736.

Bacon of Verulam, Francis, *Nova Atlantis*, London, 1627, Berlin, 1793, Reinbek / Hamburg, 1890, 1960.

Bagschik, Thorsten, *Utopias in the English-speaking world and the Perception of Economic Reality*, Frankfurt am Main and New York, 1996.

Bahrdt, Hans Paul, *Die moderne Großstadt*, Hamburg, 1969.

Baier, Lothar, *Die verleugnete Utopie*, Berlin, 1993.

Bailey, James Oster, *Pilgrims Through Space and Time: Trends and Patterns in Scientific*, New York, 1947.

Bakunin, Michael, *Selected Writings*, New York, 1974.

Baltrušaitis, Jurgis, *Imaginäre Realitäten*, Cologne, 1984.

Bammer, Angelika, *Partial Visions. Feminism and Utopianism in the 1970s*, New York, 1991.

Banham, Reyner, *Megastructure – Urban Futures of the Recent Past*, London, 1976.

Banham, Reyner, *The Visions of Ron Herron*, London, 1994.

Barloewen, Constantin von, *Der Mensch im Cyberspace*, Munich, 1998.

Barmeier, Eike (ed.), *Science Fiction*, Munich, 1972.

Barnett, Horner Garner, *Indian Shakers*, Carbondale, IL, 1957.

Batifoll, Louis, *Autour de Richelieu*, Paris, 1937.

Battisti, Eugenio, »Recuperto di un' utopia, San Leucio presso Caserta«, *Controspazio VI*, 4/1974.

Bauer, Hermann, *Kunst und Utopie*, Berlin, 1965.

Bauer, Hermann, *Wandlungen des Paradiesischen und Utopischen*, Berlin, 1966.

Baumer, Franz, *Paradiese der Zukunft*, Munich and Vienna, 1967.

Bebel, August, *Charles Fourier. Sein Leben und seine Theorien*, Stuttgart, 1888, 1921.

Becker, C. L., *Der Gottesstaat der Philosophen des 18. Jahrhunderts*, Würzburg, 1946.

Bedford, Arthur, *The Scripture Chronology Demonstrated by Astronomical Calculations*, London, 1730.

Beevers, Robert, *The Garden City Utopia: A Critical Biography of Ebenezer Howard*, New York, 1988.

Beffroy de Reigny, Louis Abel (Cousin Jacques), *Dictionnaire néologique des hommes et des choses ou notice alphabetique, par le Cousin Jacques*, London and Paris, 1801.

Behrend, Hanna, Isolde Neubert-Köpsel, and Stefan Lieske, *Rückblick auf das Jahr 2000 – Was haben Gesellschaftsutopien uns gebracht?*, Berlin, 1997.

Bellamy, Edward, *Equality*, New York, 1897.

Bellamy, Edward, *Looking Backward 2000–1887*, Boston, 1888, Cambridge, MA, 1967.

Benedict, Michael (ed.), *Cyberspace – First Steps*, London, 1991.

Benevolo, Leonardo, *The History of Modern Architecture*, London, 1971.

Benevolo, Leonardo, *The History of the City*, New York, 1986.

Benson, Timothy O., *Expressionist Utopias*, Los Angeles, n. y.

Berens, Lewis H., *The Digger Movement in the Days of the Commonwealth*, London, 1906.

Berghahn, Klaus L., and Hans Ulrich Seeber (eds.), *Literarische Utopien von Morus bis zur Gegenwart*, Königstein, 1983.

Berneri, Marie Louise, *Journey through Utopia*, London, 1950, New York, 1971.

Bestor, A. E., *Backwoods Utopias*, Philadelphia, 1950.

Bettauer, Hugo, *Die Stadt ohne Juden. Ein Roman von übermorgen*, Vienna, 1922.

Bettauer, Hugo, *The City without Jews. A Novel of our Time*, New York, 1926.

Bibliotheca Utopistica, *Utopien-Science Fiction und Phantastische Literatur*, Vienna, 1984.

Biedermann, Jacobus, pseud. Didacus Bernardinus, *Utopia Didaci Bernardini, Jacobi Bidermani*, Basel, 1640, Venice, Milan, 2004.

Biesterfeld, Wolfgang, *Die literarische Utopie*, Stuttgart, 1974.

Bird, Arthur, *Looking Forward – A Dream of the USA in 1999*, Utica, 1899.

Blanc, Louis, *Organisation du travail*, Paris, 1845.

Bloch, Ernst, *Geist der Utopie*, Munich, 1918, Frankfurt am Main, 1964.

Bloch, Ernst, *Das Prinzip Hoffnung*, 3 vol., Frankfurt am Main, 1973.

Bloch, Ernst, *Abschied von der Utopie?*, Frankfurt am Main, 1980.

Bloch, Ernst, and Arno Münster (eds.), *Verdinglichung und Utopie*, Frankfurt am Main, 1987.

Bloch, Robert N., *Bibliographie der Utopie und Phantastik 1650–1950 im deutschen Sprachraum*, Hamburg, 2002.

Blüher, Rudolph, *Moderne Utopien*, Bonn and Leipzig, 1920.

Bogner, Dieter (ed.), *Haus-Rucker-Co, Denkräume – Stadträume 1967–1992*, Klagenfurt, 1992.

Bogner, Dieter (ed.), *Friedrich Kiesler*, Vienna, 1988.

Boguslaw, Robert, *The New Utopians: A Study of System Design and Social Change*, New York, 1965.

Boller, Paul F. Jr., *American Transcendentalism 1830–1860*, New York, 1974.

Bollerey, Franziska, *Architekturkonzepte der utopischen Sozialisten*, Berlin, 1977, 1991.

Bölsche, Wilhelm, *Der Mensch der Zukunft*, Stuttgart, 1915.

Boos, Florence S., and Carole G. Silver (eds.), *Socialism and the Literary Artistry of William Morris*, Columbia, SC, 1990.

Borsano, Gabriella, *Monte Verità*, Vienna, 1979.

Borsi, Franco (ed.), *Hermann Finsterlin*, Florence, 1968.

Borsi, Franco, *Leon Battista Alberti*, Milan, 1975.

Bossle, Lothar, *Zur Soziologie utopischen Denkens in Europa von Thomas Morus zu Ernst Bloch*, Würzburg, 1993.

Boudon, Philippe, *Richelieu. Ville nouvelle*, Paris, 1978.

Bougainville, Louis-Antoine, *Voyage autour du monde par le frégate du roi Boudeuse, et la flute Ètoile, en 1766, 1767, 1768 & 1769*, Paris, 1772.

Bougainville, Louis-Antoine, *Voyage round the World*, London 1772, Amsterdam and New York, 1967.

Bowman, Sylvia E., *The Year 2000: A Critical Biography of Edward Bellamy*, London, 1958.

Bowman, Sylvia E. (ed.), *Edward Bellamy Abroad*, New York, 1962.

Bradbury, Ray, *The Martian Chronicles*, Garden City, NY, 1950.

Bradbury, Ray, *Fahrenheit 451*, New York, 1953, Zurich, 1955, 1981.

Bradstock, A., *Winstanley and the Diggers 1699* to *1999*, London, 2000.

Braghine, Colonel, A., *The Shadow of Atlantis 1940*, Stuttgart, 1939.

Brasch, Moritz, *Sozialistische Phantasie-Staaten*, Leipzig, 1887.

Brayer, Marie-Ange, Frédéric Migayrou, and Fumio Nanja (eds.), *Archilab's Urban Experiments*, Tokyo, 2004, London, 2005.

Brehmer, Arthur, *Die Welt in 100 Jahren*, Berlin, around 1900.

Brentjes, Burchard, *Atlantis, Geschichte einer Utopie*, Cologne, 1993.

Brewer, Priscilla, *Shaker Communities, Shaker Lives*, Hanover, NH, 1986.

Brooks, H. Allen, *Le Corbusier, Urbanisme, Algiers and other Buildings and Projects 1930–1933*, New York and London, 1983.

Bruckmann, Gerhard, and Helmut Swoboda, *Auswege in die Zukunft*, Vienna, Munich, Zurich, 1974.

Brugger, Ingried, and Florian Steininger (eds.), *Roy Lichtenstein*, Vienna, Wolfratshausen, 2003.

Buber, Martin, *Pfade in Utopia*, Heidelberg, 1950.

Buber, Martin, *Der utopische Sozialismus*, Cologne, 1967.

Buckingham, James Silk, *National Evils and Practical Remedies, with the Plan of a Model Town*, London, 1849.

Bulwer-Lytton, Edward George, *The Coming Race (Vril)*, Edinburgh and London, 1871.

Buonarotti, Philippe, *Babeuf und die Verschwörung der Gleichheit mit dem durch sie veranlassten Prozess und den Belegstücken*, Stuttgart, 1909.

Burden, Chris, *Beyond the Limits*, Vienna, 1996.

Bürkle, J. Christoph, *El Lissitzky. Der Traum vom Wolkenbügel*, Zurich, 1990.

Burnham, James, *The Managerial Revolution*, New York, 1941.

Butler, Samuel, *Erewhon: or over the Range*, London, 1872, 1910.

Butler, Samuel, *Erewhon Revisited*, London, 1880, 1932.

Cabet, Etienne, *Voyage en Icarie*, Paris, 1840, New York, 1848, 1973.

Cabet, Etienne, *Adresse du fondateur d'Icarie*, Paris, 1856.

Cabet, Etienne, *Colonie Icarienne aux Etats Unis d'Amérique, sa constitution, ses lois, sa situation matérielle et morale après le premiere semestre de 1855*, Paris, 1856.

Cabet, Etienne, *Travels in Icaria*, Western Illinois University Press, Macomb, IL, 1985.

Callenbach, Ernest, *Ecotopia*, New York, 1975, London, 1978.

Calvino, Italo, *Le città invisibile*, Turin, 1972.

Campanella, Tommaso, *Civitas solis idea republicae philosophicae; als Anhang zu Philosophia epilogistica realis*, Utrajecti, 1643, Altenburg, 1789.

Campanella, Tommaso, *La città del sole*, Milan, 1863.

Čapek, Carel, *WUR – Werstands Universal Robots*, Prague, 1920.

Čapek, Carel, *R.U.R. – Rossums Universal Robots*, Prague, 1922.

Carden, Maren Lockwood, *Oneida: Utopian Community to Modern Cooperation*, Baltimore, MD, 1969.

Carlyle, Thomas, *Chartism. Past and Present*, London, 1858

Carré, Rose-Marie, *Cyrano de Bergerac, voyages imaginaires à la recherche de la vérité humaine*, Paris, 1977.

Cartier, Jacques, *Navigation faites en MDXXXVI par J. C. aux Îles de Canada Hochelaga, Saguenay et autres*, Paris, 1545, 1863.

Casanova, Giacomo Chevalier de Seingalt, *Icosameron ou Histoire d'Edouard et d'Elisabeth*, Prague, 1788, 1800.

Cataneo, Pietro, *Die vier ersten Bücher über die Architektur*, Vienna, 1554.

Charlevoix, Pierre (Pater) Franciscus de, *Geschichte von Paraguay und den Missionen der Gesellschaft Jesu in diesen Ländern*, Vienna, 1830.

Choay, Françoise, *L'urbanisme, utopies et réalités*, Paris, 1965, 2001.

Choay, Françoise, *The Modern City Planning in the 19th Century*, New York, 1969.

Christ, Yvan, *Projets et divagations de Claude Nicolas Ledoux*, Paris, 1961.

Cioran, Emil Michel, *Histoire et utopie*, Stuttgart, 1960, 1965.

Clarke, J. F., *The Tale of the Future from the Beginning to the Present Day*, London, 1961.

Clausberg, K., *Kosmische Visionen*, Cologne, 1980.

Coates, Stephen, and Alex Stetter (eds.), *Impossible Worlds*, Basel, Boston, Berlin, 2000.

Cole, Margaret Isabel, *Robert Owen*, London, 1953.

Cole, Margaret, and George Douglas Howard, *The Life of Robert Owen* (Robert Owen of New Lanark), London, 1953, 1966.

Collins, George R., *Visionary Drawings of Architecture and Planning 20th Century through the 1960s*, Chicago, 1979.

Colonna, Francesco, *Hypnerotomachia Poliphili* (1499), Cambridge, MA, 1997, London, 1999.

Conrads, Ulrich, and Hans G. Sperlich, *The Architecture of Fantasy*, New York, 1962.

Considérant, Victor, *Description du phalanstère et considerations sociales sur l'architectonique*, Leipzig 1848, 1906, Vienna, 1921.

Considérant, Victor, *Fouriers System der sozialen Reform*, Leipzig, 1906.

Considérant, Victor, *Exposition abrégée du système phalanstérien de Ch. Fourier*, Paris and Vienna, 1921.

Constant (Constant Anton Nieuwenhuys), *New Babylon, art et utopie*, Paris, 1997.

Contini, Franciscus, *Adriani Caesaris in Tiburtina villa ... tabulis aeries descripta*, Rome, 1668.

Cook, Peter, *Experimental Architecture*, London, 1970.

Coop Himmelblau. Die Faszination der Stadt. The Power of the City, Darmstadt, 1988.

Coop Himmelblau. 6 Projects for 4 Cities, Darmstadt, 1990.

Croce, Benedetto, *Come il Marx fece passare il communismo dall' utopia alla scienca*, Bari, 1984.

Curcio, Carlo, *Utopisti e riformatori sociali del Cinquecento*, Bologna, 1941.

Curtis, Edith Roelker, *A Season in Utopia*, New York, 1961.

Curtis, Peter H., *Bellamy Nationalism and Later Reform Moments 1888–1940*, Indiana University, Bloomington, IN, 1973.

Cyrano de Bergerac, Savinien de, *L'autre Monde ou les états et empires de la lune*, Paris, 1656, Dresden, 1910.

Cyrano de Bergerac, Savinien de, *Voyages fantastiques de C. B.*, Paris, 1875.

Cyrano de Bergerac, Savinien de, *Die Reise zu den Mondstaaten und Sonnenreichen*, Munich and Leipzig, 1913.

Dahinden, Justus, *Stadtstrukturen für morgen*, Stuttgart, 1971.

Dahinden, Justus, *Urban Structures for the Future*, London, 1972.

Dahinden, Justus, *Urbanisme 1 cahiers du centre d'études architecturales 16*, Brussels, 1972.

Dahinden, Justus, *Mensch und Raum, Man and Space*, Stuttgart and Zurich, 2005.

Dahrendorf, Ralf, »Out of utopia«, in: *Essays in the Theory of Society*, Berlin, 1968.

Daidalos, 7/1983; 42/1991; 57/1995.

Daneshgar, Armin Mohsen, *Bits Architecture*, Vienna, 2002.

Dante Alighieri, *Divina Commedia*, Venice, 1497.

Davis, J. C., *Utopia and the Ideal Society*, New York, 1981.

De Foigny, Gabriel de, *Les aventures de Jacques Sadeur dans la découverte et le voiage de la Terre Australe*, Paris, 1692, New York, 1974.

Delabre, Guy, and Jean-Marie Gauthier, *La régeneration de l'utopie socialiste: Godin et le Familistère de Guise*, Paris, 1978.

Delon, Michel, and Catriona Seth, *Sade en toutes letters autour d'Aline et Valcour*, Paris, 2004.

De Pauli-Schimanovich, Werner, and Peter Weibel (eds.), *Europolis 1–3*, Vienna, 2003.

Derivaux, J. C., and E. Ruhstral, *Zur Geschichte der Sozialutopie*, Pfaffenweiler, 1987.

Dessauce, Marc, *Inflatable Moment*, New York, 1999.

Dethier, Jean, and Alain Guiheux, *La Ville, art et architecture en Europe 1870–1993*, Paris, 1994.

Deville, G., *Grachus Babeuf und die Verschwörung der Gleichen*, Zurich, 1887.

Dick, Philip K., *Do Androids Dream of Electric Sheep?*, New York,1968.

Diderot, Denis, *Voyage autour du monde par la frigate la Bondeuse et la flute de l'Étoile*, Paris, 1778.

Diderot, Denis, *Jacques le fataliste et son maître*, Paris, 1780.

Diderot, Denis, *Jack the Fatalist and his Master*, London, 1797, New York, 1984.

Diderot, Denis, *Supplement au »Voyage de Bougainville«*, Paris, 1796.

Dijksterhuis, Edward Jan, and Simon Stevin, *Science in the Netherlands*, Den Haag, 1970.

Dilas-Rocherieux, Yolene, Laurent Gervereau, and Thierrry Paquot, *Rêver Demain*, Paris, 1994.

Dirx, Ruth, *Sie dachten Utopia*, Gelnhausen and Berlin, 1982.

Dobbs, C. R., *Freedom's Will. The Society of Separatists of Zoar*, New York, 1947.

Documenta 11, Plattform 5, exhibition catalogue, Kassel, 2002.

Dodd, Anna Bowman, *The Republic of the Future, or Socialism as Reality*, New York, 1887.

Domenig & Huth 1963–67, Propositionen, exhibition catalogue, Graz, 1967.

Domenig, Günther, *Werkbuch*, Salzburg and Vienna, 1991.

Doni, Anton Francesco, *I mondi del Doni*, Venice, 1552.

Donnelly, Ignatius, *Caesar's Column*, (1892), Middletown, CN, 2003.

Donner, Henry Wolfgang, *Introduction to Utopia*, Uppsala, 1945.

Doren, Rudolf Alfred, *Wunschräume und Wunschzeiten*, Leipzig, 1927.

12 Villes Prospectives, 8. Congrès de l'UIA, Neuilly/Seine, 1965.

Doxiadis, Constantin, *Between Dystopia and Utopia*, Hartford, CT, 1966.

Dubois, Claude-Gilbert, »Problèmes de l'utopie«, in: *Archives des lettres modernes 1968*, Paris, 1977.

Dürer, Albrecht, *Etliche Unterricht zur Befestigung der Stett, Schloss und Flecken*, Dietikon-Nürnberg, 1527, Zurich, 1971.

Duschlbauer, Thomas, *Die Metamorphose der Kommunikation: vom Panopticon zum Cyberspace*, Vienna, 1994.

Duveau, Georges, *Sociologie de l'utopie et autres essais*, Paris, 1961.

Eaton, Ruth, *Ideal Cities: Utopianism and the (Un)built Environment*, New York, 2002.

Eberlin von Günzburg, Johann, *Ein newe ordnung weltlich standts – Der elfft bundtgnoss*, Halle a. d. Saale, 1896.

Egli, Jules, and Josef Lackner, *Die Anti-Stadt*, Wetzikon, 1966.

Eibl, Moritz, *Zwei französische Utopien aus dem 17. Jahrhundert*, n. p., 1908.

Eimer, Manfred, *Geschichte der Stadt Freudenstadt*, Freudenstadt, 1937.

1900-talets Utopia, Verklighetsflykt och teknokrati, Stockholm, 1989.

Eisfeld, Dieter, *Stadt der Zukunft*, Stuttgart, 1981.

Elias, Norbert, »Thomas Morus' Staatskritik«, in: Wilhelm Voßkamp, *Utopieforschung*, Bd. 2, Stuttgart, 1985.

Eliot, John, *The Christian Commonwealth; or The Civil Policy of the Rising Kingdom of Jesus Christ*, London, 1659.

Elliott, R. C., *The Shape of Utopia. Studies in a Literary Genre*, Chicago, 1970.

El Lissitzky, Proun und Wolkenbügel, Dresden, 1977.

El Lissitzky, 1890–1941, exhibition catalogue, Sprengel Museum Hannover, Hanover, 1988.

El Lissitzky, Architect – Painter – Photographer – Typographer, Eindhoven, 1990.

Enfantin, Prosper, *Die Nationalökonomie des Saint-Simonismus*, Leipzig, 1905.

Engels, Friedrich, *Zur Wohnungsfrage*, Leipzig, 1872, 1887, Berlin, 1930.

Engels, Friedrich, *Die Entwicklung des Sozialismus von der Utopie zur Wissenschaft*, Vienna, 1882, 1945.

Engels, Friedrich, *Der Ursprung der Familie, des Privateigentums und des Staates*, Zurich, 1884, Stuttgart, 1892, Berlin, 1953.

Engels, Friedrich, »Beschreibung der in neuerer Zeit entstandenen und noch bestehenden kommunistischen Ansiedlungen«, in: *Marx-Engels-Gesamtausgabe*, Berlin, 1932.

Erman, G., *Deutschland im Jahre 2000*, Kiel and Leipzig, 1891.

Ernst, Morris L., *Utopia 1976*, New York and Toronto, 1955.

Erste Seite, Die, 11. September 2001, Cologne, 2002.

Erzgräber, W., *Utopie und Anti-Utopie in der englischen Literatur*, Munich, 1980, 1981, 1988.

Estlake, A., *The Oneida Community*, London, 1900.

Euhemeros, (Euhemerismus), »Heilige Aufzeichnungen«, in: Johannes Hoops, *Reallexikon der Germanischen Altertumskunde*, Berlin and New York, 1994.

ex. Position, Avantgarde Tirol 1960/75, exhibition catalogue, Innsbruck, 2005.

Faßbinder, Maria, *Der »Jesuitenstaat« in Paraguay*, Halle a. d. S., 1926.

Favre, Pierre, *Sade utopiste: Aline et Valcour*, Paris, 1967.

Featherstone, Mike, and Roger Burrows, *Cyberspace/Cyberbodies/Cyberpunk*, New Delhi, 1995.

Fehlner, Gert, *Literarische Utopien als Reflexion und Kritik amerikanischer Wirklichkeit*, Meitingen, 1989.

Fénélon, François de Salignac de la Motte, *Les Aventures de Télémaque fils d'Ulysse*, Paris, 1699, Linz, 1795, Vienna, 1832, Leipzig, 1878.

Ferguson, John, *Utopias of the Classical World*, Ithaca, 1975.

Ferguson, Russell (ed.), *At the End of the Century*, Los Angeles, 1998.

Ferris Leich, Jean, *Architectural Visions*, New York 1890.

Ferrucci, Carla, *La lettura dell' utopia*, Milan, 1984.

Fetz, August, *Ein Blick in die Zukunft 2407*, Leipzig, 1907.

Feuerstein, Günther, *Urban Fiction*, exhibition catalogue, Vienna, 1966.

Feuerstein, Günther, »Verkehrs-Etagen. Otto Wagner und Antonio Sant'Elia«, *Daidalos* (Berlin), 42/1991.

Feuerstein, Günther, *Visionary Architecture in Austria in the Sixties and Seventies*, Vienna, 1996.

Fiacci, Luigi, *Giovanni Battista Piranesi. The Etchings*, Cologne, 2006.

Fichte, Johann Gottlieb, *Der geschloßne Handelsstaat*, Tübingen, 1800.

Filarete, Antonio (Averlino), *Trattato di architettura*, Florence, 1461, 1464.

Fincke, Andreas, and Matthias Pöhlmann, *Kompass.Sekten und religiöse Weltanschauungen*, Gütersloh, 2004.

Firpo, Luigi, *Lo stato ideale della Controriforma: Ludovico Agostini*, Bari, 1957.

Firpo, Luigi, *L'utopismo del rinascimento e l'età nuova*, Alpignano, 1990.

Fischer, Marie, *Die Familistère Godins*, Hamburg, 1890.

Fischer von Erlach, *Entwurff einer historischen Architektur*, Leipzig, 1725.

Fishman, Robert, *Bourgeois utopias. The Rise and Fall of Suburbia*, New York, 1987.

Fishman, Robert, *Urban Utopias in the Twentieth Century*, Cambridge, MA, 1982, 1994.

Fistetti, Francesco, *Heidegger und die Utopie der Polis*, Frankfurt am Main, 2002.

Flagge, Ingeborg, *Die Utopie der nahen Zukunft*, Bonn and Hamburg 1983.

Fleck, Robert, *Die Mühl-Kommune*, Cologne, 2003.

Fludd, Robert, *Utriusque cosmi, jamoris scilicet et minoris, metaphysica, physica atque technica historia 1617*, n. p,. 1617.

Flusser, Vilém, *Ende der Geschichte, Ende der Stadt?*, Vienna, 1991.

Flusser, Vilém, *Ins Universum der technischen Bilder*, n. p., 1985.

Flusser, Vilém, *Vom Subjekt zum Projekt*, Bensheim, Düsseldorf, 1994.

Foigny, Gabriel de, *Les aventures de Jacques Sadeur dans la découverte et le voiage de la terre Australe*, Paris, 1543, 1705, Geneva, 1676.

Fonatti, Franco, *Architekturskizzen und Zeichnungen*, Vienna, 1974.

Fontenelle, Bernhard de, *La republique des philosophes ou histoire des Ajaoiens*, Paris, 1758.

Fourier, Charles, *Le nouveau Monde amoureux*, Paris, 1808, 1967.

Fourier, Charles, *Théorie des quatre mouvements et des destinées générales*, Paris, 1808, 1841.

Fourier, Charles, *Traité de l'association domestique agricole*, Paris, 1822.

Fourier, Charles, *Le nouveau Monde industriel*, Paris, 1829.

Fourier, Charles, *Die gesellschaftliche und industrielle neue Welt mit ihren Vorteilen im Vergleich der seitherigen Civilisation. Im Geiste ihres Stifters*, Heidelberg, 1835.

Fourier, Charles, *Œuvres complètes*, Paris, 1841, 1843, Frankfurt am Main, 1966.

Fourier, Charles, *Phalanx or journal of social science*, New York, 1843, 1967.

Fourier, Charles, *Des modifications à introduire dans l'architecture des villes*, Paris, 1845.

Fourier, Charles, *L'Harmonie universelle et la Phalanstère*, Paris, 1848.

Fourier, Charles, *Contre la civilisation*, Paris, 1972.

Fourier, Charles, *Theorie of the four movements*, London, 1996.

Frankel, Boris, *The Post-industrial Utopians*, Cambridge, MA, 1987.

Fränkel, Heinrich, *Gegen Bellamy!*, Würzburg, 1891.

Frayn, Michael, *A Very Private Life*, London, 1968.

Fregna, Roberto, *Le città di utopia*, Bologna, 1987.

Frewin, Anthony, *One Hundred Years of Science Fiction Illustration: 1840–1940. A non fictional book*, London, 1974.

Freyer, Hans, *Die politische Insel*, Leipzig, 1936.

Friedell, Egon, *Die Reise mit der Zeitmaschine*, Munich, 1946.

Friedman, Yona, *L'architecture mobile*, Paris, 1970.

Friedman, Yona, *Machbare Utopien*, Frankfurt am Main 1974, 1977.

Fritsch, Theodor, *Die Stadt der Zukunft*, Leipzig, 1896, 1903.

Fuller, Richard Buckminster, *Konkrete Utopie*, Düsseldorf, Vienna, 1974.

Fuller, Richard Buchminster, *Fuller Projection Air-Ocean World Dymaxion Map*, Los Angeles, 1992.

Furlong, Guillermo, *Missiones y sus pueblos de Guaranies 1610–1813*, Buenos Aires, 1962.

Furttenbach, Joseph, *Gewerb – Statt – Gebäw*, n. p., 1650.

Gallet, Michel, *Claude-Nicolas Ledoux*, Stuttgart, 1983.

Garnier, Tony, *The Cité Industrielle*, New York, 1969.

Garnier, Tony, *Une cité industrielle*, Paris, 1917.

Gasper, Hans, and Friederike Valentin (eds.), *Endzeitfieber*, Freiburg, Basel, Vienna, 1997.

Gehrke, A., *Communistische Idealstaaten*, Bremen, 1878.

Gerbel, Karl, and Peter Weibel (eds.), *Ars Electronica 1995*, Vienna, New York, 1995.

Gerber, Richard, *Utopian Fantasy*, London, 1955.

Geretsegger, Heinz, Max Peintner, and Walter Pichler, *Otto Wagner 1841–1918. Unbegrenzte Großstadt*, Salzburg, 1964.

Gerosa, Pier Giorgio, *Le Cobusier, Urbanisme et mobilité*, Basel and Stuttgart, 1978.

Gibson, William, *Count Zero*, London, 1987.

Gibson, William, *Mona Lisa Overdrive*, London, 1989.

Gibson, William, *Neuromancer*, New York, 1989, Munich, 2001.

Gibson, William, *Idoru*, London, 1996, 1997.

Gillen, Otto (ed.), *Hortus Deliciarium des Herrad v. Landsberg*, Neustadt, 1979.

Gilman, Charlotte Perkins, *Herland*, Mineola, NY, 1998.

Girsberger, Hans, *Der utopische Sozialismus des 18. Jahrhunderts in Frankreich*, Wiesbaden, 1973.

Glasenapp, Jörn, and Claudia Lillge (eds.), *Cyberfictionen*, Munich, 2002.

Glaser, Horst Albert, *Utopische Inseln: Beiträge zu ihrer Geschichte und Theorie*, Frankfurt am Main, 1996.

Glauche, Johannes W., *Der Stupa*, Cologne, 1995.

Glenn, R. Negley, and Max J. Patrick (eds.), *The Quest for Utopia*, New York, 1952.

Gloag, John, »To-Morrow's Yesterday«, in: *First one and twenty*, London, 1932.

Glückstadt, Stadtverwaltung, Information, Glückstadt, 1984.

Göbel, Gerhard, *Poeta Faber*, Heidelberg, 1971.

Godin, Jean-Baptiste, *Solutions sociales*, Paris, 1871.

Godin, Jean-Baptiste, *La Richesse au service du peuple: Le Familistère de Guise*, Paris, 1874.

Godwin, William, *An Enquiry Concerning Political Justice, and its Influence on General Virtue and Happiness*, London, 1793.

Goldberger, Paul, *The Skyscraper*, London, 1982.

Goodwin, Barbara, *Social Science and Utopia: Nineteenth-Century Models of Social Harmony*, Sussex, 1978.

Goodwin, Barbara, and Keith Taylor, *The Politics of Utopia: A Study in Theory and Practice*, New York, 1982.

Gothein, E., »Der christlich-soziale Staat der Jesuiten in Paraguay«, in: Schmoller G. (ed.), *Staats- und sozialwissenschaftl. Forschungen*, Leipzig, 1883.

Gott, Richard J., *Zeitreisen in Einsteins Universum*, Reinbek / Hamburg, 2002.

Gott, Samuel, *Novae Solymae libri sex*, London, 1648.

Graf, Otto Antonia, *Otto Wagner, Das Werk des Architekten*, 2 (3) vol., Vienna, Cologne, Graz, 1985.

Graf, Otto Antonia, *Masterdrawings of Otto Wagner*, Vienna, 1987.

Graf, Otto Antonia, *Otto Wagner 5, 6, 7, Baukunst des Eros*, Vienna, Cologne, Weimar, 2000.

Grafton, Anthony, *Leon Battista Alberti*, New York, n. y.

Graham, C. R. B., *A Vanished Arcadia. Being some Account of the Jesuits in Paraguay*, London, 1924.

Green, Rosalie (ed.), *Herrad of Landsberg, Hortus Deliciarium*, London, 1979.

Gregorovius, Emil, *Der Himmel auf Erden in den Jahren 1901 bis 1912*, Leipzig, 1892.

Gsöllpointner, Helmuth, *Temporäre variable Raumobjekte*, Vienna, 2003.

Guadalupi, Gianni, Alberto Manguel, *Von Atlantis bis Utopia*, Munich, 1981.

The Guardian, London, 2001.

Guter, Josef, *Pädagogik in Utopia*, Neuwied, 1968.

Hadid, Zaha, and Patrik Schumacher, *Latente Utopien*, Vienna, New York, 2002.

Hajnóczi, Gábor, *Andrea Palladio*, Hanau, 1979.

Haller, Albrecht von, *Fabius und Cato*, Bern, 1774, Reutlingen, 1779.

Haller, Fritz, *totale stadt integral urban. ein modell*, Olten, 1968.

Hanak, Werner (ed.), *Eden Zion Utopia*, Vienna, 2000.

Haraway, Donna, *The Haraway Reader*, New York, London, 2004.

Harbou, Thea von, *Metropolis*, Frankfurt am Main, Berlin, Vienna, 1984.

Harrington, James, *The Commonwealth of Oceana*, London, 1656, 1700, Lund, 1924.

Harrison, John Fletcher Clews, *Robert Owen and the Owenites in Britain and America*, London, 1969.

Hartmann, Peter Claus, *Der Jesuitenstaat in Südamerika 1609 –1768*, Weißenhorn, 1994.

Hasselmann, Erwin, *Im Anfang war die Idee. Robert Owen*, Hamburg, 1958.

Hassfurther, Katalog der Auktion 30. 5. 2005, Vienna, 2005.

Haus-Rucker-Co 1967–1983, Braunschweig and Wiesbaden, 1984.

Hawken, Paul, *The Magic of Findhorn*, New York, 1975.

Hawking, Stephen, *Die illustrierte kurze Geschichte der Zeit*, Reinbek / Hamburg, 2000.

Hayden, Dolores, *Seven American Utopias*, Cambridge, MA, London, 1976.

Hecht, Konrad, *Der St. Gallener Klosterplan*, Wiesbaden, 1982.

Heimann, Jim, *Future Perfect*, Cologne, 2002.

Heindel, Max, *The Rosicrucian Cosmoconception or Mystic Christianity*, London, 1925, Oceanside, CA, 1929.

Heinisch, Klaus J., *Der utopische Staat*, Reinbek / Hamburg 1964, 1979.

Heller, Arno, Walter Hölbling, and Waldemar Zacharasiewicz, *Utopian Thought in American Literature*, Tübingen, 1988.

Hemken, Kai-Uwe, *El Lissitzky – Revolution und Avantgarde*, Cologne, 1990.

Henne am Rhyn, Otto, *Aria. Das Reich des ewigen Friedens im 20. Jahrhundert*, Pforzheim, 1895.

Hertzka, Theodor, *Freiland*, Dresden and Leipzig, 1890.

Hertzka, Theodor, *Freeland. A Social Anticipation*, New York, 1891.

Hertzka, Theodor, *Eine Reise nach Freiland*, Leipzig, 1893.

Hertzka, Theodor, *Entrückt in die Zukunft*, Berlin, 1895.

Herzl, Theodor, *Altneuland*, Berlin and Vienna, 1919.

Herzl, Theodor, *Der Judenstaat*, (reprint of the edition of Leipzig and Vienna, 1896), Osnabrück, 1968.

Herzl, Theodor, *The Jew's State*, Northvale, NJ, 1997.

Heubner, Thomas, *Die Rebellion der Betrogenen*, Berlin, 1985.

Heuermann, Hartmut, and Bernd-Peter Lange (eds.), *Die Utopie in der angloamerikanischen Literatur*, Düsseldorf, 1984.

Hexter, Jack H., *More's Utopia. The Biography of an Idea*, Princeton, 1952, New York, 1965.

Heyd, Wilhelm (ed.), *Heinrich Schickhardt, Ohngevare Verzaichnus was mit Gottes gnediger Hilff*, Stuttgart, 1902.

Higgins, Dick, *Wolf Vostell, pop architektur*, Düsseldorf, 1969.

Hilberseimer, Ludwig, *Entfaltung einer Planungsidee*, Frankfurt am Main, Berlin, 1963.

Hilberseimer, Ludwig, *Großstadtarchitektur*, Stuttgart, 1927, 1978.

Hilpert, Thilo, *Die funktionelle Stadt: Le Corbusiers Stadtvision*, Braunschweig and Wiesbaden, 1978.

Hinds, W. A., *American Communities*, Oneida, 1878.

Hine, R. V., *California's Utopian Colonies*, New Haven, 1966.

Hinterhäuser, Hans, *Utopie und Wirklichkeit bei Diderot*, Heidelberg, 1957.

History, Magazin für Geschichte, Munich, 1903.

Hodgson, William, *The Commonwealth of Reason*, London, 1795.

Höfer, Werner, and Walter Prankl, *Die vierte Haut*, Vienna, 1968.

Holberg, Ludvig, *Nicolai Klimu iter subterraneum*, Leipzig, Copenhagen, 1741.

Holberg, Ludvig, *Niels Klims Wallfahrt in die Unterwelt*, Leipzig, 1828.

Holberg, Ludvig, *Nicolai Klims unterirdische Reise*, Leipzig 1753, 1847.

Hans Hollein, Walter Pichler, Architektur, Galerie St. Stephan, exhibition catalogue, Vienna, 1963.

»Hans Hollein«, *Architecture and Urbanism* (Tokyo), 1985.

Hans Hollein, Historisches Museum der Stadt Wien, exhibition catalogue, Vienna, 1995.

Holloway, Mark, *Heaven on Earth*, London, 1951.

Höppner, Joachim, and Waltraud Seidel-Höppner, *Sozialismus vor Marx*, Leipzig, 1975, Berlin, 1987.

Howard, Ebenezer, *Garden Cities of Tomorrow*, London, 1898, 1903, 1920, 1966.

Howard, Ebenezer, *Domestic Industry as it Might Be*, London, 1906.

Hruza, Jiri, *Teorie Mešta*, Prague, 1965.

Huntemann, Georg Hermann, *Utopisches Menschenbild und utopistisches Bewußtsein im 19. und 20. Jahrhundert*, Erlangen, 1953.

Huxley, Aldous, *Brave new World*, London, 1932.

Huxley Aldous, *Brave New World – Revisited*, London, 1959.

Illing, Werner, *Utopolis*, Berlin, 1930, Frankfurt am Main, 1974.

Infield, Henrik F., *Utopia und Experiment*, Göttingen, 1956.

»Instant City in Progress – Archigram«, *Architectural Design* (London), 6/7, November, 1970.

Invontionon, Piranesi und Architekturphantasien in der Gegenwart, Hanover, 1981.

Ioannis Ravisii (Tixier de Ravisi, Johannes), ... *Elucidarium poeticum*, Basel, 1545.

Jaacks, Gisela (ed.), *Der Traum von der Stadt am Meer*, Hamburg, 2003.

Jacobelli, Angelamaria Isoldi, *Tommaso Campanella, Il diverso Filosofar mio*, Rome and Bari, 1995.

Jahn, Isabel-Dorothea, and Kaspar Stiblin, *Commentariolus de Eudaemonensium Republica*, Regensburg, 1994.

Jean, Georges, *Voyages en utopie*, Paris, 1994.

Jellicoe, G. A., *Motopia – a Study in the Evolution of Urban Landscape*, London, 1961.

Johnson, Christopher H., *Utopian Communism in France: Cabet and the Icarians 1839–1851*, Ithaca, NY, and London, 1974.

Johnson, Robbin S., *More's Utopia: Ideal and Illusion*, New Haven, CT, and London, 1969.

Jones, Lloyd, *The Life, Times and Labours of Robert Owen*, London, 1889.

Jouvé, Jean Pierre, Claude Prévost and Clovis Prévost, *Le Palais idéal du facteur cheval*, Paris, 1981.

Jünger, Ernst, *Heliopolis*, Tübingen, 1949.

Jünger, Ernst, *Gläserne Bienen*, Reinbek / Hamburg, 1960.

Jünger, Ernst, *Weltstaat, Organismus und Organisation*, Stuttgart, 1960.

Jünger, Ernst, *The Glass Bees*, New York, 1991.

Kahn, Herman, and Anthony J. Wiener, *Ihr werdet es erleben*, Munich and Vienna, 1967.

Kahn, Herman, and Anthony J. Wiener, *Year 2000: A Framework for Speculation on the next thirty-three Years*, New York, 1967.

Kahn, Herman, and B. Bruce-Briggs. *Things to Come; Thinking about the Seventies and Eighties*, New York, 1972.

Kahn, Herman, *World Economic Development, 1979 and beyond*, Boulder, CO, 1979.

Kahn, Herman, *Coming Boom: Economic, Political and Social*, New York, 1982.

Kainrath, Wilhelm, *Die Bandstadt*, Vienna, 1996.

Kamlah, Wilhelm, *Utopie, Eschatologie, Geschichtsteleologie*, Mannheim, Vienna, Zurich, 1969.

Kane, Bob, *Batman*, Frankfurt am Main, 2002.

Kateb, George, *Utopia and its Enemies*, London, 1963.

Kaufmann, Edgar, *Von Ledoux bis Le Corbusier*, Vienna, 1933.

Kaufmann, Edgar, *Three Revolutionary Architects: Boullée, Ledoux, and Lequeu*, Philadelphia, PA, 1952.

Kautsky, Karl, *Thomas More and his Utopia*, London, 1885.

Keane, A. H., *The Gold of Ophir*, London, 1901.

Kemp, J. (ed.), *Diderot: Selected Writings*, New York, 1963.

»Kiyonori Kikutake«, *World Architecture* (London), 32/1993.

Kimpel, Harald, and Gerd Hallenberger (eds.), *Zukunftsräume*, Eberberg, 1984.

King's Views of New York, New York, 1928.

Kirchenheim, Arthur, *Schlaraffia Politica, Geschichte der Dichtungen vom besten Staate*, Leipzig, 1892.

Kircher, Athanasius, *Mundus subterraneus*, Amsterdam, 1664, 1675.

Kircher, Athanasius, *Turris Babel, Sive Archontologia Qua primo priscorum post diluvium hominum vita, mores rerumque gestarum magnitudo, Secundo Turris fabrica civitatumque exstructio, confusio linguarum, & inde gentium transmigrationis, cum principalium inde enatorum idiomatum historia,*

multiplici eruditione describuntur & explicantur, Amsterdam, 1679.

Klein, Yves, *Air Architecture*, Los Angeles, Vienna, 2004.

Kleinwächter, Friedrich, *Die Staatsromane*, Vienna, 1891, Amsterdam, 1967.

Klengel-Brandt, Evelyn, *Der Turm von Babylon*, Leipzig, Vienna, Munich, 1982.

Klostermann, Michael, *Auroville – Stadt des Zukunftsmenschen*, Frankfurt am Main, 1976.

Klotz, Volker, *Die erzählte Stadt in den Werken von Lesage, Hugo, Zola, Defoe, Raabe*, Frankfurt am Main, 1985.

Klucker, Ehrenfried, *Heinrich Schickhardt. Architekt und Ingenieur*, Herrenberg, 1992.

Knoedler, Ch., *The Harmony Society*, New York, 1954.

Knortz, K., *Die christlich-kommunistische Kolonie der Rappisten in Pennsylvanien*, Leipzig, 1892.

Koch, Fritz, *Bellamy's Zukunftsstaat, Analyse und Kritik*, Bonn, 1924.

Kohn, Wendy (ed.), *Moshe Safdie*, London, 1996.

Koolhaas, Rem, *Delirious New York. A Retroactive Manifesto for Manhattan*, New York, 1978.

Kopp, Anatole, *Changer la vie, changer la ville*, Paris, 1975.

Kotzab, Gabriele, *Virtual Reality und Cyberspace*, Vienna, 1995.

Krämer, Sibylle, »Verschwindet der Körper?«, in: Maresch R., Weber N., *Raum-Wissen-Macht*, Frankfurt am Main, 2002.

Krauss, Werner (ed.), *Reise nach Utopia. Französische Utopien aus drei Jahrhunderten*, Berlin, 1964.

Kretzmann, Edwin Martin John, *The Pre-War Utopian Novel (1890–1914)*, Providence, 1936.

Kropotkin, Peter, *Landwirtschaft, Industrie und Handwerk*, Brighton, 1912, Berlin, 1921.

Kruft, Hanno-Walter, *Städte in Utopia*, Munich, 1989.

Kruse, Vinding Fr., *Community of the Future*, London and Kopenhagen, 1950.

Kumar, Krishan, *Utopia and Anti-Utopia in Modern Times*, New York, 1987.

Kurokawa, Kisho, *Das Kurokawa-Manifest*, Berlin, 1977, 2005.

Lablaude, Pierre-André, *Les Jardins de Versailles*, Paris, 1995.

Laicus, Philipp, recte Wasserburg Ph., *Etwas später!*, Mainz, 1891.

Landauer, Georg, *Zionismus im Wandel dreier Jahrzehnte*, Tel Aviv, 1957.

Lanier, Jaron, »Was heißt Virtuelle Realität?«, in: Manfred Waffender, *Cyberspace*, Reinbek / Hamburg, 1991.

Larsson, Lars Olof, *Die Neugestaltung der Reichshauptstadt*, Stuttgart, 1978.

Larsson, Lars Olof, *Albert Speer. Le plan de Berlin 1937–43*, Brussels, 1983.

Lasswitz, Kurd, *Auf zwei Planeten* (1887), Donauwörth, 1948.

Lasswitz, Kurd, *Two Planets*, (1887), Carbondale, IL, 1971.

Latent Utopias. Experiments within Contemporary Architecture, Vienna and New York, 2002.

Lauritzen, Lauritz (ed.), *Städtebau der Zukunft*, Düsseldorf and Vienna, 1969.

Lavedan, Pierre, *Histoire de la communauté Icarienne*, Nîmes, 1907.

Lazzaroni, Michele, and Antonío Munoz, *Filarete, scultore e architetto del secolo XV*, Rome, 1908.

Leary, Timothy, *Neuropolitics. The Sociobiology of Human Metamorphosis*, Los Angeles, 1977.

Le Corbusier, *Précision sur un état présent de l'architecture et de l'urbanisme*, Paris, 1930.

Le Corbusier, *Œuvre complète* (5 volumes), Zurich, 1946–1964.

Le Corbusier, *Urbanisme*, Paris, 1925.

Ledoux, Claude Nicolas, *L'Architecture de Claude Nicolas Ledoux*, Paris, 1789.

Ledoux, Claude Nicolas, *L'Architecture considérée sous le rapport de l'art, des mœurs et de la legislation*, Paris, 1804.

Le Guin, Ursula K., *The Left Hand of Darkness*, Munich, 1969, 1974.

Le Guin, Ursula K., *The Disposseded. An Ambiguous Utopia*, New York, 1974.

Le Guin, Ursula K., *Winterplanet*, Munich, 1974.

Lem, Stanislaw, *Solaris*, Krakow, 1968.

Lem, Stanislaw, *Summa teknologii* , n. p., 1968.

Lem, Stanislaw, *Bajki robotow*, Krakow, 1969.

Lem, Stanislaw, *Fantastyka i futurologia*, Krakow, 1970.

Lem, Stanislaw, *Dzienniki gwiazdowe*, Krakow, 1973.

Lem, Stanislaw, *Wysoki zamek*, Krakow, 1974.

Lem, Stanislaw, *Star Diaries*, New York 1976,

Lem, Stanislaw, *Futurological Congress*, San Diego, 1985.

Lem, Stanislaw, *Peace on Earth*, New York, 1994.

Lem, Stanislaw, *High Castle. A Remembrance*, New York, 1995.

Levering, J. M., *A History of Bethlehem / PA 1741 to 1892, with some Account of Its Founders and their Early Activity in America*, Bethlehem, PA, 1903.

Levitas, Ruth, *The Concept of Utopia*, New York 1990.

Libeskind, Daniel, with Sarah Crichton, *Breaking Ground*, Cologne, 2004.

Liebknecht, Wilhelm, *Robert Owen. Sein Leben und sozialpolitisches Wirken*, Nuremberg, 1892.

Lindo, Wilfred, *Cybermania*, Düsseldorf, 1994.

Lissitzky, El, *Die Rekonstruktion der Architektur in der Sowjetunion*, Vienna, 1930.

Lissitzky, El, *An Architecture for World Revolution*, Cambridge, MA, 1970.

Logan, George M., *The Meaning of More's ›Utopia‹*, Princeton, 1983.

Lopez, Raymond, *L'Avenir des villes*, Paris, 1964.

Lowry, Charles W., *Communism and Christ*, New York, 1952.

Lowry, Nelson, *The Mormon Village*, Salt Lake City, 1952.

Lück, Hartmut, *Fantastik, Science Fiction, Utopie: das Realismusproblem der utopisch-fantastischen Literatur*, Gießen, 1977.

Lupton, J. H., *The Utopia of Sir Thomas More*, Oxford, 1895.

Lux, H., *Etienne Cabet und der ikarische Kommunismus*, Berlin and Bonn / Bad Godesberg, 1974.

Lux, Joseph August, *Otto Wagner*, Munich and Vienna, 1914.

Maar, Christa, and Florian Rötzer (eds.), *Virtual Cities*, Basel, Boston, Berlin, 1998.

Maass, Michael, *Planstädte der Neuzeit vom 16. bis zum 18. Jahrhundert*, Karlsruhe, 1990.

Macdonald, Alexander, »Bellamy, Morris and the Great Victorian Debante«, in: Boos, Florence (ed.), *Socialism and the Literary Artistry of William Morris*, Columbia, 1990.

MacLuhan, Marshall, *Understanding Media*, Toronto, 1961.

MacLuhan, Marshall, *The Gutenberg Galaxy*, Toronto, 1962.

MacLuhan, Marshall, *Understanding Media: The Extension of Man*, New York, 1966.

MacLuhan, Marshall, *Die magischen Kanäle*, Düsseldorf and Vienna, 1968.

Magnago Lampugnani, Vittorio, *Architecture and City Planning in the Twentieth Century*, New York, 1985.

Mago, Simone, *De Paradiso Ophir*, Rostock, 1655.

Mahieu, Jacques de, *Die Templer in Amerika oder das Silber der Kathedralen*, Tübingen, 1979.

Maltese, Corrado (ed.), *Francesco di Giorgio Martini, Trattati di architettura*, Mailand, 1967.

Mang, Karl, *Die Shaker*, Vienna, 1974.

Manguel, Alberto, and Gianni Guadalupi, *The Dictionary of Imaginary Places,* Toronto, 1980, 1999.

Manguel, Alberto, Gianni Guadalupi, *Von Atlantis bis Utopia*, Munich, 1981.

Mannheim, Karl, *Ideologie und Utopie*, Bonn, 1929, 1930.

Mantegazza, Paolo, *L'Anno 3000*, Milan, 1897.

Manuel, Frank Edward (ed.), *Utopias and Utopian Thought*, Boston, 1966.

Manuel, Frank Edward (ed.), *Wunschtraum und Experiment*, Freiburg, 1970.

Marchi, Francesco de, *Della Architettura Militare, del Capitano Francesco de'Marchi, Bolognese, gentil' huomo Romano* (1599), Rome, 1810.

Marcuse, Herbert, *Das Ende der Utopie*, Frankfurt am Main, 1980.

Maresch, Rudolf, and Florian Rötzer (eds.), *Cyberhypes. Möglichkeiten und Grenzen des Internet*, Frankfurt am Main, 2001.

Maresch, Rudolf, and Niels Weber (eds.), *Raum – Wissen – Macht*, Frankfurt am Main, 2002.

Marinetti, Filippo Tommaso, *Gli Indomabili*, n. p., 1922.

Martim, Avillez (ed.), *Sites & Stations*, New York , 1995, 1996.

Martin, Eddie Owens, and Tom Patterson, *St. Eom in the Land of Pasaquan*, Columbus, GA, 1987.

Martini, Francesco di Giorgio, *Trattato di Architettura*, Florence, Turin, 1475.

Marx, Karl, and Friedrich Engels, *Das Kommunistische Manifest*, Munich, 1848, Vienna, 1932.

Marx, Carl (Karl), *Das Kapital*, (3 vol.) vol. 1, *Kritik der politischen Ökonomie*, Hamburg, 1872, 1890, 1894, 1921, Berlin, 1932.

Masereel, Frans, *Die Passion eines Menschen*, Munich, 1928.

Mavor, James W. jr., *Voyage to Atlantis*, London 1969.

Mayer, Karl, *Weihnachtskrippen*, Steyr, 2001.

Mayr, Franz Wilhelm, *Die Subkultur der Hippies*, Linz, 2000.

Mayrhofer, Maximilian, *William Gibsons Cyberspace Trilogie*, Graz, 1991.

Mazzolen, Donatella (ed.), *La città e l'immaginario*, Rome, 1985.

Mercier, Louis-Sébastien, *L'an deux mille quatre cent quarante – Rêve s'il en fut jamais*, Paris, 1771, London, 1772.

Mercier, Louis-Sébastien, *Le Nouveau Paris*, Paris, 1786.

Mercier, Louis-Sébastien, *Das Jahr Zweitausendvierhundertundvierzig*, Frankfurt am Main, 1989.

Merrill, Albert Adams, *The Great Awakening, the Story of the Twenty-Second Century*, Boston, 1899.

Metamorph, 9. International Architecture Exhibition, exhibition catalogue, Biennale Venice, 2004.

Michaelis, Richard, *Looking Further Forward; an Answer to ›Looking Backward‹*, Chicago, 1890.

Miksic, John, *Borobodur*, Munich, 1991.

Miles, *Hippies*, London, 2003, Munich, 2004.

Miller, Amy Bess, *Hancock Shaker Village*, Hancock, 1984.

Miller, Mervyn, *Raymond Unwin: Garden Cities and Town Planning*, Leicester, London, New York, 1992.

Milton, John (pseud.), *Nova Solyma* (Samuel Gott), London, 1649, 1902.

Minkowski, Helmut, *Vermutungen über den Turmbau zu Babel*, Freren, 1991.

Mitchell, William J., *City of Bits*, Basel, Boston, Berlin, 1995, 1996.

Möbus, Gerhard, *Politik des Heiligen*, Berlin, 1952.

Modrevius, Andreas Frizius (Modrzewski), *De republica emendanda*, n. p., n. y.

Moeller van den Bruck, *Das Dritte Reich*, Hamburg, Berlin and Leipzig, 1931.

Mohl, Robert von, *Geschichte und Literatur der Staatswissenschaften*, Erlangen, 1855.

Moholy-Nagy, Sibyl, *Die Stadt als Schicksal*, Munich, 1968.

Moll, J. J., *Cahier, Contenant six differentes parties de plans de villes ...*, n. p., n. y.

Molnar, Thomas, *Utopia: The Perennial Heresy*, London, 1972.

Moment, Gairdner B., Otto F. Kraushaar (eds.), *Utopias: The American Experience*, Metuchen, NJ, 1960.

Monte Verità, *Berg der Wahrheit, Lokale Anthropologie als Beitrag zur Wiederentdeckung einer neuzeitlichen sakralen Topographie*, Milan, 1979.

More, Sir Thomas, *De Insula Utopia*, Leuwen, 1516.

More, (Sir) Thomas, *De optimo reipublicae statu deque nova insula Utopia libellus vere aureus ... Thomae mori ...*, Basel, 1518, Frankfurt am Main, 1601.

More, Sir Thomas, *Ordentliche und ausführliche Beschreibung der ... Insel Utopia*, Leipzig, 1612.

More, Sir Thomas, *Utopia. Eine Konstruktion des humanen Staates*, Munich, 1960.

Morelly, Etienne Gabrielle, *Le Prince. Les délices des cœurs ...*, Amsterdam, 1751.

Morelly, Etienne Gabrielle, *Naufrages des isles flottantes*, Messine, 1753.

Morelly, Etienne Gabrielle, *Code de la nature*, Paris 1755, 1910, 1953.

Morgan, Arthur Ernest, *Begin of Modern American Poetry*, New York, 1944.

Morgan, Arthur Ernest, *Nowhere Was Somewhere: How History Makes Utopias and How Utopias Make History*, Westport, CT, 1976.

Moro, Tommaso, *L'utopia ovvero la Republica Introvabile*, Milan, 1863.

Morris, May, *The Collected Works of William Morris*, London, 1910–15.

Morris, William, *Wie wir leben und wir wir leben könnten*, n. p., n. y.

Morris, William, *The Earthly Paradise*, Boston, 1868.

Morris, William, *A Dream of John Ball*, New York, 1888.

Morris, William, *News from Nowhere*, London, 1890.

Mörtenböck, Peter, *Die virtuelle Dimension*, Vienna, Cologne and Weimar, 1998.

Morton, Arthur Leslie, *The English Utopia*, London, 1952.

Morton, Arthur Leslie, *The Story of Utopias*, London, 1941, New York, 1962.

Morus, Thomas, *Von der wunderbarlichen Insel Utopia genannt ...*, Basel, 1524.

Morus, Thomas, (Thomae Mori), *Utopiae Libri*, Basel, 1563.

Mosca, Capitale dell'utopia, Milan, 1991.

Mucchielle, M. Roger, *Le Mythe de la cité idéale*, Paris, 1960.

Muckle, Friedrich, *Die Geschichte der sozialistischen Ideen im 19. Jahrhundert*, Berlin, 1917.

Muckle, Friedrich, *Die großen Sozialisten Owen, Fourier, Proudhon*, Leipzig and Berlin, 1919.

Muehll, Emanuel v. d., *Denis Veiras et son Histoire des Sévarambes*, Paris, 1938.

Mujica, Francisco, *City of the Future*, New York, 1975.

Mujica, Francisco, *History of the Skyscraper*, New York, 1977.

Mulder, J. D., and R. van Liere (eds.), *Virtuel environment 2000*, Vienna and New York, 2000.

Müller, Ernst, *Ein Rückblick aus dem Jahre 2037 auf das Jahr 2000, Aus den Erinnerungen des Herrn Julian West*, Berlin, 1891.

Mumford, Lewis, *The City in History*, New York and London, 1961.

Mumford, Lewis, *The Story of Utopias*, New York, 1922, 1962.

Münter, Georg, *Idealstädte. Ihre Geschichte vom 15.–17. Jahrhundert*, Berlin, 1957.

Mystische Stätten, Geheimnisse des Unbekannten, n. p., 1988.

Mythos, Galerie im Stifterhaus, exhibition catalogue, Linz, 1997.

Naredi-Rainer, Paul, *Herbert Boeckl*, Graz, 1990.

Negley, Glenn R., and Max J. Patrick (eds.), *The Quest of Utopia. An Anthology of Imaginary Societies*, New York, 1952

Negley, Glenn R., *Utopian Literature*, Lawrence, 1977.

Nelson, William (ed.), *20. Century Interpretations of Utopia*, Englewood Cliffs, NJ, 1968.

Neue Stadtbauformen, Die prämierten Projekte des »Grand Prix International d'Urbanisme et d'Architecture«, Zurich, 1969.

Neumayer, Fritz, *Quellentexte zur Architekturtheorie*, Munich, Berlin, London, New York, 2002.

Neupauer, Ritter Josef von, *Oesterreich im Jahre 2020*, Dresden and Leipzig, 1893.

Neusüss, Arnhelm (ed.), *Utopie. Begriff und Phänomen des Utopischen*, Neuwied, Berlin, Frankfurt, 1986.

Niemeyer, Oscar. Eine Legende der Moderne – A Legend of Modernism, Frankfurt am Main, Basel, Boston, Berlin, 2003.

Noever, Peter (ed.), *Chris Burden – Beyond the limits – Jenseits der Grenzen*, Vienna, 1996.

Nouvelles de nulle part, Utopies urbaines 1789 to 2000, Paris, 2001.

Novak, Marcos, »Liquid Architecture in Cyberspace«, in: Michael Benedict (ed.), *Cyberspace – First Steps*, London, 1991.

Noyes, George Wallingford, and John Humphrey Noyes, *The Putney Community*, Oneida, NY, 1931.

Noyes, John Humphrey, *History of American Socialism*, Philadelphia, 1870.

Nozick, Robert, *Anarchie, Staat, Utopia*, Munich, 1974.

Oechslin, Werner, »J. J. Molls Napoléonville als „irdisches Paradies«, *Daidalos*, 7/1983.

Oestreich, P. (ed.), *Charles Fourier*, Munich, 1919.

Oettinger, Wolfgang von, *Über das Leben und die Werke des Antonio Averlino, genannt Filarete*, Leipzig, 1888, 1890.

Oncken, Hermann, *Die Utopia des Thomas Morus und das Machtproblem in der Staatslehre*, Heidelberg, 1922.

Orient, Sandra, and Alberto Terruzzi, *Città di fondazione. Le reducciones gesuitiche del Paraguay tra il XVII e il XVIII secolo*, Milan, 1982.

Ortner, Helmut, and Karl Plötzl, *Wohnmobile*, Vienna 1968, Linz, 1975.

Orwell, George, *Nineteen Eighty-Four*, London, 1949.

Österreicher, Oliver, *Räumliche Idealstadtmodelle und utopische Umsetzungsversuche – Versuch einer Einordnung der »Stadt des Kindes« in Wien*, Vienna, 2003

Owen, Gregory, *Meccania, The Super-State*, London, 1918.

Owen, Robert, *A New View of Society or Essays on the Principle of the Formation of the Human Character*, London, 1813/14.

Owen, Robert, *Report to the County of Lanark*, Glasgow, 1821.

Owen, Robert Dale, *An Outline of the System of Education at New Lanark*, Glasgow, 1824.

Owen, Robert, *Outline of the Rational System of Society ...*, London, 1832.

Owen, Robert, *The Book of the New Moral World*, London, 1836, 1842, New York, 1845.

Owen, Robert, *Life of Robert Owen, Written by Himself*, London, 1857/58.

Owen, Robert Dale, *Threading my Way. Twenty-seven Years of Autobiography*, London, 1860.

Owen, Robert, *Catalogue of an exhibition of printed books 1958*, London, 1958/59.

Pahl, Jürgen, *Die Stadt im Aufbruch der perspektivischen Welt*, Berlin, 1963.

Palladio, Andrea, *Quattro Libri dell'Architettura*, Venice, 1570.

Palladio, Andrea, *Four Books of Architecture*, London, 1738, 1742.

Paltock, Robert, *The Life and Adventures of Peter Wilkins*, London, 1751, 1973.

Parent, Claude, *Dessins utopiques*, Paris, 1990.

Parent, Claude, *Entrelacs de l'oblique*, Paris, 1981.

Parent, Michel, *Vauban, Un Encyclopédiste avant la lettre*, Paris, 1982.

Paris – Architecture et utopie, Projets d'urbanisme pour l'entrée dans le 21ème siècle, Berlin, 1989.

Parrington, Vernon Louis, *American Dreams, A Study of American Utopias*, Providence, 1947, New York, 1964.

Passer, Arnold von, recte Hoffmann, and Franz-Levy, *Menetekel! Eine Entdeckungsreise nach Europa*, Erfurt and Leipzig, 1893.

Patritio (Patrizi), Francesco, *La città felice del medesimo*, Venice, 1553, 1603.

Pavan, Gino, *Palmanova, fortezza d'Europa 1593 to 1993*, Venice, 1993.

Pavel, Thomas G., *Fictional Worlds*, Cambridge, MA, 1986.

Peck, Bradford, *The World a Department Store; a Story of Life under a Cooperative System*, Lewiston, ME, Boston, 1900.

Pedretto, Carlo, *Leonardo Architetto*, Milan, 1978.

Pehnt, Wolfgang, *Expressionist Architecture*, New York, 1973.

Peichl, Gustav (ed.), *Die Kunst des Otto Wagner*, Vienna, 1984.

Perret, Jacques, *Des fortifications et artifices*, Paris, 1601.

Peters, Carl, *Aequatorial- und Süd-Afrika nach einer Darstellung von 1719*, Berlin, 1895.

Peters, Carl, *Das goldene Ophir Salomo's*, Munich and Leipzig, 1895.

Peters, Carl, *Ophir. Nach den neuesten Forschungen*, Berlin, 1908.

Pfister, Manfred (ed.), *Alternative Welten*, Munich, 1982.

Walter Pichler, Salzburg, 1971.

Piero della Francesca, *De Prospectiva pingendi*, Firenze, n. p., n. y.

Piper, Ernst, and Julius H. Schoeps (eds.), *Bauen und Zeitgeist*, Basel, Boston, Berlin, 1998.

Pisek, Karin, *ECO – Feminism and 20th Century American Literature*, Innsbruck, 1988.

Plato, *The Republic*, Baltimore, MD, 1974.

Platonov, Andrei, *Chevengur*, Paris, 1928/29, 1971.

Pleij, Herman, *Der Traum vom Schlaraffenland*, Frankfurt am Main, 2000.

Pochat, Götz, and Brigitte Wagner, *Utopie. Gesellschaftsformen. Künstlerträume*, Graz, 1996.

Ponten, Josef, *Architektur die nicht gebaut wurde*, Stuttgart, 1925, 1987.

Poppe, Reiner, and G. Orwell, *A. Huxley: Animal Farm, Brave New World, 1984*, Hollfeld, 1980.

Popper-Lynkeus, Josef, *Phantasien eines Realisten*, Düsseldorf 1909, 1980.

Popper-Lynkeus, Josef, *Die allgemeine Nährpflicht*, Dresden, 1912.

Portoghesi, Paolo, *Bernardo Vittone. Un architetto fra Illuminismo e Rococò*, Rome, 1966.

Poster, Mark, *The Utopian Thought of Restif de la Bretonne*, New York, 1971.

Prader, Herbert, and Franz Fehringer, *Hexagonale Wohnzellen*, Vienna, 1973.

Priest, H., *More's Utopia & Utopian Literature*, Lincoln, 1975.

Proudhon, Pierre Joseph, *De la création de l'ordre dans l'humanité*, Paris 1849, 1927

Proudhon, Pierre Joseph, *Du principe de l'art et de sa destination sociale*, Paris, 1865, 1988.

Rabelais, François, *Le quart livre des faits et des dits de Pantagruel*, Paris, 1540, 1548.

Rabelais, Franz (François), *Gargantua und Pantagruel*, Strassburg, Leipzig, 1913.

Rabl, Claudia, *Virtual Reality – Eine techno-ökonomische Analyse*, Vienna, 1995.

Rahmsdorf, Sabine, *Stadt und Architektur in der literarischen Utopie der früheren Neuzeit*, Heidelberg, 1999.

Rainald, Franz, *Vincenzo Scamozzi 1548–1616*, Petersberg, 1999.

Ramm, Thilo, *Die großen Sozialisten als Rechts- und Sozialphilosophen*, Stuttgart, 1955/56.

Ramm, Thilo (ed.), *Frühsozialismus*, Stuttgart, 1956.

Ramusio, Giovanni Battista, *Delle Navigationi et Viaggi*, Venice, 1556–1606.

Rasmussen, Steen Eiler, *London: The Unique City*, London, 1937.

Redmond, James, *Introduction to »News from Nowhere«*, London, 1970.

Reich, Erna, *Der utopische Roman von 1850 bis zur Gegenwart*, Vienna, 1927.

Reichardt, A., *Das Bellamy Zeitalter 2001–2010*, Berlin, 1893.

Reiner, Thomas A., *The Place of the Ideal Community in Urban Planning*, Philadelphia, PA, 1963.

Reiner, Thomas A., *Utopia e urbanistica*, Padua, 1967.

Reinhart, C., *Die Grundsätze für die Planung und den Bau von neuen Städten*, Vienna, 1964.

Retif de la Bretonne, *La découverte Australe ou les Antipodes par un homme volant ou le Dedale français*, Paris, 1776.

Revolutionsarchitektur, Boullée, Ledoux, Lequeu, Baden-Baden, 1970.

Reybaud, Louis, *Le fer et la houille. Familistère de Guise*, Paris, 1874.

Rheingold, Howard, *Virtuelle Welten – Reisen im Cyberspace*, Reinbek / Hamburg, 1992.

Rheingold, Howard, *Virtuelle Gemeinschaft*, Bonn and Paris, 1994.

Richardson, Sir Benjamin Ward, *Hygieia, a City of Health*, London, 1876.

Richter, Dagmar, *The Architecture of Dagmar Richter*, London, 2001.

Richter, Dieter, *Schlaraffenland*, Frankfurt am Main, 1995.

Richter, Eugen, *Sozialdemokratische Zukunftsbilder*, Berlin, 1892.

Rihs, Charles, *Les philosophes utopistes*, Geneva, 1970.

Ritter, Klaus, *Start nach Utopolis*, Berlin (Ost), 1978.

Robinson, C. E., *The Shakers and their Homes: A Concise History of the United Society of Believers called Shakers*, Canterburry, NH, 1893.

Rocheleau, Paul, and June Spring, *Shaker-Architektur*, Cologne, 1996.

Rodwin Lloyd (ed.), *The Future Metropolis*, New York, 1960.

Rosario, Pavia, *L'idea di città XV – XVIII secolo*, Milan, 1982.

Rosenau, Helen, *The Ideal City. Its Architectural Evolution*, Bristol 1959, London, 1974.

Rosenau, Helen, *Vision of the Temple*, London, 1979.

Rossi, Aldo, *L'architettura della città*, Padua, 1970.

Rottensteiner, Franz, *Phantastische Welten*, Frankfurt am Main, 1984.

Rötzer, Florian, *Die Telepolis*, Mannheim, 1995, 1997.

Rötzer, Florian, *Digitale Weltentwürfe*, Munich and Vienna, 1998.

Rousseau, Jean Jacques, *Du contrat social*, Geneva, 1766, Paris, 1925.

Rousseau, Jean Jacques, *Discourse sur l'origine et les fondemens de l'inégalité parmi les hommes*, London 1755, 1782.

Rousseau, Jean Jacques, *On the Social Contract*, New York, 2003.

Ruyer, Raymond, *L'Utopie et les Utopistes*, Boston, 1950.

Rykwert, Joseph, *The Idea of a Town*, Princeton and London, 1978.

Rykwert, Joseph, and Anne Engel, *Leon Battista Alberti*, Milan, 1994.

Sade, Donatien-Alphonse-François, Comte de, (Marquis de Sade), *Aline et Valcour ou le roman philosophique*, Paris, 1790.

Saint-Simon, Claude Henri, Comte de, *Nouveau Christianisme*, Paris, 1832.

Saint-Simon, Claude Henri, Comte de, *Œuvres Choisies*, Brüssel, 1859.

Saint-Simon, Claude Henri, Comte de, *Selected Writings*, Westport, CT, 1979.

Saint-Simon, Fourier, Owen, Institutul de Filozofie al Academiei R. P R, Bukarest, 1957.

Samjatin, Jéwgenij, *Wir*, Cologne and Berlin, 1958, Munich, 1982.

St. Florian, Friedrich, *Projects*, Cambridge, MA, 1973.

St. Florian, Friedrich, *Projects 1961–1976*, Austin, TX, 1976.

San Leucio, *Entstehung der Colonie von Ferdinand IV König beyder Sizilien*, Vienna, 1791.

Sargean, Jack, and Stephanie Watson, »Fantasies of Utopia«, *Art & Design* (London), 1996.

Sargent, Lyman Tower, *British and American Utopian Literature 1516–1975*, Boston, 1979.

Scamozzi, Vincenzo, *L'Idea della Architettura Universale*, Venice, 1615.

Scenarios. Neue Arbeiten von Peter Cook, Christine Hawley, Ron Herron, London and Berlin, 1981.

Schaffer, Christen, *Daniel H. Burnham*, New York, 2003.

Schaffer, Nicole, *cyborgs @ cyberspace.com*, Vienna, 2000.

Schaik, Martin van (ed.), *Exit Utopia. Architectural Provocations 1956–76*, Munich, Berlin, London, New York, 2005.

Schaufler, Gernot, *A First Step Towards Object – Oriented Architectures for Virtual-Reality Applications*, Vienna, 1993.

Scheerbart, Paul, *Der Kaiser von Utopia* (1904) und *Das graue Tuch und zehn Prozent Weiß* (1914), Frankfurt am Main, 1988.

Scheerbart, Paul, *Glasarchitektur*, Berlin 1914, 1971, 2000.

Scheer-Schäzler, Brigitte (ed.), *Women's Fantastic Adventures*, Stuttgart, 1992.

Schempp, Hermann, *Gemeinschaftssiedlungen auf religiöser und weltanschaulicher Grundlage*, Tübingen, 1969.

Schepelmann, Wolfgang, *Die englische Utopie im Übergang: von Bulwer-Lytton bis H. G. Wells*, Vienna, 1975.

Schiffer, Herbert, *Shaker Architecture*, Exton, PA, 1979.

Schippke, Ulrich, *Das Bild der Zukunft*, Munich, Gütersloh, Vienna, 1974.

Schippke, Ulrich, *Zukunft. Das Bild der Welt von morgen*, Gütersloh, 1970.

Schirren, Matthias, *Bruno Taut – Alpine Architektur*, Munich, Berlin, London, New York, n. y..

Schmitt, Friedrich, *Die mittelenglische Version des Elucidariums des Honorius Augustodunensis*, Burghausen, 1909.

Schnabel, Johann Gottfried, *Die Insel Felsenburg*, Nordhausen, 1731–1743, Nürnberg 1828, Reinbek, 1969.

Schneider, Wolf, *Überall ist Babylon*, Düsseldorf, 1960.

Schöffer, Nicolas, *die kybernetische stadt*, Paris, 1969, Munich, 1970.

Schumpp, Mechthild, *Stadtbau-Utopien und Gesellschaft*, Gütersloh, 1971.

Schuyt, Michael, and Joost Effers, *Phantastische Architektur*, Cologne, 1980.

Anton Schweighofer. Architekt, exhibition catalogue, Vienna, 1989.

Schwarz, Egon, »Aus Wirklichkeit gerechte Träume: Utopische Kommunen in den Vereinigten Staaten von Amerika«, in: Voßkamp, W., *Utopieforschung 3*, Stuttgart, 1982, 1985.

Schwonke, Martin, *Vom Staatsroman zur Science Fiction*, Stuttgart, 1957.

Scientific American, London, 1913.

Sciolla, Gianni Carlo, *La città ideale nel Rinascimento*, Turin, 1975.

Scott, Ridley, *Blade Runner*, 1981.

Scully, Vincent, *Frank Lloyd Wright*, New York, London, 1960.

Seibt, Ferdinand, *Utopica*, Düsseldorf, 1972, Munich, 2001.

Sehm, Gunter, *Der ethnographische Reise- und Abenteuerroman des 19. Jahrhunderts*, Vienna, 1972.

Seipel, Wilfried (ed.), *Der Turmbau zu Babel*, Vienna, Milan, 2003.

Selle, Gerd, *William Morris und sein Roman*, Cologne, 1974.

Semler, H., *Geschichte des Sozialismus und Kommunismus in Nordamerika*, Leipzig, 1880.

Serlio, Sebastiano, *Il secondo libro di prospettiva*, Venice, 1566.

Serlio, Sebastiano, *Tutte l'opere d'architettura*, libri 6–8. Frankfurt am Main, 1554, Milano, 1994.

Servier, Jean, *Histoire de l'Utopie*, Paris, 1967.

Servier, Jean, *Der Traum von der großen Harmonie*, Munich, 1971.

Sharp, Dennis, (ed.), *Glass Architecture, by Paul Scheerbart; and Alpine Architecture, by Bruno Taut*, New York, 1972.

Simonds, Charles, *Schwebende Städte und andere Architekturen*, Münster, 1978.

Sinold von Schütz, and Johannes Philipp Balthasar, *Die glückseligste Insul auf der gantzen Welt, oder das Land der Zufriedenheit*, Königsberg, 1723.

Skinner, Burrhus Frederic, *Walden Two*, New York, 1948.

Skinner, Burrhus Frederic, *Futurum zwei*, Hamburg 1970.

Smith, Joseph, *History of the Church of Jesus Christ of Latter-day Saints*, Salt Lake City, 1830, 1927.

Smith, Joseph, *Das Buch Mormon*, Dresden, 1928.

Snodgrass, Mary Ellen, *Encyclopedia of Utopian Literature*, Santa Barbara, CA, Denver, CO, Oxford, GB, 1995.

John Soane, London and New York, 1983.

Sociopolis, Projekt für eine Stadt der Zukunft, Valencia, Vienna, 2004.

Soeffner, Hans-Georg, *Der geplante Mythos*, Hamburg, 1974.

Soleri, Paolo, *Fragments*, Vienna, 1985.

Soleri, Paolo, *Arcosanti, Labor für Öko-Urbanität*, Basel, 1988.

Soria y Mata, Arturo, *Ciudad lineal*, Madrid, 1910.

Soria y Mata, Arturo, La città lineare, Milan, 1968.

Lo spazio condivisio, artisti e architetti cosmorama divina proporzione, exhibition catalogue, Rome, 2000.

Speckle, Daniel, *Architectura von Vestungen, wie die zu unsern Zeiten mögen erbawen warden* etc., Strassburg 1589, 1599, 1608, 1639.

Spencer, John R. (ed.), *Antonio Filarete's Treatise on Architecture*, New Haven and London, 1965.

Sprigg, June, and David Larkin, *Shaker. Life, Work and Art*, New York, 1987.

Stadt und Utopie, Modelle idealer Gemeinschaften, Berlin, 1982.

Stamm, Rainer, and Daniel Schreiber (eds.), *Bau einer neuen Welt, Architektonische Visionen des Expressionismus*, Cologne, 2003.

Stary, Othmar, and Wim van der Kallen, *Die Seckauer Apokalypse von Herbert Boeckl*, Graz, Vienna, Cologne, 1989.

Stefanelli, Virginia (ed.), *Giorgio Vasari, La città ideale*, Rome, 1970.

Sterling, Bruce, *Islands in the Net*, New York, 1988.

Sterling, Bruce, *Mirrorshades. The Cyberpunk Anthology*, London, 1988.

Stevin, Symon, *Nouvelle manière de fortification par éscluses*, Leyden, 1618.

Stevin, Symon, *Science in the Netherlands around 1600*, Den Haag, 1970.

Stiblin(us), Caspar, *Coropaedia, sive de moribus et vita virginum sacrum libellus. Ejusdem de eudaemonensium republica commentariolus*, Basel, 1555.

Stocker, Gerfried, and Christine Schöpf, *Flesh Factor. Informationsmaschine Mensch*, Vienna and New York ,1997.

Stoloff, Bernhard, *Die Affäre Ledoux, Autopsie eines Mythos*, Braunschweig, 1983.

Ströbel, Heinrich, *Die erste Milliarde der zweiten Billion*, Berlin, 1919.

Sturm, Leonhard Christian, *Freundlicher Wettstreit der Französischen, Holländischen und Teutschen Kriegsbaukunst*, Augsburg, 1718.

Superstudio 1966–1982, Storie, figure, architettura, Florence, 1982.

Surtz, Edward, *The Praise of Wisdom*, Chicago, Cambridge, MA, 1957.

Surtz, Edward (ed.), *St. Thomas More. Utopia*, New Haven, London, 1964.

Süssmuth, Hans, *Studien zur Utopia des Thomas Morus*, Münster, 1967.

Suttner, Bertha von, *Das Maschinenzeitalter. Zukunftsvorlesungen über unsere Zeit*, Düsseldorf, 1983.

Swank, Scott T., *Shaker Life, Art and Architecture*, New York, London, Paris, 1999.

Swift, Jonathan, *Travels into several Remote Nations of the World. By Lemuel Gulliver. First a Surgeon, and then a Captain of several Ships*, London, 1726.

Swift, Jonathan, *Gulliver's travels*, Berlin, NJ, 2004.

Swoboda, Helmut (ed.), *Dichter reisen zum Mond*, Frankfurt am Main, Hamburg, 1969.

Swoboda, Helmut, *Die politische Willensbildung in den utopischen Staaten*, Vienna, 1969.

Swoboda, Helmut (ed.), *Der Traum vom besten Staat*, Munich, 1972.

Swoboda, Helmut, *Utopia*, Vienna, 1972.

Sywottek, Christian, »Was Neuland ist, wird in China betreten (Luchao Harbour City)«, *Der Standard*, (Vienna), 27 December, 2003.

Tabor, Jan (ed.), *Fuß in der Tür*, exhibition catalogue, Vienna, 2000.

Tabor, Jan, »Besser bauen, besser wohnen, besser leben«, *Du* (Zurich), 742/2003.

Tafuri, Manfredo, *Architecture and Utopia*, Bari, 1973, Cambridge, MA, London, 1976, 1999.

Tafuri, Manfredo, *Utopie et projets de l'avant-garde à la Métropole*, Paris, 1979.

Tarde, Gabriel, *Fragment d'histoire future, Das soziale Gesetz*, Lyon, 1904.

Taschen, Angelika (ed.), *Eccentric Style*, Berlin, 2002.

Bruno Taut, ABK Vienna 1980, exhibition catalogue, Vienna, 1980 .

Taut, Bruno, *Die Stadtkrone*, Jena, 1919.

Taut, Bruno, *Der Weltbaumeister*, Hagen, 1920.

Taut, Bruno, *Frühlicht*, Magdeburg, 1921.

Taylor, Anne, *Visions of Harmony*, New York, 1987.

Teatro. Eine Reise zu den oberitalienischen Theatern des 16.–19. Jahrhunderts, Marburg, 2001.

Thomas, John L., *Introduction to Looking Backward 2000–1887*, Cambridge, 1967.

Thompson, E. P., *William Morris: Romantic to Revolutionary*, London, New York, 1977.

Thomsen, Christian W., *Experimentelle Architekten der Gegenwart*, Cologne, 1991.

Thomsen, Christian W., *Visionary Architecture from Babylon to Virtual Reality*, Munich and New York, 1994.

Thomsen, Christian W., *Sensuous Architecture*, Munich and New York, 1998.

Tigler, Peter, *Die Architekturtheorie des Filarete*, Berlin, 1963.

Till, Rudolph, *Wiener Projekte und Utopien*, Vienna and Munich, 1972.

Tod, Ian, and Michael Wheeler, *Utopia*, London, 1978.

Transgalaxis, Katalog der deutschsprachigen utopisch-phantastischen Literatur 1460–1960, n. p., 1959/60.

Treyer, Hans, *Die politische Insel*, Leipzig, 1936.

trigon 69, Dreiländerbiennale Italien, Jugoslawien, Österreich, exhibition catalogue, Graz 1969.

Trousson, Raymond, *Voyages aux pays de nul part* , Brüssel, 1975.

Tupitsyn, Margarita, *El Lissitzky. Jenseits der Abstraktion*, Munich, Paris, London, 1999.

Twombly, Robert C., *Frank Lloyd Wright: His Life and Architecture*, New York ,1979.

Új Atlantisz felé, *Verso una nuova Atlantide, Towards a New Atlantis*, Venice, 2000.

Das ungebaute Wien, exhibition catalogue, Vienna 1999.

Unwin, Raymond, *Town Planning in Practice*, London, 1909.

Unwin, Raymond, Grundlagen des Städtebaus, Berlin, 1910.

Der Utopische Staat, Morus: Utopia, Campanella: Sonnenstaat, Bacon: Neu-Atlantis, Reinbek/ Hamburg, 1960.

Vairass, Denis (Veiras d'Alais), *Histoire des Sevarambes peuples qui habitent une partie du troisième continent communément appellé la terre Australe*, p. 1, Paris, 1679, Amsterdam, 1702, 1711.

Vairasse d'Allais, Dyonys, *The History of the Sevarites or Sevarambi: A Nation inhabiting part of the third continent, commonly called Terrae Australes Incognite*, London, 1675.

Vallée, Sheila de, *Architektur der Zukunft*, Paris, 1995.

Varen(io), August(o), *Paradiso Ophir*, Rostock, 1655.

Vaz, Mark Cotta, *The Art of Star Wars – Episode II – Angriff der Klonkrieger*, Stuttgart, 2002.

Veding, Gert, *Literatur ist Utopie*, Frankfurt am Main, 1978.

Venir, A., *Ein Blick nach vorn*, Leipzig, 1906.

Vercelloni, Virgilio, *Europäische Stadtutopien*, Munich, 1994.

Vergangene Zukunft, Design zwischen Utopien und Wissenschaft, Krems, 2001.

Verne, Jules, *Les cinq cents millions de la Bégum*, Paris, 1879.

Verne, Jules, *The Begum's Fortune*, London, 1887.

Verne, Jules, *L'Île à helice*, (1895), Paris, 1992.

Verne, Jules, *L'etonnante aventure de la mission Barsace*, Paris, (1880) 1977.

Verne, Jules, *Paris au XXe siècle*, (1863), Paris, 1994.

Verne, Jules, *Paris in the Twentieth Century*, (1863) Thornike, ME, 1997.

Versins, Pierre, *Encyclopédie de l'utopie, des voyages imaginaires et de la science-fiction*, Lausanne, 1972.

Vidler, Anthony, *Claude-Nicolas Ledoux*, London 1987, Basel, Boston, Berlin, 1988.

Villgradter, Rudolf, and Friedrich Krey (eds.), *Der utopistische Roman*, Darmstadt, 1973.

Virilio, Paul, and Claude Parent, *Architecture principe*, Besançon, 1996.

Visionen und Utopien, exhibition catalogue, Frankfurt am Main, 2003.

Visionen und Utopien: Geheimnisse des Unbekannten, Eltville, 2002.

Les visionnaires de l'architecture, Collection dirigée par André Parinaud, exhibition catalogue, Paris, 1965.

Vitruvius (Marcus Vitruvius Pollio), *De architectura libri decem*, (33/22 BC), Rome, 1960.

Vitruvius, *The Ten Books on Architecture*, London, 1826.

Vogt, Adolf Max, *Russische und französische Revolutions-Architektur 1917/1789*, Cologne, 1974.

Vogt, Elke, *The Double View of the Future in Ursula Le Guin's The Dispossessed and Marge Piercy's Woman on the Edge of Time*, Vienna, 1988.

Voigt, Andreas, *Die sozialen Utopien*, Leipzig, 1906.

Voltaire, François Marie Arouet de, *Micromegas*, Stuttgart, 1984.

Voltaire, François Marie Arouet de, *Candide oder der Optimismus*, Frankfurt am Main, Vienna, Zurich, 1964

Voßkamp, Wilhelm, *Utopieforschung*, vol. 1, 2, 3, Stuttgart 1982, 1985.

Waffender, Manfred (ed.) *Cyberspace. Ausflüge in virtuelle Wirklichkeiten*, Reinbek/Hamburg, 1991.

Wagner, Otto, *Moderne Architektur*, Vienna, 1895, 1899, 1902.

Wagner, Otto, *Die Baukunst unserer Zeit*, Vienna, 1914, 1979.

Wagner, Otto, *Unbegrenzte Großstadt. Beginn der modernen Architektur*, Salzburg, 1964.

Wagner, Otto, *Das Werk des Architekten*, Vienna, 1963.

Wagner, Richard Robert, *Robert Owen. Lebensroman eines Menschengläubigen*, Zurich and New York, 1942.

Wagner, Wilhelm J., *Österreichs reale Utopien*, Vienna, Munich, Zurich, 2000.

Walther, J. (ed.), *Der Traum aller Träume*, Berlin, 1987.

Ward, Colin, *Utopia: Human Space*, Harmondsworth, 1974.

Watt, Eduard Donald, *Aldous Huxley. The Critical Heritage*, London, 1975.

Wauchope, B., *Lost Tribes and Sunken Continents*, Chicago and London, 1962.

Webster, Charles (ed.), *Samuel Hartlieb and the Advancement of Learning*, Cambridge, 1970.

Wedewer, Rolf, and Thomas Kempas, *Architektonische Spekulationen*, Düsseldorf, 1970.

Wegener, Ulrike, *Die Faszination des Maßlosen. Der Turm zu Babel*, Hildesheim, 1995.

Weihsmann, Helmut, *Utopische Architektur*, Vienna, 1982.

Weihsmann, Helmut, *Bauen unterm Hakenkreuz*, Vienna, 1998.

Weiner, Monika, »Wo lag das sagenhafte Reich«, *P.M. History*, no. 6/2007

Weingärtner, W., *Historische Karten der US-Pioniersiedlungen*, n. p., 1833.

Weitling, Wilhelm, *Das Evangelium des armen Sünders. Die Menschheit, wie sie ist und wie sie sein sollte,* Hamburg, 1971.

Weller, Allen Stuart, *Francesco di Giorgio (Martini) 1439–1501*, Chicago, 1943.

Wells, Herbert George, *The Time Machine*, New York 1895, London, 1985.

Wells, Herbert George, *The Island of Doctor Moreau,* London, 1896.

Wells, Herbert George, *When the Sleeper Wakes*, London, 1899, New York 1925, 2003.

Wells, Herbert George, *Tales of Space and Time*, Leipzig, 1900.

Wells, Herbert George, *Jenseits des Sirius*, Stuttgart 1911.

Wells, Herbert George, *Men like Gods*, London, 1970.

Werner, Frank, *Die vergeudete Moderne*, Stuttgart, 1981.

Werner, Frank, *Covering + Exposing, Die Architektur von Coop Himmelb(l)au*, Basel, Berlin, Boston, 2000.

White, Frederic Randolph, *Famous Utopias of the Renaissance*, New York, 1955.

Whitwell, Stedman, *Description of an Architectural Model ... Advocated by Robert Owen*, London, 1830.

Whyte, Iain Boyd, *Bruno Taut and the Architecture of Activism*, Cambridge, 1982.

Whyte, Jennifer, *Virtual Reality and the Built Environment*, Oxford, 2002.

Wiebenson, Dora, *Tony Garnier: The Cité Industrielle*, New York, 1969.

Wiener, Norbert, *Cybernetics or Control and Communication in the Animal and the Machine*, New York 1955, 1961.

Wiener, Norbert, *The human use of human beings*, New York, 1957.

Wiener, Norbert, *Mensch und Menschmaschine*, Frankfurt am Main, 1958.

Wietek, Gerhard, *Deutsche Künstlerkolonien und Künstlerorte*, Munich, 1976.

Wigley, Mark, *Constant's New Babylon*, Rotterdam 1998.

Wilbrandt, Conrad, *Des Herrn Friedrich Ost Erlebnisse in der Welt Bellamy's*, Wismar, 1891.

Wilhelm, Karin, *Utopie heute?*, Vienna, 1993.

Wilhelm, Karin, »Auf der Suche nach der verlorenen Unsterblichkeit. Technische Utopien des 20. Jahrhunderts«, *Utopie*, Graz, 1996.

Willis, Paul, *Profane Culture*, Boston, 1978, Frankfurt am Main, 1981.

Winstanley, Gerrard, *The Digger Movement in the Days of the Commonwealth*, London, 1900.

Winstanley, Gerrard, *The Law of Freedom and Other Writings*, London, 1654, Hammondsworth, 1973.

Winstanley, Gerrard, *The True Levellers Standard Advanced*, New York, 1965.

Winter, Michael, *Compendium Utopiarum: Typologie und Bibliographie literarischer Utopien*, Stuttgart, 1978.

Winter, Michael, *Ende eines Traumes*, Stuttgart, 1993.

Wolff-Plottegg, Manfred, *Das binäre Haus & die Interaktion*, Graz, 1989.

Woods, Lebbeus, *Centricity*, Berlin, 1987.

Woods, Lebbeus, *Anarchitecture. Architecture is a Political Act*, London and New York, 1992.

World Architecture, London, 1993.

Wright, Austin Tappan, *Islandia*, New York, Toronto 1942.

Wright, Frank Lloyd, *The Disappearing City*, Taliesin, 1932.

Wright, Frank Lloyd, *Genius and the Mobocracy*, New York, 1949, 1971.

Wright, Frank Lloyd, *Living City*, New York, 1958.

Wright, Frank Lloyd, Architect, exhibition catalogue, New York, 1994.

Wuckel, Dieter, *Science Fiction*, Hildesheim, Zurich, New York, 1986.

Wunenburger, Jean-Jacques, *L'Utopie ou la crise de l'imaginaire*, Paris, 1979.

Zamyatin, Yevgeny Ivanovich, *My*, n.p., 1920, 1952.

Zehnder, Carl, *Ideal-Architekturen*, Zurich, 1981.

Zimmermann, Petra Sophie, *Die Architectura von Hans Vredeman de Fries*, Berlin, 2002.

Numbers in *italics* refer to illustrations

Photo credits